Getting Right with Reagan

Getting Right with Reagan

THE STRUGGLE FOR
TRUE CONSERVATISM,
1980–2016

Marcus M. Witcher

 University Press of Kansas

Published by the University Press of Kansas (Lawrence, Kansas 66045),
which was organized by the Kansas Board of Regents and is operated and
funded by Emporia State University, Fort Hays State University, Kansas
State University, Pittsburg State University, the University of Kansas, and
Wichita State University

Library of Congress Cataloging-in-Publication Data

Names: Witcher, Marcus M., author.
Title: Getting right with Reagan : the struggle for true conservatism,
1980–2016 / Marcus M. Witcher.
Description: Lawrence, Kansas : University Press of Kansas, [2019]
Includes bibliographical references and index.
Identifiers: LCCN 2019019363
  ISBN 9780700628773 (cloth)
  ISBN 9780700628780 (ebook)
Subjects: LCSH: Reagan, Ronald—Influence. | Reagan, Ronald—Political
and social views. | Reagan, Ronald—Public opinion. | Republican Party
(U.S.: 1854–) | Conservatism—United States—History—20th century.
| Conservatism—United States—History—21st century. | Political
culture—United States—History—20th century. | Political culture—
United States—History—21st century. | United States—Politics and
government—1981–1989. | United States—Politics and government—1989
Classification: LCC E877.2 .W58 2019 | DDC 973.927092 [B]—dc23
LC record available at https://lccn.loc.gov/2019019363.

British Library Cataloguing-in-Publication Data is available.

Printed in the United States of America

10 9 8 7 6 5 4 3 2 1

The paper used in this publication is recycled and contains 30 percent
postconsumer waste. It is acid free and meets the minimum requirements
of the American National Standard for Permanence of Paper for Printed
Library Materials Z39.48-1992.

To the women in my life:

Bobbi Turner, Lynlee Aguirre, and Takayla Witcher

Contents

Acknowledgments

Unfortunately, it would be impossible to thank all the people whose advice, encouragement, and support have made this book a reality. I begin by thanking David Beito and Kari Frederickson for agreeing to be my coadvisers in graduate school. David Beito's willingness to grant me artistic license made the project enjoyable, and his constant encouragement kept me going. Kari Frederickson's thoughtful guidance was essential to framing each chapter. I will forever be in her debt for the countless hours we spent discussing conservatism and contemporary politics. Furthermore, her willingness to tell me when I was trying to do too much made the size and scope of the book manageable. Their guidance was essential to the ultimate completion of my dissertation, and they have continued to provide support as I expanded the project into its current form.

I also thank Margaret Peacock, Lawrence Kohl, Douglas Brinkley, and George Rable for their feedback, reassurance, and thoughtful comments. Margaret Peacock pushed me to venture outside my comfort zone and constantly challenged my ideological and methodological assumptions. Her involvement has made this project much better. Larry Kohl taught me the value of clear and concise writing (which I hope comes through in the text) and ingrained in me the view that historians must make their work relevant to the public. This project is largely the application of the philosophical conversations we had in his classes. Doug Brinkley also offered insightful comments on the final draft of my dissertation and was generous with his time. I thank him for being the outside reader for my dissertation and for his continuing interest in my work. The title of this book owes its origins to George Rable, who suggested that *Getting Right with Reagan* might be an appropriate title. Likewise, he was the most forceful advocate for the current structure of the project—insisting that the first and second parts of the work would complement one another and that this story could be told in a single volume. I also thank Margaret Abruzzo, Daniel Riches, Janek Wasserman, Herold Selesky, Howard Jones, and the rest of the faculty and staff at the University of Alabama for the classes, conversations, and support they provided.

I also benefited from a supportive group of fellow graduate students while at Alabama. Chris Gasque, Katie Deale, Kevin Hughes, Derek Pryor, Jon Merritt, and Blake Ball endured countless conversations about President Reagan and provided me with friendship and support. I appreciate Chris Gasque's continued friendship and his insistence that I spend some time doing things I love, such as going to concerts and professional soccer matches. Both were essential to maintaining my sanity through the writing of this book. Kevin Hughes and I spent countless days at coffee shops working on our dissertations. His instant feedback shaped many of the ideas and sentences in this project. Likewise, Blake Ball was extremely helpful in providing feedback on the dissertation and was essential in helping me with the more mundane aspects of completing a dissertation—formatting and the like. The months we worked together proved to be instrumental to the completion of the project.

Since leaving the University of Alabama, I have been blessed with two professional appointments. I thank Josh Hall and the Economics Department at West Virginia University for having me as a postdoctoral scholar. My time at WVU afforded me the opportunity to add three chapters to the book and to refine my ideas. Furthermore, I thank the Center for Free Enterprise, and Josh specifically, for supporting the project financially. Because of the CFE, I was able to expand my source base and get feedback at conferences. Likewise, I thank Wendy Lucas for helping make my current position—as a resident scholar in the History Department at the University of Central Arkansas—a possibility. UCA has offered me an opportunity to take all that I've learned from research and apply it to the classroom. Wendy is the best "boss" a young scholar could have. She is supportive and encouraging, and she pushes me to grow, both as a scholar and as an educator. I also thank the Arkansas Center for Research in Economics for its generous support. I express my appreciation to David "Mitch" Mitchell and Christy Horpedahl for giving me the opportunity to return to UCA and for supporting this book as well as my other research initiatives. Finally, Dave Welky, Daniel Spillman, Todd Ewing, and Steven Harthorn are all exceptional educators, and each inspired me to become a historian. I am forever indebted to each of them for the countless hours they spent editing my writing and discussing ideas with me.

No piece of history is possible without the tireless work of archivists who ensure that scholars' archival trips are a success. Accordingly, I thank the archivists and staff at the Ronald Reagan Presidential Library for their patience, diligence, and unending support. Specifically, Jennifer Mandel went above and beyond to assist me while I was in the archive and continued to provide clarification and guidance through countless emails. Her expertise has made this book significantly better. Likewise, I thank Steve Branch for his help in acquiring the images for this book. I am also grateful to Blynne Olivieri at the Annie Belle Weaver Special Collections at the University of West Georgia for helping me acquire documents related to the memorialization of Ronald Reagan. Additionally, I thank the archivists and staff at the Liberty University archives, the Hoover Institution archives, the University of Kansas archives, the National Library of Medicine, the National Archives, and the Library of Congress for their support. Finally, I thank Elga Zalite for the work she did in the Hoover Institution archives on my behalf and Harry David and Carol A. Kennedy for editing the final manuscript.

The life lessons offered by my father, Rick Witcher, have shaped me into a determined individual who refuses to quit. That resilience and perseverance were essential to completing my PhD and finishing this project. Likewise, my mother, Bobbi Turner, put me on the path of education at a young age. I am privileged to have a mother who provided me with such a foundation and constantly provides me with love and support. My little sister, Lynlee Aguirre, was always there to tell a joke, to share some new music, and to make me laugh. She is a beautiful young woman who will do great things in her own right.

Finally, I want to thank my wife, Takayla. She persevered, sacrificed, and endured throughout my time in graduate school and continues to do so now that we are in search of that elusive tenure-track academic appointment. Her love and understanding enables me to be successful. Throughout this process, she has always been there to remind me of the truly important things in life. Without her, this book, and indeed all life's ventures, would be meaningless. I couldn't ask for a better partner, and I look forward to conquering the rest of life's challenges together.

Introduction: The Evolution of Conservatives' Perceptions of Reagan

Ronald Reagan was no conservative ideologue. Indeed, to many of his most ardent supporters he was not conservative enough. Reagan was a pragmatist who worked with Democrats, when possible, to pass the most conservative legislation politically achievable. In May 1980, one of Reagan's top advisers assured the press, "We don't want to dismantle the government, we want to improve its efficiency. We want a well-managed conservative welfare state. And Reagan is not Goldwater. He is not a mad ideologue."[1] In 1981, the *Washington Post* ran a story chronicling Reagan's journey to the White House. It asserted that Reagan succeeded because he was an excellent politician. The *Washington Post* declared that while Reagan was "a politician more wedded to the conservative sentiment than most," he would "always try to do what is right within the limits of what he thinks will work politically." The paper concluded that "Ronald Reagan never will willingly go down in flames for the cause."[2]

Despite such press reports, conservatives continued to believe that Reagan would usher in a conservative revolution and were deeply disappointed when their policy goals went unrealized. In 1983, columnist M. Stanton Evans had a debate with the adamantly pro-Reagan editor of *National Review*, William Rusher, about Reagan's record. Evans lamented that the "great opportunity" that was "presented in 1980 . . . has been defaulted." He concluded that "there was no Reagan Revolution in Washington and there will be no Reagan Revolution."[3] In 1988, conservative columnist Fred Barnes exclaimed that conservatives' agenda of mandating a balanced budget, achieving a line-item veto, and making education local "hasn't a prayer." He went on to defend Reagan against his critics as the most "conservative a president we're going to get" and concluded "that any conservative goal that wasn't achieved by Reagan isn't achievable."[4]

Many conservatives, however, were not willing to give Reagan a free pass. In 1988, the Republican presidential hopefuls spent much of the campaign running to the right of Reagan, assuring voters that their policies would be in line with "the old Reagan of the 'freedom fighters' and the Reagan Doctrine" instead of the conciliatory policies Reagan pursued during his second term.[5]

Lyn Nofziger, who worked with Reagan while he was governor and president, lamented in his memoir that "Ronald Reagan used to be one of us, but by the time he left the presidency he also had left us."[6] Summing up conservatives' disillusionment with Reagan in 1988, conservative activist Richard Viguerie asked what had been achieved from 1980 to 1988. His answer was "not much." According to Viguerie, Reagan had "proclaimed the passing of the 'evil empire' . . . picked supporters of détente for the Cabinet . . . bailed out Soviet agriculture . . . bailed out international banks that lent money to anti-American countries . . . and approved some of the biggest taxes in history." Many other conservatives agreed with Viguerie. Irving Kristol, a neoconservative, even penned an op-ed entitled, "The Reagan Revolution That Never Was."[7]

In the years following Reagan's departure from the White House, conservative sentiment toward the president quickly improved. One of the reasons that Reagan enjoyed such admiration among conservatives was that subsequent presidents' conservative credentials and achievements paled in comparison to those of the fortieth president.[8] President George H. W. Bush had an icy relationship with conservatives, which culminated in his violating his promise not to raise taxes. Although President William J. Clinton was significantly more conservative than Democratic hopefuls in the 1970s and 1980s, to conservatives he was a big-spending liberal only kept in check by conservative speaker of the House Newt Gingrich. President George W. Bush, whom conservatives hoped would be the next Reagan, got mired in the quagmire of Iraq, supported Medicare expansion, expanded federal control of education, proposed comprehensive immigration reform, and failed to privatize Social Security. Finally, despite President Barack Obama's attempt to offer conservatives an olive branch by praising Reagan for changing "the trajectory of America" and for restoring "a sense of optimism in our country, a spirit that transcended politics," his overtures fell on deaf ears.[9] Conservatives adamantly opposed Obama's Affordable Care Act and his attempt to phase out the Bush tax cuts, and condemned the president for not leading on the global stage.

Another reason for Reagan's increased standing among conservatives was fortuitous historical events, such as the fall of the Berlin Wall and the dissolution of the Soviet Union, that made his policies appear prescient. Reagan's cooperation with Mikhail Gorbachev, which conservatives during the 1980s condemned, was either forgotten or downplayed as part of Reagan's grand strategy to defeat global communism.[10] Likewise, the recessions of the early 1990s and the early 2000s, as well as the financial crisis of 2008, left conservatives longing for the economic policies of Reagan, which they view as responsible for the swift economic recovery from the worst economic downturn since the Great Depression. Any thoughts of Reagan's unbalanced budgets, which conservatives denounced during the 1980s, have disappeared or are considered peripheral.[11] Likewise, the moral scandals of the Clinton administration and President Obama's support for late-term abortion have led conservatives to long for what they view as the moral righteousness of the Reagan years.[12] Social conservatives have forgotten how frustrated they were with Reagan during the 1980s for his inability to pass a right-to-life amendment and a school-prayer amendment. In all these matters, time has improved Reagan's legacy among conservatives.

A final reason that conservatives' appraisal of Reagan has improved is his absence from the modern political scene. In the years immediately following his presidency, Reagan was busy framing his presidential legacy and fighting charges that he was involved in the Iran-Contra scandal. Unlike President George W. Bush, Reagan did not go into self-imposed political exile, but he also did not criticize his successor. Reagan did, however, take a controversial stand when he wrote an op-ed in support of the 1991 Brady Bill. The bill was named for Jim Brady, Reagan's press secretary, who had been paralyzed when he was hit by a bullet during John Hinckley Jr.'s assassination attempt on Reagan. The legislation imposed a seven-day wait period for the purchase of handguns, allowing law enforcement to run background checks to prevent those with a history of mental illness and those with criminal records from receiving the weapons.[13] Had Reagan remained in the spotlight, it is possible that conservatives' infatuation with the ex-president might have diminished. Sadly, Reagan did not get the opportunity to make extensive comments about public policy during his postpresidency. In 1994, he wrote a letter to the American people explaining that he had been diagnosed with Alzheimer's disease.[14] Following the letter, Reagan largely disappeared from public life, leaving conservatives to imagine how Reagan would react to contemporary political issues. Reagan's absence enabled the development of a mythical Reagan.[15] In time, Reagan came to represent the purest form of conservative principles, and his pragmatic governing style was forgotten.[16]

This book makes several arguments. First, it establishes that there were significant differences between Reagan and conservatives during the 1980s and challenges the view that the 1980s marked a triumph of conservatives. Second, it demonstrates that in the wake of the Cold War, Reagan's legacy took the place of anticommunism as the glue that held the conservative movement together. Finally, it argues that how conservatives view Reagan has shaped the conservative movement and also the Republican Party—moving both significantly to the right over the past thirty years. In reality, Reagan was a pragmatic conservative who understood that building coalitions across party lines was essential to effective governance.[17] In contrast, both conservatives and liberals have forgotten these qualities, and from 2004 to 2016 Reagan began to be framed as a conservative purist. In so framing him, conservative politicians have embraced a political discourse that is black and white and have constrained their policy prescriptions to those that will be perceived as unequivocally conservative. This lack of flexibility and the inability, or unwillingness, to compromise has significantly damaged the GOP's ability to govern effectively.

This book recasts Reagan as a shrewd political operator who often moderated his conservative positions—much to the vexation of conservatives during the 1980s.[18] It was Reagan's flexibility that allowed him to extend the sustainability of Social Security, pass comprehensive immigration reform, revitalize the American economy, restore American morale, and rebuild relations with the Soviet Union so a peaceful conclusion to the Cold War could be attained.

Dramatic music played as the camera panned across the Air Force One Pavilion at the Ronald Reagan Presidential Library in Simi Valley, California. The camera swung around and focused on CNN moderator Anderson Cooper standing next to former first lady Nancy Reagan. Cooper thanked Mrs. Reagan for hosting the final debate before Super Tuesday in the 2008 GOP primary. Governor Mike Huckabee, Congressman Ron Paul, Senator John McCain, and Governor Mitt Romney were introduced, and each was greeted by Mrs. Reagan before they took their seats with Reagan's Air Force One as a backdrop.[19] While Republican presidential hopefuls have lived in the shadow of Reagan since 1988, the 2008 primary was the first following Reagan's death, and in many ways his presence loomed larger than when he was alive. Reagan's influence on contemporary conservative politics was magnified at the Reagan Library, where every year hundreds of thousands of well-wishers from across the globe travel to commemorate his life and presidency.

From the outset, Reagan's legacy dictated the terms of the debate. Cooper invoked Reagan by asking each of the candidates whether they believed "Americans are better off than they were eight years ago." Sitting next to

President Reagan's actual diary, Cooper later cited the criticism that Reagan received from pro-life forces when he nominated Sandra Day O'Connor to the Supreme Court and asked Governor Huckabee if "she was the right choice." Huckabee responded with humor, declaring "history will have to determine that. And I'm not going to come to the Reagan Library and say anything about Ronald Reagan's decisions. I'm not that stupid. If I was, I'd have no business being president."[20]

As the debate came to an end, Cooper asked the candidates, "Would Ronald Reagan endorse you? And if so, why?" With Nancy Reagan sitting in the front row, the candidates were asked to use her husband as a political weapon against one another. Romney was first to respond, asserting that Reagan would "absolutely" endorse him. Romney went on to presume that Reagan would stay in Iraq "until we win," would "lower taxes," would "lower spending," would support "an amendment to protect marriage," would "drill in ANWR," would have been "absolutely" opposed "to McCain-Feingold," and "would say, there is no way we are having amnesty again." Romney emphasized that just like Reagan, he was a Washington outsider and concluded that the GOP had a choice regarding "what the heart and soul of this party is going to be, and it's going to have to be in the house that Ronald Reagan built." McCain retorted that "Reagan came with an unshakable set of principles" and he "would not approve of someone who changes their positions depending on what year it is." Paul conceded that he was not "sure exactly what [Reagan] would do right now" but reminded the audience that he was one of four congressmen to support Reagan in 1976 and concluded that Reagan had a solid understanding of monetary policy. When it was his turn, Huckabee turned the question on its head. Huckabee declared that "it would be incredibly presumptuous and even arrogant for me to try to suggest what Ronald Reagan would do, that he would endorse any of us against the others." Huckabee honestly exclaimed that he was "not going to pretend he would endorse me . . . but I endorse him." Huckabee continued that the greatest aspect of Reagan was his spirit and concluded that "whether he believes in us, I hope we still believe in those things which made him a great leader and a great American."[21]

The 2008 debate at Simi Valley was not the first time that GOP presidential hopefuls were asked to fill the boots of Ronald Reagan, and with each passing year those boots became bigger. Since Reagan left the public scene in 1994, it has become almost a rite of passage for Republicans to "get right with Reagan" and establish themselves as adequately conservative in relation to his faultless record. Unfortunately for the candidates, they were being compared not to the real Reagan—the man whose greatest accomplishment was to work with the opposition to change the trajectory of American politics—but rather to an idealized Reagan with few, if any, faults.

Every four years, the Republican Party attempts to re-create the "Reagan Revolution," but each year the Reagan whom candidates invoke looks less and less like the Reagan who won the presidency in 1980. Reagan has become the patron saint of conservatism whose name is frequently taken in vain. By 2016, even business mogul Donald Trump was using Reagan as a justification for his inconsistent conservative principles. Addressing his varying positions during a debate, Trump insisted "you have to have flexibility," and "Ronald Reagan" was "the great example." Trump recounted that Reagan had been "a somewhat liberal Democrat who became a somewhat, pretty strong conservative" and that "he made many of the changes that I've made." Trump's manipulation of Reagan was quickly pointed out by Governor Jeb Bush, who reminded viewers that while Reagan was a liberal in 1950, "he was a conservative reformed governor for eight years before he became president, and no one should suggest he made an evolution for political purposes." Bush then pivoted to use the language of the Reagan legacy against Trump, exclaiming that Reagan "was a conservative and he didn't tear down people like Donald Trump"; instead "he tore down the Berlin Wall."[22]

This book is about perception and identity. Specifically, it explores how conservative opinions of Ronald Reagan have evolved over the course of the past forty years. It is also a story about the development of conservatism from 1980 to 2016. Interestingly, the battle over the future of conservativism has often involved reinterpreting the past—specifically the legacy of President Reagan. Accordingly, this work is interested more in how conservatives viewed Reagan rather than what Reagan did, or did not, actually achieve.[23]

At the heart of this book is the elusive question: What is American conservatism? After years of research and study, I have concluded that there is no one definition that can encompass all the competing interpretations of conservatism. What it means to be a conservative is always in flux, just as what it means to be a liberal is constantly changing. Instead of offering a concrete definition of what conservatism is and then imposing it on my subjects, I have decided instead to demonstrate how conservatives (in all their various manifestations) attempted to answer this very question for themselves. As historian George Nash has noted, "the very quest for self-definition has been one of the most notable motifs of [conservative] thought."[24] Since I do not attempt to define conservatism, my subjects are those who self-identified as conservatives. Indeed, one of the primary contributions of this study is to trace the evolution of conservatives' own internal debate about the definition of conservatism from 1980 to 2016.[25]

Furthermore, Ronald Reagan is at the center of conservatives' own understanding of what it means to be conservative. Every branch of conservatism has claimed Reagan as one of its own over the last forty years, and his place in the conservative movement continues to influence not only how conservatives view the past, but also how they frame conservatism to address the problems facing the United States in the present. From the conservative movement's conception to 1991, anticommunism served as the glue that held it together. Following the collapse of the Soviet Union, the conservative movement ran the risk of fracturing. During the 1990s, however, President Reagan and his legacy replaced anticommunism as the glue that united most conservatives. The emergence of a useable legacy provided conservatives with common language, a series of accepted policy prescriptions, and a past that conservatives, of most varieties, could take pride in and venerate.

In time, the Reagan legacy—which was essential in encouraging GOP unity—shifted from what Reagan accomplished to how he achieved success. From 2004 to 2016, conservatives reinterpreted Reagan and created the myth that he was a dogmatic conservative whose success was a product of his rigid commitment to his conservative principles. As such, the Reagan myth served as a litmus test to determine whether Republican candidates were adequately conservative, thus limiting the potential policy responses to contemporary issues. By 2016, the Reagan legacy's positive function of binding the GOP together was outstripped by the rigidity imposed by the Reagan myth. To Donald Trump's credit, he broke away from the constraints of the Reagan myth, ran on a series of policies that were decidedly outside the parameters of the Reagan dogma, and won the presidency. It is unclear what the role of the Reagan myth and legacy will be following Trump's unexpected election. Trump is the opposite of Reagan in terms of temperament, and on many key policy issues (such as immigration and trade) the two are diametrically opposed. Despite this, the GOP and the conservative movement still desperately need a glue to hold them together. Ronald Reagan and his legacy have served that role for the last twenty-five years, and it is hard to imagine that the series of symbols, language, and useable past provided by the Reagan legacy will simply disappear following the Trump administration. Indeed, it may ultimately become more important—depending on the success or failure of Trump.

This book is split into two parts. Part 1, chapters 1 through 8, details conservative perceptions during Reagan's presidency. Part 2, chapters 9 through 14, explores the creation of Reagan's legacy and how conservatives have reimagined Reagan and created the Reagan myth to serve their contemporary political agenda. Especially in the wake of Donald Trump's surprise election in 2016, it is important to explore what conservativism is, what it has been, and where it might go.

Chapters 1 and 2 recount Reagan's economic policies and how conservatives responded to them during the 1980s. Reagan's top priority when taking office was to revitalize the economy, and he embraced supply-side economics to achieve his goals. Supply-side theory asserted that cutting taxes would encourage producers to invest more capital into their businesses and would result in economic growth. While most conservatives desired economic growth, many were also devoted to a balanced budget. This tension, between conservatives' desire to cut taxes and their belief in fiscal responsibility, led to bitter disputes.[26]

Chapters 3, 4, and 5 describe the disappointment that social conservatives felt toward Reagan for not prioritizing their agenda. While Reagan was personally pro-life and in favor of reinstating voluntary prayer in school, he did not use his political capital to pass significant legislation to restore Judeo-Christian family values. These chapters demonstrate that Reagan's relationship with the Religious Right was tenuous and question the New Right's influence during the 1980s.[27]

Chapters 6, 7, and 8 demonstrate that neoconservatives and the New Right had major problems with Reagan's foreign policy. They explore how the differences between Reagan's assertive rhetoric and his pragmatic policy confused and frustrated conservatives.[28] Although Reagan saw aggressive rhetoric as a means to bring the Soviet Union to the bargaining table, his conservative supporters embraced such rhetoric as a workable foreign policy and accordingly were disappointed when Reagan compromised with the USSR. During Reagan's first two years in office, they frequently condemned the president for not pursuing a more assertive interventionist policy to win the Cold War. When Reagan ratcheted up his rhetoric with the announcement of the

Strategic Defense Initiative and his intervention in Grenada, conservatives were momentarily satisfied with the president. In time, however, Reagan's desire to reduce nuclear weapons and his proposals to negotiate with hostile regimes such as the Sandinistas in Nicaragua resulted in some of the most severe conservative attacks on the president. Ultimately, Reagan's signature foreign policy achievement, the signing of the Intermediate-Range Nuclear Forces (INF) Treaty, brought him the ire of practically the entire conservative movement.[29] Combined, the first eight chapters tell, for the first time, the story of conservative disillusionment with Reagan during the 1980s.[30]

The second part of this work centers on how conservatives have reinterpreted Reagan's presidency to support their contemporary political proposals and, in the process, created both the Reagan legacy and myth. Chapter 9 explores how Reagan interpreted his own presidency and how he attempted to frame his legacy from 1988 to 1994.[31] The president used both his autobiography and his presidential library and museum to emphasize the revitalization of the economy, the restoration of American morale, and his role in helping bring the Cold War to an end. Unlike later conservatives, Reagan did not dramatically overstate his role in ending the Cold War. Instead, the president gave credit to Mikhail Gorbachev and the people of Eastern Europe for ending the conflict.

Chapters 10 through 12 describe how, in Reagan's absence from public life, conservative politicians attempted to claim that they represented the Reagan legacy. From Reagan's departure from the political scene in 1994 to his death in 2004, his legacy was at the center of the nation's political discourse. During the key elections of 1994, 1996, and 2000, conservatives attempted to frame each contest as an opportunity to continue the Reagan Revolution, acknowledging that the fortieth president had left some business unfinished. During these elections, however, Reagan's legacy was altered and what it meant to be a Reagan conservative changed. The process of determining Reagan's legacy, however, provided conservatives a common language, policy prescriptions, and identity. Chapters 10 and 12 focus on how the Reagan legacy evolved during the elections of 1994, 1996, and 2000. Chapter 11 traces how conservative activists began to build memorials to President Reagan—both in print and in marble. Specifically, this chapter explores the importance of Dinesh D'Souza's *Ronald Reagan: How an Ordinary Man Became an Extraordinary Leader* and details the debate over changing the name of Washington National Airport to Reagan Washington National Airport. During the political battles of the 1990s and early 2000s, conservatives reforged Reagan's legacy. Over time, however, this legacy building led to the creation of the Reagan myth. By the time of his funeral, Reagan had won the Cold War and many conservatives labeled his achievements as providential.[32]

Chapters 13 and 14 explore the development of the myth that Reagan was successful because of his dogmatic commitment to conservative principles. Drawing on a mixture of conservative politicians and commentators, these chapters trace that myth from the 2004 Republican National Convention to its culmination during the 2016 election. Chapters 13 and 14 trace the development of the Reagan myth and also track the rightward trajectory of the GOP from 2004 to the present.[33] Interestingly, the more time that passes, the more principled Reagan becomes in the minds of his acolytes. In trying to emulate the mythological Reagan, as opposed to the actual man, the GOP has forgotten many of the qualities that made Reagan a successful politician and an effective leader, such as his ability to compromise and his ability to appeal to moderates. The result of this process has led conservatives to oppose compromise, to embrace a more polarizing political discourse, and has resulted in the party's inability to govern effectively.[34] Furthermore, conservatives' embrace of the Reagan myth contributed to the GOP's crushing defeats in the 2008 and 2012 elections.

In 2016, rather than embracing conservative principles, Donald Trump won the presidency without invoking the Reagan legacy or myth. The future of conservatism is unclear following Trump's victory, as is Reagan's role in shaping the future of the GOP. Indeed, Trump's success, at least in part, was the result of his addressing the pressing issues facing the nation in a way that did not adhere to conservative orthodoxy. Perhaps the 2016 election will mark a demarcation point when conservatives quit asking "what would Reagan do" and instead began to ponder how conservative principles can be applied to an ever-changing world. Or, if Trump fails in the eyes of conservatives, perhaps the Reagan legacy will become even more critical to the identity of the Republican Party and the conservative movement. Only time will tell, but it seems clear that Reagan will continue to be an important symbol in American politics for years to come.

PART I: CONSERVATIVE FRUSTRATION WITH REAGAN, 1945–1988

1. The Origins and Evolution of Reagan's Economic Policies

Ronald Reagan smiled as he and Nancy were rushed past a group of protesters and into the Mayflower Hotel in Washington, DC. It was March 20, 1981, and a conservative had finally captured the White House. For the first time ever, a president would address the annual banquet of the Conservative Political Action Conference (CPAC). In past years, Reagan had come to CPAC to rub elbows with the nation's most powerful conservatives, and the attendees had spoken freely with him about their ideas, goals, and aspirations. This night, however, was different. The guests entered a separate room for a private meeting with the Reagans. Many were nervous, and most were quiet. As a result, the Reagans found themselves in a room alone with thirty minutes until the scheduled dinner. Nancy requested that the meal be moved up; the staff sprang into action, and a few minutes later the Reagans entered the grand ballroom. "Hail to the Chief" rang out as the president and first lady made their way into the room. Tears flowed, and the atmosphere was jubilant. To those present, forty years of hard work had been vindicated: it seemed conservatism was triumphant.[1]

Reagan took the stage to euphoric applause. He greeted his fellow "truth seekers" who had "held fast" to their vision for America, declaring that the victory of conservatism was "not so much a victory of politics" but rather "of ideas." He credited Henry Hazlitt, Russell Kirk, James Burnham, Ludwig von Mises, Friedrich A. Hayek, and Milton Friedman for shaping "so much of our thoughts." Reagan explained that those who believed in the "supremacy of the state" would be remembered "for their role in a sad, rather bizarre chapter in human history" in which "the largest planned economy in the world has to buy food elsewhere or its people would starve." The speech ended with a call to action: "If we carry the day and turn the tide, we can hope that as long as men speak of freedom and those who have protected it, they will remember us, and they will say, 'Here were the brave and here their place of honor.'"[2]

Although conservatives had high hopes for a Reagan presidency in 1981, by the fall of 1982 many questioned whether the president had abandoned his small-government principles.[3] Elected on a platform that pledged to get inflation under control, cut taxes, and revitalize America's image abroad, Reagan discovered that delivering on his campaign promises was difficult. Furthermore, the supply-side vision of cutting taxes to revitalize the economy clashed with fiscal conservatives' almost doctrinaire belief in balanced budgets. Combined with Reagan's insistence on revitalizing the US military through dramatic increases in military spending, the tax cuts made balancing the budget difficult. As a result, by the middle of the 1980s, fiscal conservatives found themselves disillusioned with Reagan and his inability or unwillingness to propose, let alone enact, a balanced budget.[4]

Historians have often assumed that Reagan's election marked the triumph of conservative ideals.[5] On further inspection, however, Reagan was unable to pacify, let alone satisfy, fiscal conservatives. The high point of the Reagan presidency, in regard to his conservative economic achievements, took place in 1981 when Congress passed the Economic Recovery Tax Act. Conservatives praised Reagan as a tax cutter and looked forward to economic growth, balanced budgets, and a continuation of his small-government economic policies.[6] In 1982, Reagan joined with them to push for a balanced-budget amendment to the Constitution. Its failure demonstrated to conservatives that revolutionizing Washington would be more difficult than they had initially thought. Reeling from the balanced-budget defeat, conservatives were infuriated by Reagan's support for tax increases in 1982 to make up for budget shortfalls. Conservatives accused the president of reneging on his fiscal principles and lamented the fact that the economy had yet to improve.[7] Even when the economy recovered in 1983 and 1984, conservatives condemned Reagan for not doing more to balance the budget.[8] Budget battles between Reagan and conservatives became a staple of Reagan's second term, and when Reagan made his final address to the nation in January 1989 he lamented that he was not able to do more to bring the budget into balance.[9] In short, far from achieving their agenda, conservatives spent the 1980s fighting with Reagan and complaining about the perceived fiscal irresponsibility of his administration.[10]

Despite conservatives' concerns, there was much more continuity between conservatives and Reagan on fiscal issues than on social or foreign policy. This was in large part due to Reagan's insistence that the economy be issue number one in his administration.[11] By the end of Reagan's first term, his tax cuts and increases in military spending, along with the Federal Reserve's policy that reined in inflation, produced a strong economic recovery.[12] Some conservatives still complained that Reagan was running massive deficits and attempted to force the president to cut spending. The complaints of budget hawks, however, paled in comparison to conservatives who prioritized social issues and believed that Reagan was overemphasizing economics at the expense of the issues they cared about the most. Many of Reagan's fiercest critics were members of the New Right, whose primary goal was to see the restoration of Judeo-Christian values in American society. Finally, Reagan's willingness to compromise, even on some of his core principles (such as his belief that lower taxes increased production and encouraged economic growth), demonstrates that he was not rigidly conservative but rather was a pragmatic conservative who did what was necessary to govern effectively. Years after Reagan left office, conservatives would reimagine Reagan as an unyielding fiscal conservative as they began to aggrandize the president's already impressive economic record.

In 1945, most Americans, including Ronald Reagan, did not unequivocally support the free enterprise system. Following World War II, Keynesian economics—credited at the time for overcoming the Great Depression—was accepted by a majority of both Republicans and Democrats.[13] Only a few politicians and academics broke ranks from the consensus that encouraged persistent government spending and regulation. The mainstream of American economic thought generally dismissed this small group of dissenters. According to historian George H. Nash, "for those Americans who believed in the creed of old-fashioned, classical, nineteenth-century, liberal individualism, 1945 was especially lonely, uncompromising, and bleak."[14]

Although the future looked uninviting for proponents of the free market, they soon discovered an articulate advocate in F. A. Hayek.[15] Hayek was an Austrian-born economist who moved to Britain in 1931 to teach at the London School of Economics.[16] During the Second World War, his book *The Road to Serfdom* (1944) became a fiscal conservative call to arms. Hayek stated the case against centralization and emphatically declared that both fascism and communism were the outcome "of the same tendencies"—namely government control of the means of production.[17] Due to British paper shortages, Hayek dubbed *The Road to Serfdom* as "that unobtainable book."[18] In the United States, however, it was a different story. A year after its original release, *Reader's Digest* published more than a million copies of the condensed version for the Book of the Month Club. Almost overnight, Hayek had "skyrocketed to national prominence."[19] Millions of Americans first discovered

Hayek through this abbreviated version that preserved his larger arguments and presented the core of Hayek's beliefs. As Nash has argued, the publication made clear that classical liberalism had "acquired an articulate voice again," and conservatives rejoiced that "at last they had a champion who made the enemy squirm."[20]

Ronald Reagan was one of millions who read *The Road to Serfdom* after its release in 1944.[21] Although remaining a committed Democrat, by the early 1950s Reagan came to identify the state's control of citizens and the economy as the primary problem in America. In 1945 and 1946, Reagan traveled around California giving speeches for progressive organizations such as the American Veterans Committee. His speeches focused on the postwar world, and he always denounced the evils of fascism. One day he decided, "at the suggestion of a minister," to add a paragraph at the end of his speech condemning totalitarian communist regimes as well. Suddenly, the audience that had cheered as Reagan lambasted Mussolini "sat sullen and silent." Reagan realized at that moment that the people he associated himself with—mainly New Deal liberals—were "curiously one-minded."[22]

Reagan's skepticism of centralized power grew during the 1950s.[23] In the fall of 1954, *GE Theater*, a nine o'clock Sunday-night radio and TV show on CBS, asked Ronald Reagan to be its host. *GE Theater* was immensely popular and became America's top-rated Sunday prime-time show. Reagan's role went beyond appearing on air; he was also contracted to tour GE's plants and give a series of speeches to promote the ideas of conservative free enterprise.[24] His work ethic made a strong impression on the president of General Electric, Ralph Cordiner, who was surprised by Reagan's habit of personally researching and preparing the remarks he delivered to the workers. According to Cordiner, Reagan was a "student" who did not "appear before an audience, write a speech, deliver a paper or even have a discussion with a very small group unless he has researched and reviewed the subject."[25]

Reagan's conversion to fiscal conservatism was cemented during his time at General Electric. Historian Thomas W. Evans argues that GE and, more specifically, its vice president Lemuel Boulware are to credit for Reagan's conversion to conservatism. Boulware created an educational program for the employees of GE that included writers such as Henry Hazlitt. Part of Reagan's job was to understand Boulware's program, and as a result he read Hazlitt's *Economics in One Lesson* as well as other fiscal-conservative books and pamphlets to prepare for his appearances. According to Evans, during this time, "Hazlitt's preachings became an important part of Reagan's economic philosophy."[26] Boulware served an important role in introducing Reagan to libertarian writers of political economy, and these libertarian economists had a profound effect on Boulware's own intellectual development. In fact, according to Kim Phillips-Fein, "Boulware was deeply influenced by writers like von Hayek and von Mises, whose books he owned."[27] In short, while businessmen were important to the rise of fiscal conservatism, they, and Reagan, were influenced by and found intellectual justification for their views in the works of free market economists.

Reagan continued to work for General Electric until 1962, during which time he completed his transformation from an opponent of totalitarianism in general to an advocate of fiscal conservatism. This was most evident in his speeches in which he emphasized lower taxes as part of ensuring the American dream. Speaker of the House Tip O'Neill later quipped that Reagan came to embrace low taxes only because he found himself paying high rates while an actor in Hollywood. Regardless of his personal interest in lower taxes, Reagan framed his opposition to high rates with principled free market rhetoric.[28] For instance, in his January 27, 1958, remarks before the House Ways and Means Committee, Reagan condemned the tax rates he paid in Hollywood as "unrealistic, confiscatory, and contrary to the principles of free enterprise." The individual freedom that Reagan had championed in 1947 as a critic of centralization had become by 1958 a fervent distaste for what he viewed as unreasonably high tax rates. In his remarks to the committee, Reagan warned that high tax rates "stifle and reduce overall production." Putting his argument into personal terms, he explained that the artist paying seventy-five to ninety-one cents on the dollar either raises his or her price dramatically or turns down the picture entirely. According to Reagan, the confiscatory tax rates in the United States resulted in unemployment in the motion picture industry and led to "a loss of tax revenue to the Government."[29] As early as 1958, Reagan was championing tax reductions as a means to increase production and overall economic output—an idea that would become central to supply-side economics.

During the late 1950s and early 1960s, Reagan did not just praise conservative principles; he also condemned Keynesian policy and endorsed legislation to reduce the size of government. In 1959, in a speech entitled "Business, Ballots, and Bureaus," Reagan complained about the burden of regulation by explaining that in his lifetime the tax code had gone "from thirty-one words to more than four hundred and forty thousand words." Reagan lambasted those who wanted to "soak the rich" to cure deficits. Reagan proclaimed that "if the Federal Government should confiscate all income over $6,000, the increased revenue wouldn't pay the interest on the national debt." During the speech, Reagan delved deep into the numbers and demonstrated the negative effects of high inflation and high taxes on Americans. He also contested the commonly held Keynesian view that unbalanced budgets were acceptable. Instead, Reagan proclaimed, "we must end deficit spending and reduce the fodder upon which government has fed and grown beyond the consent of the governed." Reagan also endorsed the 1957 Sadlak-Herlong bill to reduce taxes on top earners from 91 percent to 47 percent. Reagan concluded with a call to action, exclaiming that "freedom is never more than one generation away from extinction."[30] In "Business, Ballots, and Bureaus," Reagan adopted a more combative stance and clearly articulated his opposition to Keynesian economic policies. In fact, he even went so far as to equate freedom with lower taxes. By 1961, when John F. Kennedy came into the White House, Ronald Reagan was one of the most effective spokesmen for the free market creed.

Leonard Read, the president of the Foundation for Economic Education (FEE), was so impressed with Reagan's "Business, Ballots, and Bureaus" that he contacted Reagan personally. Read explained that his reason for writing was "that the thoughts you expressed are strikingly consistent with what we are up to here at FEE." Read sent Reagan a free copy of the organization's publication, the *Freeman*, and told the actor that he "would consider it a privilege to send [Reagan] everything" produced by FEE, including the journal and other educational materials.[31] Reagan responded by subscribing to FEE's mailing list in 1961.[32] Reagan developed a relationship with FEE and even attended a lecture by Read, where he asked "some pointed questions about the freedom philosophy and its application to the problems of America."[33] Furthermore, Reagan became a regular reader of the *Freeman*, and it is likely that the journal's content helped shape his opinions concerning free markets and the role of the state. More telling, however, is that Read, a leading libertarian intellectual, reached out to Reagan after recognizing his potential to understand and articulate the ideas promoted by FEE as early as 1960.

Arizona senator Barry Goldwater's nomination as the Republican candidate for president in 1964 demonstrated the growing power of fiscal conservatives within the party. On October 27, just a week before the general election, the Goldwater campaign agreed to allow Reagan to deliver a nationally televised speech later known as "A Time for Choosing." Reagan opened the nationwide broadcast by attacking President Lyndon B. Johnson's claim that Americans had "never had it so good." Reagan, who had switched his voter registration from Democrat to Republican in 1962, complained that the Democratic Party had left him and was on its way to becoming the "labor Socialist Party of England."[34] He insisted that present government spending levels were dangerous and that the answer to every social problem was not a government program. Instead, Reagan put the choice Americans faced in black-and-white terms: between individualism—where a small noninvasive government would lead to "man's old-aged dream, the ultimate individual freedom consistent with law and order"—and collectivism, which would lead "to the ant heap of totalitarianism."[35] He condemned the inefficiencies of government and argued that "for three decades, we've sought to solve the problems of unemployment through government planning, and the more the plans fail, the more the planners plan." Reagan attacked Social Security, urging that Americans be allowed to invest in a private plan that would enable them to retire with twice the nest egg they would receive from the government entitlement. He spoke of the great overhead in welfare, providing numbers demonstrating that recipients received only 13 percent of overall welfare spending. The problem with liberals, Reagan insisted, "is not that they're ignorant; it's just that they know so much that isn't so."[36] According to Reagan, liberal policies, while perhaps well meaning, often did not account for the unintended consequences that inevitably resulted from changing incentives. Such policies, in Reagan's view, were shortsighted and ultimately harmful to the very people liberals wanted to assist.

Viewers on both sides of the political aisle agreed that the speech was well-delivered and effective. Reagan concluded with a call to action, exclaiming, "You and I have a rendezvous with destiny. We'll preserve for our children this, the last best hope of man on earth, or we'll sentence them to take the last step into a thousand years of darkness."[37] In a single speech, Reagan detailed a free market vision for the country much like that expounded in the *Freeman*. "A Time for Choosing" was radical in its belief in the rights of the individual—so radical that many of its themes would be left behind in later years as Reagan faced the realities of governance. Reagan's speech demonstrated, in the words of Lee Edwards, a journalist and the first biographer of Reagan, "more than a superficial knowledge of ideas"; much of the speech's content was "quite profound."[38] *Time* magazine labeled Reagan's speech the "one bright spot in a dismal campaign," and it was not long before Reagan received a string of inquiries about his political intentions.[39] While Goldwater's crusade suffered a crushing defeat, Reagan's performance launched him onto the path to national political prominence.

In early October 1965, Lee Edwards and his wife, Anne, spent two days traveling across California with the Reagans.[40] Reagan had decided that the political waters were the right temperature and jumped into the governor's race. As Reagan spoke before various groups, Edwards was impressed. Reagan had "a good grip on the issues" and had solutions for "California's more pressing" political and social problems. On the afternoon of the second day, Reagan took the couple to his home overlooking Hollywood. Waiting in Reagan's office, while the Reagans prepared iced tea, Edwards browsed through the soon-to-be governor's bookshelves. Although Edwards had heard "A Time for Choosing" and understood that Reagan "obviously had some appreciation for conservatism," he was amazed to find "serious works of history, the west, of California, books on politics, and books on economics." The books that Edwards remembers being on the shelves were *Economics in One Lesson* by Henry Hazlitt, *Witness* by Whitaker Chambers, *The Law* by Frédéric Bastiat, and *The Road to Serfdom* by F. A. Hayek. Thinking that perhaps Reagan simply owned the books but had not read them, Edwards pulled *The Road to Serfdom* from the shelf and discovered that the book had been "underlined, annotated, dog eared." After interviewing Reagan, Edwards concluded that Reagan "was a thinking conservative and he had arrived at his positions himself through his own study and his own research."[41]

In searching for policy initiatives while running for governor of California, Reagan discovered the work of another libertarian economist—Milton Friedman. Friedman had joined the faculty at the University of Chicago in 1946 but had focused on academic debates rather than public policy. That changed when F. A. Hayek joined the faculty at Chicago in 1950. According to Friedman, his interest in policy was "reinforced by Hayek's powerful book *The Road to Serfdom*, by [his] attendance at the first meeting of the Mont Pelerin Society in 1947, and by discussions with Hayek after he joined the university faculty in 1950."[42] In 1962, Friedman published *Capitalism and Freedom*, which argued that the proper role of government was limited and its primary focus should be to "protect our freedom both from the enemies outside our gates and from our fellow-citizens."[43] The book outlined the government's role in regulating monopolies, distributing licenses, funding education, encouraging a sound monetary policy, and ending discrimination (in many of these cases Friedman argued that government had a very limited role). While running for governor, Reagan read Friedman's *Capitalism and Freedom*.[44] Although it is unclear what initial impact the book had on Reagan, when the two men met for the first time in 1967 Friedman came away impressed with Reagan's views on education. He happily recalled "that Reagan had thought the issue through and was fully aware of the inequity of taxing those who did not go to state universities for the benefit of those who did."[45] Perhaps Friedman was pleased because Reagan's positions reflected some of the arguments the economist made in chapter 6 of *Capitalism and Freedom*, "The Role of Government in Education."

Once elected governor of California in 1966, Reagan found that effective governance meant moderating his conservative principles. Confronted with deep deficits, Reagan did what he had to do to get the state's finances under control. He froze the hiring of government employees and signed a record $1 billion tax increase.[46] Reagan also faced social unrest during his administration. He cracked down on student protests at the University of California's Berkeley campus, made it illegal to carry a loaded gun on a public highway, and signed a bill that legalized abortions under particular circumstances.[47] During his second term as governor, Reagan attempted to return to his free market principles by supporting legislation that tightened eligibility for welfare in California, but even then, he increased the benefits for those who qualified. Furthermore, Reagan doubled public spending during his time as governor and did not decrease the size of the bureaucracy.[48] His most conservative fiscal-policy initiative was Proposition 1, a proposal to limit the total amount the state could spend in any given year to 8.3 percent of the personal income of Californians.[49] Reagan asked Friedman to travel with him across California to promote the initiative. During the campaign, Friedman "talked freely" with Reagan "about both his life and his views." According to Friedman, it was "an unforgettable experience." On the final day, when he was asked by a reporter whether he would support Reagan for president in 1976, Friedman replied that he would.[50] Proposition 1 ultimately failed, and the Reagan governorship was a mixed bag of success and failure for fiscal conservatives. His time as governor also revealed that while Reagan held conservative principles, he was willing to compromise to achieve his policy goals.

While Reagan was experimenting with free market ideas in California, a group of young intellectuals were proposing a radical new approach to address the economic malaise of the 1970s.[51] The energy crisis, combined with runaway inflation, high unemployment, and persistent economic hardships, plagued Presidents Richard Nixon, Gerald Ford, and Jimmy Carter. While all three embraced status quo Keynesian solutions, Dr. Robert A. Mundell and Dr. Arthur Laffer were creating the intellectual foundation for what would become Reaganomics.[52] Since the early 1960s, Mundell had written about the need to cut taxes to provide incentives for producers.[53] He and Laffer argued that the way to curb inflation was to produce more goods, not less, and emphasized the drag America's high tax rates had on producers.[54] In 1971, Laffer befriended a young journalist from the *National Observer*, Jude Wanniski, who two years later moved to the *Wall Street Journal*.[55] Wanniski quickly became an advocate of what he termed the "the Mundell-Laffer hypothesis," and he used his editorials at the *Wall Street Journal* to advocate lower tax rates as a means to spur production and relieve the nation of its economic woes.[56] During his time at the newspaper, Wanniski had lively debates with Robert Bartley, the editor of the *Wall Street Journal* editorial page, over the merits of supply-side economics. Originally, Bartley, an old-school fiscal conservative, argued that tax cuts, while potentially spurring economic growth, also led to higher deficits.[57]

Bartley's conversations about supply-side economics went beyond Wanniski. He and Alan Reynolds, a contributor to the libertarian publication *Reason* and William F. Buckley's conservative *National Review*, corresponded frequently about the pros and cons of tax cuts. Bartley's conversations with Reynolds led him to fully endorse supply-side economics and to use the *Wall Street Journal*'s editorial page to advocate tax cuts.[58] By 1976, Mundell's and Laffer's ideas were starting to gain powerful allies who would popularize their complicated economic theory and deliver it to a desperate audience: the American people.

While Laffer and Mundell were mobilizing a small nucleus of believers, young conservative tax cutters were establishing themselves in Congress—the most prominent being Jack Kemp.[59] Kemp was heavily influenced by the libertarian writings of Ayn Rand, Barry Goldwater, Milton Friedman, Ludwig von Mises, and F. A. Hayek.[60] He had worked for Reagan's gubernatorial campaign in 1966, while he was still quarterbacking in the American Football League. After he retired from the sport, Kemp ran for Congress, won, and hired young conservative activists, the most ardent of whom was Paul Craig Roberts.[61] Although Kemp was enthusiastic, he found that there was bipartisan opposition to his ideas. In 1974, Kemp's savings and investment act—an act aimed at doubling the investment tax credit—was defeated by Republicans who feared it would increase the national debt.[62]

Wanniski and Laffer saw Kemp as an ally, and before long were holding regular meetings with him and other like-minded congressmen such as David Stockman. Stockman, also influenced by libertarian economists, was appointed to the US House Commerce Committee, where he "did battle" with the "monster" of Keynesian government control "every day, hacking away at it with a sword forged in the free market smithy of F.A. Hayek."[63] Kemp introduced Stockman to supply-side economics, and the two formed a friendship and an alliance in Congress. According to Stockman, he, Kemp, Laffer, and Wanniski turned Kemp's office into "a kind of postgraduate seminar in supply-side economics." In that office, these free market crusaders "hammered out counter positions to every statist proposal or initiative Carter or Congress came up with."[64]

Even this tight group of like-minded tax cutters, however, had significant disagreements, particularly on the question of whether supply-side tax cuts would increase revenues. Wanniski and Laffer were bullish, arguing that the tax cuts would create enough economic growth to pay for themselves. Others, such as Roberts, believed that economic activity caused by the rate cuts would make up for only part of the lost revenue. Kemp agreed with Laffer and Wanniski that the tax cuts would pay for themselves just as, in his view, the Kennedy tax cuts had paid for themselves twenty years prior.[65] In a 1978 profile for *Fortune*, Kemp declared that he did not "worship at the shrine of the balanced budget."[66] To many traditional conservatives, such a statement was akin to sacrilege.[67] Traditional conservatives' economic policy centered on tight monetary policy, decreasing government spending, and when necessary increasing taxes to ensure a balanced budget.[68] Throughout the 1980s, the supply-side vision of cutting taxes to spur economic growth would conflict with these basic beliefs. Even among supply-side advocates, the question of which to prioritize, tax cuts or a balanced budget, would cause intense debate and disagreement.[69]

David Stockman advocated supply-side tax cuts, but he also wanted to balance the budget and was more willing than the others to cut spending. During the Carter years, Stockman partnered with Congressman Phil Gramm, a Democrat from Texas, to put together the bipartisan coalition for fiscal responsibility plan. The plan was similar to what would become the first Reagan budget, and the politicking for it gave Congress an introduction to the ideas that later came to be known as Reaganomics. Stockman and Gramm worked around the clock to get fifty congressmen to sign the budget plan. According to Stockman, the bipartisan plan brought together all the important political blocs in the House and "formed the nucleus of what would become the Reagan coalition."[70] Stockman's efforts to cut spending were in some ways opposed to the supply-side doctrine of achieving a balanced budget through economic growth. Stockman and Kemp represented two sides of the conservative vision for reviving the American economy. Both wanted lower taxes, economic growth, and a balanced budget. Disagreements about how to achieve these results, however, would create tension and dissatisfaction among conservatives during Reagan's presidency.

While Jack Kemp and David Stockman were pushing for tax and spending cuts in Congress, Laffer moved to California and formed a close friendship with Reagan—a relationship that soon established Reagan as an advocate of supply-side economics.[71] In January 1977, in one of Reagan's radio addresses, all of which he wrote and researched himself, Reagan condemned the estate tax and called for indexing tax rates so they adjusted to the inflation rate, proclaiming that "indexing is an idea whose time has not only come, it is overdue." Later that year, Reagan endorsed Kemp's efforts, arguing that his "bill would keep the inc[ome] tax progressive by cutting substantially the inc[ome] tax across the board in every bracket. People would have more of their money to spend as they wish [and] there would be more for investment to expand our industry. And gov[ernment] would reduce the deficit."[72] While embracing the supply-side view that tax cuts were essential for reviving the economy, Reagan also clung to the old fiscally conservative belief in a balanced budget. Drawing on the optimistic projections of Wanniski, Laffer, and Kemp, Reagan believed that the Kemp tax cuts would lead to such great economic activity that they would help, not hinder, in balancing the budget.[73] This interpretation allowed him to gloss over any inconsistencies or tensions that existed between conservatives who desired balanced budgets and those who pushed for tax cuts.

Although Reagan was already moving toward tax cuts as a means to encourage investment and entrepreneurship, the advent of a grass roots tax revolt reinforced his views.[74] A little over a year after Laffer arrived at the University of Southern California, Howard Jarvis introduced Proposition 13, a proposal to limit property taxes to 1 percent of market value.[75] Reagan embraced this movement with enthusiasm. According to Laffer, "Proposition 13 was enormously influential on [Reagan]. He saw a tax cut pass in a landslide against virtually every politician . . . and he watched the results of Proposition

13 when the economy took off like a jack rabbit."[76] After the success of Proposition 13, Reagan's support for Kemp-Roth appeared justified. By 1978, Reagan had the proof he needed to champion supply-side economics in his bid for the White House.[77]

President Carter struggled from 1976 to 1980 to combat the economic stagnation and inflation that gripped the country. Economic events confounded the old Keynesian tenet claiming a trade-off existed between inflation and unemployment—meaning that as inflation increased, unemployment would decline. Under Carter, inflation jumped from 4.8 percent in 1976 to 12 percent in 1980, and the unemployment rate spiked to almost 8 percent at the time of the 1980 election.[78] Stockman explained that by 1980, "the reigning Keynesian economic model of the era was being so massively invalidated by empirical events that its practitioners—especially the Carter Administration economists—had been reduced to offering blatherings and gibberish in lieu of analysis."[79] Searching for an answer to the economic downturn, Carter turned to fiscal conservatism. He appointed Paul Volcker, who, as chairman of the Federal Reserve, was determined to contract the money supply to bring inflation under control. Furthermore, Carter deregulated the airline industry, the transportation system, and key areas in the financial sector.[80]

Despite these policy initiatives, American discontent with Carter increased. The 1970s witnessed social unrest, the Watergate scandal, stagflation, and the powerlessness of the United States in the Iran hostage crisis. The cumulative effect led many Americans to accept the message of small-government individualism and supply-side economics. What began with Mundell and Laffer being ridiculed by elite economists in the early 1970s was a mass movement by the time voters cast ballots in November 1980.[81] When Reagan was sworn in, the *Wall Street Journal* editorial page featured regular defenses of supply-side economics, Jack Kemp and a significant number of other congressmen were pushing for marginal tax reductions in the House, and antitax movements were gaining traction across the nation. Although Reagan had a mandate to experiment with supply-side policies, the differences between supply-side advocates who emphasized economic growth and traditional fiscal conservatives who prioritized a balanced budget as the be-all and end-all of economic policy were brushed aside. Furthermore, Reagan's insistence on increasing military spending made balancing the budget a difficult task and earned him the ire of some fiscal conservatives.[82]

2. The Battle for Fiscal Conservatism: Supply-Siders v. Budget Hawks

Ronald Reagan wanted to cut taxes, reduce inflation, and decrease spending once elected president. Reagan's priority upon taking office was to get tax cuts through Congress, an act that conservatives believed would reinvigorate the economy. Reagan also wanted to turn over government programs to the states: what he called "new federalism."[1] Additionally, conservatives expected Reagan to propose alternatives to entitlement programs such as Social Security.[2] In short, conservatives and Reagan himself hoped to embark on a revolution to scale back the size and scope of government. Much to conservatives' chagrin, however, Reagan's first two years were spent fighting a worsening economy, a Democratic majority in Congress, and Senate Republicans who were far from revolutionaries.

As soon as the election was over, Reagan began pushing his economic agenda, arguing that "nothing was more important than getting the tax and spending cuts through Congress."[3] With the transition, and much of the administration focusing on the tax cuts, he appointed David Stockman as the director of the Office of Management and Budget.[4] Stockman immediately set to work on cutting government spending. The budget had been in deep deficit when Reagan took office, and his proposed tax cuts and increases in military expenditures meant that real spending cuts were necessary for the administration to deliver on its goal of balancing the budget by 1985.[5]

When Stockman brought his proposed budget cuts before the cabinet he faced fierce opposition. One by one, Stockman and his budget working group had to "brow-beat" the cabinet "into accepting the cuts." Stockman quickly realized that the cabinet did not consist of "revolutionaries" and that they would "largely ignore" any pruning of their departments.[6] By the first week of February, the budget working group had cut, at least on paper, $220 billion from the budget. Predictably, the reaction from the Democrat-controlled House to news of the proposed cuts was not positive. Stockman later acknowledged that he had not understood "how little weight the paper recommendations of a presidential budget carr[ied] on Capitol Hill—particularly when you've got a whole department of bureaucrats, including the top one, working for the other side."[7] In his memoir, Lyn Nofziger—who served as press secretary when Reagan was governor and was the assistant to the president for political affairs during Reagan's first year in the White House—lamented that many in the administration simply "didn't have the courage to fight for the things we came to Washington to fight for."[8] Just a month after Reagan took office, it was becoming apparent that opponents of conservative fiscal reforms, both in the administration and in Congress, were going to make balancing the budget extremely difficult.[9]

In early February, Stockman still had not provided Reagan with the necessary numbers for an upcoming speech later in the month. Indeed, the administration was dragging its feet on cutting spending. For instance, the cabinet had not addressed the necessary cuts to Social Security, Medicare, Head Start, and Supplemental Security Income for the poor, disabled, and the elderly.[10] Stockman understood that the only way to cut taxes, increase military spending, and still arrive at a balanced budget was to make cuts to middle-class entitlements. Unfortunately for Stockman, not everyone in the administration was keen on cutting spending, let alone entitlements that millions of Americans benefited from daily.[11] A misunderstanding in a cabinet meeting in early February led to the *New York Times* running a story the next day that started with the lead: "President Reagan's abrupt announcement yesterday sparing seven basic social programs from budget cuts . . ."[12] With no consensus on what should be cut, Stockman was forced to include $44 billion in "future cuts" in the figures for the president's economic address.[13] Furthermore, the budget projections assumed economic growth of 5.2 percent and an inflation rate of 7.7 percent—neither of which turned out to be accurate.[14] The final result of this confusion was President Reagan's address to the nation on February 18, in which he promised to cut taxes, cut wasteful spending, cut inflation, and balance the budget by 1985.[15] To many Americans, and indeed many conservatives, it must have seemed that Reagan had figured out how they could have their cake, by enacting tax cuts, and eat it too, by also having a balanced budget. The desire to both cut taxes and balance the budget created massive unrest in conservative ranks in the years to come.

As David Stockman fought to cut spending, President Reagan faced tough opposition from both Democrats and Republicans to his tax cuts.[16] Progress was slow in February and March as the Democratic Speaker of the House, Tip O'Neill, and his caucus were fighting the president's economic program. Likewise, Senate Republicans, concerned about potential deficits, were holding up the process. In response, Reagan and his Republican allies attempted to assemble a coalition with conservative Southern Democrats, but O'Neill frustrated their efforts. Everything changed on March 30 when John Hinckley Jr. attempted to assassinate the president. Reagan was rushed to the hospital, where he had an emergency operation. Reagan handled the ordeal with dignity and humor.[17] He pulled through the surgery and the next day signed a piece of legislation from his hospital bed causing headlines such as "Reagan Is Recovering, Signs New Dairy Law, Quips with Aides, Docs" to appear across the country.[18] The administration attempted to project a quick recovery, but in truth Reagan had almost died.[19] O'Neill visited the president and in his memoirs described the president's condition: "I suspect that in the first day or two after the shooting he was probably closer to death than most of us realized. If he hadn't been so strong and hardy, it could have been all over."[20]

Instead, Reagan recovered and found himself in a position of political strength. In the aftermath of the attack, his popularity soared "from 59 percent in mid-March to 73 percent within days of the shooting." Reagan maintained the public's support, and in May his approval rating was still in the high sixties.[21] Throughout April, support for the president's economic policy was overwhelming. The average of the NBC, ABC, and CBS polls showed 58 percent in favor of the Reagan tax cuts and 17 percent opposed.[22] Reagan was determined to capitalize on the opportunity.

Reagan decided to make his move on April 28, in his first speech following the shooting. As the president walked into the House chamber to address a joint session of Congress, he was met with a standing ovation. Reagan began by thanking the American people for their well-wishing and prayers. He explained that the tragedy was not evidence of a sick society. Instead, Reagan insisted that the incident demonstrated the resolve of the American people. He exclaimed that the sacrifices of those public servants who took bullets showed why "people like us [are] so proud to be Americans and so very proud of our fellow citizens." After addressing the tragedy, Reagan pivoted to the state of the economy. He charged that since the election, the government had done little, and insisted that "six months is long enough. The American people now want us to act and not in half-measures." Reagan concluded his remarks by prodding Congress: "All we need to do is act, and the time for action is now."[23] House majority leader Jim Wright wrote in his diary the night of the president's address that "we've been outflanked and outgunned."[24] Reagan knew he had the upper hand and after the speech joked "that reception was almost worth getting shot for."[25]

From April to July, Reagan fought for his economic package of tax cuts and spending reductions. According to House members, they heard more from Reagan in four months than they had from Carter in four years, and the grassroots pressure on O'Neill to put Reagan's proposals to a vote was mounting. Republicans were also using the rhetoric of John F. Kennedy against the Democrats. In April, Reagan's advisers released a memo entitled "Chronology and Key Elements of the 1964 Tax Cuts." It contained statements by sitting House Democrats in support of the Kennedy tax cuts. Perhaps even more troubling for Democrats was that quotations from Kennedy sounded similar to Reagan's rhetoric. Arguing for tax reductions, Kennedy had explained that "with the present high tax encumbrances imposed upon our economy it would be difficult, if not impossible, to achieve the economic expansion necessary to provide a fully employed economy."[26] The Reagan tax bill, a variation of Kemp-Roth, mirrored the Kennedy tax cuts in that it phased in the tax cuts over a three-year period. Indeed, Kemp fancied himself as "the second JFK" for proposing the legislation.[27]

The Democrats struggled to counter the administration, and as late as June 17, 1981, they had no detailed plan to counter Kemp-Roth.[28] House Democrats presented a proposal at the end of June, but less than three weeks later Senate Democrats handed the administration a significant victory by passing an amendment fifty-seven to forty to index income tax rates (ensuring that Americans would be taxed based on their income after controlling for inflation).[29] Reagan spent much of late spring and early summer "on the telephone and in meetings trying to build a coalition."[30] He instructed Republicans to "tell me who you want me to call and I'll take care of it." Responding to the last statement, O'Neill said he "would have given [his] right arm to hear those words from Jimmy Carter."[31]

O'Neill presented Reagan's tax policy, the Economic Recovery Tax Act, for a vote on July 29, and it passed overwhelmingly in both chambers.[32] Its passage was the largest tax cut in American history, reducing marginal income taxes by 23 percent and also providing significant tax relief for businesses and the oil industry.[33] After the victory, President Reagan spoke briefly to the press: "We have made a new beginning. We're back on the right road. We're making progress."[34] After his statement Reagan joined his senior staff, which included Vice President George Bush, Treasury Secretary Donald Regan, and David

Stockman, in the Oval Office. They cracked open a bottle of champagne to celebrate the momentous victory.[35]

Conservatives across the country also celebrated. For the moment, Reagan was their champion. Tax cuts were an integral part of the conservative agenda, but they were not the only issue or the most important to some conservatives.[36] Almost before the ink from Reagan's signature had dried, social conservatives began insisting that Reagan address their social agenda. School prayer, abortion, and pornography were in the New Right's crosshairs, and they expected the president, who had insisted that social issues would come after the economy was back on track, to keep his word.[37] Supply-siders, such as Kemp, worried that Reagan was going too slowly and that his economic program was not bold enough.[38] Others expressed concern about the phasing in of the tax cuts. Laffer warned Reagan after his victory that recovery might be slowed because producers would put off investment until the full range of the tax cuts went into effect in 1983.[39] In short, Laffer feared capital would stay on the sidelines while the Federal Reserve continued to contract the money supply. The result was a prolonged recession that made the 5.2 percent growth projections look like a fairy tale and placed Reagan under considerable pressure from conservatives.

In response to ballooning deficits, a continuing recession, and the prospect of a tax increase in 1982, Reagan faced opposition on the right. At the beginning of the year, forty-five conservative leaders condemned Reagan's policies as Howard Phillips, founder of the Conservative Caucus, and Richard Viguerie, publisher of *Conservative Digest*, appeared on ABC's *This Week with David Brinkley* to lambast Reagan's fiscal policies. Phillips called on Reagan to ignore aides who wanted higher taxes in 1982 as a means to reduce the deficit. Instead, he urged Reagan to cut federal spending, including Social Security's cost-of-living adjustment. Viguerie called on Reagan to "fire many of his top advisers." He said, "Reagan's rhetoric is hard, his desire is firm, but his policies are weak." He concluded that Reagan needed to "get involved in his presidency."[40] Phillips added in a separate interview that if Jimmy Carter had proposed budget deficits equal to Reagan's, "conservatives would have been up in arms." He continued, "We [conservatives] sinned by our silence during the Nixon administration . . . we ought not to sin by silence now."[41]

Conservatives in Congress heeded Phillips's suggestion, and in January and February they began to push for a balanced-budget amendment to the Constitution. The National Tax Limitation Committee (NTLC) drafted the amendment with the help of Milton Friedman and other scholars.[42] It required both that the government arrive at a balanced budget for each fiscal year and that Congress adopt a statement that "taxes cannot increase any faster than national income." The amendment also allowed Congress to waive the amendment in case of war and established that the federal government could not simply push expensive programs onto the states. The amendment was sponsored by conservative senators Strom Thurmond (R-SC) and Orrin Hatch (R-UT) and received the endorsement of many prominent conservatives representing organizations from across the country including the Moral Majority, the Heritage Foundation, the American Conservative Union, the National Association of Evangelicals, Veterans of Foreign Wars, the National Pro-Family Coalition, and the National Pro-Life PAC.[43]

The balanced-budget amendment enjoyed grassroots support from a wide range of conservative groups and businesses, and its proposal prodded Reagan to act on his conservative principles.[44] Reagan had a long history of supporting a balanced-budget amendment and had proposed a similar measure while he was governor of California in 1973.[45] Reagan, however, stayed on the sidelines at the request of the NTLC, which believed that his involvement would make the balanced-budget amendment a partisan issue.[46] Not all conservatives were convinced that Reagan should not advocate the balanced budget. Morton Blackwell, Reagan's liaison to conservatives, received one letter suggesting that Reagan's visible support for the amendment during its passage would also "be a reminder to the public of Ronald Reagan's commitment to true fiscal reform."[47] On April 29, 1982, Reagan addressed the nation about the need to rein in government spending and implement a balanced budget.[48] By the end of April, the amendment had 53 cosponsors in the Senate and 201 cosponsors in the House.[49] To be sent to the states for ratification, however, it needed a two-thirds majority in both houses.

As spring turned into summer, conservative activists began to question whether passage of the balanced-budget amendment was possible without Reagan's vocal and active support. Reagan had already called on the American people to write their representatives and urge them to support the amendment, but faced with the prospects of failure, conservative activists reached out to the administration to do more.[50] Grover Norquist, executive director of Americans for the Reagan Agenda, organized a grassroots rebellion against the

NTLC. Norquist released a memo in early June that was cosigned by the largest and most influential conservative organizations in the nation that decried the NTLC as having "no record of successful political organization."[51] Instead, Norquist insisted that "only a Presidentially-led grand coalition" could get the amendment passed. He called on Reagan to make a nationally televised speech prior to the congressional vote in which he would devote himself to the passage of the amendment.[52]

By the end of May, there was consensus among conservatives that Reagan needed to personally lead the fight for a balanced-budget amendment. While the administration had planned on Reagan fully supporting the amendment before Norquist suggested it, the vote on the fiscal year 1983 budget as well as the Memorial Day recess set them back.[53] Despite making the decision to use the presidential bully pulpit to push the amendment, the administration continued drafting memorandums on how to use Reagan effectively. In late June, the cabinet unanimously decided to schedule a speech by Reagan on the west-face Capitol steps just days before the final vote on the amendment was scheduled to take place.[54] Reagan finally delivered the speech on July 18 in the sweltering DC heat to a crowd of upward of fifteen thousand supporters. House Democratic leader Jim Wright of Texas mocked Reagan's speech, asserting that the president being for a balanced budget is "like the president of Sara Lee leading an anti-calorie crusade."[55] Shortly after Reagan delivered his speech, the Senate suspended consideration of the amendment and instead turned to a tax increase bill. Despite a July US Chamber/Gallup survey concluding that Americans supported the balanced budget by a ratio of almost three to one, Congress rejected the amendment shortly before the end of the session.[56] One conservative congressman said the opposition used "the kind of crafty tactics that gives politics a loathsome name." The vice president of the NTLC threatened that the lame duck session of Congress was "the last shot that Congress has to avoid facing a Constitutional Convention."[57] Conservatives appreciated Reagan's efforts to get the balanced-budget amendment passed; however, any goodwill that Reagan might have earned from his efforts was lost when Reagan supported a tax bill before Congress to raise taxes.[58]

In the waning days of summer, Reagan sent a new tax bill to Congress that enraged conservatives. Reagan requested an increase of $98.3 billion in taxes over three years in exchange for a disputed amount in spending cuts. Conservatives immediately rejected the measure and accused Reagan of abandoning his conservative principles.[59] Supply-side activist Paul Craig Roberts condemned the measure as "austerity with a vengeance" and as "a far cry from the supply-side policy of balancing the budget through economic growth."[60] Just weeks after fighting alongside conservatives for a balanced-budget amendment, Reagan found himself aligned with Democrats in Congress and at odds with many of his most ardent supporters.

Hoping to quell conservative resistance to the tax bill, Reagan held a meeting with his most vocal conservative critics. Far from indicating that he was backing down, the meeting was held to demonstrate that conservative opposition to Reagan's agenda "wasn't helpful" to either the president or the movement.[61] Reagan's most ardent critic in attendance was Jack Kemp. White House staff expressed great "displeasure" with Kemp and told the press that his opposition "may be an effort to position himself for a presidential run." The White House launched a full attack on Kemp to discredit the man whose tax plan gained it the admiration of conservatives just a year earlier. Assistant White House press secretary Larry Speakes publicly confirmed that "Mr. Kemp received a thorough scolding from colleagues and presidential aides during White House meetings." The White House, worried about Kemp challenging Reagan from the right or undermining the president's influence in Congress, used the meeting to demonstrate that Reagan was the leader of the Republican Party.[62] Reagan was also irritated with Kemp. In his diary, he called Kemp's opposition to the tax increase "unreasonable" and emphasized "the tax increase is the price we have to pay to get the budget cuts."[63] Reagan, unlike other, "unreasonable" supply-siders, was willing to compromise with the Democrats to achieve budget reductions.

The meeting with conservatives was designed, however, to do more than chastise Kemp: its goal was to get the original supporters of Reagan's supply-side agenda back in line. Two of Reagan's closest conservative advisers, Martin Anderson and Lyn Nofziger, as well as former Reagan Treasury Department officials Norman Ture and Paul Craig Roberts, had signed a pledge to continue to support the supply-side economic plan regardless of Reagan's intentions. Anderson, Nofziger, Ture, and Roberts, along with twenty other prominent conservatives, whom the *Washington Post* described as "the core of the original Reagan supporters," pledged to give their "best efforts to reduce spending and to oppose the tax bill now before Congress." The pledge asserted that, as "friend and supporters of Ronald Reagan," the signees "oppose the tax increase" because to "put Americans back to work, America should follow a course against high taxes and high federal spending."[64] Reagan's meeting with his conservative opposition was labeled by one press report as an "urgent conference" in which he was "firm and direct," insisting that his administration would support the tax increases. Reagan personally asked Anderson and Nofziger not to "undermine his efforts." Honoring Reagan's request, neither man was available for comment in the days following the meeting.[65]

Reagan's appeals worked on Anderson and Nofziger; however, many conservatives were still vocally opposed to the tax increases. Representative Philip Crane (R-IL), a staunch fiscal conservative, labeled the bill as an "abomination." Other conservative representatives threatened legal action, claiming that the bill did not originate in the House and was therefore unconstitutional.[66] The *Atlanta Constitution* asserted that Washington politics were turned upside down as Democrats lined up with Reagan while conservatives "pulled out all stops to defeat the tax bill."[67] Newt Gingrich (R-GA), who had formed a group in the House called the Conservative Opportunity Society to push conservative principles, asserted that the tax battle was the "opening round of a fight over the soul and future of the Republican Party" with President Reagan, presumably, on the side of moderate forces willing to compromise. When asked about the fight between Republicans, Democratic Speaker of the House Tip O'Neill replied that the GOP was "having one hell of a brawl."[68]

While the Democrats were enjoying the show, Reagan scrambled to justify tax increases to his base. Downplaying the significance of the tax bill, the administration claimed that half of the tax increases were the result of efforts to increase compliance with existing law. So in their view, the increases were not new taxes. Unfortunately for Reagan, conservatives did not accept the president's line of reasoning. Their rejection derived from the logical view that if tax cuts encouraged economic growth (as Reagan had insisted time and time again), then tax increases would hurt the economy at a time when it was still struggling. The White House worried about the political fallout from Reagan's support for the tax increase. They asserted that his "identification with the tax-increase plan . . . could undercut the political benefits he gained for pushing through" the Economic Recovery Tax Act in 1981.[69] While the administration was spinning Reagan's position, the president attempted to justify his support for the tax bill in fiscally conservative terms, asserting that he "could not stand by and see the further cuts in spending go down the drain when the price . . . gave us the biggest share of what we were seeking."[70] Reagan was so concerned with being labeled as unprincipled that he handwrote a letter to conservative columnist John D. Lofton Jr. to explain his support for the tax bill. Reagan assured Lofton that it had been difficult for him to support the tax bill and that he still believed "in supply-side" economics and realized that tax "increases slow the recovery." He also insisted that "we haven't had all the spending or tax cuts we're going to get."[71] Despite Reagan's assurances that the tax bill was not a revocation of his fiscally conservative principles, conservatives persisted in their opposition to the president until the final hour.

The White House had hoped Reagan would not be forced to personally lobby for tax increases; however, just weeks before the vote it looked like the bill would fail without Reagan's full support. As a result, the president picked up his telephone, not as an advocate of his supply-side vision for lower taxes, but rather as pragmatic leader hoping to build consensus. During his conversations with representatives, Reagan emphasized that "rather than imposing new taxes on working people, this bill tries to ensure that everyone pays a fair share of the tax burden." He added that "more than three-fourths of the revenue raised comes from increased taxpayer compliance and the closing of tax loopholes."[72] When Reagan's phone calls did not have the desired effect, he paraded "scores of congressmen through the White House for some last minute arm-twisting" in what was reported as his "busiest round of lobbying." The night before the final vote, he invited two dozen undecided representatives for dinner, and Reagan announced his public support for the tax bill in time for the nightly network news. Reagan, standing with O'Neill, insisted that "some here are Democrats, some Republicans, some are liberals, some conservatives, but all of us here today are united by something much bigger than political labels: We're all Americans. We all want to get the American economy moving."[73] Regardless of Reagan's justification for the tax increases, his public spat with supply-siders demonstrated the inconsistencies and fractures among fiscal conservatives.

At the last minute, many conservatives changed their votes and accepted the tax increases that their leader insisted were necessary. The *Baltimore Sun* reported that Reagan's victory was his "biggest triumph on Capitol Hill" and marveled at the approval of a $98.3 billion tax increase just a few months before the midterm elections. Conservatives who had publicly denounced the bill "as a desertion of supply-side economics" switched their votes at the last minute. Conservative congressman Henry Hyde (R-IL) explained that while he believed "in supply-side economics and the need to cut marginal tax rates . . .

we have a $150 billion deficit staring us in the face, and we are not able to fight deficits with a rolled up copy of *The Wall Street Journal*." Just as Reagan used the fiscal-conservative denunciation of deficits to paint himself as a fiscal conservative despite raising taxes, so too did those representatives who ultimately went along with the administration. Having ideological cover, however, did not heal the wounds that Reagan suffered with his conservative base. An aide to one of the chief opponents of the bill asserted that Reagan had "damaged himself with Republicans." For those advocates of supply-side economics who had supported Reagan and believed they were leading a revolution, O'Neill's insistence that the tax bill was a necessary "correction" for the Reagan economic program, a "correction" that their leader himself had supported, would not easily fade from memory.[74]

Following Reagan's "victory" on the tax bill and his defeat in securing a balanced-budget amendment, Reagan tried to bridge the gap between his administration and conservatives. On November 1, the White House held a meeting with thirteen fiscally conservative organizations including the US Chamber of Commerce, the American Lobby for a Balanced Budget, and the Heritage Foundation.[75] The meeting resulted in a list of twenty requests and suggestions. At the top of the list was to "take up the Balanced Budget–Tax Limitation Amendment again." The second suggestion was to "resolve Social Security as soon as possible." The organizations requested that Reagan force the Office of Management and Budget to present a balanced budget with no tax increases and to "propose draconian spending cuts, and go down fighting for them if necessary." They also chastised the president for "playing Orwellian word games" by dubbing tax increases as "accelerated taxes" as Reagan had done when justifying an increase in the rates of the Social Security payroll tax. The organizations asserted that such tactics were "fooling no one and making a laughing stock" of the administration. They also unanimously agreed that "there should be no tax increases."[76] In short, conservatives expected Reagan to get back to his fiscal-conservative roots in 1983 by pushing for a balanced budget, tax cuts, spending reductions, and reforms to entitlement programs such as Social Security.

Despite the president's almost laser focus on economic issues during his first two years in office, many conservatives looked back and saw missed opportunities. The Heritage Foundation wrote a 375-page report on Reagan's first two years that concluded that Reagan had "squandered much of his political capital." It called on the president to return to his conservative principles and quit being "a prisoner of his optimism." Heritage also insisted that Reagan recognize that deeper spending cuts were necessary and called on the administration to launch "a major assault on federal spending, especially business subsidies administered by the Departments of Agriculture, Commerce, and Transportation."[77]

Other fiscal conservatives, including Milton Friedman, agreed with Heritage that Reagan had squandered his opportunity to significantly challenge the status quo in Washington.[78] Paul Weyrich, the director of the Committee for the Survival of a Free Congress, complained that "the radical surgery that was required in Washington was not performed." Indeed, Weyrich lamented that the only campaign promise that Reagan had kept completely was his pledge not to touch entitlements. Phyllis Schlafly, the founder of Eagle Forum, said that Reagan's main problem was that "he is not a tough enough administrator." Others, such as former Reagan national security adviser Richard Allen, complained that "not enough Reaganauts were put in key positions," while John T. Dolan, head of the National Conservative Political Action Committee, downplayed even Reagan's tax cuts as "minor achievements."[79] Steve Antosh, the former national campaign chairman of Youth for Reagan, summed up many conservatives' sentiments when he wrote Morton Blackwell that "among many people who should be President Reagan's staunchest supporters, the President has received harsh criticism for not being 'Reagan' enough."[80] This statement is one of the first indications that conservatives were beginning to identify being a purist, principled, small-government advocate with Reagan himself. To be a "Reagan conservative" meant being principled and pursuing conservative policies in their pure form without compromising. As early as 1983, conservatives were beginning to differentiate between Reagan the man and Reagan the ideal, and the president was having problems fulfilling the expectations that came along with being Reagan.

Although fiscal conservatives were frustrated with Reagan's first two years, they realized that their best hope of achieving their policy goals was to steer the president to the right. The American Conservative Union insisted to its members throughout 1982 that "one of the most important ways to make this journey easier, obviously, will be to continue supporting the President wholeheartedly."[81] Furthermore, many conservative organizations were busy pushing for conservative reforms at the state and local level.[82] Regardless of their successes on smaller stages, conservatives continued to be frustrated with the lack of significant economic reforms from the administration.

Following the midterm election and the holiday season, Reagan once again addressed CPAC, this time to defend his first two years and set the stage for the next two. Reagan began his speech by acknowledging that "there is a good deal left unfinished on the conservative agenda," insisting that it would take the conservative "cleanup crew" more than a couple years "to deal with the mess left by others over a half-century." He assured the audience that he was "not disheartened" by "attempts to roll back some of the gains we have made," and he even acknowledged criticism of what he termed the "standby tax increase" of 1982. He vowed to continue pursuing his economic agenda, which would "pay off for every American in the years ahead." Nobody present reminded Reagan that he was the one who had been "rolling back" conservative accomplishments.[83] Discussing CPAC, the *Washington Post* asserted that conservatives "made it clear they don't like the Reagan deficits," the "tax hikes passed last year," or the fact that the Department of Education and the Department of State still existed. The *Post* reminded readers that conservatives had voted against Reagan's "jobs bill" and opposed the Reagan-endorsed Social Security package that extended the solvency of the program. Despite these policy differences, conservatives insisted that they were unwilling to break with the president. According to the *Post*, conservatives were like the big bad wolf, huffing and puffing but unwilling to blow the house down while Reagan was in it.[84] Although conservatives may not have been ready to throw Reagan overboard, by 1983 they were more than willing to fight with the president to establish a balanced budget.

Despite Reagan's fiscally conservative rhetoric, his commitment to altering the course of the Cold War by creating a more robust military doomed any hopes of bringing the budget into balance. Indeed, Reagan addressed his conflicting priorities on multiple occasions. When asked what he would do if he had to choose between a balanced budget and revitalizing America's defenses, Reagan always answered that he would "have to come down on the side of national defense."[85] On March 23, 1983, Reagan did just that when he announced to the nation that he would be pursuing the Strategic Defense Initiative (SDI). SDI intended to develop an anti–ballistic missile system that would protect the United States from missile attacks from hostile countries. Although many conservatives embraced Reagan's call for a missile shield, the cost of research and development would swell an already-bloated defense budget. Reagan defended himself from critics who were put off by his military budgets by conceding that "it wasn't pleasant for someone who had come to Washington determined to reduce government spending, but we had to move forward with the task of repairing our defenses or we would lose our ability to deter conflict now and in the future."[86] Discussing Pentagon spending for fiscal year 1984, Reagan insisted that "the budget request that is now before Congress has been trimmed to the limits of safety." He told the American people that the defense budget for 1984 was "necessary, responsible, and deserving of your support."[87] While many conservatives agreed with Reagan's strategy to end détente and to make mutually assured destruction a thing of the past, they were not ready to concede on the budget issue.

In fact, conservative opposition to Reagan's budgets had begun in 1982 when the president was fighting for tax increases. In April 1982, conservatives launched a million-dollar grassroots campaign to "stiffen President Reagan's spine" by proposing and promoting their own budget. The conservative alternative budget was announced by Howard Phillips, the director of the Conservative Caucus, and John T. Dolan, the chairman of the National Conservative Political Action Committee. Phillips denounced Reagan for allowing moderates and Democrats to put him on the defensive and declared that the president had allowed himself to become "a punching bag." Reagan, Phillips insisted, was "fighting a defensive battle on his enemy's terrain, our budget is an effort to recast the whole debate." Free from political considerations, Phillips and Dolan's budget proposed to "cut a large swath through what remain[ed] of the so-called Great Society" and also cut programs that benefited middle- and upper-class Americans as well as subsidies for agriculture and industry.[88] Phillips asserted that unless Reagan accepted such cuts, he would add $875 billion to the debt over the next four years, the effects of which would be "devastating" for the economy. Phillips and Dolan's conservative alternative was endorsed by the National Taxpayers Union, the Life Lobby, United Families of America, the National Pro-Life Political Action Committee, the Free Congress Foundation, and the Coalition for America.[89]

Although the Phillips-Dolan budget was a conservative pipe dream, the Reagan administration would have done well to take the concerns of conservatives seriously. The fiscal year 1983 budget turned into what one conservative organization called "a momentous struggle," and although conservative opposition to Reagan's 1983 budget was strongest among ideological grassroots activists, it was a precursor to the budget battles to come between Reagan and conservatives.[90] The grassroots and decentralized nature of the conservative movement made portraying the nuances of policy making in Washington difficult and enabled activists such as Dolan and Phillips to criticize Reagan for not pursuing a more principled conservative agenda. In reality, the proposals put forth by Dolan and Phillips were nonstarters in a Congress controlled by the Democrats. Despite the political realities, by distributing pamphlets and newsletters to millions of everyday conservatives, firebrands could incite anger and frustration among the conservative base in an attempt to move the political discourse to the right.

Conservatives continued to fight Reagan on the budget in 1984. When Reagan sent his proposals to Congress, conservatives balked at the administration's suggestion for "standby tax increases of about $150 billion over three years starting in 1986." Reagan's budget represented a compromise with Democrats who had insisted on immediate tax increases of $30 billion and wanted to end the inflation adjustments that ensured that Americans did not pay a higher tax rate as a result of inflation. Conservatives, however, opposed any tax increases, including Reagan's proposal that only nominally raised taxes in 1984 and 1985, allowed $50 billion in increases over the next three years if deficits continued, and promised further spending cuts.[91] In short, Reagan's budget proposal was designed to push the discussion of tax hikes down the road, preserve conservative gains such as the end of bracket creep, and force Congress to agree to more spending cuts. Reagan's budget represented the work of a pragmatic conservative, but conservatives both in Congress and in the grass roots were tired of compromise.

Indeed, to many conservatives, compromise was antithetical to conservative ideology and its historical purpose. Conservativism emerged as a political force in the 1960s in opposition to the liberal consensus. One of conservatives' founding documents, Phyllis Schlafly's *A Choice Not an Echo*, encapsulated in the title how conservatives understood their purpose in politics.[92] Their goal was to provide the American people with stark alternatives to the New Deal and the Great Society. In an updated edition, Schlafly explained that during the 1970s, however, conservatives found themselves "betrayed" by their political leaders. According to Schlafly, Nixon won the presidential election in 1968 because he ran as a conservative. As soon as he was in office, however, Nixon "betrayed conservatives' hopes" by freezing out "the conservatives who had nominated and elected him," capitulated "to the Eastern Establishment," and "gave the Rockefeller Republicans a hammerlock over all policies that mattered."[93] Likewise, Ford did not pursue conservatives' priorities. According to Schlafly, he was selected to be vice president because "Ford had already proved he was a man whom the Establishment could count on to take orders."[94] Schlafly emphasized conservatives' fear that when politicians, even self-proclaimed conservatives, went to Washington, they caught what she termed "Potomac fever and steadily moved left."[95] With this history of betrayal by their political leaders, conservative activists guarded diligently against any sign that their political representatives were compromising their conservative principles.

There was also a moral element to conservatives' opposition to deficits. To many social conservatives, the allocation of money to certain organizations and programs confirmed the legitimacy of social evils they vowed to end. Almost as soon as Reagan took up residence at 1600 Pennsylvania Avenue, conservative organizations began lobbying against Title X, a federal grant program that sought to provide individuals with family-planning and preventative health services, on the grounds that the program was filled with waste.[96] Judie Brown, the president of the American Life Lobby, led the fight to decrease funding for Title X, whose beneficiaries, many conservatives believed, provided antifamily advice and promoted abortion to young women and girls.

Every year during budget discussions, Brown mobilized opposition to Reagan's budget because of the administration's unwillingness to address the waste and fraud of Title X. Brown cited two reports from the Government Accountability Office (GAO) that concluded that there was around $48 million that could be saved from Title X.[97] Brown, the president of the largest pro-life organization in the country, lambasted Reagan and his appointees at the Department of Health and Human Services for their "acquiescence in what amounts to a bureaucratic cover-up of millions of dollars of waste and abuse." In 1982, Brown informed Reagan that support from her organization and its affiliates depended on his administration making significant cuts to Title X.[98] Although the cuts did not make it into the budget, the White House did ask for conservatives to help the administration prepare a study of how to reform the family-planning program.[99] The next winter, in January 1983, Brown wrote Reagan personally to remind him that cutting $50 million from Title X was of the utmost importance to conservatives.[100] If Reagan saw Brown's request, he did not deem the $50 million in budget savings worthy of starting a fight with

Democrats. When the budget for fiscal year 1984 was released, Brown was outraged. Speaking directly to the press, Brown accused the budget of "raising the white flag of surrender to government waste and abuse." She insisted that she had "repeatedly" brought this waste to the attention of the administration and concluded that Reagan's "budget as a plan to reduce deficits is a fraud." Brown was not the only conservative outraged at what they considered Reagan's lack of principles in the budget battles. In 1984, that frustration manifested itself as opposition to both the fiscal year 1985 budget and Reagan's bid for reelection.

Conservative disappointment and anger over Reagan's budgets became an all-out revolt in 1984. At the beginning of the legislative session, conservatives took the initiative against the White House. The Conservative Opportunity Society (COS), led by Newt Gingrich, drafted an alternative budget and criticized Reagan for "sidestepping significant efforts to cut spending." The COS budget placed across-the-board spending freezes on domestic programs, slowed the growth of entitlements, and cut defense spending by increasing efficiency. Gingrich condemned the administration for "feeding the liberal welfare state instead of changing it."[101] To some conservatives, Reagan seemed to have caught the very "Potomac fever" that Schlafly had warned about.

Perhaps the greatest evidence that Reagan had caught the fever was his advocacy of the Social Security Reform Act of 1983. Although Reagan had frequently denounced the federal government's involvement in Americans' retirement funds, he reversed course in 1983 and supported an overhaul of the Social Security system that would prevent its insolvency. The bill increased the Social Security payroll tax, raised the retirement age for recipients to sixty-seven, required federal employees to join the system, and placed taxes on the benefits of higher-income recipients. Upon signing the bill, Reagan hailed the measure as "a monument to the spirit of compassion and commitment that unites us as a people." The president added that "this bill demonstrates for all time our nation's ironclad commitment to Social Security."[102]

While the compromise was hailed in the *New York Times* as "a landmark in political statesmanship," conservatives were not pleased with Reagan's capitulation.[103] Indeed, many conservatives, including some in the White House, preferred radical surgery to the Social Security system rather than the rescue bill that Reagan ultimately signed into law. The year 1983 presented conservatives with the best opportunity they had ever seen to push their preferred option: voluntary social security, where "workers would be given the choice of staying in social security or 'opting out.'" This plan would allow "social security to be slowly phased out of existence," and as workers left the system, Social Security "would choke to death." Before the final vote on the Social Security Act, one prominent conservative declared, "I hope like hell the compromise package fails. I'd like to come back in a couple of years with another crisis and do something really dramatic."[104] After the reform package was passed, conservatives at the Heritage Foundation concluded that they would need to "prepare the political ground so that the fiasco of the last 18 months is not repeated."[105] True conservative reform of the Social Security system would have to wait.

Although some conservatives realized that more work was needed to pass major conservative reforms, others denounced Reagan's continued capitulations and were ready to push the president out of the White House. Condemning Reagan's "leftward drift," some New Right activists began looking for a "fresh new face" to run for president in 1984. Richard Viguerie asserted that "if Ronald Reagan continues to move to the left, I and other conservatives don't think he should run for reelection." Viguerie told the press that he was openly looking for another candidate and he "wouldn't be surprised to see someone else running on the conservative side." Many conservatives were quick to denounce Viguerie's efforts, and the only conservative that could realistically challenge Reagan, Jack Kemp, called the effort "foolhardy."[106] Regardless, while Reagan was campaigning for a second term, conservatives were divided on whether the president was the best person to lead the conservative revolution.

Ronald Reagan won reelection in a landslide in large part because of the recovering economy. Even the economic recovery in 1983 and 1984, however, was not enough to placate conservative concerns with the administration. By the time ballots were cast, it was clear that the Reagan administration's initial budget projections were incorrect. He had desired to cut taxes, cut spending, and increase the size of the military to fight the Cold War.[107] Reagan's advisers, drawing on the supply-side projections, had projected staggering growth rates from 1982 to 1984. In reality, the economy contracted by 1.5 percent in 1982. And even though there were significant economic improvements in 1983 and 1984, the results were not anywhere close to the administration's projections.[108] Indeed, from 1980 to 1984 the deficit as a percentage of GDP grew from 2.8 percent to 5 percent.[109] According to David Stockman, to achieve balanced budgets with tax cuts and military-spending increases the Reagan administration needed to enact "sweeping reform[s] of the big middle-class entitlement programs: Social Security, Medicare, and federal retirement pensions."[110] This reality was kept quiet in the Office of Management and Budget, but when Stockman's plan to cut entitlements was released, "resistance began to crop up everywhere, both within the Cabinet and on the Hill." Stockman later lamented that "in its totality," the backlash to entitlement cuts "amounted to a counter-revolution—a broad range of political signals that the free market and anti-welfare state premises of the Reagan Revolution were not going to take root."[111] Reagan was unable to usher in the comprehensive conservative fiscal revolution that many supply-siders desired. The presence of a Democratic Congress, opposition from within his own cabinet, and the president's own commitment to rehabilitating the United States' military with substantial increases in military spending made satisfying supply-side revolutionaries impossible.

Other conservatives also condemned Reagan for not achieving true spending cuts and addressing entitlement programs. Just before Christmas 1984, the Heritage Foundation released a six-hundred-page study that evaluated Reagan's first four years in office and suggested policy initiatives for his second term. It lamented that the "initial clear vision" of Reagan dimmed over the course of his term as "Reagan officials gradually appeared to lose their edge." Heritage suggested that the president rekindle the "spirit of momentum" by proposing a new round of spending cuts and proposing individual retirement accounts as an alternative to Social Security.[112] Some conservatives even criticized Reagan for not cutting military spending. The chairman of the House Republican Policy Committee, Congressman Richard "Dick" Cheney (R-WY), asserted that "the continued failure of the administration to deal with the deficit puts at risk everything Ronald Reagan believes in." Cheney went on to suggest that budget deficits were "potentially" Reagan's Vietnam and concluded that "many conservative Republicans had hoped Reagan would submit a deficit reduction package that would be salable to Congress and avoid the need to raise taxes."[113]

The Reagan agenda—cutting taxes, decreasing inflation, and increasing military spending—led to ballooning deficits. Despite Stockman's efforts to cut spending, the amount of spending cuts that would have been necessary to offset the rest of the Reagan program was never achieved. Democrats controlled the House throughout Reagan's administration, making cuts to government programs difficult. Furthermore, Reagan's increases in military spending led to a sort of quid pro quo where Democrats received funding for domestic programs while Republicans got their increases in defense spending.[114] Ultimately, Reagan was able to achieve the parts of his platform that were the most desirable for both legislators and voters: tax cuts. The politically difficult aspects of the supply-side agenda, cuts to middle-class entitlements, remained unrealized.

The lack of spending cuts frustrated fiscal conservatives, deficit hawks in Congress, and even Stockman. In his memoir, Stockman blamed the failure of the "Reagan Revolution" on Reagan himself. Stockman declared that only an "iron chancellor" could have made fiscal conservatism work, and "Ronald Reagan wasn't that by a long shot." According to Stockman, Reagan was "too kind, gentle, and sentimental." Ultimately, Reagan was unable to make the hard cuts. Stockman lamented that Reagan saw "the plight of real people before anything else." This unfortunate characteristic got in the way of his "right-wing image, his ideology and philosophy."[115] The results were skyrocketing budget deficits that made a mockery of Reagan's promise to cut the national debt.[116]

Reagan continued to pursue his pragmatic conservative agenda during his second term. Although he was able to get an additional tax-reform bill passed in 1986,[117] foreign policy concerns, Iran-Contra, and the Intermediate-Range Nuclear Forces (INF) Treaty grabbed most of the headlines and most of the ire of conservatives.[118] In early 1987, Reagan further isolated conservatives when he proposed an expansion of Medicare to include catastrophic health insurance for the elderly. Conservative columnist George Will asserted that conservatives should not be surprised that Reagan embraced the principle that government had a role in building a "social insurance state." According to Will, Reagan was a "New Deal Conservative" and the Depression was a formative influence on the president.[119]

The nuances of Reagan's economic approach and the divisions that existed between Reagan and other fiscal conservatives quickly faded after he left the White House. Conservatives embraced the economic recovery of 1983 as the product of Reagan's principled commitment to supply-side policies, and frustration with Reagan's large deficits faded from conservatives' collective conscious. The differences between conservatives and Reagan were downplayed and were replaced by a myth of an unflinching Reagan who courageously stuck to his fiscally conservative principles in the face of the worst economic downturn since the Great Depression. Although Reagan angered conservatives with his unbalanced budgets during the eighties, frustration with the president's fiscal policies paled in comparison to the betrayal conservatives felt regarding social issues.

3. The Origins of the New Right and the Seeds of Future Frustration

In September 1981, almost six thousand conservatives marched through Dallas to oppose President Ronald Reagan's nomination of Sandra Day O'Connor to the Supreme Court. The protestors, who held signs that read "O'Connor's No Conservative" and "Save A Human Life . . . Fight Abortion," were not exceptional. Leaders of the New Right, just one year after helping elect Reagan, were denouncing his appointment in mounting numbers.[1] Edward E. McAteer, the president of the Religious Roundtable, declared that O'Connor's "public record is one of consistent and unequivocal support for abortion." Howard Phillips, the national director of the Conservative Caucus, asserted that Reagan had lied to social conservatives, while Peter Gemma Jr., the executive director of the National Pro-Life Political Action Committee, declared that her nomination made the Religious Right "look like fools."[2] Furthermore, Jerry Falwell, the cofounder of the Moral Majority, declared "that all good Christians should be concerned by the appointment."[3]

The debate over O'Connor's nomination foreshadowed the dissatisfaction that conservatives felt toward Reagan throughout his administration.[4] Richard Viguerie, another conservative activist, asserted that "conservatives weren't consulted" on the appointment and that he had not spoken "to a conservative yet who wasn't disturbed by this." Howard Phillips went even further, predicting "a costly fight" for Reagan against "people who have been his most faithful supporters." Phillips also insisted that the New Right might withhold support for the president's other initiatives, chiefly his economic proposals.[5]

The O'Connor nomination was one of countless conflicts between Reagan and the New Right during the 1980s. Throughout the Reagan administration, conservatives who emphasized revitalizing America's moral character complained that their concerns were not being pursued with sufficient vigor. While most histories of the conservative movement and the rise of the New Right end with the election of Reagan, recently historians have detailed the battles that members of the Christian Right fought, and often lost, during the 1980s.[6] Although President Reagan was pro-life, for voluntary school prayer, and for imposing law and order, he often placed social issues on the back burner while the administration pushed its economic and foreign policy agendas. As a result, many conservative activists on the front lines of the so-called Reagan Revolution did not feel that Reagan's agenda was adequately revolutionary.

The tension between the New Right and Reagan began during the 1976 Republican primary and did not end until Reagan was on his way back to sunny California in January 1989. Indeed, the 1980s were a difficult time for social conservatives. The administration's failure to pass constitutional amendments banning abortion and permitting voluntary school prayer during Reagan's first term led some New Right activists to oppose Reagan in 1984. Even without this support, Reagan easily won reelection. But a second Reagan term did not prove any better for social conservatives. With the outset of the AIDS epidemic, the New Right attempted to encourage Reagan to limit the liberties of homosexuals in the name of public health. Although Reagan did not publicly utter the word "AIDS" until 1985, he refused to take legislative or executive measures that would have curtailed the rights of those with the disease. Reagan's unwillingness to do so, and the actions that the Department of Health and Human Services took to address the epidemic, enraged New Right activists such as the founder of Eagle Forum, Phyllis Schlafly. Furthermore, when Reagan did finally discuss the AIDS epidemic at length, in 1987, he empathized with the victims and insisted that America's goal was to find a cure—not to alienate those who had been stricken by the disease. Reagan's unwillingness to commit his political capital to address abortion and fight what many termed "the homosexual agenda" infuriated the New Right and encouraged those who condemned Reagan as a pragmatist who easily abandoned his conservative principles. Perhaps due to their ineffectiveness at the national level, by the end of the decade the New Right as a political movement was in disarray, leading social and political commentators to speculate on why the movement had failed.[7]

Many social conservatives felt a deep sense of betrayal toward Reagan for not prioritizing their agenda. While Reagan was personally pro-life and for reinstating voluntary prayer in school, he did not use his political capital to pass significant legislation to restore Judeo-Christian family values. The next three chapters demonstrate that Reagan's relationship with the New Right was tenuous and questions the New Right's influence during the 1980s. Focusing on the battles that social conservatives fought with the Reagan administration calls into question how revolutionary the "Reagan Revolution" really was, and also draws a sharp contrast with how social conservatives remember the fortieth president today.

The New Right emerged as a political force during the civil rights movement in the 1960s, following the Supreme Court's decision in *Roe v. Wade*, and after President Gerald Ford demonstrated his disdain for conservatives by appointing Nelson Rockefeller vice president.[8] The foundations for the movement, however, were laid years earlier in the late 1950s and the 1960s.[9] In 1955, William F. Buckley founded the conservative journal *National Review*, and in just a few years Buckley became the face of conservatism.[10] His publication brought together the divergent strands of conservative thought under one banner and gave it respectability by establishing "the boundaries of responsible conservatism." In doing so, Buckley helped make conservative ideas acceptable, and in *National Review* he provided a place for their inception and dissemination.[11] Buckley was indispensable to the emerging conservative movement. According to historian George Nash, "If *National Review* (or something like it) had not been founded, there would probably have been no cohesive intellectual force on the Right in the 1960s and 1970s."[12] Buckley's contribution to the conservative movement, however, went beyond *National Review*. On September 9, 1960, ninety-three college students from across the country gathered at Buckley's country estate in Sharon, Connecticut.[13] With Buckley's help, they founded Young Americans for Freedom, which went on to recruit and train thousands of conservative activists throughout the sixties and seventies.[14]

The movement that began in the pages of *National Review* quickly spilled over into national politics. Young conservatives were successful in drafting Arizona senator Barry Goldwater to run for president and were instrumental to his successful bid for the Republican nomination in 1964. While Goldwater lost resoundingly at the polls, thousands of conservative activists came together to raise money, campaign, and develop the necessary political connections to create a mass political movement.[15] According to Richard Viguerie, the New Right owed Barry Goldwater a great debt because "the Presidential campaign of 1964 was the first major political experience for most of us." Paul Weyrich concurred, asserting that "even if we did nothing but wear a Goldwater button or attend a rally—and some of the New Right are so young that is all they did—that campaign left an indelible mark on us."[16] Indeed, while many remember the 1960s for the large number of left-wing protests, there were also numerous young conservatives who campaigned for Goldwater and rallied in support of the war in Vietnam.[17]

Despite conservatives' success in nominating Goldwater, conservatism remained fragmented into the 1970s. The *Roe* decision in 1973 and Ford's decision to select liberal Republican Nelson Rockefeller as his vice president led Richard Viguerie, Howard Phillips, Morton Blackwell, Terry Dolan, and Paul Weyrich to mobilize conservatives and form a variety of organizations that collectively became known as the New Right.[18] Whereas Goldwater had focused on economic issues, and had even been pro-choice on abortion, the New Right was much more socially conservative and emphasized the restoration of Judeo-Christian family values. In 1973, Weyrich, with the financial backing of Joseph Coors, founded the Heritage Foundation, a conservative think tank that would address social issues.[19] Weyrich asserted that, unlike traditional conservatives like Buckley, "the New Right does not want to conserve, we want to change—we are the forces of change" and suggested that those who were "sick and tired of things in this country" should look to conservatives for leadership.[20] While Weyrich established institutions to create and disseminate conservative policy alternatives in the Beltway, Howard Phillips founded the Conservative Caucus. Phillips's goal was to mobilize conservative constituents in specific districts to put pressure on representatives to alter their voting records and make them more conservative.[21] Phillips, unlike many others in the New Right, understood the difficulties that their agenda of restoring Judeo-Christian values would face at the national level. He took the long view and believed that only an ideological groundswell could alter the course of American politics. In 1975, Phillips explained that "there's definitely a conservative majority in the country today . . . but for that majority to have influence, it must become organized where its strength exists—in the communities where people live."[22]

Other members of the New Right were equally important in mobilizing conservatives, including its principal fund-raiser Richard Viguerie, who became "radicalized" after Rockefeller's nomination.[23] Viguerie learned about direct mail techniques while he was employed at Young Americans for Freedom during the 1960s.[24] In just three years, Viguerie raised tens of millions of dollars for the New Right and created a list of thirty million potential conservative donors and activists.[25] Terry Dolan, who founded the National Conservative Political Action Committee in 1975, benefited greatly from Viguerie's efforts. In its first five years of existence, Dolan's organization contributed $1.2 million to political races across the country.[26] While Viguerie and Dolan focused on raising money and distributing it to conservative causes and candidates, Morton Blackwell was hard at work mobilizing and developing young conservatives. Blackwell worked diligently during the 1970s as the chair of the Committee for Responsible Youth Politics and later as the president of the Leadership Institute to train young conservatives how to be effective leaders. As a result, Blackwell served as a liaison between conservatives throughout the movement and those in Washington. [27]

In 1977, the New Right launched an all-out campaign against President Jimmy Carter's proposed changes to America's election laws. Carter wanted to have congressional elections financed by taxpayers, to ease restrictions on voter identification cards to enfranchise more people, to change existing law to allow federal employees to participate actively in politics, and to end the electoral college, allowing the president to be directly elected by the people.[28] While most conservatives and Republicans believed that the Carter administration's reforms would hurt them politically, they also did not think there was much they could do to stop the proposals. Weyrich and Viguerie, however, decided to mobilize against Carter's proposals. They contacted important Republican financial contributors and had them contact wavering senators. They launched a media war ensuring that op-eds appeared in prominent news publications. Most importantly, they utilized direct mail and asked the grassroots to make phone calls and send letters to Congress. Through their efforts, the New Right was at least partially responsible for stalling Carter's attempts to change the election laws. According to Viguerie, "this was probably the first major victory of the New Right. A rag-tag group of New Right conservatives had done what Republican Senators said could not be done. We had our first taste of victory. And there was no stopping us now."[29]

Combined, the efforts of Weyrich, Phillips, Viguerie, Dolan, and Blackwell resulted in some political victories and, in turn, brought the New Right both praise and scrutiny. In 1977, the *New York Times* described how members of the New Right met "in a large, luxuriously furnished suite" drinking "cocktails" as they mapped their "nationwide campaigns against busing, racial quotas, publicly funded abortions, homosexual rights and other things they believe are contributing to [the] disintegration of the American family and way of life." The *Times* portrayed the New Right as a group of elitists representing the "far-right" of American politics, but the publication admitted that they were "more tightly organized, better financed, more sophisticated and more pragmatic than their predecessors."[30] In July 1977, *U.S. News & World Report* asserted that the New Right was "a third force" that was "quietly building political apparatus that pointedly disregards party labels." Even the Republican Party had to recognize the importance of the New Right. In June 1977, a spokesman for the Republican National Committee remarked that if one ranked the importance of political institutions, organized labor would be first, the Democratic Party second, the Republican Party third, and the New Right fourth.[31] In short, in only a few years the New Right had become a major power player at all levels of American politics.

Over time, the number of organizations and people involved in the New Right grew to include socially conservative activists across the country. One of the most notable crusaders of the New Right was Phyllis Schlafly. Her national organization, Stop ERA, mobilized evangelical women against the Equal Rights Amendment. When she began her efforts, over twenty of the thirty-eight states needed to secure ratification had already done so. Through her grassroots organizational efforts, Schlafly was ultimately able to prevent the ERA from becoming law, and by the end of the 1970s she was probably the most influential woman of the New Right.[32] Evangelists such as Jerry Falwell, James Robison, and Pat Robertson also proved to be important additions to the New Right. According to Richard Viguerie, these ministers were essential because they reached more than twenty million people every week. Each of them encouraged Christians to register and get involved in politics. In fact, Robertson had created the Christian Broadcasting Network in 1960, which, by 1980, reached millions of viewers.[33]

Jerry Falwell soon became the most prominent, outspoken, and influential of the three evangelicals. Prior to the 1976 election, Falwell's weekly radio program, *Old-Time Gospel Hour,* was nonpolitical. In September, Jimmy Carter sat down for an interview with *Playboy* in which he confessed he had "committed adultery" in his "heart many times," leading Falwell to criticize him during his radio address.[34] Falwell endorsed Ford in 1976, and less than a year later he went to Miami to help Anita Bryant in her campaign to overturn a homosexual-rights ordinance that prohibited both public and private schools from discriminating against homosexuals when hiring. Bryant claimed that God had spoken to her and that he had insisted that she go to the Metro Dade County Commission meeting and oppose the measure. Bryant told the commissioners that she was "not only aflame, I'm on fire." She asserted that "homosexuality is an abomination to the Lord," that homosexuals "will recruit our children," and that in doing so they would use "money, drugs, alcohol," and any other means "to get what they want."[35] Bryant created an organization, Save Our

Children, to mobilize Christians throughout the country against measures similar to Miami's. Bryant solicited the help of evangelical ministers and appeared on Pat Robertson's *700 Club* and Jerry Falwell's *Old-Time Gospel Hour.* Bryant, and her allies—including Falwell—were ultimately successful. By a margin of two to one, Miami residents voted to overturn the ordinance.[36] Falwell's experience in Miami led him to begin "preaching a nationally televised series of sermons against homosexuality, abortion, and other such issues." It also led him to found the Moral Majority in 1979, which almost instantly became one of the most influential organizations of the New Right.[37] By the end of the decade, the New Right seemed poised to fundamentally change the country. To do so, however, the member groups would have to overcome their differences with the most well-known conservative running for president in 1980: Ronald Reagan.

Although many on the New Right supported Reagan as the conservative alternative to President Ford in 1976, by the end of the primary they began to have questions about his candidacy. To placate the GOP establishment's fears of his conservatism, Reagan announced that if he won the nomination he would select Richard Schweiker, the liberal Republican senator from Pennsylvania, as his running mate.[38] Reagan's decision had the unintended consequence of alienating the New Right, leading conservatives to meet in Chicago to discuss the possibility of forming a third party. According to Viguerie, "before Schweiker, most conservatives would not have thought for a minute of opposing Reagan in the November election" but "now they are reevaluating." Phillips told the press that "I think what will come out of this will be a renewed determination to let the Republican Party know that if it chooses a liberal at the top or the bottom of its ticket, it will face an independent candidacy in November that will cost it a decisive share of the vote." Not all conservatives abandoned Reagan; the American Conservative Union (ACU) continued to support him as "the preferred alternative to the Ford-Rockefeller-Kissinger Administration." Phillips countered the ACU by asserting that there was no difference between a "Ford and a Schweiker ticket" and added "I'd just as soon let the Democrats take the White House and get the Republican Party out of the way and start building a new party."[39] Many saw Jesse Helms as the potential conservative candidate.[40] When confronted with the idea, Helms did not dismiss the possibility out of hand, warning that "a ticket that is only fairly conservative—bland—is not going to excite people." In contrast, Helms explained what was needed was "a conservatism that leaves absolutely no doubt."[41]

While the New Right's efforts to affect the 1976 election were ultimately inconsequential, their qualms with Reagan were magnified in 1978 when California state Senator John V. Briggs introduced Proposition 6. The proposal would strike down a California law that protected homosexual teachers from discrimination and would grant school districts the authority to fire any teacher that publicly supported homosexuality. Briggs scheduled rallies across California to promote Proposition 6, but the campaign quickly turned into a circus as Briggs attempted to make the proposition "a referendum on whether gay is good." Briggs asserted that 25 percent of gay teachers were child molesters but assured the crowds that for all he cared, in their private lives, homosexuals could "practice bestiality."[42]

Just a few weeks before Californians went to the polls, Jerry Falwell joined Briggs to promote the proposal. At a stop in San Diego, supporters held their Bibles and donned their American flag pins, eager to hear the evangelist preach. Falwell proclaimed that "we need this measure—Proposition 6—to reverse the tide of moral decay that threatens California and our beloved nation." As the crowd responded with a resounding "Amen," Falwell implored born-again Christians to get involved in politics, asserting that "the government calls this political, we call it moral." Once Falwell had finished, Tim LaHaye, a prominent conservative pastor and Moral Majority board member, gave the benediction, in which he prayed "that these unfortunate people, whether they be homosexuals or lesbians, not be locked into their devastated lives."[43]

Briggs's proposal ultimately failed by more than a million votes, and many members of the New Right blamed Reagan for its defeat. Reagan opposed Proposition 6 and spoke out against it, declaring that it had "potential for real mischief" and could ruin "innocent lives."[44] When Briggs's amendment became the first antigay proposal to be defeated by popular vote, he lambasted "cocktail Republicans" who had homosexual friends in Hollywood for undermining his efforts.[45] Briggs explained "that one single endorsement—Ronald Reagan—turned the polls around." He insisted that "for Ronald Reagan to march to the drums of the homosexuals has irrevocably damaged him."[46] Briggs swore that Christians would remember Reagan's betrayal and proclaimed that "he's finished as a national politician."[47] Falwell also condemned Reagan for taking "the political rather than the moral route" and promised that Reagan "would have to face the music from Christian voters" in the 1980 election.[48] From 1976 to 1980, the New Right began to question whether Reagan was the right conduit for conservative ideas.

The New Right found its conservative alternative to Reagan when Representative Philip Crane (R-IL) announced in the summer of 1978 he would seek the GOP nomination for president. While Reagan had been unanimously seen as the conservative alternative in 1976, his age and his unwillingness "to stick to his conservative guns" gave many on the New Right pause.[49] Since 1976, Reagan had isolated conservatives by refusing to abandon the Republican Party and by supporting many moderate GOP candidates "even in the face of some conservative opposition to them."[50] According to the press, Crane was "the hope of the New Right," and his announcement capped "a long-planned campaign by the right wing of the GOP to have its own candidate and a candidate other than Ronald Reagan."[51] Crane also had a long-standing connection with the New Right. In 1977, he took over the American Conservative Union, increasing its budget by 400 percent from $1 million to $4 million and its membership by 500 percent from sixty thousand to three hundred thousand. Crane's success at the ACU led Viguerie to meet with Crane "after deciding conservatives needed someone other than Reagan." Many conservatives also doubted that the sixty-seven-year-old Reagan would opt to run again. Crane's "conservative credentials" were "at least a match for Reagan's," and he was young, articulate, and handsome.[52] Weyrich asserted that conservatives were looking for a new leader and that Crane had the "potential" to provide "that leadership."[53] Once Reagan announced his intentions to run for president, however, most conservatives gravitated into his camp. While the New Right wanted a principled alternative to Reagan, Crane's campaign was unable to gain traction and was ultimately unsuccessful.[54]

The New Right's qualms with Reagan persisted after he won the Republican presidential nomination.[55] As the Republican National Convention neared, attention turned to whom Reagan would nominate as his vice president. Many viewed this decision as "symbolic of the way Reagan would behave in the White House." The New Right wanted Reagan to select Jack Kemp. According to the press, Kemp had "important support from the 'New Right' and from advocates of the tax-cutting policy which bears his name in the Kemp-Roth bill."[56] Reagan decided that he would announce his choice for vice president during the convention itself. While many conservatives, including Strom Thurmond, believed that George Bush was needed to "broaden the base," the New Right was not about to accept a "moderate" vice president.[57] They urged

Helms to challenge Bush from the convention floor, and top conservatives present, including Phyllis Schlafly, met to discuss their options.[58] Ultimately, conservative opposition to Bush turned out to be futile, as the three conservative alternatives—Helms, Kemp, and Crane—combined received only 6 percent of the ballots cast for vice president.[59] After the vote, Phillips condemned the decision to select Bush and asserted, "Governor Reagan sounds like Winston Churchill but behaves like Neville Chamberlain."[60] Weyrich also rejected Reagan's choice, declaring that it would lead to conservatives' "destruction" and proclaimed that he would not "support a Reagan-Bush ticket."[61]

The experience of the convention fueled the New Right's fears that Reagan was not fully committed to his socially conservative principles. For instance, during the discussion over the Republican platform, Reagan had been prepared to compromise on the Equal Rights Amendment. While he personally opposed the ERA, Reagan was willing to allow support for the amendment to remain in the GOP platform. Phillips and others of the New Right were outraged. Nevada senator Paul Laxalt, Reagan's liaison to conservatives, acknowledged that "opposing the ERA and abortion is important, but we've got bigger issues to worry about," namely the declining state of the economy and the threat of Soviet expansion.[62] Such statements did not sit well with members of the New Right who viewed social issues as essential to restoring America. The New Right ultimately won on the issue of the ERA and also got the party to vow to end the IRS's investigation into independent schools.[63] Despite such victories, however, Reagan's choice for vice president and his willingness to compromise reminded the New Right of the concerns they had about a Reagan presidency.

Following the convention, the *Wall Street Journal* questioned whether a President Reagan would get along with his socially conservative friends and noted that while Reagan was "one kind of conservative," many in the movement were "more strident and assertive than he." The *Wall Street Journal* further questioned how "President Reagan, described by associates as a low-key, 9-5 kind of administrator who finds conflict uncomfortable, would get along with these fire-eaters." In reality, there were major questions and some uneasiness among members of the New Right. According to Laxalt, the New Right was "afraid of Ron, a little bit afraid of him."[64]

Despite their fears, the New Right did not attempt to form a third party as they did in 1976, and they campaigned vigorously against President Carter. Falwell asserted that the 1980s would be a "Decade of Destiny" and that if

Americans did not "come together and rise up . . . permissiveness and moral decay" would crush society. According to Falwell, the 1980s would be "the most important decade this nation has known" and nothing less than the survival of the American republic was at stake.[65] Writing in the lead-up to the presidential election, Falwell lamented that "in the last several years, Americans have literally stood by and watched as godless, spineless leaders have brought our nation floundering to the brink of death."[66] Falwell and other leaders of the New Right campaigned across the nation for conservative candidates dedicated to the moral renewal of the United States. Shortly after Election Day, they "basked . . . in the glow of their successful role in defeating key liberal members of Congress." The New Right targeted six incumbent Democratic senators and succeeded in defeating four of them. Phillips bragged that "the significance of the religious conservative movement is only beginning to be felt." Viguerie added that "we've just seen the tip of the iceberg of the Christian conservative movement in the political process."[67]

Members of the New Right also used their success to take credit for Reagan's election. Lou Harris, the Moral Majority's pollster, claimed that "Reagan would have lost the election by one percentage point without the help of the Moral Majority."[68] Other members of the New Right reminded Reagan that he had "not only a moral obligation . . . but a political obligation" to pursue their agenda. Terry Dolan, the head of the National Conservative Political Action Committee, warned that if Reagan failed to do so he would "pay a political price." Weyrich targeted the vice president, cautioning that Bush better "get with the new tidal wave which swept the country." Phillips, celebrating the decline of liberal influence, proclaimed that "the only way any liberal legislation is going to get passed in the next two years is if it is proposed by the Reagan Administration."[69] Just four years later, the New Right's declaration of victory would look foolhardy and premature.

4. The Battle for America's Soul: Conservative Disillusion with Reagan on Social Issues

Almost as soon as Reagan took office, the New Right and the administration clashed over priorities.[1] Reagan emphasized that the economy was the most important issue facing the nation and that social issues would be secondary.[2] In contrast, the New Right wanted to use the momentum of the election to push social issues through Congress. Peter Gemma, the director of the National Pro-Life Political Action Committee, told the press "our prime goal is to cut off all federal aid to abortions."[3] The other major goal of the New Right was to force Congress to vote on a human life amendment. Although Weyrich and Gemma admitted that it would "probably not pass," they wanted to "make it clear who is for the amendment and who isn't." Unfortunately for them, when the administration set the legislative agenda, social issues were not a priority.

While Reagan's tax cuts and spending cuts were making their way through Congress, he infuriated the New Right when the press reported that Reagan was considering Sandra Day O'Connor for an opening on the Supreme Court. The Ad Hoc Committee in Defense of Life accused Reagan's "Moderate Mafia" of trying to defuse "the expected opposition from anti-abortionists" by releasing her name before the start of the long Fourth of July weekend.[4] The president of the National Right to Life Committee asserted that Reagan's selection of O'Connor represented "a repudiation of the Republican platform pledge" to select only pro-life judges. He concluded that the "appointment is a grave disappointment to the pro-life public nationwide." Falwell also criticized the appointment. He complained that O'Connor had "been active in feminist causes and is a supporter of the Equal Rights Amendment." The New Right felt vindicated in its opposition to O'Connor when the president of the National Organization for Women praised Reagan's choice as "a major victory for women's rights." To further rub salt in the New Right's wounds, two of the most liberal members of Congress, Senator Edward Kennedy (D-MA) and Representative Morris Udall (D-AZ), praised the nomination.[5]

Despite the holiday break, the New Right mobilized to oppose O'Connor's nomination. Virtually every right-to-life group "howled" and used its influence, both inside and outside of Washington, to mobilize the grassroots against Reagan. Pro-life activists manned the phone banks, and by Monday morning, "thousands of anti-O'Connor messages had piled up."[6] Mrs. L. G. Graham of Pine Bluff, Arkansas, wrote Reagan, accusing him of betraying the people "who trusted you and worked so hard for you." She condemned Reagan for "supporting a Feminist-Atheist-Communist for the Supreme Court" and asserted that his decision "undermines any other good you could have done."[7] Mrs. Gilder L. Wideman, a member of the Eagle Forum of Alabama, exclaimed, "We can't understand this sudden turn to the left! We are shocked and very disappointed with the nomination of a liberal for the Supreme Court."[8] Nancy Lacke of Eau Claire, Wisconsin, lambasted Reagan's appointment as "an insult to those people who trusted your word concerning the rights of the unborn."[9] Donald Fries, of Cincinnati, Ohio, even questioned Reagan's personal position on abortion, declaring the president had "destroyed" his "credibility" and concluded that Reagan "either lied to us" during the election or was "lying to himself now."[10]

With complaints pouring in from across the country, Reagan administration officials attempted to get ahead of the controversy by quickly announcing that they were indeed nominating O'Connor to the Supreme Court. Reagan dashed conservative hopes that he would abandon his nominee.[11] He praised O'Connor as a "thoughtful, capable woman whose judicial temperament is highly appropriate for the court" and declared that her appointment would be "one of the proudest legacies of my presidency."[12] Reagan called on critics of O'Connor to "keep an open mind" until after she had testified before the Judiciary Committee. The president even phoned Falwell to assure the reverend that he was "fully satisfied" with O'Connor's past decisions.[13] One aide dismissed the administration's efforts to placate the "rabid right" as simple gestures "to allow them to vent their spleen."[14] Perhaps in part because of such press leaks, the New Right continued vehemently to oppose O'Connor's nomination.

Not everyone in the conservative movement, however, denounced Reagan's selection. Responding to Falwell's comments, Senator Goldwater (R-AZ) quipped that "every good Christian ought to kick Falwell right in the ass."[15] Goldwater went on to praise O'Connor's nomination as "a great step" and proclaimed that he had known her for years and "greatly respected and admire[d]" her.[16] Senator Strom Thurmond (R-SC) stood by Reagan, promising to "do everything" he could "to help the president." Orrin Hatch endorsed O'Connor as "an excellent choice" and reminded conservative critics that when Reagan asked O'Connor how she felt about abortion, she had responded that she found it "personally abhorrent." William F. Buckley went on the offensive, warning that it was "a grave mistake" for the New Right to launch "an all-out effort to defeat O'Connor." He cited the fact that she was going to be "confirmed by a heavy majority" and implied that opposition could undermine the New Right's political strength.[17] Although O'Connor easily won confirmation, the episode damaged the New Right's trust in Reagan.[18] As 1981 faded into 1982, the New Right became increasingly vocal in demanding that the Reagan administration push its conservative social agenda.

The Reagan administration spent much of its first year in office fighting for spending cuts and tax reductions. As a result, it put social legislation on the back burner, and by the end of the year the New Right was voicing its frustration. In August, *Lifeletter*, published by the Ad Hoc Committee in Defense of Life, asserted that the "critical moment has arrived" for "the President" to "turn his attention—and his power—to those 'other' promises." The publication quickly reminded readers, however, that passing socially conservative legislation would be difficult because there were many in the administration who were not pro-life.[19] In December, *Lifeletter* went further, asserting that "virtually all of RR's top advisers are either pro-abort or don't give a hoot about the issue . . . which means that the much improved anti-abort position depends on RR himself." Reflecting on the previous year, the publication lamented that while they had made some small progress, those victories had come with "very real defeats and disappointments."[20] Elizabeth Dole, an assistant to the president, warned members of Reagan's senior staff that if the administration did not show support for social issues in 1982, they risked losing the support of the New Right. Dole concluded that the administration had "reached the point where our passive support will be unable to hold many of the major conservative groups in line."[21]

Dole's warning proved well founded. In January 1982, forty-five conservative activists warned that "the abandonment, reversal, or blunting" of Reagan's conservative principles and policies would cost him their support. In a formal statement, they asked Reagan to renew his support for a right-to-life constitutional amendment, to push for a balanced budget, and to continue the fight against the ERA. Ronald Goodwin, the executive vice president of the Moral Majority, said he represented "morally concerned Americans" who were worried about Reagan's commitment to the socially conservative agenda. Goodwin emphasized that he understood that the economy had to come first, but added that the president did not "have endless time" before disappointing the grassroots activists who helped get him elected. The vice president of the Moral Majority, Cal Thomas, summed up the New Right's frustration when he told Reagan's chief of staff, James Baker, that "if we clean up the economy, but are still allowing the slaughter of one and one-half million babies a year, I will not be able to say that we are better off at all."[22]

Almost all the major leaders of the New Right joined Goodwin and Thomas in criticizing Reagan. Weyrich complained that "no one in the White House" advanced "social issues at a high level" and asserted that Reagan should stop ignoring important issues such as abortion. Phillips lambasted Reagan for trying to "woo his adversaries rather than mobilize his supporters," but begrudgingly acknowledged that Reagan was conservatives' "only option for the time being."[23] Viguerie was more direct in his criticism. He accused Reagan of making "a conscious decision" to keep the New Right "at arm's length" and labeled the president's appearances at conservative conventions as "window-dressing." Viguerie added that the administration was "very nice to us, taking our phone calls, but the policy positions in this Administration are not being held by people who were in the trenches with Ronald Reagan in early 1980."[24] Reagan responded by inviting the leaders of the pro-life movement to the White House. According to *Lifeletter*, Reagan "probably heard more about what is actually happening—divisions and all—in the anti-abort fight than he's heard since he took office." While the meeting raised the spirits of some of those in attendance, making promises a reality in 1982 would prove difficult.[25]

Although Reagan was committed to pushing social legislation, such proposals proved to be divisive both among the population at large and within the New Right.[26] Indeed, in early 1982 the *New York Daily News* released a poll showing that 75 percent of Americans opposed banning abortion.[27] There were also serious fault lines within the conservative ranks. At the opening of the legislative session there were three competing proposals for how to move forward with the pro-life agenda. Senator Helms proposed a human life bill to protect the unborn under the Fourteenth Amendment. Helms enjoyed broad conservative support, including that of the American Life Lobby and the

Christian Action Council. Some conservatives, however, did not feel Helms's proposal went far enough. Senator Hatch proposed a constitutional amendment to outlaw abortion and recognize the unborn baby's right to life. The Hatch Amendment enjoyed the support of many New Right and Christian organizations, including the National Conference of Catholic Bishops, the National Committee for a Human Life Amendment, and Pro Life Ministries.[28] While many on the New Right desired a right-to-life amendment, they also understood that Hatch's proposal had "little chance" to pass because it needed support from two-thirds of the Senate. Because of the improbability of passing the Hatch amendment, some turned to Senator Mark Hatfield (R-OR) for a third proposal.[29] The Hatfield bill asserted that "no funds appropriated by Congress may be used to pay for abortions or to refer women for abortions." Furthermore, the measure banned all federal agencies from performing abortions except to protect the life of the mother.[30] Conservatives hoped that the Hatfield bill could be passed, forcing a constitutional showdown in which a "more conservative" Supreme Court would have "to decide the abortion issue all over again."[31]

The New Right was divided over the three proposals, and supporters of each measure blamed one another for the failure of conservatives to pass an abortion ban in 1981. The Ad Hoc Committee in Defense of Life, for example, used *Lifeletter* to blame Hatch for dividing the pro-life forces and for not allowing the original human life bill to come up for a vote in "a strongly anti-abort atmosphere" in which "it most probably would have swept to victory in a rush." Instead, *Lifeletter* lamented, a year had been wasted.[32]

In March, Helms attempted to unify the pro-life movement by introducing a single piece of legislation that addressed their most pressing concerns. Helms's bill S-2148 defined the unborn baby as a person and ended both domestic and foreign funding for abortion. *Lifeletter* endorsed the measure as providing "a basis for unity among anti-abortion forces both in the Congress and nationwide that have been deadlocked in a bitter dispute over the Human Life Bill and the Hatch Amendment." Conservative observers hoped that Helms's "unity bill" would lead to immediate action. *Lifeletter* claimed that Helms's decision to push the compromise bill was in response to "the 'grass roots' of the anti-abort movement" that had "grown increasingly angry at the leadership's failure to agree on an 'omnibus' measure." Furthermore, many feared that without immediate action, their opportunity "might well be lost . . . if the looming Reagan budget battles stall 'social issue' action as they did all last year."[33] Helms's efforts were successful in bringing most of the pro-life movement under one tent, winning support from an array of New Right organizations including the Conservative Caucus, the Family Life League, the Ad Hoc Committee in Defense of Life, the Pro-Life Action League, the Right to Life Crusade, the Christian Action Council, and the largest Catholic pro-life organization—representing over 100,000 people—the American Life Lobby.[34]

As the cherry trees bloomed in the nation's capital, the pro-life movement enjoyed a renewed sense of hope when President Reagan personally endorsed Helms's unity bill. On April 5, Reagan wrote Helms to emphasize his support for the pro-life efforts in the Senate.[35] Reagan also wrote to Congress, expressing his "hope that we will not miss this long delayed opportunity." The president called on pro-life leaders to put aside "sharp differences" and move forward. Reagan concluded by emphasizing that Congress had "not only my best wishes but also my prayers for success." Staffers and political commentators called Reagan's letter "unprecedented." Capitol Hill observers asserted that Reagan's letter "should break the deadlock" and added that his direct approval elevated Helms's bill "to the status of something the Administration really wants passed." *Lifeletter* asserted that "the President's letter" was "an ultimatum, to the squabbling anti-abortion movement to move now, with or without unity in their ranks." The publication insisted that Reagan's first "direct appeal to Congressional leaders" on the issue of abortion set the stage for quick and decisive action and concluded that "it's hard to imagine that the anti-abortion movement will ever again have a better chance to win."[36]

Despite Reagan's public statements in support of Helms, abortion legislation took a back seat to the battle over tax increases, leading the New Right to launch an unprecedented attack on the president. In July 1982, *Conservative Digest*—a New Right monthly magazine with a circulation of 50,000—dedicated an entire issue "to a compendium of complaints by disappointed conservatives, who feel that Mr. Reagan has buried his own political beliefs and compromised unnecessarily."[37] Reagan's support for the $99 billion tax increase and frustration over his failure to promote legislation to "outlaw abortion and to re-introduce prayers in public schools" led Viguerie, the publisher of *Conservative Digest*, to run the anti-Reagan issue. In an open letter to Reagan, Viguerie insisted the president "reject the four Cs of Jerry

Ford—compromise, conciliation, communication and co-operation—and adopt the two Cs of coalition and confrontation."[38] Viguerie lambasted Reagan for pursuing "détente with liberals," asserting that "most of your major appointments are not conservatives." He urged the president to do more for conservatives and call on the "the American people . . . to make sacrifices."[39] Viguerie's attack demonstrated that many New Right activists believed that Reagan had unnecessarily compromised his conservative principles and that he was little better than other conservative politicians who had turned their back on the grassroots movement that elected them. The July edition of *Conservative Digest* also underscored the deep sense of frustration that the New Right felt toward the reality that change in Washington was often too slow and gradual. Although Reagan had succeeded in getting some conservative results, his achievements were not as revolutionary as grassroots activists such as Viguerie desired.

When Reagan saw the July issue, he was furious. He knew that Viguerie had always been critical of him, but he had not expected this kind of public betrayal. After venting his frustration with conservative columnist John Lofton, Reagan sat down at his desk in the Oval Office to pen a rebuke to Viguerie. He began by questioning whether Viguerie had really drafted his letter "in friendship." The president then defended his conservative credentials and cited the administration's commitment to "school prayer, a balanced budget amendment, anti-abortion, and tuition tax credits." Reagan flat-out denied that he was "dividing" let alone "destroying the conservative movement" as Viguerie had claimed and concluded that "if there is a setback in conservative fortunes it will be the *Conservative Digest* not my administration that brings it about." Once he finished the letter, Reagan decided against sending it. Instead, he drew a large X across the entirety of the letter and then drew wavy lines across the page. The letter was never sent.[40]

Following the July issue of *Conservative Digest*, conservatives from across the spectrum joined the chorus of complaints against Reagan. In his column, conservative pundit George Will criticized Reagan for appeasing "people who didn't vote for him" and warned that "the time is coming when he is going to have to do something for those who did."[41] John Wilkie, the president of the National Right to Life Committee, agreed. He predicted that if the Senate failed to vote on the Hatch Amendment, it would have "a very chilling effect on some of the administration's candidates this fall and would erode the administration's support from our movement in November." Reverend Edward

Bryce, of the National Conference of Catholic Bishops, seconded Wilkie's statements, saying he prayed "that by the end of this session of Congress, the accusation that our elected representatives have abdicated their responsibility will not be appropriate."[42] Near the end of July, the Moral Majority and the New Right held the second annual Family Forum at the Sheraton-Washington Hotel to discuss how "Reagan has neglected social issues dear to many conservatives." More than five hundred participants from thirty-seven states attended. The chairwoman of the National Pro-Family Coalition, Connaught Marshner, confirmed that "there is a disenchantment with Reagan." Marshner lamented that Reagan had broken his promises to pass tuition tax credits, pass legislation to restrict abortions, and pass a prayer amendment to the Constitution. She accused the president of talking about social issues during the election but then neglecting them to focus on the economy. Frustrated that Reagan had put their agenda "on the back burner," the New Right made it clear that its support for the administration depended on the success of social legislation.[43]

On August 3, Reagan tried to reassure the New Right that he supported the pro-life agenda in a speech before Catholic leaders in Hartford, Connecticut. While *Lifeletter* praised the speech as Reagan's "strongest-ever attack on legalized abortion," it lamented his lack of action, asserting that "the words have all been spoken." The publication insisted that the time for talk had passed and questioned whether Reagan's "moderate mafia" would "act on his words— to do the kind of lobbying and arm-twisting they've done on 'serious' (read money) issues." According to *Lifeletter*, it was essential that action be taken on social legislation because "enthusiasm" was "way down" and "discouragement is widespread even among the most 'activist' groups."[44] The newsletter cited Reagan's constant claims that he had "one agenda" and that it included "his anti-abortion promises." The problem with that, however, was that while "the economic half of that single whole has been knocked dizzy, the abortion half remains unbeaten—and time is running out."[45] *National Right to Life News* seconded *Lifeletter*'s sentiment. In an "open letter" to Reagan, the publication insisted that "without your all-out, up-front, full-throttled leadership, Mr. President, our progress will be either agonizingly slow or stopped in its tracks."[46] Hopes that the Reagan administration would fight for social issues with the same vigor it put toward achieving Reagan's economic policies, however, quickly proved to be misplaced.

As the summer ended, the administration's continuing focus on economic issues forced Helms to take unilateral action. Near the end of August, the Senate debated Helms's unity bill. Unfortunately for the senator, many were "uncomfortable with stringent new restrictions on abortion rights." Helms was forced to rewrite his bill without the proclamation that human life began at conception and to replace it with language that argued "that the Supreme Court had erred in 1973." Pro-choice forces proclaimed victory and asserted that the issue of abortion was "dead for the session."[47] Helms, however, refused to accept defeat. He attached his pro-life measures to the bill that increased the debt limit. Helms's strategy failed, however, when Republicans, fearing that the Senate would vote down the increase in the debt ceiling, stripped the bill of Helms's proposal.[48] In return, however, Senate majority leader Howard Baker (R-TN) fulfilled his promise to bring Helms's bill to the floor for a comprehensive debate.[49] Liberal and moderate senators quickly joined forces to filibuster Helms's proposal, forcing conservatives to seek sixty votes to enforce cloture to bring the bill up for a vote.[50] Pro-life leaders, who had criticized the Reagan administration for not lobbying forcefully earlier in the month for Helms, sought an appointment with the president to persuade him to actively "support" and lobby the Senate in order "to obtain the necessary votes."[51] Before he granted them an audience, however, Reagan went out of his way to throw his support behind the measure. During his speech at Kansas State University, Reagan reaffirmed his commitment to ending abortion, declaring "we have a sacred duty to protect the innocent human life of an unborn child." Later, from Air Force One, Reagan phoned several senators, asking them to help Helms end the pro-choice filibuster.[52]

Despite Reagan's support, Helms and his fellow conservatives were unable to break the filibuster. The sting of the defeat on abortion was magnified a few days later when Helms attached the School Prayer Amendment to an appropriation bill. Although Reagan supported the prayer amendment, he demanded it be stripped from the bill. At the president's request, the Senate voted fifty-one to forty-eight against the motion. Helms conceded to the press that abortion and school prayer would not be brought up again in 1982. He also condemned the administration, saying that "they played a little fast and loose with the situation." Helms added that he did not "know of one single vote they obtained for us."[53] Many in the press and in the conservative movement questioned the administration's commitment to the New Right's agenda. The *Boston Globe* concluded that "even when Reagan, in recent weeks, began talking about the social issues and pushing for congressional action on abortion and school prayer, the effort, in the view of many members, seemed more an attempt by the President to shore up his political support on the right than a major lobbying effort such as the White House mounted in the budget and tax battles in 1981 and this year."[54] The *New York Times* also noted that the Reagan administration's ability to balance "principle and pragmatism" continued with the prayer amendment, where "White House lobbyists were noticeably less intense in their efforts" than they had been in other legislative fights.[55] There is little doubt that the Reagan administration invested more political capital in economic and foreign policy issues than in social issues.

After numerous legislative disappointments, the New Right turned its ire on the White House. Dick Dingman, the Moral Majority consultant, wrote the administration to warn it that "prolife groups are so exasperated by the current state of affairs that they are planning legal action." Unable to pass either of the issues closest to their hearts, conservatives decided to target the federal family-planning program. Dingman urged that the White House "meet with conservative leaders in the near future to plan an agenda for reform" in order to avoid "hostile Senate oversight hearings" by the "President's own prolife movement."[56] While conservatives in the Senate were threatening hearings, the New Right suffered a setback in the 1982 midterm elections. Although the number of senators who opposed abortion remained virtually unchanged, *Lifeletter* admitted "things may be a bit tougher in the House."[57] By the fall of 1982, many in the pro-life movement resorted to trimming around the edges when it came to abortion. The American Life Lobby wrote Blackwell in the hope that Reagan might meet with them "to see what incremental actions the Administration could take to provide some incremental gains for the pro-life movement."[58] Although the New Right continued to push their social agenda throughout the Reagan era, they would never pass the type of sweeping legislation they claimed was needed to revitalize America.[59] To the revolutionaries on the front lines of the conservative movement, it was clear that the changes ushered in by Reagan were nowhere near as radical as they desired.

In 1983, shortly after the ten-year anniversary of *Roe*, Reagan decided to reassure conservatives that he had not compromised his socially conservative principles despite his administration's legislative failures. Reagan wrote an essay entitled "Abortion and the Conscience of the Nation" for the *Human Life Review*, founded by James P. McFadden, a former associate publisher of *National*

Review. The publication wrote that it was "honored that the President should choose our review in which to make his most remarkable testament of faith in the 'sacred value of human life'" and asserted that Reagan was "equally eloquent in condemning infanticide."[60] Reagan began that legal abortions were responsible for the deaths of "more than 15 million unborn children" which was "over ten times the number of Americans lost in all our nation's wars." The president compared the *Roe* decision to *Dred Scott*, reminding conservatives that "at first, only a minority of Americans recognized and deplored the moral crisis brought about by denying the full humanity of our black brothers and sisters; but that minority persisted in their vision and finally prevailed." Although Reagan acknowledged that there was uncertainty concerning when life began, he insisted that "anyone who doesn't feel sure whether we are talking about a second human life should clearly give life the benefit of the doubt." Reagan emphasized that he had supported and would continue to support all the measures in Congress to limit abortions. Concluding, Reagan promised conservatives that his administration was "dedicated to the preservation of America as a free land" and asserted that there was "no cause more important for preserving that freedom than affirming the transcendent right to life of all human beings, the right without which no other rights have any meaning."[61] Reagan consistently lent his voice to the pro-life movement, but he was unable to deliver the legislative victories that social conservatives desperately desired.

If Reagan thought his essay would put the New Right at ease, he was sorely mistaken. Without any major policy victories, many social conservatives questioned whether they should support Reagan in 1984. Conservatives met in Dallas in early 1983 to evaluate the conservative movement and determine a course of action in the 1984 elections. Clymer Wright, Reagan's Texas campaign finance chairman in 1980, was responsible for organizing the twenty hard-line conservatives—most of whom were dissatisfied with Reagan. Phillips and Viguerie, two of the most prominent members of the group, urged "Reagan not to run again in 1984." Viguerie asserted that "the conservative cause and the Republican Party would be better served if the President doesn't run for reelection." Phillips echoed Viguerie's dissatisfaction with Reagan, declaring that if the president did not "turn this thing around in the next several weeks," there would "be an all-out effort to persuade him not to run in 1984." Viguerie went further, adding that even if Reagan decided to seek reelection, there would be "a strong chance he would be opposed for the Republican nomination by a strong conservative." A conservative could easily run to the right of Reagan, Viguerie explained, because he had "done so very little" for conservatives and had "been strongly to the left on most issues."[62]

Although the conference convened without endorsing an alternative to Reagan, key leaders of the New Right continued to oppose Reagan's reelection. In November, Viguerie told the press that conservatives would be better served if Reagan lost in 1984 and asserted that a Reagan victory would lead to major losses in Congress in 1986. In contrast, he insisted that a Mondale victory would give conservatives an enemy and would result in "massive gains" for conservatives in the 1986 midterms. Viguerie justified the New Right's opposition to Reagan by claiming they were thinking "in long-range terms, 20 or 30 years" and added that "it wouldn't frighten me to have a Democratic president for four years."[63]

In July 1984, the National Conservative Political Action Committee turned Phillips's and Viguerie's words into action. Expressing dissatisfaction with Reagan, Terry Dolan, who had spent $2.1 million on advertisements in 1980, decided to cancel his organization's "campaign on behalf of President Reagan."[64] Despite the New Right voicing their concerns and cutting funding for the Reagan campaign, the president easily won reelection. The New Right's fear of four more years with Reagan proved to be well founded. During his second term, Reagan decided to govern from the center, and the New Right's ability to influence policy waned. As a result, the New Right became louder more extreme and intensified the culture war, which in the midst of the AIDS epidemic endangered the lives of thousands of Americans.

5. AIDS, the New Right, and Reagan's Response

The onset of the AIDS epidemic magnified the culture war that had raged between the New Right and the New Left since the sixties. The disease was perfectly suited to the New Right cause of restoring Judeo-Christian family values, and the groups initially affected—homosexual men, drug users, prostitutes, and Haitians—were already targets of the movement. The New Right railed against these people for behaving in "unnatural" ways, for their promiscuity, and for their "antifamily" lifestyles. The breakout of this mysterious disease among these seemingly "unclean" people provided the New Right an opportunity to use the epidemic for political purposes.[1] The New Right's crusade to restore family values by using the AIDS epidemic ultimately pitted it against the scientific community, the surgeon general, and eventually President Reagan.[2]

In 1981, the first cases of AIDS "sprang up almost simultaneously" in Los Angeles, San Francisco, and New York. In January, a thirty-one-year-old homosexual male was treated at UCLA by Dr. Michael S. Gottlieb. Gottlieb was puzzled because the man's immune system had broken down and he had lost a large amount of weight. Gottlieb did what he could for the man and believed "we'd never see someone like him again." Just a couple months later, however, two more patients with similar conditions were treated by Gottlieb, and similar cases were reported in San Francisco and New York.[3] In December 1981, the Associated Press reported that "a wave of pneumonia and cancer" was "killing homosexual men across the country." It asserted that "ninety-two percent of the patients" with this "strange disease" were homosexual men.[4] There was widespread fear and uncertainty surrounding the disease. Furthermore, rumors about how it was transmitted and who could contract it spread like wildfire. One of the initial theories was "that large amounts of sperm . . . might cause the problem if it were absorbed by the body during frequent oral or anal intercourse."[5] In October 1982, the *Saturday Evening Post* published an article entitled "Being Gay Is a Health Hazard," with a blurb under the title that read: "The 'gay plague' is a frightening epidemic because no one knows how much worse it will become before the cause is discovered."[6] Even the government contributed to the perception that this was a gay disease. The Centers for Disease Control (CDC) released its first report on AIDS in June 1981, but while the disease was on the government's radar, no one knew "what to call it, much less what it really was." Since those affected by the disease were primarily homosexual men, the Public Health Service initially labeled the disease gay-related immune deficiency (GRID).[7] As a result, from 1981 to 1983, AIDS was primarily associated with homosexual men, allowing sexual politics to mingle with public health.[8]

While most of the country was either unaware of AIDS or fearful of those who had it, the gay communities in New York and San Francisco began fighting the disease. Gay doctors, social workers, community organizers, and journalists worked with medical experts to confront and educate the public about the disease. Support systems were created to help victims, and journalists began warning that lifestyle changes were necessary to avoid contracting AIDS. By 1983, "the shared wisdom" in the gay community was that gay men needed to change their lifestyles, not their sexuality.[9] These activists also provided funding for sex-education programs that advocated safe sex and the use of condoms in all sexual encounters.[10] The efforts of the gay community saved countless lives and began a national conversation about the importance of safe sex and sex education in schools.[11]

Sex and politics were closely linked during the 1980s, and the AIDS epidemic magnified the disputes about morality, family, and the role of government in peoples' sex lives. The rights revolution that began with the civil rights movement inspired the gay community to push for equality before the law.[12] During the 1970s, there was a campaign to make sexual orientation grounds for receiving protection from discrimination. Conservative groups such as the Truth about Gays Political Action Committee wanted to prevent such protections.[13] The New Right feared groups like the Gay Alliance of New York that were dedicated to putting "an immediate end to all opposition of homosexuals and the immediate recognition" of "basic rights" for the gay community. The Gay Alliance insisted that homosexuals had a right to their own feelings, to their own bodies, to be attracted to a person of the same sex without being questioned, and "the right to make love to anyone, anyway, anytime" so long as all parties consented.[14]

While the gay-rights movement was seeking equal rights and the recognition of homosexuality as an alternative lifestyle, the New Right was dedicated to both stopping the gay-rights movement and restoring traditional concepts of morality. Phyllis Schlafly and her organization, Eagle Forum, pushed "for changes in textbooks in order to reflect traditional sex and family roles." The New Right also launched a broad attack "on teachers, textbooks, and curriculums—an attack aimed at infusing public education with conservative positions, including an opposition to abortion and in some cases, fundamentalist Christian doctrine." They also pressured "publishers, local school committees and government agencies to modify curriculum and textbooks to comply with their views."[15] In short, AIDS became a national epidemic while homosexuality was at the center of partisan debate.

In 1982, the New Right's fears that homosexuality might be recognized as an alternative lifestyle were seemingly realized when a federal judge struck down Texas's sodomy law. The decision to overturn the law, which prohibited "deviant sexual intercourse," including intercourse and oral sex between people of the same sex, was the first decision of its kind.[16] Lucia Valeska, the executive director of the National Gay Task Force, praised the ruling and predicted that "a national strategy will emerge" to combat sodomy laws across the United States. Don Baker, the president of the Dallas Alliance, described the decision as "homosexual's Emancipation Proclamation, the Magna Carta, and the Declaration of Independence" all rolled into one.[17] In contrast, conservatives condemned the decision. One conservative organization, in an early example of how some conservatives would use AIDS to their advantage, linked the removal of sodomy laws to public health. The organization warned that the ruling would "encourage promiscuity among homosexuals and the evidence to date indicates homosexuals transmit AIDS and that AIDS has appeared in blood donations, posing a threat to innocent recipients of blood transfusions."[18] Such arguments were just the beginning of the politicization of the AIDS epidemic.

The battle against AIDS was transformed in 1983 as health professionals learned more about the disease and media outlets began to run articles to raise public awareness. *Discover* magazine asserted that doctors were doubtful that AIDS would "spread to the general public," citing that "the disease appears to be present in blood and semen, and perhaps mucus and saliva," which implied that only "intimate contact" resulted in the transmission of the disease.[19] *Newsweek* also ran an informational article on the disease in which it declared that AIDS was not "a gay plague" and insisted that if it "had not developed first among homosexuals, it could well have struck some other risk group."[20] For every responsible report, however, there were alarmists. Even the *New York Times* published one article under the headline "Mere Contact May Spread AIDS."[21]

In addition to conflicting news reports, the New Right used the epidemic to dismiss homosexuals' calls for equal rights and some even used AIDS as a reason to further target the gay community. Phyllis Schlafly condemned homosexuals for blaming government for their contracting AIDS when the real reason they got the disease was "their anonymous promiscuity." Schlafly cited a news report that claimed "homosexuals with AIDS" had "an average of 1,100 sexual partners," and she concluded that "it's almost impossible for the average person to comprehend such massive promiscuity." Schlafly then pivoted to sex education. Citing a CBS documentary, she asserted that the "homosexual movement" had "a well-funded 'educational' program in the schools to present homosexuality to school children as an 'alternative normal lifestyle.'" She warned that the gay community was also seeking child custody, spousal benefits, and acceptance into the US Armed Forces.[22] By connecting AIDS and sexual promiscuity to sex education in the schools, Schlafly encouraged parents to distrust and even despise homosexuals for trying to manipulate and corrupt their children. In doing so, Schlafly hoped to discredit all the gay community's requests for equal rights.

Schlafly was not the only member of the New Right to use the AIDS epidemic to gain the high ground in the culture war. Just a year after a federal judge struck down Texas's sodomy laws, a Texas lawmaker introduced legislation to reinstate the restrictions, insisting that because of the AIDS outbreak public officials did not need to focus on what was "right or wrong" but rather on "what's good for society."[23] Alert Citizens of Texas echoed the lawmaker's sentiment in a pamphlet entitled *The Gay Plague: Homosexuality and Disease*. These Texas conservatives asserted that "the truth about homosexuality and the public health must be told." The pamphlet claimed that "homosexual conduct threatens to destroy the fabric of our culture—medically, psychologically, and sociologically." It added that all AIDS victims were gay and asserted that the disease was "transmitted by homosexual conduct." Citing "statistics," Alert Citizens of Texas accused homosexuals of being rapists, child molesters, prostitutes, and mass murders. The publication asserted that "gays are 20 times more apt to molest children than heterosexuals." It concluded by endorsing sodomy laws, citing that "homosexuality endangers the public's health, causes increased crime and threatens to destroy the foundations of our culture," and added that "homosexuality is deviant, pathological social behavior."[24] In addition to state and local efforts to fight the "gay agenda," Weyrich's Free Congress Research and Education Foundation released the "first political exposé of the homosexual movement in America," detailing its goals and its vision for the nation.[25] Despite losing key legislative battles over school prayer and abortion, in 1983 many in the New Right believed that they could win the culture war, and some looked to the administration for support.

The New Right had good reason to believe that the administration would support their position when it came to the AIDS epidemic. From 1982 to 1984, White House press secretary Larry Speakes answered questions about AIDS by deflecting and relying on homophobic humor.[26] Lester Kinsolving, a conservative news reporter for the *Globe Syndicate*, asked Speakes, in late 1982, if he was aware that the CDC had declared AIDS an epidemic and added that the disease was known as "gay plague." In a demonstration of the attitudes of the time, the press pool erupted in laughter and Speakes quipped, "I don't have it, do you?" Kinsolving followed up by asking Speakes if the White House considered "this as a great joke." Speakes responded that he was not aware of AIDS and retorted, "There's been no personal experience here, Lester."[27]

Over eight months later, in June 1983, Speakes was once again asked about AIDS. He initially took a more serious tone and responded that "the president has been . . . briefed on the AIDS situation a number of months ago in a Cabinet meeting and ordered that higher priority be given to research on it." The press secretary, however, could not contain himself when Kinsolving asked if Reagan had any suggestions on whether "gays [should] cut down on their cruising." The press pool erupted into laughter, and Speakes poked fun at Kinsolving's interest in the subject. Speakes emphasized that the administration was researching AIDS, and that if "any research . . . sheds some light on whether gays should cruise or not cruise we'll make it available to you." Laughter rang out in the briefing room, and one reporter shouted, "Back to fairy tales!" In 1984, Kinsolving was once again mocked by Speakes and the other members of the press when he cited that three hundred thousand Americans had been exposed to AIDS and erroneously added that it could be spread through saliva. He asked if Reagan would act to ban people with AIDS from working in the Armed Forces' food and medical services to protect the military from infection. Speakes responded with a simple "I don't know," and when Kinsolving pressed him, Speakes asserted that he had not heard Reagan "express concern," but added that "I must confess I haven't asked him about it." The other reporters in the room mocked Kinsolving's inquiry by sarcastically asking, "Is the president going to ban mouth to mouth kissing?" The way in which many of the nation's top reporters and the Reagan administration's top spokesman dismissed AIDS is a testament to the culture of homophobia that existed in the 1980s.[28]

While Speakes and the press pool were making light of the epidemic, other members of the Reagan administration were taking actions to combat the disease.[29] Secretary of Health and Human Services (HHS) Margaret Heckler announced in August 1983 that Reagan would ask Congress for $40 million to fund AIDS research in 1984—double the administration's initial request.[30] Sitting beside an AIDS patient, Heckler told the press that the administration endorsed the increase in funding "because scientists studying the malady said they needed more money." Explaining the venue for the announcement, Heckler said she "hoped the public would see that she did not fear an encounter with an AIDS victim and would 'cast aside the emotional reaction' that has led many to shun those who had the disease." Heckler reiterated that AIDS was "spread by sexual contact or by shared needles—not by casual contact." When Peter Justice, the patient, was asked what he thought of the visit, he responded that he was "delighted she's here, I'm delighted she cares."[31] Throughout 1983, Heckler "tried to discourage panic and encourage compassion for victims of the disease." Jeffrey Levi, the Washington representative of the National Gay Task Force, acknowledged "a greater responsiveness than there was four or five months ago." He praised Dr. Edward N. Brandt Jr., the assistant secretary of health, and Heckler for making "AIDS the No. 1 priority of the Public Health Service."[32]

Other members of the federal government were also doing their best to quell the fear and uncertainty surrounding the disease. James Curran, the head of the CDC's task force on AIDS, told the public that the disease was not found "in the co-workers of AIDS victims, or in people who have routine household contact with them."[33] By the end of 1983, many in the Reagan administration were focused on combating the AIDS epidemic, but more could have been done. Most obviously, Reagan could have used the bully pulpit of the presidency to calm the American people and perhaps even separate politics from the public health.[34]

As the country was focused on the 1984 presidential election, the Reagan administration announced a major breakthrough in AIDS research. By 1984, there were more than 5,000 reported cases of AIDS and nearly 2,300 deaths. Despite the growing number of AIDS cases outside the gay community, "there seemed to be little outcry from the public or even organized medicine for more and appropriate leadership from the government."[35] On April 23, Secretary Heckler announced that HHS resources had contributed to finding the cause of AIDS. Heckler denounced those "who disparaged this scientific search" and "those who have said we weren't doing enough." She asserted that "from the first day that AIDS was identified in 1981, HHS scientists and their medical allies have never stopped searching for the answers to the AIDS mystery." Heckler concluded that "the resources of the Public Health Service have been effectively mobilized" and announced that new research would make it possible to create a blood test "to diagnose people infected with AIDS virus, to render the blood supply safe, and to provide the basis for making a vaccine against AIDS."[36]

In 1985, the test that Heckler discussed a year earlier was developed and the death of Rock Hudson put AIDS in the public spotlight. Hudson's diagnosis increased concern about the disease, and because of Reagan's friendship with the actor, AIDS—for the first time—"touched the White House."[37] Just before Hudson's death, Reagan broke his silence. A reporter asked Reagan if children with AIDS should be allowed to attend school. The president responded that while he understood both sides of the issue, "his own medical experts stated that children infected with AIDS posed no threat to other children in school."[38]

Conservative criticism of the Reagan administration's handling of the public health increased dramatically in 1985. While some in the White House agreed with Heckler's advocacy of AIDS funding, conservative forces within the administration "charged that she failed to develop an aggressive stance on big budget issues like Medicare, Medicaid, and Social Security." According to the *Boston Globe*, Heckler was ultimately let go "for allegedly being insufficiently doctrinaire to suit hardline conservatives."[39] In midsummer of 1985, conservatives launched an organized campaign to force the Reagan administration to "unmuzzle" the conservative surgeon general, C. Everett Koop. More than five thousand postcards poured into the administration suggesting that Reagan should crack down on homosexuals and those with AIDS in the name of public safety. Conservatives accused the government of hiding the facts about the disease from the public and "conspiring with the homosexual community to 'cover up' the epidemic."[40] Shortly thereafter, the New Right got their wish and Koop was appointed to the AIDS Task Force. The surgeon general quickly became the administration's voice on the disease. In October

1985, Koop began answering questions about AIDS. In November he gave an interview to *Christianity Today* in which he leveled his "oft-repeated conclusion that in preventing AIDS the moralist and the scientist could walk hand in hand."[41] Koop, a conservative darling up until 1985 for his views on abortion, quickly isolated the New Right with his talk of science, education, and prevention.

Increased awareness of AIDS allowed public health officials an opportunity to discuss education and prevention, but it also gave national attention to conservative activists who proposed radically different solutions. Falwell announced in September 1985 that he supported increased funding for AIDS but added that while the disease was not yet curable it was "totally preventable" if only homosexuals would "stop doing those vulgar things that even animals don't perform."[42] He continued to blame the spread of AIDS on gay men throughout the fall, lambasting "the unwillingness of some homosexuals to change their lifestyles to prevent the spread of AIDS."[43]

In the spring of 1986, William F. Buckley penned an op-ed for the *New York Times* in which he discussed the AIDS epidemic and offered some solutions. Buckley suggested that all couples seeking to marry should be tested for AIDS and if either test came back positive then the marriage would only be allowed if the couple agreed "to sterilization." To protect the population at large, including gay men, Buckley suggested the use of private identification where "everyone detected with AIDS should be tattooed in the upper forearm, to protect common needle users, and on the buttocks, to prevent the victimization of other homosexuals."[44] While many scoffed at Buckley's op-ed, he was serious about his proposals. Writing to Reagan near the end of April, he mentioned his suggestion that those infected with AIDS be forced to get tattoos. Buckley told the president that he was getting a great "amount of flak" for the suggestion, but that his critics could not "answer" when he asked them why it was not "a Gay Right not to be infected by someone already infected." Buckley ended the letter by recounting that a colleague at *National Review* had "asked whether the rear tattoo might appropriately be the line from Dante, 'Abandon hope, all ye who enter here!'"[45] Reagan never responded to the letter.

Some conservatives did more than just talk about their proposals, they offered legislative solutions. In California, Lyndon LaRouche, the leader of an assortment of far-right-wing organizations, led an effort to force a statewide vote on registering and quarantining those with AIDS.[46] Supporters of the initiative claimed the measure "would require AIDS sufferers and carriers be banned from working or studying in schools or working in commercial food establishments." It also called for all AIDS cases to be registered, for the spreading of AIDS to be a misdemeanor, and for state officials to "control the activities of those with AIDS or the virus."[47] LaRouche's authoritarian solutions were echoed in Washington. Congressman William Dannemeyer—representing conservative Orange County, California—proposed mandatory AIDS testing for the entire United States and forcible quarantine for those with AIDS (as was done under Castro's regime in Cuba), and advocated making it a felony for those with the disease to "exchange body fluids."[48] Dannemeyer along with Newt Gingrich, Phil Crane, and six other congressmen wrote Reagan directly, calling for a tougher policy toward people with AIDS. They called it "appalling" that children with AIDS were "not only encouraged to attend school but to do so anonymously so that other children are precluded from taking appropriate precautions." The congressmen called medical experts in the administration "cavalier" for advising "hospitals and restaurants to refrain from testing personnel for AIDS" and for "failing to prohibit AIDS victims from working in these areas."[49] Such proposals never made it out of committee. Koop and Dannemeyer were friends, and during their conversations, Koop asked the congressman what he would do if everyone with AIDS could be identified. Dannemeyer responded that he would "wipe them off the face of the Earth!" That attitude, Koop later recalled, "although not widely voiced, was widely held."[50]

While some on the far right were proposing internment camps and mandatory testing, Reagan contemplated discussing AIDS in his 1986 State of the Union message. In January, two White House staffers gave Koop a note while he was at a dinner hosted by Treasury Secretary Jim Baker informing the surgeon general that Reagan intended to mention AIDS in the State of the Union and that the president had requested that Koop write a report on the epidemic. AIDS did not make it into the State of the Union message, the tone of which was upbeat and positive. Instead, Reagan personally made his way to DHHS on February 5 to discuss AIDS. Reagan told Dr. Otis Bowen, the newly appointed secretary of HHS, as well as the others present, including Koop, that he "wanted AIDS to be a top priority in the department and was looking forward to the day when there would be a vaccine." Reagan also announced that he wanted Koop to prepare a report on AIDS—no formal request for the report was ever made beyond Reagan's personal appeal.[51]

In late July, at Koop's request, Reagan almost tied AIDS to Nancy and his new initiative against drugs, the "Just Say No" campaign, to raise awareness about the disease. Koop called Jack Svahn, a domestic adviser to Reagan, who took the idea to the president. Svahn reported back to Koop that "Reagan had grasped the issues completely and appreciated the implications of tying the two together." Reagan arrived at his staff meeting the following morning "sold" on the idea, "but his advisers were simply not interested in the president's doing anything about AIDS." One attendee reminded Reagan that "'Just Say No' is a win-win: AIDS is a 'no-win.'"[52] The president's advisers were probably correct that there would have been a severe backlash from the New Right had Reagan decided to speak out in 1986.[53]

Conservative backlash over the administration's handling of AIDS, however, proved unavoidable. Their main target, though, was Koop and not Reagan. When Koop released his report, the New Right was "stunned" that he endorsed "sex education in the schools and the use of condoms to avoid AIDS."[54] Weyrich and Schlafly wasted little time criticizing Koop for advocating "safe sodomy" and "safe fornication with condoms" to young children.[55] New Right activists boycotted a dinner held in Koop's honor and pressured the Republican presidential hopefuls not to attend. Weyrich and Schlafly condemned the dinner for playing "right into the hands of those promoting the gay rights agenda, which is to teach children how to use condoms for premarital promiscuity with either sex."[56] Asserting that "homosexuals were editing" Koop's material, Schlafly complained that Reagan would not fire Koop as "the president has put up with a number of disloyal people." She concluded by lamenting the fact that "the president has great tolerance."[57] It seems to have never crossed Schlafly's mind that perhaps Reagan's "tolerance" also extended to those afflicted with AIDS or that the surgeon general of the United States might have been acting at the president's request.

Schlafly and Weyrich were not the only members of the New Right dissatisfied with Koop's report.[58] Judie Brown, the director of the American Life Lobby, called for Koop to resign and condemned him for being "more concerned with the civil rights of AIDS patients than the threat they posed to society." Reverend Robert Dugan of the National Organization of Evangelicals observed that because of his report, Koop was no longer a New Right "hero," but rather "a bad guy" wearing a "black hat."[59] Koop's report led to friction in the White House as well. A civil war broke out between those who did not want the administration pushing sex education, led by Secretary of Education William Bennett, and more moderate Republicans who supported Koop.[60]

Ultimately, Bennett and Koop were able to work out their differences, and the administration mailed an educational pamphlet to over 107 million Americans and distributed a guide for schools on how to accommodate students with AIDS and how to provide adequate sex education to students.[61]

Although many other members of the New Right voiced their dissatisfaction with Koop, Schlafly led the charge against the surgeon general.[62] Schlafly wrote Koop numerous times and denounced his proposals in her newsletter.[63] Koop, however, declined to comment on matters that were "judgmental in nature and which do not directly bear upon the scientific, medical and epidemiological facts of the disease of AIDS."[64] In response, Schlafly went into overdrive. She held a press conference in which she claimed Koop's report "looks and reads like it was edited by the Gay Task Force," and she reiterated that Koop wanted to teach "safe sodomy" to students in the third grade. Tired of being ignored, Schlafly finally "stormed" into Koop's "office in the Humphrey Building to hand-deliver another angry letter." Koop took the letter but refused to acknowledge Schlafly's criticisms. Koop later remarked that "Schlafly was beneath contempt" and declared that he "would not lower" himself "to respond" to her.[65]

On May 31, 1987, Reagan finally spoke on the subject of AIDS. A week or so before the speech, Koop had the opportunity to speak to Landon Parvin, who was involved in preparing Reagan's remarks. Koop "took the opportunity to fill his ear for a half hour, giving him some anecdotes for Reagan to use." Parvin discussed some of the material with Reagan, and the president asked Parvin to convey to Koop that the president "knew all too well how the press could make two people appear to be at odds when really they were allies." That was Koop's first direct indication that Reagan approved of his report and intended "to follow the path marked by health officers, not by political advisers in the White House."[66]

When Reagan delivered his speech at the awards dinner, it was clear that the president had heeded Koop's report. Reagan began by thanking Koop for his hard work on AIDS and added that he was "what every Surgeon General should be . . . an honest man, a good doctor, and an advocate for the public health." Reagan thanked all the doctors, researchers, and health professionals who "showed genuine courage" when there was little understanding of the disease. He insisted that while it was government's job to educate citizens about the danger of AIDS and to "encourage safe behavior . . . only medical science can ever truly defeat AIDS." Reagan contended that much had been done to combat the disease in a short time and announced that there would be a 30 percent increase in the funding for AIDS research in 1988. He declared that "spending on AIDS has been one of the fastest growing parts of the budget" and added that "it deserves to be."[67]

The president then turned to what the administration was doing to help the victims of AIDS. Reagan promised that he was doing everything possible to tear "down the regulatory barriers so as to move AIDS from the pharmaceutical laboratory to the marketplace as quickly as possible." He lamented that both a vaccine and a cure were years away, but insisted that Americans needed to discuss how to "protect the citizens of this nation." Reagan did not endorse any of the New Right's proposals; instead he asserted that "education" was "critical to clearing up the fears" and "to stopping the transmission of the disease." He refused to "break down the numbers and categories" of those who had died of AIDS because Reagan did not "want Americans to think AIDS simply affects certain groups." Indeed, Reagan added, "AIDS affects all of us." Reagan continued that the disease called for "urgency, not panic . . . compassion, not blame . . . and for understanding, not ignorance." Reagan insisted that it was "important that America not reject those who" had "the disease, but care for them with dignity and kindness." Seemingly speaking to the New Right, Reagan reminded the audience that "final judgment is up to God" and that Americans' duty was to "ease the suffering and find a cure." After all, Reagan asserted, "this is a battle against a disease, not against our fellow Americans."[68]

As the Reagan administration came to end, the New Right began to question who would lead conservative forces into the 1990s. In 1987, Viguerie indicated that the New Right had given up on Reagan and declared "we are now basically in the post-Reagan era. . . . We're looking beyond the next 20 months."[69] Coincidently, that same year, Weyrich's Free Congress Research and Education Foundation published *Cultural Conservatism*, which laid out the New Right's vision for the post-Reagan era.[70] The book chastised "Reagan for his failings" and discussed how to remedy "'certain shortcomings' of the religious and pro-family right."[71]

Despite the New Right's efforts to reenergize social conservatives, observers from across the political spectrum began to question whether the New Right would survive the next election. Kevin Phillips, a former conservative political analyst, declared that the New Right's influence was waning. Phillips asserted that they did not have a platform to run on, declaring, "Ramboism is played out, the tax revolt is played out, the religious right is played out because of the scandals, and opposition to big government is played out." The *Boston Globe* asserted that the New Right had "no cause, no candidate," and "no money." The publication explained that "the New Right is suffering an identity crisis, struggling to come to terms with the unfulfilled promises of the Reagan Revolution."[72] Even some members of the Religious Right began to consider their stint in politics as a failure, and books such as *The Rise and Fall of the Christian Right: Conservative Protestant Politics in America, 1979–1988* and *Fall from Grace: The Failed Crusade of the Christian Right* were published in 1988 and 1989.[73] Even right-leaning publications began to question whether the New Right as a political movement was over. The *Wall Street Journal* published an article in 1989 entitled "Why 'Moral Majority,' a Force for a Decade, Ran Out of Steam."[74]

Looking back on the Reagan years, many social conservatives believed that the Reagan Revolution had been less than revolutionary. Mitch Daniels, Reagan's former political director, described the "mood among conservatives" as "morose." Gary Bauer concluded that conservatives were "somewhat depressed" seeing George H. W. Bush as the Republican nominee in 1988. The *Wall Street Journal* explained that "a curious malaise—frustration mingled with a sense of opportunities lost—grips many conservative leaders." The *Journal* added that conservatives were even "disillusioned with Ronald Reagan himself," believing that "he ultimately betrayed or undercut their most cherished causes." Conservative activist Amy Moritz exclaimed that "Reagan lost his vision," and Gingrich concluded that conservatives who "had grown up in opposition" simply "weren't prepared for governing." Weyrich lamented that "Franklin D. Roosevelt made institutional changes that forever changed the political landscape of the country" and "we haven't done that." Weyrich dismissed the talk about a Reagan Revolution and legacy as "an illusion."[75]

6. Neoconservatives, the New Right, and Reagan's First Two Years of Foreign Policy

In the early morning hours of September 1, 1983, Soviet missiles shot down Korean Air Lines Flight 007 (KAL007), flying from New York to Seoul. Secretary of State George Shultz told the press that the plane "strayed into Soviet airspace over the Kamchatka Peninsula, the Sea of Okhotsk and over the Sakhalin Island," where "at least eight fighters" intercepted it. Shultz asserted that the fighter that shot down the airliner "was close enough for a visual inspection," and he concluded that the administration could see "no explanation whatever for shooting down an unarmed commercial airliner." All 269 persons aboard the plane perished, including 62 Americans, among whom was Congressman Larry McDonald, a conservative Democrat from Georgia.[1]

President Reagan was purposefully slow to respond to the crisis, but conservative activists immediately held a press conference declaring the act intentional.[2] The Conservative Caucus and other conservative groups praised McDonald, who had recently become the chairman of the John Birch Society, as a martyr and suggested that the attack was a Soviet attempt "to silence McDonald and other conservative lawmakers" who were on their way to attend a conference in Seoul. Conservatives bound for the conference included Senators Jesse Helms and Orrin Hatch—both of whom had booked different flights. Jerry Falwell claimed that the USSR had targeted the flight "to kill Larry McDonald." Representative Philip Crane (R-IL) concurred that the Soviets had shot down the plane to knock "out some of the foremost adversaries of communism," and McDonald's staff added that the congressman from Georgia "was simply a danger the Soviets could not afford to face."[3]

Conservatives demanded that President Reagan retaliate against the Soviet Union despite the fact that such a heavy-handed reaction would escalate Cold War tensions. Indeed, Reagan's address to the nation should have pleased conservatives. He was unequivocal that the Soviet Union had committed "an act of barbarism born of a society which wantonly disregards individual rights and the value of human life and seeks constantly to expand and dominate other nations." Reagan condemned the Soviets for denying that they shot down the plane and again reminded the world that the Soviets had demonstrated such "inhuman brutality" in Czechoslovakia, Poland, Hungary, and Afghanistan. After making this clear, however, the president altered his tone. Reagan told the audience that vengeance was "not the proper answer" and insisted that his goal would be to achieve "justice" and encourage "action to see that this never happens again."[4]

Reagan's refusal to retaliate infuriated conservatives. Conservative columnist William Safire condemned the president for "sounding off more fiercely than Theodore Roosevelt" but acting "more pusillanimously than Jimmy Carter."[5] The New Right almost unanimously denounced Reagan's response as all talk and no action. Paul Weyrich lamented that Reagan "missed this great opportunity to exercise decisive leadership."[6] Weyrich insisted that Reagan could have used the incident as a means to end loans to communist countries and demand that the USSR release 269 political and religious prisoners. Richard Viguerie proclaimed that "the American people want the President to take action, not just make nice speeches." Viguerie denounced Reagan's response as "a slap on the wrist" and asserted that "this isn't what the American people thought they were getting when they elected Ronald Reagan."[7]

When it came to foreign policy, Reagan faced criticism for talking conservatively but not acting with the same resolve. Although Reagan's rhetoric was often bombastic and assertive, his policy initiatives were usually pragmatic and moderate. Conservatives loved Reagan's rhetoric, but denounced what they saw as concessions to conservatives' enemies at home and abroad. In reality, however, Reagan's rhetoric was a means to his pragmatic ends. This disconnect often led conservatives to feel that Reagan, and his staff, had betrayed them in matters of foreign policy.

Throughout the Reagan presidency, conservatives were frustrated and disappointed with the administration's foreign policy.[8] During the first years of the Reagan administration, both the New Right and neoconservative intellectuals denounced him for what they viewed as the president's continuation of détente. Although the complaints subsided after Reagan's unilateral action in Grenada and his announcement of the Strategic Defense Initiative, conservatives were outraged when the president opened nuclear-arms negotiations with the Soviet Union during his second term. Conservatives also disagreed with Reagan's handling of Taiwan, Israel, and even Nicaragua. Often, conservatives viewed Reagan as unwilling to take the necessary steps to roll back communism across the globe and lamented the fact that Reagan's fiery rhetoric did not result in conservative policies. By 1988, the Republican presidential hopefuls were distancing themselves from the man in the Oval Office, claiming they would carry on the vision of the true Reagan, not the man who was bartering with the "evil empire."

At the heart of conservatives' frustration with the Cold War liberal consensus was détente, a policy that encouraged the United States and the Soviet Union to ease tensions with one another and focus on coexisting.[9] Détente emerged during the late 1960s in response to the global student protest movement and the threat of social revolution in Western countries. Civil unrest across Europe and the United States led global leaders to agree that international stability was needed to ease domestic pressures created by the Cold War.[10] Secretary of State Henry Kissinger described détente as a process "of managing relations with a potentially hostile country in order to pressure peace while maintain[ing] our vital interests."[11] President Richard Nixon embraced détente as another form of containment and as a tool to end the hostilities in Vietnam. Accordingly, he quickly moved to improve relations with communist China and General Secretary Leonid Brezhnev.[12] Conservatives who had believed the United States should not coexist with "godless communism," but rather defeat it were outraged by the policy of détente, and they felt betrayed by Republicans, such as Nixon, who decided to ease tensions with a nation they viewed as the principal source of evil in the world. Over time, Ronald Reagan became the most outspoken critic of détente. Once Reagan took office, however, his fiery conservative antidétente rhetoric gave way to a much more pragmatic foreign policy that often frustrated and even outraged conservatives.

Before conservatives were discouraged by Reagan negotiating with the Soviets, they were betrayed by Nixon's embrace of détente. On July 15, 1971, Nixon announced that he intended to normalize relations with China and added that he was going to visit Beijing.[13] To American conservatives, who viewed communism as unequivocally evil and considered Chiang Kai-shek's exiled forces in Taiwan as the rightful government of China, such news was anathema.[14] William F. Buckley watched Nixon's announcement with Ronald and Nancy Reagan at their Sacramento home. The room was silent while Nixon spoke, and almost as soon as he finished the phone rang—it was Kissinger. According to Buckley, "Henry Kissinger, within five minutes of the public announcement, had reached and reassured the most conspicuously conservative governor in the Union that the strategic intentions of the president were in total harmony with the concerns of the conservative community."[15] Reagan responded positively to Kissinger's assurances and agreed not to criticize the administration, thus crippling conservative opposition to Nixon's policies.

Buckley and other conservatives, however, were not so hesitant. In late July, Buckley and ten other prominent conservatives "suspended" their support for Nixon largely because of his "policies towards mainland China and on conventional and strategic arms." Buckley's group joined other conservative publications and groups, such as *Human Events* and the American Conservative Union, in opposing Nixon for "adopting an insufficiently hard line towards the Communist powers." They criticized Nixon's "overtures to Red China" without "any public concessions" by the Chinese "to American and Western causes." Buckley's group also condemned Nixon's inability to "respond to the rapid advance of the Soviet Union."[16] William Rusher, the publisher of *National Review*, went further than the others. He helped "persuade" Representative John Ashbrook (R-OH) to run as a conservative against Nixon in the 1972 Republican primary. Rusher's hopes that Ashbrook could mount a successful challenge proved to be unfounded, and Ashbrook's campaign turned out to be "remarkably unsuccessful."[17]

Conservatives were disenchanted by Nixon's insistence on working with the Soviets as a violation of their commitment to winning the Cold War. For instance, Young Americans for Freedom's founding statement declared that conservatives desired "victory over, rather than coexistence with," the "menace" of communism.[18] By the end of 1973, several of Nixon's "policies—the failed family assistance plan, détente, the opening of relations with China, wage-price controls—had hopelessly disillusioned the conservative movement."[19] Indeed, Spiro Agnew was the only reason many conservatives held back their criticism of the administration. The vice president was considered a true conservative and likely the next Republican in line for the presidency. Agnew's resignation in October 1973, due to scandal, and his replacement by Gerald Ford cemented conservatives' opposition to the Nixon administration.[20] As the Watergate investigation got underway, Buckley wrote Reagan, asserting that "there is great need to expose détente, and I hope the dangers of it will become palpable before the demonstration of its phoniness becomes too painful." He told Reagan that the governor had many skeptics when it came to his knowledge of foreign policy and asserted that "you will need in due course to take a position here." Buckley concluded by recommending that Reagan hire someone to focus on foreign policy full time and suggested that Reagan select a young staffer working with the hawkish Democratic senator from Washington, Senator Henry "Scoop" Jackson.[21]

Although Buckley and other traditional conservatives showed disdain for the Nixon administration, the most vocal critics of détente were a group of anticommunist academics who came to be known as neoconservatives.[22] The neoconservatives were "once-liberal intellectuals" who despised the New Left and its opposition to the war in Vietnam. According to Jeane Kirkpatrick, one of the most prominent neoconservatives, her "alienation from the national Democratic Party" was "rooted in the rise of the counterculture and the anti-war movement."[23] Irving Kristol, "one of the godfathers of neoconservatism," concurred. Kristol asserted that neoconservatives began their rightward drift following "the campus revolts of the 1960s, the rise of the counterculture," the "misconceived" Great Society, and the takeover of the Democratic Party "by the McGovernite wing."[24] The neoconservatives strongly opposed George McGovern in 1972, but also did not agree with the policy of détente started by Nixon and later continued by Ford. As a result, by the mid-seventies they found themselves without a party. According to the *Washington Post*, neo-conservatives wanted "a bigger defense budget, stronger support of Israel, a harsher stance toward the Soviet Union, and a reduced emphasis on human rights."[25] Few politicians from either party, however, shared their agenda in 1975.[26]

When Nixon resigned in the wake of Watergate, Ford became president and instantly isolated most conservatives by selecting Nelson Rockefeller as his vice president and retaining Kissinger as secretary of state. When the New Right activists emerged as a political force in the mid-seventies, they formed "an alliance" with neoconservatives against "the moderate Republicans, the old Ford-Kissinger people who wanted a diluted policy toward the Soviet Union." [27] One of Richard Viguerie's six essentials to being a conservative was "the recognition of Communism as an unchanging enemy of the free world."[28] For the New Right, heavily influenced by evangelical preachers, there was no compromising with godless communism.

As 1976 approached, people from across the conservative political spectrum urged Reagan to run for president. Throughout 1975, *National Review* publisher William Rusher made regular trips to California to persuade Reagan to run as a third-party candidate.[29] In February, more than five hundred conservatives held a convention to discuss their options in 1976. Reagan spoke at the conference but discouraged the idea that he would mount a conservative challenge to Ford. He also denounced the idea that a conservative should run as an independent against the president. Commenting on the conference, the *Los Angeles Times* warned that conservatives' "unfocused anger and energy . . . could blow sky-high everyone's assumptions about 1976" and concluded that "it would be a mistake for anyone to take these people for granted."[30] In April, South Vietnam collapsed, and conservatives denounced Ford for not doing more to prevent the communist takeover.[31] Furthermore, conservatives excoriated the administration for agreeing to the Helsinki Accords and for negotiating with Panama to give it control of the Panama Canal.[32] In response to what they viewed as Ford's foreign policy failures, New Right leaders visited Reagan in California to persuade Reagan to change his mind and run on a third-party conservative ticket. Even if Reagan lost, they argued, his efforts would make conservatism "politically viable." Reagan rejected the idea out of hand.[33] Instead, Reagan decided that he would challenge Ford in the Republican primary.[34]

Unsurprisingly, Reagan attacked Ford for his policy of détente. Reagan asserted that he was running for president to reduce the size and scope of government and to restore America's defenses. In his announcement speech, Reagan lamented that the United States had lost its "military superiority" and was being "surpassed by a nation that has never made an effort to hide its hostility to everything we stand for." Reagan said that he agreed with the goal of détente—to make "peace with our adversaries"—but he explained that in making peace there needed to be "a stronger indication that" the Soviet Union "also seek[s] a lasting peace towards us."[35] Ford continued to defend détente, asserting that the policy had been successful in easing tensions between the two superpowers.[36] The Soviet Union's involvement in Angola, however, led Kissinger to condemn its actions as a threat to détente.[37] The Soviet response to Kissinger, that "détente did not mean—and will never mean—a freezing of the social and political status quo in the world," only increased the number of conservatives critical of the administration's policy toward the Soviet Union.[38] At the core of conservative frustration with Kissinger was a fundamental misunderstanding of why the administration was pursuing détente. Kissinger viewed détente as a means to contain Soviet expansion and eventually win the Cold War. In contrast, conservatives detested the idea of containment, and likewise, détente. They believed that Kissinger's policies took the pressure off the USSR, legitimized the existence of the Soviets, and even enabled the expansion of communism.

Reagan's continued denunciation of détente forced Ford to reevaluate his own foreign policy. In March 1976, Ford felt the need to address Reagan's charge "that détente has favored the Soviet Union" and Reagan's declaration that if he was president "he would fire Mr. Kissinger." Ford responded by declaring that "détente no longer describes United States-Soviet relations." He told the press that he would no longer use the word "détente" and that he did not "think it is applicable anymore." Confronted with criticism of Kissinger, Ford stressed that he would stay in the cabinet "as long as he wants to be Secretary of State." Ford's support for Kissinger only fueled conservatives, on both sides of the aisle, who constantly criticized Kissinger for being "overeager" to make "deals with the Soviet Union, especially with regard to trade and a nuclear arms treaty."[39] Norman Podhoretz, a leading neoconservative, condemned Kissinger for accepting "the proposition that the United States should never go to war for any purpose other than defense of its own territory." Podhoretz asserted that Kissinger, and by extension the entire administration, had "lost the will to defend the free world—yes, the free world—against the spread of Communism."[40] While Ford was able to secure the nomination on the floor of the convention, his battle against the critics of détente had only begun.

When Jimmy Carter, the Democratic nominee for president and governor of Georgia, met President Ford for their second televised debate, disagreements over détente stood out as the principal foreign policy difference between the two candidates. Ford defended his and Kissinger's policies with the Soviets and his administration's involvement in the Middle East, Rhodesia, and South Africa. Carter, however, attacked the policy of détente from both the right and the left. On the one hand, Carter accused Ford "of giving away too much to the Russians under détente." On the other, he condemned Ford for fueling "a worldwide arms race" and for "toppling elected regimes in such places as Chile."[41]

Carter's attacks on Ford's foreign policy might have failed to gain traction had Ford not seemingly confirmed that he was in denial when it came to the Soviet Union. Early in the debate, Ford emphatically asserted that "there is no Soviet domination of Eastern Europe and there never will be under a Ford administration." When the moderator asked Ford to clarify, the president proclaimed that he did not "believe that the Poles consider[ed] themselves dominated by the Soviet Union." Carter quickly countered that Polish, Czech, and Hungarian Americans understood that their homelands lived "under the domination and supervision of the Soviet Union behind the Iron Curtain." He labeled Ford a terrible negotiator and, drawing on conservative criticisms of the president, lambasted him for refusing to meet with Aleksandr Solzhenitsyn, who Carter declared was "a symbol of human freedom recognized around the world."[42] Ultimately, Americans' frustration with Ford's pardon of Nixon, his inability to reinvigorate the economy, and what many viewed as the failures of détente narrowly secured the White House for Jimmy Carter.

If conservatives disliked Ford, they quickly came to detest Carter. Carter continued the SALT II negotiations to limit both superpowers' armaments; however, he wanted to go further and actually reduce the number of missiles in each nation's arsenal.[43] Furthermore, Carter ramped up a new foreign policy seemingly designed to isolate those who criticized him from the right. Carter insisted that America's relationship with China was "a central element of our global policy" and asserted that "China" was "a key force for global peace." Carter went on to condemn the old black-and-white thinking of the Cold War, which assumed that if a country was anticommunist they were an ally and as such were shielded from criticism regarding their violations of human rights. In contrast, Carter asserted that countries that consistently violated their citizens' rights, such as South Africa, would have to change their policies. Carter also altered US policy toward Israel by declaring that there must be a "homeland for the Palestinians" and asserting that the United States was concerned with the welfare of Palestinian refugees.[44] Combined, Carter's willingness to continue to negotiate with the Soviets and his view that human rights should be central to US foreign policy led conservatives to conclude that he was naïve about the way the world really worked.

Carter continued to infuriate conservatives throughout his administration. In the summer of 1977, he announced that he was discontinuing production of the B-1 bomber. Despite media reports that this move enhanced Carter's hand in the SALT negotiations and indicated that he was committed to the development of cruise missiles, conservatives balked.[45] Representative Phillip Crane (R-IL), who also was the chair of the American Conservative Union, exclaimed that Carter's decision was "one of the most dangerously foolish, short-sighted decisions I have ever seen."[46] During his radio program, Reagan condemned Carter for getting rid of the "B-1 Bomber without waiting for negotiations" and concluded that the president's actions confirmed that "we are negotiating the Salt II treaty from a position of weakness."[47] Likewise, neoconservatives asserted that Carter "was pandering to post-Vietnam neoisolationists."[48]

Following a series of Soviet provocations, the climax of which was the Soviet invasion of Afghanistan, neoconservatives met with Carter at the White House, hoping he would take the hard line.[49] Austin Ranney, a neoconservative political scientist associated with the American Enterprise Institute, told Carter that there were two ways of viewing the USSR. The first was that "it was a mature superpower that could be dealt with in good faith," and the other was the view that the Soviets were "dangerous, expansionists, and fundamentally hostile to the United States." Ranney lamented that Carter had held the first view during much of his administration. He and the others were pleased, however, that in the wake of Afghanistan and Iran, Carter seemed to have changed his view. Taken aback, Carter responded by telling Ranney that his "policies had not changed" at all and that he still held the same view of the Soviets as he always had. The neoconservatives left the meeting disappointed. They told the press that "it was a very unsatisfactory meeting."[50]

While Carter was isolating neoconservatives, Reagan was hard at work courting them. In the winter of 1979, Reagan read Kirkpatrick's article in *Commentary* criticizing Carter for his "very odd policy of dealing selectively with foreign strongmen of the right and left." Reagan was impressed and wrote Kirkpatrick a letter praising the article and requesting a meeting.[51] Kirkpatrick was not the only neoconservative Reagan contacted. He sent letters, set up meetings, and offered them advisory roles. As a result, neoconservatives began to identify with the Republican Party. Kirkpatrick explained that while neoconservatives were "treated quite badly by the Democratic Party," they were being "bombarded with friendly messages from Republicans." "After a certain time," Kirkpatrick added that such appeals began "to seem irresistible, especially" coming from a person who was "very likely to be the next president of the United States."[52]

Although neoconservatives differed with other conservatives on many issues, their disdain for communism ultimately led them to support Reagan. On social issues such as abortion and school prayer, neoconservatives "maintain[ed] rather traditional liberal views." Some of them, like philosopher Sidney Hook, also differed "sharply with economic libertarians of the Milton Friedman school" who sought free trade and "minimal regulations."

In contrast, many neoconservatives supported trade restrictions, especially with nations like the USSR, and some had close ties to labor unions.[53] Kirkpatrick, for example, acknowledged that she had "personal and intellectual ties to the labor movement" and added that someone with her "economic views" would not have a job as an economic adviser to Reagan.[54] When it came to the New Right, many neoconservatives viewed them as "anti-intellectual" and extreme in their opposition to federal programs.[55] On matters of foreign policy, however, neoconservatives and other conservatives were united.

The New Right and neoconservatives were united in their opposition to softening relations with the Soviets even if their reasoning differed. For the New Right, the Soviet Union was evil, and some even argued that the USSR was destined—by biblical prophecy—to assault Israel and usher in the Second Coming of Christ. Just before the 1980 election, Falwell published *Armageddon and the Coming War with Russia,* in which he argued that the "the stage is rapidly being set even today in the Middle East" for the wars prophesized in the Bible. Falwell continued that it was "almost certain" that verses in "Ezekiel refer to none other than that Red Communistic Bear, the U.S.S.R." Falwell pointed to the invasion of Afghanistan as proof that the future invasion of Israel by the Soviet Union was imminent. He concluded that "the pieces are falling into place even today before our very eyes."[56] Almost every member of the New Right was hostile to the Soviets. Viguerie asserted that living under communism was the same as living in "slavery" and condemned "liberal national defense policies" for weakening the United States militarily, the result of which was "American collapse around the world."[57] To the New Right, the Cold War was a predestined conflict between the forces of good and evil. In such a worldview, compromise was futile; there could be only victory. Combined, the New Right and neoconservatives supported an aggressive Cold War triumphalism that regarded victory and not containment as the goal of American foreign policy. Both groups placed their confidence in Reagan to embrace a hawkish foreign policy and win the Cold War.

Reagan easily defeated Carter in November 1980; nevertheless, both the New Right and the neoconservatives rapidly became disillusioned when Reagan turned from campaigning to governing in 1981.[58] Conservatives were anguished that many Nixon and Ford loyalists were given positions in the Reagan administration. Howard Phillips complained that "the early signs are that

Governor Reagan will be pursuing liberal policies economically and a policy of détente in foreign affairs."[59] Neoconservatives were also perplexed when a senior White House official told the press that there were "people" in the administration who feel "we owe very little to the neoconservatives." Aram Bakshian Jr., special assistant to the president, argued that the reason that neoconservatives were not central to Reagan's decision-making was that they were intellectuals and as such did not "have the same handle on the nuts and bolts of politics as the people heavily engaged on Capitol Hill."[60]

Such statements miffed neoconservatives. Irving Kristol, coeditor of *Public Interest*, conceded that he had no idea whether he had "influence or not." Norman Podhoretz, after seconding Kristol's sentiment, condemned the administration for diminishing its position toward the Soviets and complained that Reagan's prioritizing of the domestic economy over foreign concerns was "troublesome." Podhoretz proclaimed that Reagan's "priority ought to be on rebuilding American defenses and trying to get ground forces in the Persian Gulf." Elliott Abrams, Reagan's assistant secretary of state for international organizations and Norman Podhoretz's son-in-law, concluded that "the outcome of the alliance" between neoconservatives and Reagan "remains in doubt." When Richard Viguerie heard about neoconservatives' complaints about influence he responded, "Welcome to the party. . . . We've all got the same complaint." Paul Weyrich added, "The neoconservatives aren't on the circuit and if you're not on the circuit you're not consulted."[61]

Conservative complaints about Reagan's foreign policy dominated the president's first two years in office. The New Right and neoconservatives were initially skeptical of Reagan's proposed sale of America's airborne warning and control system (AWACS) surveillance planes to Saudi Arabia. John Terry Dolan, the director of the National Conservative Political Action Committee, asserted that Reagan had "made a mistake" in deciding to "sell sophisticated weapons to Saudi Arabia." Dolan continued that the sale of AWACS to Saudi Arabia would undercut Israel's security as the Saudis were hostile to the Jewish state. Dolan concluded that "the sale of these weapons would undermine the security of Israel, jeopardize American security and regional interests, and cast still another doubt on the value of American commitments overseas and President Reagan's personal credibility."[62] Reagan did not understand the opposition to his proposed sale of AWACS. Writing in his diary, Reagan insisted that it was "clear" that there had never been "a better friend of Israel in the W[hite] H[ouse]" than himself and concluded that the Saudis were "key" to providing "peace between Israel [and] the Arab nations." Reagan insisted that the proposed sale would not "change the balance of power between them [and] the Arabs" but would encourage Saudi Arabia to continue to work toward peace in the region.[63]

Both liberals and conservatives in the Senate initially shared Dolan's concerns, forcing Reagan to double his lobbying efforts to overcome stiff opposition to the proposed radar-plane sale.[64] The administration decided that the only way to get AWACS to Saudi Arabia was to move the conservative and moderate senators who had not firmly committed one way or another on the sale. In a memorandum, drafted just days after Dolan's editorial, the administration determined that it needed to create the perception that there was widespread grassroots support for Reagan's proposal. The administration wrote to conservative groups, many of them associated with the New Right, asking them to solicit support for the arms sale.[65] Key conservative organizations, including the American Security Council, Conservative Victory Fund, Phyllis Schlafly's Eagle Forum, Fund for a Conservative Majority, National Christian Action Coalition, and Young Americans for Freedom, drafted a joint letter to the Senate urging it to support the sale of AWACS to Saudi Arabia.[66]

Despite Reagan's arm twisting and grassroots conservatives' efforts, it was unclear up until the moment of the vote whether Reagan would win his first foreign policy showdown with Congress. The White House senior staff gathered uncertainly "to listen to the tense roll call vote." When Senator Edward Zorinsky (D-NE) switched his vote in favor of the administration, Secretary of State Alexander Haig, unable to contain himself, slapped his hand down on the table and exclaimed "That's it!" It was "an upset victory" for Reagan, who later conceded that he did not know whether he would win until his staff came into the Oval Office and "handed me the votes." Reagan won the vote by securing the support of conservative senators and by flipping a handful of moderate Republicans and Democrats. The final vote was fifty-two to forty-eight in favor of the administration, with forty-one Republicans and eleven Democrats siding with the president.[67]

Although many conservative grassroots activists supported Reagan, the battle over AWACS gave other conservatives pause. Reagan had taken on pro-Israel forces and won, a victory that brought him the ire of some neoconservatives.[68] When Israel's prime minister, Menachem Begin, spoke out against the sale, Reagan responded by declaring that "it is not the business of other nations to make American foreign policy." Podhoretz asserted that "the

President's attack on Israel for interfering" in the debate "was disturbing" and "alarming." Podhoretz concluded that "from the point of view of domestic politics [administrative officials have] done themselves some damage."[69] Reagan's rebuke of Israel gave some pause, as did the fact that Reagan was fighting so hard for an arms deal that had been set in motion by the Carter administration. Dolan condemned Reagan for following "any of the wrong-headed policies undertaken by Jimmy Carter."[70] Even more galling to conservatives was that the administration asked Kissinger, conservatives' foreign policy nemesis, to speak in favor of the arms sale.[71] In short, the AWACS sale was perceived as an example of Reagan continuing the foreign policy of past administrations instead of forging a new conservative strategy. It was the first of many foreign policy decisions in which Reagan would refuse to toe the conservative line.

Conservative frustration boiled over into full-blown anger concerning Reagan's approach to China. On May 12, 1982, the Taiwanese government condemned Reagan for ignoring its "national interests" when the president wrote a letter to China asserting that "we welcome your nine-point initiative" to arrive at a peaceful settlement concerning Taiwan. Although the Chinese proposal would allow Taiwan to "keep its present social system, its present way of life and its own armed forces," it also called on Taiwan to "abandon its claim to be an independent nation and agree to be placed under Peking's rule." Using Cold War rhetoric, the Taiwanese government asserted that China's proposals would force 18 million people to live under communism. The Nationalist Party paper, the *Central Daily News*, declared that "the United States has failed to recognize the scheme behind the Chinese Communist peace talk proposals."[72]

Conservatives, who wanted Reagan to roll back communism, were appalled that he might abandon Taiwan to communist China. Gary Jarmin, the national director for the conservative American Council for Free Asia (ACFA), wrote Morton Blackwell, Reagan's liaison to conservatives, to voice his frustration with the administration's policy.[73] Jarmin called Reagan's overtures to China "a disaster for Taiwan in the making" and asserted that the president would "deserve" the "severe backlash from conservatives" that he saw coming. Jarmin also warned that if Reagan agreed to a joint communique with China, it would mean "a total sell-out of Taiwan." If the administration decided to go forward with the communique, Jarmin concluded, Reagan would be "severely beaten over the head by conservatives" and the "ACFA will be the first to soundly attack the President should this sell-out occur."[74]

Jarmin did not stop after he wrote Blackwell; he mobilized a large number of conservative organizations to condemn Reagan and force him to reverse his overtures with China. Twenty-three conservative organizations, including the American Conservative Union, the American Council for Free Asia, Christian Voice, the Conservative Caucus, *Conservative Digest*, the Life Amendment PAC, the Moral Majority, the National Defense Council, the National Pro-Family Coalition, Young Americans for Freedom, and Richard Viguerie's National Christian Action Coalition signed the "statement of conservative leaders." These conservatives complained that Taiwan was receiving half the financial support under Reagan that it had received under Carter, and they condemned the administration for rejecting "the sale of every weapon system requested by the R.O.C."[75] They identified Secretary of State Haig as the architect of Reagan's China policy and called on the president to devise a new policy that "reflects his own views and the principles he campaigned for in 1980."[76] The "statement" reminded Reagan that there was no "grassroots pro-Communist China constituency in this nation," but there was "a broad based coalition of conservatives who helped elect Reagan and will be greatly demoralized should he adopt the Haig proposals." They accused Reagan of allowing China to make the United States' policy toward Taiwan and exclaimed that "the time for a president to uphold the law and reject Beijing's abhorrent and tactless fulminations is long overdue."[77] These conservatives warned that Reagan's Taiwan policy "could easily break apart the 1980 coalition" and promised that anyone in the administration that believed they would "be easily mollified with some pro-Taiwan statements" was "living in a fantasyland."[78] Interestingly, these conservatives appealed to Reagan's "own views," implying that the president was not living up to what it meant to be a Reagan conservative.

In addition to grassroots conservative opposition, Reagan also faced criticism from the halls of Congress. At the same time Reagan was under fire from conservatives for supporting tax increases, he was also being condemned for trying to improve relations with China by reducing American arms sales to Taiwan. Senator Barry Goldwater (R-AZ) voiced his concern with the administration's policy, asserting that "it would lead to a gradual withdrawal of arms support for Taiwan by this country."[79] Senator Gordon J. Humphrey (R-NH), a member of the Armed Services Committee, exclaimed that the Reagan administration's "abandonment" of Taiwan was because "the State Department is so full of weaklings and sissies and people with mush for brains . . . that even with a new president the State Department bureaucracy just goes on doing its own thing."[80]

Despite conservative criticism, Reagan stood fast to his Taiwan policy. Near the end of July, the president met with twenty-four congressional Republicans to address their concerns over Taiwan. One attendee, Jerry Lewis (R-CA), said it "was a very healthy meeting" and that the meeting cleared "the air" and helped "to allay fears." Ultimately Reagan signed the communique with China. The president insisted that the agreement would not decrease "the administration's concern for 'the well-being of the people of Taiwan'" and insisted that the United States would continue to provide significant military support for Taiwan. In the final agreement, it was announced that the United States "does not seek to carry out a long term policy of arms sales to Taiwan" and concluded that the United States "intends to reduce gradually its sales of arms to Taiwan, leading over a period of time to a final resolution."[81] Reagan's signing of the communique isolated conservatives, who, despite the president's assurances, felt that he had abandoned Taiwan just as he had ignored Israel's concern over the sale of AWACS to Saudi Arabia.

By the summer of 1982, neoconservatives were voicing their frustration with Reagan in articles and at gatherings such as the Committee for the Free World (an organization consisting of prominent neoconservatives). In May, Podhoretz published a column in the *New York Times* titled "The Neo-Conservative Anguish over Reagan's Foreign Policy," in which he systematically dismissed the president's accomplishments in foreign affairs. Podhoretz was disappointed in Reagan's inability to reverse the decline of American power on the world stage. He praised the president for presiding "over the refurbishing and modernization" of America's military but did not see armaments alone as enough. Podhoretz insisted that the Reagan administration had not clearly outlined a vision for what it wanted to accomplish and complained that Reagan had spent the first year of his term focusing on the economy and had not addressed "himself with an equivalent seriousness and energy to the international situation." The result, according to Podhoretz, was "a vacuum into which have come pouring all the old ideas and policies against which Ronald Reagan himself has stood for so many years."[82] Instead of a new conservative foreign policy, the country—under Reagan—was following the same path set by former presidents.

In addition to Podhoretz's displeasure with Reagan's policies across the globe, he also unequivocally condemned Reagan's Cold War policy. With regard to nuclear weapons, Podhoretz explained that Reagan "has been shaky and uncertain." He lamented that although the president opposed the nuclear-freeze movement, Reagan supported freezing the production of nuclear arms provided the Soviets no longer had nuclear superiority over the United States. Such a position, according to Podhoretz, was self-defeating because it undercut Reagan's ability to close the nuclear gap. Podhoretz also criticized Reagan's handling of the Polish crisis. Podhoretz lamented that Reagan had not supported the Polish people in the face of the Soviet-backed military crackdown. The president, Podhoretz explained, could have cut economic aid, made an effort to halt the construction of the natural gas pipeline from Siberia to Western Europe, and reimposed the embargo on technology and grain shipments to the USSR. Podhoretz declared that such actions would have forced the Soviets to "pay the full price for the consequences of the Communist system they have imposed by domestic force and terror upon the peoples of Eastern Europe." Unfortunately, according to Podhoretz, Reagan followed "a strategy of helping the Soviet Union stabilize its empire rather than a strategy aimed at encouraging the breakup of that empire from within."[83]

Podhoretz condemned Reagan by labeling his policy toward the Soviet Union as détente. Podhoretz defined détente as the idea that the USSR could "be induced to behave moderately and responsibly by means of a structure of incentives and penalties." Podhoretz acknowledged that Reagan had once been an avid opponent of such policies but exclaimed that it was difficult to "think of a term that more accurately describes his own foreign policy." Podhoretz gave Reagan credit for pursuing the sophisticated form of détente and not the "corrupted adaptation, so often indistinguishable from appeasement, pursued by the Carter Administration." The difference between the two, according to Podhoretz, was that at least Reagan held onto the threat of military force as an essential element of détente, whereas Carter had not. After pointing out how weak Carter had been, Podhoretz slammed Reagan by asserting that at least the feckless Carter had imposed the grain embargo and boycotted the Olympics, whereas Reagan took few measures and even paid the interest due on the Polish debt just after martial law was declared in the country. Podhoretz agreed with George Will that the Reagan administration "loves commerce more than it loathes Communism" and quipped that "to say that neo-conservatives were disappointed by all this understates the case to an incalculable degree."[84]

Podhoretz's problems with Reagan's foreign policy extended well beyond

Europe. He wanted Reagan to send "more and better arms to the Afghans" and provide "more political support for the Angolan guerrillas trying to expel the Cuban troops who have helped turn their country into a Soviet Satellite."[85] In totality, Podhoretz viewed Reagan as unwilling to fight communism on a global scale: "There is as little true determination to hold the line in Central America as there seems to be in the Persian Gulf." Podhoretz accused Reagan of growing "alarmed" and retreating from conflict in El Salvador, allowing "opposition both in El Salvador and in the United States to gather much greater strength than it could muster a year before." Podhoretz also denounced Reagan for toning down criticism of Nicaragua, Cuba, and El Salvador because the administration feared "that attention would be distracted from the President's economic program." He emphasized again that in all these respects Reagan's foreign policy "bears a surprisingly close resemblance to the original strategy of détente as conceived by Richard Nixon and Henry Kissinger in 1972." Podhoretz further decried Reagan's policy toward Saudi Arabia and his neglect of Israel. He worried that such an alliance would result in the United States gradually joining the Saudi "demand for a Palestinian state on the West Bank ruled by the Palestine Liberation Organization, even though the P.L.O. is sworn on the destruction of the only democratic nation in the region and is in addition bound by hoops of ideology and arms to the Soviet Union." Podhoretz agreed with foreign policy expert Robert W. Tucker's description of Reagan's policy toward the Middle East: it was "Carterism without Carter."[86]

Concluding, Podhoretz returned to Reagan's policies toward the Soviet Union. He emphasized that Reagan's "simplistic" view that the Soviet Union was to blame for most of the major conflicts across the globe was correct, and he implored the president to trust his instincts. Podhoretz declared that "the Soviets were more often than not to be found fishing in troubled waters or trying to roil the waters up." This, according to Podhoretz, offered the United States an opportunity because "it helped concentrate the mind on the global reach that Soviet imperial power has acquired in recent years through its relentless military buildup." In response, Podhoretz expected Reagan to move quickly to secure the Caribbean and the Persian Gulf, actions that Reagan himself accepted as necessary. Despite the president's own views, however, no action had been taken. Podhoretz determined that "either this administration does not in fact know what it wishes to do, or what it really wishes to do does not correspond to what the President himself has said." In conclusion,

Podhoretz explained that although there was still time for Reagan to put his stamp on foreign policy, "we neo-conservatives are not the only group in the Reagan coalition growing daily more anguished over the slipping away of a precious political opportunity that may never come again."[87]

Podhoretz's complaints prompted a telephone call from Reagan. During their conversation, the president assured Podhoretz three times that he was not following a policy of détente. Reagan's assurances, however, did not convince Podhoretz, who concluded that "it was clear . . . that he did believe in something that I would call détente."[88] Podhoretz was one of many conservatives who judged Reagan based on what they believed should be his foreign policy priorities. Conservatives often cited Reagan's "instincts" or his "beliefs" when criticizing him for not pursuing a more aggressive foreign policy. In reality, Reagan's combative rhetoric was not indicative of the policies he carried out. Indeed, conservatives often mistook Reagan's rhetoric as an end unto itself instead of as a means to achieve results that were pragmatically obtainable.[89]

The first two years of Reagan's foreign policy were a disappointment for conservatives. Conservatives viewed the Soviet Union as an imperialistic and expansionistic state that was insistent on spreading communism throughout the world. Furthermore, many conservatives viewed the Cold War as a conflict between good and evil, and some even believed that biblical prophecy explained contemporary international conflicts. According to this worldview, Reagan's unwillingness to back up his aggressive rhetoric with consistent action meant that he was compromising with what he himself would later describe as an "evil empire."[90] Many conservatives believed that the Soviets were winning the Cold War. Senator Helms, who condemned Reagan for leaving foreign policy in the control of "diplomatic retards," warned that Reagan was not acknowledging that "the Soviet strategy is and has been to encircle and surround the United States with socialist nations."[91] The Christian Anti-Communism Crusade echoed Helms's words, exclaiming that the United States needed to pursue "energetic action to defeat Communism." The organization insisted Reagan should reject "complacency and apathy, and realize that "this is the time to take the offensive."[92] Reagan heeded its words, and in 1983 he announced an assertive conservative foreign policy that conservatives praised—even as it brought the world to the brink of nuclear conflict.

7. The Year of Fear: Ronald Reagan and the Transformation of America's Foreign Policy

Although many conservatives were frustrated with Reagan's foreign policy during his first two years, in 1983 Reagan embraced the language and the policy initiatives that had led conservatives to support him in 1980. Reagan's embrace of a more aggressive foreign policy, both in rhetoric and in practice, contributed to a global climate of fear and anxiety concerning superpower relations. Ironically, the escalation of tensions in 1983, especially in the fall and winter, led President Reagan to seek reconciliation with the Soviets at the end of the year. On January 16, 1984, Reagan went out of his way to announce his commitment to eliminating nuclear weapons. For Reagan to get to this point, however, the world had to endure a year of fear.

Despite conservatives' antipathy toward Reagan during the first two years, they applauded his hostility to the nuclear freeze movement. During the early days of the Reagan administration, the global opposition to nuclear weapons organized in an attempt to encourage the major powers to freeze production of nuclear weapons. Conservatives mobilized the grassroots to discredit the peace movement and delegitimize the idea of a nuclear freeze. Major General John K. Singlaub, the former chief of staff of the American forces in South Korea, released a letter for the conservative American Council for Free Asia in which he claimed that "the worldwide 'peace movement' is being coordinated and financed by communist leaders in the Kremlin, specifically the KGB." He asserted that Moscow controlled the protesters in Washington, New York, and Los Angeles, as part of a KGB propaganda effort to "give the Soviet Union military superiority forever."[1]

Singlaub's letter was part of a prolonged and concerted effort on the part of anticommunist conservative organizations to delegitimize the nuclear freeze movement. In early March 1983, the conservative anticommunist American Security Council organized anti–nuclear freeze activities in all fifty states and in the capital.[2] The American Security Council, like other conservative organizations, opposed a nuclear freeze because it would do nothing to limit conventional weapons while freezing into place the advantage the Soviets enjoyed in their nuclear armament. Another conservative organization, the American Legislative Exchange Council (ALEC), opposed the nuclear freeze because the group regarded the Soviets as untrustworthy and unlikely "to allow the on-site inspections necessary to insure compliance." ALEC concluded that the supporters of the nuclear freeze were naïve.[3] George Will condemned the nuclear freeze movement's rhetoric as "seductively simple panaceas" designed to "pander to the widespread desire to believe that there can be an easy, cheap escape from the dangers posed by modern physics and the Soviet state."[4]

Despite polls that indicated widespread popular support for a "mutual and verifiable" nuclear freeze, President Reagan opposed the movement.[5] The president asserted in early 1982 that "a nuclear freeze at this time would legitimize a condition of great advantage for the Soviets." Echoing this point, Secretary of State Alexander Haig charged that a freeze "would perpetuate an unstable and unequal military balance," reward "a decade of unilateral Soviet buildup and penalize the United States for a decade of unilateral restraint."[6]

Although the administration's stance on the nuclear freeze encouraged conservatives, they fundamentally misunderstood the source of Reagan's opposition. Conservatives, and indeed most Americans, believed that the president took this stand because his anticommunist sentiment led him to favor escalation of the Cold War and ultimately victory over the Soviet Union. In short, they believed that Reagan's opposition to nuclear freeze meant that he was for nuclear buildup. In reality, Reagan shared conservatives' concern over the nuclear gap, but he also opposed a freeze because he wanted something much more radical: the eradication of all nuclear weapons.[7]

Few knew it at the time, but Reagan hated nuclear weapons and held on to an idealistic belief that such weapons could be eliminated.[8] In a letter to the president of Smith College, Jill Conway, Reagan assured her that he shared her "conviction that an answer must be found to the nuclear threat," but lamented that the efforts of the administration in Geneva were being "impeded by the nuclear freeze movement." Reagan closed his letter by assuring Conway that he shared her view that "our ultimate goal must be the elimination of nuclear weapons."[9] Additionally, in an interview with Reagan biographer Lou Cannon, Strobe Talbott, a nuclear-arms expert, described Reagan as "a romantic, a radical, a nuclear abolitionist."[10]

In their memoirs, Reagan's closest advisers confirm the president's deep opposition to nuclear weapons. Ed Meese, perhaps Reagan's longest-serving adviser, reflects that "what most puzzled Reagan's critics was his deep aversion to nuclear weapons and even the remotest prospect of nuclear war."[11] George Shultz, who served as secretary of state for the last six years of Reagan's administration, recalls that Reagan's deep-rooted hostility to nuclear weapons was a constant throughout his administration and notes that the public largely "did not take seriously Reagan's views about banishing nuclear weapons."[12] In his autobiography, Reagan insists that "for the eight years I was president I never let my dream of a nuclear-free world fade from my mind."[13] Reagan was an adamant anticommunist, but he also wanted to work toward nuclear reductions. These two principles, anticommunism and anti–nuclear proliferation, were often at odds with one another. The result was a somewhat confused foreign policy where the president sent mixed signals to both the Soviets and the American people.

Throughout the second half of 1982, many in the American press and public came to believe that the Reagan administration thought it could win a protracted nuclear conflict with the Soviet Union. This increased tensions leading into 1983. On May 30, 1982, the *New York Times* ran the headline "Pentagon Draws Up First Strategy for Fighting a Long Nuclear War" on the front page. The *Times* had been leaked a copy of the "first complete defense guidance" of the Reagan administration, which had been signed by Defense Secretary Caspar W. Weinberger. In the document, the Pentagon detailed a plan to participate in a nuclear conflict "over a protracted period." According to the *Times*, the document formed "the foundation of the Administration's overall strategic position." The paper argued that the document showed that the Reagan administration had determined that if a nuclear war was fought it would not be over in a matter of hours, but instead would be a protracted conflict over the course of several weeks or even months. Based on this determination, the Pentagon declared in the document that the United States "must prevail and be able to force the Soviet Union to seek earliest termination of hostilities on terms favorable to the United States."[14] The *Times* story portrayed high-ranking Reagan officials as believing that a nuclear war was survivable and showed that they were making plans on how to win a nuclear conflict should it occur. This story heightened nuclear fears and fed into the perception that the Reagan administration was acting recklessly when it came to nuclear war.

Three months later, *Los Angeles Times* columnist Robert Scheer ran a story on the front page titled "Pentagon Plan Aims at Winning Nuclear War." The lead of the story asserted that "the Pentagon last week completed a strategic master plan to give the United States the capacity of winning a protracted nuclear war with the Soviet Union." Scheer exclaimed that this "presidential directive represents the first reported time the U.S. government has declared that nuclear war with the Soviets can be won."[15] The Reagan administration's stance bothered Scheer so much that he wrote an entire book titled *With Enough Shovels: Reagan, Bush and Nuclear War,* which was published before the end of 1982. On the front cover, Scheer selected a quote from the deputy under secretary of defense for strategic and theater nuclear forces, T. K. Jones, that downplayed the casualties that would be caused by nuclear war. Scheer quoted Jones as saying, "Dig a hole, cover it with a couple of doors and then throw three feet of dirt on top. . . . It's the dirt that does it. . . . If there are enough shovels to go around, everybody's going to make it." While Scheer's concern over the prospects of a nuclear war initiated by a reckless US administration seem overblown today, he did provide many examples of officials in the Reagan administration, including Vice President Bush, indicating that nuclear war could be fought and won.[16] If nothing else, the fact that Random House was willing to publish a book about the possibility of the Reagan administration fighting a nuclear war demonstrates the deep anxiety over Reagan and his team's position on nuclear war.

Regardless of the legitimacy of such anxiety, mainstream newspapers were writing about the prospect of nuclear war, and officials in the Reagan White House were forced to address such concerns. In November 1982, the *Washington Post* explained that the Reagan administration had "generated controversy" because it had "created an impression that it is more inclined to fight than its predecessors, and that it believes a nuclear war, even possibly a protracted nuclear war, could be fought and won." Critics of the administration claimed that Reagan was lowering "the nuclear threshold by making nuclear war less unthinkable and so much more likely to occur." Top officials in the Reagan administration denied any shift in US policy and pointed to Reagan's statements that nuclear war was unwinnable. They did acknowledge, however, that "loose talk about nuclear alternatives" and tough rhetoric toward the USSR had increased tensions. Weinberger, fed up with reports that the administration was preparing for a protracted nuclear conflict, sent a letter to seventy editors across the country. He denounced "completely inaccurate" articles "that portray this administration as planning to wage protracted nuclear war or seeking to acquire a nuclear war fighting capability." Weinberger insisted that there was "nothing new" about the administration's nuclear policy.[17]

As 1982 ended, Secretary of State Shultz set about establishing a dialogue with the Soviet Union to ease tensions. He sent Reagan memos early in the year that proposed addressing "arms control, regional conflicts, trade and bilateral issues, and human rights" with the Soviets in 1983.[18] In a private discussion with Reagan on February 12, Shultz told the president that he was having a meeting with Anatoly Dobrynin, the Soviet ambassador to the United Nations, later in the week. Shultz asked Reagan what he would "think about my bringing Dobrynin over to the White House for a private chat?" Reagan responded that that would be "great," but they would "have to keep this secret." The president added that he did not "intend to engage in a detailed exchange with Dobrynin, but I do intend to tell him that if Andropov is willing to do business, so am I." Shultz received a phone call early on Monday morning, the day before Reagan was to speak with Dobrynin, from Reagan's national security adviser, William P. Clark, who informed Shultz that he had "argued against the meeting to the president."[19] Despite the opposition of Clark and Weinberger, who feared moving too quickly with the USSR, Reagan endorsed Shultz's proposal.[20]

As a result, Reagan approved a meeting with the Soviet ambassador to the United States, Anatoly Dobrynin, on Tuesday, February 15. When Dobrynin arrived at Shultz's office, he was asked, "Anatoly, how would you like to go see the president?" Shultz led him back down the elevator to the State Department basement garage, where a car, sent by Mike Deaver, was waiting.[21] The two men made their way on what Dobrynin described as a "foggy" and "frosty" evening to the White House East Gate, where Dobrynin could be brought into the White House without the press's knowledge. To Dobrynin's surprise, he did not meet Reagan in the West Wing, but rather in the president's private residence. Over coffee, Reagan asked Dobrynin to

> please tell Andropov that I am also in favor of good relations with the Soviet Union. Needless to say, we fully realize that our lifetime would not be long enough to solve all the problems accumulated over many years. But there are some problems that can and should be tackled now. Probably, people in the Soviet Union regard me as a crazy warmonger. But I don't want a war between us, because I know it would bring countless disasters. We should make a fresh start.

Reagan then turned to an issue he cared deeply about. Reagan noted "that Andropov is clearly committed to the maxim: 'More deeds, less words'" and suggested that it would be easy for the general secretary "to make the first step even if it is a symbolic one." Reagan explained that he would like for Andropov to allow seven Pentecostal Christians who were being housed in the American Embassy to leave the country. According to Reagan, the Soviets' granting them exit visas would be a great symbolic gesture and would be received "with greater enthusiasm than any other bilateral agreement" by the American people.[22]

For his part, Dobrynin responded that if Reagan truly wanted better relations, he "could rely on reciprocity from us." But the ambassador did not pull his punches; he informed Reagan that the USSR regarded "the huge rearmament program in the United States now under way amidst political tension between the two countries as a real threat to our country's security." Dobrynin acknowledged that he understood that Reagan and the American people did not want war, but insisted that America's military buildup still raised tensions. Reagan brought up his view that Marxist-Leninist ideology left no future for the United States. Reagan insisted that "we believe in our future, and we will fight for it." Dobrynin explained that Reagan's view of the Soviet Union was "unrealistic" if "sincere." He explained that the Soviets "were not going to impose our views and convictions by force of arms. . . . We are not proclaiming a world crusade against capitalism." Dobrynin explained, "We are ready to accept the verdict of history without making wars or any rash moves that might lead to a disastrous war, particularly between the United States and the Soviet Union. It is in the two countries' interests to avert it." The ambassador concluded that "to achieve that we should work jointly with a view to normalize our relations."[23]

Reagan and Dobrynin spoke for nearly two hours. As the meeting ended, Reagan asserted that they should let the delegations in Geneva "keep on working." The president repeated "that, like Andropov, I favor good relations between our countries. I want to remove the threat of war in our relations. I want a positive turn. Please communicate this to the general secretary and the whole Soviet leadership."[24]

All three men believed that the meeting had been a success and that it could potentially mark an important shift in the Cold War. Immediately following the meeting, Shultz was "impressed and reassured" by Reagan being "personally engaged." He "felt this could be a turning point with the Soviets."[25] Ambassador Dobrynin shared Shultz's sentiment. After he left with Shultz, Dobrynin told the secretary of state "this could be a historic moment." For his part, Reagan's diary entry on the subject was hopeful.[26] Unfortunately, Reagan's rhetoric and the announcement of the Strategic Defense Initiative a little more than a month later alienated the Soviets and stifled efforts to improve superpower relations.

In March 1983, Reagan undid any goodwill he had garnered with Dobrynin. He delivered a speech to the National Association of Evangelicals in Orlando, Florida, in which he praised the United States' Judeo-Christian values in contrast to the totalitarian Soviet state. Reagan painted the Cold War as a "struggle between right and wrong and good and evil." He decried those who would "label both sides equally at fault" and asserted that the United States could not ignore "the aggressive impulses of an evil empire."[27] Those words, "evil empire," would become a rallying call for conservatives who were pleased that a US president finally had the courage to frame the Cold War as a conflict between good and evil. While American conservatives applauded Reagan's rhetoric, the Soviets took the "evil empire" comment as another insult demonstrating why they could not work with the Reagan administration. In addition to Reagan's alienating rhetorical flourishes, his proposal of an antiballistic missile system further alienated the Soviets.[28]

The Strategic Defense Initiative (SDI) was at least partially the product of conservative organizations, specifically the American Security Council. In early 1981, the American Security Council drafted a memorandum in which it advocated a new strategy to win the Cold War. It complained that "the classic, costly, and present" approach to win the Cold War by "increasing spending to buy more forces and weapons" was outdated and that the president should embrace a bold new strategy.[29] Writing to Blackwell a couple of months later, the American Security Council proposed Reagan use his political capital to create a defense program based in space.[30] The American Security Council's proposal had been laid out in the spring of 1981 in the organization's publication *Strategic Review*. After praising Reagan's commitment to increasing the defense budget, the American Security Council endorsed "a space-based ballistic missile defense" initiative as "a bold stroke." They insisted that a new strategy that went beyond increased spending was needed and condemned détente as "peace through trust." Instead, the organization proposed a new strategic framework be based on peace through strength.[31]

The proposals of the American Security Council coincided with proposals that Reagan had been crafting since his radio broadcasts during the late 1970s, and the term "peace through strength" would come to define the president's foreign policy.[32] Indeed, Reagan's deep opposition to nuclear weapons and his belief that defensive systems could render them obsolete went back to his days in California. While he was governor, Reagan visited Lawrence Livermore Laboratory, where he spoke with Dr. Edward Teller about ways to defend against ballistic missiles. According to the chief of the SDI, James Abrahamson, Reagan's trip to that facility and his conversations with Teller and others "planted the idea in his mind that it might be possible" to develop strategic defense. Teller later recalled that Reagan asked many questions and must have mulled over the issue for over a decade before ultimately offering a plan in 1983. According to Teller, during that fifteen years "he had thought about the subject again and again; he had talked to people, collected information," and only after long consideration did he act.[33] Another visit, this time to the North American Aerospace Defense Command (NORAD) in the summer of 1979, had a profound effect on Reagan. While touring the facility, Reagan came to realize "to his shock and dismay that there was no defense against even a single Soviet missile fired against the United States."[34] Martin Anderson, who accompanied Reagan to NORAD, recalled that near the end of their flight back from touring the facility Reagan lamented that if the Soviets launched a nuclear missile the only options the US president would have "would be to press the button or do nothing. They're both bad. We should have some way of defending ourselves against nuclear weapons."[35]

On March 23, 1983, President Reagan announced a plan to start investing resources into the development of an antiballistic missile shield aimed at ending the policy of mutually assured destruction.[36] Speaking from the Oval Office, Reagan proposed his SDI, suggesting that the US "embark on a program to counter the awesome Soviet missile threat with measures that are defensive." The president envisioned a future in which the United States "could intercept and destroy strategic ballistic missiles before they reached our own soil or that of our allies." Reagan acknowledged that the proposal was ambitious but insisted that it "would be worth every investment necessary to free the world from the threat of nuclear war." In language that would have been condemned by conservatives as dangerously naïve if uttered by a Democrat, Reagan called on "the scientific community in our country, those who gave us nuclear weapons, to turn their great talents now to the cause of mankind and world peace, to give us the means of rendering these nuclear weapons impotent and obsolete." Reagan asserted that "this could pave the way for arms control measures to eliminate the weapons themselves." He concluded that the United States' "only purpose—one all people share—is to search for ways to reduce the dangers of nuclear war."[37] For Reagan, SDI would render nuclear weapons obsolete, as such weapons would be ineffective once both the US and USSR had a missile shield. Once the weapons were worthless, Reagan posited that the prospects for eliminating nuclear weapons would become a reality.

Conservative groups such as Citizens for America praised Reagan's proposal. In a briefing paper entitled "President Reagan's Solution to Nuclear Holocaust: Strategic Defense," Citizens for America declared SDI as "the only moral solution." It argued that under mutually assured destruction, the American people were "held hostage" in a "nuclear face-off" and that negotiations over the last twenty-five years had left the United States "worse off now than ever before." The organization explained that "for the first time in modern history, we can construct weapons that do not endanger human lives, but instead target weaponry and seek to save lives." It also praised Reagan's proposal for making "good economic sense," as "investment in new technologies" would result in private-sector growth. Citizens for America added that a defensive system would end "wasteful spending on offensive weaponry that is needed in ever-enlarging quantities, but does little to make our society more secure." It concluded that "the construction of a defensive system removes the use of hundreds of millions of civilians as hostages in a nuclear face-off of terror."[38]

While conservative organizations praised SDI, the press quickly questioned whether the initiative was "a smoke screen" to "shield his embattled 1984 defense budget" that Congress had already denounced. The *Atlanta Constitution* questioned just a few days after Reagan proposed SDI "whether Reagan honestly" wanted to replace "deterrence with Star Wars technology, or whether he frivolously threw out the idea to distract everyone's attention from his short-term astronomical defense demands."[39] Contrary to the press's allegations, Reagan truly believed that SDI held the key to ending the prospect of nuclear war.[40]

In contrast, the Soviets viewed SDI as an escalation of the Cold War. Indeed, they viewed SDI as an attempt by the Reagan administration to gain a strategic advantage that would allow the United States to launch a preemptive strike. Three days following Reagan's announcement, General Secretary

Andropov condemned SDI as "a bid to disarm the Soviet Union in the face of the U.S. nuclear threat." Two months later, George Kennan reflected that superpower relations were in "a dreadful and dangerous condition."[41] Despite Reagan's claims that SDI was designed to ward off the prospect of nuclear war, the Soviets viewed the program as an attempt by Reagan to undermine the status quo of mutually assured destruction and give the United States a strategic advantage in the deployment of nuclear weapons.

During the summer of 1983, both the US and the USSR sought to cool tensions. During Shultz's testimony before the Senate Foreign Relations Committee, he asserted that "having begun to rebuild our strength, we now seek to engage the Soviet leaders in a constructive dialogue—a dialogue through which we hope to find political solutions to outstanding issues." Likewise, on the same day, Andropov insisted that it was time for the USSR to revise its policy toward the United States. Andropov emphasized that "the threat of a nuclear war overhanging the world makes me appraise in a new way the basic meaning of the activities of the entire communist movement."[42]

In addition to his comments, Andropov wrote Reagan a personal letter on July 4 that opened the possibility of a constructive dialogue between the two leaders. For his part, Andropov emphasized the "unbending commitment of the Soviet leadership and the people of the Soviet Union to the cause of peace, the elimination of the nuclear threat and the development of relations based on mutual benefit and equality with all nations."[43] Reagan wrote a draft response on July 8 to Andropov in which Reagan reassured the general secretary that "the government and the people of the United States are dedicated to the cause of peace and the elimination of the nuclear threat." In the draft, Reagan asked whether the two countries could "achieve these goals in the meetings we are presently holding in Geneva." In his concluding remarks, Reagan added the question: "If we can agree on mutual, verifiable reductions in the number of nuclear weapons we both hold, could this not be a first step toward the elimination of all such weapons?" Had this draft been sent to Andropov, it would have been historic. Instead, at the request of Reagan's national security adviser, William P. Clark, the final paragraph of the letter was edited and all hints about eliminating nuclear weapons were eliminated.[44] The conciliatory tone of Reagan's letter created confusion in Moscow. Andropov, whose shaky handwriting indicated the severity of his health problems, responded cautiously: "I shall welcome concrete, businesslike and candid exchange of opinions with you on these and other questions."[45]

In addition to words, some actions taken in the summer of 1983 implied that superpower relations might be on the verge of improving. On July 28, the USSR and the US agreed to a $10 billion sale of US grain to the Soviet Union over five years—an agreement that was met with considerable consternation on the part of American conservatives. Furthermore, on August 20, heeding Shultz's advice, Reagan lifted controls that restricted the sale of gas pipeline equipment to the USSR. Likewise, negotiators from both countries were still involved in good-faith negotiations at Geneva over the future of intermediate missiles in Europe. Accordingly, in mid-August 1983, when Reagan took his vacation at the Rancho del Cielo in sunny California it looked as if relations might indeed be on track to improve significantly.[46]

Any hopes of substantial improvements in superpower relations disappeared when at 2:20 in the afternoon on August 31 Korean Áirline flight 007 suddenly ceased communications. Eight hours later, William Casey was informed that KAL007 might have been shot down by the USSR. Secretary of State Shultz and President Reagan were briefed the following morning. Reagan's initial reaction was one of caution. When the president was briefed by William Clark, Reagan responded, "Bill, let's pray it's not true" and added that "at this particular time we've got to be very careful that we don't overreact." Shultz spoke for the administration when he released a statement asserting "the United States reacts with revulsion to this attack. Loss of life appears to be heavy. We can see no excuse whatsoever for this appalling act." The media described Shultz's response as "controlled fury" and Assistant Secretary of State Richard Burt commented that Shultz's emotions were evident: "He really has it in his eyes."[47] Following the confirmation that the airliner had indeed been shot down, Reagan cut his vacation at his ranch short and returned to Washington.[48]

Reagan met with the congressional leadership on Sunday, September 4, 1983, to discuss the US response to KAL007. Reagan played "a tape of conversation between 2 Soviet pilots including the one who stated he had locked on his radar guiding air to air missiles, launched them and 'target destroyed.'" Reagan described the bipartisan meeting as a "very good" three-and-a-half-hour meeting. The president spent the next day revising his speech, as he had been displeased with both drafts that had been presented to him.[49]

In his public address on the KAL incident, Reagan was resolute in his denouncement of the Soviets' barbaric behavior. From the Oval Office, he called the shoot-down a "massacre," an "atrocity," and labeled the Soviets' actions as "a crime against humanity."[50] He played "excerpts from the Soviet pilot's exchanges with his ground control in a dramatic television broadcast designed to demonstrate that 'there is no way a pilot could mistake this for anything other than a civilian airliner.'" Although "a closed hearing of the Senate Foreign Relations Committee was told that NSA analysts believed the Soviet pilot did not know that his target was a civilian airliner," Reagan used the tapes and his rhetoric to condemn the Soviet Union.[51]

Reagan had decided during a National Security Council meeting that he would embrace Shultz's proposal that he present the issue as a moral failing by the USSR, hit it with harsh rhetoric, but keep other retaliatory actions limited. As a result, even though Reagan offered a thorough condemnation of the Soviet Union, it was not enough for his most ardent conservative supporters. Richard Viguerie announced that Reagan was "Teddy Roosevelt in reverse: he speaks loudly but carries a small twig."[52] Conservative commentator George Will lashed out at the president for his failure to act. Will insisted that "the administration is pathetic. . . . We didn't elect a dictionary. We elected a President and it's time for him to act." The *Manchester Union-Leader* editorial board declared that "if someone had told us three years ago that the Russians could blow a civilian airliner out of the skies—and not face one whit of retaliation from a Ronald Reagan administration, we would have called that crazy. It is crazy. It is insane. It is exactly what happened."[53] Although Reagan tried to not respond directly to such attacks from conservatives, their criticism clearly bothered him. In his diary, Reagan commented, "I'm really upset with George Will. He has become very bitter and personal in his attacks—mainly because he doesn't think I've done or am doing enough about the Russians and KAL007 massacre."[54]

The Soviets made things worse on themselves by denying responsibility for the attack for five days following the incident and then claiming that KAL007 was a US reconnaissance plane sent to spy on them.[55] Despite the absurdity of such claims, by all accounts, many Soviet officials believed their own propaganda. According to Oleg Gordievsky, a KGB double agent stationed in London, even internally the leadership was denying responsibility for the shooting down of the Korean airplane. According to Gordievsky, "the most dangerous consequence of the KAL007 tragedy was its repercussions in Moscow, where it strengthened the belief at both the Center and the Kremlin in a far-reaching anti-Soviet plot by the Reagan administration." Gordievsky concluded that many in the Soviet leadership convinced themselves "that KAL007 had been an American Intelligence mission" and continued to believe that for years to come. In response to what the USSR labeled a fabricated response by the Reagan administration, Soviet students were withdrawn from the United States for their safety and Cold War tensions were ratcheted up.[56]

On September 8, 1983, Shultz met with Foreign Minister Gromyko in Madrid, Spain. The meeting had been planned prior to the KAL tragedy as an opportunity for Shultz to begin moving toward a policy of reconciliation with the Soviets, but the tone of the meeting was dramatically changed by the events leading up to it.[57] In his opening comments, Gromyko declared that "the world situation is now slipping toward a very dangerous precipice. . . . Problem number one for the world is to avoid nuclear war."[58] Shultz, however, was interested in discussing KAL007. The result was what Shultz described as "a rock-and-sock meeting."[59] Long-time State Department translator William Krimer told Shultz after the meeting that "he had been interpreting in high-level meetings with the Soviets for seventeen years and had never seen anything remotely like it."[60] During the meeting, Gromyko declared, "We accuse the American side of carrying out a serious of premeditated actions against the Soviet Union." He expressed doubt that KAL007 had accidently strayed into Soviet airspace. It was an amazing coincidence, according to Gromyko, that the plane strayed "towards the Soviet border, over vitally important military territory in the Soviet Far East" for over two hours. He concluded, "That is why we accuse the US administration of organising a criminal act against the USSR, only one of many such attacks on us. At the same time, we object most strongly to words which have become the administration's common currency in its abuse of the USSR and our social system." Reflecting on the Madrid meeting in his memoirs, Gromyko exclaimed that "it was probably the sharpest exchange I ever had with an American Secretary of State, and I have had talks with fourteen of them."[61]

It is hard to exaggerate just how large a setback the KAL007 tragedy was for superpower relations. Immediately following the Madrid meeting, Shultz told the press that "Foreign Minister Gromyko's response to me today was even more unsatisfactory than the response he gave in public yesterday. I find it totally unacceptable." Shultz described the KAL007 incident as "the unprovoked Soviet destruction of a defenseless, unarmed Korean airliner" and condemned the Soviet response as a "preposterous explanation." Don Oberdorfer, a journalist at the time, described Shultz's response as "chilling in its implications for the fabric of dialogue between the superpowers."[62] Reagan acknowledged that relations had deteriorated because of KAL007. The day after the Madrid meeting, he noted that "the Soviets have stepped up their propaganda drive to point us as the villains, the KAL as a spy plane and themselves as protecting their rights."[63] The two powers were at an impasse. Reagan also wrote that following the incident, "a number of substantive matters" had to be put "on ice."[64] A few days following Madrid, Pope John Paul II issued a warning that the world could be entering "a new prewar phase." Seeming to confirm the pope's concern, Reagan, during his regular radio address, declared, "We can stop pretending they share the same dreams and aspirations we do. We can start preparing ourselves for what John F. Kennedy called a long twilight struggle."[65] Such rhetoric did little to ease tensions. To make matters worse, the Soviets were engaged in similar tactics.

On September 28, Andropov issued a public statement condemning the Reagan administration. He claimed that the United States was a "country where outrageous militarist psychosis is being imposed." According to Andropov, "if anyone had any illusions about the possibility of an evolution for the better in the policy of the present American administration, recent events have dispelled them once and for all." He also foreshadowed future conflict, declaring that "the Reagan administration in its imperial ambitions, goes so far that one begins to doubt whether Washington has any brakes at all preventing it from crossing the mark before which any sober-minded person must stop."[66] Andropov's rhetoric matched Reagan's when he denounced the president's "dangerous, inhuman policies" and as he proclaimed that Reagan's "militarist course" posed "a grave threat to peace."[67] In addition to Andropov's condemnations, *Time* reported that the "Soviet press abounds in descriptions of Reagan as a crypto-Nazi. Soviet cartoonists, who have long depicted the President as a gunslinging cowboy, now add swastikas and ghostly faces of Hitler to their drawings."[68] Indeed, Reagan was consistently portrayed in the Soviet press as a "madman," and the Soviet Defense Ministry did its best to portray the American administration as militaristic and intent on "world domination." To make matters worse, Andropov, who was suffering from kidney failure, diabetes, and heart issues, was moved to a suite in Kuntsevo Hospital in late September, raising questions of who was in charge in Moscow. As summer faded into fall, US-Soviet relations were approaching the worst they had been since the Cuban missile crisis.[69]

To the American people, Reagan looked resolute in his denunciations of the Soviet Union and confident in America's ability to stand against such immoral acts as the shooting down of KAL007. Behind the scenes, however, Reagan and his closest advisers were perplexed that there had been no communication between Moscow and Washington about the plane even though the Soviets had monitored it for more than two hours prior to shooting it down. Indeed, the Reagan administration was "deeply disturbed that the Soviets could have made such an error." The way they saw it, "two hundred sixty-nine lives had been lost because of a series of miscalculations and a breakdown in communications between Washington and Moscow."[70] Reagan could not help but wonder and worry whether such a breakdown might not occur on a larger scale—perhaps even with nuclear weapons. In his autobiography, Reagan recalled:

> If anything, the KAL incident demonstrated how close the world had come to the precipice and how much we needed nuclear arms control: If, as some people speculated, the Soviet pilots simply mistook the airliner for a military plane, what kind of imagination did it take to think of a Soviet military man with his finger close to a nuclear push button making an even more tragic mistake? If mistakes could be made by a fighter pilot, what about a similar miscalculation by the commander of a missile launch crew?[71]

As important as it was, the KAL007 tragedy was just one of several moments that led Reagan to reflect on the potential unintended consequences of his aggressive and somewhat reckless rhetoric toward the Soviet Union.

In October, Reagan received a copy of *The Day After*, a made-for-TV movie by ABC. While he was at Camp David, Reagan took the opportunity to watch the movie prior to its November 20, 1983, national debut. That evening, Reagan recorded in his diary that the film was "powerfully done—all $7 mil. worth. It's very effective and left me greatly depressed." Reagan worried that the film might help the "anti nukes," but his "reaction was one of our having to do all we can to have a deterrent and to see there is never a nuclear war."[72] Political scientist Beth Fischer has argued that *The Day After* "was especially well suited to Reagan's intellect. The film's format and style were perfect for impressing upon the president the reality and horrors of nuclear war." She insists that "it spoke to his fears about a nuclear Armageddon" and "presented the concept of nuclear annihilation in visual images that would stay with Reagan far longer than jargon-laden statistics."[73] In his autobiography, Reagan acknowledges the role of the film in making him "aware of the need for the world to step back from the nuclear precipice," but also notes that the film made him "more aware than ever of the urgent need for a defense against nuclear missiles."[74] Although the events of September and October 1983 had a profound effect on how Reagan viewed nuclear war, and even made him rethink some of his tactics, the president still did not realize that his desire for a missile shield increased the likelihood that the Soviets would misinterpret his policies, thus increasing the possibility of the very type of misunderstanding Reagan feared.

Reagan's fears that the Soviets might misinterpret US actions were realized in November when the US and its NATO allies carried out a test of their nuclear arsenals. From November 7 to 11, they tested "the communications and command procedures" of NATO's nuclear facilities. Although these nuclear exercises had been carried out before, Able Archer was "more extensive" and included top members of NATO. Initially, during the earliest conversations about the tests, Reagan, Bush, and Weinberger were to participate in the test. The United States, concerned about a political overreaction by the Soviets, removed top-ranking civilian and military commanders—including Reagan—from the exercise.[75] Despite their efforts, Able Archer brought the world to the brink.

The Soviets had been preparing for the possibility of a nuclear first strike by the US since Reagan took office. When Reagan was elected, the Soviets expected his anticommunist rhetoric to subside, just as Richard Nixon's had.[76] After Reagan's first press conference as president—in which he denounced the USSR as desiring a "world revolution and a one-world socialist or communist state" and insisted that their leaders thought they had "the right to commit any crime, to lie, to cheat" to achieve their goals—the Soviets realized that Reagan's "hostility to the Soviet Union derived not from campaign tactics but from deep conviction."[77] In response, Andropov (then the chairman of the KGB) declared that the United States "was actively preparing for nuclear war" and "announced that the KGB and the GRU were for the first time to cooperate in a worldwide intelligence operation code-named RYAN"—an operation intended to collect information that might indicate the launch of a preemptive first strike by the Reagan administration.[78]

It was in this climate, in which the KGB was already on high alert due to

Reagan's anti-Soviet rhetoric and the increased tensions in the wake of the KAL tragedy, that Able Archer was carried out. Accordingly, when NATO exercises commenced, "the KGB concluded that American forces had been placed on alert—and might even have begun the countdown to nuclear war." According to Gordievsky, one of the reasons that Able Archer scared the USSR was that "Soviet contingency plans for a surprise attack against the West envisaged using training exercises as cover for a real offensive. The Center was haunted by the fear that Western plans for a surprise attack on the Soviet Union might be the mirror image of its own."[79] Gordievsky, who was stationed in London, told British intelligence at the time that "some KGB units were telling Moscow that NATO was moving troops [and] to prepare for a real attack on the Soviet Union." In fact, because of the increased activity the Soviets placed several nuclear-capable fighter aircraft on high alert in Eastern Europe.[80] On November 7, Grigory Romanov, a prominent member of the Politburo who had been one of the possible successors to Brezhnev, exclaimed, "Comrades, the international situation at present is white hot, thoroughly white hot."[81] His comments, which were reported in the Western press, should have been an indication of how tense the situation had become—at least from the Soviet perspective. Instead, the *Washington Post* seemed perplexed by the comment, exclaiming Romanov was simply using "hyperbole" given that there had been no "overt act, or threat of war" on the part of the United States.[82]

Tensions reached their peak on November 8 and 9 when the KGB sent the Center intelligence that seemed to confirm that the United States was indeed preparing to launch nuclear weapons. According to Gordievsky, the KGB "in Western Europe reported a nonexistent alert at U.S. bases." In response, the Center sent a telegram that warned that it could mark "the beginning of preparations for a nuclear first strike."[83] It instructed its agents "to gather all possible information on the highest-priority basis of U.S. preparations for a surprise nuclear missile attack against the Soviet Union."[84] Luckily, Able Archer ended on November 11, 1983, and tensions in the Center and in Moscow eased a bit. Looking back, Gordievsky recalls that "during Able Archer 83 [the world] had, without realizing it, come frighteningly close—certainly closer than at any time since the Cuban missile crisis of 1962" to reaching "the edge of the nuclear abyss."[85]

When Reagan learned that the Soviets had been genuinely concerned about an American first strike during Able Archer, it deeply concerned him and encouraged him to reevaluate his foreign policy. Shortly after the exercise

ended, London informed the Reagan administration that the Soviets had believed Able Archer might be a preemptive nuclear strike by NATO. This information, along with another report that drew similar conclusions, was passed
along to Reagan by his national security adviser, Robert "Bud" McFarlane.
McFarlane doubted that the Soviets had actually feared a US nuclear strike
and told Reagan that these reports were probably the product of Soviet propaganda to ratchet up fear. Despite McFarlane's explanation, "Reagan seemed
uncharacteristically grave after reading the report." Reagan asked McFarlane,
"Do you suppose they really believe that?" Reagan continued, confounded, "I
don't see how they could believe that—but it's something to think about."[86]

Although Reagan did not explicitly mention the briefing by McFarlane,
shortly after their discussion he met with Shultz to discuss new ways to engage
the Soviet Union. In his diary, Reagan recorded on November 18, 1983:

> George Shultz & I had a talk mainly about setting up a little in house group of
> experts on the Soviet U. to help us in setting up some channels. I feel the Soviets
> are so defense minded, so paranoid about being attacked that without being in
> any way soft on them we ought to tell them no one here has any intention of
> doing anything like that. What the h—l have they got that anyone would want.[87]

Reagan added in his autobiography that he was surprised to learn after a few
years in office that "many people at the top of the Soviet hierarchy were genuinely afraid of America and Americans." The president outlined what he had
learned from his experiences from the fall of 1983, asserting that "many of
us in the administration took it for granted that the Russians, like ourselves,
considered it unthinkable that the United States would launch a first strike
against them." Over time, however, Reagan explained that he "began to realize that many Soviet officials feared us not only as adversaries but as potential
aggressors who might hurl nuclear weapons at them in a first strike."[88] On
November 18, Reagan was also briefed by Weinberger and General Vessey on
"our complete plan in the event of a nuclear attack." In his diary Reagan called
the briefing "a most sobering experience."[89] The combination of the Soviets'
reaction to the KAL tragedy, Reagan's viewing of *The Day After*, the Soviet
paranoia during Able Archer, and Reagan's own realization of the bleakness
of nuclear war after he was briefed led him to seek reconciliation with Andropov and to publicly pursue a more conciliatory relationship with the Soviet
Union.[90]

Before he could write Andropov or change US foreign policy, Reagan stood firm and deployed Pershing missiles to Western Europe. The deployment was in response to the Soviet Union's deploying SS-20 intermediate-range ballistic missiles to Eastern Europe. In fact, President Carter had approved the deployment of intermediate US missiles to counter the Soviet threat, and Reagan promised to carry out the deployment of these missiles if the Soviets did not agree to his "zero option." When the USSR refused to remove its SS-20s, the Pershing missiles were deployed. In response, the Soviet delegation pulled out of discussion in Geneva.[91] Following the Soviet withdrawal, French president François Mitterrand (who had supported the Pershing deployment) exclaimed that the situation was "comparable in gravity with the Cuban missile crisis of 1962 or the Berlin blockade of 1948–49."[92] For his part, Reagan attempted to ease tensions. He told the press that the language that the Soviets used in explaining why they would no longer engage in negotiations at Geneva implied that they would be open to taking up the negotiations at a later date. Reagan insisted that he was "very hopeful" that they would return to the negotiating table in due course.[93]

In December 1983, Reagan began to take measures to ease tensions with the Soviet Union and emphasized his commitment to eliminating the prospects of nuclear war. At a White House news conference, the president declared that he was "determined that once you start down that path [of reducing nuclear weapons], we must come to the realization that those weapons should be outlawed world-wide forever."[94] Reagan was echoing the theme that he had first articulated in a speech before the Japanese diet in the wake of Able Archer. In Japan, Reagan proclaimed that he believed "there can be only one policy for preserving our precious civilization in this modern age: A nuclear war can never be won and must never be fought. The only value in possessing nuclear weapons is to make sure they can't be used—ever." Reagan insisted that he spoke "for people everywhere when I say, our dream is to see the day when nuclear weapons will be banished from the face of this Earth. Arms control must mean arms reductions."[95]

Reagan committed himself in December 1983 to pursuing a more conciliatory policy toward the Soviet Union. Reagan spoke with Shultz about "his desire to eliminate nuclear weapons," which Shultz promised to take a look at despite the fact that "no one in the arms control community shared Reagan's view." On Saturday December 17, the two met and Reagan instructed Shultz that he "wanted to make a major Soviet speech and include in it his readiness to get rid of nuclear weapons."[96] The address was eventually scheduled for January 16, 1984.

In the meantime, Reagan wrote Andropov a personal letter in which he expressed his hope that the Soviets would return to negotiations. Reagan emphasized that he had "pledged, both publicly and privately," that "the United States seeks and will accept any equitable, verifiable agreement that stabilizes forces at lower levels than now exist." The president pushed his idea of reducing nuclear weapons, insisting that "it is only through serious negotiations that the reduction and eventual elimination of the weapons over which the Soviet Union has voiced such public concern can be achieved." Reagan reminded Andropov that the two of them had both pledged their commitment to peace and concluded that if the general secretary was serious about improving relations, Reagan would join him "in a joint search for ways to move relations between our countries in a more positive direction."[97] Andropov responded in late January that he was open to eliminating intermediate-range nuclear weapons in Europe.[98] Unfortunately, Andropov died on February 9, 1984, and Reagan once again faced the prospect of developing a relationship with a new Soviet general secretary: Konstantin Chernenko.

At home, Reagan used his interview with *Time* magazine for their "Men of the Year" edition, in December 1983, to push his belief in nuclear arms reductions and to reassure the public that superpower relations would improve. Reagan told *Time* that he yearned "to convince the Soviets that no one in the world has aggressive intention towards them. Certainly, we don't." Reagan emphasized that he "would like to make them see that it is to their best interest to join us in reducing arms." The president also downplayed tensions between the two nations and the potential for nuclear war. He told the reporters that "there is less of a risk and less of a danger today than there was a few years ago. I think the world is safer and further removed from a possible war than it was several years ago." Reagan then pivoted to discussing nuclear arms reductions. He told *Time* that he wished both sides would "start down that road of reducing" their nuclear arsenals. Reagan, somewhat idealistically, asserted that he hoped that once reductions commenced the two nations would ask themselves, "Why don't we rid the world of these weapons . . . and get back to being civilized." The most telling moment of the interview, however, occurred when Reagan was asked if he would call the USSR the "focus of evil" in the world again as he had in his speech before the National Association of Evangelicals earlier in the year. Surprisingly, Reagan responded, "No, I would not say things like that again, even after some of the things that have been done recently."[99] Following the chaotic and tense fall, Reagan attempted to reset relations with the USSR and walk back some of his more controversial statements in an attempt to mend relations and reassure a public scared of the prospects of nuclear war.[100]

Reagan's most profound statement came on January 16, 1984, when he announced that his administration was interested in resuming negotiations with the Soviet Union and wanted to reduce nuclear weapons. In his address, which was broadcast live in Europe, the president described 1984 as "a year of opportunity for peace." Reagan declared to the world that his "dream is to see the day when nuclear weapons will be banished from the face of the Earth."[101] Reflecting on his speech in his autobiography, Reagan concludes that he "was sincere in wanting arms reductions and peace" and that the speech made it clear that "the United States stood ready to undertake another attempt at negotiating an arms agreement with the Soviets."[102] There was a great deal of optimism in the administration at the beginning of 1984. Shultz described 1983 as a success for the administration despite the tension: "Our INF deployments had begun. Our allies were with us. The Soviets had suffered a severe propaganda defeat throughout Europe." The secretary of state was hopeful that "now it was time for us to try and resume a dialogue with the Soviets if we could, but on the basis Ronald Reagan advocated."[103] To engage in such a dialogue, however, Reagan would need a willing partner.

As Reagan's first term came to an end, many conservatives were hopeful, but not confident, that after being reelected Reagan might pursue a more aggressive foreign policy. Others, such as Howard Phillips, continued to denounce him. Phillips's Conservative Caucus asked a federal judge to rule that Reagan was breaking the law by adhering to the 1979 Strategic Arms-Limitations Talks treaty after the Senate decided not to approve it. Phillips declared that "President Reagan is in violation of his oath of office" and condemned Reagan's foreign policy as inconsistent.[104] Although Phillips and other New Right activists were most vocal in denouncing Reagan in 1984, the voices grew into a chorus during the president's second term.

8. The Battle for the Cold War: Conservative Frustration with the INF Treaty

Ronald Reagan is "a useful idiot for Soviet propaganda." Howard Phillips, chairman of the Conservative Caucus, doubled down on his comments in December 1987 on C-SPAN. He told the moderator that Reagan had "unwittingly advanced Soviet propaganda" leading up to the Washington Summit and therefore was a "useful idiot for Kremlin propaganda." When asked about the INF Treaty, Phillips responded that "the treaty is a bad deal" because "it can't be verified." According to Phillips, verification was impossible because the United States did not know how many missiles the Soviets had in their arsenal prior to the signing of the treaty. Furthermore, Phillips insisted that even "if it were verifiable," the Soviets had a history of "cheating on treaties" and could not be trusted.[1]

Phillips did not reserve his criticism just for Reagan's policies. He also attacked the president. According to Phillips, Reagan was a nice, charming, and bright man who "lacks a great deal of intellectual energy when it comes to public policy issues" and frequently "relies on his subordinates for information as well as counsel." Phillips concluded that "the conservative movement has been badly weakened during the presidency of Ronald Reagan because to a very great degree his policies have paralleled those which we criticized under President Carter."[2]

Phillips was just one of many conservatives who denounced Reagan's arms-reduction negotiations with Soviet general secretary Mikhail Gorbachev. Indeed, nearly everyone in the conservative movement, from traditional conservatives such as William F. Buckley to the New Right as represented by Phillips, were opposed to the INF Treaty. By Reagan's second term, many of his most ardent conservative supporters found themselves disillusioned with the Reagan presidency.[3]

Reagan was an ardent anticommunist, but he also sincerely believed in reducing, and potentially eliminating, nuclear weapons. During his first year in office he proposed a "zero option" with regard to intermediate-range nuclear missiles in Europe. Reagan suggested that the United States would not deploy its Pershing II and cruise missiles if the Soviets withdrew their intermediate-range missiles targeting Western Europe. The Soviet Union rejected this proposal.[4] In the spring of 1982, Reagan proposed a new round of talks on long-range nuclear weapons, to be held at Geneva, titled Strategic Arms *Reduction* Talks. The new talks replaced the Strategic Arms *Limitation* Talks of Presidents Nixon and Carter. According to policy analysts and journalists Morton Kondracke and Fred Barnes, "the name change signified Reagan's desire that nuclear arsenals be diminished, not merely capped."[5] At the same time, Reagan continued to make overtures to the Soviet leaders by sending them handwritten notes explaining his desire to work together to achieve ends that would benefit both nations. In his note to General Secretary Leonid Brezhnev following the attempt on Reagan's life, the president asserted that he was putting an end to the grain embargo "in the spirit of helping the people of both our nations." The president concluded that "perhaps this decision will contribute to creating the circumstances which will assist us in fulfilling our joint obligation to find lasting peace."[6] Reagan made similar overtures to General Secretaries Yuri Andropov and Konstantin Chernenko, but all three Soviet leaders rebuffed him.[7]

Reagan's rhetoric and actions during his first term were partially to blame for the Soviet leaders' rejection of his personal appeals. After all, Reagan had proposed massive increases in defense spending, he was an ardent anticommunist, and he was constantly denouncing the Soviet Union for its human rights violations. In March 1983, Reagan delivered a speech to the National Association of Evangelicals in Orlando, Florida, in which he praised the United States' Judeo-Christian values in contrast to the values of the totalitarian Soviet state. Reagan painted the Cold War as a "struggle between right and wrong and good and evil." He decried those who would "label both sides equally at fault" and asserted that the United States could not ignore "the aggressive impulses of an evil empire."[8] Just a couple of weeks later, Reagan announced the Strategic Defense Initiative, leading the Soviets to compare Reagan to Hitler. Behind the scenes, however, Andropov wrote Reagan a private letter agreeing that the two should work toward "the elimination of the nuclear threat."[9] Despite such positive back-channel communication, the Soviets withdrew from the Geneva talks to protest Reagan's deployment of the Pershing missiles to Europe.[10] As US-Soviet relations were at their most tenuous, conservatives were the happiest they had been with Reagan's foreign policy. The president continued to hope that "somewhere in the Kremlin" there were "people who realized that the pair of us standing there like two cowboys with guns pointed at each other's heads posed a lethal risk to the survival of the Communist world as well as the Free World."[11] In January 1984, the Reagan administration shifted its public tone regarding the Soviet Union. During a press conference, Reagan asserted that the two superpowers "must establish a better working relationship . . . marked by greater cooperation and understanding."[12] Such overtures, however, did not result in meaningful dialogues with his Soviet counterparts.

Relations with the Soviet Union continued to be tenuous until Mikhail Gorbachev became general secretary in 1985.[13] Gorbachev was the only Soviet leader to be born after the October Revolution, and his ascendance represented a new era and new generation of Soviet leadership. Gorbachev was a reformer who recognized that for Soviet communism to survive, it had to evolve.[14] Although it was unclear what reforms Gorbachev would institute, it was evident to Great Britain's prime minister, Margaret Thatcher, that the new general secretary was different. When Thatcher visited Reagan in the United States, she told the president that the West could do business with him.[15] Shortly after Gorbachev took office, Reagan wrote the general secretary that he hoped to "make progress toward our common ultimate goal of eliminating nuclear weapons." Reagan assured Gorbachev of his "personal commitment to work with you and the rest of the Soviet leadership in serious negotiations."[16] Despite the letter, Thatcher's assurances, and those who claimed Gorbachev was "a different type than past Soviet leaders," Reagan confided to his diary that he was "too cynical to believe that."[17]

Reagan and Gorbachev met for the first time a few months later in Geneva to discuss international diplomacy and set the stage for further discussions. The two leaders had an hour-long private meeting before their delegations joined them. Reagan began by asserting that the US and the USSR were "the only two countries that could bring peace to the world." Although Reagan hoped that the two would discuss many items in the general meeting, he believed that "the primary aim between them should be to eliminate the suspicions which each side had of the other." Gorbachev responded that he was confident that the two "could change relations for the better." Reagan agreed with Gorbachev and said that the two nations "did not get into trouble when they talked to each other, but rather when they talked about each other." Gorbachev replied that he hoped the summit would seriously address "the question of ending the arms race" and emphasized that "the Soviet side is in favor of this."[18]

When Reagan and Gorbachev joined the delegations for the larger meeting, Gorbachev challenged the president on the issue of SDI. He condemned Reagan for listening to conservative think tanks such as the Heritage Foundation that encouraged escalation of "the arms race . . . to weaken the Soviet Union," assuring the president that such a strategy was "a delusion." Reagan insisted that the United States wanted to seek arms reduction with the Soviet Union and again emphasized that "if we can go on the basis of trust, then those mountains of weapons will shrink quickly as we will be confident that they are not needed."[19] Reagan insisted that his goal was to "get rid of nuclear weapons, and with them, the threat of war." The president added that the United States was willing to share SDI technology with the Soviets, to which Gorbachev chided that SDI was "one's man's dream." Reagan questioned why "it was so horrifying to seek to develop a defense against this awful threat."[20] Despite their differences, the Geneva summit enabled Gorbachev and Reagan to build trust and begin discussions.

Reagan's negotiations with Gorbachev led conservatives, however, to fear that the president might abandon SDI for an arms-reduction treaty. Senate conservatives complained in late 1985 that Reagan was interpreting the 1972 Anti-Ballistic Missile (ABM) Treaty in a way that limited the development of SDI. Helms insisted that the administration's position was contradictory, asserting that it "doesn't even make good nonsense." Conservatives were so fearful of Reagan's impending capitulation that the president held an "unusually frank and heated" meeting with congressional conservatives, who were afraid he was "on the verge of abandoning his 'space shield' against nuclear missiles to obtain an arms agreement with the Soviets." Reagan reassured them that he wanted to deploy SDI, but he ignored the congressmen's proposal that he reject the ABM Treaty. In his opening statement, Reagan assured conservatives that SDI was "no bargaining chip" and promised he would never "cut off or delay research or testing." The most ardent supporters of SDI, including Kemp, were displeased with Reagan's many public statements that admitted that SDI technology was many years from being functional. Kemp and seven others wrote Reagan a letter in which they warned that the president's portrayal of SDI as a faraway reality might erode support for the program. Instead, they suggested that Reagan ignore the ABM Treaty and begin building what "antimissile devices we can" so "the American people" could "enjoy real and growing protection" immediately.[21]

Reagan's second meeting with Gorbachev, in Reykjavik, Iceland, caused conservatives further consternation. In July 1986, conservative groups held a meeting to voice their concern that SDI would be delayed or abandoned as part of an upcoming arms deal. Citizens for America, the Coalition for SDI (which consisted of 196 smaller conservative organizations), the Center for Peace and Freedom, former White House adviser George A. Keyworth II, and former national security affairs adviser William P. Clark all asserted their support for SDI and their fear that the program might be compromised. The Center for Peace and Freedom held a news conference entitled "SDI Sellout Danger" to discuss their discontent.[22] Kemp gave a speech at the Heritage Foundation in which he decried the State Department for trying to get the "president to negotiate away the deployment of the Strategic Defense Initiative." Howard Phillips attacked Reagan directly, insisting that "the president is at fault." He decried "agreements that would legitimize communist powers as equal generators of peace, when in reality they remain the principal threat to peace."[23]

On the eve of the Reykjavik summit, conservatives worried that Reagan might abandon his anticommunist principles. The *Washington Post* column entitled "Did the Conservatives Misjudge Their Man?" discussed widespread conservative dissatisfaction with the course of Reagan's foreign policy. Responding to conservative criticism, Reagan pointed out how odd it was that he was being forced to defend himself and denied he was "getting soft on communism."[24] But Reagan was responsible for some of conservatives' misgivings. On September 22, just three weeks before his trip to Reykjavik, Reagan held a meeting in the White House with prominent conservatives, including Weyrich. Reagan told the group that "Gorbachev was a different kind of Soviet leader, the first to say that his goal is not conquering the West" and that internal forces were pushing the general secretary to negotiate with the United States.[25] Such statements confirmed for conservatives that Reagan was serious about negotiating with what they still believed to be the "evil empire."

When the summit convened, Reagan demonstrated that conservative concern over his commitment to SDI was misplaced. Gorbachev came to Reykjavik ready to negotiate, and he was willing to agree to significant reductions in both Soviet and American strategic weapons. Reagan wanted to phase out all intercontinental ballistic missiles and offered an idealistic scenario in which he and Gorbachev would meet back in Iceland in ten years and destroy the final missile from each of their countries at that time—thus achieving the end of nuclear weapons. Furthermore, Reagan again offered to share SDI technology with the Soviets. Here was the sticking point: Gorbachev insisted that in exchange for any agreement, the United States had to limit SDI research to the laboratory. Furious, Reagan abandoned the summit.[26]

By walking away from the table at Reykjavik, Reagan reassured conservatives. The vice president of the Heritage Foundation, Burton Yale Pines, explained that conservatives "were expecting the worst from the Iceland summit," but Reagan's unwillingness to trade SDI for arms control assured conservatives he was "more committed than ever to SDI." According to the *New York Times*, "by refusing to bargain away the missile shield program and effectively selling his position to the public, Mr. Reagan has largely reunited the major factions" of the conservative movement.[27] Although Reagan had refused to bargain away SDI, he was committed to achieving an arms-reduction agreement with the Soviet Union. Accordingly, any goodwill that Reagan earned at Reykjavik quickly dissipated after the president and Gorbachev agreed to the 1987 Intermediate-Range Nuclear Forces (INF) Treaty.

Following the failure of the Reykjavik Summit to reach a deal, the United States' and the Soviet Union's delegations continued to discuss the prospect of reducing their intermediate-range nuclear forces. Throughout 1987, the two countries worked out the details for a treaty to eliminate the very missiles that had caused the Soviets to walk away at Geneva four years earlier. Even Reagan's insistence that Gorbachev tear down the Berlin Wall in the summer of 1987 did not delay progress on the treaty.[28] Gorbachev's need for domestic reforms and Reagan's desire to end the prospect of nuclear escalation pushed the two leaders to continue negotiations.[29]

Attempting to preempt and potentially alter any deal between the two countries, conservatives publicly denounced Reagan's desire for an intermediate-range nuclear forces treaty. In early April, Secretary of State George Shultz traveled to Moscow to establish the foundation for a final agreement. In response, Dan Quayle, the conservative senator from Indiana, asserted that "it's appalling that there's been no real thought about what a post-INF agreement would be." He denounced the Reagan administration as being caught with its "pants down" when the Soviets agreed to Reagan's zero-zero option. He and other conservatives were concerned that any INF agreement would expose NATO to the Soviet Union's advantage in conventional arms.[30]

Just a few weeks later, Reagan received a letter from William F. Buckley, his good friend and editor of *National Review*, which expressed Buckley's opposition to the INF deal. Buckley wrote Reagan that "for the first time, I and my colleagues need to take very serious issue with you. It is all dramatically explained in the attached issue of *NR*." Buckley added that he had "taken pains to see to it that the very first copy goes to you. You will discover in it the depths of our anxiety."[31] The edition of *National Review* that Buckley included was titled "Reagan's Suicide Pact," and it contained a searing indictment of Reagan's conciliatory policy toward the Soviet Union.[32]

"Reagan's Suicide Pact" included criticism from a wide spectrum of conservatives. Kemp penned an article titled "Arms Control Perverted," in which he insisted that "the Soviets have been trying to use arms control as a wedge to break up NATO and neutralize Western Europe." Kemp insisted that he believed that "reducing offensive nuclear arms" was a "worthwhile goal" but "in order to enhance security and peace, any agreement must include effective verification measures and compliance guarantees, and must also address the conventional imbalance of forces." He reminded readers that achieving "iron-clad" verification measures, however, would be difficult as the Soviets had a history of cheating and "the Soviets could well be hiding additional missiles in warehouses and deployment areas we don't know about." Kemp declared that "if the price of this treaty is exposing Western Europe and American troops to the overwhelming advantage of Soviet firepower, and making Europe safe for conventional war, then the price is too high." He concluded that adopting the INF Treaty "would require the United States to withdraw our front-line defenses," which would further the Soviet goal to "split the NATO alliance at the mid-Atlantic."[33]

Henry Kissinger and former president Richard Nixon also criticized the Reagan administration's proposed agreement with the Soviets. They condemned Gorbachev for knowing that "the Soviet cuts do not reduce in any significant manner the Soviet nuclear threat to Europe, and that they increase the Soviet conventional threat." Kissinger and Nixon asserted that the general secretary was "seeking to weaken the ties between the United States and Western Europe and between Germany and the Atlantic Alliance." They told readers that they were issuing their first joint statement in *National Review* because they were "deeply concerned" that the United States might "strike the wrong kind of deal" and accordingly "could create the most profound crisis of the NATO alliance in its forty-year history." Taking direct aim at Reagan's declarations that he wanted to see the abolition of nuclear weapons, Nixon and Kissinger insisted that abolishing nuclear weapons would "create a far more dangerous world." They added that "any Western leader who indulges the Soviets' disingenuous fantasies of a nuclear-free world courts unimaginable perils." The former statesmen concluded that while every president wanted to be remembered as a peacemaker, Reagan needed to "remember that however he may be hailed in today's headlines, the judgement of history would severely condemn a false peace." They suggested that Reagan insist on a reduction of conventional weapons and the complete elimination of intermediate nuclear weapons. If he was able to achieve that, Nixon and Kissinger insisted, Reagan would "be able to sign the right agreement and make a significant step toward real peace."[34] Combined, Kemp, Kissinger, and Nixon offered a tough rebuttal to Reagan's proposals to eliminate intermediate-range nuclear weapons, but they refrained from insulting Reagan personally.

National Review also ran an article by John P. Roche, a professor of foreign affairs at Tufts University and former advisor to President Johnson, that mocked Reagan's policy toward the Soviets. Roche began by offering a not so subtle comparison of Reagan to Neville Chamberlain by asserting that the president was seeking to "bring peace in our time." Roche went on to compare Gorbachev to Hitler while quoting Hitler's lofty rhetoric about his desire for peace in front of the Reichstag in February 1933. Roche cheekily wrote that "maybe the Russians have been born again as peace-lovers," but then asserted that when "dealing with aggressive totalitarians, perhaps there is something to be said for an arms race." In case readers were unsure where Roche stood concerning Reagan's proposal, he concluded that INF was "a recipe for long-term disaster."[35]

Other contributors to the edition also compared Reagan to Chamberlain and attacked his arms-control policies. Evan G. Galbraith, who had served as Reagan's ambassador to France from 1981 to 1985, concluded his article by declaring that "perhaps [Shultz] and President Reagan both feel this pact with the Soviets will entitle them to a revered page in history. They are wrong. The umbrella of nuclear deterrence is being exchanged for the umbrella of Munich."[36] *National Review* also featured an interview in which William Jackson, who had served as the director of a panel for the Arms Control and Disarmament Agency and was a former Senate aide. He accused Reagan of negotiating from a place of weakness and not strength. Jackson insisted that any discussion of "a coherent defense strategy" emanating from the White House was "nonsense." According to Jackson, "The Reagan administration has simply blown it when it comes to any overall defense or arms-control strategy or plan to advance the national interest of the United States. . . . The European deal is a last effort by a weakened Administration."[37]

After reading conservatives' assault on his foreign policy, Reagan wrote a response to Buckley in which he attempted to address some of the criticism found in *National Review*. He began by thanking Buckley for the early edition and acknowledged that he understood Buckley's "anxiety." Reagan contended, however, that "the essays on possible arms agreements with the Soviets overstate the risks and understate my own awareness of the Soviet conventional threat." Reagan reassured Buckley that he had "not changed my belief that we are dealing with an 'evil empire.' In fact, I warned the General Secretary in Reykjavik that his choice was to join in arms reductions or face an arms race he couldn't win." Reagan concluded by reminding Buckley that the United States had more than four thousand short-range nuclear weapons to counter the Soviets' conventional-forces advantage.[38]

Traditional conservatives were not the only ones questioning Reagan's stance toward the Soviet Union. In the early spring of 1987, Reagan sat down with the editors of the New Right publication *Conservative Digest* in the Oval Office for an interview. In the wake of the Iran-Contra scandal, the editors noted that "some young conservatives are disheartened" and asked Reagan if he could offer them some words of encouragement. Reagan insisted that "just as America's future has never been brighter, the greatest days of the conservative movement lie ahead."[39] The editors asked Reagan about his agenda for the final eighteen months of his presidency, and he emphasized his commitment to seeing the Soviets withdraw their forces from Afghanistan and his hope that democracy would triumph in Angola and Nicaragua. Any hopes that Reagan had abandoned his goal for nuclear-weapon reductions following Reykjavik were dashed as the president exclaimed that he was "looking forward to completing arms-control negotiations with the Soviets without abandoning our Strategic Defense Initiative."[40]

The interview transitioned to questions about Reagan's newly appointed chief of staff, Howard Baker, and his lack of conservative credentials. Reagan responded that he would "welcome Howard Baker" to his staff and insisted to the editors that Baker was a conservative. Just in case *Conservative Digest* readers were unsure who was calling the shots in the White House, Reagan emphatically explained that "the chief policy maker and final arbiter of policy disputes around here has pretty good movement conservative credentials, too. His initials are R.R."[41] Throughout his administration, Reagan was perplexed by conservative criticism of his policies. Often, conservative critics did not condemn the president personally, but would instead attack the more moderate members of his administration. Reagan constantly insisted that he, and not his staff, was responsible for the policy of the administration.

In the summer of 1987, the editors of *Conservative Digest* chose to ignore Reagan's insistence that he was making policy. Instead, they launched an offensive against his advisors for the administration's foreign policy. The reason for not attacking Reagan personally was twofold. First, many conservatives genuinely cared for the president and did not believe he could be responsible for a foreign policy strategy that seemed at odds with their, and his, anticommunism. Additionally, the New Right had discovered firsthand after the KAL007 incident that if they attacked Reagan personally, fund-raising would suffer.[42] As a result, during July and August 1987, *Conservative Digest* attacked the State Department, insisting that Secretary Shultz was undermining Reagan's vision. In one article, titled "George P. Shultz Continues to Earn His Liberal Stripes," *Conservative Digest* publisher William R. Kennedy Jr. claimed that "conservatives remain distressed over the repeated undercutting of the Reagan Doctrine by Secretary Shultz and his State Department." Kennedy quoted Representative Jack Kemp's warning that "if left unchecked, the State Department détentists and others would substitute false diplomacy for the victory we all want for freedom and democratic capitalism throughout the world."[43]

The divisions that existed between pragmatists and conservatives in the media regarding the desirability of a nuclear arms reduction treaty were also present in the White House. Secretary of Defense Caspar Weinberger believed that Reagan was not adhering to his conservative principles and had developed too close a relationship with Gorbachev.[44] In a September 8, 1987, National Security Planning Group meeting, Reagan placed himself squarely in support of Secretary of State Shultz's desire for another summit meeting to reach a nuclear deal. In response, Weinberger warned Reagan of the dangers of "reaching quick decisions under the pressure of a meeting." When Reagan spoke, he emphatically asserted:

> You've got to remember that the whole thing was born of the idea that the world needs to get rid of nuclear weapons. We've got to remember that we can't win a nuclear war and we can't fight one . . . if we could just talk about the basic steps we need to take to break the log jam and avoid the possibility of war. I mean, just think about it. Where would the survivors of the war live? Major areas of the world would be uninhabitable. We need to keep it in mind that's what we're

about. We're about bringing together steps to bring us closer to the recognition that we need to do away with nuclear weapons.[45]

Reagan's position alienated Weinberger and confirmed the fears of conservatives within the administration that the president was serious about making a deal with Gorbachev to reduce both nations' nuclear stockpiles. Disagreements over Reagan's engagement with the Soviet Union had been raging throughout his time in office. In 1987, however, it seemed clear that Reagan would embrace negotiation, engagement, and arms control. In March 1987, Richard Perle, the assistant secretary of defense for international security policy, resigned, and in November Weinberger followed.[46]

Despite conservatives' public criticism, Reagan continued to insist both privately and publicly that he had not violated his principles and that his foreign policy was not a new détente. In the fall of 1987, Reagan and Buckley had a long telephone call in which the president insisted multiple times that he had not gone "soft" as many on the right had claimed. Reagan explained to his close friend that he was "determined that for the sake of the world we need, if possible, to eliminate nuclear weapons." He added, however, that he was "not going to do it at the expense of leaving us out weighted by them— and I haven't softened up a bit."[47] At a speech to a conservative audience in Denver, Reagan declared that SDI would "not be traded away" to get the INF Treaty. Following his speech, a beaming Reagan announced to the press that Secretary Shultz had reached a deal with his Soviet counterpart, Foreign Minister Eduard A. Shevardnadze, to move forward with the INF Treaty. Reagan smiled as he declared that "the treaty will be finalized when General Secretary Gorbachev and I meet in Washington next month." When asked if he would consider delaying the deployment of SDI, Reagan deflected and refused "to discuss that right now."[48]

Despite the success of the Washington Summit, the warm welcome that Americans gave Gorbachev, and the public signing of the INF Treaty, conservatives both inside and outside Washington vowed to oppose the ratification of the treaty. Conservatives in the Senate were so upset that the president would ultimately have to counter hold-back amendments and modifications. Furthermore, with the exception of Vice President George Bush, every GOP presidential hopeful opposed the treaty.[49] Kemp was probably the most forceful. In

May 1987, he had blasted the proposal during a speech at the Heritage Foundation. He labeled Reagan's treaty "a nuclear Munich" and insisted that his Senate colleagues vote against the president.[50]

The New Right agreed with Kemp and denounced both the treaty and Reagan. Weyrich labeled Reagan "a weakened president, weakened in spirit as well as clout, and not in a position to make judgments about Gorbachev." Weyrich noted that it was ironic that "the great conservative dream was that Ronald Reagan, in his last two years, not having to worry about the election or any further aspirations, would set the stage for the conservative revolution. On the contrary, we have Ronald Reagan, who, freed from all constraints, is endangering what he has already accomplished and behaving in a way that will have a harmful effect on the future."[51]

Following the bombardment of criticism from conservatives, Reagan attempted to placate them with a series of interviews and meetings. At a meeting in the White House, he told conservative leaders that he believed that the Soviet Union was "still an evil empire." Reagan also used his weekly radio address to quiet those who claimed he had gone soft on the Soviets. He cautioned his audience to "make no mistake, the Soviets are and will continue to be our adversaries, the adversaries of all who believe in human liberty."[52]

The next day, on December 3, 1987, Reagan gave an interview in the Oval Office and undid any progress he had made the previous days. During the interview, the president asserted that some in the conservative movement "were ignorant of the advances that had been made in verification." Other conservatives refused to accept that the USSR could be trusted. Reagan delivered what was taken as a stinging indictment of conservatives when he added that "in their deepest thoughts," some conservatives "have accepted that war is inevitable and that there must come to be a war between the superpowers."[53]

The outrage among conservatives toward Reagan's comments was swift. The next day, Senators Malcolm Wallop, Jesse Helms, Steve Symms, Larry Pressler, and Dan Quayle all announced that they opposed the treaty. A few days later, Senate Republican leader and GOP presidential hopeful Bob Dole gave an interview in which he declared he did not "trust Gorbachev" and accused Reagan of "stuffing the treaty down the throats of the allies." Quayle confronted Reagan directly, denouncing the president's comments as "totally irresponsible." Quayle added that he was "appalled" by Reagan's interview and insisted that amendments to the proposed treaty would be needed to address the disparity in conventional weapons (Quayle and other conservative senators understood that the adoption of such an amendment would kill the treaty, as the USSR would not accept such limitations).[54]

The New Right also responded to Reagan's interview with indignation. Howard Phillips exclaimed that "Ronald Reagan is a very weak man with a strong wife and a strong staff" and added that Reagan was "a useful idiot for Soviet propaganda." Viguerie asserted that Reagan "is now aligned with his former adversaries, the liberals, the Democrats, and the Soviets. . . . We feel alienated, abandoned, and rejected by the president."[55] Viguerie called Reagan "an apologist" for Gorbachev and exclaimed that INF represented "a splitting of the blanket—conservatives will file for divorce and never reconcile again."[56] The Anti-Appeasement Alliance declared that INF would "result eventually in the neutralization of Western Europe and a shift to reliance on conventional arms for defense against the Soviets." They concluded that with Reagan's insistence that Gorbachev was "a 'new kind' of Soviet leader 'no longer interested in world domination,' the Administration is plunging headlong into another Munich."[57] While some conservatives used fear to denounce Reagan, Cal Thomas, a conservative columnist, mocked Reagan's newfound belief in nuclear disarmament. Thomas praised Gorbachev, who had "done a brilliant job of blurring the distinction between good and bad, or what Reagan used to call 'evil' before he was born again by accepting an INF agreement as his political savior."[58]

Although Reagan and Gorbachev met at the Washington Summit and signed the INF Treaty on December 8, 1987, it did not weaken conservatives' opposition to the agreement. Indeed, conservatives geared up for a battle in the Senate over ratification. Tom Wicker at the *New York Times* wrote an article after the Washington Summit questioning why conservatives were so upset with the INF Treaty. Wicker explained that most conservatives understood that the treaty would be ratified by a healthy margin, but that they were raising hell to deter Reagan from pursuing any further deals with Gorbachev. Wicker insisted that Reagan's move toward "treaty-making with the hated Soviet Union and Godless Communism is a clear signal to Howard Phillips and the American right that their moment in the sun is passing; if there ever was a Reagan Revolution, in their eyes it's ending not with a bang but with a whimper." Wicker concluded that perhaps worst of all, "Ronald Reagan—the hero of the right, the man who led the progeny of Bill Buckley and Barry Goldwater out of the wilderness and into Washington—has betrayed the faith by entering into a pact with the keepers of the Evil Empire."[59]

Indeed, conservatives both inside and outside the administration continued to voice their opposition to working with the Soviets. Peggy Noonan, a long-time Reagan speechwriter, speaking on National Public Radio, praised Gorbachev's ability to humanize communism, but she urged listeners to remember that he oversaw a Soviet system that committed numerous human rights abuses. She asked her audience whether they had "heard of the Gulag." "Well," Noonan exclaimed, "he is the warden. You have heard of the toy bombs that the Afghan children pick up, and lose their hands? He is the foreman of the toy-bomb factory. You have read of the psychiatric prisons? He is the man in the white coat holding the needle. See those teeth? Those are the bars Christians and Jews cannot get past." Noonan concluded by comparing Gorbachev to Hitler and Stalin. After all, Noonan reminded her listeners, "Stalin loved to sing, and Hitler loved to dance." She insisted, however, that "when bad men humanize themselves and their systems it gives us a terrible case of cognitive dissonance." Noonan feared that Gorbachev's exemplary performance at the Washington Summit, and the American people's "Gorby fever" (as it was called), would make it "harder to form consensus" the next time the USSR did "something bad."[60]

For her part, Noonan stopped short of condemning either the president or the INF Treaty; however, Howard Phillips did not mince words and launched a full-scale assault on both Reagan and the treaty. In a scathing op-ed in the *New York Times*, Phillips declared that "the United States has never been in more danger than now, during the final 13 months of the Reagan Administration." He lamented that "conservative influence is absent from the top decision-making councils of the executive branch, and conservative policies have been comprehensively abandoned." Phillips directly denounced Reagan, declaring that "President Reagan is little more than the speech reader-in-chief for the pro-appeasement triumvirate of Howard H. Baker Jr., George P. Shultz, and Frank C. Carlucci." Phillips decried the "summit meetings and so-called arms control treaties" as "cover for the treasonous greed of those who manipulate the Administration" and declared that if the treaty was ratified, "a major battle of World War III will have been lost by default, without a shot having been fired." He condemned Reagan's assertion that Gorbachev was "a new kind of Soviet leader." Claiming that Reagan had betrayed his conservative supporters, Phillips exclaimed that "Mr. Reagan is no longer in any way accountable to the millions who recognize that we are in a deadly, strategic end-game with the Soviet Union, militarily the most powerful regime in world history." Phillips concluded his diatribe by issuing a warning to conservatives: "If the treaty is ratified—especially if it is approved without significant opposition—the Administration can be expected to push forward with economic and strategic policies that are even more dangerous to America's interests." Calling conservatives to action, Phillips explained that "we—you and I—have our work cut out for us. It won't be easy, but we can prevail. We must defeat the Regachev Doctrine."[61]

Reagan chose not to address the criticism of New Right leaders, such as Phillips, publicly. The president did, however, respond to many of conservatives' criticisms in a private letter to Nackey Loeb—a conservative publisher of both the *Union Leader* and the *New Hampshire Sunday News.* Loeb had written an op-ed on December 3, following Reagan's comments about some conservatives believing that war with the Soviets was inevitable. In her op-ed, Loeb asserted that Reagan was "promoting an agreement that will give communism the advantage, accompanied by a Hollywood show of smiles and handshakes with the leader of what the original Reagan called 'the evil-empire.'" Frustrated with Reagan, Loeb had sent her op-ed and a personal letter to the president.[62] In typical Reagan fashion, the president sent Loeb a hand-written response on December 18 assuring her that "I'm still the Ronald Reagan I was and the evil empire is still just that." He guaranteed her that "I wasn't talking about you or people like you when I spoke of 'inevitable war.'" Reagan insisted he had been talking "about those individuals giving up on any effort to influence history and accepting permanent hatred and enmity as the only future for the two greatest superpowers." Reagan added that "the probability of disaster is too great to accept that without making an effort."[63] Despite the criticism from conservatives, Reagan's approval rating after the Washington Summit and the signing of the INF Treaty soared to 67 percent, with 81 percent of Americans approving of his policy toward the Soviet Union.[64]

Just before Congress adjourned for winter recess, Reagan met with eight conservative GOP senators in the Cabinet Room in the hopes that he could secure an easy victory for the INF Treaty. Reagan pitched the treaty, how it eliminated an entire class of missiles, and asked them to allow "a clean treaty" to make its way through the Senate. After Reagan finished speaking, Senator Helms responded, "Well, Mr. President, I look around this table and I don't see a yes man." Continuing in his North Carolina drawl, Helms told the president that he "was certainly not a yes man, and you've never been a yes man. I have no intention of being frivolous about it. But if a treaty needs a reservation or an amendment, it's going to be offered in the Senate." Reagan stiffened as Helms continued, "I haven't made up my mind what to do about the treaty except to find out what's in it and try to correct the defects."

Helms cautioned Reagan that the president should not expect the treaty to be "rushed through, 'cause a lot of folks in the Senate are going to take their time about it, including me." Senator Dole then asked the others to voice their concerns to the president. Senator Wallop (R-WY) intensely reminded Reagan that "the Soviets have broken most every treaty they have ever signed. How do we assure compliance with the new treaty? And if they don't comply, what do we do about it?" Reagan responded, "For one thing, we'd just start building Pershings again." Wallop hostilely rebuked the president: "Is Europe on board on that? Has anyone at Defense studied this or is that just a throwaway line?" There was a long silence that was finally broken by Chief of Staff Howard Baker reminding the senators that INF was "a very popular treaty."[65] Despite Reagan's overtures, it was clear after the meeting that the administration would face opposition from many of the people who considered themselves part of the Reagan Revolution.

As 1987 turned into 1988, conservatives ramped up their efforts to defeat the INF Treaty in the Senate. Senator Helms said that INF represented a great threat to US security. Helms believed that dismantling the Pershing II missiles would result in NATO being an alliance "in name only" and would open those countries to an invasion by the Soviet Union. Speaking to reporters, Helms concluded, "We're talking about, perhaps, the survival of Europe." Conservative Republican senator Jim McClure of Idaho insisted that Reagan tie the INF Treaty to other humanitarian issues: "Let them get out of Afghanistan, let them tear down the Berlin Wall." Conservative senators also used Reagan's own tough criticism of Soviet noncompliance to undermine the president's call for a clean approval of INF. These senators, citing Reagan's assertion that any new treaty with the USSR should force Soviet compliance with past treaties, hoped to tie its passage to the "dismantling of the Krasnoyarsk radar," which even the Reagan administration argued was "a violation of the ABM treaty."[66]

Conservative activists also increased their efforts to undermine Reagan. The New Right, who had decided in May to not use the pages of *Conservative Digest* to challenge Reagan personally, founded the Anti-Appeasement Alliance to fight the INF Treaty.[67] John M. Fisher, the chairman of the National Security Council, mailed his 110,000 members a letter urging them to contact their senators and voice their opposition to the treaty. Thomas Moore, along with more than two thousand other retired generals and admirals, signed a position opposing the treaty. They claimed the agreement "would lock" the United States "into strategic" and "military inferiority," and would "make our allies more vulnerable." Sixty conservative organizations, including Citizens for Reagan, endorsed the petition and circulated it to their members. Daniel L. Casey of the American Conservative Union and Paul Weyrich of the Free Congress Foundation lobbied senators to try to derail the treaty by attaching poison pill amendments. Weyrich reminded conservatives that "the only way these campaigns work is when the inside and the outside work together." Richard Viguerie declared that conservatives had "to battle the whole East-West relationship. Fighting this battle will have the effect of fighting the next treaty, the loans and credits that Gorbachev wants, the whole détente apparatus that Reagan has signed on to." In an attempt to rally the grassroots, prominent conservative activists mailed close to three hundred thousand letters expressing their opposition to INF and more than five thousand cassette tapes of General Bernard Rogers, the former supreme commander of NATO, denouncing the treaty.[68]

The most dramatic expression of conservative opposition to Reagan and the INF Treaty, however, came in the form of a one-page newspaper advertisement that the Conservative Caucus, led by Howard Phillips, bought in papers across the country including the *Washington Times* and New Hampshire's *Manchester Union-Leader*. The ad ran under the title "Appeasement Is as Unwise in 1988 as in 1938." Below the headline, there was a picture of Ronald Reagan directly under a picture of Neville Chamberlain. Across from their images, Gorbachev appeared directly under the image of Adolf Hitler. Phillips and the Conservative Caucus implored readers to HELP US DEFEAT THE REAGAN GORBACHEV INF TREATY.[69] Conservative anti-Reagan rhetoric reached its zenith when Phillips compared the INF Treaty to the Munich agreement, in which the prime minister of Great Britain, Neville Chamberlain, infamously traded away parts of Czechoslovakia in exchange for Adolf Hitler's guarantee of peace. Of course, Hitler continued his expansion, and Munich became the embodiment of the failure of appeasement as a policy. The equation of INF with Munich, and by extension Reagan with Chamberlain, was the strongest possible denunciation conservatives could have lobbed at the president, and it is in sharp contrast with future conservatives' comparisons of Reagan to Prime Minister Winston Churchill.

Under a barrage of attacks from conservatives, Reagan stood his ground, supported the treaty, and even defended Gorbachev. In a private letter,

Reagan insisted that "the treaty we have just signed calls for the destruction of medium-range nuclear missiles. The verification provisions are the most stringent ever signed in an arms reduction treaty. I assure you we'll carry them out." Reagan also defended Gorbachev, explaining that the general secretary was the first Soviet leader to "agree to destroy weapons they already have" and the first not to embrace "the Marxian concept of a one-world Communist State."[70] Responding to William F. Buckley's continued opposition to INF, Reagan stood fast. He tried to reassure Buckley that "we are on solid ground on the INF Treaty based on our verification provisions and on the fact that Gorby knows what our response to cheating would be—it's spelled Pershing."[71]

Conservatives continued to oppose the INF Treaty throughout the spring, but the treaty was ultimately ratified by a vote of ninety-three to five in the Senate.[72] An attempted filibuster by Helms was unsuccessful.[73] Reagan's and Gorbachev's efforts resulted in the destruction of 2,692 weapons (846 US and 1,846 Soviet weapons) and went a long way to achieving Reagan's "zero option."[74] The INF Treaty was one of Reagan's principal foreign policy achievements.

To get an agreement from the Soviets, however, Reagan had to ignore his most ardent supporters' complaints that he was selling out on his conservative principles. Writing in *Newsweek* near the end of Reagan's second term, George Will lamented "how wildly wrong he is about what is happening in Moscow. . . . Reagan has accelerated the moral disarmament of the West—actual disarmament will follow—by elevating wishful thinking to the status of political philosophy."[75] Furthermore, Will exclaimed that "December 8"—the day the INF Treaty was signed—would "be remembered as the day the Cold War was lost."[76] Jim Kuhn, executive assistant to the president, recounted how frustrated Reagan had been that conservatives did not support his negotiations with Gorbachev, but concluded that "with or without them, the president was determined to carry on and serve America's best interests." Kuhn explained that "while [Reagan's] core belief system was strongly conservative, he was a pragmatist who didn't let his ideology deter him from embracing what he believed was best for the United States and the world as a whole."[77]

Despite some conservatives' accusing Reagan of pursuing an arms agreement simply to secure a favorable legacy, Reagan's closest advisers insisted that the president always favored nuclear arms reduction and the eventual elimination of nuclear weapons. Just days before the INF Treaty was signed, Lou Cannon of the *Washington Post* reported that according to "longtime advisers and friends," Reagan had "nurtured the idea of nuclear arms reduction for at least seven years and is not going to be diverted from his goal even by those who consider themselves his core constituents." Martin Anderson recalled that Reagan surprised strategists during the 1980 election by pushing for large-scale reductions to the nuclear arsenals of both the US and the USSR, an idea "far more radical than a nuclear freeze." According to Anderson, during those early meetings Reagan made it clear that the United States should pursue military buildup "designed to force the Soviets to the bargaining table." The White House conceded that Reagan was not "going to convert the right-wingers," but insisted that the president could "go over their heads and speak directly to their constituency." Polling demonstrated that most Americans agreed with the president's treaty. Seventy-four percent of Republicans and 69 percent of Democrats supported INF. Ultimately, despite conservative fears that the new détente between the US and the USSR would "lead to reduced defense spending, the emasculation of the Strategic Defense Initiative and the abandonment of the Nicaraguan contras," INF became law.[78]

The signing of the INF Treaty was key to bringing a peaceful end to the Cold War. In his memoir, Secretary of State George Shultz explained that "the INF agreement was important in the many precedents set by its terms, which were almost exactly what Ronald Reagan, to the scoffing of arms control experts, had proposed back in 1981: reductions to the point of elimination of an entire class of nuclear weapons!"[79] Jack Matlock, the US ambassador to the Soviet Union from 1987 to 1991, insisted that INF was important because of the "precedents it set. For the first time, both countries agreed to reduce the number of their nuclear weapons."[80] Perhaps most powerfully, Gorbachev asserted that "the INF treaty set the whole process in motion. It is doubtful whether we would ever have been able to sign the subsequent agreements without it—the INF treaty represented the first well-prepared step on our way out of the Cold War, the first harbinger of the new times."[81]

Ronald Reagan deserves credit for working with Gorbachev to ease tensions between the United States and the Soviet Union. Reagan played an important role in the end of the Cold War, and he did so over the opposition of conservatives during 1987 and 1988. Ironically, just a few years later conservatives hailed Reagan for winning the Cold War. In praising Reagan, they asserted that Ronald Reagan won the Cold War by sticking to his conservative principles. The fact that Reagan was condemned by many conservatives for doing just the opposite during the 1980s has faded from conservatives', and Americans', collective memory.

———————

In addition to their anger over the INF Treaty, conservatives were enraged by what they saw as Reagan's abandonment of the Nicaraguan Contras in the wake of the Iran-Contra scandal.[82] Over the course of Reagan's first term, one aspect of his foreign policy became known as the "Reagan Doctrine," the policy that the United States would provide aid to anticommunist "freedom fighters" to roll back Soviet-backed governments across the globe.[83] Part of Reagan's strategy was to provide aid to the Contra opposition in Nicaragua so that the Sandinistas would hold free elections.[84] Although both the Contras and the Sandinistas used brutal tactics on one another and Nicaraguan citizens, Reagan insisted that the United States send aid to the Contras. Congress went along with the president until October 1984, when it passed an amendment forbidding the administration from providing military assistance, direct or indirect, to the Contras. In November 1986, *Ash-Shiraa*, a Lebanese magazine, published a story that the Reagan administration was selling weapons to Iran and was also trying to purchase the release of Americans being held hostage by Hezbollah in Lebanon. Some of the proceeds from the arms sales to Iran were being diverted, against the direct order of Congress, to the Contras in Nicaragua, who were fighting the left-wing revolutionary Sandinista government of Nicaragua.[85] When the news broke that the Reagan administration not only had sold weapons to the Iranians but also had used the proceeds to illegally fund the Contras, conservatives—as well as most other Americans—were furious.

Although the Iran-Contra scandal fueled conservative anger, conservatives had long been skeptical of Reagan's goal to bring the Sandinistas to the negotiating table. Instead of negotiations, conservatives desired military victory for the Contras. In 1986, Reagan sent Philip C. Habib as a special envoy to Central America with the goal of arriving at a settlement. Conservative GOP congressmen complained that Reagan was "trying to negotiate an 'illusory peace' in Central America." Furthermore, they condemned Habib for saying that "the Contras can't win" and promising that the administration would end support for the Contras if Daniel Ortega, the Nicaraguan president, signed the treaty with other Central American leaders.[86] Kemp blasted Habib for attempting to establish "a false peace" that "will lead to diplomatic disaster."[87] Frustrated, Kemp wrote a letter to Reagan arguing that the peace would lead to "an illusory peace much as you saw in Vietnam." The White

House responded that Ortega would not sign the treaty, which would indicate that the Sandinistas, and not the United States, were responsible for continued warfare in Nicaragua.[88]

After Iran-Contra broke in November, conservatives were once again fearful that Reagan would abandon the Contras and yield to political pressure. In the midst of the scandal, Howard Phillips told the press that many conservative activists were criticizing the president for "impotence and weakness."[89] In the aftermath of the revelations, it was unclear what Reagan had known or what he had ordered with regard to the arms sales to Iran or the proceeds going to the Contras. Lieutenant Colonel Oliver North quickly became the center of the scandal. North had established the networks necessary to channel the funds from Iran to the Contras. Reagan moved quickly to dismiss North and set up a three-person committee to investigate the illegal arms sale.[90]

Conservatives praised North as a martyr and condemned the Reagan administration for making him "the fall guy." Michael Waller, the publications director for the conservative Council for Inter-American Security, praised North, saying he was "very proud of what he's done." Weyrich argued that North's actions were necessary, asserting that "if North tried to help the Contras while Congress turned their backs, then I don't think he should be made a scapegoat." Howard Phillips was thrilled that conservatives were calling for renewed support for the Contras and denouncing Reagan's decision to dismiss North. Phillips asserted that "we're seeing a psychological liberation from Ronald Reagan that we saw from Richard Nixon in 1974." Phillips explained that conservatives were discovering that Reagan was unable "to provide the leadership they were seeking."[91] By 1988, Reagan recognized that the Contras were a hopeless cause. Learning that conservatives were making attempts to provide the Contras with more aid without his support, he lashed out at his chief of staff, exclaiming, "Those sonsofbitches won't be happy until we have 25,000 troops in Managua, and I'm not going to do it!"[92] As Reagan's second term was coming to a close, many conservatives were beginning to view his presidency in the same way they viewed Richard Nixon's: as a failure for the conservative revolution.

Conservatives continued to criticize Reagan's policies toward Nicaragua, and as the 1988 presidential primary began to heat up, many of the candidates criticized the president's foreign policy to appeal to disenchanted conservative voters. The *Los Angeles Times* ran a story on the front page in the fall of 1987 entitled "Angry Conservatives Accuse Reagan of Betraying Ideals." The

newspaper reported that "President Reagan's progress toward an arms reduction agreement with the Soviets, coupled with his diplomatic initiative in
Central America, has provoked a torrent of criticism from many of his most
conservative supporters."[93] The *Hartford Courant* questioned whether conservatives would turn out in 1988, writing that "when Reagan muddies the
message, as he did by selling arms to the ayatollah and now by seeming ready
to subordinate the Contras' cause to a negotiated settlement in Nicaragua,
the morale of his most ardent supporters suffers." The *Courant* concluded
that "the first challenge facing Reagan's would-be Republican successor is to
restore a sense of confidence and coherence to the conservative activists. And
it may be tougher than anyone supposed."[94]

Looking back on the Reagan years, conservatives lamented their missed
opportunities, and the press reported that conservative primary voters desired
a candidate more conservative than Reagan. R. Emmett Tyrrell Jr. of the conservative *American Spectator* condemned conservatives, proclaiming that "in
six years of presidential power, the conservatives never significantly affected
the climate of American ideas." The September 1987 edition of the *Spectator*
focused on "disillusionment" and offered a "roundtable" where eight prominent conservatives discussed "the coming conservative crack-up."[95] Conservative frustration led the GOP candidates to move to Reagan's right. The *New
York Times* reported that conservative primary voters were calling for the candidates' "outright support for the government of South Africa, a flat commitment to the earliest possible deployment of the space-based missile defense
program, and overt, not covert support for anti-Communist groups like the
Nicaraguan rebels." The *Times* concluded that conservative voters were "looking for a candidate who takes an even tougher line than Mr. Reagan."[96]

For their part, the Republican hopefuls tried to find a way to embrace parts
of Reagan's record while denouncing what they viewed as his foreign policy
capitulation. Kemp declared that the administration has "no strategy to deal
with the Soviet threat in Central America." Vice President George Bush reassured a Miami audience that the United States would "not leave the Contras
twisting in the wind, wondering whether they are going to be done in by a
peace plan." While the candidates denounced certain parts of Reagan's record,
they attempted to differentiate "true Reagan policies" from those deemed inadequately conservative. Senator Dole and former Delaware governor Pierre
S. du Pont IV declared that "they believed in the old Reagan of the 'freedom
fighters' and the Reagan Doctrine, not this newly minted substitute." In their

view, the Reagan of 1987 was an imposter who did not represent what it meant to be a Reagan conservative.[97]

In the first manifestation of the Reagan myth making, 1988 GOP candidates began to parse the Reagan record, picking and choosing the positions and issues that would come to define Reagan's presidency. They labeled him an ardent Cold Warrior who had the guts to stand up to the Soviets. Over time, Reagan would become the man who won the Cold War, not by negotiating with the Soviets, but rather because of his steadfast commitment to America's moral superiority over the "evil empire."[98] Throughout the 1990s and the 2000s, conservatives tried to reimagine the Reagan presidency as a triumph of conservatism, forgetting the many qualms they once had with the fortieth president. In due course, Reagan's arms agreements, his tax increases, his granting of citizenship to millions of illegal immigrants, his willingness to negotiate with his adversaries, and his pragmatic conservative approach to politics would fade away and would be replaced by a myth based on a good deal of forgetting and the exploitation of half-truths.

President Reagan meeting with Senator Barry Goldwater in the Oval Office. In many ways, Goldwater provided the foundation for Reagan's election in 1980. Goldwater's failed presidential bid in 1964 offered many young conservatives their first taste of electoral politics and catapulted Reagan onto the national political scene. 2/23/81. Courtesy Ronald Reagan Library.

President Reagan exiting the US Capitol after his economic speech to Congress. The speech offered Reagan an opportunity to pitch his tax cuts to the American people. House Majority Leader Jim Wright wrote in his diary after Reagan's address: "We've been outflanked and outgunned." 4/28/81. Courtesy Ronald Reagan Library.

President Reagan and Vice President George Bush meet with House Speaker Tip O'Neill, Robert Byrd, Jim Wright, and Dan Rostenkowski to discuss the tax bill in the Oval Office. Despite their sometimes bitter disagreements, O'Neill and Reagan worked together to govern effectively. 6/1/81. Courtesy Ronald Reagan Library.

President Reagan addresses the nation from the Oval Office on tax reduction legislation. Reagan often took his case directly to the American people, believing—often correctly—that they would support his initiatives. 7/27/81. Courtesy Ronald Reagan Library.

President Reagan addressing the Ninth Annual Conservative Political Action Conference (CPAC) Dinner at the Mayflower Hotel in Washington, DC. Despite the Reagan administration's inability to fully enact the conservative agenda, conservative activists continued to support Reagan, often exclaiming that his advisors needed to simply "let Reagan be Reagan." 2/26/82. Courtesy Ronald Reagan Library.

President Reagan and House Speaker Thomas "Tip" O'Neill exiting the Oval Office for a press conference regarding the Federal Tax and Budget Reconciliation Act in the Rose Garden. Despite Reagan's legacy as a tax cutter, he angered many supply-side conservatives by increasing taxes in 1982. 8/18/82. Courtesy Ronald Reagan Library.

President Reagan addresses the annual convention of the National Association of Evangelicals in Orlando, Florida. In his "Evil Empire" speech, Reagan silenced many conservatives' complaints that he was not being aggressive enough in the Cold War. 3/8/83. Courtesy Ronald Reagan Library.

President Reagan meeting with Phyllis Schlafly in the Oval Office. Schlafly was one of the most effective conservative grassroots activists. At times she would criticize Reagan for not doing more to implement the social agenda that many conservatives believed was essential to revitalizing the United States. 3/21/83. Courtesy Ronald Reagan Library.

President Reagan meeting with Jack Kemp and a group of Republican members of Congress to discuss the 1984 budget in the Cabinet Room. Kemp was often labeled as Reagan's heir; however, at times the two men locked horns over legislative priorities. 3/22/83. Courtesy Ronald Reagan Library.

President Reagan addresses the nation from the Oval Office on national security. In 1983, Reagan announced the Strategic Defense Initiative (SDI). Although Reagan offered to share the technology with the Soviets, the USSR believed SDI would allow the United States to launch a preemptive nuclear strike on the Soviet Union. 3/23/83. Courtesy Ronald Reagan Library.

President Reagan makes an address to the nation from the Oval Office on the Soviet attack on Korean Air Liner KAL007. While many conservatives called for retribution, Reagan was cautious not to escalate tensions with the Soviets. 9/5/83. Courtesy Ronald Reagan Library.

President Reagan addresses the nation on US-Soviet relations in the East Room. Following what many labeled as the "year of fear" in 1983, Reagan decided to take a more conciliatory approach to the Soviet Union. This speech marked a major shift in US policy. 1/16/84. Courtesy Ronald Reagan Library.

President Reagan meeting in the Yellow Oval Room with George Bush, Howard Baker, Jesse Helms, Strom Thurmond, Fred Fielding, Jim Baker, and M. B. Oglesby to discuss the upcoming debate in the Senate on the proposed school prayer amendment. 3/2/84. Courtesy Ronald Reagan Library.

President Reagan meeting with Congressman Newt Gingrich and other "core" members of the Conservative Opportunity Society (COS) in the Oval Office. Gingrich and the COS would push Reagan to be more conservative throughout his presidency. 5/20/85. Courtesy Ronald Reagan Library.

President Reagan addressing the nation from the Oval Office on the Iran-Contra controversy. The scandal almost wrecked the Reagan presidency and may have provided the president with an added incentive to sign the INF Treaty. 3/4/87. Courtesy Ronald Reagan Library.

President Reagan addressing the American Foundation for AIDS Research at Potomac-on-the-River Restaurant in Washington, DC. Often condemned for not speaking out on the AIDS epidemic, Reagan took this opportunity to praise doctors, activists, and his surgeon general, C. Everett Koop, for their work in fighting the disease. 5/31/87. Courtesy Ronald Reagan Library.

President Reagan giving his famous Berlin Wall speech in front of the Brandenburg Gate in the Federal Republic of Germany. When Reagan called on Secretary Gorbachev to "tear down this wall," he couldn't have imagined it would be gone just two years later. 6/12/87. Courtesy Ronald Reagan Library.

President Reagan giving a speech at Moscow State University in the USSR. Reagan's trip to the Soviet Union represented the incredible progress that he and Gorbachev had made in easing tensions and laying the groundwork for the end of the Cold War. 5/31/88. Courtesy Ronald Reagan Library.

President Reagan giving his Farewell Address to the nation from the Oval Office. When Reagan left Washington, not all conservatives were satisfied with what the administration had achieved. 1/11/89. Courtesy Ronald Reagan Library.

President Reagan talking with Donald Trump and Ivana Trump at a state dinner for King Fahd of Saudi Arabia in the Blue Room. Trump would later win the presidency without embracing the Reagan legacy and by proposing many policies at odds with Reagan conservatism. 2/11/85. Courtesy Ronald Reagan Library.

PART II: THE LEGACY AND EVOLVING
MYTHOLOGY OF PRESIDENT RONALD
REAGAN, 1988–2016

9. Recasting Reagan: How the Fortieth President Framed His Legacy, 1989–1994

At their 1988 national convention, Republicans attempted to unify the party by appealing to the legacy of Ronald Reagan. The lights went dim in the Superdome, and the boisterous crowd of activists went silent. Everyone's attention turned to the jumbotron, where a video tribute to President Reagan played. It began with British prime minister Margaret Thatcher thanking Reagan for his leadership and for his "testament of belief." Following this were happy images of the Reagan years with "America the Beautiful" playing in the background. Reagan's calm and resolute voice recalled his eight years in office. While enterprising Americans building homes flashed across the screen, Reagan asserted, "We said we intended to reduce interest rates and inflation and we have; we said we would reduce taxes to get our economy moving again and we have." The images shifted to the president walking with American soldiers as Reagan declared, "We said we would once again be respected throughout the world and we are; we said we would restore our ability to protect our freedom on land, sea, and in the air and we have." Images of Americans, both black and white, smiled and laughed as Reagan avowed, "We came together in a national crusade to make America great again, and to make a new beginning."[1] As Republicans gathered in New Orleans for the nomination of George H. W. Bush, their goal was to unify the party behind Bush—especially the conservatives who had supported other candidates.[2] The one man who brought most Republicans together was Reagan, and the tribute reminded Republicans of their shared pride for the successes of the 1980s.[3]

The tribute, produced by the Republican National Committee, made it clear that Reagan believed his greatest achievements were revitalizing the economy, negotiating arms reductions with the Soviet Union, and rebuilding American morale. Looking back on the administration's economic achievements, Reagan proclaimed, "We made headway in getting government off the backs of the people, we breathed new life into our economy, and put more people to work than ever before in history." He then pivoted to the military, declaring, "We rebuilt our military strength and brought the world a little closer together in peace." Citing the Intermediate-Range Nuclear Forces (INF)

Treaty, Reagan proudly pronounced that "the era of nuclear arms reductions had finally begun and for the first time I thought we could actually look forward to a future not clouded by the threat of nuclear war." Reagan concluded that "above all, more than anything else, we got America to stand tall again" and "I'd like to think that's the thing I'm proudest of." The tribute ended with Reagan humbly asserting, "I guess we did okay."[4]

The video was the first public opportunity for President Reagan to shape his own legacy, but he would continue to comment on his presidency until he was diagnosed with Alzheimer's disease in 1994. Reagan's emphasis on his economic agenda and his foreign policy continued throughout his postpresidency. Social issues such as abortion, school prayer, and the administration's reaction to the AIDS epidemic, however, were not discussed—just as they were not present in the tribute video.

Using his postpresidential speeches, Ronald Reagan's and Nancy Reagan's autobiographies, and the exhibits at the Ronald Reagan Presidential Library, it is possible to reconstruct how Reagan—himself—wanted to be remembered.[5] The Reagan legacy, at least according to Reagan, centered around economic recovery, rebuilding the military, reducing the threat of nuclear war, and restoring Americans' belief in their country. Contentious social issues, and the people who were at the heart of the culture wars of the 1980s, were not present in his account.

Reagan viewed his economic policies as overwhelmingly successful, even while acknowledging the recession of 1981–1982. By contrast, supply-siders often begin their analysis of the Reagan years in 1983, glossing over Reagan's role in the recession that marked the early years of his administration, preferring to shift the blame to Carter and the failed policies of the 1970s. In doing so, fiscal conservatives exaggerate the president's good economic record.[6] In contrast, Reagan's understanding of his role in ending the Cold War ran counter to many conservative interpretations—including those of the Reagan-victory school.[7] Whereas conservatives attributed the end of the Cold War to the president's policies, Reagan credited Secretary General Mikhail Gorbachev and the people of Eastern Europe. On social issues, Reagan was silent. Neither his autobiography nor the museum mentions the controversial issues of abortion, gay rights, the AIDS epidemic, or school prayer. Reagan was very aware of the importance of presenting his legacy in a positive light and was frustrated with the press and others who seemed "bent on denying us our victories and rewriting history."[8] Accordingly, Reagan decided to focus on his economic and foreign policy achievements and to recount his two terms as a time that all Americans could look back on positively. Furthermore, Reagan's conception of his presidency provides critical context for the evolution of how conservatives perceived him from 1994 to 2016.

President Reagan was extremely proud of the economic recovery that took place during his time in office, but he was hesitant to personally take credit for the achievements of the 1980s. As the 1988 RNC video came to an end, Reagan acknowledged that the "tribute really belongs to the 245 million citizens." He emphasized that it was "really the American people who endured the great challenge of lifting us from the depths of national calamity, renewing our economic strength, and leading the way to restoring our respect in the world." Although Reagan humbly diverted the credit for the economic successes to the American people, he did frame his administration's economic policy as overwhelmingly successful. His 1988 convention speech included "a friendly reminder" of what the country had faced when he took office: mortgage interest rates at 21 percent, lagging industrial production, family income decreasing by almost 6 percent, and a misery index (a combination of the unemployment and inflation rate) of 21 percent. Reagan concluded that the Democrats had not mentioned the index at their convention "because right now it's less than 9.2 percent. Facts are stubborn things."[9]

Reagan told the friendly audience that conservatives were the change agents, cutting, indexing, and reforming taxes. He touted that the top 5 percent of earners were paying a larger percentage of the total government revenues, praised his administration for overseeing sixty-eight straight months of job growth, and celebrated the creation of almost 18 million jobs. Reagan also noted that inflation had fallen from 18 percent to 4 percent. Reagan asserted that "new homes are being built. New car sales reached record levels. Exports are starting to climb again. Factory capacity is approaching maximum use." Reagan paused and concluded, "You know, I've noticed they don't call it Reaganomics anymore."[10]

Despite this glowing review of his administration's economic policies, Reagan acknowledged that during his tenure deficits had gotten out of control. He reminded the convention audience, however, that "the President doesn't vote for a budget, and the President can't spend a dime," adding "only the Congress can do that." Reagan pushed back against critics who claimed his requests for increases in defense spending were to blame for the deficits, explaining that "defense spending today, in real dollars, is almost exactly what it was 6 years ago." Reagan claimed that if Congress "had passed my first budget, my first spending plan in 1982, the cumulative outlays and deficits would have been $207 billion lower by 1986." Reagan then emphasized that he had always "supported and called for a balanced budget amendment to the Constitution, and the liberals have said no every year." He said he also supported a "line-item veto, which 43 Governors have, to cut fat in the budget, and the liberals have said no." Continuing to blame the Democratic Congress, Reagan declared that "every year I've attempted to limit their wild spending sprees, and they've said no."[11] Reagan was very aware that the most visible strike against his economic record was the near tripling of the national debt under his watch.

A few months later, from the Oval Office, Reagan emphasized the economic successes of his administration during his farewell address. Reagan opened by telling the American people that he had "been reflecting on what the past eight years have meant and mean" and that the economic recovery was one of the "two great triumphs" of his presidency (the other being the recovery of American morale). As for the recovery, he declared that "the people of America created—and filled—19 million new jobs." Reagan continued, "Our economic program brought about the largest peacetime expansion in our history: real family income up, the poverty rate down, entrepreneurship booming, and an explosion in research and new technology." Reagan emphasized that "we're exporting more than ever because American industry became more competitive and at the same time, we summoned the national will to knock down protectionist walls abroad instead of erecting them at home." For all the successes of the economic recovery, however, Reagan did admit that he had his regrets. Reagan frankly explained that he regretted the budget deficit but then passed on the opportunity to blame Congress. Instead, he simply asserted that "tonight isn't for arguments, and I'm going to hold my tongue."[12]

Almost as soon as Reagan's term ended, he and his accomplishments came under attack. The day Reagan left office, the *New York Times* declared that "no one credits Mr. Reagan with much of an intellect . . . nor does anyone call him a hard worker or active leader. . . . As President, his strength lay in delivering the lines that were arranged for him." The *Times* article was the first of many attacks on Reagan for simply being actor-in-chief.[13]

Many others called his postpresidential activities into question. Reagan was widely criticized for accepting $2 million to speak to Japan's Fujisankei

Communications Group.[14] According to the *Los Angeles Times*, Reagan's trip to Japan "was widely interpreted as the shameless huckstering of a President's prestige." A *New York Times* editorial asserted that no other president had "plunged so blatantly into pure commercialism." The money Reagan received from the Japanese company made him a punchline. In early 1990, he sat silently and grinned while business mogul Donald Trump "made a crack about the Japanese millions from the podium at the Hebrew University Scopus Awards dinner."[15]

Criticism of Reagan went beyond his trip to Japan. The president was lambasted for his normal $50,000 speaking fee, for his book deal reportedly worth $5 to $7 million, for receiving a $150,000 annual subsidy for his staff from the Republican Party, for the over $1 million the federal government paid for transition expenses, and for his $99,500 pension. Reagan was also criticized for choosing a penthouse suite on the outskirts of Beverly Hills as his office space. The federal government paid for all ex-presidents' office space, but Reagan's was the most expensive of any of them.[16] For a president who had emphasized the importance of individual responsibility and limiting government subsidies, and who frequently spoke out against deficits, such extravagance—some of which was on the government's dime—gave his critics ample ammunition to use against him.

In addition to attacks on Reagan's postpresidential activity, conservatives questioned the revolutionary nature of the Reagan Revolution. Looking back on the Reagan administration in early 1989, the *Wall Street Journal* asserted that "the fact that Ronald Reagan left office as the most popular president in modern history means that he settled for less change than either he or his supporters wanted or could have gotten." Conservative political commentator Robert Novak quipped that many conservatives lived by the motto "Reagan: Our leader, right or left." The *Wall Street Journal* reminded readers that Reagan had been "supremely pragmatic" while in office and concluded that "for those—Ronald Reagan included—who hoped for a genuine Reagan Revolution, the Reagan years offer some lessons."[17] In short, despite Reagan's acceptance of the term "Reagan Revolution" and his claim that "the men and women of the Reagan revolution . . . brought America back," many commentators questioned just how much conservative change was enacted during the Reagan years.[18]

Reagan released his autobiography in 1990, which gave him another opportunity to define and shape his legacy. Discussing the economy, Reagan reminded readers that when he took office the country was experiencing "what many economists called its greatest economic emergency since the Great Depression." Reagan recited his belief that it was the "policies of the federal government reaching back for decades that were mostly responsible for the problems."[19] Describing the vision for the economy he had implemented, Reagan "believed that if we cut tax rates and reduced the proportion of our national wealth that was taken by Washington, the economy would receive a stimulus that would bring down inflation, unemployment, and interest rates." The result of this vision, Reagan argued, "would be such an expansion of economic activity that in the end there would be a net increase in the amount of revenue to finance the important functions of government."[20] Reagan traced the evolution of his ideas on economics from being taxed 94 percent during his time in Hollywood, to his readings of the philosopher Ibn Khaldun, to President Calvin Coolidge's ability to cut taxes and increase revenues, and to President John F. Kennedy's support for lowering tax rates as a means to increase economic production and revenues in the 1960s.[21] Reagan, following up on his lifetime of experience and belief, with the help of the American people, was able to get his tax cuts passed into law. Of course, according to Reagan, his 1981 tax cuts were essential to revitalizing the American economy and bringing about the boom of the 1980s.

Just as he had in his 1988 convention speech and in his farewell address, Reagan used his autobiography to discuss what he viewed as the major criticism of his economic record: his failure to balance the budget. Reagan conceded that there was tension between doing "whatever it took to make men and women proud to wear their uniforms again" and balancing the budget. To critics who claimed he failed to deliver on his campaign promise to balance the budget, Reagan responded that "during the campaign, the people of America told me nothing mattered more to them than national security." Reagan continued that "time and again, when I went around the country calling for a balanced budget, I'd get this question: 'But what if it comes down to a choice between national security and the deficit?' Every time, I answered: 'I'd have to come down on the side of national defense.' And every time I did, the audience roared." Reagan insisted that "nobody wanted a second-class army, navy, or air force defending our country." Reagan concluded that while he "wanted a balanced budget," he "also wanted peace through strength."[22] By recalling his discussions on the campaign trail, Reagan insisted that he had not broken a campaign promise by failing to balance the budget. Instead, Reagan placed the deficits of the 1980s in the context of the rebuilding of America's military, declaring that a balanced budget, while important, was secondary to protecting the United States.

Although Reagan's autobiography forcefully defended his economic record, the Reagan Library and Museum, which opened in November 1991, continues to provide a living manifestation of President Reagan's legacy to millions of visitors. Unlike the autobiography, which had a limited readership, the museum is accessible to a wide audience. The library and museum were created by the Ronald Reagan Presidential Foundation, which Reagan founded to continue "his legacy" and "carry out his work of inspiring freedom at home and abroad."[23] President Reagan played an active role in creating the library and museum and visited frequently until he was diagnosed with Alzheimer's in 1994. He attended monthly meetings to discuss captions, pick photographs, and review the exhibit designs. According to one museum designer, "the exhibits tell the story from the President's point of view." She explained that the museum was "not going to be totally objective, nor highly critical."[24] Indeed, the museum's purpose is to present Reagan's conception of his presidency and capture his legacy through photographs, exhibits, and text. From the first day the museum opened, Americans from across the nation have traveled to Reagan Country to visit the museum and relive the legacy of America's fortieth president.[25] Through the numerous exhibits, videos, and informative captions, Reagan continues to speak to each visitor.

Reagan's economic achievements are at the heart of the museum. Visitors who make their way through it begin with Reagan's early life, his time in Hollywood, his work as a spokesman for General Electric, his speech in 1964 for Barry Goldwater, and his two terms as governor of California. Moving from the exhibit on his governorship to his time as president the hallway walls contain tumultuous images from the 1970s with large words: "Shortages," "Protests," "Frustration," "Recession," "Unemployment," "Foreclosures," "Olympic Boycott," "A Nation in Crisis," "Stagflation," "Misery Index," "Unemployment," and "Layoffs." The dimly lit and somewhat claustrophobic hallway establishes the mood of the years leading up to the Reagan administration as miserable, bleak, hopeless, dark, and casts the American people as desperate for a change of direction. A small exhibit labeled "The Turbulent 1970s" explained that "at home, Americans suffered through factory closings, high energy prices, gas lines, and a ten-year battle with inflation." The hallway ends with a quotation from Reagan asking, "Are you better off than you were four years ago?"[26]

The exhibit, more than any of Reagan's speeches or his autobiography, demonstrates the dismal condition of the economy when he took office. Capturing the mood of the 1970s and juxtaposing it against the hope and optimism that Reagan's economic achievements gave the American people is essential for framing the president's legacy. Missing from the museum, however, is any acknowledgement that President Carter implemented some free market policies that set the stage for Reagan's success. Carter reduced regulations in the airline industry, in the transportation system, and in the financial sector.[27] Most importantly, however, Reagan did not acknowledge Carter's role in appointing Paul Volcker as chairman of the Federal Reserve.[28]

President Reagan's economic accomplishments are detailed in an exhibit titled "Rebuilding America." According to the exhibit, "Reagan inherited a country in the midst of a disastrous recession, with sky-high interest rates, out-of-control inflation, massive unemployment, and other problems that tested America's resolve." The museum also contains an economic scorecard that summarized Reagan's achievements. During Reagan's time in office, "inflation fell from 12.4% to 4.6%," "unemployment fell from 7.4% to 5.2%," "the top individual tax payer rate was cut by 50% to 28%," and "mortgage interest rates dropped from 15.4% to 10.3%." It also documents that the "total tax receipts doubled from $517 billion to $1,030 billion" and "income tax receipts rose from $347 billion to $549 billion." The report card adds that "the Dow Jones Industrial Average rose from about 970 to 2,235" and "the economy grew for 96 consecutive months."[29] In short, according to the exhibit, Reagan earned an A+ for the economic recovery. In typical Reagan fashion, however, the exhibit does not give the credit to Reagan alone. Indeed, it explains that Reagan "was determined to bring about recovery by liberating the native energy, ingenuity, and entrepreneurial spirit of the American people."[30]

Reagan deserves some credit for revitalizing the economy, but some aspects of his economic record are not present in the museum. Most obvious, Reagan failed to acknowledge Volcker's role in reducing inflation. Despite being a Carter appointee, Volcker gave Reagan credit for not interfering with his policies even when advisers urged the president to challenge the independence of the Federal Reserve.[31] Reagan also did not address critics who claimed that his policies disproportionately benefited the wealthiest Americans while hurting the poor.[32] Similarly, Reagan did not confront the assertions that his policies disproportionately hurt African Americans.[33] Finally, the museum does not defend Reagan's deregulation of the financial industry, which some scholars have claimed caused the savings and loan crisis at the end of the decade.[34]

Despite such omissions, Reagan still presented his economic legacy with more nuance than supply-siders and conservatives would in the future. In contrast to supply-siders and conservatives who used data from 1983 to 1989 to overstate Reagan's economic successes, the museum cites data from 1981 to 1989, thus including the recession of 1981–1982.[35]

Just as Reagan had addressed the budget deficit in speeches and in his autobiography, the museum also acknowledges it. An exhibit titled "Give and Take" recognizes that while Reagan was in office, he was "concerned about the rising federal deficit." The museum noted that he had "raised some taxes" and "in return, Congress pledged three dollars in spending cuts for every dollar of the tax increase." The exhibit emphasizes that "spending cuts on that scale never passed Congress, but new spending bills did." As a final note on the deficit, the museum explains that Reagan's "inability to persuade Congress to rein in domestic spending was one of the president's chief regrets."[36] Throughout his postpresidency Reagan consistently deflected criticism about budget deficits by blaming Congress and citing the importance of rebuilding America's military. Summing up Reagan's economic legacy, an exhibit titled "Economic Recovery" concludes: "Ronald Reagan's economic plan yielded remarkable results. The country experienced one of the longest peacetime expansions in history—96 straight months. Almost 20 million new jobs were created. Inflation was tamed, and interest rates fell dramatically. The stock market nearly tripled in value. Americans saw their taxes cut by almost a third. With prosperity at home, President Reagan could focus on his lifelong mission to end communism abroad."[37]

The second pillar of Reagan's legacy, as promoted by the former president himself, was rebuilding America's military forces and reducing the threat posed by nuclear weapons. Speaking at the 1988 Republican National Convention, Reagan reminded the audience that when he was elected, "our national defense had been so weakened, the Soviet Union had begun to engage in reckless aggression, including the invasion and occupation of Afghanistan." Reagan denounced Carter's decision to respond to Soviet aggression by boycotting the Olympics and imposing a grain embargo. Furthermore, he condemned Carter's claim that "our people were at fault because of some malaise." Recounting his administration's achievements, Reagan proudly declared that "we rebuilt our Armed Forces." He continued, "We liberated Grenada . . . we struck a firm blow against Libyan terrorism . . . [we have] seen a growth of democracy in 90 percent of Latin America . . . and for the first time in 8 years we have the prospects of peace in southwest Africa and the removal of Cuban and other foreign forces from the region." Reagan emphasized that "in the 2,765 days of our administration, not 1 inch of ground has fallen to the communists." Pivoting to his role in reducing the number of nuclear weapons, Reagan proudly recounted that "today we have the first treaty in world history to eliminate an entire class of U.S. and Soviet nuclear missiles."[38]

Although Reagan deserves credit for rebuilding America's military might, he failed to acknowledge President Carter's investments in the military and the policies he had put into effect to address Soviet expansion. According to Robert Gates, the Reagan administration's deputy director of the CIA, the Soviets had viewed Carter as a "committed ideological foe" and a "geopolitical adversary." Indeed, according to Gates, Carter "prepared the ground work for Reagan in the strategic arena" and "in confronting the Soviets" across the world.[39] Furthermore, Reagan mocked Carter's response to Soviet aggression in Afghanistan, but Reagan rolled back the grain embargo that Carter had put into place to punish Soviet intervention.[40] Reagan also failed to mention that many of the weapons his administration invested in did not result in meaningful military advancements.[41] Despite such omissions, however, Reagan's overarching claims that he rebuilt America's armed forces and reduced the threat of nuclear war were accurate.[42]

During his farewell address, Reagan confronted conservative critics of arms reductions and insisted that his foreign policy legacy centered on rebuilding America's defenses and reducing the threat of nuclear war. Many conservatives had been critical of Reagan's decision to pursue nuclear arms reductions with the Soviets, viewing Reagan's willingness to negotiate with the "evil empire" as a dangerous proposition.[43] From the Oval Office, Reagan told the audience that he had been asked if negotiating with the Soviets was not "a gamble," but Reagan insisted that it was not, "because we're basing our actions not on words but deeds." For those who condemned him for pursuing détente with the Soviet Union, Reagan declared that "the détente of the 1970s was based not on actions but promises" and emphasized that "this time, so far, it's different." Reagan praised Gorbachev as "different from previous Soviet leaders" in that he realized that there were "things wrong with his society and is trying to fix them." Reagan told the American people that he wanted the new relationship with the Soviet Union to continue and hoped they would continue to "act in a helpful manner." But, Reagan insisted, "if and when they don't, at first pull your punches. If they persist, pull the plug." The president emphasized that "it's still trust but verify. It's still play, but cut the cards. It's still watch closely. And don't be afraid to see what you see."[44]

Unsure of how his policies would affect the Cold War, or how that conflict would unfold, Reagan desired to laud his accomplishments while still being mindful that the trust he had developed with Gorbachev might dissolve and tensions between the two nations might increase again. Initially on leaving office, Reagan was cautious in framing his foreign policy legacy. In later years, when events transpired that made him appear prescient, he would reconsider his foreign policy successes and accept a much more grandiose legacy.

After Reagan left the White House, he was intent on presenting his foreign policy in a positive light, but the fallout over the Iran-Contra affair called the president's legacy into question. During the trial of Reagan's national security adviser, John M. Poindexter, the defense requested that Reagan hand over specific diary entries to the court and even testify. These requests seemed to contradict Poindexter's earlier testimony before Congress, in which he had insisted that the president "was not briefed on every little issue involved in coordinating this effort" and implied Reagan did not have knowledge of the affair. For his part, Reagan had told the Presidential Review Board in 1987 that he was not aware "that the N.S.C. staff was engaged in helping the contras" but clarified in May that he "was very definitely involved in the decisions about the freedom fighters." Poindexter went to trial in early 1990 facing five criminal charges, including obstructing congressional inquiries and making false statements to Congress. While he was a member of the administration, Poindexter had said that "it's always the responsibility of a staff to protect their leader," but as his trial began he changed his tune, declaring that "the former president's role in the affair should be fully explored in court."[45]

Poindexter got at least part of what he desired. Reagan was subpoenaed by the defense to give videotaped testimony on Iran-Contra. Altogether, Reagan replied "I don't remember" or "I don't recall" eighty-eight times during his eight hours of testimony. The transcript of his testimony was released to the public, and it was quickly dissected. Poindexter's defense relied, in part, "on the theory that Reagan either approved of or knew about his aides' secret activities on the contras' behalf." Reagan denied that he had any knowledge of the exchange of weapons but reiterated that he had asked his staff to aid the Contras by any possible legal means. Addressing Oliver North, another member of Reagan's National Security Council who had been incriminated in the Iran-Contra affair, Reagan explained that he "never had any inkling" of the illegal activity. Reagan said that he and North "did not meet frequently or anything of that kind" and added that he could not recall "ever having a single meeting with him." Although Reagan's testimony did not reveal any involvement in the affair, the *Chicago Tribune* concluded that the deposition revealed "startling gaps in the memory of the 79-year-old former president."[46]

The Iran-Contra affair continued to define Reagan's foreign policy and detract from his legacy. In October 1991, just weeks before the opening of the Reagan Library, excerpts from Oliver North's memoir were released. North emphatically asserted that "President Reagan knew everything. . . . I have no doubt that he was told about the use of residuals for the Contras and that he approved it. Enthusiastically." According to the *Los Angeles Times*, however, North's claims were offered with "no concrete evidence to support his charge and conceded that he never spoke to Reagan about the diversion."[47] North's and Poindexter's accusations detracted from Reagan's efforts to frame his foreign policy in a positive light. Even in August 1992, when Reagan was informed that he was no longer under investigation for his connection to the Iran-Contra prosecutions, the ordeal haunted his legacy and threatened how future generations would view his foreign policy.[48]

While the outcome of the Iran-Contra prosecution was still unclear, events around the world enabled Reagan to adjust and enhance his legacy in foreign affairs. On November 9, 1989, East Berliners gathered at the Berlin Wall's crossing points demanding to be admitted to the West. The guards, who had no directions, did not fire on the crowds, and some even opened the gates. Germans from East and West danced and cheered; many brought hammers and chisels and began to tear down the wall.[49] The collapse of the Berlin Wall was a powerful image that the people of Eastern Europe would determine their own destiny, but it also became a symbol of Reagan's prescience. After the wall was torn down, pieces of it were spread across the world.

President Reagan was given one piece of the wall, and in April 1990 the Reagan Library held an outdoor ceremony to unveil the 6,338-pound concrete mass. Standing in front of the wall, Reagan told the audience that his 1987 call for Gorbachev to "tear down this wall" was not "merely a polite suggestion."[50] Reagan asserted that the wall "shattered dreams and crushed hopes," "made us angry," and "seemed to be impenetrable." When the wall did come down, Reagan declared that "all freedom-loving people in the world were

Berliners." Reagan said he was pleased to accept the section of the Berlin Wall "with solemn remembrances of the past and the resolution of what happened must never happen again." Reagan concluded that he hoped "our children and grandchildren come here and see this wall and reflect on what it meant to history. Let them understand that only vigilance and strength will deter tyranny."[51] Although Reagan mentioned his 1987 call for Gorbachev to tear down the Berlin Wall, Reagan did not claim responsibility for its collapse. Instead, he was more interested in explaining what the fall of the Berlin Wall meant for people who had been trapped in East Berlin. In time, conservatives would assert that Reagan's 1987 speech was prophetic and that it proved that his foreign policy vision led to the end of the Cold War.

As the Soviet Union began to collapse, Reagan recognized his role in the conflict but gave the credit to the people of Eastern Europe, Gorbachev, and his allies in Western Europe. One year after the fall of the Berlin Wall, Reagan dedicated a statue constructed from eight sections of the Berlin Wall in Fulton, Missouri.[52] Discussing the fall of the wall, Reagan credited the "brave men and women on both sides of the iron curtain who devoted their lives—and sometimes sacrificed them—so that we might inhabit a world without barriers." Looking back at his time in office, Reagan traced the events that made the fall of the Berlin Wall possible. He began by explaining that when faced with the threat of intermediate-range missiles and the prospect of nuclear war, the United States could not "lower its profile" or its "flags." Instead, Reagan explained that with the development of the Strategic Defense Initiative he had hoped "to hasten the day when the nuclear nightmare was ended forever, and our children's dreams were no longer marred by the specter of instant annihilation." Reagan said that in his attempts to stand up to the Soviets and establish peace, he was not alone. He praised "leaders like Helmut Kohl and Margaret Thatcher" who reinforced the "message that the West would not be blackmailed and that the only rational course was to return to the bargaining table in Geneva and work out real and lasting arms reductions for both sides." Reagan then pivoted to Mikhail Gorbachev, whom he credited with putting an "end" to "numbing oppression." He insisted that glasnost and perestroika had opened up Soviet society and offered the Soviet people "the promise of a better life, achieved through democratic institutions and a market economy." Reagan praised Gorbachev for enabling "real arms control" to move forward and declared that their negotiations resulted in "an entire class of weapons" being "eliminated for the first time in the atomic age."[53]

Addressing the end of the Cold War, Reagan credited the people within the Soviet Union for rising up and demanding freedom. Reagan asserted that "within months" of the implementation of Gorbachev's policies, "the Soviet Empire began to melt like a snowbank in May." Reagan declared that "one country after another overthrew the privileged cliques that had bled their economies and curbed their freedoms." While Reagan was not sure Gorbachev had listened when he had called for the Berlin Wall to be torn down, "neither he nor the rulers of Eastern Europe could ignore the much louder chants of demonstrators in the streets of Leipzig and Dresden. . . . In the churches and the schools, in the factories and on the farms, a once silent people found their voice and with it a battering ram to knock down walls, real and imagined." Reagan concluded, "Because of them, the political map of Europe has been rewritten."[54]

Reagan did use his autobiography, however, to recast his plan for the Cold War as consistent and coherent from the moment he took office. Although Reagan had been interested in reducing the number of nuclear weapons prior to the attempt on his life in March 1981, he credited the assassination attempt for motivating him to seriously work toward this goal. Reagan wrote that while he was in the hospital, he pondered that "perhaps having come so close to death made me feel I should do whatever I could in the years God had given me to reduce the threat of nuclear war; perhaps there was a reason I had been spared."[55] Reagan recalled that in front of the National Press Club in November 1981 he declared his "commitment to reducing the risk of nuclear war" and asking "the Soviet Union to join us in doing so." That speech, Reagan wrote, was the product of months of discussions with key members of the administration. But to achieve his ultimate goal of nuclear reduction, Reagan "knew it had to begin with an increase in arms" and that "we had to bargain with them from strength, not weakness."[56] According to Reagan, his strategy to reduce nuclear weapons depended on him "sending a powerful message" that "we weren't going to stand by anymore while they armed and financed terrorists and subverted democratic governments." Reagan wrote that he "wanted peace through strength, not peace through a piece of paper."[57]

In order to achieve the reductions, Reagan claimed that he "deliberately set out to say some frank things about the Russians, to let them know there were some new fellows in Washington who had a realistic view of what they were up to and weren't going to let them keep it up." Reagan wrote that it was essential to let the Soviets "know that we were going to spend whatever it took to stay ahead of them in the arms race."[58] But according to Reagan, his aggressive rhetoric was only one part of his plan. He also sought to reassure the Soviets that he "realized the nuclear standoff was futile and dangerous for all of us" and that he "wanted to reduce the tensions that had led us to the threshold of a nuclear standoff."[59] Reagan insisted that his military buildup, his antagonistic language, and the creation of a missile defense shield were partially responsible for bringing the Soviets to the negotiating table. Observers and critics, from both the right and left, failed, in Reagan's view, to realize that his anticommunist rhetoric was not an end unto itself but rather a means to achieve his ultimate goal of reducing, and potentially eliminating, the threat of nuclear war.

Although Reagan may have had a comprehensive plan to bring the Soviets to the negotiating table, those within his administration often pursued contradictory policies. James Baker, Reagan's chief of staff during his first term and later secretary of the treasury, described Reagan's foreign policy from 1981 to 1987 as "a witches' brew of intrigue" in which competing factions fought to promote their own agendas.[60] This infighting was compounded by the fact that Reagan was often unwilling to settle the differences that existed between his staff members. General Colin Powell, the president's national security adviser, noted he was unnerved that when "contrasting views" on foreign policy were presented to Reagan, the president would "merely acknowledge" the recommendations "without saying yes, no, or maybe." Reagan was even ambivalent about some arms control issues, causing Frank Carlucci, the secretary of defense, to exclaim to Powell, "My God, we didn't sign on to run this country!"[61] If Reagan had a grand strategy to bring the Soviets to the negotiating table, he did not share it with the secretary of defense or the National Security Council. In reality, the president gave his subordinates significant power to determine important elements of the administration's foreign policy.

In addition to the lack of a clear and consistent policy within the Reagan White House, Reagan announced a more conciliatory policy toward the Soviets during a public address in January 1984. Robert McFarlane explained that the purpose of Reagan's address was to declare his intention "to solve problems with the Soviet Union and to improve the state of this crucial relationship."[62] Diplomat Jack Matlock asserted that the January address was designed as a pivot in the administration's strategy for engaging Moscow. The new strategy was "a process which we hoped conceivably could end in the end of the cold war, but we couldn't be confident that it would."[63] Despite what Reagan himself remembered, his administration—both publicly and privately—pursued multiple policies, which eventually resulted in a more conciliatory public tone toward the Soviet Union. Indeed, Reagan's two foreign policy goals of defeating communism and reducing the threat of nuclear weapons were often at odds with one another. Instead of acknowledging that his goals conflicted, and at times inhibited one another, Reagan chose to present his foreign policy as a coherent strategy.[64] Doing so allowed the president to cast himself as a prescient leader and enabled him to ignore the fact that his critics were correct that his rhetoric often alienated the Soviets and hurt his attempts to reduce nuclear weapons.

When the Reagan Library opened in November 1991, five presidents gathered to celebrate not only its dedication but also America's victory in the Cold War.[65] The *Los Angeles Times* reported that the presidents' speeches demonstrated that "they considered America's Cold War triumph to be a team effort with plenty of credit for several commanders-in-chief—not just Reagan or Bush." As a brisk breeze snapped the flags and rustled the presidents' thinning hair, each delivered his thoughts on the Cold War. Nixon recounted his meeting with Nikita Khrushchev thirty-two years earlier, during which Khrushchev pushed his finger in Nixon's chest and said, "Your grandchildren will live under communism," to which Nixon responded, "Your grandchildren will live in freedom." Nixon continued, "At the time, I was sure he was wrong. But I was not sure I was right. And now we know—thanks in great part to the strong, idealistic leadership of President Ronald Reagan, Khrushchev's grandchildren will live in freedom." For his part, George H. W. Bush praised Reagan's prescience and asserted that "he predicted that communism would land in the dustbin of history. And history proved him right." In delivering his speech, Reagan exclaimed that "visitors to this mountaintop will see a great jagged chunk of yes—an evil empire, that spied on and lied to its citizens, denying them their freedom, their bread, even their faith." Reagan triumphantly declared that "the Iron Curtain has rusted away."[66] Reagan expressed satisfaction that the Soviet Union was collapsing, but he was still unwilling to accept the credit.

Although the museum is meant to showcase the two pillars of Reagan's legacy—his role in revitalizing the economy and ending the Cold War—it also addresses Iran-Contra. The museum contains a large room detailing the global challenges that the Reagan administration faced when taking office. As visitors move through the foreign policy exhibit, they make their way toward a statue of Reagan and Gorbachev. If the statue was not enough to draw the visitors' attention, a film about the evolution of Reagan and Gorbachev's relationship plays directly behind the two world leaders. By choosing a statue of Reagan and Gorbachev involved in pleasant conversation, the museum emphasizes Reagan's role as pragmatic diplomat willing to work with his adversaries to reduce the threat of nuclear weapons. Before visitors arrive at the statue, however, there is an exhibit to its right titled "Iran-Contra." The exhibit is not hidden, but it is in a place where visitors' eyes might jump to the film or to the statue of Reagan and Gorbachev sitting and speaking. The purpose of this placement suggests that the museum seeks to emphasize Reagan's role in working with Gorbachev to help bring an end to the Cold War rather than draw attention to scandals that would detract from Reagan's legacy.

Furthermore, the Iran-Contra exhibit downplays the role of the president in the scandal. The description of the Iran-Contra affair begins with a quotation from Reagan taking "full responsibility" for his "own actions" and for the actions of those in his administration. The exhibit description explains that because "Ronald Reagan was determined to free hostages held and tortured by terrorists in the Middle East," the president "reluctantly approved a plan that allowed the sale of U.S. arms from Israel to a moderate faction in Iran in exchange for help in releasing the hostages." The description then addresses the transfer of funds to the Contras, emphasizing that "without the President's knowledge a small group of his subordinates siphoned funds from the sale to support anti-Communist Contra fighters in Nicaragua." It concludes that "a scandal erupted when news of the 'Iran-Contra' connection surfaced, badly damaging the president's credibility at the time."[67] The centerpiece of the exhibit is a video of President Reagan addressing the American people from the Oval Office. Although the exhibit presents the affair as regrettable, it shifts the blame for the ordeal onto John Poindexter and Oliver North. By placing Reagan's apology to the American people at the center of the exhibit, Reagan comes across as a leader willing to accept responsibility for the actions of his subordinates while promising transparency and accountability by appointing the Tower Commission to investigate the scandal.[68]

Like Reagan's autobiography, the museum presents Reagan as having a coherent strategy to win the Cold War from the outset of his presidency. One exhibit, titled "The Reagan Strategy," asserts that "Ronald Reagan came to the leadership of the free world with a new strategy for securing peace and transcending communism." According to the exhibit, Reagan's strategic vision included "rebuilding America's military might," "fearlessly pointing out the evils of communism, promoting democracy, and reaffirming America's moral leadership on the international stage," "ending the policy of containment and supporting freedom fighters to roll back communism around the world," "protecting the American people through the Strategic Defense Initiative (SDI)," and "the reduction and eventual elimination of the threat of nuclear weapons through face-to-face diplomacy and improved communication."[69] Far from being a coherent and prescient strategy to end the Cold War, Reagan's foreign policy—like that of all presidents—was largely determined by external factors, the give and take of policy making, and the pragmatic application of principles to changing circumstances.

Unlike later conservatives who would credit Reagan's dogmatic commitment to principle for ending the Cold War, the museum emphasizes the president's willingness to engage with his adversaries. The emphasis on diplomacy is present in the "Four Summits" exhibit, which details Reagan's and Gorbachev's role in bringing an end to the Cold War. In this exhibit, Reagan offers his interpretation of the arms reduction negotiations and their larger meaning for the world. The exhibit emphasizes that Reagan had always believed that meeting a Soviet leader face to face would enable him to make progress toward peace. It also emphasizes that the buildup of America's armed forces was designed "to bring the Soviet Union to the negotiating table."[70] Summarizing Reagan and Gorbachev's nuclear negotiations, the "Four Summits" exhibit concludes that "between November 1985 and May 1988, they . . . negotiated dramatic reductions in nuclear arms, and began to bring the Cold War to an end."[71]

The museum emphasizes the importance of Reagan and Gorbachev's willingness to sit down and discuss their differences. At Geneva, the two developed a relationship with one another, and at Reykjavik their emerging friendship was tested. The "Reykjavik Summit" exhibit explains that the meeting was historic because both leaders were considering "the possibility of eliminating nuclear weapons." No deal was reached, however, because "Gorbachev conditioned any agreement on ending SDI." According to the exhibit, Reagan asked Gorbachev "to reconsider and offered to share the technology" with the Soviet Union. When Gorbachev refused, "the president left the summit furious."[72] The museum explains that "the unknowable effect of SDI ultimately helped convince Gorbachev to end the arms race and agree to reductions in nuclear weapons."[73]

Although Reagan left Reykjavik, he did not cut off communication or negotiations with the Soviet Union. Indeed, it was his and Gorbachev's continued efforts that resulted in the elimination of intermediate- and short-range missiles. The museum's "Washington Summit" exhibit argues that "as Ronald Reagan predicted, the Soviets had concluded that they could not compete in the arms race."[74] In short, according to the museum, Reagan's comprehensive plan to build up the military and create a missile defense system was successful, just as he had planned, in bringing the Soviets to the negotiation table. The museum also praises the Moscow Summit, where he and Gorbachev agreed to a joint statement in which they "said in part that both nations were determined to prevent any war between them and disavowed 'any intention to achieve military superiority.'" That exhibit then asserts that "the next year, the Berlin Wall came down" and "the Soviet Union fell apart by the end of 1991."[75] By linking Reagan's negotiations with Gorbachev to the collapse of the Soviet Union, the museum directly connects Reagan to the end of the Cold War.

The museum presents Reagan's policies as incentives designed to force the Soviet Union to negotiate, but in reality his behavior did not always elicit a conciliatory response from the Kremlin. Throughout his administration, but especially during his first term, Reagan often used inflammatory rhetoric when discussing the "evil empire." Far from inducing the Soviets to come to the negotiating table, such rhetoric at times actually hindered his professed goal of eliminating nuclear weapons and fed Soviet fears that made the prospect of nuclear conflict more likely.[76] Indeed, Reagan's denunciation of the Soviet Union undercut Gorbachev with hard-liners within the Politburo and convinced them that the general secretary's efforts to negotiate with Reagan were senseless.[77]

Likewise, Reagan's uncompromising commitment to SDI, a program that his generals conceded was decades away from actualization, threatened his goal of nuclear disarmament. At Reykjavik, Gorbachev insisted—as part of the agreement to reduce nuclear weapons—that the United States limit SDI research to the laboratory and abide by the Anti-Ballistic Missile (ABM) Treaty for an additional ten years. Reagan and his delegation were willing to accept the ten years of ABM compliance, but the president refused to limit SDI to the laboratory.[78] Reagan walked out of the conference. His unwillingness to compromise on SDI, especially in light of the fact that the Pentagon believed that implementing the system would take decades, unnecessarily put his stated goal of nuclear reduction at risk. Also absent from the museum is any discussion of the opportunities to further nuclear reductions after the INF Treaty—opportunities that Reagan showed little to no interest in pursuing.[79] In the museum, Reagan attempts to bring his anticommunism and his belief in nuclear reductions into line with one another. He presents the two ideas as working in tandem instead of acknowledging the reality that the two were often at odds with one another.

Reagan used his 1992 speech at the Republican National Convention to praise President Bush and remind Americans that Republicans were the ones who had believed victory was possible in the Cold War. Reagan happily declared that "after generations of struggle, America is the moral force that defeated communism and all those who would put the human soul itself into bondage." Reagan reminded the audience that it was Republicans that "stood tall and proclaimed that communism was destined for the ash heap of history" while liberals ridiculed them. He continued that Republicans knew that "the sky would not fall if America restored her strength" or "if an American President spoke the truth." Reagan added, "The only thing that would fall was the Berlin Wall." Reagan ridiculed the Democrats for saying that "we won the Cold War." The president concluded by "wondering, just who exactly do they mean by 'we'?"[80] Reagan's message at the convention was more explicit in crediting the United States, the Republican Party, and by extension himself for winning the Cold War. Perhaps it was the nature of the speech, partisan and overtly political, that forced Reagan to shed his nuanced view that Gorbachev and the people of Eastern Europe and the Soviet Union deserved much of the credit for bringing the Cold War to an end. Or perhaps Reagan decided that if someone in the United States had to take credit for winning the Cold War, it might as well be the Republican Party.

In one of Reagan's final public appearances, the celebration of his eighty-third birthday in 1994, he once again refused to explicitly take credit for ending the Cold War. It was clear, however, that Reagan felt vindicated by the dissolution of the Soviet Union. He asserted that "there was nothing foolish in my prediction that communism was destined for the ash-heap of history." But when it came to distributing credit, Reagan proclaimed that "after decades of struggle, and with the help of the bold leadership of Margaret Thatcher, democracy won the Cold War and the Berlin Wall came tumbling down." Although Reagan did not take credit for winning the Cold War, he did proclaim that "we put our house in order and took our rightful place as the most dynamic country in the world."[81]

President Reagan never claimed he won the Cold War. Indeed, Reagan consistently gave credit to others, especially the people in Eastern Europe and in the Soviet Union, for demanding an end to the status quo of the Cold War. Over the course of the 1990s, however, many conservatives began to claim that Reagan single-handedly confronted the "evil empire," demanded that the Berlin Wall be torn down, stuck to his principles, and won the Cold War.

When Ronald Reagan framed his legacy, he emphasized his economic and foreign policy achievements while ignoring social issues almost entirely. In fact, the absence of any significant discussions of abortion, school prayer, or homosexuality in any of his major speeches, in his autobiography, or in his museum speaks volumes. The few times he addressed his vision for American society during his postpresidency, he promoted an inclusive, tolerant, and welcoming country, a shining city on a hill to all those who would come and be a part of the American experience. It is clear Reagan did not want his legacy to be defined by the debate over school prayer, abortion, or the proper response to the AIDS epidemic. For Reagan, those issues were not at the heart of the Reagan Revolution in same way as revitalizing the economy and restoring America's military.

During his farewell address, Reagan did not discuss contentious social issues, but he did lay out a vision for the country that was tolerant and inclusive. Near the end of his address, Reagan shared his vision of the shining city on a hill that he had invoked throughout his political career. In his mind, Reagan asserted, "it was a tall, proud city built on rocks stronger than oceans, windswept, God-blessed, and teeming with people of all kinds living in harmony and peace; a city with free ports that hummed with commerce and creativity." Reagan insisted that "if there had to be city walls, the walls had doors and the doors were open to anyone with the will and the heart to get here." He concluded, "That's how I saw it, and see it still."[82] Reagan's vision of the city on a hill welcomed immigrants, encouraged toleration, believed in free markets, and supported free trade.

After Reagan left office, he did not advocate socially conservative values; instead he became a spokesman for children with AIDS. While he was still in the White House, Reagan met Elizabeth Glaser, who had contracted HIV during a blood transfusion. Glaser lost her daughter at the age of six, and her five-year-old son also tested positive for the disease. Like many other activists,

Glaser wished the Reagan administration had acted sooner to confront AIDS. Glaser acknowledged that "there are people who feel very angry at him," but insisted that she and her husband were thankful that Reagan agreed to speak on behalf of the Pediatric AIDS Foundation, which they had founded. Glaser explained that "as the Great Communicator, he has an open line to a large section of the country that possibly no one else can reach." After Reagan left office, he took Christmas presents to children with AIDS at UCLA's Medical Center and he also cut a commercial for Glaser's foundation. In the commercial, Reagan asserted that "we all grow and learn in our lives, and I've learned that all kinds of people can get AIDS, even children." He emphasized that "it's the disease that's frightening, not the people who have it," and "you know, you can't catch AIDS from hugging someone." Reagan told the audience he was not asking for their money. Instead, Reagan asked them "for something even more important," their "understanding." He concluded that "maybe it's time we all learn something new."[83] Reagan's work for the Pediatric AIDS Foundation enabled him to address the AIDS crisis without forcing him to acknowledge the issue of homosexuality.

In addition to being a spokesman for children with AIDS, Reagan also advocated for tougher gun laws. In March 1991, Reagan spoke near the hospital where he almost died ten years earlier. He was there to announce his support for the Brady Bill, a piece of legislation that required a seven-day waiting period for those purchasing handguns. Reagan called the waiting period "plain common sense." Reagan, a lifetime member of the National Rifle Association, urged Congress to adopt the Brady Bill because "with the right to bear arms comes a great responsibility to use caution and common sense." Advocates of the bill asserted that Reagan's endorsement might just push it across the finish line. Representative Charles (Chuck) Schumer, the Democrat from New York and chairman of the Criminal Justice Subcommittee of the House Judiciary Committee, asserted that Reagan's endorsement "could make the difference." Sarah Brady, the wife of Reagan's press secretary James Brady, called Reagan's endorsement "tremendous." The NRA released a statement that rejected the Brady Bill as unconstitutional but acknowledged that Reagan "has an understandable loyalty to James Brady."[84]

Some critics pointed out that the Reagan administration had opposed the legislation in 1988 and asked why Reagan was supporting it in 1991. Reagan responded that he had not changed his views since 1988, explaining that he "was opposed to a lot of ridiculous things that were proposed . . . with regard to gun control." When Ed Meese III, Reagan's attorney general, was asked about the apparent inconsistency, he reminded them that Reagan was "a strong supporter" of California's fifteen-day waiting period.[85] Reagan did not stop his outspoken support for the Brady Bill after his announcement in Washington. Returning to Sacramento, his first appearance at the state capital since being governor, Reagan spoke forcefully in support of the Brady Bill. By doing so, Reagan offered Republican congressmen cover from the GOP and the NRA to vote for the bill.[86] It took two more years, but in 1994 it became law.

In November 1990, while speaking in Fulton, Missouri, Reagan once again declared that diversity, pluralism, and inclusiveness were the qualities that defined America. While dedicating the sculpture made from sections of the Berlin Wall, Reagan declared that "in dedicating this magnificent sculpture, may we dedicate ourselves to hastening the day when all God's children live in a world without walls." Reagan added, "That would be the greatest empire of all." Reagan went on to speak about the Cold War and the fall of the Berlin Wall, but he finished by praising American pluralism. Reagan told the audience that "the truth of the matter is, if we take this crowd and if we could go through and ask the heritage, the background of every family represented here, we would probably come up with the names of every country on earth, every corner of the world, and every race." Reagan asserted that the United States was "the one spot on earth where we have the brotherhood of man." He concluded that if "we continue with this proudly, this brotherhood of man [will be] made up from people representative of every corner of the earth, maybe one day boundaries all over the earth will disappear as people cross boundaries and find out that, yes, there is a brotherhood of man in every corner."[87] Reagan's "Brotherhood of Man" speech was another example of the former president emphasizing the need for Americans to recognize that diversity and individuality were what made America exceptional.

When Reagan released his autobiography, social issues were barely even mentioned in its pages. *An American Life* did not recount the struggles over abortion, school prayer, or other culture battles, and the president never mentioned Richard Viguerie, Howard Phillips, Paul Weyrich, Jesse Helms, Phyllis Schlafly, or Jerry Falwell.[88] Furthermore, according to the index, the words "school prayer," "abortion," and "AIDS" were not present in the book. Reagan emphasized that his first priority was his economic agenda and that his other goal was to reduce "the threat of nuclear war."[89] His autobiography offered extensive commentary on Reagan's views of economic and foreign policy, and it recounted the legislative battles that he fought to achieve his policy agenda. On social issues, however, such commentary is lacking. It is hard to imagine that Reagan unconsciously excluded social issues from his autobiography. The absence of these issues demonstrates that fiscal and foreign policy were the most important issues to Reagan and that they were the accomplishments he wanted to build his legacy around. Furthermore, by excluding any discussion of contentious social issues, Reagan framed himself as a president who brought the country together to revitalize the economy and restore the American military. Reagan thus established his achievements as American achievements and recast himself as a leader that all Americans, Democrats included, could celebrate.

Like her husband, Nancy Reagan did not discuss social issues at length in her memoir. When Mrs. Reagan described her husband's "top priorities," she explained that "economic recovery," "greater economic freedom," "a strong defense," and "less government" were the most important and that "other things had to wait."[90] Although the First Lady's memoir did not address social issues in a meaningful way, she adamantly denounced those who labeled Reagan a bigot. Nancy recounted how Reagan's father deplored discrimination and had passed those beliefs on to his sons. She exclaimed that it was "ridiculous" that just because "Ronnie" was "a conservative Republican," he was "probably a bigot." Indeed, Mrs. Reagan asserted that Reagan "just doesn't believe that social problems should—or can—be solved by government."[91] Mrs. Reagan's explanation of how Reagan viewed social issues perhaps explains why his administration did not fight for school prayer or antiabortion measures with the ferocity that it fought for its fiscal and foreign policy agenda. Combined, the memoirs of Ronald and Nancy Reagan reveal that the Reagans did not prioritize social issues and did not believe that the contentious culture wars should be a part of Reagan's legacy.

The Reagan Library and Museum is also devoid of any mention of social issues. As visitors move through the museum, what is striking is the lack of exhibits on the New Right, Jerry Falwell, abortion, or school prayer. An exhibit titled "The Campaign Trail" explains that the themes of Reagan's campaign were "the economy, national defense, and hope for a brighter future."[92] Likewise, an exhibit that discusses his "vision for America" declares that "from the first day of his presidency, he began to implement his core philosophy of smaller government, lower taxes, and a strong national defense."[93] The museum presents Reagan's legacy as one of economic recovery, restoring the American military, and negotiating nuclear arms reductions. In short, the museum emphasizes that Reagan succeeded in "Making America Great Again" just as he had promised to do in 1980 when he inherited, in his view, a fledgling economy, a military in decline, and an America inflicted by malaise. The lack of any exhibits explaining the president's relationship with the New Right, or his positions on social issues, indicates that Reagan did not want to be remembered as an overtly partisan president. Indeed, the exhibit on the 1980 debate recalls that "Ronald Reagan gave a confident, relaxed performance that thwarted President Carter's attempts to portray him as a right-wing extremist."[94] Reagan is portrayed throughout as a statesman, not as an ideologue, who did what was necessary to revitalize and reinvigorate the country he loved.

The Republican National Convention in 1992 offered America two contrasting visions for the future of the nation and the trajectory of the Republican Party. As it happened, Reagan spoke after Patrick Buchanan, who told the audience that "every American President" was remembered with a single sentence. Buchanan declared that "George Washington was the father of his country," "Abraham Lincoln freed the slaves and saved the Union," "and Ronald Reagan won the Cold War." After praising Reagan and his policies, Buchanan pivoted and delivered a diatribe on the status of America's culture wars. Buchanan painted a dark picture of America at a crossroads. Americans could elect either Bush, a "defender of right-to-life, and a champion of the Judeo-Christian values and beliefs upon which America was founded," or the Democratic nominee Governor Bill Clinton who believed in "unrestricted abortion on demand" and endorsed militant homosexuality, and whose wife believed in "radical feminism." The election, Buchanan explained, was about the identity of America. According to Buchanan, the United States was at war with itself. There was "a religious war going on . . . it is a cultural war" and he declared that it was "as critical to the kind of nation we shall be as the Cold War itself."[95]

For his part, Reagan emphasized the pluralistic and accepting nature of American society. Striking a very different tone from that of Buchanan, Reagan reminded the audience that "whether we come from poverty or wealth; whether we are Afro-American or Irish-American; Christian or Jewish, from big cities or small towns, we are all equals in the eyes of God." According to Reagan, however, that was "not enough." He insisted that as Americans, "we must be equal in the eyes of each other." Reagan explained that "in America, our origins matter less than our destinations." While Reagan praised the work that had been done, he asserted that "with each sunrise we are reminded that millions of our citizens have yet to share in the abundance of American prosperity." He emphasized to the audience that "many languish in neighborhoods riddled with drugs and bereft of hope" and "still others hesitate to venture out on the streets for fear of criminal violence." Reagan called for the delegates to join him in pledging "ourselves to a new beginning for them." Concluding his thoughts, Reagan urged the convention to "apply our ingenuity and remarkable spirit to revolutionize education in America so that everyone among us will have the mental tools to build a better life."[96] Instead of building on Buchanan's theme of a nation at war with itself, Reagan insisted that only by working together for a brighter tomorrow could the convention capture the essence of what it meant to be American. Almost as if he sensed the profound difference that existed between himself and Buchanan, Reagan concluded that "whatever else history may say about me when I'm gone, I hope it will record that I appealed to your best hopes, not your worst fears, to your confidence rather than your doubts."[97]

The differences between the two speeches were not lost on political commentators. According to the *Washington Post*, Reagan's speech "was a model of sensitivity compared with the hate-filled harangue of Pat Buchanan that preceded it." It called Buchanan's speech a "spectacle" where his supporters constantly interrupted him and "took up fist-waving refrains at every opportunity." According to the *Washington Post*, the networks cut "to shots of a satisfied-looking Jerry Falwell . . . and conservative activist Phyllis Schlafly with that eerie frozen smile." The activists who seemed most satisfied with Buchanan, the article concluded, were "the people Nancy worked hard to keep at arm's length from Ronnie."[98] The *Wall Street Journal* praised the former president for being "almost solely preoccupied with forward movement, driven by the country's intellectual, technical and economic skills . . . he is a relentless apostle of progress." Comparing Reagan's and Buchanan's addresses, the *Wall Street Journal* argued that it was "impossible to imagine Ronald Reagan talking in the way Pat Buchanan does about keeping foreign people and foreign products out of the U.S." Reagan, the article explained, would never "give the impression that his political actions drew their energy from reservoirs of bitterness and antipathy." The *Wall Street Journal* concluded that "during the years of the Reagan presidency his and the party's personality were defined in terms of tomorrow's potential, not today's problems."[99]

Ronald Reagan used his postpresidential speeches, his autobiography, and his museum to define his legacy as revitalizing the American economy, rebuilding the American military, reducing the threat of nuclear war, and restoring American morale. Reagan's view of his economic legacy remained relatively constant during the five years that he was in the public sphere during his postpresidency. In contrast, Reagan adjusted his foreign policy legacy as the Berlin Wall fell, as the Cold War came to an end, and in the wake of the dissolution of the Soviet Union. Looking back on 1981, Reagan presented his foreign policy as coherent, consistent, and prescient. In contrast to many conservatives and the Reagan-victory school of historians, Reagan gave Gorbachev, Kohl, Thatcher, and especially the people of Eastern Europe and the Soviet Union the credit for ending the Cold War. Perhaps he was being humble. Or perhaps he realized that he was just one part, albeit an important part, of a process that made the world a safer place.

Missing from Reagan's legacy was any mention of social issues. His desire to distance himself from the controversial positions that many of his supporters—and historians—believed were at the heart of the Reagan Revolution demands an explanation. Unfortunately, Reagan did not provide any commentary on why social issues are conspicuously absent from his autobiography and the museum tasked with carrying on his legacy. It could be that Reagan was upset that he had failed to deliver significant victories on social issues and therefore did not want to discuss them. More likely, Reagan realized that he did not have the political capital to address many contentious social issues. Stu Spencer, an adviser to Reagan, recalled that when Reagan met with Falwell during a trip to Liberty University, the pastor spoke for almost the entire meeting, insisting that Reagan prioritize social issues. Reagan sat silently and politely listened. When the meeting was over, Spencer asked Reagan if he was "giving any serious thought" to Falwell's suggestions. Reagan "deadpanned" and responded, "Do you think I'm crazy."[100] By omitting contentious issues such as abortion, school prayer, and the administration's response to the AIDS epidemic, Reagan attempted to frame his legacy in terms that all Americans could embrace. In short, Reagan wished to present himself as a nonpartisan visionary leader who rehabilitated the United States.

Regrettably, Ronald Reagan's time to present his legacy was cut short by Alzheimer's disease. Following the 1994 midterm election, which was partially a referendum on Reagan's economic policies, Reagan decided to write a letter to the American people informing them that he had Alzheimer's. Reagan wrote that he and Nancy hoped that by opening their hearts they "might promote greater awareness of this condition." He told the American people that he felt fine and intended to "continue to share life's journey with my beloved Nancy and my family." He explained that as the disease progressed, it was the family that had to bear the "heavy burden." Reagan lamented that he could not "spare Nancy from this painful experience." He thanked the American people for allowing him to serve as their president and asserted that "when the Lord calls me home, whenever that day may be, I will leave with the greatest love for this country and eternal optimism for its future." Reagan concluded, "I now begin the journey that will lead me into the sunset of my life," but "I know that for America there will always be a bright dawn ahead."[101] Following his announcement, Reagan receded from the public eye. His legacy, which he had done so much to shape, was now in the hands of others.

10. Remembering Reagan: The Reagan Legacy in Conservative Politics, 1994–1996

The crowd applauded as Jack Kemp took the podium. The former secretary of housing and urban development traveled to the Reagan Library just before the 1994 midterm elections to announce that the "Reagan Revolution" was "still on."[1] Kemp noted that "debates over the Reagan legacy run on the front pages" of the newspapers and that Reagan remained "current," "controversial," and "relevant." The former congressman explained that the debate over Reagan was "not just an argument about the past" but a predictor of "our entire view of political and economic challenges" facing the nation. Kemp exclaimed that "if Reagan was right, liberals will always be wrong" and added that "the argument over his legacy is never ancient history; it is always current." In declaring his support for the Contract with America, Kemp explained he agreed with the Democrats' assessment that it was "everything Republicans ran on during Reagan's heyday."[2] He concluded with a call to action: "The Reagan Revolution is not a relic to be presented and admired. It's a banner to be taken into battle in 1994 and 1996 and on into the next century."[3]

Although there were significant differences between the Contract with America and Reagan's own policies during the 1980s, Kemp used Reagan's legacy as a call to arms for conservatives. Following what many conservatives viewed as the failures of the Bush administration, and after two years of a democratic president, conservatives looked back on the Reagan years with some nostalgia. Reagan became the champion that conservatives and Republicans lacked. After all, what other Republican president could they embrace as the manifestation of their values and views? Nixon had been disgraced by Watergate, and indeed many conservatives had soured on his administration during its second term. Likewise, Ford accomplished little in conservatives' view and had never been one of them. Accordingly, Reagan and the 1980s served as a foundation for the conservative movement, a moment in history when they could look back and be proud of what they had accomplished. Admittedly, what the various factions of the conservative movement and the GOP envisioned as Reagan's accomplishments varied, but nonetheless the fortieth president provided them with a common language, an array of acceptable policy prescriptions, and a usable past that conservatives could point at to validate their policies and positions in the present.

Conservative understanding of the Reagan legacy was at the center of the political discourse of the 1990s and early 2000s. In many ways, the elections of 1994, 1996, and 2000 were contests over whether Reagan's vision for the country should determine its course in the twenty-first century. In the process of those political conflicts, however, Reagan's legacy was altered and his vision for the country became malleable. In arguing with their liberal counterparts—who frequently discounted Reagan's legitimate contributions—conservatives created a mythology around the fortieth president.[4] During the 1990s, conservatives framed Reagan's legacy in terms of what he did and did not achieve. At the time of his death in the summer of 2004, however, conservatives forgot that the Reagan Revolution had been left unfinished and instead focused on Reagan's "larger-than-life" accomplishments. Furthermore, conservatives began to cite Reagan's dogmatic commitment to principles as the reason for his success. When Reagan passed away, conservatives framed his legacy in ideological terms and proclaimed his achievements as providential.

Conservatives were generally successful during the 1990s and early 2000s in persuading voters that conservatives' conception of Reagan Republicanism would improve the United States.[5] And indeed the Democrats had moved significantly to the right during the 1990s—perhaps one of the greatest achievements of Reagan and the conservative movement. Of the three elections that altered the course of American politics—the midterm elections of 1994, the 1996 presidential election, and the 2000 presidential election—conservatives won two. Even in defeat, a conservatism wedded to the values and beliefs of Ronald Reagan, if somewhat amorphous, offered Americans a respectable and dignified worldview. The darkest elements of conservative populism—xenophobia, anti-immigration, intolerance, protectionism, and an uncompromising commitment to principles—were kept at bay.[6] Indeed, conservative politicians such as Robert Dole and George W. Bush attempted to capture the positive and optimistic nature of Reagan, while Newt Gingrich embraced Reagan's rhetoric and legacy in discussing the critical issues of the 1990s.

Likewise, conservative scholars and activists began to craft Reagan's legacy with ink and marble. Following Dole's defeat in 1996, Dinesh D'Souza published his tribute to Reagan, and combined with Michael Reagan's and Peter Hannaford's works it established a conservative counternarrative to interpretations of the Reagan presidency offered by professional historians—which were overwhelmingly critical. Likewise, Grover Norquist founded the Ronald Reagan Legacy Project in 1997 and set about memorializing Reagan across the United States. One of his greatest successes was the renaming of Washington National Airport to Ronald Reagan Washington National Airport in 1998. This process of memorializing Reagan in books and on street signs went a long way toward keeping Reagan in the national conversation and crafting an overwhelmingly positive legacy for the Gipper.

Although Reagan had begun in 1994 "the journey that [would] lead [him] into the sunset of [his] life," the debate over the nature of his legacy continued to shape the politics of the 1990s and 2000s.[7] Consequentially, the Reagan legacy—like a memory that is slightly altered each time it is recalled—was fundamentally changed by ensuing political debates. The evolution of Reagan's legacy culminated in his death in June 2004. At his funeral, for better or worse, Reagan entered the pantheon of American political mythology.

As Reagan began his decade-long struggle with Alzheimer's, he became the focus of the 1994 midterm elections. Specifically, "Reaganomics" came under fire from Democrats eager to tie Newt Gingrich's Contract with America to what they viewed as the failed trickle-down economics of the 1980s.[8] Reagan's economic legacy became a subject of rigorous debate among conservatives and liberals alike. The result of that debate, however, was just as important to the future direction of the country as it was to framing the president's legacy.

Newt Gingrich, the House minority whip, designed the Contract with America to provide House members a comprehensive agenda that would make the 1994 midterms national in scope. In writing the Contract, Gingrich hoped to reach out to voters who had supported Ross Perot in the 1992 presidential election. Accordingly, he attempted to deemphasize party distinctions and instead focused on policy prescriptions that were seemingly nonideological.[9] House Republicans offered Americans "a detailed agenda for national renewal, a written commitment with no fine print." They framed the 1994 election as an opportunity, "after four decades of one-party control," to elect a Republican majority. The Contract asserted that "government is too big, too intrusive, and too easy with the public's money" and offered a "Congress that respects the values and shares the faith of the American family." Invoking President Abraham Lincoln, the Contract swore to "restore accountability," to end the "cycle of scandal and disgrace," and to make Americans "proud again of the way free people govern themselves." If elected, House Republicans promised to introduce ten bills that would restore the country within the first one hundred days of the Congress. At the center of that legislation was the balanced budget amendment, anticrime legislation, welfare reform, and term limits. It also included a series of small-business tax incentives, capital gains tax reductions, legal reforms, and an end to the tax hikes on Social Security recipients.[10] Interestingly, in these years before the Reagan legacy had been created, Gingrich chose to invoke another Republican—Abraham Lincoln.

Although the Contract demonstrated a belief in smaller government, it made no reference to President Reagan. Indeed, its emphasis on a balanced budget was a departure from the supply-side policies of the 1980s that put economic growth before deficit reduction. In time, however, conservatives would decide that the core of what the Contract wanted to achieve was in line with the vision, if not the policies, of Reagan. Despite Gingrich's attempts to make the Contract appeal to Americans from across the political spectrum, the press began to interpret it as a restoration of Reagan-era policies. In September, the *Washington Post* ran a headline on its front page that read "GOP Offers a 'Contract' to Revive Reagan Years." The article explained that House Republicans aimed to "resurrect the Reagan agenda that drove the party's success in the 1980s—promises of balanced budgets, tax cuts and defense buildups."[11] Indeed, linking the Contract to Reagan came naturally because the president had spent much of his postpresidency advocating a balanced budget amendment. Furthermore, many of the provisions in the Contract were policies that conservatives had wanted to implement during the Reagan administration.[12] Despite the similarities between the Contract and Reagan's vision, Gingrich had no intention to make the election a referendum on Reagan's record. Democrats, however, welcomed the opportunity to rehash the battles of the 1980s.

Almost as soon as the Contract with America was released, Democrats began devising ways to present the document as a return to Reaganomics. In early October, the Democratic National Committee announced a plan to spend $2 million on ads to paint the Contract with America as more of what President Clinton described as the "failed policies of the past." The ads tried to link the Contract to the most negative aspects of the Reagan administration. They used language and terms such as "trickle-down economics" and "explode the deficit" to persuade Americans that the Contract would disproportionately help the rich and would be fiscally reckless. One ad featured a senior citizen explaining that "the Republican Contract is designed to return to the Reagan years. . . . But why would we go back to that?"[13]

Democratic surrogates across the country attempted to turn the midterm elections into a referendum on President Reagan's economic record. President Clinton, campaigning at a sparsely attended rally in Detroit, declared that "no one would want us to go back to the days when the deficit was exploding and our economy was going downhill." Leon Panetta, Clinton's chief of staff, emphasized the rising income gap under Reagan, and Laura Tyson, the chairwoman for Clinton's Council of Economic Advisers, labeled the Contract "Voodoo Two."[14] Stanley Greenberg, the White House pollster, explained that the Democrats' strategy was to turn out their base by linking the Contract to Reagan.[15]

Shifting the election from a referendum on Clinton's first two years in office to a referendum on President Reagan's policies, however, was a risky strategy for Democrats. As the *Christian Science Monitor* explained, "Reagan remains the most highly regarded president in a generation, according to the polls."[16] The Republican National Committee responded to the Democrats' strategy, pointing out that "the DNC's pre-election day advertising blitz makes no mention of President Clinton, his policies or the record of the failed Clinton Congress—But can you blame them?"[17] The *New York Times*, agreeing with the RNC and the *Christian Science Monitor*, concluded that Democrats' insistence on making the election a referendum on Reagan was dangerous as he was a "far more popular figure than Mr. Clinton."[18] Celinda Lake, a Democratic pollster, admitted that the strategy was risky because "Reagan is very popular; he's the most popular living American among young voters," but explained that the plan was to "refer to the stale policies of the '80s" instead of attacking Reagan himself.[19] The distinction between Reagan and his policies, however, would be lost on the electorate, and the 1994 midterms partially became a referendum on Reagan's legacy.

The Democrats' insistence on making the 1994 midterms about Reagan gave Gingrich pause, and Republican surrogates were initially tentative. Eventually, however, some conservatives realized that they could not ignore the Democrats' metaphorically placing Reagan on the ballot; they decided to go out there and "win one more for the Gipper." David McIntosh, a Republican running for Congress in Indiana, asserted in mid-October that his race was "going to be a referendum on Clintonism versus a more conservative agenda that Ronald Reagan and Dan Quayle articulate." William Kristol, Dan

Quayle's former chief of staff, gleefully declared that "the Republican Party is more Reaganite through its ranks today than when Ronald Reagan was president."[20] Kristol did not define exactly what he meant by "Reaganite." The Democrats' attacks on Reagan led the GOP to circle the wagons and defend the fortieth president, ironically beginning the reformulation of the Reagan legacy in American national politics.

Within a week of the Democrats' attacks, Republicans began to embrace the midterm elections as a referendum on Reagan. Bruce Bartlett, supply-side advocate and former domestic adviser to President Reagan, frustrated with the *Washington Post*'s "effort to discredit the House Republican 'Contract with America'" by connecting it with Reagan's economic record, penned an op-ed in early October. Bartlett defended Reagan's economic legacy, asserting that the tax cuts were not responsible for the deficits of the 1980s. Bartlett pointed out that government revenues as a percentage of GDP were 18.97 percent in the 1980s while they were 18.45 percent during the 1970s. Bartlett concluded that "the *Post*'s implication—that the national debt would be far lower had Mr. Reagan not proposed a tax cut in 1981—is clearly false."[21] By defending the Reagan record, Bartlett hoped to dispel the idea that the Contract's embrace of Reagan's policies was a bad idea. Instead, Bartlett blamed excess spending by Congress for the budget deficits, thus adding legitimacy to Gingrich's and Reagan's insistence on a balanced budget amendment and blaming the Democrat-controlled House for the deficits during the Reagan years.

By the middle of October, prominent Republicans joined Bartlett in labeling the Contract as a continuation of Reagan's economic policies. On October 18, Congressman John Kasich (R-OH) wrote an op-ed in the *Wall Street Journal* titled "Sign Here to Complete the Reagan Agenda." He insisted that Republicans should welcome Democrats' attempts to make the election "a referendum on the goals and policies of Ronald Reagan vs. Bill Clinton." According to Kasich, "Reagan's message was straight forward—government is the problem, not the solution"—and his solutions were "common-sense proposals" including "tax cuts, sound monetary policy, spending restraint, and deregulation." The congressman insisted that on three of the four, Reagan had succeeded. Kasich argued that the result of Reagan's policies was tremendous economic growth with the creation of nineteen million new jobs from 1982 to 1989, two-thirds of which were "high-paying and managerial jobs." Kasich acknowledged that spending was not cut by either party during the 1980s but claimed that "if Congress had held the growth of all nondefense spending to the rate of inflation during the 1980s, the deficit in 1989 would have been $23 billion—not $152 billion."[22] In short, Kasich argued that Reagan's economic policies had been incredibly successful and the president's inability to balance the budget was just as much Congress's fault as Reagan's. In doing so, Kasich took Clinton and the Democrats' most effective criticism of Reagan's economic record—the soaring deficit—and used it against congressional Democrats.

Shifting to the midterms, Kasich framed the Contract as fulfilling the goals of the Reagan Revolution. Kasich declared that "through Contract with America, House Republicans are offering to re-create the positive developments of the 1980s, while finishing the job on spending restraint that Congress failed to do back then." Kasich summarized the Contract as offering "10 proposals to limit and hold government accountable, to promote economic opportunity and individual responsibility for families and businesses, and to maintain security both at home and abroad." He concluded that "the American people clearly want a government that works better and costs less—to complete the job that President Reagan started."[23] Interestingly, during the 1994 midterms, conservatives acknowledged that the Reagan Revolution was unfinished and that Reagan had fallen short in limiting spending and decreasing the size and scope of government. Framing themselves as the descendants of Reagan, the Republican House promised to fulfill his legacy.

By the end of October, conservative commentators and politicians alike were defending the Reagan record and linking the Contract with America to the fortieth president's legacy. Lawrence Kudlow, the assistant director of economics and planning in the Office of Management and Budget during Reagan's first term, wrote an op-ed in *National Review* encouraging conservatives to connect the Contract with Reagan. Kudlow insisted that the GOP needed to "set the record straight" and defend "the longest peacetime expansion in history and the economic policies that propelled it." The key to electoral success in 1994, according to Kudlow, was distinguishing "between Reaganism, which liberated entrepreneurship by lowering tax, regulatory, and inflation burdens, and Bushism, which suppressed growth by raising taxes, re-regulating business, and extinguishing consumer, real-estate, and business credit."[24] For Kudlow and other conservatives, the Democrats' insistence on running against Reagan's record gave the GOP an opportunity to remind voters that they were the party of Reagan and not Bush—in short, to embrace a history of success rather than the unusable past offered by the Bush years.

Kudlow encouraged Republicans to embrace the comparisons of the Contract with the Reagan years, arguing that the Reagan economy was far superior to the economy that existed under Bush and Clinton. Kudlow asserted that three and a half years from the height of each recession, Reagan had created 10.4 million jobs compared to Clinton's 5.8 million. GDP growth was 4.9 percent under Reagan and only 2.9 percent with Clinton. Furthermore, real disposable income had increased by 3.8 percent in the first thirteen recovery quarters with Reagan compared to 2.4 percent with Bush and Clinton. Kudlow acknowledged that "the deficit and debt story will forever be the Achilles heel of Reaganomics." Kudlow exclaimed, however, that "given Reagan's success in restoring growth, slaying inflation, and ending the Cold War, the debt story amounts to nothing more than liberal ankle biting." He concluded that "if Democrats continue to attack the Gingrich Contract as 'Reaganomics,' the GOP should take it as high praise."[25] The article was accompanied with a brilliant sketch depicting Reagan as a muscular bodybuilder manhandling the scrawny and weak Clinton. The image was meant to portray the differences in Reagan's and Clinton's economic recoveries. One was strong and robust, while the other was weak, fragile, and effeminate.[26] According to Kudlow, with the powerful and vibrant Reagan record on their side, the GOP would be foolish not to embrace the fortieth president.

On election day Americans overwhelmingly voted in support of Gingrich's Contract with America. Republicans picked up fifty-four seats in the House and nine seats in the Senate. Conservatives were in a state of euphoria, and in January, when Gingrich took the gavel, the floor of Congress was electric. The Republicans' side of the House was full of laughs and handshakes. They were rowdy and pleased with themselves. In contrast, the Democrats sat gloomily as a somber Dick Gephardt gave the Speaker's gavel to Gingrich and sadly proclaimed, "So ends 40 years of Democratic control."[27] There was little time to enjoy the victory, however, as Gingrich and his conservative caucus began to draft the bills that they had promised to have to the House floor within the first one hundred days.[28]

Immediately following the election, conservatives and their critics began comparing Gingrich to Reagan. In a scathing attack on Republicans, the *New York Times* complained that "the beauty of Ronald Reagan, Newt Gingrich and so many other Republicans is that they make it all sound so simple."[29] The *Washington Post* warned liberals not to underestimate Gingrich as they had Reagan.[30] Replying to criticism that he was "a rabid right-winger," Gingrich responded by linking himself to the larger conservative movement: "Reagan went through it. Goldwater went through it." Jude Wanniski, the supply-side advocate, praised Gingrich for fighting alongside the president for income tax reductions during the 1980s and hoped he would continue the fight as Speaker.[31] Peggy Noonan, a speech-writer and special assistant to President Reagan, declared that "Gingrich dominates the day and captures the imagination as no leader has since Ronald Reagan."[32] Gingrich was the first conservative leader to endure the burden of Reagan's emerging legacy, and he ultimately proved to be much less affable than the fortieth president.[33]

The expectations for Gingrich's speakership were daunting, but the representative from Georgia accepted the mantle and publicly embraced the challenge of completing the Reagan Revolution. Gingrich charged Kasich with balancing the budget, which the representative from Ohio viewed as his personal responsibility. Kasich declared that he and his colleagues were given "precious opportunity . . . to rewrite and re-route government." The *Wall Street Journal* asserted that "Congress's post-Reagan revolutionaries vow to do what their idol never did—to go beyond trimming the branches of government and uproot federal programs whole."[34] When the new revolutionaries set out to complete the revolution, however, they had to confront the inconsistencies of balancing the budget while also cutting taxes and preserving Reagan's defense initiatives. In February 1995, the House, under Gingrich's leadership, voted to end the Strategic Defense Initiative. Twenty-four House Republicans "defied their leader" and refused to vote for the measure, asserting that SDI was "an emotional issue that is the legacy of Ronald Reagan."[35] To Gingrich's credit, he realized that to implement some of Reagan's unfinished goals he would need to undermine some aspects of Reagan's legacy.

By April, Gingrich and the House Republicans had finished their work on every provision of the Contract. They held a celebration on the west steps of the Capitol, where six months before House Republicans had signed the Contract. The "sun-splashed festivities" drew more than 160 members of Congress and their relatives. According to the *Washington Post*, the day was "filled with speeches that also sought to evoke memories of the glory days of the Reagan administration." The event was carefully choreographed to tie the accomplishments of the 104th Congress to President Reagan. Representative John David Hayworth (R-AZ) declared in the first of many references to Reagan that it was "once again morning in America." Majority Leader Richard K. Armey (R-TX) lauded the accomplishments of the Republican-led Congress and, using Reagan's language, promised Americans, "You ain't seen nothing yet."[36] Both Hayworth and Armey drew on the litany of one-liners provided by Reagan during his long career in the public eye. The development of a common conservative language wrapped up in Reagan's legacy was essential to holding conservatives together for the next two decades.

Although the House Republicans used Reagan's language to connect themselves to the 1980s, they did not acknowledge the difficult decisions that had to be made about what elements of the Reagan legacy they were going to keep and which aspects were downplayed or ignored in the Contract. The process of forgetting certain accomplishments of Reagan's—such as immigration reform and ensuring the solvency of Social Security—would play an important role in the form the Reagan legacy eventually took.

In preparing for his nationally televised speech upon the completion of the Contract, Gingrich enlisted the help of former Reagan deputy chief of staff Michael K. Deaver, who had been essential in creating Reagan's image.[37] Deaver helped Gingrich choose the proper backdrop, props, and camera angles to use during the speech. In his thirty-minute speech, Gingrich evoked Reagan, promised a balanced budget and a revamping of federal programs, and hinted that he was open to implementing a "flat" tax. The Speaker used charts and graphs, just as Reagan had, to make his case to the American people. Gingrich declared that approving the Contract was "the preliminary skirmish to the battle yet to come."[38] Gingrich explained that Congress had passed a balanced budget amendment and a line-item veto, the two reforms that Reagan had advocated in his postpresidency, but that the Senate had blocked both provisions. Gingrich channeled the optimism of Ronald Reagan, declaring that in the "spirit of committing ourselves idealistically, committing ourselves romantically, believing in America, that we celebrate having kept our word." Gingrich concluded that "together we and the American people can give our children and our country a new bit of freedom."[39]

Much of Gingrich's success resulted from his pragmatic application of Reagan's principles to the problems of the 1990s. Faced with growing budget deficits, the Speaker emphasized the need to cut spending, including programs such as SDI. Likewise, Gingrich understood that much of Reagan's success had come from working across the aisle and from his optimistic tone. Unlike future appropriators of the Reagan legacy, Gingrich emphasized the need to complete the Reagan Revolution rather than just carry it forward. Unfortunately for the bellicose Speaker, working with Democrats and continuing to use the common optimistic language provided by Reagan proved impossible and undermined some of his reforms.

After the midterm elections of 1994, President Clinton moved to the political center and appropriated many of conservatives' key issues. Clinton had already signed legislation that expanded trade, decreased crime, and reduced the deficit. In addition to these accomplishments, almost two-thirds of Gingrich's Contract became law before the 1996 presidential election.[40] Although the passage of much of the Contract was a victory for conservatives, it actually hurt Republicans in 1996. Many of the key issues that conservatives ran on in midterms were at least partially achieved, allowing Clinton to take the credit and therefore bolstering the president's record. Despite the negation of many of their key issues, Republicans hoped to nominate a candidate to embrace Reagan's legacy and convert it to electoral victory in 1996.

The question of who would carry the Reagan mantle dominated the conversation of who should run in the Republican primary. In the summer of 1995, there were rumors that Gingrich would run for president. Many political commentators proclaimed that the Speaker was the "dominant politician in America today" and was "to 1996 what Ronald Reagan was to 1980."[41] Others, such as the *Wall Street Journal*, disagreed, asserting that "rather than being a contemporary Reagan, Newt Gingrich is almost the exact opposite." Their major issue with the Speaker was his "exceedingly flexible principles."[42] Perhaps thinking he would be more effective as Speaker, Gingrich ultimately declined to run.

Jack Kemp, widely seen as Reagan's natural successor in 1988, was also speculated to be considering a run for president. Of all the other potential candidates, he had the most plausible claim to the supply-side legacy of Reagan. He decided early in the process, however, that his "passion for ideas" was "not matched with a passion for partisan or electoral politics" and declined to run. Indeed, Kemp's opposition to two tenets of the Contract, the balanced budget amendment and term limits, along with his opposition to California's anti-immigration Proposition 187, put him at odds with much of the GOP. Vin Weber, the former secretary of the House Republican Conference, explained that while Kemp was seen in 1988 "as the logical successor to Ronald Reagan," the party had become "more protectionist" and "austerity" had "replaced growth."[43]

The absence of Gingrich and Kemp opened the door for Senate majority leader Bob Dole to embrace the Reagan legacy. At a Republican National Committee meeting in Philadelphia, Dole told the party he was "willing to be another Ronald Reagan" to win the nomination and the White House.[44] Despite such proclamations, Dole's lifetime commitment to balanced budgets and his opposition to supply-side economics made convincing GOP primary voters he was Reagan's heir difficult. Taking Kemp's advice, Dole tried to ease the "mutually contemptuous relations with the supply-side camp" by discussing "radical tax simplification," including "flatter" tax rates. For all his efforts, however, many former Reagan stalwarts, including Dick Fox, who was Reagan's Pennsylvania state chairman in 1980, dismissed Dole as just "playing around with buzzwords."[45] Amid headlines like "Where Dole Is No Reagan," convincing voters he could lead Reagan's party would take more than a shift in the way Dole discussed fiscal policy.[46]

Patrick Buchanan also attempted to frame himself as the true Reagan Republican. Buchanan emphasized his commitment to Christian values, American exceptionalism, and his opposition to globalism. He decried Senator Phil Gramm as being unfit to carry the Reagan mantle because of his vote to confirm Justices Ruth B. Ginsburg and Stephen G. Breyer. But Gramm's worst sin, according to Buchanan, was his endorsement of "world government."[47] The *Wall Street Journal* denounced Buchanan's attempts to campaign as Reagan's heir. In an op-ed titled "We Knew Reagan and Pat Buchanan Is No Gipper," the *Wall Street Journal* argued that Buchanan "better resembles modern pillars of the European right" than Reagan. Although Buchanan, like Reagan, relied on nationalistic symbols, the article explained that Reagan's nationalism "was muscular but also optimistic." In contrast, "Buchanan's darker nationalism flows from a perception of national decline." The *Journal* reminded readers that Reagan had hailed "America's immigrant past and future," whereas "Buchanan wants a five-year halt in legal immigration." The article concluded that rather than being Reagan's heir, Buchanan was "the political heir to the myth of American decline popularized by liberal intellectuals."[48] Despite all his claims, Buchanan's embrace of the culture wars, protectionism, anti-immigration, and the dark picture that he painted of the United States was not at all in line with the policies of Ronald Reagan. Buchanan would ultimately fail to craft the emerging Reagan legacy to match his own political positions, and as a result would leave the GOP in 2000, taking a segment of paleoconservatives with him.[49]

The absence of an advocate for supply-side economics, with its emphasis on economic growth, led businessman Steve Forbes to enter the primary. The *Wall Street Journal* viewed Forbes as Kemp's "disciple," and it hoped that his presence would "force the campaign debate beyond Robert Dole's dour orthodoxy, Phil Gramm's barbed-wire conservatism, and Pat Buchanan's culture war cries, and toward his own sunny vision of uncharted economic prosperity." In many ways, Forbes was a less charismatic version of Reagan, and his optimistic message of unleashing American productivity did not resonate with voters. Instead, the budget hawks controlled the fiscal message, the cultural conservatives had become a larger and more influential portion of the electorate, and social upheavals cast a dark mood over the GOP primary. Despite key endorsements and a plethora of praise from the *Wall Street Journal*, Forbes's "Reagan-style mood music" did not result in electoral success.[50]

Just as Superman's 1993 death in DC comics left a void that countless "super men" unsuccessfully tried to fill, each Republican primary challenger channeled a specific element of the Reagan legacy, but none fully represented his vision. Dole presented himself as a fiscal conservative and budget hawk. Buchanan emphasized the cultural issues that Reagan paid lip service to during his tenure, and Forbes fully embraced Reagan's optimistic rhetoric and supply-side economic policies. By 1996, Reagan had, in many ways, become the Republican Superman. Unlike the comic book, however, the GOP could not resurrect Reagan to fill the void. Instead they were left with imperfect candidates, none of whom could don Superman's cape.[51]

By February, Dole had established himself as the frontrunner, and he used the primary debate to reassure voters that he was a Reagan conservative—a concept that was still developing and evolving. Dole reminded the audience that "he had carried the flag for Reagan and Bush and now was battling Clinton's vetoes of Republican welfare and budget bills." Dole depicted his election as the culmination of the Reagan Revolution, proclaiming that "we're just one election away from history, from getting all of these things done." Following the debate, the *Washington Post* concluded that while Dole did not stumble, he also did not "dominate the stage the way Reagan did in 1980." Luckily for Dole, none of his competitors shined. Forbes "showed less animation than any of his rivals, delivering his comments in deadpan fashion, with no rhetorical flourishes."[52] In the end, Dole's lack of luster did not hurt him, and he won by default.

With the nomination all but clinched, Dole turned his attention to the general election with hopes of reproducing the Reagan coalition. In March, Dole went on a four-day swing through the Midwest. He began making his "case against President Clinton," "explicitly urging Democrats who strayed to Ronald Reagan in the 1980s to vote again for a Republican."[53] Dole reassured voters that he was willing "to be Ronald Reagan" by emphasizing his intention to cut taxes and balance the budget. In an article titled "Bob Dole Alias Ronald Reagan," the *Baltimore Sun* reminded readers that Dole did not possess "Mr. Reagan's immense personal appeal" that enabled him to transcend "public concern over his fiscal promises." The newspaper also emphasized that Dole was "a long way from conveying" the "rosy, optimistic promise" that Reagan sold so convincingly. Instead, the *Sun* explained that Dole continued "to labor under his image as a harsh naysayer."[54]

Determined to tap into the tremendous popularity of President Reagan, Dole made "a political pilgrimage" to the Reagan Library to meet with the Reagans.[55] Elizabeth Dole brought Nancy a chocolate cake to celebrate her birthday, and the two men shook hands and posed for pictures.[56] Dole described the meeting with Reagan as "a shot in the arm" for the campaign. He added that the meeting reminded him "of the great things that President Reagan had done for America—tax cuts, a good economy, strong defense." The *Orlando Sentinel* noted, however, that Dole spoke of Reagan with "reverence," papering "over the pair's early clashes on tax cuts and Supply-side economics." As could be expected given the fact that he was battling Alzheimer's, Reagan sat comparatively subdued and did not say much during the meeting. But according to Ken Khachigian, Dole's top strategist, the former president "listened very intently and seemed to really enjoy the tales from the campaign, and he laughed at some of the stories they had to tell."[57] Dole hoped that the images of himself and President Reagan shaking hands would reinforce his rhetoric that he was the man to continue the Reagan Revolution.

As Dole pivoted to the general election, William F. Buckley urged him to select his long-time rival Jack Kemp as vice president. Writing in June, Buckley advised Dole to embrace Kemp's economic proposals and "make a second equally exciting move by announcing that he intended to name Jack Kemp as his vice-presidential candidate." Buckley concluded that "Ronald Reagan aside, it has been for many years Jack Kemp who has the ability to ignite enthusiasm in those whom he addresses."[58] The selection of Kemp might bring excitement, but it also meant addressing years of conflict between the two. Kemp's biographers label Dole as "Kemp's political nemesis, [and] a die-hard enemy of Supply-side economics." Kemp himself had denounced Dole as the ultimate "root canal" deficit-concerned Republican. In fact, the disagreements between the two men were not ancient history. During the 1996 primary, when Dole attacked the flat tax in Kemp's home state of New York, Kemp quipped, "I'm surprised he didn't call it voodoo economics." For his part, Dole decried Kemp for pushing "painless solutions . . . while some of us do all the dirty work."[59] Despite their long-standing and deep-rooted differences, Dole selected Kemp as his vice president and went further by fully embracing the supply-side vision for economic growth.

Speaking to the Chicago Chamber of Commerce, Dole delivered a public profession to supply-side economics. He promised to "finish the job Ronald Reagan started so brilliantly." Dole explained that his administration would "balance the budget, cut taxes and remove the dead weight of government to unleash the full potential of the American people once again."[60] Heading into his convention, Dole attempted to recreate himself in Reagan's image by selecting the most well known supply-sider in the country as his vice president, by using snippets of Reagan's rhetoric, and by promoting dramatic tax cuts to stimulate the economy. The 1996 election cemented tax cuts as an essential part of the emerging Reagan legacy. The fact that Reagan raised taxes in 1982, 1983, 1984, and 1986 in various forms had conveniently been forgotten.[61]

Dole's willingness to abandon his life-long opposition to supply-side economics for what seemed to be political expediency did not earn him universal praise. The press questioned why "a longtime skeptic of the so-called Supply-side economics championed by Ronald Reagan" had suddenly abandoned his long-standing convictions.[62] Further criticism came from some of Reagan's economic advisers. Murray L. Weidenbaum, Reagan's chief economic adviser from 1981 to 1983, asserted that he and Reagan had "learned the hard way" that Congress was more likely to cut taxes than reduce spending. He worried "that proposed tax cuts will not be offset by new expenditure cuts." Appearing at the National Association of Business Economists in Boston, Weidenbaum insisted that the economists present learn from the Reagan administration, not copy it verbatim. He testified that "on the basis of experience—I also bear the scars of the 1981–1982 cycle—those deficits can lead to a variety of negative effects" including "a diminution of investment capital available for private business expansion" and "scaring the Federal Reserve into tightening the flow of money and credit." Instead, Weidenbaum encouraged policy makers to focus on passing regulatory reform, shifting to a consumption tax, and cutting subsidies to businesses and the middle class.[63] Although many questioned the genuineness of Dole's shift, and some even the prudence of the move, Dole used his convention to present himself as a born-again believer in the supply-side creed.

Arriving in San Diego to a spectacle of fireworks, boats, and partisan politics, Dole constantly evoked Reagan.[64] In prime time, on the first night of the convention, Nancy Reagan delivered a tribute to her husband. Before she spoke, the convention played a video produced by the Republican National Committee, saluting the fortieth president. It began by celebrating Reagan's economic record. Kemp recounted how "Reagan had to confront the worst economic crisis of any president since Franklin Roosevelt" and Reagan's "combination of cutting taxes and regulations led to the fastest growth without inflation in the century."[65] There was no mention of Volcker's monetary contraction, Carter's important deregulations, or the global decline in oil prices, all of which contributed to the economic recovery of the 1980s.

As should be expected, nuance was also missing when the video shifted to Reagan's role in ending the Cold War. Former secretary of state Henry Kissinger told the audience that "Ronald Reagan ended the Cold War" and "stopped the Soviet advance by building up a military establishment and by developing the concept of strategic defense, which provided a huge incentive for the Soviets to come to the bargaining table." The video played Reagan emphatically calling on Gorbachev to "tear down this wall" and then flashed to Berliners taking sledge hammers to the Berlin Wall—implicitly linking the two events. While one can appreciate the political considerations behind connecting Reagan's speech and the actual events that led to the fall of the wall, doing so is complicated to say the least. Although the video implied that Reagan caused many of the key events, including the fall of the Berlin Wall, it did not claim that Reagan single-handedly won the Cold War. In fact, it even stressed the importance of Reagan's working with Gorbachev. Kissinger described Reagan's success as "the greatest diplomatic victory of the modern period."[66]

The RNC tribute established Reagan as a seminal figure in the American political tradition. Near the end of the video, Lee Iacocca, who had served as Chrysler Corporation CEO during the 1980s, declared, "Mr. President, you're like the guys you played in the movies. You're a hero." Kemp thanked "the Gipper" for all he "did for America and the whole wide world," and Kissinger assured Reagan, "Your country will never forget you." The video also celebrated Ronald and Nancy Reagan's marriage and enduring love for one another.[67] Although perhaps not intended, the images of the Reagans walking happily hand in hand were a stark contrast to the sexual scandals of the Clinton administration. The video ended with Reagan's voice humbly asserting, "I guess we did ok."[68] Combined, the statements of Kemp, Kissinger, and others—along with the masterfully placed images and voiceover by the president—in the video provided viewers with a clear understanding that Reagan, his optimism, and his policies had revitalized the economy, helped end the Cold War, and renewed the American spirit. There was little doubt for the thousands of conservatives gathered in San Diego that Reagan deserved to be discussed with Washington, Jefferson, Lincoln, and FDR as one of the greatest presidents in American history.

By the time the video ended and Mrs. Reagan took the stage, many in the convention hall were in tears. The former first lady added to the sadness present in the room, lamenting that "Ronnie said it could be his last speech at a Republican Convention" four years before and "sadly, his words were too prophetic."[69] Although Reagan was not physically present, one of the central focuses of the convention was imbuing Dole in the Reagan legacy and contrasting the seemingly happy and joyous 1980s with the Clinton administration. Interestingly, however, in 1996 Reagan was portrayed as a pragmatic conservative whose accomplishments came from working with his adversaries and putting his country first.

When Dole took center stage, one of his primary goals was to present his candidacy as a continuation of the Reagan Revolution. Indeed, Dole opened his speech on the final night of the convention by declaring "we're going to win one for the Gipper." He asserted that "one man, Ronald Reagan, really did start it all" and emphasized, "now it's up to us to finish the job and win the Reagan revolution once and for all." Dole touted his newfound belief in supply-side economics as the principal reason he would carry on Reagan's legacy. Dole proclaimed that together "we're going to cut taxes, tax rates across the board for every working person in the country."[70] The tribute to Reagan, Nancy Reagan's speech, and Dole's proclamations legitimized Dole's claims to Reagan's legacy. Lyn Nofziger, assistant to the president on political affairs under Reagan, asserted that the convention "reminded people that Reagan was not only the great communicator but the great unifier." Nofziger concluded that Dole "must indeed come as close as possible to being Ronald Reagan, if not in substance or on the issues, then at least in getting his message across to the electorate."[71] For better or worse, the convention had inextricably tied Dole's image to Reagan and especially his legacy of supply-side economics.[72]

Following his convention speech, conservatives praised Dole for invoking Reagan. Robert Bartley, the editor of the *Wall Street Journal*, wrote an article titled "Dole as Reagan's Heir," in which he asserted that it was no surprise that Reaganomics had been revived. Citing data from 1983 to 1990, Bartley praised Reagan's 3.6 percent growth rate and 20 percent increase in per capita income. Bartley embraced the developing mythology around Reagan, declaring that during the Reagan administration, "an inflationary crisis was subdued, the Cold War won and American morale restored." Bartley blamed Clinton's and Bush's tax increases for what he viewed as the anemic 2.5 percent growth rate and condemned the two presidents for creating a "repressed economy, with citizens worrying about progress for their children." He endorsed Dole's 15 percent reduction in income taxes and significant cuts in capital gains taxes as a means to achieve higher levels of economic growth. Bartley euphorically concluded that with Dole's shift, "the GOP has returned to the tradition of Ronald Reagan."[73] *National Review* praised Dole's tax plan to "satisfy all the factions of the GOP, and unite them around a common rallying point." Furthermore, according to the journal, the plan was "a victory for Reaganism," made "all the sweeter since Bob Dole has long been a skeptic." *National Review* predicted that Dole would "take a hammering for representing Reagan redux," but asserted it was "criticism he should welcome." The publication insisted that Dole needed to advance his tax plan "with conviction and passion" to fend off Democratic accusations that Dole would "abandon his principles to win an election."[74] These conservative voices were explicitly acknowledging that the Reagan legacy was the glue that could hold a fractured movement and party together. Unfortunately for conservatives, and the GOP, Americans were not ready to reembrace supply-side economics, and while the Reagan legacy proved to be unifying for Republicans, it did not deliver victory in November.

Indeed, by endorsing supply-side economics, Dole inadvertently conceded the budget issue to Clinton and caused many Americans to question his consistency. With Dole trailing in the polls, Americans for a Republican Majority—a political action committee directed by House majority whip Tom DeLay—released a 103-page analysis of the electorate. Conservative pollster Frank Luntz, who had worked with Gingrich to develop the Contract, found that instead of tax cuts the electorate wanted fiscal responsibility and balanced budgets. Ironically, the data that Luntz compiled showed that what voters wanted was "entirely consistent with Bob Dole's own career-long record as a deficit hawk." Instead of being himself, however, the *New York Times* explained that Dole built "his candidacy instead around exactly the kind of tax-cut promise that Mr. Luntz predicted would leave voters incredulous." The *Times* concluded that the lesson of Luntz's analysis was that "if Bob Dole had been true to his own economic convictions, he wouldn't now be trying to sell a 15 percent tax-cut plan few Americans are buying, and he wouldn't have enabled a Democratic president, however preposterously and disingenuously, to steal the balanced-budget banner from the Republicans."[75] Trying to justify why Dole was trailing Clinton by a "Secretariat-style margin," *National Review* explained that "the economy is in recovery" and Dole was handicapped by the Republican "Congress's unpopularity." The publication lamented that although Dole would make a good president, "campaigning puts a premium on verbal, intellectual, and imaginative skills—the 'vision thing'"—and Dole lacked Reagan's charisma.[76]

As the campaign came to a close, it was clear that Dole's embrace of supply-side economics had not led to recreating Reagan's electoral success. Though he had unimaginatively embraced some of Reagan's policies, he could not transform himself into the Gipper. An internal memorandum of the Dole campaign described why Dole was not gaining any momentum heading into November. It explained that the economy was too "good," Dole had not "defined" himself, his economic plan had gained "no traction," moral and character issues were not polling, the "gender gap still persists," the campaign had no "wedge issue," and on top of it all there was only a little more than fifty days to the election. With few remaining options, the campaign decided to attack President Clinton "on character and trust."[77] Unfortunately for Dole, his claims that the Clinton administration had "more investigations, prosecutions and convictions than any administration in two decades" were false. CNN quickly pointed out that the Reagan administration had more prosecutions and convictions than Clinton. Despite being forced to defend the Reagan-era scandals, the ethics strategy closed the gap significantly.[78] On election day, however, it was not enough to push Dole over the top. Clinton's landslide victory demonstrated that Dole's attempts to ride Reagan's popularity to victory were not successful.

Although Dole lost the election, 1996 was an important year for the development of the Reagan legacy. Common themes began to emerge as conservatives revisited the history of the Reagan years. According to conservatives,

Reagan had revitalized the economy by cutting taxes, had won the Cold War, and had boosted America's morale by renewing the country's belief in itself. Likewise, the common language, history, and policy prescriptions (while at times limiting) enabled paleoconservatives, neoconservatives, libertarian conservatives, traditional conservatives, and others to continue to work together.[79] The conservative movement, which had been held together by its anticommunism since its conception, had found a new unifier: the legacy of Ronald Reagan.

11. Memorializing Reagan: Enshrining the Reagan Legacy, 1996–2000

In the wake of Dole's dismal defeat, conservatives doubled their efforts to cement Reagan's legacy. Without a contemporary champion for conservatism, they looked to the past. Accordingly, Reagan could serve as a rallying point for conservatives following the 1996 election in a way that no other living figure could. Indeed, after the collapse of the Soviet Union, his legacy was the only glue strong enough to hold the disperate parts of the conservative coalition together. In 1997, conservative scholars began to push back against the negative narratives provided by professional historians about the Reagan presidency.[1] Dinesh D'Souza led the charge with his tribute to Reagan titled *Ronald Reagan: How an Ordinary Man Became an Extraordinary Leader.*[2]

At the same time conservatives were reevaluating Reagan's legacy in print, conservative activists, led by the president of Americans for Tax Reform, Grover Norquist, began partnering with local government to name streets, parks, schools, and even airports after the fortieth president. Norquist founded the Ronald Reagan Legacy Project (RRLP) in 1997 to preserve "the legacy of one of America's greatest presidents throughout the nation and abroad."[3] Or in the words of the executive director, Michael Kamburowski: "We want to create a tangible legacy so that 30 or 40 years from now, someone who may never have heard of Reagan will be forced to ask himself, 'Who was this man to have so many things named after him?'"[4] The combined effect of these efforts reestablished Reagan at the center of the conservative movement and the Republican Party. While President Clinton was mired in scandal, conservatives reforged Reagan's legacy, creating a wellspring of positive sentiment that Texas governor George W. Bush would eventually draw from.

In 1996, historian Arthur Schlesinger Jr. released an article ranking the presidents from Washington to Clinton. President Reagan received "low average" marks in the survey, which ranked him as the twenty-eighth-most-effective president of the thirty-nine presidents appraised. Schlesinger explained that while some of the survey's participants thought that Reagan should be elevated to the "near great" category, many others believed he was either "below average" or a "failure." These critics asserted that Reagan's "priorities—his attack on government as the root of all evil and his tax reductions that increased disparities between rich and poor while tripling the national debt—[were] a disaster for the republic."[5] As a result, Reagan ended up in the "low average" category along with President Carter.

The Schlesinger survey enraged conservatives and confirmed their view that academic historians were not interested in giving Reagan and his legacy a fair trial. Accordingly, James Piereson, the executive director of the John M. Olin Foundation, and the Intercollegiate Studies Institute (ISI) commissioned their own presidential survey to challenge Schlesinger.[6] Once the survey was complete, Piereson published the results in the *Weekly Standard.* He began by criticizing Schlesinger's survey for its liberal bias. Surprisingly, Schlesinger had included Mario Cuomo (former Democratic governor of New York) as well as Paul Simon (former Democratic senator from Illinois) as members of the survey. Piereson asserted that "it hardly came as a surprise, then, when the results of the study fell along predictable ideological lines." Piereson concluded that conservatives who did not promote the liberal conception of an activist state "were punished with low rankings (Ronald Reagan), regardless of their actual accomplishments."[7] The Schlesinger survey created an opening for conservatives who had long believed that academic historians harbored a bias against conservative ideas, positions, and politicians. In many ways, these conservative activists were correct. As Alan Brinkley acknowledged in 1994, initially the historical profession did a poor job of taking conservative ideas and the conservative movement seriously. Indeed, it took until the late 1990s and early 2000s for historians to provide a more balanced interpretation of the conservative movement.[8]

In the fall of 1997, the poor treatment of Reagan in the Schlesinger survey enabled conservative activists to present their own presidential rankings to the media and the public. Gary Gregg, director of academic development at the ISI, went on the C-SPAN program *Washington Journal* to present the findings of the ISI survey. Gregg told the audience that Schlesinger's survey suffered from "an overwhelming liberal bias" and that most of those surveyed were "liberal Democrats" and some were even Democratic politicians. To counter Schlesinger, Gregg asserted that "ISI decided to do a poll of our own testing the Schlesinger hypothesis of who ranks where in history." Gregg was pressed by the host of the show to admit that his poll leaned right, but he insisted that it was "a bit more balanced than the Schlesinger poll" and reiterated that the ISI poll did not "have any national Republican figures" surveyed. Gregg added that all the academics surveyed by ISI were "top-flight scholars" and that he was not aware of their political affiliation. There was a great deal of overlap among the two polls, especially in how they rated nineteenth-century presidents. Gregg noted, however, that "one of the main differences is Reagan's place." In the Schlesinger poll, Reagan was labeled as "low average" whereas in the ISI poll he was placed in the "near great" column. Gregg insisted that it was "really hard to believe that any objective look at the Reagan record could put him in the low-average category." Gregg explained that the scholars surveyed believed Reagan deserved to be labeled as "near great" because they were "willing to give Reagan credit for winning the Cold War, for setting that process in motion, and for standing up to the Soviet Union." The ISI scholars also gave Reagan credit for "rebuilding" the Republican Party in the wake of Watergate, for reviving "the American spirit," and for delivering "eight years of peace and prosperity."[9]

The foray of conservative intellectuals and activists into the battle over presidential rankings was new and demonstrated that conservatives were willing to fight for Reagan's place in history. In 2000, the Federalist Society, in coordination with the *Wall Street Journal*, conducted a similar poll. The 2000 survey, however, carefully selected a survey sample with an equal number of conservatives and liberals. Once again, Reagan was ranked "near great;" however, there was a large range of opinions about the fortieth president. For instance, Reagan was "named the most 'underrated' president" and was also deemed "the second most 'overrated' president" by those surveyed. The author of the survey concluded that Reagan's position was "in part" due "to a growing appreciation of his accomplishments and in part to the study's balanced panel of scholars."[10] By countering the Schlesinger survey, conservatives were able, both in 1997 and in 2000, to offer a countermeasure of what made a successful president. In disagreeing with the metrics used by the scholars in the Schlesinger rankings, conservatives challenged the role of academic historians in evaluating and writing the legacies of key figures in American history—especially Ronald Reagan.

In addition to ISI's efforts, conservative scholars realized that they would need to challenge academic historians' narratives about the 1980s. Dinesh

D'Souza became one of the most important conservatives in revitalizing Reagan's legacy. D'Souza, an immigrant from Bombay, had served in the Reagan administration as a senior domestic policy analyst from 1987 to 1988. In 1991, D'Souza became a US citizen and published *Illiberal Education: The Politics of Race and Sex on Campus* to widespread acclaim. The book was even praised by prominent historian C. Vann Woodward in the *New York Review of Books*.[11] D'Souza joined the American Enterprise Institute (AEI) in the early 1990s, where he continued to publish. His reputation as a conservative intellectual who was interested in engaging academia and offering thoughtful analysis took a hit after the release of *The End of Racism: Principles for a Multiracial Society* in 1995. The book had forty-six pages of footnotes, but some of D'Souza's claims, including the assertion that "the African slave was treated like property, which is to say, pretty well," drew virtually unanimous ire.[12] Despite D'Souza's citing renowned historians, such as Eugene Genovese, to support his case, critics largely denounced and dismissed *The End of Racism*, which led him to shift further to the right and write for a more conservative audience.[13]

In 1997, Dinesh D'Souza published *Ronald Reagan: How an Ordinary Man Became an Extraordinary Leader*. With his evaluation of the Reagan years, D'Souza directly challenged mainstream historians' interpretations of the fortieth president's legacy. In chapter 1, "Why Reagan Gets No Respect," he attacked historians directly, concluding that they were "hardly objective and balanced."[14] In his critique, D'Souza asserted that "since many of these pundits disapproved of Reagan's views from the outset, regarding his policies as wrongheaded and destructive, we cannot expect them to applaud his success in enacting his agenda." D'Souza insisted that "it is human nature to judge the effectiveness of a leader based on whether we approve of what he put into effect."[15] D'Souza also criticized Reagan's "former lieutenants" and the president's "ideological allies" for not launching "a ferocious counteroffensive for the Gipper." Instead, most of Reagan's allies had "responded for the most part with a deafening silence." In reasoning similar to Norquist's, D'Souza concluded that conservatives' "failure to defend Reagan naturally reinforces the liberal critique" and that their silence largely derived from the fact that "they are a little embarrassed by him."[16]

Unlike future conservative authors, D'Souza remembered how conservatives were disenchanted by Reagan's presidency. He recalled that near the end of Reagan's second term, "*Policy Review*, the flagship magazine of the Heritage

Foundation, polled leading conservative politicians, intellectuals, and activists to ask them how the President was doing. Eight out of eleven were highly critical." D'Souza admitted that he was "one of those conservatives" who "portrayed Reagan as a conventional Republican whose lackadaisical governing approach could not be expected to fulfill his promise to change fundamentally the landscape of American politics."[17] Because of conservatives' harsh criticism of Reagan during the 1980s, D'Souza posited that they had been slow to embrace, build, and protect the Reagan legacy.

But following Dole's dismal defeat, it was time—according to D'Souza—for conservatives to recognize they had been wrong about Reagan and to embrace Reagan's legacy.[18] D'Souza insisted that the Reagan legacy was deserving of conservatives', and Americans', admiration. D'Souza explained that "Reagan will be remembered in the following way: 'He won the cold war, revived the American spirit, and made the world safe for capitalism and democracy.'" According to D'Souza, "No American president other than Washington, Lincoln, and FDR can claim a legacy of comparable distinction."[19] The ultimate purpose of D'Souza's book was to establish that "Ronald Reagan did more than any other single man in the second half of the twentieth century to shape our world" and to begin the process of properly paying tribute to his legacy.[20]

At the center of D'Souza's framing of the Reagan legacy were Reagan's economic achievements. D'Souza reminded readers of the dismal economic conditions that Reagan inherited—high inflation, high unemployment, and a stagnant economy—and praised Reagan's response. According to D'Souza, Reagan's economic achievement stemmed from supporting "monetary policies that practically eliminated the problem of inflation, and his tax cuts produced a juggernaut of economic growth and corporate restructuring that continued through the 1980s and whose effects persist in the 1990s."[21] Although D'Souza credited Volcker's tight monetary policy, and Reagan's support for it, for contributing to the economic recovery, he gave a large amount of the credit for economic recovery to the Reagan tax cuts. According to D'Souza, it was following "1983, the final year that the Reagan tax cuts went into effect, the U.S. economy commenced a seven-year period of uninterrupted growth." These seven years were "the biggest peacetime economic boom in U.S. history" with "a growth rate of 3.5 percent."[22] D'Souza continued to list the impressive accomplishments of the Reagan economy: double-digit inflation disappeared, the energy crisis disappeared, interest rates declined, and over twenty million jobs were created.[23]

D'Souza dismissed many of the criticisms that both the Left and Right leveled against the Reagan years. Democrats during the 1990s criticized the Reagan economy for benefiting the wealthy, increasing income inequality, and creating a culture that venerated greed as good. D'Souza countered that tax cuts had actually made the income tax more progressive and that median family income had increased by 15 percent. Far from the United States being a nation driven by the ethos of Gordon Gekko where middle-class Americans became poorer, charitable giving increased by 57 percent during the Reagan years and "millions of middle-class Americans disappeared into the ranks of the affluent."[24] In short, the rising tide of the Reagan expansion lifted all boats. Both Democrats and Republicans also condemned the Reagan deficits. On this point, D'Souza blamed Congress for not embracing Reagan's spending cuts and acknowledged that Reagan faced trade-offs and ultimately "reconciled himself to presiding over a large federal government as the price worth paying for his defense policy."[25] D'Souza insisted, however, that the deficits during the 1980s turned out to be inconsequential. According to D'Souza, "none of the dire warnings about the deficit came true. . . . Deficits were supposed to retard growth and choke off the economic recovery; this too did not happen in the 1980s, nor has it occurred in the 1990s."[26]

D'Souza did not simply refute criticism and reinforce established conservative views of Reagan's economic successes; he attributed the economic prosperity of the 1990s to Reagan. In 1994, conservatives had condemned the Bush and Clinton economic records, but by the time D'Souza was writing the United States was experiencing technological and economic growth. Accordingly, D'Souza credited the prosperity of the 1990s to Reagan's economic policies. In the wake of the technology boom, D'Souza traced the doubling of venture capital from 1981 to 1983 to Reagan's economic policies. According to D'Souza, entrepreneurs whom he spoke with "credited Reagan's policies of limited government, deregulation, and open markets with creating an atmosphere in which the [tech] revolution could flourish." He also quoted T. J. Rodgers, the founder of Cypress Semiconductor, who exclaimed that "without Reagan the technological surge of the past two decades 'would not have happened this way, and this fast.'"[27]

Perhaps the most surprising assertion, however, was D'Souza's claim that Reagan was to credit for the budget surpluses of the 1990s. According to D'Souza, "during the 1990s, largely due to a continuation of the Reagan economic boom as well as huge defense savings resulting from the end of the cold war, the deficit evaporated, and the federal budget actually saw a surplus." D'Souza audaciously declared that "thus, even on the objectives that proved most elusive throughout his administration—controlling the rate of growth of government and limiting the deficit—Reagan achieved, in the end, a measure of success."[28] For D'Souza, Reagan's economic legacy was clear: Reagan got inflation under control, he decreased interest rates, he decreased taxes, he increased economic growth, and his policies helped create twenty million new jobs. Or as D'Souza put it, during the Reagan years "the United States reaffirmed its position as the world's preeminent economy" and "became the vanguard of technology at a time of breathtaking progress."[29]

In addition to Reagan's revitalization of the American economy, D'Souza credited the fortieth president for ending the Cold War. Like later scholars of the Reagan-victory school, D'Souza emphasized that Reagan foresaw the collapse of the Soviet Union when all the experts, on both sides of the political aisle, believed that the US had to find a way to tolerate the USSR's existence. For instance, in 1981 Reagan prophetically proclaimed at the University of Notre Dame that "the West won't contain Communism. It will transcend Communism. It will dismiss it as some bizarre chapter in human history whose last pages are even now being written." Reagan's statements emanated from his deep belief in the superiority of capitalism and free enterprise to command economies. Indeed, perhaps better than anyone, Reagan seemed to grasp the inadequacies of the Soviet economic system. In 1987, during his speech before the Brandenburg Gate, Reagan insisted, "In the Communist world, we see failure, technological backwardness, declining standards. . . . Even today, the Soviet Union cannot feed itself." Just as conservatives at the 1996 Republican National Convention attempted to tie Reagan's rhetoric to actual world events, D'Souza claimed that "not long after this, the wall did come tumbling down, and Reagan's prophecies all came true." According to D'Souza, Reagan did more than just foresee the collapse of the Soviet Union, "he advocated policies that were aimed at producing it. He was denounced for those policies. Yet, in the end, his objective was achieved."[30]

Unlike later conservative scholars, however, D'Souza realized that while Reagan was a "visionary," he was also "an intensely practical man." For instance, D'Souza asserts that "although Reagan was resolute in principle, he was creative and flexible about his ideas in practice." D'Souza also recognized the distinction between conservatives and Reagan. According to D'Souza, Reagan, like most "good leaders," understood that you "often have to work with people who don't" share your vision. Accordingly, "unlike his conservative critics, Reagan recognized the value of pragmatists in the White House; despite their disagreements with him, they helped him get his agenda through." D'Souza emphasized that Reagan had his own vision regarding both his domestic and foreign policy objectives and that the "conventional wisdom" that Reagan was a puppet to his advisors "must be turned on its head: he wasn't their pawn; they were his." In the end, many of Reagan's aides realized that "there was no inner circle—just Reagan."[31]

In fact, D'Souza asserted that Reagan had a well thought-out plan to confront the Soviet Union from the moment he took office. According to D'Souza, Reagan "developed a complex, often counterintuitive strategy for dealing with the Soviet Union that hardly anyone on his staff fully endorsed or even understood, and which he implemented over the objections of hawks as well as doves." Like later proponents of the view that Reagan won the Cold War, D'Souza claimed that Reagan's first term was designed to bring the Soviets to the table. His harsh rhetoric and military buildup were designed to provide the United States with leverage in any negotiations. In D'Souza's interpretation, Reagan's rhetoric—from his first press conference, where he accused the Soviets of being willing to "commit any crime, to lie, to cheat," to his labeling the Cold War as a "struggle between right and wrong, good and evil" in 1983— all contributed to the end of the conflict. D'Souza even goes so far as to claim that Reagan's "evil empire" speech "was the single most important speech of the Reagan presidency, a classic illustration of what Václav Havel terms 'the power of words to change history.'"[32]

In reality, Reagan's hostile rhetoric toward the Soviet Union increased the likelihood of an armed conflict between the two superpowers because it confirmed the fears of Soviet officials and KGB operatives.[33] Indeed, it was Reagan's evolving understanding of the Soviet Union in late 1983 and 1984 that enabled him to transition toward a more conciliatory foreign policy to pull the two rival nations back from the brink of conflict. If any speech could be labeled the most important of Reagan's presidency, it has to be the January 1984 address in which he signaled a shift in US foreign policy and embraced a cooling of tensions with the Soviet Union. Far from pursuing a continuous policy from the start, Reagan's approach to the Soviet Union developed over the course of his presidency, and he was deeply influenced by the events of the fall of 1983. By denying Reagan's openness to challenge his own ideological preconceptions, D'Souza rejected what was undoubtedly Reagan's greatest achievements: his open-mindedness and willingness to change his views when presented with new information.

Although D'Souza may be incorrect about Reagan having a clear plan from the outset, he should be credited for recognizing that Reagan's willingness to negotiate with Gorbachev set the stage for the end of the Cold War. Unlike many conservative hawks, Reagan believed that under the right circumstances he could negotiate with the Soviet Union. According to D'Souza, "these conditions were realized during Reagan's second term" and conservatives were "critical, and some even denounced Reagan as a "useful idiot," when he changed course in his dealings with the new Soviet leader, Mikhail Gorbachev." This disagreement, according to D'Souza, stemmed from Reagan's belief that the USSR was rotten at its core, whereas many hawkish conservatives "did not see how Soviet communism could possibly go away" short of "a nuclear war."[34] D'Souza detailed some of the criticism that conservatives leveled at Reagan during his negotiations with Gorbachev and credited the president for "pursuing his own distinctive course."[35] D'Souza acknowledged that it was ultimately Gorbachev's reforms that caused "the entire system to blow up," yet he still insisted that Reagan and not Gorbachev deserved the credit for the dissolution of the Soviet empire.[36] In D'Souza's view, it was Reagan who "judiciously encouraged Gorbachev's reform efforts while applying constant pressure on him to move faster and further."[37] D'Souza concluded that "Reagan proved correct not only in his moral condemnation of communism but also in his analysis of the Soviet threat and the policies he devised to counter it . . . Reagan won and Gorbachev lost. If Gorbachev was the trigger, Reagan was the one who pulled it."[38]

D'Souza did not stop at establishing how conservatives should remember Reagan. He also provided some thoughts on how the GOP and conservative movement could use the Reagan legacy to change the trajectory of American politics. According to D'Souza, despite the hopes of conservatives that Gingrich would be able to complete the Reagan Revolution, by 1997 the Republican Congress's progress had been "halted in its tracks" as the "reluctant custodian of the Reagan revolution"—President Clinton—"reconciled the Democratic party to the new political landscape created by Reagan." Although acknowledging that welfare reform had been a tremendous success, D'Souza worried that the conservative movement had lost its way. Politically, Dole had led the party to an "ignominious defeat," and in 1997 "the Republican party and the conservative intellectual movement are now aimless and frustrated."

Indeed, according to D'Souza the conservative movement was divided and fragmented, but Reagan and his legacy offered a means to unite the divided movement. D'Souza condemned social conservatives for promoting "cultural renewal through public moralizing," and paleoconservatives for embracing Pat Buchanan's narrow and "xenophobic vision" of America. In contrast, D'Souza reminded readers that "Reagan's America was a generous and inclusive place" and insisted that "Reagan would have been appalled at the schoolmarm tone in which the pundits of the right lecture the American people." After all, "unlike many Republican politicians and conservative intellectuals, Reagan did not condescend to the American people or consider them as foolish or depraved."[39]

D'Souza concluded by providing a road map for how conservatives should use Reagan's legacy to unite the GOP and achieve electoral success:

> The single most important reason for the failure of the Republicans and conservative intellectuals is that both groups have lost their faith in the American people. In the 1980s Reagan converted the right, traditionally the party of pessimism, into an optimistic movement. So perhaps it is not surprising that once Reagan left, the GOP and the conservative leaders reverted to their old familiar ways. If the Republicans fail to learn from Reagan's lesson, they will lose their congressional majority and once again become a minority party and a marginal political movement.

D'Souza insisted that there was "no point in pining for 'another Ronald Reagan,'" but encouraged conservatives, "in every situation that arises," to ask themselves "What would Reagan have done?"[40] According to D'Souza, conservatism would prosper if conservatives learned and applied the Reagan legacy. Ultimately, conservatives followed D'Souza's advice, and Reagan became the glue that held the conservative movement and the Republican Party together for the next twenty years.

As D'Souza revitalized Reagan's legacy through written word, Grover Norquist was hard at work cementing Reagan in physical memorials across the country. Norquist founded the Ronald Reagan Legacy Project (RRLP) in 1997 following Dole's defeat, and the organization quickly moved to get local and state governments to remember Reagan in their communities. As Norquist explained,

"Conservatives have been reticent to promote their heroes, and liberals have been aggressive. If you want to contend for the future, you have to contend for the public understanding of the past."[41] Over the next four years, conservative activists and legislators attempted to have Reagan replace Alexander Hamilton on the ten-dollar bill and replace FDR on the dime, and to carve Reagan's image into Mount Rushmore (a plan that was geologically impossible).[42] They also attempted to get a monument of Reagan on the Washington Mall, but ironically conservatives were stymied by Reagan himself, who had signed a law in 1986 that prohibited monument construction until twenty-five years after the person being commemorated had died.[43] The most successful undertaking of the Reagan Legacy Project, at least in its early years, was the renaming of Washington National Airport to Ronald Reagan Washington National Airport. Even in this victory, those who were attempting to rehabilitate Reagan's image and enshrine him in the minds of contemporary Americans found the intersection of history and memory to be perilous waters to navigate. To achieve the name change, conservatives would have to push back against a tenet that Reagan held dear: the idea of local control.[44]

On October 23, 1997, Representative Bob Barr and Senator Paul Coverdell, both Republicans from Georgia, introduced legislation to rename Washington National Airport in honor of President Reagan.[45] Barr was joined by Speaker Gingrich and Norquist for a news conference at the Capitol to explain why Reagan deserved to have Washington National Airport named after him. Barr acknowledged Norquist and asserted that it was "through the hard work of groups like Americans for Tax Reform and their Ronald Reagan Legacy Project that this nation will continue to remember and honor one of our nation's greatest presidents." Barr explained that "Ronald Reagan reshaped America and in particular Washington DC, the home of our government. It is only fitting that the gateway to the city that still enjoys the Reagan legacy of smaller government and lower taxes, be named after this American hero." Barr did not stop there; he recited the litany of achievements that conservatives had bestowed on the fortieth president. Seemingly echoing D'Souza, Barr exclaimed that "Reagan displayed the leadership and tremendous courage that brought the cold war to an end and helped democracy flourish around the world." Barr concluded that it was "entirely appropriate to name the airport of the capital of the free world after the man who stood before the symbol of communism, the Berlin Wall, and proclaimed, 'Mr. Gorbachev, tear down that wall!'" For his part, Speaker Gingrich dubbed Reagan "one of the greatest figures of American history—a man who changed the history of the entire world." According to Gingrich, Reagan was largely responsible for "the period of peace and prosperity currently sweeping the world," and he concluded that the airport would provide "a lasting reminder of Ronald Reagan's enduring legacy."[46]

Barr and Norquist provided the enthusiasm and organization necessary to make the renaming of the airport a possibility. In a Dear Colleague letter, Barr explained that Reagan remained "a symbol of hope and opportunity" and insisted that "Reagan was a great leader who guided our nation to victory in the Cold War and set our country back on firm economic ground. His achievements will outlast all of us."[47] At the same time, Norquist—through Americans for Tax Reform and the Ronald Reagan Legacy Project—created the grassroots support for the measure. Americans for Tax Reform used its mailing list to inform conservatives. In a promotional mailing, the group asserted that "the newly-renamed airport will honor one of America's greatest and most popular presidents." The mailing insisted that if successful, Ronald Reagan Washington National Airport would "be a highlight of Americans for Tax Reform's campaign to honor our 40th president and his legacy by naming more buildings, airports, highways, schools, mountains, national parks and monuments, libraries and museums after our nation's greatest president." Americans for Tax Reform urged recipients "to contact your governor, mayor, state legislator and city council members in an effort to name more things after President Reagan."[48] Through the efforts of Barr and Norquist, conservatives who supported renaming the airport were much more organized than those who wanted the name to remain the same.

The debate over renaming Washington National led, however, to some uncomfortable discussions of the nature of Ronald Reagan's legacy. On December 1, 1997, James Brady, Reagan's press secretary who had survived a gunshot wound to the head during the failed assassination attempt on Reagan, wrote to Barr to remind the congressman of Reagan's support for some forms of gun control. Brady attached Reagan's March 29, 1991, op-ed, which was published in *New York Times* and titled: "Why I'm for the Brady Bill." In his letter to Barr, Brady began by praising the congressman's attempt to memorialize Reagan, exclaiming that the fortieth president was "an inspiration to all Americans—Republicans and Democrats alike." Brady's tone then shifted, and he reminded Barr that Reagan's legacy included support for gun control measures. Brady insisted that Reagan "was a great help to us in our fight to pass the Brady law and the federal ban on semi-automatic assault weapons, personally calling and writing Members of Congress in the crucial days prior to the votes to talk about the merits of those lifesaving pieces of legislation."[49] With his letter, Brady challenged Barr's position on gun control by challenging the representative's conception of what defined Reagan's legacy.

Barr, who was a long-standing opponent of gun control, responded to Brady's challenge by agreeing that he too was a "great admirer of the 'Great Communicator.'" Unfortunately, the two men disagreed over what it was that Reagan communicated on the issue of guns. Barr explained that he was "mystified" by Brady's references "to gun control, which has nothing to do with renaming National Airport." Barr reminded Brady that during Reagan's eight years in office, the president "did not support or sign any gun control legislation into law." Chastising Brady's close relationship with President Clinton, Barr suggested that perhaps the former press secretary should use his "considerable influence with this president to urge his support of this well-deserved honor for President Reagan."[50] The implication of Barr's words was that Brady was not a true conservative because of his closeness with a Democratic president and perhaps also because of his support of nonconservative positions such as gun control. Unfortunately, Brady did not write back to Barr, and the two did not resolve what Reagan's legacy, as memorialized through the airport, would ultimately represent. Brady and Barr's correspondence contained one of many arguments that would be waged between not only Democrats and Republicans, but also self-proclaimed admirers of Reagan's, over what his true legacy was and how it should be preserved and promoted.

In early January 1998, the name change picked up critical support. Both Michael and Nancy Reagan publicly supported the proposal, and the Republican Governors Association voted unanimously in support of the measure. The Republican governor of Virginia (where the airport was located) explained that when lawmakers arrived at Reagan National in the future, "they'll be reminded they're here to serve the people, even though they're far from home." Trying to anticipate Democratic criticisms, Norquist offered to pay to replace the signs after Washington National was renamed in honor of Reagan. Such gestures did not silence the growing opposition to the renaming of the airport. Liberal *Washington Post* columnist Mary McGray exclaimed that the idea should be "nipped in the bud" because Reagan "didn't only rail against Washington, he genuinely despised it."[51]

On January 15, renowned journalist Albert R. Hunt penned an op-ed in the *Wall Street Journal* arguing that a memorial to Reagan would serve as a reminder to conservatives of the decency and pragmatism of the fortieth president. Hunt asserted that although he was "not enamored with many of Ronald Reagan's policies," Reagan should be remembered for practicing "a politics of civility . . . a trait that more than a few of his conservative confreres have forgotten." Hunt reminded his readers that "President Reagan proved that government could work" in the wake of the numerous failures of the federal government in the 1970s. Hunt insisted that "Reagan proved that with courage of convictions, an able White House staff and the ability to communicate with the American public, the system worked just fine. Some of us might not have liked the outcomes, but it was a vitally important lesson: one of the great beneficiaries has been Bill Clinton." In stark contrast to conservatives' conceptions of what Reagan's legacy represented—the end of the era of big government—Hunt argued that indeed it was Reagan who had restored credibility to the federal government. Hunt concluded that renaming the airport in honor of Reagan might be a nice olive branch from Clinton to Republicans—"it'd be something like we used to see in the 1980s."[52] Hunt's column represented the improving approval of Reagan among the American public near the end of the millennium and demonstrated that despite some partisan opposition, the renaming of Washington National would probably pass Congress.[53]

Supporters of renaming Washington National insisted that Reagan was one of the country's most successful presidents and as such deserved significant memorials in his honor. Prior to the final vote, the House Republican Conference (HRC) released a set of talking points for members. The message from the HRC was that Reagan was one "of the greatest presidents of modern times." Accordingly, "naming our country's national airport after him is one small way of recognizing his contribution to the United States and the world." The HRC reminded members that on October 30, 1986, Reagan transferred the "National Airport to local control," which "resulted in long-overdue modernization, exemplified by the new terminal." Trying to justify why Reagan should have an airport named after him, the HRC concluded that "a modern, efficient National Airport is a result of Ronald Reagan's vision of moving power and influence back to localities. Its name should be a tribute to him."[54]

In addition, Senate majority leader Trent Lott (R-MS) insisted that renaming the airport was an easy decision. He exclaimed that "history will show clearly that [Reagan] is one of the greatest Presidents of the century, and in my opinion, the greatest by far." Norquist appealed to Democrats' belief in fairness, asking for equality in honoring past presidents. He argued that "Ronald Reagan's legacy is at least as powerful as John F. Kennedy's, his greatness is at least as identifiable as John F. Kennedy's, so we should be looking for the same number of things named after Reagan as Kennedy."[55] Norquist's implication was that since JFK had an airport named after him in New York, it was only fair that Reagan receive the same honors in Arlington, Virginia.

Despite Norquist's appeals, the debate over renaming Washington National did result in some partisan bickering and some interesting disagreements about Reagan's true legacy. One Democratic representative, James Oberstar (MN) exclaimed that he did not "see why we would name an airport for the president who fired 11,000 air traffic controllers."[56] Randy Schwitz, the executive vice president of the National Air Traffic Controllers Association, agreed. Schwitz colorfully insisted that he would "rather have a hot poker in my eye" and insisted that renaming the airport after Reagan was "like dumping salt on [the] wound" that was created when Reagan "fired 11,000 controllers."[57] While some argued that Reagan did not deserve an airport named after him because of his treatment of the air traffic controllers in 1981, Senate minority leader Tom Daschle (D-SD) took a different approach. Daschle pointed out that the localities near the airport opposed the name change. The senator invoked Reagan and insisted that the federal government's renaming Washington National in defiance of the local constituents marked "the kind of federal intrusion" that Reagan himself found "abhorrent."[58]

On February 5, 1998, on the eve of Reagan's birthday, the legislation to rename Washington National passed both the House and the Senate.[59] President Clinton, who had agreed to sign the bill, released a gracious statement: "As the nation celebrates President Reagan's 87th birthday, we wish him and his family well. He is in our thoughts and prayers." Nancy Reagan was grateful and described the renaming of Washington National in honor of her husband "a wonderful gift."[60] Republicans were ecstatic, and the leaders to rename the airport imbued the legislation passing with meaning. Coverdell insisted that "as he celebrates his 87th birthday, Ronald Reagan will know just how much the American people appreciate his enormous contribution to the cause of freedom."[61] Gingrich exclaimed that renaming the airport was about more than just thanking Reagan. Indeed, he insisted that it would encourage "millions of visitors to Washington each year will see Ronald Reagan's name—a fitting symbol for the man who initiated the concept of responsive, smaller government, as well as a worldwide movement of freedom."[62] Barr, with his statement, hinted that the renaming of the airport was inadequate to truly honor Reagan. More work needed to be done. Barr declared that "although naming our national airport in his honor pales in comparison to the immense legacy President Reagan gave to all of us, it is a positive and well-deserved step toward honoring one of the greatest Americans of this century."[63] Over the next two decades, the Ronald Reagan Legacy Project, Republican lawmakers, and conservative activists would continue to create physical reminders of Reagan across the American landscape.

With the victory of Ronald Reagan Washington National Airport behind them, the RRLP and conservative lawmakers turned their attention to engraving Reagan into the American psyche in other ways. Although they failed to get Reagan on Mount Rushmore, to erect a monument to him on the National Mall, or to get Reagan's image engrained on US currency, they did celebrate other successes. In 2001, the USS *Ronald Reagan* was christened, and in 2003 many state governors signed onto the organization's proposal and celebrated February 6 (Reagan's birthday) as Ronald Reagan Day.[64]

By 2000, the efforts of the RRLP and conservative scholars had gone a long way in creating a clear legacy for Reagan. Furthermore, their efforts had provided the GOP with a shared past, a common language, and a joint commitment to the principles espoused by the Gipper. As early as March 1998, conservatives began to recognize the role that Reagan's legacy could play in uniting the GOP. Jack Pitney, a Republican activist, encapsulated how important Reagan's legacy was in an interview with the *Philadelphia Inquirer*: "Ronald Reagan has already become the Shroud of Turin for the Republicans. Every political movement needs its heroes, and who else can Republicans turn to: Richard Nixon? Gerald Ford? George Bush? Ike was a hero, but that was because of the war. This Reagan-worship is also happening because there's a leadership vacuum in the party right now. When people can't see the future, they look to the past."[65]

During the late 1990s, conservatives created the Reagan legacy and did their best to enshrine the fortieth president into the very essence of America. In doing so, conservatives were addressing the very real problem that they had lost their identity and the issue that had held the various factions of the GOP together—anticommunism. The dismal showing by Republicans in the 1998 midterm elections only strengthened the view that conservatives needed to channel Reagan if they wanted to achieve political success. In the lead-up to the 2000 election, the Reagan legacy became not only the glue that held the disparate parts of the conservative movement together, but also the road map for how Texas governor George W. Bush could capture the presidency.

12. Reinventing Reagan: George W. Bush and the Emergence of the Reagan Myth, 2000–2004

In 2000, Texas governor George W. Bush boldly embraced the Reagan legacy and framed his candidacy as a campaign for a third Reagan term.[1] Before the first primary contest, Bush made the pilgrimage to the Reagan Library to deliver a major foreign policy speech. George Shultz, Reagan's secretary of state, introduced Bush, and the candidate mentioned Reagan six times during the speech while referring to his father only once.[2] Bush emphasized that the United States needed "a distinctly American internationalism." In an article titled "George W. Reagan," the *New York Post* praised Bush for distancing himself from the "isolationist" policies of Buchanan and the "drift" of Clinton.[3] The *Post* concluded that Bush "demonstrated his understanding of Reagan's 'peace through strength' philosophy with a full-throated advocacy of missile-defense systems."[4] After his speech, the press concluded that Bush was "sending a message that if he is the next president of the United States he will give America the third Reagan term voters thought they were getting when they elected his father president in 1992." They observed that Bush signaled to the audience "a George W. Bush presidency . . . will be Reagan III, not Bush II." Bush explained that his agenda included "entitlement reform, lower taxes to keep the economy growing, a stronger military to keep the peace, and education reform."[5] Bush's principal primary opponent, John McCain, did not make a serious attempt to frame himself as Reagan's heir. As a result, Bush claimed his candidacy represented the Reagan Revolution and dismissed McCain by asserting, "It is not Reaganesque to say one thing and do another."[6] Unlike Dole, however, Bush benefited from four years of memorialization and legacy building by the likes of Norquist and D'Souza.

After Bush bested McCain, Nancy Reagan publicly endorsed Bush. The former First Lady said Bush was a candidate "Ronnie would be proud of." She declared she was "proud to endorse George W. Bush" because he was "doing a fine job of carrying on Ronnie's legacy." Specifically, Mrs. Reagan praised "his agenda of tax cuts, smaller government, and a strong national defense" as building "pride in America just as it did when my husband was President." Using the common language provided by her husband's time in office, she concluded that "George W. Bush will help America once again become a 'shining city on a hill.'" Bush responded that he was "delighted to have Mrs. Reagan's support." He thanked her for the endorsement and pledged himself to "an optimistic, positive campaign, in the Reagan tradition, to renew America's spirit and encourage a new era of personal responsibility and freedom."[7] With Reagan unable to comment on contemporary politics, Mrs. Reagan's endorsement legitimized Bush and passed the torch of the Reagan Revolution to the governor of Texas.

Following Bush's convention, conservatives who viewed themselves as the protectors of Reagan's legacy praised him and accepted Bush as Reagan's heir. The *Wall Street Journal* commended Bush's optimistic campaign and defended the Republican nominee from conservative criticism of his toughness and commitment to principle. While the *Journal* praised Bush's convention, it noted that Ronald Reagan loomed "over the shoulder of the GOP's current nominee." Although Reagan could not comment on Bush or his strategy, the *Wall Street Journal* reported that "those who knew him best said at this week's Reagan Library reception that he would find it both politically savvy and respectful of his legacy."[8] *National Review* celebrated Bush's convention speech as "impeccably conservative" for making "the moral case for school choice, missile defense, tax cuts, restrictions on abortion, and free market reform of Social Security."[9] Larry Kudlow and Stephen Moore, the president of the Club for Growth, admired Bush for adopting "Reagan's principles" with his plan to lower personal tax rates across the board. They also complimented Bush for giving Reagan's principles a populist flair by arguing that excess government revenues should be redistributed to the people because after all "the surplus is the people's money."[10]

As the presidential campaign entered its final month, Bush channeled Reagan and used the fortieth president's legacy to propel his bid for the presidency. Bush deflected questions about his lack of experience by declaring, "That's what they said about Ronald Reagan when that good man was running for President." Bush used his speeches to emphasize the "greatness of America" and need for a president "who unites this nation and lifts this country's spirits." In interview after interview, Bush used Reagan as a defense against criticisms of his intellectual prowess and his preparedness to be president. He reminded "the press that they had belittled Reagan saying 'oh, he can't possibly be smart enough to be President. He is simply an actor.'" Bush then emphatically exclaimed that Reagan "turned out to be a great President." One of Bush's central themes was his opposition to "big government" and his insistence that he would "trust the people, not the government." This theme was clearly in the vein of Reagan, who often emphasized that government was the problem, not the solution. Indeed, evoking Reagan was a Bush campaign strategy. Scott McClellan, a spokesman for the Bush campaign, frequently made reference to Reagan. He told the press that "like Ronald Reagan, Governor Bush understands that the role of a leader is to set a clear agenda to get things done and bring people together." In another instance, McClellan asserted that "like Ronald Reagan, Governor Bush is setting a positive, uplifting tone for the country, in stark contrast to Al Gore, who is playing upon fear."[11] One of the goals of the campaign was to link Bush to Reagan in the minds of American voters and to use the success, as established by the legacy builders, of the 1980s as a shield against criticism and as a justification for Bush's policy agenda.

In the final days before the election, the press explained that if Bush won, it would be in large part because of his embrace of Ronald Reagan. Conservative columnist Charles Krauthammer asserted that temperament mattered, and implied that Bush's optimistic campaign and his genuineness, like Reagan's, would win him a narrow victory over Gore.[12] The *Independent*, in Great Britain, declared that "if Bush wins it will because he has something of Ronald Reagan's gift for allowing Americans to feel it's 'morning in America.'"[13] The 2000 election was one of the closest and most controversial contests in American history. Ultimately, the Supreme Court ruled five to four to end the recounts in Florida. All of Reagan's judicial appointments supported the position that granted Bush the presidency.[14] Bush successfully rode the Reagan legacy to the White House.

After Bush was sworn in as the forty-third president, he continued to cite Reagan to justify his policy initiatives, and he played a pivotal role in further cementing the Reagan legacy. Shortly after taking office, President Bush offered a tribute to Reagan in celebration of his ninetieth birthday. In a recorded message for *Larry King Live*, Bush gave Reagan credit for revitalizing America's spirit and for bringing peace to the world. Bush recounted that Reagan made the United States "strong again." He praised Reagan for prophetically declaring "that the evil empire would pass, and that freedom would prevail" and concluded, "Your resolve made it happen." After giving Reagan credit for winning the Cold War, Bush lauded "the good heart that always guided" Reagan and "the unbending principles that always defined" the president. Bush finished by thanking Reagan for his service and declaring that Americans loved and honored him.[15]

By the beginning of the twenty-first century, it was well established in conservative circles that Reagan had won the Cold War, revitalized the US economy, and restored America's morale after the debacle of the Carter presidency. Bush's use of the most powerful platform in the world to legitimize these conservative conceptions established them as mainstays in America's political discourse. However, Bush attempted to add another element to the Reagan legacy—the idea that Reagan had "unbending principles" that he adhered to throughout his administration. While it was true that Reagan was a principled politician, he was also pragmatic. In time, this emphasis on Reagan's "unbending principles" would evolve into the myth that Reagan's success was a result of his unyielding commitment to conservative principles.

Just a few months after Bush's tribute, he was given an opportunity to approve stem cell research that hoped to find cures for debilitating diseases like Alzheimer's. The question of whether embryonic stem cell experiments should be legal threatened Bush's image as the next Reagan. On the one hand, Bush's opposition to abortion encouraged him to reject such research, while on the other, many, including Nancy Reagan, favored allowing such experiments in the hope that they would result in significant scientific advancements.[16] Mrs. Reagan wrote Bush in April, urging him to support the "miracle possibilities" that embryonic stem cell research could produce for people with Alzheimer's like her husband. The former first lady concluded, "Mr. President, I have some personal experience regarding the many decisions you face each day . . . I'd be very grateful if you would take my thoughts and prayers into your consideration on this critical issue."[17]

Ironically, some news outlets determined that the Reagan thing to do would be to stand on principle and reject stem cell research. The *Daily Telegraph* concluded that Bush's decision would determine "whether Mr. Bush is sticking to principles like Ronald Reagan or trimming like another George Bush." Instead of embracing political expediency and "invoking Mr. Reagan's medical plight" and "announcing federal funding for embryonic stem cell research," Bush stuck to his principles and rejected the proposal.[18] Paradoxically, for Bush to retain his legitimacy as Reagan's heir, he had to denounce medical research that could have helped people like Reagan who suffered from Alzheimer's disease.[19]

Bush's primary domestic policy achievement during his first term was his $1.35 trillion tax cut. Initially, the Bush administration justified this proposal as returning to taxpayers money that belonged to them. As the economy moved into recession, however, it "took on a new urgency," and Bush "pressed Congress to move quickly" to pass the tax cuts to stimulate economic activity.[20] The *Chicago Tribune*, in an article titled "George W. Reagan," questioned whether "Bush's tax reduction plans" would bring the "return of the kind of runaway deficits that defined the Reagan years and forced the shrinking of government."[21] In contrast, the administration preferred to emphasize the economic recovery and sustained economic growth of the 1980s when comparing their tax cuts to Reagan's. Vice President Cheney later explained that Reagan's "tax cuts helped spur one of the longest sustained waves of prosperity in our history," the result of which was "peace," "increased federal revenues, and, eventually, lower deficits."[22] Similarly to Reagan, Bush dramatically cut taxes while also increasing military spending to fight the war on terror. The result was ballooning deficits. As Bush attempted to establish his own legacy, he proudly explained that in June 2001 he "signed a $1.35 trillion tax cut, the largest since the one Ronald Reagan signed during his first term."[23] The revenue lost due to the Bush tax cuts might have been offset by his reforms to Social Security, but on September 11, 2001, the Bush administration's priorities turned to combating international terrorism.

President Bush used his State of the Union address in January 2002 to explain America's post-9/11 foreign policy. Bush emphasized his commitment to preserving the United States' security and told the American people that a new "axis of evil" threatened the Western world. According to Bush, North Korea, Iran, and especially Iraq posed an imminent threat. Bush claimed that Saddam Hussein desired to produce nerve gas, anthrax, and even nuclear weapons. Bush also detailed how Hussein had committed crimes against his own citizens—leaving women and children dead in the streets. The United States, according to Bush, would not wait for these evil nations to attack. Rather, his administration would pursue a preemptive foreign policy that addressed threats to the national security of the United States before Americans could be harmed.[24]

Following the speech, many political commentators compared Bush's rhetoric to Reagan's. Conservative columnist Charles Krauthammer asserted that Bush's speech was an "astonishingly bold address" and that any internal debate about what to do in regard to Iraq was over as "the speech was just short of a declaration of war."[25] Bob Woodward wrote shortly thereafter that Bush's "'Axis of evil' seemed to echo President Ronald Reagan's provocative declaration in 1983 that the Soviet Union was an 'evil empire.'" According to Woodward, just as "Reagan asserted that there was no moral equivalence between totalitarian Soviet Russia and the United States," Bush was claiming the moral high ground against rogue nations. Woodward concluded that "since Reagan, no president had so blatantly rattled the sword."[26] The *New York Times* also linked Bush's rhetoric to Reagan. The publication emphatically proclaimed that "Bush should leave the Reagan style to its own era." The *Times* concluded that "even those who thought Ronald Reagan's rhetorical flourishes well suited to the demands of the cold war era have reason to think that President Bush's rhetorical approach is a mistake."[27] Those involved in writing the speech had consciously channeled Reagan. Colin Powell, Bush's secretary of state, had asked Bush to include several "uplifting paragraphs" because he believed that Reagan's success had been due, in large part, to his optimism. Bush's national security adviser, Condoleezza Rice, thought that the media headline the next morning would be about democracy and political change in the Middle East. Instead, the news media focused on "the force of the phrase" "axis of evil" with its "echoes to World War II and Ronald Reagan."[28]

When Bush announced that the United States was going to invade Iraq in 2003, conservative commentators deflected any criticism of Bush by invoking the emerging Reagan myth. Conservative advocate and writer Ann Coulter was one of the most outspoken defender of Bush. In 2002 she published *Slander: Liberal Lies about the American Right*, in which she defended President Bush from his critics who questioned his ability to lead the nation after September 11. Coulter reminded her readers that liberals had bashed Reagan for being "an idiot" just as they did Bush, but "stupid old Reagan won the Cold War."[29] Coulter's point, beyond reinforcing the view that Reagan won the Cold War, was to dismiss criticisms of Bush because the same type of unfair attacks had been leveled at Reagan and he turned out to be a great president.

Coulter built on this theme of defending Bush by citing Reagan in her 2003 book titled *Treason: Liberal Treachery from the Cold War to the War on*

Terrorism. In *Treason*, Coulter asserted that "just as liberals went into panic when Ronald Reagan referred to Russia as an 'evil empire,' they were in a state of frenzy over Bush's 'axis of evil' speech."[30] Coulter spent much of the book detailing how many liberals did not believe that the Cold War was winnable. After demonstrating how liberal scholars and pundits were wrong about the Cold War, she mocked historian Walter LaFeber for predicting that the war on terror would be "a continual war . . . to 'lead the world' to continual peace." Coulter concluded that "liberals expect everyone to forget not only what they said during the Cold War, but the fact that there *was* a Cold War and that they were rooting for the other side."[31] Coulter insisted that the American public should dismiss LaFeber's and other liberals' criticism of Bush and the war on terror because they had been shortsighted during the Cold War. Through her manipulation of Reagan's legacy, Coulter hoped to delegitimize those who were concerned about US intervention in the Middle East.

Of course, the history surrounding the end of the Cold War and Reagan's views on preemptive strikes were much more complicated than conservative commentators like Coulter cared to admit.[32] During his presidency, Reagan was very careful not to get the United States bogged down in another Vietnam. His major foreign policy intervention was in Grenada, where few US troops were needed to secure the objective. Even though National Security Decision Directive 75 stated that "US policy will include active efforts to encourage democratic movements and forces to bring about political change inside these countries," Reagan did not send troops to Nicaragua, Angola, or Afghanistan.[33] Instead, he sent other forms of assistance to challenge what he viewed as the spread of communism. Although Reagan stationed US marines in Lebanon, when they were bombed he quickly withdrew them rather than get caught in the middle of a quagmire. In his autobiography, President Bush recognized that his decision to take aggressive action against al Qaeda was different from what Reagan had done after Hezbollah bombed the US Marine barracks and embassy in Lebanon. Bush explained, simply, that Reagan's decision was made in "a different time."[34]

Paradoxically, Reagan's commitment to conservative principles and his harsh rhetoric did not result in the successes that conservatives constantly cited. Conservative commentators, such as Ann Coulter, embraced the developing myth that Reagan won the Cold War by using harsh rhetoric, engaging in economic warfare, and refusing to compromise. In reality, Reagan's fiery rhetoric during his first term actually isolated those who wanted to negotiate in the Soviet politburo and propped up those who wanted to prolong the Cold War.[35] Furthermore, during his postpresidency Reagan countered such claims that he won the Cold War, instead crediting Gorbachev and the people of Eastern Europe. Indeed, Reagan was very proud of the INF Treaty and his negotiations with Gorbachev. In order to get a deal to reduce nuclear weapons, Reagan moderated his language and pragmatically engaged the Soviet Union.[36] It was personal diplomacy between Reagan and Gorbachev that engendered the trust that enabled the two men to fight off the reactionary elements in both their countries and strike a deal that made the world a safer place.[37]

By 2003, however, most conservatives were ready to embrace George W. Bush as the heir to the Reagan legacy. Michael Deaver explained that Bush was "the most Reagan-like politician we have seen, certainly in the White House." Deaver concluded that George H. W. Bush "was supposed to be the third term of the Reagan presidency—but he wasn't. This guy is." Martin Anderson, Reagan's domestic policy adviser, drew up public policy tutorials for Bush and concluded that "on taxes" and "on education," Bush's positions were exactly the same as Reagan's. He continued that on "Social Security, Bush's position was exactly what Reagan always wanted and talked about in the 70s." Anderson concluded that he could not "think of any major policy issue on which Bush is different." Grover Norquist, the president of Americans for Tax Reform, explained that Bush was "a post-Reagan president." The younger Bush, Norquist insisted, had "come of age watching Reagan succeed and his father fail." As a result, Bush understood conservatism: "With Bush, this stuff is visceral."[38]

As they defended Bush, many conservatives went beyond Reagan's legacy to embrace the myth that it was Reagan's commitment to principle that was the reason for his success. By doing so, they justified the continuation of George W. Bush's policies in the face of criticism. Condoleezza Rice asserted that Reagan and Bush were similar in that the two framed international tensions in moral certainties. Rice praised Bush's ability to "delegitimize the enemy" and "to speak in black-and-white terms."[39] Peter J. Wallison, President Reagan's legal counsel from 1986 to 1987, recalled that Reagan succeeded because "the president stood firm" and shrugged "off advice to change his economic and foreign policies." Wallison insisted that if Bush stood firm on principle regarding taxes and Iraq, he would prove "he is truly like Mr. Reagan."[40] For his part, Bush asserted that Reagan had "combined the moral clarity and conviction to cut taxes, strengthen the military, and face down the Soviet Union despite withering criticism throughout his presidency." Bush "learned from Ronald Reagan" to stick to his vision and principles despite any criticism he might endure.[41] Journalist Bill Keller concluded in his article titled "Reagan's Son" that if Bush failed it would "be a failure not of caution but of overreaching," which meant it would "be on a grand scale." If Bush were to succeed, according to Keller, he would "move us toward an America Ronald Reagan would have been happy to call home."[42]

As 2003 came to an end, the conservative myth that Reagan's success was due to his dogmatic commitment to conservative principle had replaced any nuanced view of why Reagan had been a successful president. Gone were any memories of conservatives complaining as Reagan compromised on taxes, Social Security, immigration, and the budget. Missing as well was any recollection that Reagan had fallen short in delivering a school prayer amendment, a right-to-life amendment, or a federalization of welfare. Likewise, many conservatives forgot that they had condemned Reagan for negotiating with Gorbachev and that some even compared their mythical hero to Neville Chamberlain. Also absent from these conservative interpretations was the realization that Reagan was a pragmatic conservative who had worked across the political aisle to achieve his goals. The unyielding commitment to principle was never a significant part of the Reagan governing philosophy, and the belief that he achieved greatness through his commitment to conservative dogma is nothing more than a myth. When Reagan's administration embraced the interventionist and hardline positions that conservatives in 2003 praised, it resulted in Iran-Contra, an increase in tension in the Cold War, and congressional gridlock.

Not all conservatives were comfortable with using the Reagan legacy to justify US intervention in Iraq. In October of 2002, Patrick Buchanan, Taki Theodoracopulos, and Scott McConnell launched the *American Conservative.* The publication's purpose was to offer conservative readers an alternative to the neoconservative views that dominated the *Weekly Standard* and *National Review.* The *American Conservative* presented paleoconservative critiques of the Bush administration and its decision to invade Iraq.[43] In addition to opposing the war in Iraq, the publication encouraged an "America First" approach—this included decreasing immigration and putting an end to free trade. In its first volume, "Iraq Folly: How Victory Could Spell American Defeat," the magazine made good on its mission to criticize the "imperialistic" and "interventionist" longings of the neoconservatives.[44]

In a critique that would come to look prescient, Pat Buchanan lambasted Bush's decision to invade Iraq. In an article titled "After the War," Buchanan warned that the United States should be careful not to get overextended militarily. Furthermore, he argued that the "invasion will not be the cakewalk neoconservatives predict." Buchanan went further to predict that the war would probably become a "bloody mess." Buchanan also commented on the potential that the war had of destabilizing the region and enflaming anti-American sentiment. He wrote that "pro-American autocrats will be targeted by assassins" and that the US invasion will delegitimize pro-American regimes. American troops, Buchanan predicted, "will be tied down for decades" in Iraq. Most importantly, he argued that the American presence in Iraq would lead to resentment across the region and would encourage "calls for jihad from Morocco to Malaysia."[45] Buchanan's opposition to the Bush administration's actions in Iraq, as well as the denouncements of libertarians, demonstrates the limits of the Reagan legacy in holding the conservative movement together in the face of contentious policy decisions.[46] In the wake of the Cold War, conservatives had not established a consensus about what defined a "conservative" foreign policy, and the use of preemptive strike in Iraq threatened to undermine the unity that propagators of the Reagan legacy had built in the 1990s.

Despite some dissent in the conservative ranks, conservatives largely embraced the emerging Reagan myth—that Reagan was successful because he did not deviate from conservative principles—and encouraged Bush to stay the course on taxes, Iraq, and his other domestic policy initiatives regardless of the outcomes. In his autobiography, Bush explained that the "one lesson" he took from "Reagan was to lead the public, not chase the public opinion polls." This belief led him to "push for sweeping reforms, not tinker with the status quo."[47] Although in the Reagan myth was in its infancy in 2003, the potential damage of viewing Reagan as an uncompromising principled conservative crusader was already evident. The myth that Reagan was uncompromising would only intensify from 2004 to 2016.

Ronald Reagan's eyes closed for the last time on June 5, 2004. Two days later, Reagan's body was taken to the Reagan Library, where it lay in repose. There was a private service where Mrs. Reagan and the rest of the Reagan family gathered. When the family left, the library opened to the public, and more than one hundred thousand people paid their respects.[48] On June 9, one of the two Boeing 747-200s that served as Air Force One arrived in California to fly the body and Reagan's family to Washington. Just before noon, the plane touched down at Andrews Air Force Base. The casket was removed and driven by hearse through the Maryland and Virginia suburbs on its way to the capital. Near the Ellipse at President's Park, Mrs. Reagan got out of her limousine as Reagan's casket was transferred to a horse-drawn caisson for the procession down Constitution Avenue to Capitol Hill.

Thousands of people lined the street to pay their respects, and millions more watched the live proceedings at home. The cortege began its forty-five-minute journey just after six o'clock eastern time. Military units escorted the caisson as the sound of muffled drums echoed through the mournful streets. Behind the carriage, a riderless horse named Sargent York trotted, carrying Reagan's riding boots reversed in the stirrups. The caisson paused at the intersection of Fourth Street and Constitution as twenty-one Air Force F-15s flew over in missing-man formation. On the procession's arrival at Capitol Hill, military units removed Reagan's casket and "Hail to the Chief" was played amid a twenty-one-gun salute. The casket was carried up the west steps of the Capitol in a symbolic gesture to Reagan's earlier wishes that he be inaugurated facing west. As the casket reached the top of the steps, the Reagan family met it, and Nancy broke away from her escort and placed her hand gently upon it. The casket was then set under the rotunda "atop a plain pine catafalque that was first used for the funeral of Abraham Lincoln," where it lay in state.[49]

The eulogies delivered at the invitation-only ceremony in the Capitol Rotunda emphasized Reagan's place in history. As the sun set in the West, the ceremony began. Vice President Cheney, Senate pro tempore Ted Stevens (R-AK), and House Speaker J. Dennis Hastert (R-IL) offered eulogies. Hastert praised Reagan's "story and his values as quintessentially American." Stevens declared that "by the time President Reagan left office, he had reversed the trend of ever increasing government control over our lives, restored our defense capabilities, guided us through the worst economic downturn since the Great Depression and set in motion policies which ultimately led to the collapse of the 'evil empire.'"[50] To Stevens, Reagan was not just a great president but the savior of the nation, single-handedly reversing the trend toward bigger government and prophetically implementing policies that would end the Cold War.

Although both Stevens and Hastert reinforced the conservative legacy of the Reagan presidency, Vice President Cheney declared that Reagan's achievements transcended history. Cheney lamented that knowing that this day would come had not made it easy to "see the honor guard" or "the flag draped before us." The vice president lauded Reagan's accomplishments and his place in history. Cheney reminded those present that before Reagan came to office, the Cold War had raged for decades and "few believed it could possibly end in our own lifetimes." According to Cheney, "Reagan was one of those few," "and it was the vision and the will of Ronald Reagan that gave hope to the oppressed, shamed the oppressors, and ended the evil empire." He declared that "more than any other influence, the Cold War was ended by the perseverance and courage of one man who answered falsehood with truth, and overcame evil with good."[51]

Cheney did not stop with Reagan's achievements. He asserted that Reagan was "more than an historic figure"; indeed "he was a providential man, who came along just when our nation and the world needed him." Cheney concluded that "believing as he did that there is a plan at work in each life, he accepted not only the great duties that came to him, but also the great trials that came near the end." Cheney emphasized that even in those final years, facing the onset of Alzheimer's, Reagan was courageous and selfless: thinking only of others who would be affected by his ailments—especially his beloved Nancy. In Cheney's eulogy, Reagan came across as prophetic in regard to the Cold War. Reagan, standing virtually alone, had the courage to face evil and defeat it. Along the way, Reagan gave hope to the hopeless and inspired millions to live freely—he offered ideas and beliefs that would transcend the suffering of those behind the Iron Curtain. Finally, Cheney implied that Reagan was God's tool in ending the Cold War and uplifting the United States. In accomplishing greatness, however, Reagan suffered greatly, but even in his suffering his concern was not for himself but for those he loved and his focus was on the future of America. In many ways, Cheney presented Reagan as having had messianic qualities.[52]

The GOP leaders laid three large wreaths near the casket, and Cheney escorted Mrs. Reagan out of the rotunda. The former first lady paused, once again, and knowingly patted the casket while Michael Reagan leaned down and kissed his father goodbye. Once the Reagans and the other guests left the rotunda, the doors were opened to the public. Police estimated that between one hundred thousand and two hundred thousand people paid their respects during the thirty-four hours that Reagan lay in the rotunda before his official state funeral ceremony in the National Cathedral.[53]

More than any other dignitary, Lady Thatcher's eulogy for Reagan emphasized his prophetic role in ending the Cold War and the providential nature of his presidency. In her recorded comments, Thatcher asserted, "We have lost a great president, a great American, and a great man, and I have lost a dear friend." She insisted that Reagan confronted "daunting historic tasks" such as mending "America's wounded spirit," restoring "the strength of the free world," and freeing "the slaves of communism." Thatcher insisted that it was "hard to deny that Ronald Reagan's life was providential when we looked at what he achieved in the eight years that followed." According to Thatcher, Reagan "inspired America and its allies with renewed faith in their mission of freedom," "he transformed a stagnant economy into an engine of opportunity," and "he won the Cold War . . . without firing a shot." The former prime minister praised Reagan for "knowing his own mind," for holding "firm principles," and for possessing a resolve that "was firm and unyielding." Thatcher labeled Reagan "the great liberator" and insisted that at that very moment, Reagan was being mourned by millions across Eastern Europe. Thatcher concluded that those present "still move in twilight" but that the example of Ronald Reagan now served as a "beacon to guide us."[54] Similarly to Cheney, Thatcher painted Reagan's achievements in providential terms, arguing that his accomplishments were so great that it was hard to contemplate them being achieved by a mere mortal.

In his eulogy, President George W. Bush emphasized Reagan's commitment to principles and his willingness to address evil on the world stage. Bush began with a warm tribute to Reagan in which he lamented that "Ronald Reagan belongs to the ages now, but we preferred it when he belonged to us." Bush then turned to Reagan's accomplishments and the characteristics that enabled Reagan to succeed. The president praised the "clarity and intensity of Ronald Reagan's convictions," declaring that "he spoke to communist rulers as slave masters, of a government in Washington that had overstepped its proper limits, of a time for choosing that was drawing near." Bush explained that Reagan believed "in the power of truth in the conduct of world affairs" and that "when he saw evil camped across the horizon, he called that evil by its name." The president exclaimed that "there were no doubters in the prisons and gulags, where dissidents spread the news, tapping to each other in code what the American President had dared to say." Bush continued, "There were no doubters in the shipyards and the churches and secret labor meetings, where brave men and women began to hear the creaking and rumbling of a collapsing empire," and "there were no doubters among those who swung hammers at the hated wall as the first and hardest blow had been struck by President Ronald Reagan." The president concluded that communism viewed history as unfolding according to cold and impersonal rules, whereas "Reagan believed instead in the courage and triumph of free men."[55] Although Bush did not include any biblical allusions to tie Reagan to a providential mission, he insisted that Reagan's success in foreign affairs was due to his moral courage. According to Bush, who was implementing a similar policy in 2004, it was Reagan's willingness to paint foreign policy in terms of good and evil that granted the United States the moral clarity to win the Cold War.[56]

Although many of the eulogies insisted that Reagan won the Cold War through his unflinching commitment to his conservative principles, President George H. W. Bush reminded those present of Reagan's use of diplomacy in foreign affairs. Bush acknowledged that Reagan "believed in freedom so he acted on behalf of its values and ideals" to become "the great liberator." Bush insisted, however, that it was through Reagan's "relationship with Mikhail Gorbachev" that "the Gipper, and yes Mikhail Gorbachev, won one for peace around the world." Bush concluded that although Reagan "fought hard for his beliefs" and "led from conviction," he "never made an adversary into an enemy."[57] Bush, unlike most of the other speakers, maintained that Reagan's accomplishments were possible because of his willingness to engage in diplomacy and develop personal relationships with those who disagreed with him. Furthermore, Bush offered those present a more nuanced, and accurate, reason for why the Cold War ended. As Reagan had done a decade earlier, Bush gave credit to Gorbachev and his policies for bringing the seemingly endless conflict to an end.

Former secretary general Mikhail Gorbachev also emphasized the importance of diplomacy when he delivered his eulogy for Reagan at the Russian Embassy. He praised Reagan as "an extraordinary political leader" and lauded him for deciding "to be a peacemaker." Gorbachev did not find it "serious," however, to claim that Reagan won the Cold War. Instead, Gorbachev explained that both sides had "lost the Cold War, particularly the Soviet Union," because both sides "lost $10 trillion." Gorbachev insisted that "we only won when the Cold War ended." He also dismissed "all that talk that somehow Reagan's arm race" forced him and the Soviets "to look for some arms reductions." Gorbachev insisted, perhaps for his own reasons, that "the Soviet Union could have withstood any arms race." Reagan did deserve credit, according to

Gorbachev, for embracing a more conciliatory tone toward the Soviet Union in his second term. In the former secretary general's view, it was Reagan's willingness to change his views and work diplomatically with the Soviet Union that made him a great leader and contributed to the end of the Cold War. Gorbachev recalled that Reagan's views on the Soviet Union changed so much that when Reagan visited Moscow in 1988, the president told reporters that he no longer regarded "the Soviet Union as an evil empire."[58] To Gorbachev, it was Reagan's willingness to change, adapt, and be flexible when addressing foreign affairs that was admirable. In short, Gorbachev believed that Reagan's foreign policy legacy, and his role in ending the Cold War, should emphasize his pragmatic willingness to compromise and negotiate with those whom he saw as his adversaries.[59]

The two conflicting reasons for Reagan's success, his political pragmatism versus his dogmatic commitment to principle, continued to be debated after his death. In time, however, those who lived during the Reagan presidency and those who were present when the Cold War ended were drowned out by ideologues who believed Reagan's greatness could be found in his bellicose rhetoric and his unfailing commitment to conservative principles. From 2004 to 2016, the Reagan legacy would take a back seat to the Reagan myth as conservatives shifted from an emphasis on what Reagan achieved to how he achieved it. Indeed, Reagan would be resurrected as a conservative purist whose unflinching rigidity and commitment to principle were the keys to his greatness.

13. Reconstructing Reagan: How Conservatives Created a Mythical Reagan, 2004–2008

Shortly after what would have been President Reagan's one-hundredth birthday, in 2011, he became the center of rigorous debate on the floor of Congress. Democratic representative Mike Quigley (D-IL) invoked Reagan's support for raising the debt ceiling as evidence of how unreasonable Quigley's Republican, and specifically Tea Party, colleagues had become. Quigley read a 1983 letter that Reagan wrote to Congress in which the president asserted, "The full consequences of default—or even the serious prospect of default—by the United States are impossible to predict and awesome to contemplate." Quigley declared that "in the year of his 100th birthday, the Great Communicator might be amazed at how far his own image has shifted from the original." The Democratic congressman continued, "He'd see his most dedicated followers using his name as justification for saying no to honoring our debts" and "he'd see his legacy used to play chicken with the world's greatest economic engine."[1]

During the 2011 debate over the debt ceiling, Republicans attempted to use Reagan's antigovernment rhetoric as a justification for not fully funding the government. Representative Trent Franks (R-AZ) avowed that implementing budget caps would enable the United States to become "that great city on a hill that Ronald Reagan spoke of." Representative Marsha Blackburn (R-TN), justifying her opposition to the debt-ceiling increase, reminded Congress that Reagan was correct when he declared, "The closest thing to eternal life on Earth is a federal government program." Texas Republican congressman Kevin Brady insisted that the Reagan thing to do would be to not raise the debt ceiling, as he cited Reagan's joke that "the nine most terrifying words in the English language are 'I'm from the government and I'm here to help.'"[2] Instead of simply passing another continuing resolution on the budget, which would allow wasteful federal programs to persist, Franks, Blackburn, Brady, and others called for Republicans to embrace Reagan and force President Obama to cut spending.

During the ensuing battle, congressional Democrats continued to maintain that Reagan would support the increase in the debt ceiling. John Larson, the House Democratic Caucus chairman, played an audio recording from Reagan to prove that the Gipper was on the Democrats' side. In the recording, Reagan began by condemning Congress for constantly bringing "the government to edge of default before facing its responsibility." Reagan continued that "this brinkmanship threatens the holders of government bonds and those who rely on Social Security and veterans' benefits." The president insisted that if the debt ceiling was not raised, "interest rates would skyrocket, instability would occur in financial markets, and the federal deficit would soar." Reagan concluded, in a tone very similar to President Obama's admonishment of Congress, that "the United States has a special responsibility to itself and to the world to meet its obligations." In an op-ed for the *Washington Post*, columnist Dana Milbank concluded that it was "clear that the Tea Party Republicans have little regard for the policies of the president they claim to venerate."[3]

Milbank's observation that the Tea Party's conception of Reagan did not correspond with Reagan's actual policy positions is correct. From Reagan's death in 2004 to the candidacy of Ted Cruz in 2016, some conservatives created a mythical Reagan whose dogmatic commitment to twenty-first-century conservative principles enabled him to win the Cold War and revitalize the American economy. From 2004 to 2016, what it meant to be a conservative, or at least who qualified as one, radically changed. Conservative purists rebuked George W. Bush for attempting to pass immigration reform in 2006.[4] Furthermore, in 2008 Bush's support for the Troubled Asset Relief Program (TARP) and his embrace of Keynesian stimulus as a means to combat the Great Recession also infuriated them.

In response to what they viewed as Bush's betrayal of his conservative principles, conservatives began to contemplate leaving the Republican Party. Only John McCain's choice of Alaska governor Sarah Palin as his running mate ensured that many grassroots conservatives supported the 2008 GOP ticket.[5] In the wake of President Obama's election as the first black president, the passage of the American Recovery and Reinvestment Act, the federal government's bailout of the auto industry, and the passage of the Affordable Care Act, grassroots conservatism flourished. The rise of the Taxed Enough Already movement, the Tea Party, reinvented American conservatism and reinvigorated the debate over President Reagan's legacy—shifting it significantly to the right.[6]

From 2010 to 2016, conservatives engaged in a civil war over the future of the Republican Party, and at the center of that debate were disagreements concerning Reagan's legacy. Conservative purists defended their dogmatic commitment to conservative principles and their unwillingness to compromise by reinforcing the myth of Reagan as an unrelenting conservative. Reagan's success, which these purists attributed to his rigid adherence to conservative principles, became a powerful weapon against those Republicans who claimed governance required compromise. The Tea Party was not a monolith. Some Tea Party advocates and candidates—such as Michael Reagan and Rand Paul—argued that Reagan was successful because of his ability to engage with the opposition to find solutions.[7] Most of the Tea Party, however, embraced Ted Cruz and his portrayal of Reagan as a dogmatic conservative.[8]

At the heart of the argument over Reagan's legacy was the debate concerning the future of the Republican Party. Pragmatic conservatives, those who argued that the GOP must reach out to Latinos, African Americans, and women and shift its positions on social issues to correspond with the changing culture, insisted that Reagan was a successful president because of the pragmatic and strategic application of his conservative principles. Conservative pundits, intellectuals, and politicians such as David Frum, Arthur Brooks, Matt Lewis, Rand Paul, John Boehner, Paul Ryan, Marco Rubio, and others (while undoubtedly having differences themselves) fought for the legacy of Reagan as a pragmatic conservative who understood the necessity of compromise.[9] In contrast, Ann Coulter, Rush Limbaugh, Sean Hannity, Phyllis Schlafly, Richard Viguerie, Glenn Beck, Laura Ingraham, Ted Cruz, and others (although once again having significant differences among themselves) fought for a legacy of Reagan as dogmatically committed to conservative principles.[10] This struggle for the meaning of Reagan's legacy and the future of the Republican Party divided the GOP and resulted in many voters and political commentators doubting whether conservatives were capable of governing.[11]

The definition of Reagan's legacy, which had held conservatives together in the wake of the Cold War, was itself hotly debated and as such threatened to tear apart an already deeply fractured conservative coalition. Furthermore, the advent of dogmatic principled conservatism and the Reagan myth alienated segments of the American population that were essential to the GOP's quest to win the White House. While conservatives were arguing whether Marco Rubio, Rand Paul, or Ted Cruz represented true Reagan conservatism, Donald Trump almost completely ignored Reagan, although at one point he did quip that Reagan had admired him.[12] Trump capitalized on the frustration and dissatisfaction that many of the Reagan purists, including those in talk radio, had helped stoke for over a decade.[13] In Trump, the GOP nominated neither a pragmatic conservative who could appeal to minority voters nor a dogmatic politician committed to conservative principles.[14] Instead, they got a brash billionaire businessman and reality TV star who did not have the faintest interest in conservatism or the legacy of Ronald Reagan.[15]

Even before Reagan was entombed at his library in Simi Valley, the *New York Times* began discussing how President Bush would link himself to Reagan in the 2004 presidential election. The *Times* declared that "the White House's efforts to follow the Reagan playbook have been nothing if not relentless" despite the fact that "no politician in his right mind would even invite comparisons to the Great Communicator." Yet, "no one has more strenuously tried to emulate the 40th president in both style and substance than George W. Bush." The *Times* noted that "Reagan's body was barely cold" when Republican chairman Ed Gillespie declared that "the parallels" between Reagan and Bush were "there" and exclaimed that he did not "know how you miss them." The *Times* concluded that Bush was "eradicating his patrician one term father to adopt the two-term Gipper as his dad instead."[16]

The next day, during his eulogy for his father, Reagan's liberal son and namesake, Ron Reagan, delivered a devastating critique to those who would claim his father's mantle. Ron Reagan began by reminding the audience that his dad "treated everyone with the same unfailing courtesy—acknowledging the innate dignity in us all." Reagan continued that "the idea that all people are created equal was more than mere words on a page, it was how he lived his life." In what was interpreted as an attack on President Bush, Ron Reagan exclaimed that while his dad was "a deeply, unabashedly religious man," "he never made the fatal mistake of so many politicians—wearing his faith on his sleeve to gain political advantage." Reagan concluded that it was true that after his father "was shot and nearly killed early in his presidency, he came to believe that God had spared him in order that he might do good. But he accepted that as a responsibility, not a mandate. And there is a profound difference."[17] Much to Ron Reagan's chagrin, President Reagan was too important a symbol for Republicans to let his legacy be buried with him in those peaceful western mountains. Instead, the meaning of Reagan conservatism would become the center of the debate over the future of the Republican Party.

Two weeks after Reagan was laid to rest, conservatives paid tribute to

Reagan in a memorial edition of *National Review*. In doing so, however, two very different versions of Reagan's legacy emerged. Dinesh D'Souza, conservative author and commentator, wrote that "the secret of Reagan's success was that throughout his career he pursued his convictions with bold disregard for the two most powerful forces in politics: the American people and the elites." D'Souza concluded that "Reagan was willing to go against the polls, and take on the elites—these were the crucial elements of his success."[18] Larry Kudlow, the assistant director of economics and planning in the Office of Management and Budget during Reagan's first term, wrote that Reagan "never faltered" in his "unequivocal belief in freedom and democracy." Kudlow concluded with a quasi-religious reverence for the fortieth president: "Reagan saved America. His passing is a sad occasion. But as his soul gazes down from the heavens, he will see that his ideas will live forever."[19] Rush Limbaugh, in his tribute titled "The Great One," presented Reagan as a relentless advocate of conservative principles who "rejected socialism and big government." According to Limbaugh, Reagan "slashed taxes," "rejected communism, détente, and containment," and "set us on a course to win—not manage—the Cold War." Limbaugh then explained that he had often wondered what Reagan would say about the war on terror. To justify his conclusion that Reagan would have supported Bush, the conservative commentator cited Reagan's speech on the fortieth anniversary of D-Day, in which Reagan asserted that "there is a profound moral difference between the use of force for liberation and the use of force for conquest." Limbaugh concluded that "Reagan was right, as George W. Bush is right today. And I believe that if President Reagan had been able, he would have put his hand on President's Bush's shoulder and said to him, 'Stay the Course, George.'"[20] Together, D'Souza, Kudlow, and Limbaugh venerated Reagan and concluded that his success should be attributed to his commitment to conservative principles.

Other conservatives attributed Reagan's success to his willingness to pragmatically apply conservative principles and his willingness to work with those who disagreed with him. William F. Buckley reprinted a keynote address he delivered in 1999 in which he praised Reagan's ability to switch gears between moral indignation and diplomacy when dealing with the Soviet Union. According to Buckley, Reagan's dual strategy resulted in him "bringing peace in our time!"[21] *National Review* in its official tribute explained that Reagan was "the first, so far the only, president drawn from the conservative-movement ranks." It characterized Reagan as "a conservative statesman" who tailored his "program" to suit "the circumstances he found," and as someone who "set priorities, which meant that lower priorities were sacrificed." For example, *National Review* explained Reagan "correctly judged it more important to win the Cold War than shrink the state." The publication concluded that conservatives had "correctly judged his successes as more important than his disappointments and defeats."[22]

Although both Buckley and *National Review* emphasized the importance of Reagan's diplomacy and pragmatism to Reagan's success, neither was as forceful as Victor Davis Hanson, a senior fellow at the Hoover Institute, in dismissing Reagan's commitment to conservative principles. Hanson declared that "Ronald Reagan's legacy is not one of ideological purity." He reminded conservatives that Reagan "raised taxes and signed liberal abortion legislation in California" and insisted that "despite his 'evil empire' speech, he was not the preeminent Cold Warrior." Hanson emphasized that it "was Barry Goldwater who laid the foundations of sagebrush conservatism" and recalled that "federal spending went up during Reagan's two presidential terms."[23] Unlike Buckley and *National Review*, Hanson lamented Reagan's halfhearted commitment to conservative principles. In time, critiques like Hanson's largely faded from the conservative discourse surrounding Reagan's legacy, and two versions remained: Reagan as a purist conservative and Reagan as a pragmatic conservative.

Both interpretations of President Reagan's legacy were present at the 2004 Republican National Convention, but Michael Reagan—a conservative talk show host—attempted to place his father above partisan politics. On the third night of the convention, Michael Reagan set the stage for a tribute to his father produced by the Reagan Foundation. He began by thanking Americans across the country for the outpouring of love "during the week we laid my father to rest." Reagan told the audience that one well-wisher, Jorge Rodriguez, left his passport at the Reagan Library with a message for the Reagan family. Rodriguez wrote that "because of President Reagan, my family and I were able to achieve the American Dream. God bless Ronald Reagan!" The inclusion of Rodriguez's story seems strategically placed to remind Latino voters that Reagan, and by extension Republicans, had passed comprehensive immigration reform in the 1980s. Its presence, however, marked a deviation from the interpretation that Reagan was a committed conservative who never strayed from what right-wing commentators viewed as true Reagan conservatism. Michael Reagan insisted that because of his dad, "we are that shining city on a hill and we shine a little bit brighter tonight." He concluded that it was "with pride, ladies and gentlemen, I present to you a video tribute to the Fortieth President of the United States, my dad, Ronald Wilson Reagan."[24]

The 2004 video tribute to President Reagan presented both conceptions of Reagan's legacy and began the process of viewing Reagan as a mythic figure who renewed America. The lights dimmed and taps played as the video titled *The Final Journey* began. Images of Reagan's funeral panned to the president riding his white horse as the commentator said "America bids farewell to a hero." According to the video, "Reagan's greatest legacy was giving America back its optimism and its sense of pride." As the tribute flashed back to the 1980s, New York mayor Rudy Giuliani asserted that "Reagan was a statesman of the first order, persuasive, disarming, instinctive. He inspired America and the entire world with the clarity of his vision and his sense of direction and purpose." Henry Kissinger, in the same clip from the 1996 tribute, declared that "Ronald Reagan ended the Cold War." He was immediately followed by Reagan demanding that Gorbachev "tear down this wall." Images of the Berlin Wall being ripped apart panned across the screen as Reagan recalled "the Iron Curtain came down for good and the special joy I felt was that the answer came in my own lifetime." The video then pivoted and emphasized Reagan's diplomatic prowess, showing images of Reagan and Gorbachev signing the INF Treaty. Howard Baker, Reagan's former chief of staff, explained that "Reagan was one superb negotiator. . . . Indeed he could charm the birds out of the trees, but it was his idealism and his endless strength and courage that put America and the world on the road to lasting peace."[25] The first half of the tribute implied the importance of both Reagan's bellicose rhetoric and his diplomacy in ending the Cold War. There was tension, however, between what Giuliani and Baker chose to emphasize, and the question of whether it was Reagan's principles or his willingness to compromise that led to his success was left unanswered.

As the video returned to the funeral, Reagan was presented as a mythic figure, and President Bush was tied to his legacy. Reverend Daniel Coughlin, chaplain of the House of Representatives, exclaimed that "with his style and grace [Reagan] made it seem easy, with his compassion and sense of timing, he brought strength of character to the nation and enkindled hope in a darkened world." Speaker of the House Dennis Hastert proclaimed that "while others worried, President Reagan persevered," "when others weakened, President Reagan stood tall," "when others stepped back, President Reagan stepped forward, and he did it all with great humility, with great charm, and with great humor." The tribute showed Vice President Cheney delivering his eulogy for Reagan and standing by Mrs. Reagan. Later, the video flashed to the National Cathedral, where George W. Bush delivered his eulogy to Reagan. Images of Bush escorting Nancy Reagan to her seat and comforting her played as Bush lamented that "Ronald Reagan belongs to the ages now, but we preferred it when he belonged to us." As the video came to an end, a final bit of text, "Ronald Wilson Reagan, An American Hero, 1911–2004," appeared on the screen as "I'm proud to be an American" rang triumphant throughout the convention hall. The delegates cheered and held up signs that read "Win One for the Gipper."[26]

The purpose of the tribute video was not only to celebrate President Reagan's life, but also to establish Bush as Reagan's heir and capitalize on the outpouring of goodwill that America had showed during the funeral. The convention organizers followed up the Reagan tribute with a video of Bush titled "President Bush: Fulfilling America's Promise" in a further attempt to tie Bush to Reagan.[27] Although it is unclear whether linking himself with Reagan helped Bush win reelection, the 2004 convention showcased the two competing understandings of Reagan's legacy. The debate between those who viewed Reagan's success as a product of his rigid commitment to principle and those who emphasized his willingness to compromise continued into Bush's second term.

Reagan's death sparked a renewed interest in what it meant to be a Reagan conservative. In 2005, Michael Deaver edited a volume titled *Why I Am a Reagan Conservative* featuring prominent conservatives from across the country and occupational spectrum.[28] He dedicated the book "to Ronald Reagan, who changed all our lives," and in the introduction Deaver asserted that "all of us who describe ourselves, for various reasons, as conservatives, stand on the shoulders of Ronald Reagan because he made conservatism respectable, acceptable, and now mainstream."[29] The volume was a testament to the extent to which Reagan and his legacy had indeed become the glue that tied the various strands of conservatism together. Although most of the contributors had different views of what it meant to be a Reagan conservative, all agreed that Reagan represented their values and that they looked to the fortieth president as the foundation for the evolution of the conservative movement.

Although the contributors disagreed on what it meant to be a Reagan conservative, they predominately credited Reagan's commitment to conservative principles as the reason for his success. Conservative journalist Robert Novak asserted that to be a conservative, one had to "think the government always is the problem rather than the solution." Novak insisted that "Ronald Reagan and Calvin Coolidge" were "the only presidents of the Twentieth and Twenty-First centuries who agree with that."[30] The implication was that George W. Bush was not a true conservative because he had worked with Democrats to use government to address problems he believed needed to be addressed. Ken Mehlman, the chairman of the Republican National Committee, contended that "Ronald Reagan, Margaret Thatcher, and John Paul II . . . promoted peace by their moral, military, and intellectual campaign against international communism." These principled "conservative leaders," according to Mehlman, "by speaking truth . . . brought down the Berlin Wall without firing a shot." Turning to the war on terror, Mehlman insisted that Republicans needed to embrace "the path of Reagan and Churchill" and reaffirm the conservative commitment to "the mandate of freedom." Mehlman concluded that a "peaceful ending" to the war on terror depended—"as always—on our renewed commitment" to the conservative principle of resistance to tyranny.[31] Both Novak and Mehlman agreed with Donald J. Devine, the vice chairman of the American Conservative Union, when he concluded that the United States needed to "return to the original vision of conservatism" as embodied by Reagan.[32]

Despite disagreements about Reagan's views on specific issues, the compilation demonstrated that a wide range of conservative politicians and intellectuals had embraced the myth that Reagan was successful because of his relentless commitment to conservative principles. Edwin Meese III, Reagan's attorney general, insisted that Reagan's "leadership and advocacy demonstrated that conservative principles worked in practice and promoted economic growth, individual freedom, and political success."[33] Martin Anderson, Reagan's domestic policy adviser, mockingly quipped that how Reagan won the Cold War, revitalized the economy, and restored America's morale "is still somewhat of a mystery to historians." Anderson insisted Reagan's success began with his "brilliant mind" and "tireless work" ethic but added "if you don't have the courage and toughness to stick with what you believe, no matter what happens, you will never have a chance of doing what Reagan did." Anderson concluded that the answer to politicians who ask themselves, "What Would

Reagan Do?" was "obvious"—they needed to commit themselves to conservative principles.[34] Just a year after Reagan's death, a powerful myth was created to explain why President Bush was failing where Reagan succeeded. According to the fifty-four conservatives who contributed to Deaver's compilation, Reagan's legacy was defined by his commitment to conservative principles, and any deviation from the conservative creed would result in failure.

In 2006, during the debate over President Bush's proposed comprehensive immigration reform, Reagan's position in the 1980s became central to the discussion.[35] William Bennett, Robert Bork, Ward Connerly, Newt Gingrich, David Horowitz, David Keene, and Phyllis Schlafly issued an open letter to Republican members of Congress opposing any sort of "amnesty" and demanding the passage of enforcement-only legislation. Other conservatives—including Grover Norquist, Jack Kemp, J. C. Watts, Steve Forbes, and Jeane Kirkpatrick—according to one press report, "pulled out the big guns by boldly claiming the mantel of the GOP's patron saint: Ronald Reagan." These conservatives insisted that Republicans should "remember the counsel of the great conservative standard-bearer, Ronald Reagan," who "constantly reminded us that America must remain a 'beacon' and a 'shining city on a hill' for immigrants who continually renew our great country with their energy and add to the nation's economic growth and prosperity." Although they agreed that border security was important, Norquist, Kemp, Watts, Forbes, and Kirkpatrick insisted that "the best way—the only way—to realize President Reagan's vision is through comprehensive immigration reform legislation."[36] Many conservatives, including President Bush, attempted to use Reagan's pragmatic application of conservative principles on immigration as justification for comprehensive immigration reform. These conservatives believed that for the GOP to be successful in the upcoming presidential election, the party needed to reach out to Latino Americans by presenting itself as more inclusive and reasonable on the issue of immigration.

Responding to those who were using Reagan's legacy to promote a pathway to citizenship, conservatives who attributed his success to a dogmatic commitment to conservative principles dismissed Reagan's pragmatic views on immigration reform. Edwin Meese III penned an op-ed explaining that although "it is very difficult to directly translate particular political decisions to another context, in another time," he believed Reagan would oppose comprehensive immigration reform. Meese insisted that Reagan "would not repeat the mistakes of the past, including those of his own administration." Meese asserted that Reagan understood the importance of "secure borders" and "would now insist on meeting that priority first." Furthermore, Reagan "would seek to strengthen the enforcement of existing immigration laws." Far from violating conservative principles, Meese declared that conservatives should embrace Reagan's "principled policy" of "humanely regaining control of our borders" and preserving "the value of one of the most sacred possessions of our people: American citizenship."[37]

While Meese insisted that conservatives meet the challenge of immigration by keeping "open the door of opportunity," other conservatives insisted on a hardline approach.[38] Responding to Republicans and conservatives who were for immigration reform, Howard Phillips, Phyllis Schlafly, Richard Viguerie, and other prominent conservative purists held a press conference. They declared they would "dedicate [themselves] to defeating any presidential candidate" who supported legislation "that provides legalization for illegal immigrants or substantially increases legal immigration."[39] For conservatives who believed that the best way to govern was to replicate President's Reagan's commitment to principle, the fortieth president's support for comprehensive immigration reform and praise of immigration posed problems. The best way to overcome this apparent contradiction was to declare that Reagan would "not repeat" his "amnesty mistake" and instead claim that he would have embraced a hardline position in 2006.[40]

Regardless of what Reagan would have done in 2006, Bush lost the debate over immigration reform. Members of the GOP leadership undermined his efforts, and grassroots activists rebelled against the president. House minority leader John Boehner, speaking at a private reception for the Republican Rapid Responders, made headlines when he told the audience that he "promised the president today that I wouldn't say anything about . . . this piece of shit bill."[41] Furthermore, as Richard Viguerie noted, "'comprehensive immigration reform' cost [Bush] whatever support he had left with the conservative grass roots."[42] As the Bush administration came to a close, many conservatives felt as though they had been betrayed. Bush had presented himself as a true Reagan conservative, but after six years he had expanded the size and scope of government and had done little to advance the conservative agenda.[43]

———————

As George W. Bush's presidency unraveled in 2006, conservatives looked to Reagan for answers about how he would approach contemporary issues. Conservatives began using the acronym WWRD (What Would Reagan Do?) in the early 2000s, but it was in Bush's second term that its use became widespread. In September 2005, Ann Coulter wrote an article in which she urged Bush to ask himself "WWRD?" when selecting a replacement for Justice Sandra Day O'Connor. Coulter explained to readers that "for Christians, it's 'What Would Jesus Do?'" but "for Republicans, it's 'What Would Reagan Do?'" Coulter insisted that "Bush doesn't have to be Reagan he just has to consult his WWRD bracelet." She acknowledged that there was a "'Sandra Day O'Connor bylaw' to the WWRD guidelines: Never appoint anyone like Sandra Day O'Connor to any court at any level."[44] The presence of bylaws to the WWRD mantra demonstrated that conservative purists, if unknowingly, recognized that Ronald Reagan—the man—would also have needed a goofy bracelet to remind him to live up to the example set by Ronald Reagan—the myth.

The use of WWRD increased in the lead-up to the 2008 presidential election. Determined to usher in the second coming of Ronald Reagan, the Heritage Foundation collaborated with talk radio conservative commentators Sean Hannity and Laura Ingraham to wage a one-year crusade to encourage voters and candidates to consider what Reagan would do in 2008.[45] The Heritage Foundation dedicated a section of its website to videos and articles detailing "What Would Reagan Do?," and Sean Hannity used his program on Fox News to deliver segments exploring the same question. Before long, T-shirts, bracelets, posters, and bumper stickers were widely available. Trying to explain this phenomenon, the *New York Times* asserted that the conservative movement had "lost its way." It noted that "across the spectrum of the right, writers and thinkers have turned their relentless analysis inward, a kind of political EST seminar aimed at self-transformation." According to the *Times*, many conservatives had concluded that "the conservative decline" was "simply the result of veering away from the golden age of Ronald Reagan." Jonathan Rauch of the Brookings Institute agreed that many conservatives were exclaiming: "Reagan got it right and the party strayed too far."[46]

The 2008 Republican primary debates demonstrated Rauch's point. According to the *Weekly Standard*, "the first two GOP presidential debates" proved that "Reagan remains emblematic of American conservatism." At a debate held at the Reagan Library, the candidates invoked Reagan's name nineteen times. The *Weekly Standard* concluded that "conscious of their vulnerability on the right, Rudy Giuliani, John McCain, and Mitt Romney have all made bids for the Reagan mantle," and "their fallback question seems to be: 'What Would Reagan Do?'"[47] Imbuing Reagan's legacy with quasi-religious language and acronyms, complete with memorabilia, enabled those who viewed Reagan as a conservative purist to imprint their conception of Reagan's legacy on the national consciousness.

Purist conservatives were pleased that Republicans were trying to emulate Reagan's legacy of sticking to his conservative principles. The conservative website *Townhall*, in an article titled "What Would Reagan Do?," insisted that candidates were invoking Reagan's name "because they sense that Americans are looking for true leadership based on the bedrock principles of our Founding Fathers" including "limited government, a strong national defense, traditional values and individual freedom." *Townhall* exclaimed that "Ronald Reagan proved that when you govern according to these conservative principles—when you do not waver—when you are steadfast and true to freedom—America flourishes." The website concluded that "Ronald Reagan's legacy is defined by timeless principles, fearless leadership and visionary solutions."[48] The creation of the myth that Reagan was successful because of his unwavering commitment to conservative principles ignored many of Reagan's accomplishments that were the product of compromise—such as Social Security reform, immigration reform, and the INF Treaty especially. Likewise, the Reagan myth provided a convenient way to separate the conservative movement from an unpopular president and to claim that Bush's failure stemmed from his deviation from unchanging conservative principles. In short, conservatism had not failed during the Bush years, Bush had failed conservatives.

The president of the Heritage Foundation, Ed Feulner, reinforced the myth that Reagan was successful because of a rigid commitment to conservative principles. Feulner declared that "Ronald Reagan secured victory because he spoke powerfully to the American people about conservative principles—which he would not compromise!" Feulner concluded that Reagan "governed by conservative principles," never "compromising" or "giving into pressure."[49] In the wake of the Bush administration, Feulner and others were outlining a way forward and it was simple: return to the principles that made Reagan successful. Unfortunately, as Feulner and other conservatives resurrected Reagan to guide the GOP into the future, they forgot the rigorous debates between Reagan and conservatives during the 1980s—debates in which many of them had participated and which revolved around Reagan's own deviation from conservative orthodoxy.

Not all conservatives agreed with the presentation of Reagan as a conservative purist. The *Weekly Standard* acknowledged that "in big-picture terms, Reagan was a very conservative—and very successful—chief executive, who dragged the entire political spectrum rightward." But, the publication explained, the contemporary presentation of "Reagan tends to be somewhat one-dimensional." According to the *Weekly Standard*, had Reagan "truly been as doctrinaire and unwavering as many now seem to imagine he was, chances are he would have been less popular." The journal concluded by recounting neoconservative Norman Podhoretz's recollections on President Reagan:

> Ronald Reagan was much more of a conventional politician than he was taken to be. It is this that explains why he could so often compromise and sometimes violate even key elements of his putatively rock-bottom convictions; or why he tried mightily to pretend both to his friends and his opponents (and in some instances to himself as well) that he was doing no such thing; or why he was even willing to reverse course altogether for the sake of victory.[50]

Other conservatives went beyond simply correcting conservative purists' conceptions of Reagan. After Senator John McCain's loss to President Obama, conservative columnist and author David Frum declared that "the nub of the problem" facing the GOP was "not deviance from the 1980s agenda but worshipful adherence to it."[51] In the wake of the 2008 election, Frum attempted to become the spokesman for a twenty-first-century pragmatic conservatism. His commentary drew the ire of Sean Hannity and other conservatives who desired a more principled conservatism. At the heart of the debate between Frum's and Hannity's conflicting visions for the future was their differing understandings of Reagan's legacy and the reasons for his success.

Following McCain's defeat, Frum wrote *Comeback: Conservatism That Can Win Again*, in which he argued that conservatives needed to stop harkening back to Reagan and instead create an agenda that confronted the issues of the day. Frum, a neoconservative speech writer for President George W. Bush, recalled that "Bush often told aides that his top political priority was to 'change the party,' that is, to move it away from the Reagan-style conservatism of the 1980s towards a new, softer centrism." This strategy, according

to Frum, led to Bush's political alienation from his base because conservatives had believed "that he was leading the nation back toward Reagan-style
conservatism." But, Frum insisted, it had been the correct strategy. Despite
Bush's failure in changing the GOP, Frum insisted that the GOP could not
return "to Reaganism, because Reagan Republicanism offers solutions to the
problems of forty years before, not to those of the twenty-first century." He
argued that "both the country and the party have to work forward from the
Bush experience, not back to some mythical golden past."[52] Discussing how
the GOP primary candidates all attempted to take up Reagan's mantle, Frum
lamented that not one of them had asserted that "what made [Reagan] great
was his ability to respond to the demands of his times" and added, "we must
respond to the demands of ours."[53] By embracing Reagan as a pragmatic conservative, Frum explained that conservatives could take up the Reagan mantle
without being confined by it. Frum exclaimed that "from Lincoln to Churchill
to Reagan, the greatest conservatives have recognized that sometimes the only
way to conserve is to change."[54] Frum then outlined how conservatives should
apply their principles to education, environmentalism, health care, trade, social issues, and more. Frum's insistence that conservatives leave Reagan and
his legacy in the past and focus on a new conservative vision was prudent, if a
bit naïve. Frum quickly came under fire from purist conservatives who viewed
him as an apostate.

Sean Hannity emerged as one of the most vocal critics of Frum. In his
2010 book *Conservative Victory: Defeating Obama's Radical Agenda*, Hannity
denounced Frum and those who agreed with him as "self-serving attention
seekers desperately trying to be loved by the mainstream media."[55] Hannity
decried Frum's mistaken belief "that the time has passed for traditional Reagan conservatism" and belittled his willingness to "capitulate to the inevita-
bility of big government." Hannity summed up Frum's new conservativism
as "wrongheaded, cynically pragmatic, and ultimately destructive to our first
principles and the timeless ends of American constitutional governance."[56]
The Fox News commentator explained that "the arrival of modern times"
does not require "us to abandon timeless principles," adding that this belief
was his "main philosophical difference" with Frum. Hannity denounced "the
purveyors of this new brand of conservatism" for "abandoning, modifying,
or diluting traditionally conservative principles, primarily because they don't
believe in them to the extent that mainstream conservatives do." Indeed,
Hannity exclaimed, for these "big-government conservatives . . . there are

few conservative hills to die on." Hannity concluded that "the logical conclusion—and, if widely adopted, the destiny—of Frumism is a surrender to liberalism, through the slow abandonment of core principles and the ceding of political turf."[57] Hannity easily dismissed Frum as abandoning conservative principles and instead insisted that the future of conservative success rested on its return to Reagan conservatism.

Hannity did more than just repudiate Frum in *Conservative Victory*; he also laid out a vision for how conservatives could defeat President Obama and "his socialism."[58] For Hannity, the future of the GOP depended on returning to the timeless principles that made Reagan successful. According to Hannity, Reagan's legacy was defined by his commitment to principle. In the wake of the 2008 defeat, Hannity insisted that conservatives embrace Reagan, who himself had "felt strongly that the best path forward for Republicans must involve a rigorous adherence to conservative principles, not a softening of their resolve or a dilution of their core convictions in the service of compromise." Hannity declared that conservatives who desired the party to grow needed to remember that Reagan, "by clearly laying out his commonsense principles," attracted "the widest grouping of Americans to this 'new' Republican Party *without* compromising fundamental principles." Hannity added that "modern polls continue to speak to the timelessness of his approach."[59] In short, conservatives did not need to compromise their principles to grow the party as Frum and others insisted. For Hannity, the recipe for conservative success was simple—return to the true conservative principles as embodied by Ronald Reagan.

Although Frum attempted to get conservatives to think beyond their first principles to address contemporary political issues, the way he framed his argument made it too easy for conservative purists to dismiss him for abandoning conservative principles. Furthermore, Frum's new conservatism too often embraced the federal government as a means to address social and economic problems. This made it incompatible with the conservative worldview that individuals, not government, are most capable to address the problems in their communities. Frum was correct, however, that conservative principles needed to be applied in new and innovative ways to contemporary issues. Instead of rejecting Reagan as a point of reference, Frum's cause would have been better served by emphasizing Reagan's willingness to compromise and build coalitions to govern. By ceding Reagan's legacy to Hannity, Frum opened himself up to charges that he was a shill of the "mainstream media" and a "big-government conservative," a label that was purposefully designed to be an oxymoron.[60]

As a result, Hannity's insistence that the GOP double down on conservative principles carried the day. In many ways, Hannity's case was the easier of the two to make. It confirmed for his conservative audience their belief in the righteousness of their principles and reinforced the myth that Reagan's success was a result of his uncompromising commitment to conservative principles. As Hannity was finishing his book, a dramatic grassroots conservative movement transformed American politics. The emergence of the Tea Party seemed to confirm Hannity's belief that the United States was still "a center-right nation" that rejected President Obama's promise of "fundamental change."[61] In the immediate wake of the Tea Party, the conversation about the nature of conservatism in the twenty-first century was pushed aside, and conservatives embraced the role of the principled opposition to Obama and big-government Republicans.

14. Resurrecting Reagan: The Tea Party Movement and the Manifestation of the Reagan Myth, 2008–2016

In the aftermath of the 2008 financial crisis, President Bush called for a series of policies that alienated conservatives and led to the rise of the Tea Party. Bush's support for comprehensive immigration reform, his expansion of Medicare, and the passage of the No Child Left Behind Act had already isolated him from conservatives. But it was Bush's decision to bail out the housing market with the Troubled Asset Relief Program (TARP) and his embrace of Keynesian deficit spending in the Economic Stimulus Act of 2008 that sparked widespread outrage on the right.[1]

Conservative frustration with out-of-control government spending continued after President Obama was inaugurated. On February 19, 2009, Rick Santelli, a CNBC news reporter, went on a tirade about the Homeowner Affordability and Stability Plan, which provided $75 billion to subsidize homeowners who had fallen behind on their mortgages. Santelli exclaimed that "the government is promoting bad behavior! This is America! How many of you people want to pay for your neighbor's mortgage?" Santelli condemned Obama's policies and concluded with a call to action: "We're thinking of having a Chicago Tea Party in July. All you capitalists that want to show up at Lake Michigan, I'm going to start organizing!" Video clips of Santelli went viral, and his idea of holding a Chicago Tea Party spread across the country. Before long there were Tea Party organizations being founded in every state.[2] On Tax Day (April 15) of 2009, rallies were held across the country and continued to occur spontaneously up until July 4.[3] Although the Tea Party began as a grassroots social movement, it was quickly supported by conservative organizations in the Beltway. Furthermore, conservative news commentators, especially on Fox News, ran numerous stories about the Tea Party, thereby providing much-needed news coverage for the emergent movement.[4]

As the 2010 midterms approached, the Tea Party emerged as one of the most powerful forces in American politics. New Right conservatives, such as Richard Viguerie, were ecstatic at the advent of a grassroots conservative movement. At a Tea Party leadership conference in Dallas, Viguerie exclaimed, "Hi. Where have you been? I've been waiting for you. I've been waiting for fifty years for you people."[5] Tea Party conservatives launched an all-out offensive against establishment Republicans in the primaries. Not only did the Tea Party win numerous primaries, Tea Party candidates also had success in the general election. In all, the Republicans picked up sixty-three seats in the House, forty-two of which went to Tea Party candidates.[6] In addition to their success in the House, five Tea Party candidates—Mike Lee, Marco Rubio, Rand Paul, Pat Toomey, and Ron Johnson—were elected to the Senate.[7]

Viguerie and others took the Tea Party victory as affirmation that the key to Republican electoral success was fealty to conservative principles. After the midterms, Viguerie wrote that "Big Government Republicans [should] take their place in the dustbin of history beside the slavery-accommodationist wing of the Whig Party, it is time for Tea Partiers to take the next logical step in the development of their movement." Viguerie insisted that the Tea Party should not attempt "to influence the Republican Party"; rather, it should "become the Republican Party."[8] Although the Tea Party was successful in many races, some of its candidates proved too conservative for moderate voters in their respective states. The defeat of Christine O'Donnell in Delaware, Sharron Angle in Nevada, Ken Buck in Colorado, and Joe Miller in Alaska foreshadowed the danger that the GOP faced as the Tea Party pulled Republicans further to the right—especially in presidential elections.[9]

After the 2010 midterms, conservatives attempted to frame the Tea Party as the natural successor to Ronald Reagan. Conservative journalist and activist John Hawkins's *Right Wing News* declared that "in many ways Reagan is the father of the Tea Party Movement." The website insisted that "the Reagan effect is responsible for giving Tea Partiers the feeling that they could affect government like Reagan did and that without Reagan there'd be no Tea Party movement at all."[10] Michael Reagan legitimized attempts to tie Reagan to the Tea Party when he wrote that his dad "was the tea party of his time" and that President Reagan "would have seen today's tea party as the proper response to the threat to our individual liberties represented by such legislation as so-called Obamacare." Michael Reagan went even further, asserting that Reagan "would have been in the forefront of the tea party movement, urging it on and devoting every last ounce of his energy to its progress in restoring America."[11] Conservative historian Steven F. Hayward also agreed that Reagan "would have been an enthusiastic supporter of the tea party movement." According to Hayward, "Reagan would have seen them as reviving the embers of what he called the 'prairie fire' of populist resistance against centralized big government." Hayward concluded that Reagan "would probably have cheered" Governor Sarah Palin "on and surely would have had no problem voting for her should she secure the GOP presidential nomination."[12]

Although most conservatives agreed that Reagan would have supported the Tea Party, not all were convinced that the new movement, known for its inflexible loyalty to conservative principles, would have embraced Reagan had he been a candidate in 2010. During an interview with Bill Hemmer on Fox News, Mike Huckabee declared that "Ronald Reagan would have a very difficult, if not impossible time being nominated in this atmosphere of the Republican Party." Huckabee explained that Reagan had "raised taxes as governor, he made deals with Democrats, he compromised on things in order to move the ball down the field." Huckabee continued: "As president he gave amnesty to 7 million illegal immigrants," and many of his other policies "would have been anathema." Huckabee concluded that although conservatives often claimed Reagan stood "absolutely steadfast" to his principles, in reality "you have to govern" differently "than the way you campaign."[13] Conservative representative Duncan Hunter (R-CA) shared this view. He told the San Diego chapter of Eagle Forum that Reagan was a "moderate" and a "former liberal . . . who would never be elected today."[14] Others, such as former Republican senator Bob Bennett of Utah, argued that the Tea Party was manipulating Reagan's legacy. After his defeat in the primary, Bennett exclaimed that "Ronald Reagan would probably not recognize the description of Ronald Reagan that is coming out of a lot of the Tea Party blogs."[15]

Almost as soon as the Tea Party emerged, conservatives began to debate its relation to Reagan and his legacy. Some viewed the Tea Party's success as proof that Republicans needed to follow Reagan's example of strict adherence to conservative principles. Other conservatives, and even some members of the Tea Party, were wary of the Tea Party's resistance to compromise and continued to stress the need to pragmatically apply conservative principles to contemporary issues.

These two conflicting interpretations of Reagan's legacy were present in Michael Reagan's *The New Reagan Revolution* (2010), intended as a road map for how the Tea Party could achieve its goals. Michael Reagan agreed with conservative purists who believed that the GOP needed to return to the principles of Reagan, but he also recognized that some of the reasons for his father's success—such as President Reagan's willingness to work across the aisle and compromise when necessary—had been ignored by some members of the Tea Party. In the foreword, former Speaker Newt Gingrich asserted that "this book proves that the timeless principles of Reagan conservatism are as valid today as they ever were." Gingrich added a caveat, however, that Reagan succeeded because he "built winning coalitions" and "understood that he needed to build a transpartisan majority in order to govern America effectively."[16] This nuanced narrative, that conservative principles still worked, but also that conservatives needed to compromise at times to govern effectively, was present throughout the book.

Ultimately, Michael Reagan sided with conservatives who argued that compromise and coalition building were central to President Reagan's legacy. Like most other movement conservatives, Michael Reagan fully embraced the Reagan legacy and insisted that conservatives' "next leader must be a leader of bold, unmistakable colors, waving a banner of bold principles."[17] Despite these similarities, however, Michael Reagan differed from conservative purists when it came to the practical implementation of conservative principles into policy. Michael Reagan insisted that many conservatives had forgotten that "the key to" Reagan's "phenomenal success as a president was his ability to work with opponents in his own party, opponents in the Democratic Party, and even opponents in the Kremlin."[18] He lamented that "when Ronald Reagan left, the idea of coalition building left with him. Today, conservatives take pride in their ideological purity and their unwillingness to work with others who are less than 'pure.'" As a result, the conservative "cause goes down in flames." Michael Reagan emphasized that the way to "advance your agenda" was "by incremental steps" that are achievable only "by building a coalition." He concluded that "if we subject one another to ideological litmus tests, we will never advance our cause."[19]

Michael Reagan also criticized conservatives for imposing unrealistic standards on Republican candidates. Following the 2008 election, in which many conservatives brutally condemned Republican nominee John McCain and constantly compared the Republican presidential hopefuls to the mythical Ronald Reagan, Michael Reagan flatly declared that conservatives were "not going to find a perfect candidate." He reminded conservatives that "Ronald Reagan had his flaws" and "was not 100 percent pure." He added that "despite all the respect he has garnered from conservatives" in talk radio, "Ronald Reagan couldn't win the GOP nomination today." Michael Reagan recounted that his dad "raised taxes, . . . signed a bill legalizing abortions," and "signed the first no-fault divorce law in the country." He insisted that "if Ronald Reagan were running for president today," he "would not be considered ideologically pure enough to be the standard-bearer of the party." Michael Reagan concluded that conservatives were right to "revere Ronald Reagan as the patron saint of the GOP . . . but if conservatives in 1980 had applied the same standards to Ronald Reagan that they apply to John McCain, we might never have had the economic recovery of the 1980s or the fall of the Berlin Wall."[20]

In *The New Reagan Revolution*, Michael Reagan outlined and presented an alternative vision of his father's legacy to that of conservative purists. He emphasized that to govern, conservatives needed to build coalitions and pragmatically apply Reagan's principles to contemporary issues. Instead of taking Michael Reagan's advice and building coalitions to govern effectively, pragmatic conservatives and conservative purists continued to fight over the meaning of Reagan's legacy and the future of the GOP.

Although the Tea Party won a historic victory during the 2010 midterms, John Boehner and other "establishment" conservatives controlled the GOP leadership positions. Boehner, who had been a member of the Conservative Opportunity Society during the Reagan administration, became Speaker of the House. Furthermore, the so-called conservative "young guns"—Eric Cantor, Kevin McCarthy, and Paul Ryan—who received leadership roles in the Republican-controlled House all predated the Tea Party movement.[21] Almost immediately after being sworn in, the newly elected Tea Party members clashed with conservatives who had been in Washington for years over priorities and strategy.

Many of the Tea Party conservatives had campaigned against "business as usual" in Washington and had been elected by rank-and-file conservatives who would "tolerate no politics-as-usual compromise, moderate Republican lawmakers, or negotiation with political adversaries."[22] One of the most conservative members of the Republican caucus during the 1980s, Boehner now found himself being criticized for not being fully committed to conservative principles. Many establishment Republicans and long-time conservative politicians recognized the influence that the Tea Party had during the midterms and feared that if they opposed the movement, they might face challengers from their right in the primaries. As a result, the newly elected Tea Party conservatives had substantial power, which enabled them resist Boehner's attempts to whip them into line for votes that violated their conservative principles.[23] The result was political stagnation and a Congress that became ultrapartisan.[24]

As the specter of a government shutdown loomed in 2011, political commentators attempted to use the celebration of Ronald Reagan's one-hundredth birthday to remind conservatives and the country that the Tea Party was violating his legacy. National Public Radio exclaimed that conservatives who invoked Reagan to justify a potential government shutdown misunderstood the fortieth president. NPR reminded listeners that "Reagan was a president who held firm beliefs but was also willing to work with his ideological opponents." Such pragmatic governance, however, was "the sort of thing that doesn't much lend itself to mythmaking." Historian and editor of the *Reagan Diaries* Douglas Brinkley reminded listeners in an interview that "Reagan was never afraid to raise taxes. . . . He knew that it was necessary at times." Brinkley concluded that "there's a false mythology out there about Reagan as this conservative president who came in and just cut taxes and trimmed federal spending in a dramatic way. . . . It's false."[25]

Despite the history lessons of political pundits and the Democrats citing Reagan's support for raising the debt ceiling, conservatives continued to threaten the shutdown of the federal government if Democrats did not agree to substantial spending cuts. Speaker Boehner in his negotiations with President Obama explained that while he wanted to arrive at a deal to keep the government functioning, he also had to satisfy the "wild-eyed bomb-throwing freshmen" who required significant reductions in government spending.[26] Many conservatives agreed with Representative Mike Pence (R-IN) when he exclaimed that if President Obama and the Democrats refused "a modest down payment on fiscal discipline and reform, I say, 'Shut it down!'" The several hundred Tea Party attendees erupted in agreement, chanting, "Shut it down! Shut it down!" Ultimately, Republicans got $38 billion in cuts, over half of what they had originally requested. Billions of dollars in cuts was not enough for fifty-nine conservative purists who refused to support Boehner and his compromise legislation.[27] The government almost defaulted again during the summer of 2011. Only a last-minute agreement to cap federal spending and appoint a commission to find $1.2 trillion in spending cuts prevented a government shutdown.[28]

Political commentators decried the 112th Congress for its unwillingness to compromise, while conservative purists denounced Boehner for doing just that. The *Washington Post* declared in 2012 that the GOP was "ideologically extreme; scornful of compromise; unmoved by conventional understanding of facts, evidence and science; and dismissive of the legitimacy of its political opposition." The publication lamented that "when one party moves this far from the mainstream, it makes it nearly impossible for the political system to deal constructively with the country's challenges."[29] Richard Viguerie offered a very different assessment. He asserted that the compromise represented an abandonment of "conservative principles" and was "a complete cave-in by the House Republican leadership." Viguerie denounced Boehner for giving "Obama and the Democrats a free pass on the spending, deficit, and debt issue until after the 2012 election."[30] To conservative purists, any compromise with Democrats was viewed as capitulation. As the 2012 presidential election approached, Congress's approval rating stood at 17 percent; most Americans agreed that the government was dysfunctional.[31]

Beginning with his announcement speech, Governor Mitt Romney attempted to recreate the Reagan Revolution with his presidential bid. In June 2011, the *Washington Post* asserted that Romney was "channeling Reagan rhetorically" as he "seeks to draw a direct line from the rebirth of the Republican party under Reagan to what Romney hopes to do with his campaign in 2012 and beyond." Romney invoked Reagan's optimism as he painted a positive vision of the country and called for voters to "Believe in America." He emphasized the importance of a free market economy, states' rights, and American exceptionalism.[32]

During the primaries, however, Romney was relentlessly attacked by Texas governor Rick Perry and former Speaker Newt Gingrich and forced to the right on important issues, especially immigration. In the Republican debates, Romney praised Arizona's SB1070, which "would require police officers to check the status of anyone they stop should they have a 'reasonable suspicion' that the person is in the US without permission." Critics feared the provision would lead to racial profiling of Latino Americans. Ultimately, Romney promised conservative primary voters that under his administration illegal immigrants would find life so difficult that those who were in the country illegally would "self-deport."[33] Romney's self-deportation policy provided him adequate cover during the primary; however, it alienated Latino voters that he needed if he hoped to defeat President Obama. On election day, Romney received only 27 percent of the Latino vote, losing them "58 to 40 in Florida, 87 to 10 in Colorado, 80 to 17 in Nevada, and 66 to 31 in Virginia." After Romney's defeat, *National Review* concluded that "Republicans were clobbered among Hispanics because . . . in the midst of discussion of border guards, moats, and 'self-deportation' during the Republican primaries, there was precious little appreciation for the contributions of legal Hispanics to American life and culture."[34]

Despite Romney's embrace of Reagan's optimistic vision for the country, his economic message did not resonate with minority voters. Tea Party senator Marco Rubio summed up Romney's troubles in an interview with Fox News commentator Juan Williams: "It's very hard to make the economic argument to people who think you want to deport their grandmother."[35] In the wake of the 2012 election, the debate over the future of the GOP intensified. Conservative purists claimed that Romney had lost because he was not adequately conservative. Others argued that the GOP needed to work across the aisle, form coalitions, govern, and pragmatically apply conservative principles where possible.

Immediately following Romney's defeat, many conservatives accepted that they needed to consider working with the Democrats to pass comprehensive immigration reform. In an interview with Diane Sawyer, Speaker Boehner said he would address the question of immigration and explained that after the election, "Obamacare is the law of the land." He downplayed the divisions in his own party, wishfully claiming that "all of us who were elected in 2010 were supported by the Tea Party." On immigration, Boehner asserted that "a comprehensive approach is long overdue, and I'm confident that the president, myself, and others can find the common ground to take care of this issue once and for all." Asked if the GOP was "too white, too old and too male," Boehner replied that Republicans needed to learn how to "speak to all Americans." He added that the GOP believed "in empowering all citizens" and that the party's message resonated "with all Americans, but we need to do a much more effective job in communicating it."[36]

Boehner was not the only Republican searching for answers following Romney's defeat. The Republican National Committee underwent the "most comprehensive post-election review" ever conducted after a presidential loss. Describing the so-called autopsy, Chairman Reince Priebus told the National Press Club that the Republicans' "policies are sound, but in many ways the way we communicate can be a real problem." The report emphasized the importance of campaigning "among Hispanic, black, Asian, and gay Americans to demonstrate" that the GOP cared "about them, too." Sally Bradshaw, a Florida GOP strategist, insisted that the Republican Party needed "to stop talking to itself" and asserted that the "standard should not be universal purity, it should be a more welcoming form of conservatism." The theme that the GOP needed to be more inclusive and apply its principles to the problems faced by minority communities dominated the news conference, and the report was especially critical of Romney's "self-deportation" policy.[37] For many conservatives, the future of the Republican Party depended on softening their often harsh rhetoric and using conservative principles to address issues in minority communities.[38]

Even some conservative purists realized that the GOP needed to reach out to minorities. On his radio program, Sean Hannity told his audience that he had "evolved" on the issue of immigration. Hannity exclaimed that conservatives had "to get rid of the immigration issue altogether." He explained that if illegal immigrants had "criminal records you can send them home, but if people are here, law-abiding, participating for years, their kids are born here, you know, it's first secure the border, pathway to citizenship, done."[39] Anna Navarro, a Republican pundit and consultant who often criticized conservatives for not addressing immigration reform, tweeted: "Monkeys evolved into humans. Hannity has evolved on immigration. Keeping hope alive."[40] Hannity's reaction to the 2012 election proved short-lived and he condemned Senator Marco Rubio and others who proposed comprehensive immigration reform less than a year later.[41]

In contrast to those who believed the GOP needed to appeal to minority voters, conservative purists claimed that millions of conservatives did not vote in 2012 because Romney was inadequately conservative. They insisted that minority outreach was unnecessary and instead that the GOP simply needed to nominate a candidate who adhered to conservative principles. On November 6, 2012, Jeffrey Lord, former White House associate political director for President Reagan, asserted "that it wasn't Ronald Reagan and his conservatism that lost" presidential elections, it was the "seemingly endless stream of very nice moderate Republicans" who failed to win the White House. Lord condemned conservative commenters who charged that Reagan conservatism could not work because "it's not 1980 anymore." He blamed Romney's defeat on the nominee's unwillingness to embrace conservative principles. Lord claimed that "3 million base GOP voters simply refused to vote for Romney" and reasoned that had these missing conservatives showed up at the polls, Romney would have won the national popular vote by 180,661 votes. Lord concluded that the problem "isn't appeals to Hispanics, blacks or women"; the true "problem is that we nominate too many Republicans—no matter how nice, decent, and good they may be—for whom conservatism is a second language. And then they lose. What we need are more of the New Reagans. And fortunately, they are here."[42]

Lord was just one of many conservative activists who believed that the Republican Party needed to embrace the Reagan myth and the belief that a dogmatic commitment to conservative principles was necessary to win elections. Rush Limbaugh asserted that "three million predominately white voters stayed home" on election day. According to Limbaugh, these missing Republican voters were "tired of moderate nominees" and believed that the Republican Party had abandoned its conservative principles. Limbaugh imagined that these voters had exclaimed, "To hell with it. If you're gonna eschew conservatism, I'm not giving you any money, and I'm not voting for you." Limbaugh insisted that those who believed that Republicans were "not winning presidential races" because they were "not for amnesty" were wrong. He concluded that if the GOP moderated its position on immigration, they would "cease to exist" because the conservative base would "abandon" the Republican Party.[43] Numerous other conservatives joined Lord and Limbaugh in embracing the view, which conservative political strategist Karl Rove vehemently denounced, that millions of conservatives had refused to vote for Romney.[44] As a result, conservative purists insisted that the future of the Republican Party depended on emulating Reagan's commitment to conservative principles and not in reaching out to minority communities.

In an otherwise dismal election, conservatives celebrated Tea Party candidate Ted Cruz's Senate victory. Cruz, whom *National Review* labeled "the next great conservative hope," fully embraced conservative principles. His commitment to the conservative creed led the *New York Times* to lament that Cruz was "expected to join Senator Jim DeMint of South Carolina and other Tea Party icons as an uncompromising irritant of mainstream Republicans and Democrats alike."[45] Richard Viguerie applauded Cruz's "grassroots campaign based on the clear and unafraid advocacy of limited-government constitutional conservative principles." According to Viguerie, Cruz's election was "a game changer for conservatives" and his "youthful energy, intellect, and constitutional scholarship" were "like adding an entire division to the small, but rapidly growing army of conservatives in the US Senate."[46]

When discussing his political philosophy, Cruz labeled himself as a true Reagan conservative. Cruz admired Reagan so much that his wedding party picnicked at the Reagans' Rancho del Cielo the day before his wedding. According to Cruz, "It was a moving, even spiritual experience." For nearly thirty minutes, Cruz stood behind the chair where Reagan did much of his work. He almost treated the chair as a religious relic, refusing to sit in it out of reverence for Reagan. Cruz recalled that he stood there "looking out that window and soaking up the ambiance of a man I've admired my whole life for having the courage to stand by his deep principles and the ability to lay out a vision that transformed this country and the world."[47] Almost as soon as Cruz arrived in Washington, he alienated much of his party with his unwillingness to compromise. In time, Cruz would become the standard-bearer for conservatives who believed that the future of the GOP depended on emulating the mythical Ronald Reagan's commitment to conservative principles.

Following the 2012 election, the two conflicting conceptions of Reagan's legacy and their respective visions for the future of the GOP clashed. Over 140 movement conservatives, including Morton Blackwell, Phyllis Schlafly, Ed Meese, Erick Erickson, Brent Bozell, Gary Bauer, and Richard Viguerie, signed a letter to all the Republican members of the House and Senate insisting that they had "a mandate to fight for conservative principles." Blackwell, who wrote the letter, exclaimed that "united you can stop any bill which violates the principles you publicly committed to support." He urged Republicans not to work with Democrats, because any compromise would be "a disaster for conservative principles" as it "would result in permanent advances for the 'fundamental changes' the left wants to impose on our country." Blackwell then issued a thinly veiled threat: "Let us also remind you that a great many potent conservative organizations and millions of conservative and liberty-loving voters do not believe in the divine right of incumbents to be renominated. Conservatives know how to recruit and support candidates." Blackwell concluded that it was in Republicans' interest and the interest of the country for "you to use the power you unquestionably have now to stand firm and not surrender your conservative principles, no matter how loud the clamor of people whose central interest is to advance the left's agenda."[48] Although it is impossible to know how much influence Blackwell's letter had on Republican legislators, in 2013 principled conservatives, led by Senator Ted Cruz, decided to force a government shutdown rather than compromise on a continuing resolution that would temporarily fund the government.[49]

In the wake of the shutdown, pragmatic conservatives lambasted purists who refused to compromise and govern. Indeed, the Reagan legacy, which had united conservatives for over twenty years, was quickly becoming a source of disagreement, and differing interpretations threatened to undermine the unity of the conservative movement. The *Wall Street Journal* declared that the Republicans were getting "a far larger share of the blame" for the shutdown than their Democratic colleagues. Writing for the neoconservative magazine *Commentary*, conservative columnist Peter Wehner exclaimed that "the image of the GOP fell to a record low in the aftermath of the shutdown." He blamed conservative commentators such as Mark Levin for "spending more and more of their time and energy targeting those they perceive as heretics" instead of encouraging lawmakers to govern. Wehner lamented that "these self-appointed enforcers of conservative purity often invoke Ronald Reagan and claim to be his heirs," but "in many respects they don't understand him very well at all." He continued that "they twist Reagan this way and that, like Stretch Armstrong, to make him appear to match their own dispositions and patterns of thought and biases." Wehner insisted that if these conservative purists' "absolutist mindset" were "applied to the Reagan record," the fortieth president "would have drawn their wrath." He added that "by their own logic, Reagan would have been deemed a RINO (Republican in Name Only)." Wehner asserted that even Reagan could not "approach the standards of purity embraced by today's radicals on the right." He concluded that if purists wanted to, they could, "in the words of Reagan, go over the cliff with all flags flying. That's up to them. They just shouldn't try to take Reagan's party down with them."[50] Conservatives' understanding of Reagan's legacy continued to dictate the course that they believed the Republican Party should take. Wehner and other pragmatic conservatives continually reminded conservative purists of Reagan's true record. By recalling how Reagan compromised and negotiated with his political opponents, these pragmatists hoped the GOP would embrace a conservatism that governed effectively and still held true to conservative principles.

By 2014, it was clear that the Republican Party was in disarray. Speaker Boehner could not control his own caucus, and the rift between conservative purists and conservative pragmatists was growing. Some Tea Party conservatives, such as Senators Marco Rubio (R-FL) and Jeff Flake (R-AZ), drew the ire of conservative purists for embracing comprehensive immigration reform. Others, such as Ted Cruz, became darlings of conservative purists for standing on principle. As conservatives began to discuss potential presidential nominees, conflicting views of Reagan's legacy were often at the center of their debates.

At the annual gathering of conservatives at CPAC in 2014, the different conceptions of Reagan's legacy were on full display. ABC News reported that although "Reagan died nearly 10 years ago," the president was "very much alive for many of the speakers" at CPAC. Fittingly, on the opening day of the conference, the conservative *Washington Times* ran the headline "ACU at 50: Strong, Looking Ahead" with a large picture of Reagan on the front page.[51] The implication was that the future for conservative organizations such as the American Conservative Union depended on channeling Reagan. Senator Cruz agreed with the newspaper. In his speech, Cruz insisted that conservatives should "stand for principle" just as Reagan did. Cruz contended that McCain and Romney "didn't win the White House because they didn't draw a clear enough contrast between themselves and the Democrats they ran against."[52] Senator Rubio, who delivered a devastating critique of President Obama's foreign policy, asserted that conservatives could learn from Reagan's engagement with the USSR. Rubio insisted that "Reagan dealt with the Soviet Union because they had nuclear weapons and he wanted peace, but he never accepted the Soviet Union." Likewise, the United States could engage with its enemies but should never accept the existence of evil.[53]

In contrast to the other Tea Party conservatives, Rand Paul delivered a blistering indictment of the National Security Agency's (NSA) monitoring of US citizens' communication. Instead of invoking Reagan, Paul likened the NSA's behavior to the "British soldiers writing their own warrants" in the years leading up to the American Revolution. Paul insisted that "there is a great battle going on for the heart and soul of America" and implored conservatives to recognize that "the Fourth Amendment is equally as important as the Second Amendment." Paul applied the libertarian-conservative defense of individual liberty to contemporary issues. Rather than be paralyzed by asking whether Reagan would have supported NSA surveillance, he boldly exclaimed that any conservative constitutionalist needed to consistently defend the entirety of the Constitution—not just the parts they agreed with. Paul implored conservatives to not "trade our liberty for security. Not now, not ever." Paul also attacked President Obama for "equivocating on civil liberty issues," emphasizing that no "minority of thought, color, creed, or religion" should be imprisoned wrongfully. Paul's speech was "starkly libertarian," but it also attempted to apply conservatives' principle of individual liberty beyond the economic sphere.[54] Despite not directly invoking Reagan, Paul won the CPAC straw poll for president with 31 percent, whereas Cruz finished a distant second with 11 percent.[55]

Paul's victory at CPAC made him a target. As soon as the conference ended, Cruz used Reagan to criticize Paul's foreign policy. Although Cruz agreed with Paul that "we should be very reluctant to deploy military force abroad," Cruz argued that just like Reagan he believed there was "a vital role" for the US military. Cruz tied himself to Reagan and asserted that when "Ronald Reagan called the Soviet Union an evil empire, when he stood in front of the Brandenburg Gate and said, 'Mr. Gorbachev, tear down this wall,' those words changed the course of history." Cruz concluded that it was clear that "the United States has a responsibility to defend our values."[56] By channeling Reagan's rhetoric and in asserting that Paul's views on foreign policy were not in line with those of the fortieth president, Cruz attempted to delegitimize his colleague. Furthermore, Cruz attempted to link Paul's noninterventionist foreign policy to President Obama, thereby implying that Paul was inadequately conservative. The message to conservative voters was clear: Cruz was the true Reagan conservative.

In response, Paul dismissed Cruz's interpretation of Reagan as simplistic and instead argued that Reagan was a pragmatic conservative who was wary of foreign conflict. He insisted that "every Republican likes to think he or she is the next Ronald Reagan . . . but too often people make him into something he wasn't in order to serve their own political purposes." Paul acknowledged that Cruz was correct that "Reagan clearly believed in a strong national defense and in 'Peace Through Strength,'" and that Reagan "had stood up to the Soviet Union" and had "pushed back against Communism." But Paul reminded Cruz, and his readers, that Reagan's foreign policy was much more complicated than a few soundbites. Paul emphasized that "Reagan also believed in diplomacy and demonstrated a reasoned approach to our nuclear negotiations with the Soviets." In fact, he explained it was "Reagan's shrewd diplomacy" that "eventually lessened the nuclear arsenals of both countries." Paul added that "many forget today that Reagan's decision to meet Mikhail

Gorbachev was harshly criticized by the Republican hawks of his time, some of whom would even call Reagan an appeaser." Paul framed Reagan's foreign policy legacy as one of careful negotiation and reluctance to engage in conflict. The senator exclaimed that he "greatly admire[d] that Reagan was not rash or reckless with regard to war." Paul did not "claim to be the next Ronald Reagan," nor did he "disparage fellow Republicans as not being sufficiently Reaganesque." Instead, Paul concluded that "today's Republicans should concentrate on establishing their own identities and agendas, as opposed to simply latching onto Ronald Reagan's legacy—or worse, misrepresenting it."[57]

Conservative commentator and author Matt Lewis shared Rand Paul's assessment that Reagan's willingness to compromise with his adversaries was central to his success. Lewis reminded conservatives that Reagan nurtured his relationship with Democratic House Speaker Tip O'Neill and built "strong friendships and relationships with colleagues on both sides of the aisle."[58] Lewis also condemned the "us-versus-them approach to politics" that had "eliminated compromise from the vocabulary of modern conservatives." He recounted that the Constitution that conservatives loved to invoke would not exist without compromise. Lewis concluded that "the very people most likely to don tri-cornered hats and genuflect at the Founding Fathers and Ronald Reagan (who cut deals with Tip O'Neil [sic] and Mikhail Gorbachev) most vociferously oppose compromise."[59] According to Lewis, conservatives needed to strategically identify policy areas where they could compromise with Democrats without abandoning their principles. Furthermore, Lewis emphasized the importance of compromise to Reagan's legacy, thus providing conservatives with an intellectual justification to form coalitions and govern effectively.

Similarly, Arthur Brooks, the president of the American Enterprise Institute, argued that much of Reagan's success derived from his ability to demonstrate how his policies helped those who needed it most. Brooks lamented in *The Conservative Heart* that conservatives often discussed their economic policies without mentioning the people their policies were designed to help. In contrast, Brooks noted that "Ronald Reagan talked about the poor in two-thirds of his public pronouncements" and "spent most of his speech talking about who he was fighting for."[60] Throughout the book, Brooks demonstrated how conservatives could apply their principles to issues that would help broaden their appeal among voters from all walks of life. Brooks asserted that the Tea Party still had time to win over many Americans, but it needed to adopt Reagan's optimism. Brooks explained that Reagan's rhetoric was "optimistic, aspirational, and resoundingly pro-people." He lamented that "many of today's angriest voices who scramble to claim Reagan's mantle" did not realize how important Reagan's optimism was to his success.[61] Brooks wrote that while it was very clear "what the Tea Party is against—big government, taxes, regulation, spending, deficits, debt, and Obamacare"—it was unclear what they stood for. He concluded that the Tea Party had an opportunity to demonstrate how "the power of free enterprise" could "help Americans escape poverty and dependency by creating good-paying jobs, restoring upward mobility, and creating a new culture of opportunity."[62]

According to Lewis and Brooks, conservatives did not need to abandon their principles to reach out to minority voters and those who lived in poverty. Indeed, the problem with conservative purists was not their fixation with conservative principle, but rather the negative tone that they deployed when discussing their vision of the country. Furthermore, both commentators demonstrated that compromise and optimism were essential components of the Reagan legacy, and they powerfully used Reagan to espouse a more inclusive conservatism. Combined, Lewis and Brooks offered a pragmatic conservatism that appealed to Americans of all creeds and colors without compromising principle.

In the two years before the 2016 primaries, racial unrest, resurgent radical Islamic terrorism, and increased concern about illegal immigration dominated the national headlines. Rather than promoting conservative solutions to the emerging social problems, conservatives resorted to condemning those who called for justice and equal treatment under the law. In this environment, Tea Party pragmatists such as Rand Paul—who had been one of the first politicians to travel to Ferguson after the death of Michael Brown and call for criminal justice reform—and Marco Rubio—who had compromised with Democrats to try and solve America's immigration problem—found themselves trailing conservative firebrand Ted Cruz in the polls.[63]

Conservative purists lined up and supported Ted Cruz during the 2016 primaries. On January 11, 2016, Morton Blackwell wrote an open letter to conservatives titled "Please Join Me in Supporting Ted Cruz." Blackwell asserted that although there were "many presidential candidates" who were "more conservative than anyone the Republican Party has nominated since Ronald Reagan," he decided to endorse Cruz. According to Blackwell, Cruz had "consistently demonstrated his deep commitment to conservative principles" and conservatives could "be confident that Ted Cruz will make superb judicial nominations."[64] Sean Hannity echoed Blackwell's praise for Cruz. Although Hannity did not formally endorse Cruz, the conservative commentator labeled him as "a Reagan-conservative constitutionalist" who would "fight for his core principles, values, and beliefs."[65] Conservative radio-show host Mark Levin also endorsed Cruz, explaining that the senator supported "the Constitution, the Republic, individual sovereignty, separation of powers, the Bill of Rights, family, faith, a secure border," and "our national security."[66]

Ted Cruz's most vocal supporter during the 2016 campaign, however, was Glenn Beck. The conservative media entrepreneur endorsed Cruz early and even campaigned with him across the country, likening the Texas senator to Reagan.[67] Beck was so insistent on the similarities between Cruz and Reagan that one publication ran with the headline "Glenn Beck Declares Ted Cruz the Second Coming of Ronald Reagan." Beck consistently told conservative audiences that Cruz was the principled leader they had been praying for. Beck even contended that "Ted Cruz may be Ronald Reagan" because he was smart, truthful, clean, and ethical.[68] Beck's exuberance, however, sometimes got the best of him on the campaign trail. At one stop, he spent over half an hour weeping and shouting at the crowd. Beck asserted that "God has a plan to save this nation but it requires Christians to do everything they can to elect Ted Cruz."[69] At another campaign event, Beck declared that those who did not vote for Cruz would ultimately be to blame for "the blood of the people who could have been saved."[70] Although Beck carried his enthusiasm for Cruz beyond that of other conservatives, most conservative purists agreed that Cruz's dogmatic commitment to conservative principles made him the natural heir to Reagan and the best candidate in 2016.

Ted Cruz's consistent invocation of the Reagan myth on the campaign trail failed to result in electoral victories. One news outlet exclaimed that "Cruz discusses Reagan's victory in the 1980 general election so often that a casual listener might think the Texas Senator is preparing himself to run against Jimmy Carter and not Hillary Clinton." According to conservative-leaning columnist Ross Douthat, Cruz built his campaign on the assumption that primary voters "wanted Reagan, or at least a fantasy version of Reagan." Although Cruz did everything he could to emulate the Gipper, he lost to businessman Donald Trump. Douthat explained that Cruz's defeat demonstrated that "Republicans didn't want true conservatism." According to Douthat, Trump's victory "proved that movement conservative ideas and litmus tests don't really have any purchase on millions of Republican voters." After all, Douthat concluded, Cruz and others had "stressed that Trump wasn't really a conservative; they listed his heresies, cataloged his deviations, dug up his barely buried liberal past," and yet he still won.[71]

One of the great ironies of the 2016 election was that after more than six years of arguing about the future of the Republican Party and Ronald Reagan's proper legacy, conservatives failed to nominate one of their own. Pragmatic conservatives who wanted to appeal to minority voters were appalled as Trump lambasted illegal immigrants in his announcement speech as "bringing drugs," "bringing crime," and being "rapists."[72] Likewise, Trump's praise for President Eisenhower's infamous Operation Wetback and Trump's proposed Muslim ban horrified those who wanted to soften the party's rhetoric.[73] Conservative purists also denounced Trump. They were disturbed that Trump had once been pro-choice, for universal health care, for eminent domain, that he had owned casinos, had been married three times, faced multiple sexual-assault allegations, and was on the record disrespecting women and joking about his sexual proclivities.[74] Other conservatives were aghast that Trump opposed free trade, discussed raising the minimum wage, praised Planned Parenthood, and proposed six weeks of paid maternity leave.[75] Trump's nomination, far from ending the debate between pragmatic conservatives and conservative purists, only added a sense of despair and urgency to their arguments. More than ever, it was essential to unite conservatives behind a common understanding of Reagan's legacy and mobilize the entire movement to shape the future of the Republican Party.

Conclusion: Beyond Reagan?

It was improbable. All the experts said it was almost impossible, but at 2:36 a.m. (eastern time) the Associated Press declared Donald Trump the president-elect of the United States of America.[1] The Empire State Building lit up the New York skyline with Trump's photo and deep crimson lights.[2] At Democratic candidate Hillary Clinton's watch party, her supporters clutched tiny American flags and cried under the glass ceiling of the convention hall. The ceiling was cracked but still unbroken.[3] In the end, the public polling, the media, the GOP "establishment" were all wrong, and even members of Trump's own campaign, who anonymously acknowledged that they would lose earlier in the day, were awestruck by the results.[4] When the nation awoke on Wednesday, November 9, 2016, Republicans controlled the House, the Senate, and the presidency for just the third time since 1928.[5]

Conservatives were quick to compare Trump's victory to Ronald Reagan's 1980 win and declare a mandate for their ideas. Conservative author Lee Edwards celebrated Trump's victory, declaring it "a golden opportunity for conservatism," and reflected that Trump's victory was the result of "Reagan Democrats" being "brought back into the GOP." Edwards, having lived through the ups and downs of the Reagan administration, cautioned that "the Trump administration will face many powerful pressures to compromise, to settle for less, and to cut deals."[6] For its part, right-wing website *Breitbart* published an article exclaiming that Trump had "an opportunity to follow President Reagan's four point pro-growth plan for economic growth that reversed falling family incomes, raised millions out of poverty, and led to the doubling of stock prices during his term."[7] Conservative columnist Charles Krauthammer declared on election night that Trump's victory was an "ideological and electoral revolution the kind we have not seen since Reagan." Krauthammer, however, acknowledged that Trump did not run on Reagan's agenda and was not a conservative. Indeed, according to Krauthammer, Trump's victory meant that "the Republican Party has become a populist party and the country is going to be without a classically conservative party" moving forward.[8]

Krauthammer was correct in that Trump did not invoke Reagan's name or run on his platform during the primary or general election. Indeed, Trump showed little to no inclination to embrace Reagan's legacy at all, and many of his policy positions were directly at odds with Reagan's.[9] When he accepted the GOP nomination, Trump made no mention of the fortieth president, and instead of channeling Reagan's optimistic rhetoric Trump embraced a dark and menacing tone. In his acceptance speech, instead of empowering the American people to confront the nation's problems, Trump insisted that only he could rescue the country from its dismal condition. The differences between Reagan's acceptance speech in 1980 and Trump's were striking.[10] Indeed, all of the anger and frustration that conservative purists had stoked from 2004 to 2016 fueled the uncompromising, if not conservative, candidacy of Donald Trump.

By contrast, the Democratic nominee, Hillary Clinton, not only mentioned Reagan but also referred to the fact that the Gipper was absent from Trump's rhetoric. Clinton quipped that Trump had "taken the Republican Party from 'Morning in America' to 'Midnight in America.'" Clinton concluded that "he wants us to fear the future and fear each other."[11] President Obama also embraced Reagan during the Democratic National Convention, asserting that "Reagan called America 'a shining city on a hill'" while "Donald Trump calls it 'a divided crime scene' that only he can fix."[12] For the first time since Reagan left the White House, it was the Democrats that were the party of American exceptionalism while the Republicans framed America as a nation in decline.[13]

In fact, Democrats who had fought to dismiss Reagan's legitimate achievements for over thirty-five years discovered a newfound appreciation for him during the 2016 election. As the Republican primary candidates were taking turns denouncing Obama's Iran nuclear deal, the president enraged conservatives by comparing his negotiations with Reagan's. Obama insisted that while he had "a lot of differences with Ronald Reagan," he "completely admired him" for negotiating "with the evil empire that was hell-bent on our destruction." The president added that the Soviet Union during Reagan's time "was a far greater existential threat to us than Iran will ever be."[14]

During the primary, the Clinton campaign compared the rigidity of the GOP hopefuls to the pragmatic Reagan record. Her staff created posters at their headquarters in New York that juxtaposed the 2016 candidates' positions with Reagan's. Taking a shot at Senator Marco Rubio's opposition to what it viewed as a "fairer tax system," the Clinton campaign quoted Reagan. In June 1985, while defending his tax-reform package, Reagan had asserted that "what we're trying to move against is institutional unfairness. We want to see that everyone pays their fair share and no one gets a free ride." In contrast to Trump, the campaign cited Reagan's October 1984 declaration that he believed "in amnesty for those who have put down roots and who have lived here even though some time back they may have entered illegally." Reporting on the Democratic frontrunner using Reagan as a weapon against the GOP hopefuls, the *Guardian* explained that "Clinton's message is that the GOP has moved far to the right and left Reagan, the real Reagan, behind." The newspaper concluded that Clinton's attempt at "appropriating Reagan for her campaign" was "an audacious heist."[15]

Although Trump did little beyond coopting Reagan's "Make America Great Again" slogan, some of his surrogates attempted to tie the nominee to Reagan. Jeffrey Lord, former White House associate political director for President Reagan and one of Trump's top surrogates, constantly compared Trump to Reagan during his numerous appearances on CNN.[16] In an article for the *American Spectator*, Lord insisted that Trump, like Reagan, was "a fighter" and that both men were "disdained by the establishment." Lord encouraged a Trump/Cruz alliance, explaining "between the two they represent a revival of serious Reagan-style conservatism."[17]

The attempts of Trump surrogates to connect Trump to Reagan, however, were dismissed by Reagan's two sons. Before the GOP presidential debate at the Reagan Library, both Michael and Ron Reagan denounced comparisons of their father to Trump. Ron asserted that he could not "think of two people who are more diametrically opposed" and added that his father "would recoil" at Trump's bigotry. Michael Reagan agreed with Ron that "Ronald Reagan would never take 11 million people . . . and throw them out of the United States of America." As for "Trump being the next Ronald Reagan," Michael Reagan dismissed that as "ridiculous."[18] Although Ron and Michael Reagan were often at odds over politics, the brothers agreed that the Republican nominee did not resemble their father in the least.

With the Democrats embracing Reagan and Republicans struggling to claim his legacy, Nancy Reagan passed away in March 2016. Her death led many commentators to question whether the Reagan era had ended with her passing. Conservative columnist Peter Wehner, writing for *Time* magazine, questioned "if the party" the Reagans "took such care in shaping" had "passed into history." Wehner described Trump as the "antithesis of so much that Ronald Reagan stood for: intellectual depth and philosophical consistency, respect for ideas and elevated rhetoric, civility and personal grace." He lamented that "the fact that Trump is the favorite to win the Republican presidential nomination shows how far the GOP has drifted from the animating spirit of the most consequential and revered Republican since Abraham Lincoln." Wehner concluded that "when the mantle worn by Reagan" settles "on the likes of Trump," it is "an end-of-an-era moment."[19] Other conservatives agreed that Trump posed a fatal threat to Reagan's Republican Party. Conservative columnist George Will insisted before the conventions that Trump had no hope of winning the general election. Citing Trump's terrible numbers with minority voters and his numerous unpresidential antics, Will questioned how many Republicans would "follow Trump off the cliff."[20]

As Trump struggled to build a broad coalition to challenge Secretary Clinton, conservatives questioned how such a poor general-election candidate managed to secure the Republican nomination. At least one commentator, Peter Wehner, asserted that conservative purists and their firebrand allies in talk radio were to blame for Trump's success.[21] Wehner explained that conservatives' tactic of "employing apocalyptic rhetoric" to issues facing the country as well as their view that "compromise" was "a synonym for capitulation" had bolstered Trump. According to Wehner, somewhere along the way conservatives had decided "to replace reason with rage, to deny science when it was at odds with ideology and to cheer mindless stunts like shutting down the federal government." The result of these tactics, according to Wehner, was that conservative voters confused "cruelty, vulgarity, and bluster with strength and straight talk." He went further, asserting that "political and intellectual sclerosis"—the inability to take conservative principles and apply them to a changing world—had set in. Wehner emphasized that Reagan had been excellent at adjusting "to the realities of his time," but his would-be successors had "been decidedly less skilled" in applying conservative principles to modern times. Instead, conservatives had "placed themselves in an ideological straightjacket, trying to be more Reagan than Reagan." As a result, the GOP "was unable to explain, let alone address, huge structural changes caused by globalization, advances in technology and automation." According to Wehner, this led "blue collar Americans in particular" to feel "unheard, ignored, [and] abandoned." In the void created by a Republican Party fixated with the Reagan myth "emerged an opportunistic and populist by the name of Trump."[22] Wehner was correct that the Reagan myth had laid the foundation for Trump's appeal to the anger, frustration, and despair that many conservative voters, and Rust Belt voters, felt. Indeed, by 2016, the Reagan myth had undermined the true legacy of Ronald Reagan and had paved the way for a politician whom many considered a strongman to challenge the neoliberal order that Reagan had created.

Wehner and many other conservative commentators, however, failed to realize that Trump was, in a way, doing exactly what they called for—ignoring the Reagan legacy and policy prescriptions—and forging his own path to electoral success. Trump offered policy prescriptions for contemporary issues, and although his solutions were often ineloquent and sometimes violated conservative principles, he spoke to many Americans who felt left behind economically during the Obama administration.[23] Pragmatic conservatives condemned Trump for alienating minority voters, but on election day his economic-protectionist platform and his promise "to make America great again" resonated, and he did slightly better than Governor Romney.[24] Trump succeeded because he was able to mobilize white working-class voters in the Rust Belt better than Romney, because the Republican National Committee made significant improvements to its get-out-the-vote effort, and because Secretary Clinton was unable to motivate the base of the Democratic Party.[25] Scholars will undoubtedly debate the reasons for Trump's victory for generations to come.[26] What is clear, however, is that he was never beholden to Reagan's legacy. In fact, Trump ignored Reagan's optimistic campaign style and instead embraced the politics of fear. Trump's improbable victory presents the question: Is the party of Reagan, for better or worse, now the party of Trump?

Notes

INTRODUCTION. THE EVOLUTION OF CONSERVATIVES' PERCEPTIONS OF REAGAN

1. "The Republicans: A Government Waits in the Wings," *Washington Post*, May 27, 1980, A1.

2. "For Reagan, Crucial Choices Also Worked Politically," *Washington Post*, February 23, 1981, A1.

3. David S. Broder, "Conservatives Make a Stink," *Washington Post*, March 9, 1983, A25.

4. Fred Barnes, "A Realistic Agenda for Conservatives," *Chicago Tribune*, May 1, 1988, C3.

5. "Discontented Conservatives Rumble to Reagan's Right," *Hartford Courant*, August 19, 1987, B9E.

6. Lyn Nofziger, *Nofziger* (Washington, DC: Regnery, 1992), 266.

7. Richard Viguerie, "What Reagan Revolution? A Conservative Laments a Lost Chance to Alter the Political Balance," *Washington Post*, August 21, 1988; Irving Kristol, "The Reagan Revolution That Never Was," *Wall Street Journal*, April 19, 1988. As quoted and cited in Laura Kalman's *Right Star Rising: A New Politics, 1974–1980* (New York: W. W. Norton, 2010), 366.

8. Lou Cannon and Carl M. Cannon have made similar observations in their book *Reagan's Disciple: George W. Bush's Troubled Quest for a Presidential Legacy* (New York: Public Affairs, 2008), xii.

9. "Reconsidering Reagan's Legacy, Obama Lauds Triumph While Some Republicans Take a Critical Look Back," *International Herald Tribune*, June 15, 2009, 2. President Obama actually looked to Reagan as a guide for how to be a transformational leader. Indeed, the February 7, 2011, issue of *Time* was titled, "Why Obama Loves Reagan: And What He's Learned from Him." The article recounts how President Obama invited historians to the White House for a working dinner in which the president asked them questions. Obama was most interested in how Reagan "sparked a revolution" and how Obama could replicate that type of success. According to *Time*, historian Douglas Brinkley left the dinner with the impression that the president had "found a role model." Brinkley concluded that "Obama is approaching the job in a Reaganesque fashion." Michael Scherer and Michael Duffy, "The Role Model," *Time*, February 7, 2011, 26.

10. For an excellent analysis of Reagan's role in ending the Cold War and how

his involvement has been remembered see Michael Schaller's chapter, "Reagan and the Cold War," in Kyle Longley et al., *Deconstructing Reagan: Conservative Mythology and America's Fortieth President* (New York: M. E. Sharpe, 2007), 3–40.

11. John W. Sloan has written about the mythology of Reagan's economic record. See his chapter "The Economic Costs of Reagan Mythology," in Longley et al., *Deconstructing Reagan*, 41–70.

12. Kyle Longley has addressed how Reagan has been remembered in regard to morality and social issues in his chapter "When Character Was King? Ronald Reagan and the Issues of Ethics and Morality," in Kyle Longley et al., *Deconstructing Reagan*, 90–119.

13. Ronald Reagan, "Why I'm for the Brady Bill," *New York Times*, March 29, 1991.

14. Letter from Ronald Reagan to the American people, November 5, 1994. The full text is available at http://reagan2020.us/speeches/announcement_of_alzheimers.asp; "Reagan Illness Afflicts Millions, in Varying Ways," *New York Times*, November 7, 1994, A16.

15. The same could be said for Richard Nixon, John F. Kennedy, Franklin D. Roosevelt, Abraham Lincoln, and Thomas Jefferson—all of whom have been mythologized by their political allies and opponents alike. Indeed, there is extensive scholarship devoted to how former presidents have been invoked by later generations. A few excellent examples include: Merrill D. Peterson, *The Jefferson Image in the American Mind* (Charlottesville: University Press of Virginia, 1998); Andrew Burstein, *Democracy's Muse: How Thomas Jefferson Became an FDR Liberal, A Reagan Republican, and a Tea Party Fanatic, All the While Being Dead* (Charlottesville: University of Virginia Press, 2015); Merrill D. Peterson, *Lincoln in American Memory* (Oxford: Oxford University Press, 1994); Paul H. Santa Cruz, *Making JFK Matter: Popular Memory and the Thirty-Fifth President* (Denton: University of North Texas Press, 2015); David Greenberg, *Nixon's Shadow: The History of an Image* (New York: W. W. Norton, 2003).

16. In thinking about memory, I draw from the constructivists and their arguments that every act of recollection is a re-creation, reconstruction of a memory. Every time we "recall" a memory, we relive the event that caused it, emotionally relate to it, remake that memory, and store a new version, overwriting the old one. Recalling something is essentially similar to making a new, original memory. We don't really remember the original event; we remember our last recollection of that event. The more we remember and the more often we recall something, the more we reconstruct and alter that memory, getting farther and farther from the original. In addition, narrative psychology argues that the formation of the self is dependent upon our ability to link our memories together into a coherent narrative. The rewriting of memories serves a purpose—to edit the revised past

all the time to square with the needs of the self that we have now. This applies to collective memory as well. The more a group—such as American conservatives—remember an event, the more they mythologize that memory. It is that myth that makes our collective culture. Having written this, I have decided to keep the theory to a minimum in the text. Several books were important in formulating my understanding of memory. They include: Frederick Bartlett's *Remembering: A Study in Experimental Social Psychology* (Cambridge: Cambridge University Press, 1932); Daniel L. Schacter's *Memory Distortion: How Minds, Brains, and Societies Reconstruct the Past* (Cambridge, MA: Harvard University Press, 1995); Schacter's *Searching for Memory: The Brain, the Mind, and the Past* (New York: Basic Books, 1996); Jerome S. Bruner's *Acts of Meaning* (Cambridge, MA: Harvard University Press, 1990); Uric Neisser and Robyn Fiyush's *The Remembering Self: Construction and Accuracy in the Self-Narrative* (Cambridge: Cambridge University Press, 1994); Paul John Eakin's chapter "Autobiography, Identity, and the Fictions of Memory," in *Memory, Brain, and Beliefs*, ed. Daniel Schacter and Elaine Scarry (Cambridge, MA: Harvard University Press, 2000), 290–306; and Thomas Butler's *Memory: History, Culture and the Mind* (New York: Blackwell, 1989). In respect to how societies form collective memory I am indebted to all the excellent scholars who came before including: Alon Confino and Peter Fritzsche, *The Work of Memory: New Directions in the Study of German Society and Culture* (Chicago: University of Illinois Press, 2002); Paul Connerton, *How Societies Remember* (Cambridge: Cambridge University Press, 1989); John R. Gillis, *Commemorations: The Politics of National Identity* (Princeton, NJ: Princeton University Press, 1994); Pierre Nora, *Realms of Memory: The Construction of the French Past* (New York: Columbia University Press, 1992); Jeffrey K. Olick, *The Politics of Regret: On Collective Memory and Historical Responsibility* (New York: Routledge, 2007); Eviatar Zerubavel, *Time Maps: Collective Memory and the Social Shape of the Past* (Chicago: University of Chicago Press, 2003). There are also several excellent works that grapple with memory in the United States: Michael Kammen, *Mystic Chords of Memory: The Transformation of Tradition in American Culture* (New York: Vintage, 1991); John Bodnar, *Remaking America: Public Memory, Commemoration, and Patriotism in the Twentieth Century* (Princeton, NJ: Princeton University Press, 1992); Richard M. Gamble, *In Search of the City on a Hill: The Making and Unmaking of an American Myth* (New York: Continuum, 2012); Edward T. Linenthal and Tom Engelhardt, *History Wars: The Enola Gay and Other Battles for the American Past* (New York: Henry Holt, 1996); Edward T. Linenthal, *The Unfinished Bombing: Oklahoma City in American Memory* (New York: Oxford University Press, 2001); and Emily S. Rosenberg, *A Date Which Will Live: Pearl Harbor in American Memory* (Durham, NC: Duke University Press, 2003).

17. For a comprehensive account of President Reagan and Speaker Tip O'Neill's

relationship consult Chris Matthews, *Tip and the Gipper: When Politics Worked* (New York: Simon & Schuster, 2013).

18. In discussing the ways in which Reagan moderated his conservative principles I do not wish to imply that Reagan was not a conservative. Indeed, he believed deeply in conservative principles and policies. Reagan should not be recast as a moderate or liberal Republican despite the fact that he was often pragmatic in implementing policy.

19. CNN Republican Debate, Simi Valley, California, January 30, 2008. For the full transcript of the debate see "Transcript of GOP Debate at Reagan Library," CNN, January 30, 2008, http://www.cnn.com/2008/POLITICS /01/30/GOPdebate .transcript/index.html.

20. "Republican Debate in Simi Valley, California," *New York Times*, January 30, 2008.

21. "Republican Debate in Simi Valley, California," *New York Times*, January 30, 2008.

22. "The CBS News Republican Debate Transcript, Annotated," *Washington Post*, February 13, 2016.

23. Many of the best histories of modern conservatism end with the election of Reagan in 1980. Kim Phillips-Fein's *Invisible Hands* foreshadows the frustration that many conservatives would feel toward Reagan. Phillips-Fein concludes, "In the end, it would prove easier for conservatives to share such a broad and sunny faith when they were out of power." Once in power, conflicts "between the businessmen and the social and religious conservatives—would emerge." Likewise, Lisa McGirr and Laura Kalman both end their studies of the rise of conservatism in 1980. This work is the next step in the historiography of the conservative movement, and it challenges the implication that Reagan's election marked a "triumph of conservatism." Instead, it demonstrates that regardless of whether there was a "right turn" in American politics, conservatives were disappointed with the accomplishments of the "Reagan Revolution." Kim Phillips-Fein, *Invisible Hands: The Making of the Conservative Movement from the New Deal to Reagan* (New York: W. W. Norton, 2009), 262; Lisa McGirr, *Suburban Warriors: The Origins of the New American Right* (Princeton, NJ: Princeton University Press, 2001); Kalman, *Right Star Rising*. Historians have thoroughly debated whether America experienced a right turn following the election of Reagan. For the full debate consult William C. Berman's *America's Right Turn: From Nixon to Clinton* (Baltimore: John Hopkins University Press, 1994), and David T. Courtwright's *No Right Turn: Conservative Politics in Liberal America* (Cambridge, MA: Harvard University Press, 2010).

24. George H. Nash, *The Conservative Intellectual Movement in America: Since 1945* (Wilmington, DE: ISI Books, 1976).

25. In determining not to attempt to define conservatism, I am following in

the lead of George H. Nash. In his 1976 seminal work *The Conservative Intellectual Movement in America*, he insisted that "an a priori effort" to define conservatism "is misdirected." Nash continued: "I doubt that there is any single, satisfactory, all-encompassing definition of the complex phenomenon called conservatism, the content of which varies enormously with time and place. It may even be true that conservatism is inherently resistant to precise definition. Many right-wingers, in fact, have argued that conservatism by its very nature is not an elaborate ideology at all" (xviii).

26. In detailing such tensions between Reagan and conservatives on fiscal policy, this work builds on the work of Brian Domitrovic and numerous historians such as Laura Kalman who have written, if only briefly, about the frustration that existed among different camps of fiscal conservatives while Reagan was in office. Brian Domitrovic, *Econoclasts: The Rebels Who Sparked the Supply-Side Revolution and Restored American Prosperity* (Wilmington, DE: ISI Books, 2009) and Kalman, *Right Star Rising*, 364–365.

27. Although historians such as Dan Carter, Thomas and Mary Edsall, Darren Dochuk, and Donald T. Critchlow have emphasized the importance of evangelical conservatives to electing Reagan in 1980, they have not fully addressed the disconnect that exists between the New Right's alleged importance during the electoral process and their lack of influence in shaping Reagan's legislative agenda. Dan Carter, *The Politics of Rage: George Wallace, the Origins of the New Conservatism, and the Transformation of American Politics* (Baton Rouge: Louisiana State University Press, 1995); Thomas Edsall and Mary Edsall, *Chain Reaction: The Impact of Race, Rights, and Taxes on American Politics* (New York: W. W. Norton, 1992); Daren Dochuk, *From Bible Belt to Sunbelt: Plain-Folk Religion, Grassroots Politics, and the Rise of Evangelical Conservatism* (New York: W. W. Norton, 2010); Donald T. Critchlow, "Mobilizing Women: The 'Social' Issues," in *The Reagan Presidency: Pragmatic Conservatism and Its Legacies*, ed. W. Elliot Brownlee and Hugh Davis Graham (Lawrence: University Press of Kansas, 2003), 293–326. This work, building on Daniel K. Williams's scholarship, demonstrates that Reagan's relationship with the Religious Right was tenuous and questions the New Right's influence during the 1980s. Daniel K. Williams, *God's Own Party: The Making of the Christian Right* (Oxford: Oxford University Press, 2010).

28. I am indebted to historian James Graham Wilson for shaping how I think about these issues. James Graham Wilson, *The Triumph of Improvisation: Gorbachev's Adaptability, Reagan's Engagement, and the End of the Cold War* (Ithaca, NY: Cornell University Press, 2015).

29. Conservative outrage at the INF Treaty was widespread. William F. Buckley even ran an entire edition of *National Review* entitled "Reagan's Suicide Pact" denouncing the treaty. "Reagan's Suicide Pact" *National Review*, May 22, 1987.

30. Many historians have mentioned that conservatives were, at times, frustrated with the administration. For example, Steven Hayward wrote in 2009 that "the extent to which conservatives were frustrated with Reagan much of the time, particularly during his second term, is another aspect of the Reagan years that has receded from view." Likewise, W. Elliot Brownlee has written, "The true believers in the Reagan program of permanently slowing government, reforming welfare, and rolling back regulation found little to applaud in other policy areas, especially after 1981." The goal of the first part of this book is to discuss, in a comprehensive way, the conservative frustration that other historians have noted. Steven Hayward, *The Age of Reagan: The Conservative Counterrevolution, 1980–1989* (New York: Crown Forum, 2009), 6; W. Elliot Brownlee, "Introduction: Revisiting the 'Reagan Revolution,'" in *The Reagan Presidency*, 9.

31. This chapter draws on historians' understanding of how museums shape public memory. There is a plethora of good works on how museums shape public memory. A few examples include: Susan A. Crane, ed., *Museums and Memory* (Stanford, CA: Stanford University Press, 2000); Jerome de Groot, *Consuming History: Historians and Heritage in Contemporary Popular Culture* (New York: Routledge, 2009); Kendall R. Phillips, ed., *Framing Public Memory* (Tuscaloosa: University of Alabama Press, 2004); Jo Blatti, ed., *Past Meets Present: Essays about Historic Interpretation and Public Audience* (Washington, DC: Smithsonian Institution Press, 1987). Likewise, for analysis of how politics and memory intersect see Sue Campbell, ed., *Our Faithfulness to the Past: The Ethics and Politics of Memory* (Oxford: Oxford University Press, 2014); Bradford Vivian, *Public Forgetting: The Rhetoric and Politics of Beginning Again* (University Park: Pennsylvania State University Press, 2010); Meili Steele, *Hiding from History: Politics and Public Imagination* (Ithaca, NY: Cornell University Press, 2005); Max Paul Friedman and Padraic Kenney, *Partisan Histories: The Past in Contemporary Global Politics* (New York: Palgrave MacMillon, 2005).

32. "Eulogy for President Reagan," June 11, 2004, Margaret Thatcher Foundation, margaretthatcher.org/Document/110360; Rush Limbaugh, "The Great One," *National Review* 56, no. 12 (June 28, 2004): 36–37, and William F. Buckley, "Ronald Reagan 1911–2004: The Keynote Address," *National Review* 56, no. 12 (June 28, 2004): 14–17 (as well as several others in that issue of *National Review*); Dick Cheney, *In My Time: A Personal and Political Memoir* (New York: Threshold, 2011), 180; Sean Hannity, *Conservative Victory: Defeating Obama's Radical Agenda* (New York: Harper, 2010), 138; Ann Coulter, *Slander: Liberal Lies about the American Right* (New York: Crown, 2002); Ann Coulter, *Treason: Liberal Treachery from the Cold War to the War on Terrorism* (New York, Crown, 2003), 190; Peter Schweizer, *Victory: The Reagan Administration's Secret Strategy That Hastened the Collapse of the Soviet Union* (New York: Atlantic Monthly Press, 1994); Peter Schweizer,

Reagan's War: The Epic Story of His Forty-Year Struggle and Final Triumph over Communism (New York: Doubleday, 2002), 280–285. There are also several examples in Michael K. Deaver, ed., *Why I Am a Reagan Conservative* (New York: William Marrow, 2005). As well as countless more.

33. These final chapters draw on the following works: Will Bunch, *Tear Down This Myth: The Right-Wing Distortion of the Reagan Legacy* (New York: Free Press, 2009); Craig Shirley, *Last Act: The Final Years and Emerging Legacy of Ronald Reagan* (New York: Nelson Books, 2015); Longley et al., *Deconstructing Reagan*. Portions of chapters 5 and 6 also build on Lou Cannon and Carl M. Cannon's *Reagan's Disciple*.

34. In the wake of President Obama's impressive demographic victories there was an emerging consensus that the Republican Party had hurt itself by becoming much more conservative and polarizing since Reagan left office. This was thought to be the result of Newt Gingrich's partisan politics and the emergence of the Tea Party in 2010. It will be interesting to see if this consensus remains the same following Donald Trump's shocking victory in 2016. The Republican Party does not seem to be as dead as some journalists and historians previously believed, but the demographics that propelled Obama to the presidency continue to be of great concern to the GOP. Geoffrey Kabaservice, *Rule and Ruin: The Downfall of Moderation and the Destruction of the Republican Party, from Eisenhower to the Tea Party* (Oxford: Oxford University Press, 2013); E. J. Dionne Jr., *Why the Right Went Wrong: Conservatism from Goldwater to the Tea Party and Beyond* (New York: Simon & Schuster, 2016); Lewis L. Gould, *The Republicans: A History of the Grand Old Party* (Oxford: Oxford University Press, 2014); John Kenneth White, *What Happened to the Republican Party?: And What It Means for American Presidential Politics* (New York: Routledge, 2015). In a similar vein, Heather Cox Richardson has detailed how there are cycles of failure and rebirth for the GOP; it is unclear, right now, if Trump's election will mark such a period of rebirth. Heather Cox Richardson, *To Make Men Free: A History of the Republican Party* (New York: Basic Books, 2014).

CHAPTER 1. THE ORIGINS AND EVOLUTION OF REAGAN'S ECONOMIC POLICIES

1. "CPAC over 30 Years: Conservatives Have Come a Long Way," *Human Events*, February 3, 2003, http://www. humanevents.com/2003/02/03/cpac-over-30 -yearsbrconservatives-have-come-a-long-way/.

2. "Remarks at the Conservative Political Action Conference Dinner," March 20, 1981, http://reagan2020.us/speeches/remarks_at_cpac_dinner.asp, accessed

January 15, 2013. The full text of the speech is available at https://patriotpost.us/pages/435-ronald-reagan-remarks-at-cpac-dinner, accessed May 9, 2019. For all of Reagan's remarks at CPAC see *Reagan at CPAC: The Words That Continue to Inspire a Revolution*, ed. Matt Schlapp (Washington, DC: Regnery, 2019).

3. This chapter builds on historical scholarship that explores the origins of Reagan's economic philosophy. The most detailed account of supply-side economics is Brian Domitrovic's *Econoclasts: The Rebels Who Sparked the Supply-Side Revolution and Restored American Prosperity* (Wilmington, DE: ISI Books, 2009). W. Elliot Brownlee and C. Eugene Steuerle have also detailed Reagan's economic policies in an informative and concise chapter entitled "Taxation" in *The Reagan Presidency: Pragmatic Conservatism and Its Legacies*, ed. W. Elliot Brownlee and Hugh Davis Graham (Lawrence: University Press of Kansas, 2003), 155–181. There is also a considerable amount of scholarship on the transnational origins of what some historians have termed "neoliberal" economic policies. These accounts include Stedman Jones's *Masters of the Universe: Hayek, Friedman, and the Birth of Neoliberal Politics* (Princeton, NJ: Princeton University Press, 2012), and Angus Burgin's *The Great Persuasion: Reinventing Free Markets since the Depression* (Cambridge, MA: Harvard University Press, 2015). Although these historians have provided detailed analysis of the origins of supply-side economics and "neoliberal" economics, I seek to explain how conservatives responded to these policies, both positively and negatively, and detail the often rocky relationship that existed between fiscal conservatives and President Reagan. "Reagan Seeks to Reassure Conservatives Upset by His Support for Tax Increase," *Wall Street Journal*, August 6, 1982, 6; "Reagan Moves to Quell Conservatives' Tax Revolt," *Washington Post*, August 6, 1982, A1; "House Conservatives File Lawsuit to Stop Reagan Tax Bill," *Atlanta Constitution*, August 19, 1982, 14A; "Reagan's Victory Meant Anguish for Some GOP Conservatives," *Baltimore Sun*, August 20, 1982, A13.

4. "Conservatives Rebuff Reagan on Budget Counter-Offer," *Washington Post*, April 21, 1983, A4; "Press Release from the American Life Lobby," January 29, 1983, "American Life Lobby (2)" folder, box 1, Morton Blackwell Files, Ronald Reagan Library, Simi Valley, California (hereafter RRL); "Conservatives Offer Their Own Budget," *Washington Post*, April 17, 1982, A8; "GOP Conservatives Hit Reagan for the Less-Than-Hefty Cuts in Defense," *Christian Science Monitor*, December 20, 1984, 3; "GOP Conservatives Join to Assail Reagan on Budget Strategy, Prepare Alternative," *Wall Street Journal*, January 24, 1984, 5.

5. Many excellent accounts of the rise of the conservative movement conclude with the election of Ronald Reagan in 1980. Among these are Lisa McGirr's *Suburban Warriors: The Origins of the New American Right* (Princeton, NJ: Princeton University Press, 2001), Kim Phillips-Fein's *Invisible Hands: The Making of the Conservative Movement from the New Deal to Reagan* (New York: W. W.

Norton, 2009), Darren Dochuk's *From Bible Belt to Sunbelt: Plain-Folk Religion, Grassroots Politics, and the Rise of Evangelical Conservatism* (New York: W. W. Norton, 2010), and Laura Kalman's *Right Star Rising: A New Politics, 1974–1980* (New York, W. W. Norton, 2010). While these works have done a great deal to further our understanding of how and why the conservative movement was able to gain national prominence, they do not explore at length how conservatives reacted to the Reagan presidency. There are some notable works that do examine conservatives during the Reagan administration. These works include Daniel K. Williams's *God's Own Party: The Making of the Christian Right* (Oxford: Oxford University Press, 2010), Geoffrey Kabaservice's *Rule and Ruin: The Downfall of Moderation and the Destruction of the Republican Party, from Eisenhower to the Tea Party* (Oxford: Oxford University Press, 2013), Daniel T. Rodgers's *Age of Fracture* (New York: Belknap Press, 2011), Domitrovic's *Econoclasts*, Morton Kondracke and Fred Barnes's *Jack Kemp: The Bleeding-Heart Conservative Who Changed the World* (New York: Sentinel, 2015), and Brownlee and Graham's compilation *The Reagan Presidency*.

6. American Legislative Exchange Council, "The Reagan Plan for Tax Reform," *State Factor*, June 1981, "American Legislative Exchange Council (1)" folder, box 1, Blackwell Files, RRL; "Moving toward Policies of Economic Growth: The First 1000 Days," Briefing Paper by Citizens for America, October 27, 1983, "Citizens for America" folder, box 1, Blackwell Files, RRL; "ACU Ratings Reveal Support for Reagan Program," American Conservative Union, *Battleline* 16, no. 2 (February–March 1982), "American Conservative Union" folder, box 1, Blackwell Files, RRL.

7. "Conservatives Offer Their Own Budget," *Washington Post*, April 17, 1982, 8; Letter from Judie Brown, President American Life Lobby, to Margaret Heckler, Secretary of Health and Human Services, September 15, 1983, "American Life Lobby (4)" folder, box 1, Blackwell Files, RRL.

8. "GOP Conservatives Hit Reagan for the Less-Than-Hefty Cuts in Defense," 3; "Think-Tank of Conservatives Has Advice for Reagan," *Los Angeles Times*, December 9, 1984, OC-C1A; "GOP Conservatives Join to Assail Reagan on Budget Strategy," 5.

9. President Ronald Reagan, "Farewell Address to the Nation," January 11, 1989.

10. In addition to the historical accounts of the Reagan economic agenda, there are several noteworthy memoirs including David Stockman's *The Triumph of Politics: How the Reagan Revolution Failed* (New York: Harper & Row, 1986), Martin Anderson's *Revolution: The Reagan Legacy* (Stanford, CA: Hoover Institute Press, 1988), Paul Craig Roberts's *The Supply-Side Revolution: An Insider's Account of Policymaking in Washington* (Cambridge, MA: Harvard University Press, 1984), Edwin Meese III's *With Reagan: The Inside Story* (Washington, DC: Regnery Publishing, 1992), Donald T. Regan's *For the Record: From Wall Street to Washington*

(San Diego: Harcourt Brace Jovanovich, 1988), William A. Niskanen's *Reaganomics: An Insider's Account of the Policies and the People* (New York: Oxford University Press, 1988), and Robert L. Bartley's *The Seven Fat Years: And How to Do It Again* (New York: Free Press, 1992). The standard guide to Reagan's economic reforms is Martin Feldstein, ed., *American Economic Policy in the 1980s* (Chicago: University of Chicago Press, 1994).

11. In fact, the presidential transition team, especially the Fiscal and Monetary Task Force, spent much of its time putting together a comprehensive plan to restore the economy. "Fiscal and Monetary Policy Task Force, Issue Briefing Book," Fall 1980, Annelise Anderson Papers, "Ronald Reagan Presidential Transition Team, 1980–1981: Fiscal and Monetary Task Force" folder, box 26, Hoover Institution Archives, Stanford University, Stanford, California.

12. John B. Taylor argues that while Volcker deserves credit for getting inflation under control, Reagan deserves to be lauded for not interfering with policies at the Federal Reserve. John B. Taylor, "Changes in American Economic Policy in the 1980s: Watershed or Pendulum Swing?" *Journal of Economic Literature* 33, no. 2 (June 1995): 777–784. Volcker also gave Reagan credit for not interfering with his tight monetary policy in his memoirs. Paul Volcker and Toyoo Gyohten, *Changing Fortunes: The World's Money and the Threat of American Leadership* (New York: Random House, 1992), 175.

13. Keynesian economics emphasizes the government's ability to stimulate economic growth by spending money on infrastructure, war, professional development, or any other form of economic activity. Those who adhere to Keynesian theory vary on what they would like government to spend money on, but they are generally in agreement that government is needed to inject funds into the economy and to provide jobs to individuals so that aggregate demand does not decrease.

14. George H. Nash, *The Conservative Intellectual Movement In America: Since 1945* (Wilmington, DE: ISI Books, 1976), 1.

15. Proponents of the free market in 1945 wanted to return to an economy with low taxes, minimal regulations (usually put in place to protect capital owners), and minimal government intervention with the market forces of supply and demand. They usually longed for the economy of the 1920s if not the economy prior to the Progressive Era.

16. Nicholas Wapshott, *Keynes, Hayek: The Clash That Defined Modern Economics* (New York: W. W. Norton, 2011), 80.

17. F. A. Hayek, *The Road to Serfdom* (London: University of Chicago Press, 2007), 79.

18. Alan Ebenstein, *Friedrich Hayek: A Biography* (Chicago: University of Chicago Press, 2003), 128.

19. Lawrence K. Frank, "The Rising Stock of Dr. Hayek: American Business Has Found a Shining New Prophet," *Saturday Review*, May 12, 1945, 5.

20. Nash, *Conservative Intellectual Movement*, 11.

21. Lee Edwards, phone interview with author, February 11, 2013, audio recording in author's possession.

22. Lee Edwards, *Reagan: A Political Biography* (San Diego: Vintage Books, 1967), 52.

23. For more on the evolution of Reagan's thinking consult David T. Byrne's *Ronald Reagan: An Intellectual Biography* (Lincoln, NE: Potomac Books, 2018).

24. Thomas W. Evans, *The Education of Ronald Reagan: The General Electric Years and the Untold Story of His Conversion to Conservatism* (New York: Columbia University Press, 2008), 57.

25. Edwards, *Reagan*, 71.

26. Evans, *Education of Reagan*, 77.

27. Kim Phillips-Fein, "'If Business and the Country Will Be Run Right': The Business Challenge to the Liberal Consensus, 1945–1964," *International Labor and Working Class History* 72, no. 1 (Fall 2007): 202.

28. Tip O'Neill, *Man of the House: The Life and Political Memoirs of Tip O'Neill* (New York: Random House, 1987), 332.

29. Ronald Reagan, *Actor, Ideologue, Politician: The Public Speeches of Ronald Reagan*, ed. David W. Houck and Amos Kiewe (London: Greenwood Press, 1993), 10–17.

30. Reagan, *Actor, Ideologue, Politician*, 23–27.

31. Leonard E. Read to Ronald Reagan, August 16, 1960, Series 2.1: General File, Correspondence, box 25, folder 43, Foundation for Economic Education Archives, Irvington-on-Hudson, New York (hereafter FEEA).

32. Edmund A. Opitz to Mrs. Joe Emenhiser, January 31, 1983, Series 2.2: People File, box 27, folder 28, FEEA.

33. Richard Ebeling, "The Lasting Legacy of the Reagan Revolution," *Freeman* 54, July 1, 2004, http://www.fee.org/the_freeman/detail/the-lasting-legacy-of-the-reagan-revolution#axzz2McVi5GFx.

34. Edwards, *Reagan*, 74.

35. Ronald Reagan, "A Time for Choosing," October 27, 1964, http://www.reagan.utexas.edu /archives/reference/ timechoosing.html.

36. Reagan, "A Time for Choosing."

37. Reagan, "A Time for Choosing."

38. Edwards, interview.

39. Lee Edwards, *Goldwater: The Man Who Made a Revolution* (Washington, DC: Regnery Publishing, 1995), 336; H. W. Brands, *Reagan: The Life* (New York: Doubleday, 2015), 5–6.

40. For a detailed description of Lee Edward's life as a conservative intellectual and activist, see his memoir *Just Right: A Life in Pursuit of Liberty* (Wilmington, DE: ISI Books, 2017).

41. Edwards, interview; Steven F. Hayward, *The Age of Reagan: The Fall of the Old Liberal Order, 1964–1980* (New York: Three Rivers Press, 2001), xxii; Matt K. Lewis, *Too Dumb to Fail: How the GOP Betrayed the Reagan Revolution to Win Elections (and How It Can Reclaim Its Conservative Roots)* (New York: Hachette Books, 2016), 29.

42. Milton Friedman and Rose Friedman, *Two Lucky People: Milton and Rose D. Friedman* (Chicago: University of Chicago Press, 1998), 333.

43. Milton Friedman, *Capitalism and Freedom* (Chicago: University of Chicago Press, 2002), 2.

44. Friedman and Friedman, *Two Lucky People*, 389.

45. Friedman and Friedman, *Two Lucky People*, 388.

46. "Reagan Guest Stars before the California Assembly," *New York Times*, May 7, 1991, A18; Lou Cannon, *Ronald Reagan: The Presidential Portfolio* (New York: Public Affairs, 2001), 47–51.

47. Cannon, *Ronald Reagan: The Presidential Portfolio*, 47–51; Joe Street, *Dirty Harry's America: Clint Eastwood, Harry Callahan, and the Conservative Backlash* (Gainesville: University Press of Florida, 2016), 47.

48. Sean Wilentz, *The Age of Reagan: A History 1974–2008* (New York: Harper Perennial, 2001), 134; Street, *Dirty Harry's America*, 47.

49. Howard Jarvis, *I'm Mad As Hell* (New York: Times Books, 1979), 39.

50. Friedman and Friedman, *Two Lucky People*, 389.

51. There are extensive historical accounts of the 1970s. For more information on stagflation, as well as American culture generally, consult Jefferson Cowie, *Stayin' Alive: The 1970s and the Last Days of the Working Class* (New York: New Press, 2010); Edward D. Berkowitz, *Something Happened: A Political and Cultural Overview of the Seventies* (New York: Columbia University Press, 2006); Meg Jacobs, *Panic at the Pump: The Energy Crisis and the Transformation of American Politics in the 1970s* (New York: Hill & Wang, 2016); Judith Stein, *Pivotal Decade: How the United States Traded Factories for Finance in the Seventies* (New Haven, CT: Yale University Press, 2010). For more on conservatives in the 1970s, see Bruce J. Schulman and Julian E. Zelizer's comprehensive compilation *Rightward Bound: Making America Conservative in the 1970s* (Cambridge, MA: Harvard University Press, 2008).

52. Domitrovic, *Econoclasts*, 9. The term "Reaganomics" originated from a title that a copyeditor placed on an article that Paul Craig Roberts wrote for the *New York Times* shortly after Reagan was elected. Paul Craig Roberts, "Reaganomics:

A Change?," *New York Times*, November 9, 1980, as discussed in Roberts's *The Supply-Side Revolution*, 93.

53. There has actually been very little historical scholarship dedicated to the advent of supply-side economics. Recently, Jason Stahl in *Right Moves* dismisses the intellectual foundations of supply-side theory, asserting that "the barrier for entry in the marketplace was now so low that drawings on napkins and large block quotes from David Hume were taken seriously by many, including the president of the United States (100–101)." Stahl also contends that no peer-reviewed academic papers existed supporting supply-side theory. Contrary to Stahl's claims, Domitrovic's *Econoclasts* traces the intellectual origins of supply-side economics, including the policies of Treasury Secretary Andrew Mellon, President John F. Kennedy's tax cuts, and the academic papers of Dr. Robert Mundell during the 1960s. Jason Stahl, *Right Moves: The Conservative Think Tank in American Political Culture since 1945* (Chapel Hill: University of North Carolina Press, 2016); Domitrovic, *Econoclasts*. The Heritage Foundation released a short book that outlined the economists who influenced supply-side economics. It detailed the influences of classical economists Adam Smith and Jean Baptiste Say as well as Carl Menger, Alfred Marshall, and others. David G. Raboy, ed., *Essays in Supply-Side Economics* (Washington, DC: Institute for Research on the Economics of Taxation, 1982).

54. Domitrovic, *Econoclasts*, 110.

55. Domitrovic, *Econoclasts*, 103, 110.

56. Jude Wanniski, "It's Time to Cut Taxes," *Wall Street Journal*, December 11, 1974. Supply-side economics did not get its name until 1976 when Herbert Stein mocked the "supply-side fiscalists" at a symposium in Virginia. Word got back to Wanniski, who thought the term had promise. He rebranded "the Mundell-Laffer hypothesis" as "supply-side economics." Domitrovic, *Econoclasts*, 125–126.

57. Domitrovic, *Econoclasts*, 117.

58. Domitrovic, *Econoclasts*, 123–124.

59. For a comprehensive study on Jack Kemp's contribution to the conservative movement consult Kondracke and Barnes's *Jack Kemp*.

60. Kondracke and Barnes, *Jack Kemp*, 29; Domitrovic, *Econoclasts*, 134.

61. For Roberts's detailed account of the supply-side movement, see his memoir *The Supply-Side Revolution*.

62. Domitrovic, *Econoclasts*, 134–135. Domitrovic and Kondracke and Barnes seem to disagree as to whether the Savings and Investment Act represented a belief in supply-side stimulus. Kondracke and Barnes cite Laffer himself, who labeled the 1974 measure "an 'old line, right-wing' capital formation act." Kondracke and Barnes insist that Kemp wasn't converted to supply-side economics until Kemp came "under Wanniski's influence" in 1975. Regardless, by 1975, "Kemp became

a tax cutter first and a budget balancer hardly at all." Kondracke and Barnes, *Jack Kemp*, 31, 39.

63. Stockman, *The Triumph of Politics*, 42.

64. Stockman, *The Triumph of Politics*, 43.

65. Kondracke and Barnes, *Jack Kemp*, 42–43.

66. "Jack Kemp Wants to Cut Your Taxes—A Lot," *Fortune*, April 10, 1978, 38.

67. The pro-business forces that controlled the GOP prior to the supply-side movement emphasized balanced budgets as the top priority of the party.

68. For a complete study of tax issues from 1950 to the present consult Lawrence Kudlow and Brian Domitrovic's *JFK and the Reagan Revolution: A Secret History of American Prosperity* (New York: Portfolio, 2016).

69. One example of this conflict emerged when Reagan's budget deficit in 1981 was $79 billion. David Stockman immediately began asserting that high interest rates, which were driving the recession, were being caused by budget deficits (a common view among budget hawk Republicans at the time). In response, Stockman launched an offensive to cut spending and raise taxes. Paul Craig Roberts, a more principled supply-side advocate, asserted that Stockman's policies were "austerity with a vengeance—a throwback to the policies of the 1930s and a far cry from the supply-side policy of balancing the budget through economic growth." Roberts, *The Supply-Side Revolution*, 171.

70. Stockman, *The Triumph of Politics*, 60.

71. Domitrovic, *Econoclasts*, 159–160. For a description of Reagan's changing policy views and his relationship to the conservative movement, consult Ted V. McAllister's chapter "Reagan and the Transformation of American Conservatism," in Brownlee and Graham, *The Reagan Presidency*, 40–60.

72. Kiron K. Skinner, Annelise Anderson, and Martin Anderson, eds., *Reagan in His Own Hand* (New York: Free Press, 2001), 274.

73. Other scholars have also noticed that Reagan seemed to paint a rosy picture of the effect the supply-side tax cuts would have on deficits. Even when in the White House, Reagan continued to argue that tax cuts would spur revenues. In 1984, over lunch, Reagan told his advisers that "there has not been one tax increase in history that actually raised revenue. And every tax cut, from the 1920s to Kennedy's to ours, has produced more." His economic advisers quickly corrected him—as recounted in W. Elliot Brownlee and C. Eugene Steuerle's "Taxation" in *The Reagan Presidency*, 167. It appears clear, however, that Reagan's economic advisors realized that significant spending cuts would be necessary to make up for decreased revenue as a result of cutting taxes. The Fiscal and Monetary Task Force during the transition concluded its study on Kemp-Roth by declaring that "federal taxes can be cut substantially, and the budget can be balanced if the growth rate of Federal spending is restrained." They also believed that the tax cuts would

spur economic initiative. The task force concluded that "Roth-Kemp cannot be viewed simply as a large tax cut which cuts Federal revenues. Roth-Kemp is a supply-side tax cut which increases economic incentives, reduces the use of tax shelters; and stimulates the savings and investments needed to increase productivity and economic growth. Roth-Kemp will lead to more employment; higher real income, fewer lives wasted on welfare, and a rekindling of the work effort and entrepreneurial spirit." "The Fiscal and Monetary Task Force: Roth-Kemp and the Budget," Fall 1980, Annelise Anderson Papers, box 26, "Ronald Reagan Presidential Transition Team, 1980–1981: Fiscal and Monetary Task Force" folder, Hoover Institution Archives.

74. Brownlee and Steuerle, "Taxation," 157.

75. For a full account of the California tax revolt consult Howard Jarvis's *I'm Mad As Hell.* Brian Domitrovic credits Jude Wanniski's *The Way the World Works* and William Simon's *Time for Truth* for helping incite the national tax revolt. He asserts that both books were best sellers and "were often consulted" by the leaders of the tax revolt. Domitrovic, *Econoclasts,* 154. Jude Wanniski, *The Way the World Works: How Economies Fail and Succeed* (New York: Basic Books,1978); William Simon, *Time for Truth* (New York: Berkley, 1978). Arthur Laffer and Jan Seymour have provided historians with a convenient anthology of important documents associated with the tax revolt. Arthur B. Laffer and Jan P. Seymour, *The Economics of the Tax Revolt: A Reader* (New York: Harcourt Brace Jovanovich, 1979).

76. Dr. Arthur Laffer, phone interview with author, February 12, 2013, audio recording in author's possession.

77. There is some disagreement as to when Reagan fully endorsed supply-side economics. Morton Kondracke and Fred Barnes discuss the question of who "converted" Reagan to supply-side economics at length and give Jack Kemp at least part of the credit for his LAX meeting with Reagan. Kondracke and Barnes, *Jack Kemp,* 62–64. Reagan's numerous pre-supply-side speeches indicate that he had long been arguing that marginal tax rates were so high that they discouraged productivity. For instance, in his January 27, 1958, remarks before the House Ways and Means Committee, Reagan condemned the tax rates he paid in Hollywood as "unrealistic, confiscatory, and contrary to the principles of free enterprise." Reagan, *Actor, Ideologue, Politician,* 10–17. Edwin Meese III has also discussed this issue in his memoir *With Reagan,* 121–124. Martin Anderson also addresses the question of Reagan's conversion to supply-side economics in *Revolution,* 161. Finally, Reagan explains in his autobiography that "my own experience with our tax laws in Hollywood probably taught me more about practical economic theory than I ever learned in a classroom or from an economist, and my views on tax reform did not spring from what people called supply-side economics." Ronald Reagan, *An American Life: The Autobiography* (New York: Threshold, 1990), 231.

78. "Jimmy Carter on Budget and Economy," http://www.ontheissues.org/Ce leb/Jimmy_Carter_ Budget_&_ Economy.htm, accessed August 12, 2015.

79. Stockman, *The Triumph of Politics*, 45.

80. Jones, *Masters of the Universe*, 217. For a more complete analysis of Carter's economic policies see W. Carl Biven, *Jimmy Carter's Economy: Policy in the Age of Limits* (Chapel Hill: University of North Carolina Press, 2002).

81. In 1971, Nobel laureate and MIT economist Paul Samuelson gave a talk at the University of Chicago entitled "Why They Are Laughing at Laffer." According to Martin Anderson, a former student of Samuelson's, "what [Samuelson] did to Laffer that day in Chicago, even by academic standards of morality, was an extraordinary example of intellectual bullying." Anderson, *Revolution*, 148. Another event that demonstrated the lack of respect that supply-side ideas endured during the 1970s took place in the spring of 1976 during an economic symposium where American Enterprise Institute economist Herbert Stein described a new economic theory that was making noise in Washington. He discredited what he termed the "supply-side fiscalists" who among economists numbered "maybe two." Domitrovic, *Econoclasts*, 125–126.

82. There are some exceptional histories of the election of 1980. For more on the election itself see Craig Shirley's *Rendezvous with Destiny: Ronald Reagan and the Campaign That Changed America* (Wilmington, DE: ISI Books, 2009), and Andrew E. Busch's *Reagan's Victory: The Presidential Election of 1980 and the Rise of the Right* (Lawrence: University Press of Kansas, 2005).

CHAPTER 2. THE BATTLE FOR FISCAL CONSERVATISM: SUPPLY-SIDERS V. BUDGET HAWKS

1. President Reagan outlined his plan for the economy on February 18, 1981. Ronald Reagan, "White House Report on the Program for Economic Recovery," February 18, 1981, http://www.presidency.ucsb.edu/ws/?pid=43427. For a look at the administration's economic priorities consult "Fiscal and Monetary Policy Task Force, Issue Briefing Book," Fall 1980, Annelise Anderson Papers, box 26, "Ronald Reagan Presidential Transition Team, 1980–1981: Fiscal and Monetary Task Force" folder, Hoover Institution Archives, Stanford University, Stanford, California.

2. "No Quick Fix for Social Security," *Policy Report*, CATO Institute 3, no. 2 (February 1981), box 1, "CATO" folder, Blackwell Files, Ronald Reagan Presidential Library, Simi Valley, California (hereafter RRL). For an in-depth analysis of how the Reagan administration dealt with Social Security see Martha Derthick and Steven M. Teles's chapter "Riding the Third Rail: Social Security Reform," in *The*

Reagan Presidency: Pragmatic Conservatism and Its Legacy, ed. W. Elliot Brownlee and Hugh Davis Graham (Lawrence: University Press of Kansas, 2003), 182–208. Derthick and Teles demonstrate that the Reagan administration was unable to significantly change Social Security. Instead, Reagan embraced bipartisan legislation that "confirmed the existing program, contrary to conservative preferences" (184).

3. Ronald Reagan, *An American Life: The Autobiography* (New York: Threshold, 1990), 279.

4. David Stockman, *The Triumph of Politics: How the Reagan Revolution Failed* (New York: Harper & Row, 1986), 80.

5. The deficit for FY1980 was almost $60 billion. Furthermore, reducing inflation and ending bracket creep (whereby individual tax rates would be indexed to inflation) would decrease the revenue that the government was receiving from taxation. In short, if it had not been for high inflation during the Carter years, the deficit would have been much higher during his administration. Although ending bracket creep and addressing inflation were net positives for the economy, they did result in increased deficits. Reagan, "White House Report on the Program for Economic Recovery," February 18, 1981.

6. Stockman, *The Triumph of Politics*, 124. Stockman lamented in his memoir that there were early warnings that even members of the administration opposed necessary spending cuts to make the supply-side program work. Stockman asserted that soon after taking office he realized "I was faced with cabinet colleagues who were ill-schooled in even the basic tenets of the Reagan Revolution" (113). Additionally, Stockman tried to end funding to the Export-Import Bank, a longtime goal of conservatives. In 1981 he cut its funding by 40 percent, but just as with the cabinet, those agreed-upon figures were never hard and fast, and Congress increased the bank's budget each year.

7. Stockman, *The Triumph of Politics*, 126.

8. Lyn Nofziger, *Nofziger* (Washington, DC: Regnery, 1992), 268. Nofziger validates Stockman's criticism of Reagan in regard to the budget. According to Nofziger, despite his faults, Stockman "did come into the administration determined to balance the federal budget, more so, it turned out, than Reagan" (267).

9. It should be noted that conservative priorities were also at odds with one another. For instance, while Stockman was cutting social programs and trimming government waste in numerous federal departments he was also proposing a 160 percent increase in the defense budget by 1986. Stockman, *The Triumph of Politics*, 118.

10. Stockman, *The Triumph of Politics*, 141.

11. Stockman discusses the push back against significant cuts at length in chapter 3 of his memoir, entitled "The Counter-Revolution Begins," 147–172. He specifically discusses the problems with cutting Social Security on pages 196–208.

12. Stockman, *The Triumph of Politics*, 142.

13. Stockman, *The Triumph of Politics*, 144.

14. Indeed, the projections were a compromise between two different economic worldviews—those of David Stockman and Murray Weidenbaum. Stockman believed that supply-side economics would result in incredible economic growth of around 7 percent. Stockman also believed that such growth, along with the actions of the Federal Reserve, would lead to low levels of inflation. If the forecast had been based just on supply-side theory, it would have demonstrated that the administration was going to run large deficits. Likewise, had Weidenbaum gotten his way and decreased the forecast for economic growth, deficits would have appeared. However, the compromise to go with Stockman's growth numbers (slightly modified) and Weidenbaum's inflation numbers resulted in a rosy picture. In reality, the US economy contracted by 1.2 percent. As a result, the Reagan administration ran large deficits when its forecasts had predicted a balanced budget by 1985. Stockman, *The Triumph of Politics*, 98–108.

15. Reagan, "White House Report on the Program for Economic Recovery," February 18, 1981.

16. Jack Kemp was so frustrated with the slowness of the process and the prospect that the administration might compromise the tax cut that he rebelled by going to the press. The *New York Times* cited Kemp calling Reagan's tax proposals "timid." The article went on to quote Kemp saying he was "no longer bound" to the president and asserting that he would pursue his "own program." After his statements appeared in the press, Kemp called Reagan and the two spent twenty minutes repairing their relationship. *New York Times*, February 17, 1981, 1. As cited in Morton Kondracke and Fred Barnes's *Jack Kemp: The Bleeding-Heart Conservative Who Changed the World* (New York: Sentinel, 2015), 89–90.

17. Lyn Nofziger's handwritten notes from the hospital record Reagan's quips. He "told Nancy: 'Honey, I forgot to duck'" and to the surgeon he joked "pls tell me you're Republicans." Lyn Nofziger Handwritten Notes on Reagan Assassination Attempt," March 30, 1981, Lyn Nofziger Papers, box 10, "Nofziger's Notes re: Reagan's Assassination Attempt" folder, Hoover Institution Archives.

18. "Reagan Is Recovering, Signs New Dairy Law, Quips with Aides, Docs," *Schenectady Gazette*, April 1 1981, 1.

19. Herbert L. Abrams, *"The President Has Been Shot": Confusion, Disability, and the 25th Amendment in the Aftermath of the Attempted Assassination of Ronald Reagan* (New York: W. W. Norton, 1992), 137.

20. Tip O'Neill, *Man of the House: The Life and Political Memoirs of Tip O'Neill* (New York: Random House, 1987), 336.

21. Del Quentin Wilber, *Rawhide Down: The Near Assassination of Ronald Reagan* (New York: Henry Holt, 2011), 219.

22. Tax Cuts: Polling Results, "Tax Bill 1981 II" folder, box OA 9425, David Gergen Files, RRL.

23. "Address before a Joint Session of Congress on the Program for Economic Recovery," April 28, 1981, http://www.reagan.utexas.edu/archives/speeches /1981/42881c.htm accessed 03/15/2013.

24. Wilber, *Rawhide Down*, 217; Kondracke and Barnes, *Jack Kemp*, 93.

25. Reagan, *An American Life*, 285.

26. Chronology and Key Elements of the 1964 Tax Cuts, From Marty Asher to Jim Burnham, box OA6730, "Reagan Tax Proposal 3 01/20/1981—07/28/1981" folder, Council of Economic Advisers—Staff Economic Records (Michael Mckee) Files, RRL. Consulting President Reagan's phone records indicates that he spent an enormous amount of time and energy courting Congress to pass his economic program. The same cannot be said on social issues. See box 1, Presidential Handwriting File, Series IV: Presidential Telephone Calls (1/01/82–8/5/82), RRL. For a complete analysis on the ways that President Reagan's and President Kennedy's tax cuts mirrored one another, see Lawrence Kudlow and Brian Domitrovic's *JFK and the Reagan Revolution: A Secret History of American Prosperity* (New York: Portfolio, 2016).

27. Jack Kemp's middle name was "French." Arthur Laffer, February 12, 2013, phone interview, audio recording in author's possession.

28. Background on Democratic Tax Proposals for Testimony This Morning, Susan Nelson to Murray Weidenbaum, box OA6730, "Reagan Tax Proposal 2 01/2/1981—07/28/1981" folder, Council of Economic Advisers: Staff Economist Records (Michael McKee) Files, RRL.

29. Memo from the House Ways and Means Committee to Its Democratic Members, July 16, 1981, box OA6730, "Reagan Tax Proposal 1 01/20/1981—07/28/1981" folder, Council of Economic Advisers: Staff Economist Records (Michael McKee) Files, RRL. To be sure, indexing tax rates was one of the administration's top economic priorities. "Fiscal and Monetary Policy Task Force: Tax Indexing," Fall 1980, Annelise Anderson Papers, box 26, "Ronald Reagan Presidential Transition Team, 1980–1981: Fiscal and Monetary Task Force" folder, Hoover Institution Archives.

30. Reagan, *An American Life*, 284.

31. O'Neill, *Man of the House*, 341.

32. ERTA passed by a vote of 89–11 in the Senate and 323–107 in the House. "Both Houses Give Reagan a 3-Year Tax Cut Victory," *Atlanta Constitution*, July 30, 1981, 1A.

33. "Senate Rejects Kennedy's Pleas, Approves Tax Cuts," *Los Angeles Times*, August 4, 1981, A10; "Both Houses Give Reagan a 3-Year Tax Cut Victory," *Atlanta Constitution*.

34. Remarks of the President Following Passage of Tax Legislation in the House and Senate," July 29, 1981, box OA9425, "Tax Bill 1981 II" folder, Gergen Files, RRL.

35. Internal document, "In the Oval Office after the Tax Cut Vote," July 30, 1981, box OA8159, "Economic Policy—Congressional Tax Vote 07/30/1981" folder, Gergen Files, RRL.

36. In the run up to the tax vote, conservative groups such as the American Conservative Union were pivotal in using their grassroots networks to contact congressmen across the country. Furthermore, conservative groups from across the spectrum praised the Reagan tax cuts, asserting that Reagan's plan "invigorates the incentive for people to create." Letter from Suzanne Scholte, Affiliates Liaison/Projects Director, to ACU Board of Directors and Conservative Leaders, August 28, 1981, box 1, "American Conservative Union" folder, Blackwell Files, RRL; *The State Factor*, American Legislative Exchange Council. June 1981, "American Legislative Exchange Council (1)," "The Reagan Plan for Tax Reform" folder, box 1, Blackwell Files, RRL.

37. "Reagan's Next Contest Is to Disarm the New Right Extremists" *Los Angeles Times*, August 16, 1981, E1.

38. "Mantle of Success Rests Uneasily on Kemp; Conservatives' Heir Apparent under Pressure," *Baltimore Sun*, March 10, 1981, A6. Jack Kemp even contemplated a public break with Reagan in the spring of 1981. Both Laffer and Kemp attempted to persuade Reagan to expand the tax cuts and make them deeper. Reflecting on the 1981, the American Conservative Union asserted that while progress had been made in the conservative voting record of Congress, there was "still a long way to go in the fight against irresponsible and overbearing government." "ACU Ratings Reveal Support for Reagan Positions," *Battleline* 16, no. 2 (February –March 1982): 2, "American Conservative Union" folder, box 1, Blackwell Files, RRL.

39. Laffer, interview; "No Shrinking Supply-Sider: Economist Arthur Laffer Keeps the Faith," *Barron's*, December 21, 1981.

40. "Conservatives Hit Reagan Policy," *Washington Post*, January 25, 1982, A2.

41. "Reagan, Top Officials Woo Conservatives at Conference," *Washington Post*, February 26, 1982, A3. Many conservatives believed that President Nixon had pursued liberal policies while in office, and they partially blamed themselves for not challenging the administration for fear that they would lose influence within the GOP. For a complete analysis on the ways that Nixon has been imagined see David Greenberg's *Nixon's Shadow: The History of an Image* (New York: W. W. Norton), 2003.

42. Memorandum from Morton Blackwell to Red Cavaney, "Grover Norquist's Group," June 7, 1982, 1, box 2, "Balanced Budget Amendment (1 of 3)" folder, Blackwell Files, RRL.

43. Memorandum "Balanced Budget Constitutional Amendment," White

House, April 28, 1982, 1, box 2, "Balanced Budget Amendment (1 of 3)" folder, Blackwell Files, RRL.

44. Numerous conservative activists and groups endorsed the balanced budget amendment including Richard Viguerie, Ron Goodwin (Moral Majority), Bill Billings (National Christian Action Coalition), Dr. Edwin J. Feulner Jr. (president of the Heritage Foundation), Howard Phillips (national director of the Conservative Caucus), Veterans for Foreign Wars, American Legion, American Security Council, National Association of Evangelicals, National Pro-Family Coalition, National Pro-Life PAC, Americans for the Reagan Agenda, and American Conservative Union. "Conservative Support List for Balanced Budget Amendment," box 2, "Balanced Budget Amendment (2 of 3)" folder, Blackwell Files, RRL; Businesses from across the country also endorsed the amendment. Memorandum to Bob Moss from Bill Tobin, vice president of the National Tax-Limitation Committee, May 18, 1982, box 2, "Balanced Budget Amendment (1 of 3)" folder, Blackwell Files, RRL.

45. Press release, "Bipartisan Support Grows for Tax Limitation/Balanced Budget Amendment—Senator Cannon Signs on as Cosponsor—Presidential Endorsement Welcomed," National Tax-Limitation Committee, May 14, 1982, 3, box 2, "Balanced Budget Amendment (1 of 3)" folder, Blackwell Files, RRL.

46. Memorandum "Grover Norquist's Group" from Morton Blackwell to Red Cavaney, June 7, 1982, box 2, "Balanced Budget Amendment (1 of 3)" folder, Blackwell Files, RRL.

47. "A Push for a Balanced Budget Amendment to the U.S. Constitution," from Patrick Pizzella to Morton Blackwell, February 1981, box 2, "Balanced Budget Amendment (2 of 3)" folder, Blackwell Files, RRL.

48. "Address to the Nation on the Fiscal Year 1983 Federal Budget," April 29, 1982. Full text is available at https://www.reagan.utexas.edu/archives/speeches/1982/42982b.htm.

49. Of the 201 cosponsors in the House, 147 were Republicans and 54 were Democrats. In the Senate, 39 cosponsors were Republicans and 14 were Democrats. Memorandum "Balanced Budget Constitutional Amendment," April 28, 1982.

50. Press release, "Bipartisan Support Grows for Tax Limitation/Balanced Budget Amendment"; Memorandum "Grover Norquist's Group."

51. Cosigners to Norquist's memorandum included Paul Weyrich, director of the Committee for Survival of a Free Congress; Rev. Jerry Falwell, president of the Moral Majority; John T. Dolan, national director of the National Political Action Committee; Karen Davis, director of the Christian Women's National Concerns Committee; Phyllis Schlafly, chairman of Eagle Forum; Howard Philips, chairman of the Conservative Caucus; and Don Todd, executive director of the American Conservative Union. Memorandum, "Grover Norquist's Group."

52. Memorandum, "Grover Norquist's Group."

53. Memorandum, "Balanced Budget Amendment," [date unknown (early to mid-May 1982)], box 2, "Balanced Budget Amendment (2 of 3)" folder, Blackwell File, RRL.

54. Schedule proposal, "U.S. Capitol Steps Balanced Budget Speech," Elizabeth Dole to Fred Ryan, deputy director Presidential Appointments and Scheduling, June 28, 1982, box 2, "Balanced Budget Amendment (1 of 3)" folder, Blackwell Files, RRL.

55. "President Reagan in Blistering Heat on Capitol Steps," *United Press International,* July 19, 1982.

56. The poll found that 64 percent favored such an amendment, 20 percent opposed, 17 percent had no opinion. Interestingly, union members favored it 63–24, while nonunion supported it 64–19. Families making less than $15,000 a year were for the amendment 58–17, while those who made over $15,000 supported the amendment 68–22. Press release "New Chamber/Gallup Survey Finds Americans Favor Balanced Budget Amendment by Three to One," Chamber of Commerce of the United States, July 15, 1982, box 2, "Balanced Budget Amendment (1 of 3)" folder, Blackwell Files, RRL.

57. "Congress Rejects Balanced Budget Amendment: Pressure Shifts to States," *First Reading* 8, no. 10 (October 1982): 6, box 1, "American Legislative Exchange Council (2)" folder, Blackwell Files, RRL.

58. "Reagan Seeks to Reassure Conservatives Upset by His Support for Tax Increase," *Wall Street Journal,* August 6, 1982, 6. Reagan went to great lengths to garner support for the balanced budget amendment. The president made numerous phone calls during the summer and fall of 1982 lobbying Congress to support the amendment. Reagan also supported the grassroots organization in support of the amendment. In a phone call to Donald Kendall for example, he asked Kendall to be the national finance chairman of an independent citizen organization to promote the balanced budget amendment. Telephone call from President Ronald Reagan to Donald Kendall, June 14, 1982, box 2, Presidential Handwriting File, Series IV, Presidential Telephone Calls (5/25/82–6/14/82), RRL.

59. "Reagan Seeks to Reassure Conservatives Upset by His Support for Tax Increase," 6. Supply-side advocates also lambasted David Stockman, who had "turned into one of the leaders of anti-supply-side, deficit-hawk, tax-raising, and budget-balancing conventional Republican forces. Supply-siders, including Kemp allies who got jobs in the Treasury Department, considered Stockman a turncoat and a traitor." Kondracke and Barnes, *Jack Kemp,* 79.

60. Paul Craig Roberts, *The Supply-Side Revolution: An Insider's Account of Policymaking in Washington* (Cambridge, MA: Harvard University Press, 1984), 171.

61. "Reagan Seeks to Reassure Conservatives Upset by His Support for Tax Increase," 6.

62. Such concerns were not new among Reagan's advisers. Reagan's campaign manager, John Sears, feared that Kemp would run in the 1980 GOP primaries and undercut Reagan's conservative appeal. To undercut this possibility, Sears did everything he could to bring Kemp into the Reagan camp, including encouraging Reagan to endorse Kemp-Roth and run on a supply-side agenda. For a detailed account of Kemp's relationship with Reagan's 1980 presidential run including internal considerations, see Kondracke and Barnes, *Jack Kemp*, 55–65.

63. Ronald Reagan, *The Reagan Diaries*, ed. Douglas Brinkley (New York: HarperCollins, 2007), 96. Reagan and Kemp had been discussing the prospect of tax increases for months, and Reagan had encouraged Kemp to try to reach a compromise with the Democrats that would increase taxes by less than the $95 billion. As the process evolved, however, Kemp remained opposed to any deal that increased taxes, while Reagan decided that compromise was preferable. Phone call from Ronald Reagan to Jack Kemp, May 16, 1982, box 2, folder 24, Presidential Handwriting File, Series IV: Presidential Telephone Calls (1/01/82–8/5/82), RRL.

64. "Reagan Moves to Quell Conservatives' Tax Revolt," *Washington Post*, August 6, 1982, A1.

65. "Reagan Moves to Quell Conservatives' Tax Revolt," A1. In his memoir, Nofziger recalls that he changed his mind again. According to Nofziger he not only stopped publicly undermining the tax bill, he also "spent two weeks helping to pass the bill." Nofziger, *Nofziger*, 249. Nofziger actually put together the public relations plan in the week leading up to the passage of the bill. "Tax Bill P.R. Plan," box 11, "TEFRA Bill, 1982: P.R. Plan and Correspondence" folder, Lyn Nofziger Papers, Hoover Institution Archives.

66. In reality, the Senate bill was an amendment of a bill that did originate in the House and had been sent over to the Senate some months earlier. Therefore, House conservatives had little ground to pursue legal action. "Reagan Seeks to Reassure Conservatives Upset by His Support for Tax Increase," *Wall Street Journal*, August 6, 1982, 6; "House Conservatives File Lawsuit to Stop Reagan Tax Bill," *Atlanta Constitution*, August 19, 1982, 14A.

67. "House Conservatives File Lawsuit to Stop Reagan Tax Bill," 14A.

68. "Reagan Moves to Quell Conservatives' Tax Revolt," *Washington Post*, August 6, 1982, A1; Newt Gingrich, "Notes on Self-Government: The President's Speech Sketches a Conservative Opportunity Society," *Atlanta Daily World*, February 5, 1984, 4.

69. "Reagan Seeks to Reassure Conservatives Upset by His Support for Tax Increase," 6.

70. "Reagan Moves to Quell Conservatives' Tax Revolt," A1.

71. "Reagan Moves to Quell Conservatives' Tax Revolt," A1.

72. "Topics of Discussion for Phone Call to Representative Gene Atkinson (R-Pennsylvania)," box 3, folder 38, Presidential Handwriting File, Series IV: Presidential Telephone Calls (8/6/82–12/31/82), RRL. This folder contains numerous phone calls between Reagan and members of Congress requesting their support for the tax increase bill. The same White House talking points are emphasized, in varying degrees, in many of the phone conversations. The president ultimately went on the radio, sent key administration officials on the television shows, and delivered a public speech. "Tax Bill P.R. Plan," Lyn Nofziger Papers, box 11, "TEFRA Bill, 1982: P.R. Plan and Correspondence" folder, Hoover Institution Archives.

73. "House Conservatives File Lawsuit to Stop Reagan Tax Bill," *Atlanta Constitution,* August 19, 1982, 14A. Reagan discusses how he phoned "Boll Weevils" (Southern Conservatives) and had dinner with "a group of undecideds at the White House." Reagan, *The Reagan Diaries,* 98–99.

74. "Reagan's Victory Meant Anguish for Some GOP Conservatives," *Baltimore Sun,* August 20, 1982, A13.

75. Memorandum, "Tax Limitation Coalition Meeting," November 1, 1982, box 1, "American Legal Foundation" folder, Blackwell Files, RRL.

76. Memorandum, "'Requests and Suggestions' from Tax Limitation Coalition Meeting," November 1, 1982, box 1, "American Legal Foundation" folder, Blackwell Files, RRL.

77. "Conservatives Bid Reagan Cut More: Get the Rich and Big Business 'Off Welfare,' Says a Study by Heritage Foundation," *New York Times,* January 22, 1983, 7. For a complete discussion of the development of conservative think tanks see Jason Stahl's *Right Moves: The Conservative Think Tank in American Political Culture since 1945* (Chapel Hill: University of North Carolina Press, 2016).

78. Milton Friedman and Rose Friedman, *Tyranny of the Status Quo* (New York: Harcourt Brace Jovanovich, 1984), 2, 9.

79. "Conservatives Give Reagan Mixed Review," *Harford Courant,* December 11, 1983, A11.

80. Letter from Steve Antosh, executive director for the Center for National Labor Policy, to Morton Blackwell, special assistant to the president, June 3, 1982, box 3, "Center for National Labor Policy" folder, Blackwell Files, RRL.

81. "ACU Ratings Reveal Support for Reagan Program."

82. For example, the American Legislative Exchange Council was actively involved in encouraging the continuation of the tax revolt that had begun in California with Proposition 13. Despite Reagan asking for tax increases at the federal level in 1982, there were sixteen measures on the 1982 statewide ballots to limit taxes. One leader of ALEC asserted that "these ballot measures are a very significant indicator of the trend of the times and we're going to see more of them

throughout the eighties." "Tax Revolt Alive and Well in the States," *First Reading* 8, no. 10 (October 1982) American Legislative Exchange Council, box 1, "American Legislative Exchange Council (2)" folder, Blackwell Files, RRL.

83. "Reagan Tells Conservatives His Program Is Succeeding," *Baltimore Sun*, February 19, 1983, A7.

84. "Conservatives Make a Stink," *Washington Post*, March 9, 1983, A25.

85. Reagan, *An American Life*, 235.

86. Press release, "Address by the President to the Nation," Oval Office, White House, March 23, 1983, 1, box 4, "Citizens for America" folder, Blackwell Files, RRL.

87. Press release, "Address by the President to the Nation," March 23, 1983, 6.

88. The budget proposed massive across-the-board cuts to spending. It would have

> cut all highway construction and improvements, community development block grants, agricultural price supports, federal education programs, food stamps and federal revenue sharing, eliminate[d] the Rural Electrification Program, Small Business Administration, Civil Aeronautics Board, National Science Foundation and Federal Election Commission; slice[d] Medicaid and Medicare by ten percent, dismantle[d] the Veterans' Administration hospital system, cut the National Institutes of Health by fifty percent, cut Aid to Families with Dependent Children and eliminate[d] the Social Security minimum benefit, the Export-Import Bank and the Agency for Internal Development.

"Conservatives Offer Their Own Budget," *Washington Post*, April 17, 1982, A8.

89. "Conservatives Offer Their Own Budget," A8.

90. "Congress Reviews ALEC Federalism Plan," *First Reading* 8, no. 5 (May 1982) , American Legislative Exchange Council, box 1, "American Legislative Exchange Council (2)" folder, Blackwell Files, RRL. It is also important to note that even in 1981 just days after Reagan was shot, he had to wrangle with conservatives in the Senate Budget Committee over his proposed budget for the fiscal year 1982. From his hospital bed, Reagan met with Stockman, Vice President Bush, and his congressional lobbyist "to furnish additional information on future spending cuts to the conservative Republicans" on the Senate Budget Committee. The committee had voted 12–8 against his budget, with three conservatives voting against. These early efforts to fight Reagan on budget issues were not widespread, as most of the conservative movement was willing to give Reagan time to reach a balanced budget. "Reagan to Send More Budget Data to G.O.P. Conservatives in Senate," *New York Times*, April 15, 1981, A26.

91. "Conservatives Rebuff Reagan on Budget Counter-Offer," *Washington Post*, April 21, 1983, A4.

92. Phyllis Schlafly, *A Choice Not an Echo* (Pere Marquette Press, 1964).

93. Phyllis Schlafly, *A Choice Not an Echo: 50th Anniversary Edition* (New York: Regnery, 2014), 143–145.

94. Schlafly, *50th Anniversary Edition*, 153.

95. Schlafly, *50th Anniversary Edition*, 170.

96. On September 28, 1981 eight conservative organizations—the American Life Lobby, Coalitions for Americans, the Conservative Caucus, Concerned Women for America, the Moral Majority, the National Christian Action Coalition, the National Pro-Family Coalition, and United Families of America—wrote the House and Senate to reduce funding to Title X in the FY1982 Labor/HHS Appropriation Bill. Memorandum, "HR4560, FY1982 Labor/HHS Appropriation Bill," To the United States Senate and House of Representatives from Conservative Groups, September 28, 1981, box 1, "American Life Lobby (3)" folder, Blackwell Files, RRL.

97. Judie Brown, president of the American Life Lobby, to Richard S. Schweiker, secretary of the Department of Health and Human Services, November 19, 1982, box 1, "American Life Lobby (2)" folder, Blackwell Files, RRL.

98. Memorandum, "Budget Briefing of February 10, 1982," Judie Brown, president of the American Life Lobby, to Morton Blackwell, special assistant to the president, February 11, 1982, box 1, "American Life Lobby (3)" folder, Blackwell Files, RRL.

99. Memorandum, "Reform of Family Planning Program," Dick Dingman to Ed Meese, October 28, 1982, box 1, "American Life Lobby (2)" folder, Blackwell Files, RRL.

100. Memorandum, "Proposed Action Items for Presidential Consideration," Judie Brown, president of the American Life Lobby, to Ronald Reagan, January 21, 1983, box 1, "American Life Lobby (1)" folder, Blackwell Files, RRL. Brown also wanted the current law rewritten "to prohibit any funds from being used to perform abortions, abortion related services or lobbying particularly in favor of pro-abortion legislation and prevent children under 18 from getting prescriptions or birth control devices requiring a prescription without notifying parents." Judie Brown, president of the American Life Lobby, to John F. Cogan, associate director of the Office of Management and Budget, October 20, 1983, "American Life Lobby (4)" folder, box 1, Blackwell Files, RRL.

101. "GOP Conservatives Join to Assail Reagan on Budget Strategy, Prepare Alternative," *Wall Street Journal*, January 24, 1984, 5.

102. "Pension Changes Signed into Law," *New York Times*, April 20, 1983, A1. The bill had large bipartisan support and passed the House 243–102 and the Senate 58–14. In phone conversations with the House and Senate leadership, Reagan asserted that he was "delighted that the ambitious objective of completing action on this legislation was achieved." "Phone Call from President Ronald Reagan to

Senator Bob Dole," March 25, 1983, box 4, "Folder 57 (3/21/83 cont.—3/30/83)" folder, Presidential Handwriting File: Presidential Telephone Calls, RRL.

103. "A Triumph of Bipartisan Negotiating," *New York Times*, January 23, 1983, F2.

104. Paul Light, *Artful Work: The Politics of Social Security Reform* (New York: Random House, 1985), 110.

105. "The 80-Year Conservative War on Social Security Is Back for More" *Talking Points Memo*, January 14, 2015, https://talkingpointsmemo.com/dc/conservative -war-on-social-security-history.

106. "Some Conservatives Shop for a 'New Face,'" *Washington Post*, February 4, 1983, A2.

107. Many fiscal conservatives, including Jack Kemp and David Stockman, initially supported an increase in defense spending. While fiscal conservatives generally oppose deficits and increasing government spending, the military is generally seen as one of the few genuinely necessary functions of government. Other fiscal conservatives such as Martin Anderson, the head of the Office of Policy Development and a longtime adviser to President Reagan, opposed dramatic increases in defense spending. Stockman, *Triumph of Politics*, 117.

108. Stockman, *Triumph of Politics*, 107.

109. W. Elliot Brownlee and C. Eugene Steuerle, "Taxation," in Brownlee and Graham, *The Reagan Presidency*, 161.

110. Stockman, *Triumph of Politics*, 136.

111. Stockman, *Triumph of Politics*, 148.

112. "Think-Tank of Conservatives Has Advice for Reagan," *Los Angeles Times*, December 9, 1984, OC-C1A.

113. "GOP Conservatives Hit Reagan for the Less-Than-Hefty Cuts in Defense," *Christian Science Monitor*, December 20, 1984, 3.

114. Dinesh D'Souza, *Ronald Reagan: How an Ordinary Man Became an Extraordinary Leader* (New York: Free Press, 1997), 102.

115. Stockman, *Triumph of Politics*, 12.

116. Reagan did request the Private Sector Survey on Cost Control, more commonly known as the Grace Commission, to address "waste, fraud, and abuse" in government. While its conclusions were dramatic, the commission was not without its flaws, and its suggestions were not pursued by Congress. Steven Kelman, "The Grace Commission: How Much Waste in Government?," *Public Interest*, no. 39 (Winter 1985): 62–82.

117. It should be noted that House Republicans almost torpedoed the tax reform package. The best account is still Jeffrey Birnbaum's *Showdown at Gucci Gulch: Lawmakers, Lobbyists, and the Unlikely Triumph of Tax Reform* (New York: Vintage, 1988).

118. The Tax Reform Act of 1986 cut individual income tax rates but offset those reductions by increasing corporate taxes. For a description of the Tax Reform Act of 1986 see Brownlee and Steuerle's "Taxation," 168–173; "Reagan SDI Talk Leaves Conservatives Uneasy: Trade Off for Soviet Arms Pact Feared," *Washington Post*, August 7, 1986, A30; "Hard-Line Conservatives Set to Oppose Arms," *Sun*, December 5, 1987, 1A; "U.S. Conservatives Assail Reagan over Arms Treaty," *Los Angeles Times*, December 6, 1987, 1; "Zero Option Evokes Zero Honesty in Some Conservatives," *Chicago Tribune*, June 19, 1987, 25; "GOP Conservatives Could Stop Senate Ratification of Treaty," *Hartford Courant*, November 24, 1987, A11J; "Reagan's Arms-Control Dream Is Nightmare Conversation," *Washington Post*, November 30, 1987, A1; "Discontented Conservatives Rumble to Reagan's Right," *Hartford Courant*, August 19, 1987, B9E; "Contras' Situation Sparks Battles among Conservatives," *Los Angeles Times*, March 26, 1988, 12; "Conservatives Fear for Contras: White House Seen Betraying Rebels, Making North Its Scapegoats," *Washington Post*, November 28, 1986, A32.

119. George F. Will, "Reagan's Health-Care Plan: A Product of His New Deal Roots," *Hartford Courant*, February 19, 1987, C13. For a good analysis of how Reagan borrowed certain aspects of his populist appeal from Democratic presidents FDR and Truman, see Terri Bimes's chapter "Reagan: The Soft-Sell Populist," in *The Reagan Presidency: Pragmatic Conservativism and Its Legacy*, 61–81. For a comprehensive analysis of the ways in which Reagan's early political beliefs shaped his presidency, see Henry Olsen's *The Working Class Republican: Ronald Reagan and the Return of Blue-Collar Conservatism* (New York: Broadside Books, 2017).

CHAPTER 3. THE ORIGINS OF THE NEW RIGHT AND THE SEEDS OF FUTURE FRUSTRATION

1. The label "New Right" refers to the collection of groups such as Paul Weyrich's Committee for the Survival of a Free Congress, John Terry Dolan's National Conservative Political Action Committee, Howard Phillips's grassroots mobilization group the Conservative Caucus, and many other groups that later joined the cause, including the Moral Majority. The New Right was united around the need for a moral revival in the United States and emphasized the importance of social issues to restore America. The term "New Right" was first used in a different context by Lee Edwards in 1962 when, in an article entitled "The New Right: Its Face and Future" for *The New Guard*, he proposed a new platform for Young Americans for Freedom. In 1969, the term was used by conservative columnist M. Stanton Evans to describe the emergence of conservative students on campuses as the New Right in contrast with the New Left. It was not until 1975 that political

columnist Kevin Phillips used "the term in talking about 'social conservatives' and was the first to use it in regard to the collective efforts of Paul Weyrich, Howard Phillips, Terry Dolan," Richard Viguerie, and others. These men were collaborating to align conservatives on political issues and challenge the existing political parties. Richard Viguerie, *The New Right: We're Ready to Lead* (Falls Church, VA: Viguerie Company, 1980), 55.

2. "Nomination of Judge O'Connor Protested by Abortion Foes at Rally," *New York Times*, September 4, 1981. A8.

3. "Conservative Feud in Wake of O'Connor Choice," *Washington Post*, July 9, 1981. A1.

4. Throughout his administration, Reagan constantly reassured the New Right that he was supportive of their agenda, and ironically, given the New Right's outrage over Reagan's first Supreme Court nominee, he did the most to advance their agenda through his appointment of federal judges. For a detailed account of Reagan's role in advancing the New Right agenda through the appointment of federal judges, consult David O'Brien's chapter "Federal Judgeships in Retrospect," in *The Reagan Presidency: Pragmatic Conservatism and Its Legacies*, ed. W. Elliot Brownlee and Hugh Davis Graham (Lawrence: University Press of Kansas, 2003), 327–353.

5. "Conservative Feud in Wake of O'Connor Choice," A1.

6. The best account of the Christian Right's conflicts with the Reagan administration is found in Daniel K. Williams's *God's Own Party: The Making of the Christian Right* (Oxford: Oxford University Press, 2010). Robert O. Self also provides a detailed analysis of the New Right and its relationship with the Reagan administration in *All in the Family: The Realignment of American Democracy since the 1960s* (New York: Hill and Wang, 2012). Robert Nesmith recounts how evangelicals came to support Reagan in *The New Republican Coalition: The Reagan Campaigns and White Evangelicals* (New York: Peter Lang, 1994). Other historians have done an excellent job in explaining the rise of the Christian Right, including William C. Martin, *With God on Our Side: The Rise of the Religious Right in America* (New York: Broadway Books, 1996), and Darren Dochuk's *From Bible Belt to Sunbelt: Plain-Folk Religion, Grassroots Politics, and the Rise of Evangelical Conservatism* (New York: W. W. Norton, 2010). For an analysis of the Christian Right's relationship with the legislative branch consult Matthew C. Moen's *The Christian Right and Congress* (Tuscaloosa: University of Alabama Press, 1989). Finally, for the differences that existed in the Religious Right, see Neil J. Young's *We Gather Together: The Religious Right and the Problem of Interfaith Politics* (Oxford: Oxford University Press, 2016).

7. Steve Bruce, *The Rise and Fall of the Christian Right: Conservative Protestant Politics in America, 1979–1988* (Oxford: Oxford University Press, 1988); Michael

D'Antonio, *Fall from Grace: The Failed Crusade of the Christian Right* (New York: Farrar, Straus and Giroux, 1989); "Why 'Moral Majority,' a Force for a Decade, Ran Out of Steam," *Wall Street Journal,* Sept 25, 1989, A1.

8. "Can 'New Right' Replace GOP?," *Atlanta Constitution,* March 7, 1976, 10B; Viguerie, *The New Right,* 51–54. For an analysis that places race at the center of the emergence of the New Right, consult Dan Carter's *The Politics of Rage: George Wallace, The Origins of the New Conservatism, and the Transformation of American Politics* (Baton Rouge: Louisiana State University Press, 1995), and his *From George Wallace to Newt Gingrich: Race in the Conservative Counterrevolution, 1963–1994* (Baton Rouge: Louisiana State University Press, 1996).

9. Historians have done an excellent job detailing the rise of conservatism in American politics. While less has been done specifically on the New Right, there are some excellent works on the subject. Sociologist Sara Diamond's *Roads to Dominion* provides a comprehensive study of right-wing movements in American politics including the New Right. Sara Diamond, *Roads to Dominion: Right-Wing Movements and Political Power in the United States* (New York: Guilford Press, 1995). Historian Donald T. Critchlow is one of the leading experts on the rise of the New Right in American politics. Critchlow's *Phyllis Schlafly and Grassroots Conservatism* details how New Right activists, specifically Schlafly, positioned themselves within the GOP. Donald T. Critchlow, *Phyllis Schlafly and Grassroots Conservatism* (Princeton, NJ: Princeton University Press, 2005). Critchlow has also written a fine chapter entitled "Mobilizing Women: The 'Social' Issues" in Brownlee and Graham, *The Reagan Presidency.* For a similar historical account of Jerry Falwell see Michael Winters's *God's Right Hand: How Jerry Falwell Made God a Republican and Baptized the American Right* (New York: Harper, 2012).

10. Numerous histories detail the importance of William F. Buckley to the conservative movement. One such work is Carl T. Bogus's *Buckley: William F. Buckley Jr. and the Rise of American Conservatism* (New York: Bloomsbury Press, 2011).

11. Bogus, *Buckley,* 11–13.

12. George H. Nash, *The Conservative Intellectual Movement in America: Since 1945* (Wilmington, DE: ISI Books, 1976), 233. Richard Viguerie explains that "through his wit, intelligence, and willingness to stand up for conservative principles, Bill Buckley, almost single-handedly, made the word 'conservative' respectable and acceptable." Viguerie continues that "when Bill Buckley started *National Review,* you did not shout your conservatism from the roof tops—you whispered it behind closed doors." Viguerie, *The New Right,* 41.

13. "For Reagan, Crucial Choices Also Worked Politically," *Washington Post,* February 23, 1981, A1.

14. Bogus, *Buckley,* 189. One example of later prominent conservatives who got their start through Young Americans for Freedom was Richard Viguerie, who

would later perfect the conservative direct mail campaigns that would mobilize millions of conservatives at the grassroots. Viguerie, *The New Right*, 25. Furthermore, Howard Phillips, then a student at Harvard University, was one of the ninety-three students that founded Young Americans for Freedom. "For Reagan, Crucial Choices Also Worked Politically," A1.

15. For more on how the conservative movement began in the 1960s, see Lisa McGirr's *Suburban Warriors: The Origins of the New American Right* (Princeton, NJ: Princeton University Press, 2001); Rebecca E. Klatch's *A Generation Divided: The New Left, the New Right, and the 1960s* (Berkeley: University of California Press, 1999); and Gregory L. Schneider's *Cadres for Conservatism: Young Americans for Freedom and the Rise of the Contemporary Right* (New York: New York University Press, 1998).

16. Viguerie, *The New Right*, 42.

17. For a detailed treatment of the divide that existed between young Americans on the left and right of the political spectrum see Klatch's *A Generation Divided.*

18. "Can 'New Right' Replace GOP?," *Atlanta Constitution*, March 7, 1976, 10B; Viguerie, *The New Right*, 51–54, 66.

19. "Coors' Capital Connection: Heritage Foundation Fuels His Conservative Drive," *Washington Post*, May 7, 1975, A1. Historians have done an excellent job on tracing the role of businessmen in promoting the conservative movement. For a comprehensive account see Phillips-Fein's *Invisible Hands: The Making of the Conservative Movement from the New Deal to Reagan* (New York: W. W. Norton, 2009); Bethany Moreton's *To Serve God and Wal-Mart: The Making of Christian Free Enterprise* (Cambridge, MA: Harvard University Press, 2009); and Kevin M. Kruse's *One Nation under God: How Corporate America Invented Christian America* (New York: Basic Books, 2015). For an analysis of the rise of conservative think tanks and specifically how the Heritage Foundation overtook the American Enterprise Institute as the predominant conservative think tank, consult Jason Stahl's *Right Moves: The Conservative Think Tank in American Political Culture since 1945* (Chapel Hill: University of North Carolina Press, 2016).

20. Viguerie, *The New Right*, 60.

21. "Politics & People: Crusader," *Wall Street Journal*, May 29, 1975, 12; Viguerie, *The New Right*, 62.

22. "Politics & People: Crusader," 12.

23. "Can 'New Right' Replace GOP?," 10B.

24. "Fund Raiser Becomes New Kind of Power Broker," *New York Times*, May 23, 1975, 16.

25. "The New Right's Strong Ambition Is Fueled by Huge Mail Campaign," *New York Times*, December 4, 1977, 73.

26. Viguerie, *The New Right*, 60.

27. Viguerie, *The New Right*, 64. Once Ronald Reagan was elected president, he selected Morton Blackwell to be the administration's liaison to conservative organizations and groups. Blackwell lobbied for conservative causes within the administration until his departure in 1984.

28. "Those Carter Election Reforms," *Washington Post*, March 24, 1977, A18. Republicans opposed Carter's election reforms because there is a long-standing assumption that those who do not have driver licenses tend to be from a lower socioeconomic background and as such would vote for Democrats. Furthermore, Republicans tend to oppose ending the electoral college because of their admiration for the original intent of the founders in drafting the Constitution, where the electoral college is outlined.

29. Viguerie, *The New Right*, 76–78. Republicans'–Southern Democrats' filibuster forced Democrats to delete the public-finance section of Carter's proposal in the Senate, and the House refused to schedule a watered-down version of Carter's reforms in 1977. Carter's proposals ultimately failed. The relative importance of the New Right in the process is up for debate. "Carter's Election-Funds Bill Dies," *Chicago Tribune*, August 3, 1977, 6.

30. "The New Right's Strong Ambition Is Fueled by Huge Mail Campaign," *New York Times*, December 4, 1977, 73.

31. Viguerie, *The New Right*, 78, 79.

32. Critchlow, "Mobilizing Women," 299–300; Beverly LaHaye also played an important role in organizing women and advocating for family values. In 1979 she helped found Concerned Women for America. The organization's top priority was to ensure that ERA did not become law in the 1980s. Williams, *God's Own Party*, 145.

33. Viguerie, *The New Right*, 159.

34. Williams, *God's Own Party*, 126–127.

35. "Anita Bryant's Battle with Gays Turns into a Holy War," *Chicago Tribune*, May 2, 1977, B1.

36. Williams, *God's Own Party*, 149. Anita Bryant published a memoir in 1977 recounting her experience. Anita Bryant, *The Anita Bryant Story: The Survival of Our Nation's Families and the Threat of Militant Homosexuality* (Old Tappan, NJ: Fleming H. Revell, 1977).

37. Williams, *God's Own Party*, 151.

38. Reagan's decision to select Schweiker as his vice president was a strategic move to attract the more moderate elements in the GOP and sway the Pennsylvania delegation to support him at the convention. Richard "Dick" Cheney, then President Ford's chief of staff, asserts in his autobiography that Reagan's decision to take Schweiker allowed Ford to sway the conservative Mississippi delegation to support him. In addition to losing Mississippi, Reagan was also unable to shore up

the support of the Pennsylvania delegation. According to Cheney, in a single move "we managed to deny Reagan the extra delegates he was hunting in Pennsylvania and had nailed down our own additional votes in Mississippi." Cheney, *In My Time: A Personal and Political Memoir* (New York: Threshold, 2011), 97–98.

39. "Conservatives Weigh Third Party," *Chicago Tribune*, August 3, 1976, B8.

40. For a detailed analysis of Jesse Helms and his influence on modern conservatism, see Bryan Hardin Thrift's *Conservative Bias: How Jesse Helms Pioneered the Rise of Right-Wing Media and Realigned the Republican Party* (Gainesville: University Press of Florida, 2014).

41. "Conservatives Seek New Party if Reagan Loses," *Chicago Tribune*, August 18, 1976, 10.

42. "On Both Sides: Prop. 6 Battle a Bit Bizarre," *Los Angeles Times*, November 6, 1978, B1.

43. "Prop. 6 Will 'Draw a Moral Line'—Briggs,'" *Los Angeles Times*, October 31, 1978, A16; Both Falwell and LaHaye published memoirs in 1978 in which they condemned homosexuality. Falwell condemned homosexuality in no uncertain terms, labeling it "abnormal," "against nature," "a perversion," and a "mental sickness," all in the space of a single page. Falwell went on to assert that homosexuals "prey on children," adding that homosexuality was not a victimless crime as "little children are exploited and their bodies are ravaged by human animals." He also claimed that homosexuals "seek out young boys" and if given free rein would exploit American students. Jerry Falwell, *How You Can Help Clean Up America* (Lynchburg, VA: Liberty, 1978), 70–71. LaHaye also believed that children were at risk. He endorsed the Briggs proposal, asserting that it "does not discriminate against homosexuals, but it does protect school children from being taught perverted sex by a homosexual." LaHaye continued that homosexual teachers would "brainwash our children" and warned that "you can expect homosexual teachers single-handedly to double the homosexual community within ten years, not by recruiting, but by preparing youngsters mentally for the recruiters." If Americans allowed that to happen, LaHaye concluded, it would be the "bottom line of our culture" and once passed would mean the United States had "descended to the ultimate in abominations." Tim LaHaye, *The Unhappy Gays: What Everyone Should Know About Homosexuality* (Wheaton, IL: Tyndale House, 1978), 177–178, 197.

44. "After Low-Key Campaigns, Comeback Seen for Gay Rights," *Washington Post*, October 27, 1978, A5.

45. "Battle Is Not Over, Briggs Vows to Prop. 6 Supporters," *Los Angeles Times*, November 8, 1978, OC_A1; "Where Dole Is No Reagan," *Washington Post*, September 2, 1995, A19.

46. "Briggs to Try Antigay Move Again in 1980: Says Reagan's Stand against Proposition 6 Turned Polls Around," *Los Angeles Times*, November 9, 1978, B21.

47. "Battle Is Not Over, Briggs Vows to Prop.6 Supporters," OC_A1.

48. Williams, *Gods Own Party*, 153.

49. "Reagan Loyalist Rising as '80 Contender," *Los Angeles Times*, June 2, 1978, C1.

50. "Elephant Master?," *Christian Science Monitor*, March 9, 1979, 24. Reagan was urged to run as a third party conservative candidate in 1976. In a 1979 letter, Reagan explained that Kevin Phillips "was one of a small group who tried to persuade me to go along with a third party movement in '76 and has been rather unforgiving of me for not doing that." Ronald Reagan, *Reagan: A Life in Letters* (New York: Free Press, 2003), ed. Kiron K. Skinner, Annelise Anderson, and Martin Anderson, 227.

51. "The Republican Road is Now a Two-Lane Street," *New York Times*, August 6, 1978, E3; "New Right Gets Candidate as Crane Dives in for 1980," *Atlanta Constitution*, August 6, 1978, 14C.

52. "New Right Gets Candidate as Crane Dives in for 1980," 14C; "Reagan Loyalist Rising as '80 Contenders,'" *Los Angeles Times*, June 2, 1978, C1.

53. "Reagan Loyalist Rising as '80 Contender," C1. Lyn Nofziger recounts Crane's entry into the presidential race in his memoir. Nofziger concluded that the New Right's concerns about Reagan's age demonstrated that "they just did not understand Reagan's appeal." Nofziger, *Nofziger* (Washington, DC: Regnery, 1992), 230–231.

54. Crane did cause Reagan some problems, especially in Iowa, where Crane's 7 percent "contributed to Mr. Reagan's defeat." "Crane to Withdraw from Contest and Support Reagan: Support Begins to Fade," *New York Times*, April 17, 1980, D17. Not every member of the New Right shifted their support to Reagan after Crane dropped out. Indeed, Viguerie shifted his support to "John B. Connally, before joining the Reagan camp." "Trying to Turn a Collective Sentiment into a Government," *Washington Post*, February 24, 1981, A4. Williams mentions that many conservative evangelicals did not initially support Reagan in 1980. Williams, *God's Own Party*, 188.

55. Despite the fact that Carter personally reflected the New Right's religious beliefs, his unwillingness to legislate abortion, to oppose homosexuality, and to reinstate school prayer led them to denounce him. Instead, they threw their support to a man who had been divorced, who had legalized abortion in California, and whose church attendance was sparse. For a detailed description of the way conservatives have attempted to overemphasize President Reagan's moral and ethical qualities, see Kyle Longley's chapter "When Character Was King? Ronald Reagan and the Issues of Ethics and Morality," in Kyle Longley et al., *Deconstructing Reagan: Conservative Mythology and America's Fortieth President*. New York: M. E. Sharpe, 2007, 90–119.

56. "Reagan Campaign Looks to Running Mate," *Washington Post*, May 13, 1980, A4.

57. "Reagan Woos Ford as Top Republicans Denounce President," *New York Times*, July 16, 1980, A1. For a detailed analysis of Strom Thurmond's role in the modern conservative movement, see Joseph Crespino's *Strom Thurmond's America* (New York: Hill and Wang, 2012).

58. "Disgruntled Conservatives Caucus: Senator Helms Ponders a Bush Challenge," *Los Angeles Times*, July 17, 1980, A2.

59. "U.S. Vice President, Republican Convention," *Our Campaigns*, http://www.ourcampaigns.com/RaceDetail.html? RaceID=59877. Jerry Falwell endorsed Jack Kemp, while Howard Phillips endorsed Jesse Helms.

60. "Disgruntled Conservatives Caucus: Senator Helms Ponders a Bush Challenge," *Los Angeles Times*, July 17, 1980, A2.

61. "Reagan and the Conservatives," *Wall Street Journal*, July 28, 1980, 10.

62. "Reagan and the Conservatives," 10.

63. Williams, *God's Own Party*, 189–190.

64. "Reagan and the Conservatives," 10.

65. Jerry Falwell, *Listen America!* (New York: Bantam, 1980), 6, 8.

66. Jerry Falwell, "Introduction," in Viguerie's *The New Right*, np.

67. "'New Right' Leaders Bask in Their Success," *Los Angeles Times*, November 6, 1980, A15. Of the six Democratic senators targeted by the New Right, only Alan Cranston of California and Thomas F. Eagleton of Missouri retained their seats. Senators Birch Bayh of Indiana, John C. Culver of Iowa, George S. McGovern of South Dakota, and Frank Church of Idaho all lost their reelection bids.

68. Jerry Falwell, *Strength for the Journey* (New York: Simon & Schuster, 1987), 365. Goodwin's statements seem dubious. According to Daniel Williams, "Carter's unpopularity probably would have allowed Reagan to win regardless of whether or not Falwell and the Moral Majority supported him. In any case, most voters who cast their ballots for the Republicans had little regard for Falwell. A survey taken during the fall of 1980 showed that only 6 percent of whites 'felt close' to the Moral Majority and other Christian Right organizations" (193). Indeed, the Moral Majority and Jerry Falwell were extremely unpopular with most Americans. For example, "sixty-two percent of people in Falwell's home state disapproved of him" (198). Williams later asserts that although "a majority of American voters approved of Reagan," they did not share "the Religious Right's vision of a Christian moral order" (203). Although Goodwin was incorrect in his assertions, the fact that he and other members of the New Right believed they had won the day for Reagan would heighten their sense of betrayal when the administration did not pursue social issues with vigor. Williams, *God's Own Party*.

69. "'New Right' Leaders Bask in Their Success," A15.

CHAPTER 4. THE BATTLE FOR AMERICA'S SOUL:
CONSERVATIVE DISILLUSION WITH REAGAN
ON SOCIAL ISSUES

1. When Reagan made his appointments, the New Right was the only conservative "group without real representation in the executive branch." Viguerie mournfully explained that the New Right was "good at getting people elected, not taking people to lunch." "Trying to Turn a Collective Sentiment into a Government," *Washington Post,* February 24, 1981, A4.

2. Ronald Reagan, *An American Life: The Autobiography* (New York: Threshold, 1990), 279.

3. While the Hyde Amendment, passed in 1976, blocked Medicaid-funded abortions, many conservatives argued that federal dollars were still going to organizations that encouraged and/or performed abortions.

4. *Lifeletter'81 #10* by the Ad Hoc Committee in Defense of Life, July 16, 1981, 1, box 1, "The Ad Hoc Committee in Defense of Life" folder, Blackwell Files, Ronald Reagan Presidential Library, Simi Valley, California (hereafter RRL).

5. "Reagan Choice for Court Decried by Conservatives but Acclaimed by Liberals," *Washington Post,* July 18, 1981, A7.

6. *Lifeletter'81 #10,* 1.

7. Letter from Mrs. L. G. Graham, July 8, 1981, box 70, "[Mail Sample] 07/16/1981 Nomination of Sandra Day O'Connor" folder, Anne Higgins—Mail Samples, RRL.

8. Letter from Mrs. Gilder L. Wideman to President Reagan, July 8, 1981, box 70, "[Mail Sample] 07/16/1981 Nomination of Sandra Day O'Connor" folder, Anne Higgins—Mail Samples, RRL.

9. Letter from Nancy Lacke to President Ronald Reagan, July 8, 1981, box 70, "[Mail Sample] 07/16/1981 Nomination of Sandra Day O'Connor" folder, Anne Higgins—Mail Samples, RRL.

10. Letter from Donald Fries to President Ronald Reagan, July 9, 1981, box 70, "[Mail Sample] 07/16/1981 Nomination of Sandra Day O'Connor" folder, Anne Higgins—Mail Samples, RRL.

11. *Lifeletter'81 #10,* 1–2.

12. "Reagan Defends Foreign Policy Plans," *Hartford Courant,* July 8, 1981, A10.

13. "Reagan Urges 'Open Mind' by O'Connor Critics," *Sun,* July 9, 1981, A1.

14. "Reagan's O'Connor Gambit," *Sun,* July 15, 1981, A18.

15. "Conservative Feud in Wake of O'Connor Choice," *Washington Post,* July 9, 1981. A1.

16. "Reagan Choice for Court Decried by Conservatives but Acclaimed by Liberals," A7.

17. *Lifeletter'81 #10*, 2.

18. Conservatives continue to dispute Reagan's trust in O'Connor. She voted with the minority in 1983 when the Supreme Court voted 6–3 to reaffirm *Roe* by striking down the Akron Ordinance. O'Connor wrote the dissent, in which she argued "the government has a compelling interest in protecting human life at all stages of a woman's pregnancy." "Supreme Court Strikes Down Akron Ordinance," *ACCL Update* 9, no. 3 (Summer 1983): 3, box 1, "American Citizens Concerned for Life" folder, Blackwell Files, RRL. Despite this ruling, conservatives continued to be critical of O'Connor for her role in upholding *Roe* during the 1990s. Ann Coulter in 2005 asserted that "O'Connor was a terrible mistake and will forever mar Reagan's record, but at least he only did it once." Ann Coulter, "What Would Reagan Do?," September 21, 2005, http://www.anncoulter.com/col umns/2005-09-21.html.

19. *Lifeletter'81 #11* by the Ad Hoc Committee in Defense of Life, August 12, 1981, 2–3, box 1, "The Ad Hoc Committee in Defense of Life" folder, Blackwell Files, RRL.

20. *Lifeletter'81 #16* by the Ad Hoc Committee in Defense of Life, December 14, 1981, 1–2, box 1, "The Ad Hoc Committee in Defense of Life" folder, Blackwell Files, RRL.

21. "Conservative Issue Initiatives for 1982," Memorandum from Elizabeth H. Dole to Michael Deaver, December 16, 1981, box 20, "Conservatives-General-1982 [1 of 6]" folder, Elizabeth Dole Files, RRL.

22. Daniel K. Williams, *God's Own Party: The Making of the Christian Right* (Oxford: Oxford University Press, 2010), 196.

23. "President Warned by Conservatives: 45 Leaders Say Abandonment of Policies That Elected Him Will Cost Support," *New York Times*, January 22, 1982, A20.

24. "Again, President Is Drawing Conservatives' Ire," *New York Times*, January 13, 1982, A14.

25. Judie Brown, president of the American Life Lobby, to Morton Blackwell, special assistant to the president, January 19, 1982, box 1, "American Life Lobby (3)" folder, Blackwell Files, RRL.

26. On the issue of abortion, Reagan was emphatically pro-life, at least following his governorship. He had passed a law in California that legalized abortion in cases where the mother's life was endangered. It was a decision that haunted Reagan. In a letter to his friend Charles Schulz, the *Peanuts* columnist, Reagan asserted that when the California legislation was being debated he "probably did more studying on that subject at the time than on anything else before or since." Reagan told Schulz that he had concluded that abortion was defensible only in cases where the mother could claim self-defense. He asserted that "our religion does justify the taking of life in self defense." After signing the bill, however, Reagan

discovered that some psychiatrists were writing that the mother-to-be was having "suicidal tendencies" after "a five-minute diagnosis." Reagan lamented that California's "medical program will finance more than fifty thousand abortions of unwed mothers in the coming year on such flimsy diagnosis." Reagan's experience in California resulted in the president being firmly pro-life and rejecting mothers' health as a valid excuse for the termination of the pregnancy. Converting his convictions into public policy, however, proved to be more difficult. Ronald Reagan to Charles Schulz, August 6, 1970, "Schulz 952" folder, RRL.

27. *Lifeletter'82 #2* by the Ad Hoc Committee in Defense of Life, 2, box 1, "The Ad Hoc Committee in Defense of Life" folder, Blackwell Files, RRL. It should be noted, however, that over 50 percent of Americans were for allowing abortion in cases that involved rape or incest, or endangered the life of the mother. "When Reagan's Ex-, Conservatives Won't Be," *New York Times*, October 3, 1982, E17.

28. "Abortion Foes Hint Retaliation if Senate Skips Vote," *Chicago Sun-Times*, July 21, 1982, box 1, "The Ad Hoc Committee in Defense of Life" folder, Blackwell Files, RRL.

29. "Reagan: Time Is Now to Explore Abortion Ban," *Washington Post*, July 21, 1982, box 1, "The Ad Hoc Committee in Defense of Life" folder, Blackwell Files, RRL.

30. "Hatfield Bill Would Bar Federal Abortion Funds," *New York Times*, May 24, 1982, A11.

31. "Reagan: Time Is Now to Explore Abortion Ban."

32. *Lifeletter'82 #5* by the Ad Hoc Committee in Defense of Life, April 7, 1982, box 1, "The Ad Hoc Committee in Defense of Life" folder, Blackwell Files, RRL.

33. *Lifeletter'82 Extra* by the Ad Hoc Committee in Defense of Life, March 2, 1982, box 1, "The Ad Hoc Committee in Defense of Life" folder, Blackwell Files, RRL.

34. Supportive Conservative Groups to Senator Helms, April 19, 1982, box 1, "American Life Lobby (2)" folder, Blackwell Files, RRL; Judie Brown, president of the American Life Lobby, to the Office of General Council Legal Service Corporation, November 24, 1982, "American Life Lobby (1)" folder, box 1, Blackwell Files, RRL.

35. Ronald Reagan to Jesse Helms, April 5, 1982, box 1, "American Life Lobby (2)" folder, Blackwell Files, RRL; Reagan's letter to Helms may have been in response to Elizabeth Dole's continued insistence that the administration address the concerns of the New Right. On March 9, 1982, Dole circulated another memorandum, in which she recommended that the administration pick a couple of social issues to reenergize "the conservative grassroots." Dole asserted that this action would get them ready to help the administration with the upcoming legislative battles. "To do little or nothing," Dole continued, "will lead to greater

conservative dissatisfaction and diminish active support for the economic bat-tles." "Conservative Social Agenda" Memorandum from Elizabeth Dole to Edwin Meese III, James A. Baker, Ed Harper, March 9, 1982, box 20, "Conservatives-General-1982 [2 of 6]" folder, Dole Files, RRL.

36. *Lifeletter'82 #5*, 1–3. Despite conservatives' criticism of Reagan on the is-sue of abortion, he opted to endorse constitutional amendments that would have made abortion illegal. This was by far the most conservative option of the seven options outlined by his transition task force in the fall of 1980. "Social Is-sues: Abortion (Constitutional Amendment)," Fall 1980, box 26, "Ronald Reagan Presidential Transition Team, 1980–1981: Social Issues/Task Force on Defense and Foreign Policy" folder, Annelise Anderson Papers, Hoover Institution Archives, Stanford University, Stanford, California.

37. "Has Reagan Deserted the Conservatives?," *Conservative Digest* 8, no. 7 (July 1982), box 49: July 1982 Part 2, "16c July 1982 #2 'Newspapers, Newsletters and Journals Part 1'" folder, Correspondence of Howard Phillips, Record Group 1, Records of the Conservative Caucus, Liberty University Archive, Lynchburg, VA; "Conservatives Itch for Reagan's Remedy," *Globe and Mail* (Toronto, Ontario), September 2, 1982, 12.

38. "Conservatives Itch for Reagan's Remedy," 12.

39. Richard Viguerie, "An Open Letter to President Reagan," *Conservative Di-gest* 8, no. 7 (July 1982): 46–47, box 49: July 1982 Part 2, "16c July 1982 #2 'Newspa-pers, Newsletters and Journals Part 1'" folder, Correspondence of Howard Phillips, Record Group 1, Records of the Conservative Caucus, Liberty University Archive.

40. Ronald Reagan, *Reagan: A Life in Letters* (New York: Free Press, 2003), ed. Kiron K. Skinner, Annelise Anderson, and Martin Anderson (New York: Free Press, 2003), 621–622.

41. "Conservatives Itch for Reagan's Remedy," 12.

42. "Abortion Foes Hint Retaliation if Senate Skips Vote."

43. "New Right Meeting Grumbles about Reagan," *Washington Post*, July 28, 1982, A5.

44. *Lifeletter'82 #10* by the Ad Hoc Committee in Defense of Life, box 1, "Ad Hoc Committee in Defense of Life" folder, Blackwell Files, RRL.

45. *Lifeletter'82 #11* by the Ad Hoc Committee in Defense of Life, box 1, "Ad Hoc Committee in Defense of Life" folder, Blackwell Files, RRL.

46. Press release, "Abortion," by the American Life Lobby, August 27, 1982, box 1, "American Life Lobby (1)" folder, Blackwell Files, RRL.

47. "Social Legislation Push by Conservatives Runs Out of Gas," *Christian Sci-ence Monitor*, August 20, 1982, 5.

48. *Lifeletter'82 #11*.

49. Baker had promised Helms that he would allow Helms's proposals to be

brought to the floor of the Senate earlier in the year in exchange for Helms dropping his filibuster against the extension of key provisions of the Voting Rights Act of 1965. "The Nation; Setbacks for the Right; Congress Has Resisted Reversal of Laws on Busing, Abortion, Prayer," *Boston Globe*, September 19, 1982, 1.

50. "Power Balance in Favor of Abortion," *New York Times*, September 20, 1982, B10.

51. *Lifeletter '82 #11*; Judie Brown, president of the American Life Lobby, to James A. Baker III, chief of staff, Edwin Meese III, counsellor to the president, and Kenneth M. Duberstein, assistant to the president, box 1, "American Life Lobby (1)" folder, Blackwell Files, RRL.

52. "Senate Conservatives Fail to Curb Abortion Filibuster," *Los Angeles Times*, September 9, 1982, A1. Reagan made several phone calls from September 7 to September 9 to try to shore up support for Helms. There is, however, a handwritten note by Reagan in the file that reads: "only got a few of these made and time ran out on us." Box 3, folder 42, Presidential Handwriting File, Series IV: Presidential Telephone Calls, RRL.

53. "Defeat of School Prayer Ends New Right Crusade," *Chicago Tribune*, September 24, 1982.

54. "The Nation; Setbacks for the Right; Congress Has Resisted Reversal of Laws on Busing, Abortion, Prayer," 1. Despite conservatives' criticism of Reagan on the issue of abortion, he opted to endorse a constitutional amendment that would have made voluntary school prayer legal. This was by far the most conservative option of the five options outlined by his transition task force in the fall of 1980. "Social Issues: School Prayer, Options," Fall 1980, box 26, "Ronald Reagan Presidential Transition Team, 1980–1981: Social Issues/Task Force on Defense and Foreign Policy" folder, Annelise Anderson Papers, Hoover Institution Archives.

55. "Conservatives Hope to Link Abortion with Overseas Aid," *New York Times*, June 24, 1984, E3. It should be noted that antibusing legislation, cosponsored by Helms, was approved 57–37 in the Senate but was buried in the Democrat-controlled House. *Lifeletter '82 Extra*, March 2, 1982, box 1, "Ad Hoc Committee in Defense of Life" folder, Blackwell Files, RRL. Reviewing the records of Reagan's phone conversations demonstrates that the president made far more phone calls to congressmen and senators concerning his economic proposals than he did in regard to the right-to-life amendment or legislation that would allow prayer in public schools. This might have been because Reagan realized that the amendments had little chance of passing, or it might be an indication of his priorities. Boxes 1–11, Presidential Handwriting File, Series IV: Presidential Telephone Calls, RRL. Reagan for his part seems to have believed that he had adequately fought for the pro-life cause. His entry from September 14, 1982, asserts that he "met briefly with a group of anti-abortion leaders" and that "they recognize the effort I've

made to end the Weicher-Packwood filibuster of the Helms amendment." Reagan, *The Reagan Diaries*, ed. Douglas Brinkley (New York: HarperCollins, 2007), 100.

56. "Reform of Family Planning Program," Memorandum from Dick Dingman to Ed Meese, October 28, 1982, box 1, "American Life Lobby (2)" folder, Blackwell Files, RRL.

57. *Lifeletter'82 #15*, November 15, 1982, 4, box 1, "Ad Hoc Committee in Defense of Life" folder, Blackwell Files, RRL.

58. Gary L. Curran, legislative consultant for the American Life Lobby, to Morton Blackwell, special assistant to the president, October 6, 1982, box 1, "American Life Lobby (2)" folder, Blackwell Files, RRL.

59. Despite suffering large legislative defeats, the pro-life movement continued to be active at all levels of government. Furthermore, the Human Life Amendment and the human life bill were back on the Senate calendar in 1983. There was recognition, however, that there was little hope of passing this legislation because there were "not enough votes in the Senate to pass any amendment." "Status of Legislation Report: September 26, 1983," memorandum from the American Life Lobby to group members, September 26, 1983, box 1, "American Life Lobby (4)" folder, Blackwell Files, RRL.

60. In April 1982, a baby was born with Down syndrome and a digestive-tract disorder in Bloomington, Indiana. The parents decided, when presented their medical options, that they would prefer to pursue no treatment for the baby. The Indiana Supreme Court allowed the parents to pursue no treatment, and as a result the baby was "allowed to die of starvation in the very hospital in which he was born only a week earlier." The "Baby Doe" case (also known as the Bloomington baby) infuriated conservatives like few other issues during the 1980s. George Will wrote an op-ed in which he declared that infanticide was a natural result of the reasoning behind *Roe*. Will declared that the "values and passions, as well as the logic of some portions of the 'abortion rights' movement, have always pointed beyond abortion, toward something like the Indiana outcome, which affirms a broader right to kill." Reagan assured conservatives that he had "directed the Departments of Justice and Health and Human Services to apply civil rights regulations to protect handicapped newborns" in his essay in the *Human Life Review*. Reagan worked vigilantly during both his terms to implement policies that would prevent a replication of the Baby Doe case. During Reagan's second term, the *Wall Street Journal* asserted "one is hard put to identify another issue the Reagan administration has pursued with such single-minded persistence in the face of repeated defeat. Despite Reagan's consistent efforts, the New Right condemned the slowness with which changes were implemented." Henry J. Hyde, Jesse Helms, Orin G. Hatch, and Mark O. Hartfield to President Ronald Reagan, April 20, 1982,

box 1, "Ad Hoc Committee in Defense of Life" folder, Blackwell Files, RRL; *Life-letter'82 #6*, April 29, 1982, box 1, "Ad Hoc Committee in Defense of Life" folder, Blackwell Files, RRL; Ronald Reagan, *Abortion and the Conscience of the Nation* (New York: Thomas Nelson Publishers, 1984), 22–23; "Conservatives and Babies," *Wall Street Journal*, January 15, 1986, 26; Press release, "Pro-Life Group Commends and Warns DHHS on Anti-Infanticide Regulations" American Life Lobby, March 9, 1983, 2, box 1, "American Life Lobby (2)" folder, Blackwell Files, RRL.

61. Reagan, *Abortion and the Conscience of the Nation*, 8–9, 15, 19, 21, 31, 38.

62. "Hard-Line Conservatives to Air Complaints on Reagan," *Los Angeles Times*, January 18, 1983, A2.

63. "Conservatives: A Reagan Loss in '84 May Help GOP Retain Senate," *Christian Science Monitor*, November 25, 1983, 10.

64. "Conservatives Cancel Campaign for Reagan," *New York Times*, July 1, 1984, 16. It is important to note that not all of the organizations in the New Right followed Phillips's and Viguerie's lead. The Ad Hoc Committee in Defense of Life voiced its frustration with Reagan's advisers. They condemned "the hard-core of the 'New Right'" which they claimed "never supported Reagan," for using "the few pro-life groups it controls to stir up bogus 'anti-abortion opposition' as part of its current break-with-Reagan campaign." *Lifeletter'83 #3* by the Ad Hoc Committee in Defense of Life, February 18, 1983, 3, box 1, "Ad Hoc Committee in Defense of Life" folder, Blackwell Files, RRL.

CHAPTER 5. AIDS, THE NEW RIGHT, AND
REAGAN'S RESPONSE

1. For a detailed account of the interconnectedness between gay and lesbian activism and the New Right see Tina Fetner's *How the Religious Right Shaped Lesbian and Gay Activism* (Minneapolis: University of Minnesota Press, 2008).

2. For an accessible overview of the AIDS epidemic see Victoria A. Harden's *AIDS at 30: A History* (Washington, DC: Potomac Books, 2012). The best historical account of the AIDS epidemic and the New Right can be found in Robert O. Self's *All in the Family: The Realignment of American Democracy since the 1960s* (New York: Hill and Wang, 2012), 385–397. For a comprehensive contemporary account of the epidemic see Randy Shilts's *And the Band Played On: Politics, People, and the AIDS Epidemic* (New York: St. Martin's Griffin, 1987). Historians have almost uniformly denounced Reagan's handling of the AIDS epidemic. Self asserts that "the silence of President Reagan, who was not himself temperamentally antigay, allowed conservative voices to grow more confident between 1984 and 1987." Self concludes that "the absence of presidential leadership and the silence of the

national political class permitted the consolidation of what can only be called a poisonous homophobia." Self, *All in the Family*, 389, 393. Historian Alan Brandt has gone further, asserting that a more active president "could have changed the meaning of the epidemic in important ways." Brandt went on to imagine a scenario where Reagan had gone on national television and denounced the treatment of AIDS victims, suggesting that the president could have invited the victims to live with him and Nancy in the White House to discourage discrimination. Allan M. Brandt, "AIDS: From Public History to Public Policy," in *AIDS and the Public Debate: Historical and Contemporary Perspectives*, ed. Caroline Hannaway, Victoria A. Harden, and John Parascandola (Washington, DC: IOS Press, 1995), 128. While Brandt himself concedes, we can never know what would have occurred had Reagan been more active, such fanciful "what if" quandaries do little to help us understand why historical agents behaved the way that they did. Instead of asking what Reagan could have done differently, it is the job of the historian to ask what he did the context of the times in which he lived. When historians address tragedies, like the AIDS epidemic, it is tempting to rely on ahistorical notions and desires to reinterpret the past. In contrast, responsible historians use contextualization not only to determine what a historical agent did but to determine the historical constraints on their action. As Self notes, there was tremendous pressure on Reagan to pursue the New Right's agenda. The president rejected the proposals of the New Right, and the administration did more than historians acknowledge to fight the AIDS epidemic. Furthermore, it is important to note what Reagan did not do. He did not implement mandatory testing, he did not ask those with AIDS to get identification tattoos, and he supported his surgeon general against relentless attacks from the New Right.

3. "The AIDS Epidemic: The Search for a Cure," *Newsweek*, April 18, 1983, 74, box 11, "Homosexuals (3 of 5)" folder, Blackwell Files, Ronald Reagan Presidential Library, Simi Valley, California (hereafter RRL).

4. "Strange Disease Striking Gay Men: Immunity Loss Suspected," *Associated Press*, December 12, 1981, box 11, "Homosexuals (3 of 5)" folder, Blackwell Files, RRL.

5. "The AIDS Epidemic: The Search for a Cure," 76.

6. "Being Gay Is a Health Hazard," *Saturday Evening Post*, October 1982, 73, box 11, "Homosexuals (3 of 5)" folder, Blackwell Files, RRL.

7. C. Everett Koop, *Koop: The Memoirs of America's Family Doctor* (New York: Random House, 1991), 194–195.

8. In his memoir, C. Everett Koop, the surgeon general, blamed both the New Right and gay-rights activists for politicizing the epidemic. He regretted that the gay community combined health issues with political issues into a "single package of grievances" that included concern about AIDS as well as "access to jobs and housing as well as protection against social discrimination." Koop asserted

that their demands "generated more public confusion and anger than they did understanding and sympathy." The result of the New Right's and gay activists' efforts was that AIDS "became needlessly mired in the sexual politics of the early eighties," which cost lives. Koop, *Koop*, 197–198.

9. "The AIDS Epidemic: The Search for a Cure," 80.

10. "Lessons of AIDS: Racism, Homophobia Are the Real Epidemic," *Listen Real Loud*, April 12, 1987.

11. For the latest on how historians view the AIDS epidemic and those who fought the disease in the early 1980s see "HIV/AIDS and U.S. History," *Journal of American History* 104, no. 2 (September 1, 2017): 431–460.

12. For a detailed analysis of homosexuality in the United States in the early twentieth century, see Nancy Boyd's *Wide-Open Town: A History of Queer San Francisco to 1965* (Berkeley: University of California Press, 2003) and George Chauncey's *Gay New York: Gender, Urban Culture, and the Making of the Gay Male World, 1890–1940* (New York: Basic Books, 1994). For an account of the origins of the gay-rights movement see Dudley Clendinen and Adam Nagourney's *Out for Good: The Struggle to Build a Gay Rights Movement in America* (New York: Simon & Schuster, 1999); David Carter's *Stonewall: The Riots That Sparked the Gay Revolution* (New York: St. Martin's Griffin, 2004); Randy Shilts's *The Mayor of Castro Street: The Life and Times of Harvey Milk* (New York: St. Martin's Griffin, 2010); and C. Todd White's *Pre-Gay L.A.: A Social History of the Movement for Homosexual Rights* (Chicago: University of Illinois Press, 2009). For a detailed account of the role of the federal government in regulating homosexuality see Margot Canaday's *The Straight State: Sexuality and Citizenship in Twentieth-Century America* (Princeton, NJ: Princeton University Press, 2011).

13. "An Urgent Message from: Truth about Gays Political Action Committee," advertisement, date unknown [1982–1983], box 10, "Homosexuals (2 of 5)" folder, Blackwell Files, RRL.

14. "Preamble to the Constitution of the Gay Activists Alliance of New York," box 10, "Homosexuals (2 of 5)" folder, Blackwell Files, RRL.

15. "New Right Organizes Effort to Reshape Education in U.S.," *Boston Globe*, November 29, 1982, 1.

16. "Judge Voids Texas Ban on Gay Sex Acts," *Dallas Morning News*, August 18, 1982, box 10, "Homosexuals (2 of 5)" folder, Blackwell Files, RRL; "Judge Voids Texas Homosexual Law," *Dallas Times Herald*, August 18, 1982, box 11, "Homosexuals (3 of 5)" folder, Blackwell Files, RRL.

17. "Gay Activists Say Ruling May Start Nationwide Effort," *Dallas Morning News*, August 18, 1982, box 11, "Homosexuals (3 of 5)" folder, Blackwell Files, RRL.

18. "Consequences of Court Decision Striking Texas Sodomy Statute," date unknown [fall 1982], box 11, "Homosexuals (3 of 5)" folder, Blackwell Files, RRL.

19. "AIDS: A Plague of Fear," *Discover*, July 1983, 75, box 10, "Homosexuals (2 of 5)" folder, Blackwell Files, RRL.

20. "The AIDS Epidemic: The Change in Gay Life-Style," *Newsweek*, April 18, 1983, 80, box 11 "Homosexuals (3 of 5)" folder, Blackwell Files, RRL.

21. "AIDS: A Plague of Fear," 74.

22. Phyllis Schlafly, "What Homosexuals and Lesbians Want," *Texas Tribune*, June 9, 1983, 3, box 10, "Homosexuals (2 of 5)" folder, Blackwell Files, RRL.

23. "Lawmaker, Takes on Gays, Blue Laws," *United Press International*, April 25, 1983, box 10, "Homosexuals (2 of 5)" folder, Blackwell Files, RRL.

24. "The Gay Plague: Homosexuality and Disease," pamphlet by Alert Citizens of Texas, 1983, box 11, "Homosexuals (3 of 5)" folder, Blackwell Files, RRL.

25. "Homosexual Network," *Digest*, Church League of America, March 1983.

26. Speakes's official title was assistant to the president and principal deputy press secretary because James Brady (who was shot in the failed attempted assassination of President Reagan) retained the title of press secretary throughout the administration. Despite not having the title, Speakes served as the official spokesman for the White House for most of the administration.

27. *When AIDS Was Funny*, directed by Scott Calonico, 2015, film, https://video.vanityfair.com/watch/the-reagan-administration-s-chilling-response-to-the-aids-crisis. Larry Speakes did not address the questions about AIDS in his memoir but did briefly mention Kinsolving, describing him as a "pest," "a stellar character," and "a thorn in the side of press secretaries" Larry Speakes, *Speaking Out: The Reagan Presidency from Inside the White House* (New York: Charles Scribner's Sons, 1988), 238, 260.

28. Calonico, *When AIDS Was Funny*.

29. Although most historians denounce the Reagan administration's handling of the epidemic, the administration did take significant (although perhaps not satisfactory) measures to address AIDS. One major policy undertaken by Reagan that is generally ignored was his insistence on removing regulations that prohibited AIDS victims from using experimental drugs. For an in-depth analysis of how the Reagan administration did address the AIDS crisis, see Peter W. Huber's "Ronald Reagan's Quiet War on AIDS: His FDA Accelerated the Delivery of Lifesaving Drugs—Providing a Template for Fighting Devastating Illnesses Today," *City Journal*, Autumn 2016, https://www.city-journal.org/html/ronald-reagans-quiet-war-aids-14783.html.

30. Heckler failed to mention that the money would be taken from other programs and transferred to AIDS. The Reagan administration was hesitant, probably because of concerns over domestic spending, to ask for large increases from Congress for HHS. After Rock Hudson's death in 1985, Congress allocated additional resources specifically to combat AIDS. Harden, *AIDS at 30*, 104. Many historians

criticize the Reagan administration for not funding AIDS adequately. However, it is important to acknowledge that "Democratic Governor Michael Dukakis enraged gay leaders by submitting a $3.3 billion health and human services budget that did not earmark one cent for AIDS." Similarly, Mario Cuomo, the Democratic governor of New York, whom many praised for his "liberal credentials," was also "accused of shortchanging AIDS research." Shilts, *And the Band Played On*, 559.

31. "Heckler Says Increased Funds to Be Sought for AIDS Research," *Boston Globe*, August 18, 1983, 1.

32. "Mrs. Heckler, As Seen by Both Sides," *New York Times*, November 10, 1983, B10.

33. "AIDS: A Plague of Fear," 75.

34. According to the surgeon general, C. Everett Koop, the social climate that existed in the early 1980s made it really difficult to discuss how AIDS was spread. Many AIDS patients told health officials that they often had sex with multiple partners and that they frequently had such sexual encounters. The sexual practices of some patients "shocked and dismayed" health officials. They also shocked the White House, where "more than one White House source" decided to use the vague phrase "exchanging bodily fluids" to explain the spread of AIDS, thus "slowing down the public's understanding of how AIDS" was "transmitted." Koop, *Koop*, 198.

35. Koop, *Koop*, 198.

36. Shilts, *And the Band Played On*, 450–451; Harden, *AIDS at 30*, 64.

37. Koop, *Koop*, 199, 202.

38. Harden, *AIDS at 30*, 105.

39. "Heckler to Plead Her Case with Reagan," *Boston Globe*, September 30, 1985, 1.

40. Koop, *Koop*, 201–202.

41. Koop, *Koop*, 202–203.

42. "Falwell Draws Out Pro-Lifers, Protesters," *Sun Sentinel* (Fort Lauderdale), September 29, 1985, 1B; "Hundreds Protest Peacefully as Falwell Speaks at Church," *Orlando Sentinel*, September 29, 1985, B7.

43. "Pickets March as Falwell Attacks Spreading of AIDS," *Orlando Sentinel*, October 22, 1985, D11.

44. William F. Buckley, "Crucial Steps in Combating the AIDS Epidemic; Identify All the Carriers," *New York Times*, March 18, 1986.

45. William F. Buckley, *The Reagan I Knew* (New York: Basic Books, 2008), 196. Buckley later explained his proposal:

The record is pretty clear that the effort was never to "stigmatize homosexuals," though that charge has been made, over and over. In due course, having been told that the mere mention of "tattoo" brings to mind Nazi extermination camps (my response: Because they used barbed wire in Buchenwald to keep men and women from freedom ought not to stigmatize ranchers who used barbed wire to separate, say, bulls from cows), I formally withdrew the suggestion even though it was never more than hypothetical. But I have permitted myself to wonder how many men and women have died, or have been sentenced to death, since 1985, by society's failure to come up with a means of protecting the uncontaminated and unknowing from the contaminated who knew.

William F. Buckley Jr., *On the Firing Line: The Public Life of Public Figures* (New York: Random House, 1989), 212. Buckley and *National Review* continued to criticize Koop and his decision to emphasize sex education. Although Koop did not respond, several doctors wrote Buckley in his defense. James C. Neely, M.D., to William F. Buckley, January 22, 1987; John "Dick" Woolman to William F. Buckley, March 27, 1987, box 55, Series II: Sequential Files, "AIDS" folder, Koop, C. Everett Papers. History of Medicine Division, National Library of Medicine, Bethesda, MD.

46. To be fair, LaRouche's group held a rather odd collection of beliefs that defy easy left-right characterization.

47. "LaRouche Forces a Vote on AIDS in California," *Newsday* [Long Island, NY], June 24, 1986, 24.

48. Koop, *Koop*, 208. Dannemeyer insisted that knowingly transmitting AIDS could be prosecuted "under theories of homicide, manslaughter, attempted murder and criminal assault." Letter from William E. Dannemeyer to US Attorney General Edwin Meese, October 28, 1986, box 54, Series II: Sequential Files, "AIDS" folder, Koop, C. Everett Papers. History of Medicine Division, National Library of Medicine; "Cuba's AIDS Quarantine Center Called 'Frightening,'" *Los Angeles Times*, November 4, 1988.

49. Congressmen William E. Dannemeyer, Newt Gingrich, Phillip M. Crane, Ralph M. Hall, Thomas F. Hartnett, Don Sundquist, Robert K. Dornan, Mark D. Siljander, and Robert S. Walker to President Ronald Reagan, November 22, 1985, box 47, Series II: Sequential Files, "AIDS" folder, Koop, C. Everett Papers. History of Medicine Division, National Library of Medicine.

50. Koop, *Koop*, 208.

51. Koop, *Koop*, 203–204.

52. Koop, *Koop*, 211–212.

53. Terry Dolan, the long-time New Right activist, passed away on December 28, 1986, from complications arising from AIDS. Dolan, who kept his homosexuality a secret, claimed that he was suffering from diabetes. Shilts, *And the Band Played On*, 407, 586. For the complete report as well as the revisions that took place, see "The Surgeon General's Report on AIDS," box 54, Series II: Sequential

Files, "S.G.'s Report on Acquired Immune Deficiency Syndrome [Drafts]" folder, Koop, C. Everett Papers, History of Medicine Division, National Library of Medicine.

54. "Who, What Will Follow Reagan? New Right Casts about for a Candidate, Causes," *Boston Globe*, April 12, 1987, A21.

55. "AIDS Stand Assailed Conservatives Split as Some Attack Koop," *Los Angeles Times*, May 14, 1987, 1. The administration did take some measures to protect Americans from AIDS exposure by denying immigrants entry into the United States if they tested positive for AIDS. In a statement, Attorney General Ed Meese asserted that AIDS was "one of the most serious public health issues faced by our nation" and added that "it is imperative that the federal government do everything it can to combat this rapidly growing health problem." "Immigrants to Be Barred if Tests Show AIDS Exposure" *Los Angeles Times*, June 9, 1987, 1, box 113, "INS/AIDS" folder, Ed Meese Papers, Hoover Institution Archives, Stanford University, Stanford, California.

56. "Review and Outlook: AIDS and Dr. Koop," *Wall Street Journal*, May 19, 1987, 1.

57. "Point Man in AIDS Battle," *Boston Globe*, April 15, 1987, 1.

58. Shortly after delivering his report on AIDS, Koop began to receive letters and petitions for him to reverse course and use the "full force of your office as Surgeon General to limit the spread of AIDS by reporting and identifying those who are carriers of the disease, instead of protecting them under a blanket of confidentiality at the cost of risking millions of lives." "Petition: Surgeon General of the United States, C. Everett Koop," box 55, Series II: Sequential Files, "AIDS: Evangelical Opposition" folder, Koop, C. Everett Papers, History of Medicine Division, National Library of Medicine.

59. "Point Man in AIDS Battle," 1.

60. "Review and Outlook: AIDS and Dr. Koop," *Wall Street Journal*, May 19, 1987, 1; "Bennett, Koop End AIDS Feud," *Washington Times*, May 29, 1987, box 7, "AIDS" folder, Franklin Lavin Files, RRL.

61. "What You Should Know About AIDS," US Public Health Service and Centers for Disease Control, box 59, Series II: Sequential Files, "AIDS" folder, Koop, C. Everett Papers, History of Medicine Division, National Library of Medicine; "AIDS and the Education of Our Children," US Department of Education, box 60, Series II: Sequential Files, "AIDS" folder, Koop, C. Everett Papers. History of Medicine Division, National Library of Medicine; Koop, *Koop*, 235.

62. Schlafly did not represent the views of all conservatives, and some vocally criticized her for attacking Koop. Elizabeth Whelen, the executive director of the American Council on Science and Health, said that while she had much in common with Schlafly, "she is wrong about Dr. Koop." Whelen compared Schlafly's

newsletter to Koop's actual statements and was appalled by the discrepancies. Whelen lamented that "a lot of people out there would be with Dr. Koop if they didn't have their information filtered through Phyllis Schlafly." Another conservative, Douglas O. Lee, the chairman of Americans for Nuclear Energy, denounced Schlafly and Weyrich, asserting that "as a conservative, I resent your self-appointed intrusion into this discussion" and adding that "this is a medical problem." "AIDS Stand Assailed Conservatives Split as Some Attack Koop," 1.

63. Koop, *Koop*, 218.

64. "Schlafly Lambasts Koop on Education Sex Classes Called Pornographic," *Chicago Tribune*, March 14, 1987, 4.

65. Koop, *Koop*, 218. Koop did work hard to repair his relationship with the various religious organizations that denounced his report. He believed that he "could reason with the large conservative pro-life constituency, people who knew me and had supported my confirmation." Falwell allowed Koop to come and speak at Liberty University about his proposals on AIDS. Koop tried to persuade conservatives that they had "a unique opportunity" to work with him "to produce a morally based sex education program that would conform to their moral standards and also serve to protect a generation of youngsters from AIDS." Unfortunately, Koop concluded, "all too many fell back on old fears and prejudices." Koop, *Koop*, 209.

66. Koop, *Koop*, 228–229.

67. "Remarks by the President to the American Foundation for AIDS Research Awards Dinner," [Potomac Restaurant, Washington D.C.], May 31, 1987, box OA 17989, "AIDS (1)" folder, Webber Hildred Files, RRL.

68. "Remarks by the President to the American Foundation for AIDS Research Awards Dinner." While Reagan opposed mandatory testing, which the New Right desired, he did call on Americans who thought they might have the disease to voluntarily get tested. Furthermore, while Reagan endorsed sex education, he encouraged that it be carried out "with the guidance of the parents" and with the "commitment" that such education would "not be value-neutral." The president also approved mandatory AIDS testing for immigrants coming to the United States and for federal prisoners (to protect those prisoners without AIDS from contracting it from involuntary sexual activities). Reagan also disavowed those who wanted to discriminate against those with AIDS, declaring that "we mustn't allow those with the AIDS virus to suffer discrimination." Vice President Bush's speech the following day also emphasized sex education and understanding for the victims of AIDS. Bush was emphatic, declaring, "We must wage an all-out war against the disease. Let me repeat: an all-out war against the <u>disease</u>—not against people. Not against the victims of AIDS, but an all-out war against the disease itself." "Remarks for Vice President George Bush: Third International Conference

on AIDS," June 1, 1987, box OA 17989, "AIDS (1)" folder, Hildred Files, RRL. The *Washington Post* called the speech "sensible" and emphasized that "compassion was the keynote" of the address. "Mr. Reagan on AIDS," *Washington Post*, June 2, 1987, A18, box OA18263, "AIDS" folder, Lavin Files, RRL. Not everyone, however, enjoyed Reagan's speech, Randy Shilts—writing in 1987—complained that there was little talk of education and a lot of talk about testing. He condemned Reagan in no uncertain terms, declaring the speech was "not meant to serve the public health; it was a political solution to a political problem." Shilts continued that "the words created a stance that was politically comfortable for the president and his adherents; it was also a stance that killed people." Shilts concluded that "saving lives had never been a priority of the Reagan administration" and proclaimed that Reagan would be remembered as "the man who had let AIDS rage through America." Shilts, *And the Band Played On*, 595.

69. "Who, What Will Follow Reagan?," A21.

70. *Cultural Conservatism*, Institute for Cultural Conservatism (Lanham, MD: Free Congress Research and Education Foundation, 1987).

71. Self, *All in the Family*, 397.

72. "Who, What Will Follow Reagan?," A21.

73. Steve Bruce, *The Rise and Fall of the Christian Right: Conservative Protestant Politics in America, 1979–1988* (Oxford: Oxford University Press, 1988); Michael D'Antonio, *Fall from Grace: The Failed Crusade of the Christian Right* (New York: Farrar, Straus and Giroux, 1989).

74. R. Gustav Niebuhr, "Why 'Moral Majority,' a Force for a Decade, Ran Out of Steam," *Wall Street Journal*, September 25, 1989; Daniel K. Williams, *God's Own Party: The Making of the Christian Right* (Oxford: Oxford University Press, 2010), 222.

75. "Politics and Policy: GOP Conservatives, after 8 Years in Ascendency Brood over Lost Opportunities, Illusory Victories," *Wall Street Journal*, August 17, 1988, 44. It should be noted that not all conservatives viewed the Reagan years as a disappointment. Indeed, conservative reviews of Reagan's time in office were mixed. "A Fond Farewell to the 'Gipper,'" *Human Events*, January 21, 1989.

CHAPTER 6. NEOCONSERVATIVES, THE NEW RIGHT, AND REAGAN'S FIRST TWO YEARS OF FOREIGN POLICY

1. "U.S. Says Soviets Shot Down Airliner: Soviets' Missile Downed Korean Plane, U.S. Says," *Washington Post*, September 2, 1983, A1. For detailed accounts of the KAL 007 incident see R. W. Johnson's *Shootdown: Flight 007 and the American Connection* (New York: Viking, 1986); Seymour M. Hersh, *The Target Is Destroyed:*

What Really Happened to Flight 007 and What America Knew about it (New York: Random House, 1986); and Alexander Dallin, *Black Box: KAL 007 and the Superpowers* (Berkeley: University of California Press, 1985).

2. George Shultz praised Reagan's response, asserting that the way the president handled the incident "was the classic way it should be done." Stephen F. Knott and Jeffrey L. Chidester, *At Reagan's Side: Insiders' Recollections from Sacramento to the White House* (New York: Rowman and Littlefield, 2009), 99.

3. "Rep. McDonald Hailed as Right-Wing Martyr," *Washington Post*, September 2, 1983, A1. In reality, the United States had a spy plane off the Soviet coast monitoring what the administration described as planned missile tests. The Soviets apparently believed that KAL007 was the spy plane and took it out. Reagan, however, asserted that it "was a clear night with a half moon" and that the plane's strobe light was flashing. Reagan cited a plethora of evidence that led the administration to dismiss assertions that the Soviet pilots did not know they were shooting down an airliner. Historian Vladislav Zubok asserts that Reagan's tough stand against the Soviets resulted in a "war of nerves" that "reached its climax in the KAL-007 affair." Zubok concludes that "the nervous air-defense command mistook it for an American spy plane and ordered Soviet jet fighters to destroy it." Furthermore, General Secretary Yuri Andropov's denial of the incident came while he was in the hospital and the advice of counsel assured him that the "Americans would never find out about it." The incident, coupled with Andropov's denials, sharply intensified the distrust between the Soviet Union and the Reagan administration. "Transcript of President Reagan's Address on Downing of Korean Airliner," *New York Times*, September 6, 1983; "The KAL Flight 7 Crisis; Politics; Reagan Presidency on the Line," *Boston Globe*, September 11, 1983, 1; Vladislav M. Zubok, *A Failed Empire: The Soviet Union in the Cold War from Stalin to Gorbachev* (Chapel Hill: University of North Carolina Press, 2007), 274.

4. "Transcript of President Reagan's Address on Downing of Korean Airliner."

5. "The KAL Flight 7 Crisis; Politics; Reagan Presidency on the Line," 1.

6. "Reagan Moves Get Bipartisan Support but New Right Voices Disappointment," *Sun*, September 6, 1983, A2.

7. "Conservatives Disagree with Reagan's Decision," *Chicago Tribune*, September 6, 1983, 8.

8. For a comprehensive analysis of Reagan's foreign policy and those who shaped it, see Francis Marlo's *Planning Reagan's War: Conservative Strategists and America's Cold War Victory* (New York: Potomac Books, 2012). James Mann does an excellent job of detailing some of this frustration with Reagan's nuclear policy in *The Rebellion of Ronald Reagan: A History of the End of the Cold War* (New York: Penguin Books, 2009).

9. For an analysis of the Cold War liberal consensus following World War II,

consult Wendy L. Wall's *Inventing the "American Way": The Politics of Consensus from the New Deal to the Civil Rights Movement* (Oxford: Oxford University Press, 2008); Elaine Tyler May's *Homeward Bound: American Families in the Cold War Era* (New York: Basic Books, 2008); Lizabeth Cohen's *A Consumer's Republic: The Politics of Mass Consumption in Postwar America* (New York: Vintage Books, 2003); and Benjamin Fordham's *Building the Cold War Consensus: The Political Economy of U.S. National Security Policy, 1949–51* (Ann Arbor: University of Michigan Press, 1998). For more on the critics of détente see Jeremi Suri's chapter "Détente and Its Discontents," in *Rightward Bound: Making America Conservative in the 1970s,* ed. Bruce J. Schulman and Julian E. Zelizer (Cambridge, MA: Harvard University Press, 2008), 227–245.

10. While historians have written countless volumes debating when détente became policy (or if it ever existed), this account is interested in how American conservatives viewed détente and when they believed it became US policy. For a complete analysis of this interpretation of the rise of détente see Jeremi Suri's *Power and Protest: Global Revolution and the Rise of Détente* (Cambridge, MA: Harvard University Press, 2003). Historians have debated détente at length. Some important works on the subject include Michael Bowker and Phil William's *Superpower Détente: A Reappraisal* (New York: SAGE Publications, 1988); M. E. Sarotte's *Dealing with the Devil: East Germany, Détente, and Ostpolitik, 1969–1973* (Chapel Hill: University of North Carolina Press, 2001); Craig Daigle's *The Limits of Détente: The United States, the Soviet Union, and the Arab-Israeli Conflict, 1969–1973* (New Haven, CT: Yale University Press, 2012); Jussi Hanhimaki's *The Rise and Fall of Détente: American Foreign Policy and the Transformation of the Cold War* (New York: Potomac Books, 2012).

11. "What Is Détente," *Hartford Courant,* July 13, 1980, 34A.

12. For a complete account of Nixon and Kissinger's relationship and also their attempts to remake US foreign policy, see Robert Dallek's *Nixon and Kissinger: Partners in Power* (New York: HarperCollins, 2007). For a detailed biography of President Nixon, including his ambition to be remembered for his decisions regarding foreign policy, consult Rick Perlstein's *Nixonland: The Rise of a President and the Fracturing of America* (New York: Scribner, 2008). For an account of the Vietnam War that demonstrates the North Vietnamese unwillingness and resistance to Sino and Soviet influences, see Lien-Hang T. Nguyen's *Hanoi's War: An International History of the War for Peace in Vietnam* (Chapel Hill: University of North Carolina Press, 2012).

13. Margaret MacMillan has written an accessible and comprehensive analysis of Nixon's trip to mainland China. *Nixon and Mao: The Week That Changed the World* (New York: Random House, 2007).

14. Chen Jian offers a comprehensive overview of Mao's China including the

tensions between Mao and Taiwan. Chen also chronicles how the United States' commitment to Chiang Kai-shek placed it at odds with mainland China. Chen Jian, *Mao's China and the Cold War* (Chapel Hill: University of North Carolina Press, 2001). Jay Taylor's biography of Chiang Kai-shek offers a detailed account of the exiled leader and his relationship with the United States and Mao Zedong. Jay Taylor, *The Generalissimo: Chiang Kai-shek and the Struggle for Modern China* (Cambridge, MA: Belknap Press, 2009).

15. William F. Buckley Jr., *The Reagan I Knew* (New York: Basic Books, 2008), 52–53.

16. Other signees of Buckley's letter were James Burnham, editor of *National Review*; Allan H. Ryskind, Capitol Hill editor of *Human Events*; Jeffrey Bell, editor of *Battle Line*; Thomas S. Winter, vice chairman of the American Conservative Union; Anthony Harrigan, executive vice president of the Southern States Industrial Council; Neil McCaffrey, president of the conservative publishing company Arlington House; J. Daniel Mahoney, chairman of the New York Conservative Party; Frank S. Meyer, vice chairman of the New York Conservative Party; Randal C. Teague, executive director of Young Americans for Freedom; and William A. Rusher, publisher of *National Review*. "Buckley, 10 Colleagues Suspend Nixon Support," *Los Angeles Times*, July 29, 1971, 4.

17. "For Reagan, Crucial Choices Also Worked Politically," *Washington Post*, February 23, 1981, A1. For a detailed history of how conservative publications such as *Human Events*, *Commentary*, and *National Review* helped define conservatives' foreign policy positions consult Laurence R. Jurdem's *Paving the Way for Reagan: The Influence of Conservative Media on Foreign Policy* (Lexington: University Press of Kentucky, 2018).

18. "The Sharon Statement," Young Americans for Freedom, September 11, 1960, https://www.yaf.org/news/the-sharon-statement/, accessed May 8, 2019.

19. "For Reagan, Crucial Choices Also Worked Politically," A1.

20. "For Reagan, Crucial Choices Also Worked Politically," A1.

21. Buckley, *The Reagan I Knew*, 61. Reagan took Buckley's advice. Reagan became deeply involved in matters of foreign policy during the 1970s. According to historian Chester J. Pach Jr., "candidate Reagan read extensively about defense and national security matters, discussed these issues on trips to East Asia, Africa, and Europe, and frequently wrote about them. Between 1975 and 1979, Reagan drafted hundreds of scripts for a regular weekly radio program of political commentary. Many of them concerned national security, including nuclear balance, arms control, defense spending, and new weapons systems." Chester J. Pach Jr., "Sticking to His Guns: Reagan and National Security," in *The Reagan Presidency: Pragmatic Conservatism and Its Legacies*, ed. W. Elliot Brownlee and Hugh Davis Graham (Lawrence: University Press of Kansas, 2003), 85.

22. The term "neoconservative" was "a term of rebuke apparently coined by Michael Harrington, the veteran socialist, in 1973." Neoconservative intellectuals included Jeane Kirkpatrick, Seymour Martin Lipset, Irving Kristol, James Q. Wilson, Norman Podhoretz, Robert A. Nisbet, Midge Decter, Sidney Hook, and Nathan Glazer (among others). "Neoconservatives Today, They Explain All Their Yesterdays," *New York Times*, December 28, 1980, E5. There are numerous histories of neoconservatives. Two comprehensive studies are Justin Vaïsse's *Neoconservatism: The Biography of a Movement* (Cambridge, MA: Belknap Press, 2010) and John Ehrman's *Neoconservatism: Intellectuals and Foreign Affairs 1945–1994* (New Haven, CT: Yale University Press, 1995). For an overview of conservative intellectuals during the Reagan administration, including many neoconservatives, see J. David Hoeveler Jr.'s *Watch on the Right: Conservative Intellectuals in the Reagan Era* (Madison: University of Wisconsin Press, 1991). Neoconservatives, while important during the 1980s, became more prominent during the George W. Bush administration. For an overview of the origins of neoconservatism and its influence on conservative presidents beyond Reagan, see James Mann's *Rise of the Vulcans: The History of Bush's War Cabinet* (New York: Penguin Books, 2004).

23. "Reagan's Brain Trust: Font of Varied Ideas," *New York Times*, December 1, 1980, A1.

24. "Neoconservatives Today, They Explain All Their Yesterdays," E5.

25. "Trying to Turn a Collective Sentiment into a Government," *Washington Post*, February 24, 1981, A4.

26. The neoconservatives identified most with Senator Henry M. Jackson (D-WA) and Senator Daniel Patrick Moynihan (D-NY). If either had become the leader of the Democratic Party or if the party had moved in their direction, neoconservatives might never have aligned with the Republicans. "The Republicans: A Government Waits in Wings," *Washington Post*, May 27, 1980, A1.

27. "Reagan's Brain Trust: Font of Varied Ideas," A1.

28. Richard Viguerie, *The New Right: We're Ready to Lead* (Falls Church, VA: Viguerie Company, 1980), 11.

29. "For Reagan, Crucial Choices Also Worked Politically," A1. For a complete history of William Rusher and *National Review*, consult David B. Frisk's *If Not Us Who? William Rusher, National Review, and the Conservative Movement* (Wilmington, DE: ISI Books, 2012).

30. "The Restless Conservatives Can't Be Taken for Granted," *Los Angeles Times*, February 19, 1975, D5.

31. For his part, Reagan sided with Ford in condemning Congress for not sending support for the South Vietnamese. Reagan asserted that "this Congress is the most irresponsible and dangerous I've ever known." Reagan continued that the

failure of Congress to assist South Vietnam had created "a worldwide belief that the US breaks its promised word and abandons its allies." "Reagan Shares Ford View of Congress in Viet Congress," *Los Angeles Times*, April 2, 1975, 9. Reagan's unwillingness to condemn Ford over Vietnam combined with the perception that he was a "backsliding conservative" led the United Republicans of California, a grassroots volunteer organization, to repudiate Reagan. "GOP Volunteer Unit Repudiates Reagan," *Los Angeles Times*, May 5, 1975, B21.

32. "U.S. Is Criticized in Vietnam's Fall" *New York Times*, August 19, 1975, 13; "Tactics for Détente" *Wall Street Journal*, February 13, 1976, 8; "Reagan Charges Denied," *Washington Post*, April 24, 1976, A1.

33. "For Reagan, Crucial Choices Also Worked Politically," *Washington Post*, February 23, 1981, A1.

34. "Reagan's Challenge for Leadership of Republican Party," *New York Times*, November 21, 1975, 21; "Reagan Is Set to Run—as Opponent of 'Executive Drift,'" *Chicago Tribune*, November 18, 1975, A2.

35. "Ronald Reagan Announcement for Presidential Candidacy," November 20, 1975, http://www.reagan.utexas.edu/archives/reference/11.20.75.html.

36. "President Vows to Back Détente: Indicates He Won't Abandon It Because of Criticism," *New York Times*, January 4, 1976, 21.

37. For the most detailed analysis of Angola's role in the Cold War consult Piero Gleijeses's two volumes on the subject. Gleijeses demonstrates that the USSR and the US were often pulled into conflicts by their allies in the region. Piero Gleijeses, *Conflicting Missions: Havana, Washington, and Africa, 1959–1976* (Chapel Hill: University of North Carolina Press, 2002); Piero Gleijeses, *Visions of Freedom: Havana, Washington, Pretoria, and the Struggle for Southern Africa, 1976–1991* (Chapel Hill: University of North Carolina Press, 2013).

38. "Russ Deny That Aid to Angola Is Threat to Détente," *Los Angeles Times*, December 2, 1975, 1. By the end of 1975, "many liberals" were "joining with conservatives in questioning the United States' moves towards détente with the Russians." Some of those liberals concerned with the administration's policy were pro-Israel and for the United States confronting the USSR in the Middle East on "behalf of Israel." Others were simply opposed to a "conservative" carrying out détente—they questioned "whether a Nixon or a Ford could really have his heart in bringing about a rapprochement between the US and a Communist nation." Some liberals even agreed with conservative critics and asserted "that the U.S. isn't getting any real quid pro quo for its concessions to the Soviets." The *Christian Science Monitor* concluded in December that "there appears to be a growing number among those who once supported détente who express reservations about it today." "Washington Letter: Why 'New Liberals' Oppose Détente," *Christian Science Monitor*, December 15, 1975, 32.

39. "Ford Eschews Détente: Says U.S. Will Now Deal from Strength," *Baltimore Sun*, March 2, 1976, A1.

40. "Looking Past the Churchillian Rhetoric," *Chicago Tribune*, April 25, 1976, A6; "The Will to Resist," *New York Times*, April 23, 1976, 35.

41. "Dividing Point Was Détente," *Washington Post*, October 7, 1976, A1.

42. "The Second Carter-Ford Presidential Debate," *Commission on Presidential Debates*, October 6, 1976, accessed October 5, 2015, http://www.debates.org/index.php?page=october-6-1976-debate-transcript.

43. Laura Kalman, *Right Star Rising: A New Politics, 1974–1980*. New York, W. W. Norton, 2010.

44. "Carter's New World," *Christian Science Monitor*, June 2, 1977, 27. For more on Carter's foreign policy consult Derek N. Buckaloo's chapter "Carter's Nicaragua and Other Democratic Quagmires," in *Rightward Bound: Making America Conservative in the 1970s*, ed. Bruce J. Schulman and Julian E. Zelizer (Cambridge, MA: Harvard University Press, 2008), 246–264.

45. "Carter Kills B-1—Picks Cruise Missile," *Christian Science Monitor*, July 1, 1977, 1.

46. "Carter's B-1 Decision 'Dangerously Foolish,'" *Human Events*, July 9, 1977, 4. As cited in Kalman's *Right Star Rising*, 283.

47. Ronald Reagan, "SALT Talks I," March 13, 1978, and Ronald Reagan, "SALT Talks II," July 31, 1978, in *Reagan, in His Own Hand*, ed. Kiron K. Skinner, Annelise Anderson, and Martin Anderson (New York: Free Press, 2001), 76, 84.

48. Kalman, *Right Star Rising*, 283.

49. After Soviet troops invaded Afghanistan, the *Washington Post* declared "détente is dead." Conservative columnists such as George Will quickly reminded Americans that in their view détente had never existed, and many "liberal columnists became hard-liners overnight" insisting the United States boycott the Olympic games, a measure Carter embraced and conservatives mocked. "What Is Détente," 34A. For his part, Falwell lamented that "the only 'severe political consequence' Mr. Carter took" in response to the invasion "was to boycott the 1980 Summer Olympic games in Moscow, a very mild slap on the wrist to say the least!" Jerry Falwell, *Armageddon and the Coming War with Russia* (Self-published, 1980), 21. Many neoconservatives had supported Carter in the hope that he would take a hard line against the Soviet Union. They were ultimately disappointed and in 1980 supported Reagan. Norman Podhoretz, "The Neo-Conservative Anguish over Reagan's Foreign Policy," *New York Times*, May 2, 1982, SM30.

50. "The Republicans: A Government Waits in the Wings," *Washington Post*, May 27, 1980, A1. For more on conservatives, Carter, and foreign policy see Julian E. Zelizer's chapter "Conservatives, Carter, and the Politics of National Security" in *Rightward Bound: Making America Conservative in the 1970s*, ed. Bruce

J. Schulman and Julian E. Zelizer (Cambridge, MA: Harvard University Press, 2008), 265–287.

51. "Neoconservatives Today, They Explain All Their Yesterdays," E5.

52. "The Republicans: A Government Waits in Wings," A1. For another perspective on why some neoconservatives switched political parties see Norman Podhoretz's *Breaking Ranks: A Political Memoir* (New York: Harper and Row, 1979).

53. Neoconservatives were even internally divided over issues such as "homosexual rights and the equal rights amendment." Whatever their view on social issues, they all put a priority on strongly opposing communism and were repulsed by "the New Left's attacks on the United States." "Neoconservatives Today, They Explain All Their Yesterdays," E5.

54. "Reagan's Brian Trust: Font of Varied Ideas," A1. Neoconservatives were often at odds with traditional Republicans "who favored trade with the Soviet Union." They also differed from the New Right. One neoconservative explained that the New Right was "different from us" because they believed that unionization would lead to a Soviet-like state. He quipped that "they believe the Soviet Union is one giant OSHA with nuclear weapons." "The Republicans: A Government Waits in Wings," A1.

55. "Trying to Turn a Collective Sentiment into a Government," *Washington Post*, February 24, 1981, A4.

56. Falwell, *Armageddon*, 2, 5, 20, 21.

57. Viguerie, *The New Right*, 4.

58. Conservatives in Great Britain also hoped that Reagan would pursue an aggressive foreign policy. Margaret Thatcher, the prime minister of Great Britain, declared that Reagan shared her view that the Soviets were not interested in "genuine détente." She continued that the West needed to be strong and unified when facing the USSR. She declared that when "the Americans face difficulties, we need to say to them more clearly: 'We are with you.'" "Thatcher Doubts Moscow Interest in Real Détente," *Los Angeles Times*, January 30, 1981, B15. Thatcher would become one of Reagan's strongest allies, reinvigorating the special Anglo-American relationship that had been waning. Reagan and Thatcher's relationship was more difficult, however, than the public or the press realized at the time. For a comprehensive analysis of their relationship see Richard Aldous's *Reagan and Thatcher: The Difficult Relationship* (New York: W. W. Norton, 2012). Interestingly, the Soviet Union saw the 1980 election as a choice "between two Goldwaters." Both Carter and Reagan were "equally unpalatable to the Kremlin." *Pravda*, the Communist Party newspaper, concluded that Reagan and Carter were in competition to see "who will place more nuclear mines under the foundations of international security that were established in the 1970s." The Soviets publicly

credited the anti-Soviet mood in the United States to "reactionary forces" who were perpetuating the "myth" of the Soviet threat. In reality, however, "Moscow was completely surprised by the intensity of American reaction to the Afghanistan invasion." "Soviets Paint Carter and Reagan with Anti-Détente Brush," *Washington Post*, August 20, 1980, A2.

59. "Reagan's Heart and Mind," *Baltimore Sun*, November 16, 1980, K4.

60. "Neoconservatives and Reagan: Uneasy Coalition," *New York Times*, September 28, 1981, A16.

61. "Neoconservatives and Reagan: Uneasy Coalition," A16. Some neoconservatives realized they would have more effect on conservative thought than the Reagan administration itself. Leslie Lenkowsky, the neoconservative director of research for the Smith Richardson Foundation, asserted that "Norman and Irving's views will have long-term impact . . . they will have their effect on how educated people think about public affairs, not on the specific details of the issue of the day." It is also important to note that some neoconservatives did find positions in the Reagan administration. The most prominent of them were: Jeane Kirkpatrick, United States representative to the United Nations; Eugene V. Rostow, director of the Arms Control and Disarmament Agency; Richard N. Perle, assistant secretary for international security policy; and Charles E. Horner, deputy secretary of state for science and technology. "Neoconservatives and Reagan: Uneasy Coalition," A16. The New Right realized that they did not have the same authority on foreign policy that they had on social issues. As the administration was being formed, Morton Blackwell drew up a memorandum entitled "A New Right Foreign Policy Offensive," in which he lamented that "in the foreign policy area" the New Right was where it was "in domestic politics fifteen years ago." He suggested that the New Right take a page out of its domestic playbook and begin to "build coalitions, start new groups, undermine communist areas of strength, run international political action seminars etc." "A New Right Foreign Policy Offensive," memorandum by Morton C. Blackwell, August 29, 1980, box 1, "American Security Council and Coalition for Peace Through Strength" folder, Blackwell Files, Ronald Reagan Presidential Library, Simi Valley, California (hereafter RRL).

62. John T. Dolan, "A Conservative's Opposition to AWACS," *Hartford Courant*, October 22, 1981, A25.

63. Reagan, *The Reagan Diaries*, ed. Douglas Brinkley (New York: HarperCollins, 2007), 14.

64. "What Defeat on AWACS Would Mean to White House," *Christian Science Monitor*, September 25, 1981.

65. "White House Meeting for Organizations and Associates Supporting AWACS," memorandum from Rick Sellers to Richard Allen, Max Friedersdorf, and Diana Lozana, assistants to the president, October 26, 1981, 2, box 1,

"American Security Council and Coalition for Peace Through Strength" folder, Blackwell Files, RRL.

66. Telegram from leaders of nongovernment organizations to Senator Jeremiah Denton, box 1, "American Security Council and Coalition for Peace Through Strength" folder, Blackwell Files, RRL.

67. "How Reagan Won on AWACS," *Chicago Tribune*, October 29, 1981, 1. While convincing Senators Cohen (R-ME), Gorton (R-WA), and Zorinsky (D-NE) at the White House, Reagan said he emphasized "that Saudi Arabia was beginning to play a positive role in the peace process, especially in Lebanon." Reagan asserted that he conveyed to the senators that he considered the sale of AWACS to Saudi Arabia as "essential for the security of Israel, for the entire Middle East and for ourselves on the world scene." "How Reagan Won on AWACS," 1.

68. Jewish leaders "bitterly opposed the sale," and after it passed they called on "Reagan to 'heal the wounds' inflicted by the months of debate, which several said have brought on signs of anti-Semitism." "How Reagan Won on AWACS," 1. Tension between the United States and Israel continued during Reagan's first term. In late 1982, Lyn Nofziger wrote a memo to Bill Clark and Ed Meese describing the frustration of Moshe Arens, the Israeli ambassador, with his lack of access. Memorandum from Lyn Nofziger to Bill Clark, December 23, 1982, Lyn Nofziger Papers, box 5, "Correspondence: Clark, William 1983" folder, Hoover Institution Archives, Stanford University, Stanford, California.

69. "AWACS Sale Costing Reagan Support among Jews," *New York Times*, October 22, 1981.

70. Dolan, "A Conservative's Opposition to AWACS," A25.

71. "Saudis Bar Compromise on AWACS, Haig Says," *Los Angeles Times*, October 6, 1981, B1. Kissinger endorsed the proposal despite having some misgivings. He told the press that he believed "the sale is in the national interests of the United States. . . . It is compatible with the security of Israel; it is essential for the peace process in the Middle East." Kissinger was one of sixteen top aides of past presidents, including many of the East Coast liberal elites that conservatives condemned, who were consulted. Those consulted included former defense secretaries (Harold Brown, Elliot L. Richardson, Melvin R. Laird, and Robert S. McNamara); former national security advisers (Gordon Gray, Walt W. Rostow, McGeorge Bundy, and Zbigniew Brzezinski); chairmen of the Joint Chiefs of Staff (Adm. Thomas H. Moorer, Gen. Lyman L. Lemnitzer, and Gen. Maxwell D. Taylor). The AWACS sale had been approved under President Carter, and President Nixon publicly supported the deal, causing controversy when he declared that the sale would have easily gone "through were it not for the opposition of Israeli Prime Minister Menachem Begin and 'parts of the American Jewish community.'" "Saudis Bar Compromise on AWACS, Haig Says," B1.

72. "Taiwan Criticizes Reagan's View," *Washington Post*, May 13, 1982, A18.

73. The American Council for Free Asia (ACFA) described itself as "a pro-defense organization concerned with communist aggression—primarily in Asia" and also opposed to the worldwide "threat of nuclear freeze." Major General John K. Singlaub, former chief of staff of American Forces in South Korea, to ACFA's contributors, June 1982, box 1, "American Council for Free Asia" folder, Blackwell Files, RRL.

74. Gary L. Jarmin, national director for American Council for Free Asia, to Morton Blackwell, June 16, 1982, box 1, "American Council for Free Asia" folder, Blackwell Files, RRL.

75. "Statement of Conservative Leaders," from conservative leaders to Morton Blackwell, July 8, 1982, 1, box 1, "American Council for Free Asia" folder, Blackwell Files, RRL.

76. Haig actually resigned his post a few days before "Statement of Conservative Leaders" sent their letter to Reagan. Haig resigned over internal conflicts between himself and other members of the administration over the course of US foreign policy. In his resignation letter, Haig recalled that when he was brought on as secretary of state, "we agreed that consistency, clarity and steadiness of purpose were essential to success." He continued, "In recent months it has become clear to me that the foreign policy on which we embarked together was shifting from that careful course that we had laid out." President Reagan accepted his resignation and nominated George P. Shultz to the post. "Haig Resigns over Foreign Policy Course, but Cites No Issues; Reagan Names Shultz," *New York Times*, June 26, 1982.

77. "Statement of Conservative Leaders," 30.

78. "Statement of Conservative Leaders," 1.

79. "Reagan Reassures Taiwan Supporters on Arms Sales," *Los Angeles Times*, July 31, 1982, A1.

80. "Reagan Draws Fire of Conservatives," *Hartford Courant*, August 18, 1982, A1.

81. "Reagan Draws Fire of Conservatives," A1.

82. Podhoretz, "The Neo-Conservative Anguish over Reagan's Foreign Policy," SM30.

83. Podhoretz, "The Neo-Conservative Anguish over Reagan's Foreign Policy," SM30. We now know that Reagan approved CIA operations in Poland following the crackdown in Poland. Consult Seth G. Jones's *A Covert Action: Reagan, the CIA, and the Cold War Struggle in Poland* (New York: W. W. Norton, 2018).

84. Podhoretz, "The Neo-Conservative Anguish over Reagan's Foreign Policy," SM30.

85. For a complete discussion of Reagan's policy toward intervening in

countries across the globe, see James M. Scott, *Deciding to Intervene: The Reagan Doctrine and American Foreign Policy* (Durham, NC: Duke University Press, 1996).

86. Podhoretz, "The Neo-Conservative Anguish over Reagan's Foreign Policy," SM30.

87. Podhoretz, "The Neo-Conservative Anguish over Reagan's Foreign Policy," SM30.

88. Thomas L. Jeffers, *Norman Podhoretz: A Biography* (New York: Cambridge University Press, 2010), 215.

89. The *Chicago Tribune* made this point in 1991. Looking back on the Reagan administration, the *Tribune* concluded that "realism often ruled." The article explained that

> Reagan was largely removed from the unending debate that raged within his administration on the distinctions between speeches and policy or even whether there was a distinction between speeches and policy. He never confused a speech with a fact-finding expedition. Instead, Reagan recognized the salesman's truth that salesmen sell themselves before they sell their products, and he used his speeches to reaffirm his personal relationship with the American audience. This point was often lost on his bickering disciples, who battled among themselves about the purposes and meaning of the "Reagan Revolution."

"Despite Reagan's Rosy View, Realism Often Ruled," *Chicago Tribune*, May 5, 1991, G1.

90. To comprehend conservatives' antagonistic view of the Soviet Union, one should consult Barry Goldwater's *Why Not Victory? A Fresh Look at American Foreign Policy* (Washington, DC: MacFadden Capital Hill Books, 1963).

91. "Conservatives Favor Reagan: Not His Policies: Texas Meeting Calls for Tougher Anti-USSR Stance," *Christian Science Monitor*, February 8, 1982, 9.

92. Memorandum, "Soviet Problems—Cause for Complacency or Incentive for Action," by the Christian Anti-Communism Crusade, September 15, 1982, 2, box 4, "Christian Anti-Communism Crusade" folder, Blackwell Files, RRL.

CHAPTER 7. THE YEAR OF FEAR: RONALD REAGAN AND THE TRANSFORMATION OF AMERICA'S FOREIGN POLICY

1. Major General John K. Singlaub, former chief of staff of the American Forces in South Korea to ACFA contributors, June 1982, 2, box 1, "American Council for Free Asia" folder, Blackwell Files, Ronald Reagan Presidential Library, Simi Valley, California (hereafter RRL).

2. David E. Spray, special projects director for the American Security Council, to Morton Blackwell, special assistant to the president, February 16, 1983, box 1, "American Legislative Exchange Council (2)" folder, Blackwell Files, RRL.

3. "Nuclear Freeze: Deceptively Simple, Dangerously Misleading," *First Reading* 8, no. 10 (October 1982), box 1, "American Legislative Exchange Council (2)" folder, Blackwell Files, RRL.

4. "Nuclear Freeze: Deceptively Simple, Dangerously Misleading."

5. "Nuclear Freeze: Deceptively Simple, Dangerously Misleading."

6. "Haig Warns against a Push for Freeze on Nuclear Arms," *Washington Post*, April 7, 1982. A1.

7. For a detailed account of Reagan's desire to reduce and eradicate nuclear weapons, consult Paul Lettow's *Ronald Reagan and His Quest to Abolish Nuclear Weapons* (New York: Random House, 2006). Other historians agree that "the need to eliminate the threat of nuclear weapons was one of Ronald Reagan's most strongly held beliefs." Samuel F. Wells, "Reagan, Euromissiles, and Europe," in *The Reagan Presidency: Pragmatic Conservatism and Its Legacies*, ed. W. Elliot Brownlee and Hugh Davis Graham (Lawrence: University Press of Kansas, 2003), 141. James Graham Wilson notes that Reagan "was not the cowboy his critics alleged" and asserts that Reagan had "long dreamed of a world without nuclear weapons, and he had a strategy to meet this evolving vision." Wilson, *The Triumph of Improvisation: Gorbachev's Adaptability, Reagan's Engagement, and the End of the Cold War* (Ithaca, NY: Cornell University Press, 2015), 4.

8. Reagan had given speeches prior to becoming president that should have indicated to the public that he was opposed to nuclear weapons. Despite his speech at the 1976 RNC, and other public speaking events, many continued to ignore Reagan's pleas to end nuclear proliferation, perhaps believing such sentiment to be disingenuous.

9. President Ronald Reagan to Miss Jill Conway, president of Smith College, October 25, 1982, in *Reagan: A Life in Letters* (New York: Free Press, 2003), 390.

10. Wells, "Reagan, Euromissiles, and Europe," 141; William E. Pemberton, *Exit with Honor: The Life and Presidency of Ronald Reagan* (New York: M. E. Sharpe, 1998), 131.

11. Ed Meese, *With Reagan: The Inside Story* (Washington, DC: Regnery Gateway, 1992), 187.

12. George Shultz, *Turmoil and Triumph: My Years as Secretary of State* (New York: Scribner's, 1993), 189.

13. Ronald Reagan, *An American Life: The Autobiography* (New York: Threshold, 1990), 550.

14. "Pentagon Draws Up First Strategy for Fighting a Long Nuclear War" *New York Times*, May 30, 1982, 1.

15. Robert Scheer, "Pentagon Plan Aims at Winning Nuclear War" *Los Angeles Times*, August 15, 1982, 1.

16. Robert Scheer, *With Enough Shovels: Reagan, Bush, and Nuclear War* (New York: Random House, 1982).

17. "Administration's Nuclear War Policy Stance Still Murky" *Washington Post*, November 10, 1982, A21.

18. Don Oberdorfer, *The Turn: From the Cold War to a New Era* (New York: Poseidon Press, 1991), 35.

19. Shultz, *Turmoil and Triumph*, 164.

20. Oberdorfer, *The Turn*, 35. Shultz would continue to struggle with Weinberger and Clark throughout 1983, but things got a bit better for Shultz when Jack Matlock was brought into the administration as the chief Soviet policy official on the National Security Council in the summer of 1983.

21. Shultz, *Turmoil and Triumph*, 164.

22. Anatoly Dobrynin, *In Confidence: Moscow's Ambassador to America's Six Cold War Presidents* (New York: Times Books, 1995), 517–518.

23. Dobrynin, *In Confidence*, 518–519.

24. Dobrynin, *In Confidence*, 520.

25. Shultz, *Turmoil and Triumph*, 165.

26. Ronald Reagan, *The Reagan Diaries*, ed. Douglas Brinkley (New York: Harper and Collins, 2007), 131.

27. Ronald Reagan, "March 8, 1983: 'Evil Empire' Speech," to the National Association of Evangelicals in Orlando, Florida, *Presidential Speeches*, UVA Miller Center, http://millercenter.org/president/speeches/speech-3409.

28. The extent to which each of these events in and of itself alienated the Soviets is a subject of debate. For instance, Beth Fischer warns against scholars overemphasizing how much of an effect Reagan's "evil empire" speech had on the Soviets. Beth A. Fischer, *The Reagan Reversal: Foreign Policy and the End of the Cold War* (Columbia: University of Missouri Press, 1997).

29. Memorandum, "Summary of the Situation," by the American Security Council, May 5, 1981, 1–2, box 1, "American Security Council and Coalition for Peace through Strength" folder, Blackwell Files, RRL.

30. Daniel O. Graham, lt. general (ret) of the American Security Council to Morton Blackwell, July 21, 1981, box 1, "American Security Council and Coalition for Peace through Strength" folder, Blackwell Files, RRL.

31. "Towards a New U.S. Strategy: Bold Strokes Rather than Increments," *Strategic Review* 2, no. 9 (Spring 1981): 9–11, box 1, "American Security Council and Coalition for Peace through Strength" folder, Blackwell Files, RRL.

32. Reagan hinted at the idea of a missile defense system in a speech to the Republican Convention of Kansas in August 1976. While Reagan never outlined a

comprehensive plan to develop a missile defense system until 1983, he did hint at the possibility in two of his radio addresses. In his September 11, 1979, broadcast Reagan reminded listeners that

> there once was the beginning of a defense; an anti-ballistic missile system which we had invented and which the Soviets didn't have. We bargained it away in exchange for nothing. Instead of a defense against their missiles we settled for something called mutual destruction. The idea was that if both the Soviets & ourselves knew we could blow each other up then neither of us could afford to push the button knowing the other side would retaliate.

Reagan's opposition to mutually assured destruction and his belief that a missile defense system could render nuclear weapons obsolete are both present in embryotic form in the late 1970s. Ronald Reagan, "Defense IV" September 11, 1979, in *Reagan, in His Own Hand*, ed. Kiron K. Skinner, Annelise Anderson, and Martin Anderson (New York: Simon & Schuster, 2001), 117, 119–120. The origins of SDI are complex. For a complete analysis see Frances Fitzgerald's *Way Out There in the Blue: Reagan, Star Wars and the End of the Cold War* (New York: Simon & Schuster, 2000), 114–146. Lee Edwards had documented Reagan's embrace of SDI in *To Preserve and Protect: The Life of Edwin Meese III* (Washington, DC: Heritage, 2005), 60–63.

33. Deborah Hart Strober and Gerald S. Strober, *Reagan: The Man and His Presidency* (New York: Houghton Mifflin, 1998), 231–232.

34. Oberdorfer, *The Turn*, 25.

35. Martin Anderson, *Revolution: The Reagan Legacy* (Stanford, CA: Hoover Institute Press, 1988), 83. For Anderson's full account of SDI see *Revolution*, 80–108. The oral history on SDI within the administration is also fascinating. See Strober and Strober, *Reagan*, 231–249.

36. For a detailed analysis of the politics of Reagan's Strategic Defense Initiative see Michael Rogin, *Ronald Reagan, The Movie: And Other Episodes in Political Demonology* (Berkeley: University of California Press, 1987); William Board, *Teller's War: The Top Secret Story behind the Star Wars Deception* (New York: Simon & Schuster, 1992); and Fitzgerald, *Way Out There in the Blue*.

37. Press release, "Address by the President to the Nation," the Oval Office, the White House, March 23, 1983, box 4, "Citizens for America" folder, Blackwell Files, RRL.

38. Briefing paper, "President Reagan's Solution to Nuclear Holocaust: Strategic Defense," by Citizens for America, November 14, 1983, box 4, "Citizens for America" folder, Blackwell Files, RRL.

39. "High-Tech 'Shield' Just a Reagan Trick?," *Atlanta Constitution*, March 27, 1983, 1D.

40. Indeed, Reagan was the only person in his administration that believed that SDI could become a reality and avert nuclear war. Many viewed the program as leverage that could be used in negotiations with the Soviets. Most, including the Pentagon, understood that deploying the missile defense system could take several decades to implement. President Reagan was the only true believer, contrary to what the press claimed. Michael Schaller, "Reagan and the Cold War," in Kyle Longley, Jeremy D. Mayer, Michael Schaller, and John W. Sloan, *Deconstructing Reagan: Conservative Mythology and America's Fortieth President* (New York: M. E. Sharpe, 2007), 14, 37–38.

41. Oberdorfer, *The Turn*, 29–30.

42. Oberdorfer, *The Turn*, 37, 39.

43. *Reagan: A Life in Letters*, 742–743.

44. Draft letter from Ronald Reagan to Yuri Andropov, July 8, 1983, in *Reagan: A Life in Letters*, 742–743. A detailed account of this exchange of letters is found in Oberdorfer, *The Turn*, 37–39.

45. Oberdorfer, *The Turn*, 39.

46. Oberdorfer, *The Turn*, 21, 46.

47. Oberdorfer, *The Turn*, 50–53; "The U.S.-Soviet War of Words Escalates," *Washington Post*, November 21, 1983, A1.

48. Reagan, *The Reagan Diaries*, 175.

49. Reagan, *The Reagan Diaries*, 176.

50. Oberdorfer, *The Turn*, 59.

51. Christopher Andrew and Oleg Gordievsky, *KGB: The Inside Story* (New York: Harper Perennial, 1990), 596. Lieutenant Colonel Genadi Osipovich, the Soviet pilot who shot down KAL007, later recalled that he "never thought for a moment" that he was firing on a civilian airliner. He acknowledged it was odd to him at the time that an American spy plane would have lights and flashers. Oberdorfer, *The Turn*, 51.

52. Oberdorfer, *The Turn*, 59.

53. "Reagan and KAL007," *Washington Post*, July 18, 2014.

54. Reagan, *The Reagan Diaries*, 180.

55. Oberdorfer, *The Turn*, 54–57.

56. Andrew and Gordievsky, *KGB*, 594–595, 597.

57. Oberdorfer, *The Turn*, 58.

58. Andrew and Gordievsky, *KGB*, 598.

59. Oberdorfer, *The Turn*, 58.

60. Shultz, *Turmoil and Triumph*, 370.

61. Andrei Gromyko, *Memoirs* (New York: Doubleday, 1989), 300–301.

62. Oberdorfer, *The Turn*, 61.

63. Reagan, *The Reagan Diaries*, 178.

64. Reagan, *The Reagan Diaries*, 223.

65. Oberdorfer, *The Turn*, 61–62.

66. Andrew and Gordievsky, *KGB*, 598.

67. Oberdorfer, *The Turn*, 64.

68. "Reagan and Andropov," *Time*, January 2, 1984, 16.

69. Oberdorfer, *The Turn*, 63–65.

70. Fischer, *The Reagan Reversal*, 114.

71. Reagan, *An American Life*, 584, quoted in Fischer, *The Reagan Reversal*.

72. Reagan, *The Reagan Diaries*, 186.

73. Fischer, *The Reagan Reversal*, 118–119.

74. Reagan, *An American Life*, 585.

75. Oberdorfer, *The Turn*, 65.

76. In the immediate aftermath of Reagan's election, the "Soviet media . . . nourished hopes for a normalization of the U.S.-Soviet dialogue by interpreting the presidential election as in part a rejection by the electorate of President Carter's alleged turn away from détente and cooperation with the USSR." *Pravda* represented "Moscow's cautious optimism about the election results by reporting that Governor Reagan's statements had become more 'moderate' toward the end of the campaign but adding that only 'time and concrete action' will show whether his statements truly represent a 'sober view of the future.'" Internal memorandum, "Foreign Media Reaction to the 1980 U.S. Presidential Election: Soviet Union," November 12, 1980, 3, William J. Casey Papers, box 301, "Election Post-Mortem" folder, Hoover Institution Archives, Stanford University, Stanford, California.

77. Andrew and Gordievsky, *KGB*, 582; Lou Cannon, "Ronald Reagan: Foreign Affairs" UVA Miller Center, https://millercenter.org/president/reagan/foreign-affairs; "Reagan and Andropov," *Time*, January 2, 1984, 14.

78. Andrew and Gordievsky, *KGB*, 583; "Defector Told of Soviet Alert," *Washington Post*, August 8, 1986, A1.

79. Andrew and Gordievsky, *KGB*, 599–600.

80. Oberdorfer, *The Turn*, 65–66.

81. "Defector Told of Soviet Alert," A1; "The U.S.-Soviet War of Words Escalates," A1.

82. "The U.S.-Soviet War of Words Escalates," A1.

83. Andrew and Gordievsky, *KGB*, 600.

84. Oberdorfer, *The Turn*, 66.

85. Andrew and Gordievsky, *KGB*, 605.

86. Oberdorfer, *The Turn*, 67; McFarlane's meeting with Reagan is also recounted in Beth Fischer's *The Reagan Reversal*, 134.

87. Reagan, *The Reagan Diaries*, 199.

88. Reagan, *An American Life*, 588.

89. Reagan, *The Reagan Diaries*, 199.

90. Reagan continued to collect information about how paranoid the Soviets were about an American first strike. On February 1, 1984, Reagan met with President Mika Špiljak of Yugoslavia. Reagan recounts in his diary that during the meeting he "picked his brains about the Soviet Union. He believes that coupled with their expansionist philosophy they are also insecure and genuinely frightened of us. He also believes that if we opened them up a bit their leading citizens would get braver about proposing change in their system. I'm going to pursue this." Reagan, *The Reagan Diaries*, 217. Also quoted in *An American Life*, 589.

91. J. Peter Scoblic, *U.S. vs. Them: Conservatism in the Age of Nuclear Terror* (New York: Penguin Books, 2008), 121–123; "Reagan and Andropov" *Time*, January 2, 1984, 15.

92. "Reagan and Andropov," 8; "The U.S.-Soviet War of Words Escalates," A1.

93. "Reagan Finds a Lesser Evil in Indefinite Recess of Talks," *New York Times*, December 9, 1983, A16.

94. "Reagan Suggests Ending All Nuclear Arsenals," *Wall Street Journal*, December 15, 1983, 3.

95. "Excerpts from President's Speech in Japan," *New York Times*, November 11, 1983, A7.

96. Shultz, *Turmoil and Triumph*, 376.

97. Jason Saltoun-Ebin, *The Reagan Files: The Untold Story of Reagan's Top-Secret Efforts to Win the Cold War* (Middletown, DE: Self-published, 2010), 203–204.

98. Saltoun-Ebin, *The Reagan Files*, 208–210.

99. "An Interview with President Reagan," *Time*, January 2, 1984, 21.

100. It is hard for us today to imagine just how scary the events of 1983 were. The following description from *Time* captures the global climate in the wake of the "year of fear:" "Still, there is a grave danger: if not of war tomorrow, then of a long period of angry immobility in superpower relations; of an escalating arms race bringing into U.S. and Soviet arsenals weapons ever more expensive and difficult to control; of rising tensions that might make every world trouble spot a potential flash point for the clash both sides fear." "Reagan and Andropov," 8. Reagan may also have been motivated by his upcoming reelection campaign to ease tensions. Public opinion polls showed that the public was concerned about superpower relations. Having said that, it seems clear that the escalation of tensions in the fall of 1983 is primarily responsible for his shift in policy. Oberdorfer, *The Turn*, 71.

101. Oberdorfer, *The Turn*, 72.

102. Reagan, *An American Life*, 591.

103. Shultz, *Turmoil and Triumph*, 377.

104. "Conservatives Denounce Reagan," *New York Times*, January 19, 1984, A5.

CHAPTER 8. THE BATTLE FOR THE COLD WAR:
CONSERVATIVE FRUSTRATION WITH THE INF TREATY

1. Howard Phillips, Interview on C-SPAN Live, December 23, 1987, http://www.c-span.org/video/?299-1/status-conservative-movement-us&start=322.

2. Howard Phillips, Interview on C-SPAN Live.

3. "GOP Conservatives Could Stop Senate Ratification of Treaty," *Hartford Courant*, November 24, 1987, A11J; "Hard-Line Conservatives Set to Oppose Arms," *Sun*, December 5, 1987, 1A; "Reagan's Arms-Control Dream Is Nightmare for Conservatives," *Washington Post*, November 30, 1987, A1; "U.S. Conservatives Assail Reagan over Arms Treaty," *Los Angeles Times*, December 6, 1987, 1; "Conservatives Fear 'Illusory Peace' in Central America," *Los Angeles Times*, May 16, 1986, A24; "Conservatives Fear for Contras: White House Seen Betraying Rebels, Making North Its Scapegoat," *Washington Post*, November 28, 1986, A32.

4. Morton Konracke and Fred Barnes, *Jack Kemp: The Bleeding Heart Conservative Who Changed America* (New York: Sentinel, 2015), 183–184.

5. Konracke and Barnes, *Jack Kemp*, 183.

6. Ronald Reagan, *An American Life: The Autobiography* (New York: Threshold, 1990), 273.

7. Konracke and Barnes, 194. Reagan liked to quip that he had wanted to negotiate with the Soviets long before Gorbachev, but his efforts were slowed because the Soviet leaders "kept dying on me." "Reagan's Arms-Control Dream Is Nightmare for Conservatives," A1; Vladislav M. Zubok, *A Failed Empire: The Soviet Union in the Cold War from Stalin to Gorbachev* (Chapel Hill: University of North Carolina Press, 2007), 272–274.

8. Ronald Reagan, "March 8, 1983: 'Evil Empire' Speech," to the National Association of Evangelicals in Orlando, Florida, *Presidential Speeches*, UVA Miller Center, http://millercenter.org/president/speeches/speech-3409.

9. General Secretary Yuri Andropov to President Ronald Reagan, August 1983, *The Reagan* Files, http://thereaganfiles.com/19830800.pdf.

10. Kondracke and Barnes, *Jack Kemp*, 184.

11. Reagan, *An American Life*, 268.

12. Ronald Reagan, "The U.S.-Soviet Relationship," *Department of State Bulletin* 84:2083, January 16, 1984, 1–4, cited and quoted in Beth A. Fischer's "Reagan and the Soviets: Winning the Cold War?," in *The Reagan Presidency: Pragmatic Conservatism and Its Legacies*, ed. W. Elliot Brownlee and Hugh Davis Graham (Lawrence: University Press of Kansas, 2003), 117. Suzanne Massie, a Russian expert and concerned American citizen, was influential in changing the way that Reagan viewed the USSR. Massie met with Reagan several times from 1984 to 1988 and even played a role in briefing the president prior to his summits with

Gorbachev. Suzanne Massie, *Trust but Verify: Reagan, Russia, and Me* (Rockland, ME: Maine Authors Publishing, 2013).

13. For more on Reagan and Gorbachev's relationship, see James Graham Wilson's *The Triumph of Improvisation: Gorbachev's Adaptability, Reagan's Engagement, and the End of the Cold War* (Ithaca, NY: Cornell University Press, 2015); and Jack F. Matlock's *Reagan and Gorbachev: How the Cold War Ended* (New York: Random House, 2005). Reagan was never able to establish a positive working relationship with Chernenko during his short stint as general secretary. The Soviets were interested in waiting out the Reagan administration in 1984—hoping the president would not be reelected. Furthermore, Reagan perhaps made matters worse on August 11, 1984 when he jokingly asserted, "My fellow Americans, I'm pleased to tell you today that I've signed legislation that will outlaw Russia forever. We begin bombing in five minutes." The private remark during a mic check quickly leaked to the press, "turning what Reagan believed to be a harmless private quip into an international embarrassment, precipitating dismay among America's allies and providing fodder for Soviet propaganda mill." "Reagan 'Jokes' about Bombing Soviet Union, Aug. 11, 1984," *Politico*, August 12, 2017.

14. John Lewis Gaddis, *The Cold War: A New History* (New York: Penguin Books, 2005), 229–230; Zubok, *A Failed Empire*.

15. Ronald Reagan, *The Reagan Diaries*, ed. Douglas Brinkley (New York: HarperCollins, 2007), 289; Margaret Thatcher, *The Downing Street Years* (New York: Harper Press, 1993), 466–468.

16. President Ronald Reagan to Secretary General Mikhail Gorbachev, March 11, 1985, *The Reagan Files*, http://thereaganfiles.com/19850311.pdf.

17. Reagan, *The Reagan Diaries*, 337.

18. Memorandum of conversation, "Reagan-Gorbachev Meetings in Geneva," November 19, 1985, 1–7, *The Reagan Files*, http://thereaganfiles.com/geneva-summit-transcripts.pdf.

19. Memorandum of conversation "Reagan-Gorbachev Meetings in Geneva."

20. Gaddis, *The Cold War*, 230.

21. "Reagan SDI Talk Leaves Conservatives Uneasy: Trade Off for Soviet Arms Pact Feared," *Washington Post*, August 7, 1986, A30.

22. "Reagan SDI Talk Leaves Conservatives Uneasy: Trade Off for Soviet Arms Pact Feared," A30.

23. "Reagan SDI Talk Leaves Conservatives Uneasy: Trade Off for Soviet Arms Pact Feared," A30; "Kemp Issues Tough Advice about Summit," *Washington Times*, October 9, 1986, 1; Jack Kemp Papers, box 364, "Speeches and Statements: 1986, Sept–Oct." folder, Library of Congress, Washington, DC.

24. "Did the Conservatives Misjudge Their Man?," *Washington Post*, October 10, 1986, A27.

25. "Reagan's Arms-Control Dream Is Nightmare for Conservatives," A1.

26. Gaddis, *The Cold War*, 231–232. The entire Reykjavik summit discussions are available at *The Reagan Files*, http://thereaganfiles.com/reykjavik-summit -transcript.pdf; Don Oberdorfer, *From the Cold War to a New Era: The United States and the Soviet Union, 1983–1991* (Baltimore: Johns Hopkins University Press, 1998), 203–204. For a detailed account of the Reykjavik Summit consult Ken Adelman's *Reagan at Reykjavik: Forty-Eight Hours That Ended the Cold War* (New York: Broadside Books, 2014).

27. "Reagan Military Stand Uniting Conservatives: The Political Campaign," *New York Times*, October 25, 1986, 7.

28. Gaddis, *The Cold War*, 234–236.

29. John Patrick Diggins, *Ronald Reagan: Fate, Freedom, and the Making of History* (New York: W. W. Norton, 2007), 12; "Politics Puts U.S., Soviets into Summits" *Wall Street Journal*, November 2, 1987, 2.

30. "White House Is Criticized for Rushing to Reach Arms Pact That May Leave Europe Vulnerable," *Wall Street Journal*, April 10, 1987, 46.

31. William F. Buckley to President Ronald Reagan, April 29, 1987, in *Reagan: A Life in Letters*, ed. Kiron K. Skinner, Annelise Anderson, and Martin Anderson (New York: Free Press, 2003), 418.

32. "Reagan's Suicide Pact" issue, *National Review* 39, no. 9 (May 22, 1987).

33. Jack Kemp, "Arms Control Perverted," *National Review* 39, no. 9 (May 22, 1987): 30.

34. Richard Nixon and Henry Kissinger, "A Real Peace," *National Review* 39, no. 9 (May 22, 1987): 32.

35. John P. Roche, "From Reykjavik All Roads Led Down," *National Review* 39, no. 9 (May 22, 1987): 27.

36. Evan G. Galbraith, "Softening Up the Germans," *National Review* 39, no. 9 (May 22, 1987): 34.

37. "What Strategy?" *National Review* 39, no. 9 (May 22, 1987): 28.

38. Ronald Reagan to William F. Buckley, May 5, 1987, in *Reagan: A Life in Letters*, 418.

39. "Our Editors Interview President Reagan," *Conservative Digest*, May 1987, 5.

40. "Our Editors Interview President Reagan," 7.

41. "Our Editors Interview President Reagan," 11.

42. "The Right against Reagan" *New York Times*, January 17, 1988, SM 36. In the fall of 1983, the USSR shot down a Korean air liner. All 269 passengers, including 69 Americans, died. Reagan took a few days to deliver a searing indictment of the Soviets. Conservatives thought that the administration moved too slowly and were upset that Reagan's only response was harsh words and not sanctions. "Reagan Moves Get Bipartisan Support but New Right Voices Disappointment," *Sun*,

September 6, 1983, A2; "Conservatives Disagree with Reagan's Decision," *Chicago Tribune*, September 6, 1983, 8.

43. William R. Kennedy Jr., "George P. Shultz Continues to Earn His Liberal Stripes," *Conservative Digest*, July/August 1987, 125–128.

44. Stephen F. Knott and Jeffrey L. Chidester, *At Reagan's Side: Insiders' Recollections from Sacramento to the White House* (New York: Rowman and Littlefield, 2009), 200.

45. Robert Service, *The End of the Cold War, 1985–1991* (New York: Public Affairs, 2015), 285–286.

46. Knott and Chidester, *At Reagan's Side*, 201; "Weinberger, as Expected, Resigns Post" *New York Times*, November 6, 1987, A1. The *New York Times* reported that Weinberger "was leaving government to spend more time with his wife, who has been ill." Weinberger denied that his resignation was in response to the administration's policy–specifically the INF agreement. When pressed, Weinberger insisted "I'm all for it and I have been for it from the beginning." "Weinberger as Expected, Resigns Post" *New York Times*, November 6, 1987, 16.

47. Lee Edwards, *William F. Buckley: The Maker of a Movement* (Wilmington, DE: ISI Books, 2010), 150–151.

48. "U.S., Soviets Reach Accord on Weapons," *Wall Street Journal*, November 25, 1987, 2.

49. "GOP Conservatives Could Stop Senate Ratification of Treaty," *Hartford Courant*, November 24, 1987, A11J.

50. "Speech to the Heritage Foundation," May 22, 1987, box 365, folder 2, Jack Kemp Papers , Library of Congress, cited in Kondracke and Barnes, *Jack Kemp*, 187.

51. "Reagan's Arms-Control Dream Is Nightmare for Conservatives," A1.

52. "Summit Problems: Reagan and Gorbachev Hint at Lasting Thaw but Face Difficulties," *Wall Street Journal*, December 2, 1987, 1.

53. Carl T. Bogus, *Buckley: William F. Buckley Jr. and the Rise of American Conservatism* (New York: Bloomsbury Press, 2011), 342–343.

54. George P. Shultz, *Turmoil and Triumph: My Years as Secretary of State* (New York; Charles Scribner's Sons, 1993), 1007.

55. Hard-Line Conservatives Set to Oppose Arms," *Sun*, December 5, 1987, 1A.

56. Hard-Line Conservatives Set to Oppose Arms," 1A; "Reagan's Arms-Control Dream Is Nightmare for Conservatives," A1.

57. "U.S. Conservatives Assail Reagan over Arms Treaty," *Los Angeles Times*, December 6, 1987, 1.

58. Cal Thomas, "Americans Are Listening to the Wrong Man" *Los Angeles Times*, December 6, 1987, Cal Thomas Papers, PP 3:1, box 1: "Column Indexes and Syndicated Columns—1984–1987," "Columns: July–December 1987" folder, Jerry Falwell Library, Liberty University, Lynchburg VA.

59. Tom Wicker, "Fury on the Right: What Really Riles Critics of the Treaty," *New York Times*, December 10, 1987, A31.

60. The transcript of Noonan's December 10, 1987, appearance on NPR was reprinted in *National Review*. Peggy Noonan, "Gorbachev Glad Hand," *National Review* 40, no. 2 (February 5, 1988): 21.

61. Howard Phillips, "The Treaty: Another Sellout," *New York Times*, December 11, 1987, A39.

62. *Reagan: A Life in Letters*, 384.

63. Ronald Reagan to Mrs. William Loeb, December 18, 1987, in *Reagan: A Life in Letters*, 384.

64. Richard Aldous, *Reagan and Thatcher: The Difficult Relationship* (New York: W. W. Norton, 2012), 260.

65. "The Right against Reagan," *New York Times*, January 17, 1988.

66. "The Right against Reagan."

67. "The Right against Reagan."

68. "The Right against Reagan."

69. "Appeasement Is as Unwise in 1988 as in 1938," *Washington Times*, January 25, 1988.

70. Ronald Reagan to John J. Tringali, January 6, 1988, in *Reagan: A Life in Letters*, 420.

71. Ronald Reagan to William F. Buckley, February 1, 1988, in *Reagan: A Life in Letters*, 421.

72. Service, *The End of the Cold War*, 296.

73. Bogus, *Buckley*, 342–343.

74. Kondracke and Barnes, *Jack Kemp*, 187

75. J. Peter Scoblic, *U.S. vs. Them: Conservatism in the Age of Nuclear Terror* (New York: Penguin Books, 2008), 145; Frances FitzGerald, *Way Out There in the Blue: Reagan, Star Wars and the End of the Cold War* (New York: Simon & Schuster, 2000), 467.

76. Richard Reeves, *President Reagan: The Triumph of Imagination* (New York: Simon & Schuster, 2005), 446. As quoted in Niels Bjerre-Poulsen's "The Road to Mount Rushmore," in *Ronald Reagan and the 1980s: Perceptions, Policies, Legacies*, ed. Cheryl Hudson and Gareth Davies (New York: Palgrave Macmillan, 2008), 220.

77. Jim Kuhn, *Ronald Reagan in Private: A Memoir of My Years in the White House* (New York: Sentinel, 2004), 232.

78. "Reagan's Arms-Control Dream Is Nightmare for Conservatives," A1.

79. Shultz, *Turmoil and Triumph*, 1006.

80. atlock, *Reagan and Gorbachev*, 276.

81. Mikhail Gorbachev, *Memoirs* (New York: Bantam Books, 1995), 570–571.

82. For a detailed account of the Iran-Contra scandal and the administration's response, see Robert Busby's *Reagan and the Iran-Contra Affair: The Politics of Presidential Recovery* (New York: St. Martin's Press, 1999).

83. The "Reagan Doctrine" was outlined fully on January 17, 1983, in NSDD number 75, "U.S. Relations with the USSR," National Security Decision Directive 75, January 17, 1983 (declassified July 16, 1994), https://www.reagan.utexas.edu/ar chives/reference/Scanned%20NSDDS/NSDD75.pdf.

84. There was massive disagreement within the administration on the goal of aiding the Contras. Reagan's national security adviser, William Clark, CIA director William Casey, and UN ambassador Jeane Kirkpatrick labeled Secretary Shultz's plan to provide aid until the Sandinistas negotiated as "appeasement." Many conservatives outside the White House agreed with them, including Representative Jack Kemp. Reagan, however, sided with Shultz, and it was his policy to support the Contras in order to force the Sandinistas to hold free elections. Steven F. Hayward, *The Age of Reagan: Conservative Counterrevolution 1980–1989* (New York: Crown Forum, 2009), 301; Kondracke and Barnes, *Jack Kemp*, 179.

85. Kondracke and Barnes, *Jack Kemp*, 181.

86. "Conservatives Fear 'Illusory Peace' in Central America," *Los Angeles Times*, May 16, 1986, A24.

87. "Reagan Defends Habib in Clash with Conservatives," *Los Angeles Times*, May 23, 1986, SD1.

88. "Conservatives Fear 'Illusory Peace' in Central America," A24.

89. "Conservatives Fear for Contras: White House Seen Betraying Rebels, Making North Its Scapegoat," *Washington Post*, November 28, 1986, A32.

90. Kondracke and Barnes, *Jack Kemp*, 182. National security adviser John Poindexter resigned after correspondence linked him to the scandal.

91. "Conservative Fear for Contras: White House Seen Betraying Rebels, Making North Its Scapegoat," A32.

92. "Despite Reagan's Rosy View, Realism Often Ruled," *Chicago Tribune*, May 5, 1991, G1.

93. "Angry Conservatives Accuse Reagan of Betraying Ideals," *Los Angeles Times*, September 6, 1987, 1.

94. "Discontented Conservatives Rumble to Reagan's Right," *Hartford Courant*, August 19, 1987, B9E.

95. "Discontented Conservatives Rumble to Reagan's Right," B9E.

96. "Conservatives Pressing 1988 G.O.P. Contenders for a Rigid Foreign Agenda," *New York Times*, February 23, 1987, A3.

97. "Discontented Conservatives Rumble to Reagan's Right," B9E.

98. For an overview of the different historical interpretations of the role of the Reagan administration in ending the Cold War, with special emphasis on the

"Reagan Victory School," see Beth A. Fischer's "Reagan and the Soviets?," 113–132. For a comprehensive analysis of the end of the Cold War, consult Robert Service's *The End of the Cold War, 1985–1991.*

CHAPTER 9. RECASTING REAGAN: HOW THE FORTIETH
PRESIDENT FRAMED HIS LEGACY, 1989–1994

1. "President Reagan Tribute and Speech," August 15, 1988, C-SPAN, C-Span. org/video/?3813-1/president-reagan-tribute-speech.

2. Dan Morgan, "Evangelicals a Force Divided," *Washington Post*, March 8, 1988; Maureen Dowd, "Is Jack Kemp Mr. Right?," *New York Times*, June 28, 1987, SM19; Philip Lentz, "Kemp's Base among Conservatives May Be Crumbling," *Chicago Tribune*, December 7, 1987, 2.

3. There is a need for further work to be done on the evolution of Reagan's legacy. The second half of this project hopes to be an important first step at analyzing the emerging legacy of Reagan from the point of view of conservatives. The existing historiography is slim but important. See Craig Shirley, *Last Act: The Final Years and Emerging Legacy of Ronald Reagan* (New York: Nelson Books, 2015), and Will Bunch, *Tear Down This Myth: The Right-Wing Distortion of the Reagan Legacy* (New York: Free Press, 2009).

4. "President Reagan Tribute and Speech."

5. For more information on how museums shape public memory, consult Susan A. Crane, ed., *Museums and Memory* (Stanford, CA: Stanford University Press, 2000); Jerome de Groot, *Consuming History: Historians and Heritage in Contemporary Popular Culture* (New York: Routledge, 2009); Kendall R. Phillips, ed., *Framing Public Memory* (Tuscaloosa: University of Alabama Press, 2004); Jo Blatti, ed., *Past Meets Present: Essays about Historic Interpretation and Public Audience* (Washington, DC: Smithsonian Institution Press, 1987). For more on how politics and memory intersect see Sue Campbell, ed., *Our Faithfulness to the Past: The Ethics and Politics of Memory* (Oxford: Oxford University Press, 2014); Bradford Vivian, *Public Forgetting: The Rhetoric and Politics of Beginning Again* (University Park: Pennsylvania State University Press, 2010); Meili Steele, *Hiding from History: Politics and Public Imagination* (Ithaca, NY: Cornell University Press, 2005); Max Paul Friedman and Padraic Kenney, *Partisan Histories: The Past in Contemporary Global Politics* (New York: Palgrave MacMillan, 2005).

6. For an article detailing how some overstate Reagan's economic record, see John W. Sloan, "The Economic Costs of Reagan Mythology," in *Deconstructing Reagan: Conservative Mythology and America's Fortieth President*, ed. Kyle Longley et al. (New York: M. E. Sharpe, 2007), 41–69.

7. For an overview of the historiography on Reagan's role in ending the Cold War, especially the Reagan-victory school, seeBeth A. Fischer's "Reagan and the Soviets: Winning the Cold War?" in *The Reagan Presidency: Pragmatic Conservatism and Its Legacies*, ed. W. Elliot Brownlee and Hugh Davis Graham (Lawrence: University Press of Kansas, 2003), 113–132. Also consult Michael Schaller, "Reagan and the Cold War," in Longley et al., *Deconstructing Reagan*, 3–40. J. Peter Scoblic also does a solid job of outlining the problems with the Reagan Victory School in his chapter "President," in *U.S. vs. Them: Conservatism in the Age of Nuclear Terror* (New York: Penguin Books, 2008), 112–153.

8. Ronald Reagan to Lyn Nofziger, August 14, 1991, Lyn Nofziger Papers, box 9, "Correspondence: Ronald Reagan Related Materials" folder, Hoover Institution Archives, Stanford University, Stanford, California.

9. Ronald Reagan, "Farewell Address at the Republican National Convention," August 15, 1988, http://millercenter.org/president/speeches/speech-5469, accessed June 12, 2016.

10. Reagan, "Farewell Address at the Republican National Convention."

11. Reagan, "Farewell Address at the Republican National Convention."

12. Ronald Reagan, "Farewell Address," January 11, 1989, http://millercenter.org/president/Reagan/speeches/speech-3418, accessed June 12, 2016. Many of the claims that Reagan made in his farewell address are open to debate. See Sloan, "The Economic Costs of Reagan Mythology," 41–69.

13. This myth, created by the Left, has largely been dispelled. Most serious scholars today recognize that Reagan was widely read and much more informed than initially thought. The discovery and publication of Reagan's correspondence, handwritten speeches, and radio addresses have done a great deal to end claims that he was simply an "actor-in-chief." Kiron K. Skinner, Annelise Anderson, and Martin Anderson, eds., *Reagan in His Own Hand* (New York: Free Press, 2001); Kiron K. Skinner, Annelise Anderson, and Martin Anderson, eds., *Reagan: A Life in Letters* (New York: Free Press, 2003); "Reagan in Retrospect, on 'Frontline,'" *New York Times*, January 19, 1989, C26.

14. "Reagan Says He Forgives, Prays for Assailant Hinckley," *Sun*, January 12, 1990, A6; "Reagan's Fall from Grace," *Los Angeles Times*, March 4, 1990, SM1A.

15. When confronted with criticism of his speaking fees, Reagan responded, "I just thought that in 16 years I hadn't made any kind of money." Reagan also reasoned that the fees enabled him to give more to charity, allowing him "to help more than I have." "Reagan's Fall from Grace," SM1A.

16. "GOP Helps Reagan's Expenses with a $150,000 Yearly Subsidy," *Hartford Courant*, January 29, 1989, A23B.

17. "The Secret of Reagan's 'Success,'" *Wall Street Journal*, January 23, 1989, A15.

18. Reagan, "Farewell Address."

19. Ronald Reagan, *An American Life: The Autobiography* (New York: Threshold, 1990), 231.

20. Reagan, *An American Life*, 232.

21. Reagan, *An American Life*, 233, 244. For a complete analysis of the similarities between the Reagan tax cuts and the Kennedy tax cuts, consult Lawrence Kudlow and Brian Domitrovic's *JFK and the Reagan Revolution: A Secret History of American Prosperity* (New York: Portfolio, 2016).

22. Reagan, *An American Life*, 235.

23. "The Ronald Reagan Presidential Foundation," *After the Presidency* exhibit, Ronald Reagan Presidential Museum, Simi Valley, California.

24. A recent article about Donovan and Green, the firm that designed the museum, details Reagan's involvement in the design of the museum. It reads:

> The designers place a high value upon personal relationships, entering into decades-long partnerships with their clients. Both principals embrace a hands-on approach: When planning the Ronald Reagan Presidential Library in the late 1980s, Green worked side by side with President and Mrs. Reagan three days a month for 18 months. The firm designed the space, created the narrative, selected the artifacts and wrote and produced media, including a three-screen video of the Berlin Wall coming down and an early interactive theater. At the time of its dedication in 1991, it was the largest of the presidential libraries, housing 50 million pages of documents and other archives. Green says, "It was a memorable experience to enter into a conversation with a president about his legacy and walk him through the finished exhibition on his life and presidency for the first time."

Unfortunately, the records of Donovan and Green belong to the Reagan Foundation and are not open for researchers. "Michael Donovan and Nancye Green," *AIGA*, March 1, 2014, https://www.aiga.org/medalists-michael-donovan-and-nancye-green; "Designers Bracing for Reagan Exhibit Reviews," *Los Angeles Times*, November 1, 1991, VCB1.

25. When the Reagan Library opened, almost 600 people arrived in the first hour. By the end of the first day 2,636 people visited the museum. In the first year of being open, the Reagan Library documented over 300,000 visitors. "Public Gets Its Turn to See Reagan Library," *Los Angeles Times*, November 7, 1991, VCB1; "History Has Its Price at Reagan Library Gift Shop," *Los Angeles Times*, November 29, 1992, SDA3.

26. "The Turbulent 1970s," *A Nation in Crisis* exhibit, Ronald Reagan Presidential Museum, Simi Valley, CA.

27. Stedman Jones, *Masters of the Universe: Hayek, Friedman, and the Birth of Neoliberal Politics* (Princeton, NJ: Princeton University Press, 2012), 217.

28. Sloan, "The Economic Costs of Reagan Mythology," 62.

29. "President Reagan's Economic Scorecard 1981 to 1989," *Rebuilding America* exhibit, Ronald Reagan Presidential Museum, Simi Valley, CA.

30. Ronald Reagan Presidential Museum, *Rebuilding America* exhibit. Simi Valley, CA.

31. Paul Volcker and Toyoo Gyohten, *Changing Fortunes: The World's Money and the Threat of American Leadership* (New York: Random House, 1992), 175. Indeed, the Reagan transition team was well aware that the expansion of the money stock was the primary cause of inflation, and the administration and Reagan were committed to reducing the money stock. In a memo from the transition, Reagan's economic team insisted that Reagan should "encourage the Fed to stay its course. This credit restraint is probably appropriate at this time. There is no reason to overly criticize the Fed for past excesses." "Task Force on Fiscal and Monetary Policy: Inflation, Cause and Effect," Fall 1980, 2, box 26, "Ronald Reagan Presidential Transition Team, 1980–1981: Fiscal and Monetary Task Force" folder, Annelise Anderson Papers, Hoover Institution Archives. See also "Fiscal and Monetary Policy Task Force: Monetary Policy and Interest Rates," box 26, "Ronald Reagan Presidential Transition Team, 1980–1981: Fiscal and Monetary Task Force" folder, Annelise Anderson Papers, Hoover Institution Archives.

32. Robert Pier, "Rich Got Richer in 80s," *New York Times*, January 11, 1991; Sylvia Naser, "The Rich Get Richer," *New York Times*, August 16, 1992; Sylvia Naser, "Fed Report Gives New Data on Gains by Richest in 80s," *New York Times*, April 21, 1992. As cited in Sloan's "The Economic Costs of Reagan Mythology," 66–67.

33. For more on Reagan's relationship with the African American community see Jeremy D. Mayer, "Reagan and Race: Prophet of Color Blindness, Baiter of the Backlash," in Longley et al., *Deconstructing Reagan*, 82–83.

34. Despite these scholars' attempts to simply blame deregulation, the causes of the savings and loan crisis are complex. It is unclear that Reagan's deregulation in 1982 precipitated the crisis. Indeed, in 1980 when Carter began deregulation, the S&L industry's liabilities outnumbered its assets by $110 billion. Having said that, weak restraints combined with strong government guarantees are historically a bad combination, and that was borne out in the S&L debacle at the end of the decade. For more on the savings and loan crisis, see David L. Mason's *From Buildings and Loans to Bail-Outs: A History of the American Savings and Loan Industry, 1831–1995* (New York: Cambridge University Press, 2004); James R. Barth, Suzanne Trimbath, and Glenn Yago, eds., *The Savings and Loans Crisis: Lessons from a Regulatory Failure* (New York: Springer, 2004); Lawrence J. White, *The S&L Debacle: Public Policy Lessons for Bank and Thrift Regulation* (Oxford: Oxford University Press, 1991); Bert Ely and Vicki Vanderhoff, *Lessons Learned from the S&L Debacle: The Price of Failed Public Policy* (Lewisville, TX: Institute for Policy Innovation,

1991); and for the figures cited in this footnote see Catherine England's concise article "Lessons from the Savings and Loan Debacle: The Case for Further Financial Deregulation," *Regulation*, Summer 1992, 37–43.

35. Many supply-siders and conservatives emphasize the years from 1983 to 1990 and discount the economic downturn of 1981–1982 in their analysis of Reagan's supply-side policies. Robert Bartley even titled his memoir on the growth from 1983–1990 *Seven Fat Years*, a thinly veiled allusion to the story in Genesis. Some examples of supply-side advocates who emphasize the data from 1983 to 1990 include Robert L. Bartley, *The Seven Fat Years: And How to Do It Again* (New York: Free Press, 1992); Brian Domitrovic, *Econoclasts: The Rebels Who Sparked the Supply-Side Revolution and Restored American Prosperity* (Wilmington, DE: ISI Books, 2009), 257. For his part, Paul Craig Roberts argues that supply-side policies "fell victim in part to the failure of monetary policy, in part to the ego struggle that senior aides carried on against the President, and in part to a campaign conducted against supply-side economics by elements of the media." Roberts asserts that despite all these restraints, supply-side economics is to credit for the economic growth that ensued after 1983. Paul Craig Roberts, *The Supply-Side Revolution: An Insider's Account of Policymaking in Washington* (Cambridge, MA: Harvard University Press, 1984), 305.

36. "Give and Take," *Rebuilding America* exhibit.

37. "Economic Recovery," *Rebuilding America* exhibit.

38. Reagan, "Farewell Address at the Republican National Convention."

39. Robert Gates, *From the Shadows: The Ultimate Insider's Story of Five Presidents and How They Won the Cold War* (New York: Simon & Schuster, 2007), 177–178.

40. Norman Podhoretz, "The Neo-Conservative Anguish over Reagan's Foreign Policy," *New York Times*, May 2, 1982, SM30.

41. Schaller, "Reagan and the Cold War," 11.

42. Daniel Wirls, *Buildup: The Politics of Defense in the Reagan Era* (Ithaca, NY: Cornell University Press, 1992).

43. "Reagan SDI Talk Leaves Conservatives Uneasy: Trade Off for Soviet Arms Pact Feared," *Washington Post*, August 7, 1986, A30; "Did the Conservatives Misjudge Their Man?," *Washington Post*, October 10, 1986, A27; "Reagan's Arms-Control Dream Is Nightmare for Conservatives," *Washington Post*, November 30, 1987, A1; "Zero Option Evokes Zero Honesty in Some Conservatives," *Chicago Tribune*, June 19, 1987, 25; "GOP Conservatives Could Stop Senate Ratification of Treaty," *Hartford Courant*, November 24, 1987, A11J; "Speech to the Heritage Foundation," May 22, 1987, box 365,folder 2, Jack Kemp Files, Library of Congress, Washington, DC.

44. Reagan, "Farewell Address." Reagan was first introduced to the Russian

proverb "Doveryai, no proveryai" (Trust but verify) by Suzanne Massie during their meeting on September 23, 1986, prior to the Reykjavik Summit. Suzanne Massie, *Trust but Verify: Reagan, Russia, and Me* (Rockland, ME: Maine Authors Publishing, 2013), 232.

45. "Reagan Depicted by Poindexter as Guiding Contra Aid Efforts," *New York Times*, February 1, 1990, A20.

46. "Reagan Hazy on Iran-Contra: Knowledge of Diversion Is Denied," *Chicago Tribune*, February 23, 1990, N1. There have been studies done on Reagan's rhetoric that demonstrate that there were "subtle changes in Mr. Reagan's speaking patterns linked to the onset of dementia . . . years before doctors diagnosed his Alzheimer's disease in 1994." These studies' findings, however, "do not prove that Mr. Reagan exhibited signs of dementia that would have adversely affected his judgement and ability to make decisions in office." "Parsing Ronald Reagan's Words for Early Signs of Alzheimer's," *New York Times*, March 30, 2015, http://www.nytimes.com/2015/03/31/health/parsing-ronald-reagans-words-for-early-signs-of-alzheimers.html, accessed June 13, 2016.

47. "North Says Reagan Knew of Funds Diversion," *Los Angeles Times*, October 20, 1991, A4A. For a full account of North's involvement consult his memoir *Under Fire: An American Story* (Grand Rapids, MI: Zondervan, 1991).

48. "Iran-Contra Prosecutor Will Not Charge Reagan," *Los Angeles Times*, August 5, 1992, SDA1.

49. John Lewis Gaddis, *The Cold War: A New History* (New York: Penguin Books, 2005), 246.

50. "Piece of Berlin Wall for Reagan Library: Souvenir of Former President's Challenge to Gorbachev: 'Tear Down this Wall,'" *San Francisco Chronicle*, A2. Reference copy from vertical file, Ronald Reagan Presidential Library, Simi Valley, California (hereafter RRL).

51. "Off the Wall: Chunk of the Berlin Barrier Unveiled at Reagan Library," *Los Angeles Times*, April 13, 1990. Reference copy from vertical file, RRL.

52. The statue, created by Edwina Sandys, is titled *Breakthrough*.

53. Ronald Reagan, "The Brotherhood of Man," November 19, 1990, http://pbs.org/wgbh/americanexperience/features/primary-resources/Reagan-brotherhood, accessed June 15, 2016.

54. Reagan, "The Brotherhood of Man." Of course, the Bush administration as well as people in the Soviet Union also deserved credit for the peaceful disillusionment of the Soviet Union. For a detailed analysis of the collapse of the USSR see Serhii Plokhy's *The Last Empire: The Final Days of the Soviet Union* (New York: Basic Books, 2015), and David Remnick's *Lenin's Tomb: The Last Days of the Soviet Empire* (New York: Vintage Books, 1994).

55. Reagan, *An American Life*, 269.

356 Notes to Pages 170–175

56. Reagan, *An American Life*, 293–294.

57. Reagan, *An American Life*, 267.

58. Reagan, *An American Life*, 267.

59. Reagan, *An American Life*, 268.

60. James A. Baker III, *The Politics of Diplomacy: Revolution, War and Peace, 1989–1992* (New York: G. P. Putnam, 1995), 26–27.

61. Colin Powell with Joseph E. Persico, *My American Journey* (New York: Ballantine Books, 1995), 334.

62. Fischer, "Reagan and the Soviets," 119. Reagan's Cold War foreign policy shift is detailed in Beth A. Fischer's *The Reagan Reversal: Foreign Policy and the End of the Cold War* (Columbia: University of Missouri Press, 1997).

63. Fischer, "Reagan and the Soviets," 119.

64. For instance, Reagan's antagonistic rhetoric during his first four years in office angered conservative members of the Soviet politburo, giving them justification to pursue a more hostile policy toward the United States. Strained relations between the US and the Soviet Union closed the door to potential nuclear negotiations. Vladislav M. Zubok, *A Failed Empire: The Soviet Union in the Cold War from Stalin to Gorbachev* (Chapel Hill: University of North Carolina Press, 2007), 276; Anatoly Dobrynin, *In Confidence: Moscow's Ambassador to America's Six Cold War Presidents* (New York: Random House, 1995), 482; Scoblic, *U.S. vs. Them*, 152.

65. The dedication of the Reagan Library was the first time in history that five presidents were gathered together: Richard Nixon, Gerald Ford, Jimmy Carter, Ronald Reagan, and George H. W. Bush. "Nostalgic Ceremony Opens Reagan Library," *Los Angeles Times*, November 5, 1991, OCA1.

66. "Nostalgic Ceremony Opens Reagan Library," OCA1.

67. "Iran-Contra," *Global Issues* exhibit, Ronald Reagan Presidential Museum, Simi Valley, CA.

68. "Iran-Contra," *Global Issues* exhibit.

69. "The Reagan Strategy," *Global Issues* exhibit.

70. "What Role Could Diplomacy Play," *Global Issues* exhibit.

71. *Four Summits* exhibit, Ronald Reagan Presidential Museum, Simi Valley, CA.

72. "Reykjavik Summit," *Four Summits* exhibit.

73. "The Soviets and SDI," *Four Summits* exhibit. For a detailed analysis of how Gorbachev actually viewed Reagan see Mikhail Gorbachev's *Memoirs* (New York: Doubleday, 1996).

74. "Washington Summit," *Four Summits* exhibit.

75. "The Cold War Ends," *Four Summits* exhibit.

76. Zubok, *A Failed Empire*, 276; Dobrynin, *In Confidence*, 482; Scoblic, *U.S. vs.*

Them, 152; Christopher Andrew and Oleg Gordievsky, *KGB: The Inside Story* (New York: Harper Perennial, 1990), 582–583.

77. There is an entire school of historians who argue that Reagan's policies prolonged the Cold War rather than ending the conflict. Fischer, "Reagan and the Soviets," 115. Another example of Reagan's rhetoric and policies enflaming tensions with the Soviets came when he announced the Strategic Defense Initiative. According to Robert Gates, "For a leader like Andropov already half-persuaded the United States was preparing for a nuclear conflict with the Soviet Union, SDI likely added to his paranoia." Gates, *From the Shadows*, 266.

78. Don Oberdorfer, *From the Cold War to a New Era: The United States and the Soviet Union, 1983–1991* (Baltimore: Johns Hopkins University Press, 1998), 203–204.

79. Schaller, "Reagan and the Cold War," 14, 37–38.

80. Ronald Reagan, "Address at Republican National Convention," Houston, Texas. August 17, 1992, http://cnn.com/SPECIALS/2004/Reagan/stories/speech.archive/mc.speech.html, accessed June 15, 2016.

81. Ronald Reagan, "Speech at the 1994 Gala—On the Occasion of His 83rd Birthday," February 3, 1994, http://let.rug.nl/usa/presidents/ronald-wilson-reagan/president-reagans-speech-at-the-1994-gala.php, accessed June 15, 2016.

82. Reagan, "Farewell Address."

83. "Reagan's Fall from Grace," SM1A.

84. "Reagan Backs 7-Day Wait for Pistol Buyers," *Los Angeles Times*, March 29, 1991, SDA1.

85. "Reagan Backs 7-Day Wait for Pistol Buyers," SDA1. In his autobiography, Reagan wrote about guns that he had "never liked hunting, simply killing an animal for the pleasure of it, but I have always enjoyed and collected unusual guns; I love target shooting, and have always kept a gun for protection at home." Reagan, *An American Life*, 276.

86. "Reagan Guest Stars before the California Assembly," *New York Times*, May 7, 1991, A18.

87. Ronald Reagan, "The Brotherhood of Man."

88. Reagan, *An American Life*.

89. Reagan, *An American Life*, 288.

90. Nancy Reagan, *My Turn: The Memoirs of Nancy Reagan* (New York: Random House, 1989), 113.

91. Nancy Reagan, *My Turn*, 107.

92. "The Campaign Trail," *A New Vision for America* exhibit, Ronald Reagan Presidential Museum, Simi Valley, CA.

93. *A New Vision for America* exhibit.

94. "The Great Debate," *A New Vision for America* exhibit.

95. Patrick J. Buchanan, "Address to the Republican National Convention," Houston, Texas, August 17, 1992, *American Rhetoric Online Speech Bank,* http:// americanrhetoric.com/speeches/patrickbuchanan1992rnc.htm.

96. Reagan, "Address at Republican National Convention."

97. Reagan, "Address at Republican National Convention."

98. "Reagan, Back in from the Sunset," *Washington Post,* August 18, 1992, D1.

99. "Reagan's Secret," *Wall Street Journal,* August 19, 1992, A12.

100. Shirley, *Last Act,* 29.

101. Ronald Reagan, "Announcement of Alzheimer's Disease," November 5, 1994, http://cnn.com/SPECIALS/2004/Reagan/stories/speech.archive/alzheimer .announcement.html,accessed June 16, 2016.

CHAPTER 10. REMEMBERING REAGAN: THE REAGAN LEGACY IN CONSERVATIVE POLITICS, 1994–1996

1. "Kemp Says Reagan Revolution Is Still On," *News Chronicle,* September 30, 1994, copy from vertical file, Ronald Reagan Presidential Library, Simi Valley, California (hereafter RRL).

2. Jack Kemp, "The Relevance of the Reagan Revolution for the 1990s," September 29, 1994, at the Reagan Forum, Ronald Reagan Presidential Library, copy from vertical file, RRL.

3. "Kemp Says Reagan Revolution is Still On"; Kemp, "The Relevance of the Reagan Revolution for the 1990s."

4. For more on the development of the Reagan legacy, consult Craig Shirley's sympathetic account: *Last Act: The Final Years and Emerging Legacy of Ronald Reagan* (New York: Nelson Books, 2015). For a somewhat antagonistic view of how conservatives created the Reagan myth see Will Bunch, *Tear Down This Myth: The Right-Wing Distortion of the Reagan Legacy* (New York: Free Press, 2009).

5. Although President Clinton was a Democrat, he was constrained by the conservative climate in which he governed. Many of his greatest accomplishments were modified forms of what conservative leaders in the House and Senate were proposing. Far from being a paradigm-shifting president, Clinton was a liberal who was confined by the reality that the United States in the 1990s was much more conservative than it had been before President Reagan took office. For more on the Clinton administration and its relation to the political and cultural forces released in the 1980s, see Sean Wilentz, *The Age of Reagan: A History 1974–2008* (New York: Harper Perennial, 2001); John Micklethwait and Adrian Wooldridge, *The Right Nation: Conservative Power in America* (New York: Penguin, 2004); John F. Harris, *The Survivor: Bill Clinton in the White House* (New York: Random House,

2005); Patrick J. Maney, *Bill Clinton: New Gilded Age President* (Lawrence: University Press of Kansas, 2016); Steven Gillon, *The Pact: Bill Clinton, Newt Gingrich, and the Rivalry That Defined a Generation* (Oxford: Oxford University Press, 2008). Daniel T. Rodgers details the shift toward individualism and the creation of a new individualistic political and cultural climate in *Age of Fracture* (New York: Belknap Press, 2010).

6. This point is debatable; however, the fact that George H. W. Bush defeated Pat Buchanan in 1992 and Senator Bob Dole defeated him in 1996 meant that the xenophobic tendencies of Buchanan were kept at bay. Indeed, in 1996, Dole used his acceptance speech to point to the exits and implored any bigoted delegates to leave the hall and by extension the party. Likewise, in 2000 Buchanan formally left the GOP. His exit was a victory for those, like George W. Bush, who desired a kinder, more compassionate conservatism. The anger and frustration with immigrants and trade deals, however, continued to fester in the Republican Party and emerged with a vengeance in 2016 with the election of Donald Trump. Bob Dole, "Text of Robert Dole's Speech to the Republican National Convention," August 15, 1996, http://www.cnn.com/ALLPOLITICS/1996/concvention/san.diego/transcripts/0815/dole.fdch.shtml, accessed July 5, 2016; Peggy Noonan, "Welcome to Hard Truths," *Time*, August 26, 1996; "Dole's Appeal for Tolerance Could Turn Away Hard-Liners," *Detroit News*, June 14, 1996; "Buchanan Tries to Spoil the Party-Again," *Wall Street Journal*, September 20, 1999, A28.

7. Ronald Reagan, "Announcement of Alzheimer's Disease," November 5, 1994,http://cnn.com/SPECIALS/2004/Reagan/stories/speech.archive/alzheimer.announcement.html, accessed July 5, 2016.

8. "Democratic Ads to Stress Downside of Reagan Era," *Washington Post*, October 13, 1994, A9.

9. For a detailed account on the effect that Ross Perot's candidacy had on the two-party system, see Ronald B. Rapoport and Walter J. Stone's *Three's a Crowd: The Dynamic of Third Parties, Ross Perot, and Republican Resurgence* (Ann Arbor: University of Michigan Press, 2005). For information specifically on the Contract see 150–163.

10. Republican National Committee, *Contract with America: The Bold Plan by Rep. Newt Gingrich, Rep. Dick Armey, and the House Republicans to Change the Nation* (New York: Random House, 1994).

11. "GOP Offers a 'Contract' to Revive Reagan Years," *Washington Post*, September 28, 1994, A1.

12. Indeed, even Rapoport and Stone cite that "all of the proposals [in the Contract] had long been floating in the GOP's primeval policy soup." Rapoport and Stone, *Three's a Crowd*, 151. For example, welfare reform was on the Reagan administration's to-do list during the transition. "Social Issues: Welfare, Welfare

Reform, the Republican Way," Fall 1980, box 26, "Ronald Reagan Presidential Transition Team, 1980–1981: Social Issues/Task Force on Defense and Foreign Policy" folder, Annelise Anderson Papers, Hoover Institution Archives, Stanford University, Stanford, California. Reagan also wrote a letter to Ed Meese in 1986 in which he asked Meese for any ideas he might have regarding restructuring welfare. The president had asked his Domestic Policy Council to address welfare reform. Reagan insisted that "reforms should promote the work ethic, stronger family and community ties, and increased self and group responsibility." Ronald Reagan to Ed Meese, March 21, 1986, 2, box 120, "Presidential Correspondence, 1986" folder, Ed Meese Papers, Hoover Institution Archives.

13. "Democratic Ads to Stress Downside of Reagan Era," *Washington Post*, October 13, 1994, A9.

14. Larry Kudlow, "There They Go Again," *National Review* 46, no. 21 (November 7, 1994): 28–30.

15. "Reagan Redux: Democrats, GOP Fight over 1980s," *Christian Science Monitor*, October 19, 1994, 1.

16. "Reagan Redux: Democrats, GOP Fight Over 1980s," 1.

17. "Democrat Ads to Stress Downside of Reagan Era," A9.

18. "Republicans' Campaign Trail Turns Right, Towards Reagan," *New York Times*, October 17, 1994, A1.

19. "Democrats Run a Risk in Running against '80s," *Washington Post*, October 12, 1994, A1.

20. "Republicans' Campaign Trail Turns Right, Towards Reagan," A1.

21. Bruce Bartlett, "Ronald Reagan and Red Ink," *Washington Post*, October 7, 1994, A24. Federal revenues during the 1980s almost doubled (1990 revenues 1.996 times 1980). During the 1970s, however, revenues increased by over 250 percent (1980 revenues 2.68 times 1970). As a percentage of GDP, federal revenues averaged 17.37 percent in the 1970s (1970–1979). Interestingly, during the 1980s federal revenues as a percentage of GDP actually averaged 17.76 percent. As a percentage of GDP, federal revenues increased during the 1980s. This runs counter to the historical narrative that Reagan's tax cuts dramatically altered the amount of revenue the government was collecting. Now, it is possible that the government might have collected more revenue if the tax cuts had not been signed into law, but it is equally possible that the United States might have experienced smaller GDP numbers as well. The data seems to confirm Reagan's view that the United States did not have a revenue problem during the 1980s but rather a spending problem. Whereas Reagan would like to blame Congress for the increases in spending, the truth is that his increases in military spending combined with the Democratic Congress's domestic spending caused the budget deficits. For the data that this analysis was based on consult "Federal Receipt and Outlay Summary,"

Statistics, Tax Policy Center, http://www.taxpolicycenter.org/statistics/federal
-receipt-and-outlay-summary.

22. John Kasich, "Sign Here to Complete the Reagan Agenda," *Wall Street Journal*, October 18, 1994, A18.

23. Kasich, "Sign Here to Complete the Reagan Agenda," A18.

24. Kudlow, "There They Go Again," 28.

25. Kudlow, "There They Go Again," 30.

26. Kudlow, "There They Go Again," 28–30.

27. Peggy Noonan, "Bliss to Be Alive," *Wall Street Journal*, January 9, 1995, A14.

28. Even after Gingrich's historic victory, the conservatives faced divisions. Deficit hawks were still at odds with supply-siders, social issues still divided the GOP, and the New Right wanted "its payback." "The Gingrich Challenge," *Washington Post*, November 15, 1994, A19.

29. "A Simple Case of Fraud: G.O.P. Policies Will Help the Rich," *New York Times*, November 13, 1994, E15.

30. "Misplaying Gingrich Those Who Insist on Fighting Their Worst Fantasy of the Man Will Lose," *Washington Post*, December 12, 1994, A23.

31. Jude Wanniski, "Gingrich's Politics Didn't Follow Fashion," *New York Times*, December 1, 1994, A32.

32. Noonan, "Bliss to be Alive," A14.

33. Although President George H. W. Bush had to endure the Reagan legacy perhaps more than any other politician, he was not considered a conservative by conservatives. Indeed, many conservatives disliked Bush, and his administration purged many key conservatives from the government once it took office in 1989.

34. "John Kasich Wields the Mighty Budget Ax Granted by Gingrich," *Wall Street Journal*, January 27, 1995, A1.

35. "Erase the Nation," *Washington Post*, February 19, 1995, C1.

36. "Gingrich: 'Contract Is Only a Start," *Washington Post*, April 8, 1995, A1.

37. Deaver downplays his role in crafting Reagan's image, but by all other accounts, he played an important role during Reagan's first term and before in carefully cultivating the president's image. Michael K. Deaver, *Behind the Scenes: In Which the Author Talks about Ronald and Nancy Reagan . . . and Himself* (New York: William Morrow, 1987); Michael K. Deaver, *A Different Drummer: My Thirty Years with Ronald Reagan* (New York: Perennial, 2001).

38. "Gingrich: 'Contract' Is Only a Start," A1; "Text of Address to the Nation by House Speaker Newt Gingrich," April 7, 1995, *The HyperText Books: Thirty Years: 1986–2016*, http://papyr.com/hypertextbooks/comp2/newt4.htm.

39. "Text of Address to the Nation by House Speaker Newt Gingrich."

40. Memorandum, "Accomplishment of the Common Sense Congress," October 7, 1996, Sub Series 2: Caucus/Party Records, box 203, folder 12: "GOP Agenda,"

Robert J. Dole Presidential Campaign Papers, University of Kansas Archives, Lawrence, Kansas.

41. "Down Deep, Gingrich's Presidential Candidacy Is Shallow," *Wall Street Journal*, June 8, 1995, A13.

42. "California, Reagan and the GOP," *Minneapolis Star Tribune*, March 26, 1996, A1.

43. "Kemp Won't Enter 1996 Primaries," *Washington Post*, January 31, 1995, A5.

44. "Where Dole Is No Reagan," *Washington Post*, September 2, 1995, A19.

45. "Supply-Side Optimism is Scarce in the GOP Six Years After Reagan," *Wall Street Journal*, September 20, 1995, A1.

46. "Where Dole Is No Reagan," *Washington Post*, September 2, 1995, A19.

47. "Gingrich, Buchanan Differ Sharply on Visions of Conservatism," *Washington Post*, July 15, 1995, A9.

48. "We Knew Reagan, and Pat Buchanan Is No Gipper," *Wall Street Journal*, February 23, 1996, A12.

49. The deep disagreements between paleoconservatives and neoconservatives over how to frame the Reagan legacy and over what the Republican Party would look like demonstrate the limits of the Reagan legacy in providing the conservative movement with a new fusionism. Even though many paleoconservatives rejected the more internationalist and interventionist version of the Reagan legacy that neoconservatives would cast—especially after 9/11—I think the Reagan legacy has played a critical and important role in holding the conservative movement together from the 1990s to the present. After all, just because the John Birchers and others were excluded from the original fusionism by William F. Buckley doesn't mean that anticommunism didn't still hold large swaths of the conservative movement together.

50. "Supply-Side Optimism Is Scarce in the GOP Six Years after Reagan," *Wall Street Journal*, September 20, 1995, A1. Supply-side activist Jude Wanniski, former Reagan campaign adviser John Sears, and Jack Kemp all endorsed Forbes (Kemp's endorsement came at the end of the primary when it had little effect).

51. "An Oral History of the Original Death and Return of Superman, 25 Years Later," *SYFY Wire*, August 10, 2018, https://www.syfy.com/syfywire/an-oral-history -of-the-original-death-and-return-of-superman-25-years-later.

52. "Dole Fends Off Foes but Fails to Dominate Forum," *Washington Post*, February 16, 1996, A13.

53. "Dole Courts Democrats," *New York Times*, March 15, 1996, A1.

54. "Bob Dole, Alias Ronald Reagan?," *Baltimore Sun*, June 5, 1986, 17A.

55. "Dole Makes Political Pilgrimage," *San Diego Union-Tribune*, July 4, 1996, A1.

56. "Dole Calls Meeting with Reagan 'Shot in the Arm' for Campaign," *Baltimore Sun*, July 4, 1996, 3A.

57. "Dole Meets with Reagan during California Stop," *Orlando Sentinel*, July 4, 1996, A14.

58. William F. Buckley, "The Kemp Manifesto: A Plan Right for Dole," *New York Post*, June 24, 1996, Subseries Campaign Committees: box 193, folder 13: Jack Kemp, Robert J. Dole Presidential Campaign Papers.

59. "Dole, in Choosing Kemp Buried a Bitter Past Rooted in Doctrine," *New York Times*, September 29, 1996, 1; "Maybe Kemp Did Dole a Favor," *Wall Street Journal*, March 8, 1996, A10; Morton Kondracke and Fred Barnes, *Jack Kemp: The Bleeding-Heart Conservative Who Changed the World* (New York: Sentinel, 2015), 198.

60. "Dole Vows to Finish Reagan's Job, Once a Supply-Side Critic Candidate Says Tax Cuts, Deficit Both Come First," *Milwaukee Journal Sentinel*, August 6, 1996, 7.

61. Bunch, *Tear Down This Myth*, 51; Matthew Dallek, "Not Ready for Mt. Rushmore: Reconciling the Myth of Ronald Reagan with the Reality," *American Scholar* 78, no. 3 (June 2009): 18.

62. "Dole Vows to Finish Reagan's Job," 7.

63. "Ex-Reagan Economic Aide Criticizes Dole Plan to Cut Taxes," *New York Times*, September 11, 1996, D2.

64. "Dole Hoists Banner of Reagan Revolution," *Worcester Telegram & Gazette*, August 12, 1996, A1.

65. "Republican Convention Evening Session," C-SPAN, August 12, 1996, https://www.c-span.org/video/?74304-1/republican-convention-evening-session; for just the tribute see "Reagan Tribute Video '96," https://www.bing.com/videos/search?q=reagan+tribute+2004+rnc&view=detail&mid=AAD5B2F92AFF691098 D2AAD5B2F92AFF691098D2&FORM=VIRE14, accessed July 12, 2016.

66. "Republican Convention Evening Session"; "Reagan Tribute Video '96."

67. "Republican Convention Evening Session"; "Reagan Tribute Video '96."

68. "Republican Convention Evening Session"; "Reagan Tribute Video '96."

69. "Nancy Reagan Pays Tribute to Husband, GOP[;] Others at Podium Bring Patriotism of Party and Dole into Spotlight," *Milwaukee Journal Sentinel*, August 13, 1996, 8.

70. "Dole Hoists Banner of Reagan Revolution," A1.

71. Lyn Nofziger, "The Republican Convention: Dole Must Learn to Play Reagan," *Newsday*, August 14, 1996, A37.

72. Interestingly, President Clinton patterned his campaign after Reagan's 1984 strategy. The press reported that "Clinton has used variations of 'stay the course' that marked Reagan's motto and tries to maintain the appearance of being 'presidential' as though he were above politicking even as he campaigned for office." Even chief GOP operatives conceded that "Clinton is winning the Reagan

contest." "Both Parties Go for the Gipper's Gold: Clinton, Dole Try to Emulate Reagan," *Houston Chronicle,* August 10, 1996, 2; "Clinton Staff Annoys Republicans by Tapping Successful Reagan Style," *Baltimore Sun,* June 2, 1996, 12A.

73. Robert L. Bartley, "Dole as Reagan's Heir," *Wall Street Journal,* August 15, 1996, A10.

74. "Seeing the Right Light," *National Review* 48, no. 16 (September 2, 1996): 16–20.

75. "How Dole Fell," *New York Times,* Subseries Campaign Committees, box 197, folder 21: Strategy, Robert J. Dole Presidential Campaign Papers.

76. "No Doubt," *National Review* 48, no. 21 (November 11, 1996): 10–14.

77. "Strategy," Memorandum from Jerry Jones and Rick Fore to Donald Rumsfeld, September 9, 1996, Subseries Campaign Committees, box 197, folder 21: Strategy, 1996, Robert J. Dole Presidential Campaign Papers.

78. "Dole's Ethics Tactics Back Fire Turns Out Reagan Scandals Outnumber Clinton's," *Milwaukee Journal Sentinel,* October 27, 1996, 17. After the Lewinsky scandal, some conservatives attempted to exalt Reagan's virtue in relation to Clinton's scandals. The most prominent representation can be found in Peggy Noonan's *When Character Was King: A Story of Ronald Reagan* (New York: Penguin, 2002). For a complete analysis of this myth, consult Kyle Longley's "When Character Was King? Ronald Reagan and Issues of Ethics and Morality," in Longley et al., *Deconstructing Reagan: Conservative Mythology and America's Fortieth President* (New York: M. E. Sharpe, 2007), 90–119.

79. As I mentioned before, this coalition—while united by the Reagan legacy—was extremely fragile, and the disparate strands of the conservative movement often disagreed with one another. After the invasion of Iraq in 2003, and with the growing national debt of the George W. Bush administration, many paleoconservatives and libertarian-leaning conservatives abandoned the movement.

CHAPTER 11. MEMORIALIZING REAGAN: ENSHRINING THE REAGAN LEGACY, 1996–2000

1. For a detailed account of how historians viewed the Reagan administration see George H. Nash's chapter "Ronald Reagan's Legacy and American Conservatism," in *The Enduring Reagan,* ed. Charles W. Dunn (Lexington: University Press of Kentucky, 2009), 61–69; Gil Troy's chapter "Toward a Historiography of Reagan and the 1980s: Why Have We Done Such a Lousy Job?," in *Ronald Reagan and the 1980s: Perceptions, Policies, Legacies,* ed. Cheryl Hudson and Gareth Davies (New York: Palgrave Macmillan, 2008), 229–247.

2. Dinesh D'Souza, *Ronald Reagan: How an Ordinary Man Became an Extraordinary Leader* (New York: Free Press, 1997).

3. "About the Ronald Reagan Legacy Project," *RRLP News*, accessed April 15, 2019, http://www.ronaldreaganlegacyproject.org/about.

4. Quoted in Niels Bjerre-Poulsen's chapter "The Road to Mount Rushmore: The Conservative Commemoration Crusade for Ronald Reagan," in Hudson and Davies, *Ronald Reagan and the 1980s*, 214.

5. Arthur M. Schlesinger Jr., "Rating the Presidents: Washington to Clinton," *Political Science Quarterly* 112, no. 2 (Summer 1997): 184.

6. For a complete history of the Intercollegiate Studies Institute, consult Lee Edwards's *Educating for Liberty: The First Half-Century of the Intercollegiate Studies Institute* (Washington, DC: Regnery Publishing, 2003).

7. "Historians and the Reagan Legacy," *Weekly Standard*, September 29, 1997, 22. This article also has a complete list of the ISI and Schlesinger survey.

8. Alan Brinkley, "The Problem of American Conservatism," *American Historical Review* 99, no. 2 (April 1994): 409–429. Reagan's accomplishments and personal quality were recognized by many historians following the publication of *Reagan, in His Own Hand* in 2001 and *Reagan: A Life in Letters* in 2003. Nash, "Ronald Reagan's Legacy and American Conservatism," 61–69.

9. Gary Gregg interview, *Washington Journal*, C-SPAN, September 25, 1997, https://www.cspan.org/video/?91534-1/presidential-rankings, accessed July 15, 2018.

10. "Rating the Presidents of the United States, 1789–2000: A Survey of Scholars in History, Political Science, and Law," *Federalist Society*, November 16, 2000, https://fedsoc.org/commentary/publications/rating-the-presidents-of-the-united-states-1789-2000-a-survey-of-scholars-in-history-political-science-and-law.

11. "What Happened to Dinesh D'Souza?," *Atlantic*, July 25, 2014, https://www.theatlantic.com/politics/archive/2014/07/what-happened-to-dinesh-dsouza/374939/; Dinesh D'Souza, *Illiberal Education: The Politics of Race and Sex on Campus* (New York: Vintage Books, 1991).

12. Dinesh D'Souza, *The End of Racism: Principles for a Multiracial Society* (New York: Free Press, 1995),

13. "What Happened to Dinesh D'Souza?"

14. Dinesh D'Souza, *Ronald Reagan: How an Ordinary Man Became an Extraordinary Leader* (New York: Free Press, 1997), 12.

15. D'Souza, *Ronald Reagan*, 18.

16. D'Souza, *Ronald Reagan*, 18–19.

17. D'Souza, *Ronald Reagan*, 21.

18. D'Souza, *Ronald Reagan*, 264.

19. D'Souza, *Ronald Reagan*, 23–24.

20. D'Souza, *Ronald Reagan*, 7.

21. D'Souza, *Ronald Reagan*, 128.

22. D'Souza, *Ronald Reagan*, 109.

23. D'Souza, *Ronald Reagan*, 109–115. For D'Souza's view on how Reagan's executive orders ending price controls ended the energy crisis, see 89.

24. D'Souza, *Ronald Reagan*, 113.

25. D'Souza, *Ronald Reagan*, 102.

26. D'Souza, *Ronald Reagan*, 125–126.

27. D'Souza, *Ronald Reagan*, 124.

28. D'Souza, *Ronald Reagan*, 127.

29. D'Souza, *Ronald Reagan*, 26.

30. D'Souza, *Ronald Reagan*, 4–5.

31. D'Souza, *Ronald Reagan*, 30–31.

32. D'Souza, *Ronald Reagan*, 134–135. D'Souza claims "Reagan had a conscious strategy to impose intolerable strains on the Soviet regime, perhaps bankrupting it altogether" (140).

33. See chapter 7 of this volume.

34. D'Souza, *Ronald Reagan*, 138–139.

35. D'Souza, *Ronald Reagan*, 192.

36. D'Souza, *Ronald Reagan*, 184.

37. D'Souza, *Ronald Reagan*, 193.

38. D'Souza, *Ronald Reagan*, 196–197.

39. D'Souza, *Ronald Reagan*, 259–263.

40. D'Souza, *Ronald Reagan*, 264.

41. Quoted in Bjerre-Poulsen, "The Road to Mount Rushmore," 219.

42. "Will the Gipper Ever Get a Piece of the Rock," *New York Times*, February 11, 2001, wk5; "Have You Got Two Reagan's for a Twenty," *New York Times*, June 9, 2004, A20; Bjerre-Poulsen, "The Road to Mount Rushmore," 217.

43. Will Bunch, *Tear Down This Myth: The Right-Wing Distortion of the Reagan Legacy* (New York: Free Press, 2009), 160.

44. President Reagan believed in the merits of federalism and local control. His administration issued a statement of principles on federalism that encouraged each department of the federal government to acknowledge that "in the absence of clear constitutional or statutory authority, the presumption of sovereignty should rest with the individual state." Having said that, Reagan did at times violate his belief in federalism—one such case was the imposition of twenty-one as the national drinking age. "Federalism: Statement of Principles," box 120, "Presidential Correspondence: 1986" folder, Ed Meese Papers, Hoover Institution Archives, Stanford University, Stanford, California.

45. Press release, "Bob Barr and Senator Paul Coverdell Announce Legislation to Rename National Airport after Ronald Reagan," October 23, 1997, box 588, folder 6, Bob Barr Papers, Office Files, Ingram Library, Annie Belle Weaver Special Collections, University of West Georgia, Carrollton, Georgia.

46. "Barr, Coverdell to Rename National Airport," October 23, 1997, box 588, folder 6, Bob Barr Papers, Office Files, Ingram Library, Annie Belle Weaver Special Collections, University of West Georgia.

47. Dear Colleague letter from Bob Barr, "Ronald Reagan Washington National Airport," October 14, 1997, box 588, folder 6, Bob Barr Papers, Office Files, Ingram Library, Annie Belle Weaver Special Collections, University of West Georgia.

48. Americans for Tax Reform mailing, "Let's Rename Washington National Airport the 'Ronald Reagan Washington National Airport' and Honor a Great American President," box 588, folder 6, Bob Barr Papers, Office Files, Ingram Library, Annie Belle Weaver Special Collections, University of West Georgia. When this piece of direct mail was sent out, the Ronald Reagan Legacy Project had already had some small victories, including: the Reagan Center at Eureka College; the Ronald Reagan Bridge in Dixon, Illinois; the Ronald Reagan Institute of Emergency Medicine at George Washington University in Washington, DC; Ronald Reagan Boulevard in Warwick, NY; the Ronald Reagan Federal Building in Washington, DC; and six other memorials.

49. James Brady to Representative Bob Barr, December 1, 1997, box 588, folder 6, Bob Barr Papers, Office Files, Ingram Library, Annie Belle Weaver Special Collections, University of West Georgia.

50. News clipping, December 4, 1997, box 588, folder 6, Bob Barr Papers, Office Files, Ingram Library, Annie Belle Weaver Special Collections, University of West Georgia.

51. "Reagan National Airport," *Wall Street Journal*, January 5, 1998, A22.

52. Albert R. Hunt, "Should It Be Washington's Reagan Airport?," *Wall Street Journal*, January 15, 1998, A19.

53. Reagan's approval rating with the American public, which had been at 50 percent in 1992, was polled at 71 percent in 1999. This increase in Reagan's approval rating was the result of the scandals of the Clinton administration, the booming economy of the 1990s (in which the Reagan deficits looked less important), the outpouring of goodwill that Reagan received following his diagnosis with Alzheimer's, and to some extent the efforts of conservative activists in promoting the Reagan legacy. For the polling data, see M. J. Heale's "Epilogue: Ronald Reagan and the Historians," in Hudson and Davies, *Ronald Reagan and the 1980s*, 249.

54. "H.R. 2625—Ronald Reagan Washington National Airport" Newsmaker Alert, House Republican Conference, February 4, 1998, box 588, folder 6, Bob Barr

Papers, Office Files, Ingram Library, Annie Belle Weaver Special Collections, University of West Georgia.

55. G.O.P. Tries to Wrap Up an Airport for Reagan," *New York Times*, February 4, 1998. Conservative activists often held up Kennedy as a marker for how many memorials Reagan should ultimately have named in his honor. There is also an excellent study of JFK, Reagan, and their legacies—see Scott Farris's *Kennedy and Reagan: Why Their Legacies Endure* (Guilford, CT: Lyons Press, 2013).

56. "Bill Renames Washington National Airport after Reagan," *Spokesman-Review*, January 28, 1998, A3, https://news.google.com/newspapers?id=CbsyAAA AIBAJ&sjid=DPIDAAAAIBAJ&pg=6744%2C4755927.

57. "G.O.P. Tries to Wrap Up an Airport for Reagan."

58. "The Ronald Reagan Airport," *Wall Street Journal*, February 5, 1998, A22.

59. Press release, Office of Senator Paul Coverdell, "Coverdell Bill Honoring Reagan Clears Final Hurdle in Congress," February 5, 1998, box 588, folder 6, Bob Barr Papers, Office Files, Ingram Library, Annie Belle Weaver Special Collections, University of West Georgia.

60. "It's Reagan Airport Now," *McCook Daily Gazette*, February 7, 1998, http://news.google.com/newspapers?id=K6cgAAAAIBA&sjid=6WgFAAAAIBAJ &pg=4387,3903666, accessed July 22, 2018.

61. Press release, Office of Senator Paul Coverdell, "Coverdell Bill Honoring Reagan Clears Final Hurdle in Congress."

62. Press Release, Office of Representative Bob Barr, "Barr Bill Honoring Reagan to Become Law," February 5, 1988, box 588, folder 6, Bob Barr Papers, Office Files, Ingram Library, Annie Belle Weaver Special Collections, University of West Georgia.

63. "Congress Votes for Reagan Airport," *Washington Post*, February 5, 1998, A1.

64. Bunch, *Tear Down this Myth*, 160; Bjerre-Poulsen, "The Road to Mount Rushmore," 213.

65. Quoted in Bunch's *Tear Down this Myth*, 157.

CHAPTER 12. REINVENTING REAGAN:
GEORGE W. BUSH AND THE EMERGENCE OF
THE REAGAN MYTH, 2000–2004

1. For a comprehensive analysis of how George W. Bush tied himself to Reagan throughout his political career, consult Lou Cannon and Carl M. Cannon's *Reagan's Disciple: George W. Bush's Troubled Quest for a Presidential Legacy* (New York: Public Affairs, 2008). Interestingly, George W. Bush's first political encounter with Reagan came in 1977 when Bush ran for Congress against Jim Reese, who had been

Reagan's point man in West Texas when Reagan challenged Ford. Reagan endorsed Reese, and a Reagan-affiliated political action committee, Citizens for the Republic, donated money to Reese. Although Reagan called George H. W. Bush to assure him that he was not opposed to his son and assure Bush that Reagan would endorse W. in the general, that did not satisfy the older Bush. Reagan surrogates spoke on Reese's behalf, leading George H. W. Bush to exclaim, "I'm not interested with getting into an argument with Reagan. But I am surprised what he is doing here, in my state. . . . They are making a real effort to defeat George." Bush won the runoff, but Reese refused to endorse him, and Bush's Democratic foe used Reese's playbook to defeat Bush in the general election. "Texas Runoff Strains GOP Relations: Some Sour Feelings in Bush Camp over Reagan's Role," *Washington Post*, June 3, 1978. As cited in Cannon and Cannon, *Reagan's Disciple*, 10.

2. "George W. More Reagan III, Than Bush II," *York (PA) Daily Record*, November 29, 1999, A6.

3. During the 2000 election Pat Buchanan left the Republican Party. In September of 1999 the *Wall Street Journal* attempted to discredit Buchanan's continued assertions that he was the true heir to Reagan. The *Journal* asserted that Reagan was "a friend of Israel and American Jews" while Buchanan had time and again used derogatory language about "Jewish influence in foreign policy." The publication also declared that Buchanan's protectionism differed significantly from Reagan's belief in free trade and free markets. The *Journal* concluded that Buchanan had it backward: "He has not rejected the Republican Party. It has rejected him." "Buchanan Tries to Spoil the Party—Again," *Wall Street Journal*, September 20, 1999, A28.

4. "George W. Reagan," *New York Post*, November 23, 1999, 38.

5. "George W. More Reagan III, than Bush II," A6. For a full analysis of the relationship between George W. Bush and George H. W. Bush, see Mark K. Updegrove's *The Last Republicans: Inside the Extraordinary Relationship between George H. W. Bush and George W. Bush* (New York: Harper, 2017).

6. "Bush Says He Is Reagan's Heir and Candidate of Future," *New York Times*, February 26, 2000, A12.

7. "Nancy Reagan Endorses George W. Bush for President," *PR Newswire* (New York), May 17, 2000, 1.

8. "Bush's Party Has Learned Reagan's Lessons," *Wall Street Journal*, August 3, 2000, A14.

9. "The Big Speech," *National Review* 52, no. 16 (August 28, 2000): 12–14.

10. Larry Kudlow and Stephen Moore, "Tax Cuts: A Comeback," *National Review* 52, no. 16 (August 28, 2000): 24–25.

11. "I'm Pretty Much Like Reagan, Says Bush," *Daily Telegraph* (UK), November 2, 2000, 16.

12. Charles Krauthammer, "A Genuine George W. Bush Tops an Inauthentic Al Gore," *Washington Post*, November 4, 2000.

13. "The Call of a Second Reagan with His Country-Club Values, George W. Bush Promises It Can Be 'Morning in America Again,'" *Independent* (London), November 5, 2000, 27.

14. "George W. Bush, et al., Petitioners v. Albert Gore, Jr., et al. On Writ of Certiorari to the Florida Supreme Court," December 12, 2000, *Legal Information Institute*, http://www.law.cornell.edu/supct/html/00-949.ZPC.html. For a historical account of *Bush v. Gore* and the 2000 election see James T. Patterson's *Restless Giant: The United States from Watergate to Bush v. Gore* (Oxford: Oxford University Press, 2007).

15. "Tribute to Former President Ronald Reagan by President George W. Bush, as Recorded for CNN's Larry King Live," *US Newswire* (Washington, DC), February 6, 2001, 1.

16. "A Test of Principle Could Make or Break Bush," *Daily Telegraph* (UK), July 23, 2001, 18.

17. Former First Lady Nancy Reagan to President George W. Bush, April 11, 2001, "Stem Cell Research," *The First Lady* exhibit, Ronald Reagan Presidential Museum, Simi Valley, California; George W. Bush, *Decision Points* (New York: Crown, 2010), 106.

18. "A Test of Principle Could Make or Break Bush," 18.

19. Bush later acknowledged that his decision was affected by his reading of Aldous Huxley's *Brave New World*, the meaning of which, according to Bush, was that "the quest to perfect humanity ended in the loss of humanity." Bush, *Decision Points*, 106.

20. Bush, *Decision Points*, 442.

21. "George W. Reagan? Bush Seems to be Walking in Another President's Boots," *Chicago Tribune*, September 2, 2001, http://articles.chicagotribune.com /2001-09-02/news/0109020218_1_tax-bill-deficits-trillion.

22. Dick Cheney, *In My Time: A Personal and Political Memoir* (New York: Threshold, 2011), 311.

23. Bush, *Decision Points*, 442.

24. George W. Bush, State of the Union Address, January 29, 2002, *American Rhetoric Online Speech Bank*, http://www.americanrhetoric.com/speeches /stateoftheunion2002.htm.

25. Bob Woodward, *Plan of Attack: The Definitive Account of the Decision to Invade Iraq* (New York: Simon & Schuster, 2004), 89.

26. Woodward, *Plan of Attack*, 89.

27. "New Rules of Political Rhetoric: Bush Should Leave the Reagan Style to Its Own Era," *New York Times*, February 24, 2002, D13.

28. Woodward, *Plan of Attack*, 91–93.

29. Ann Coulter, *Slander: Liberal Lies About the American Right* (New York: Crown, 2002), 145.

30. Ann Coulter, *Treason: Liberal Treachery from the Cold War to the War on Terrorism* (New York: Crown, 2003), 14.

31. Coulter, *Treason*, 188.

32. For a detailed account of how foreign policy was determined during the 1980s, see James M. Scott's *Deciding to Intervene: The Reagan Doctrine and American Foreign Policy* (Durham, NC: Duke University Press, 1996).

33. Scott, *Deciding to Intervene*, 21.

34. Bush, *Decision Points*, 191.

35. Vladislav M. Zubok, *A Failed Empire: The Soviet Union in the Cold War from Stalin to Gorbachev* (Chapel Hill: University of North Carolina Press, 2007), 276; Anatoly Dobrynin, *In Confidence: Moscow's Ambassador to America's Six Cold War Presidents* (New York: Random House, 1995), 482.

36. Beth A. Fischer, *The Reagan Reversal: Foreign Policy and the End of the Cold War* (Columbia: University of Missouri Press, 1997).

37. William D. Jackson, "Soviet Reassessment of Ronald Reagan, 1985–1988," *Political Science Quarterly* 113, no. 4 (Winter 1998–1999): 617–644; James Graham Wilson, *The Triumph of Improvisation: Gorbachev's Adaptability, Reagan's Engagement, and the End of the Cold War* (Ithaca, NY: Cornell University Press, 2015).

38. Bill Keller, "Reagan's Son," *New York Times*, January 26, 2003, SM26.

39. Keller, "Reagan's Son," SM26.

40. Peter J. Wallison, "Bush's Reagan Moment," *New York Times*, October 26, 2003, WK11.

41. Bush, *Decision Points*, 272.

42. Keller, "Reagan's Son," SM26.

43. "We Take Our Stand," *American Conservative*, October 7, 2002 (edition 1, vol. 1).

44. "Iraq Folly: How American Victory Could Spell American Defeat," *American Conservative*, October 7, 2002 (edition 1, vol. 1).

45. Patrick Buchanan, "After the War," *American Conservative*, October 7, 2002 (edition 1, vol. 1).

46. Libertarians were also extremely critical of the Bush administration's decision to invade Iraq. For more on the subject, see Marcus M. Witcher's "Two Visions, One Future: How Neoconservative Preemptive War Isolated Libertarians," *Journal of Peace, Prosperity, and Freedom* 3 (Summer 2014): 57–67.

47. Bush, *Decision Points*, 272.

48. "Mourners Gather for First of Farewells," Associated Press, June 8, 2004,

http://www.sptimes.com/2004/06/08/Worldandnation/Mourners_gather_for_f
.shtml, accessed July 22, 2016.

49. "Plane Carrying Reagan's Casket Leaves for Washington for His State
Funeral," Associated Press, June 9, 2004, https://www.highbeam.com/doc/1P1
-95354412.html, accessed July 24, 2016; "Reagan Ceremonies to Shift to Nation's Capital," *USA Today*, June 8, 2004, http://usatoday30.usatoday.com/news
/washington/2004-06-08-funeral-usat_x.htm; "GOP Leaders Eulogize the 40th
President," *Washington Post*, June 10, 2004, A21.

50. "GOP Leaders Eulogize the 40th President," A21.

51. Richard Cheney, "Vice President Cheney's Remarks at State Funeral Ceremony," US Capitol Rotunda, Washington, DC, June 9, 2004, http://georgewbush
-whitehouse.archievs.gov/news/releases/2004/06/20040609-48.html, accessed July
24, 2016.

52. Cheney, "Vice President Cheney's Remarks at State Funeral Ceremony."

53. "GOP Leaders Eulogize the 40th President," A21.

54. Margaret Thatcher, "Eulogy for President Reagan," June 11, 2004, *Margaret Thatcher Foundation*, http://margaretthatcher.org/speeches/displaydocument
.asp?docid=110360.

55. George W. Bush, "President Bush's Eulogy at Funeral Service for President
Reagan," National Cathedral, Washington, DC, June 11, 2004, http://georgewbush
-whitehouse.archives.gov/news/releases/2004/06/20040611-2html, accessed July 25,
2016.

56. Interestingly, even Patrick Buchanan—one of Bush's most ardent paleoconservative critics—argued in a tribute to Reagan in 2004 that Reagan was successful because of his "refusal to compromise." Buchanan also praised Reagan's
"determination to challenge the Soviet Union philosophically" and implied that
Reagan's ideological consistency "led us to a bloodless victory in the Cold War."
Patrick J. Buchanan, "Goodbye to 'the Gipper,'" *Human Events*, June 14, 2004, 18.

57. George H. W. Bush, "Reagan's Vice President Remembers His Good
Friend," National Cathedral, Washington, DC, June 11, 2004, *CNN.com*, http://
cnn.com/2004/ALLPOLITICS/06/11/bush.sr.transcript.

58. "Gorbachev: 'We All Lost Cold War,'" *Washington Post*, June 11, 2004, A1.

59. Many historians grant that Reagan's pragmatism and willingness to negotiate played an important role in ending the Cold War. These historians give
Reagan, among others, credit for the de-escalation that made the dissolution of
the Soviet Union possible. See William D. Jackson, "Soviet Reassessment of Ronald Reagan, 1985–1988," *Political Science Quarterly* 113, no. 4 (Winter 1998–1999):
617–644. Also consult Beth A. Fischer's *The Reagan Reversal*.

CHAPTER 13. RECONSTRUCTING REAGAN: HOW
CONSERVATIVES CREATED A MYTHICAL REAGAN,
2004–2008

1. Dana Milbank, "The New Party of Reagan," *Washington Post,* July 19, 2011, washingtonpost.com/opinions/the-new-party-ofreagan/2011/07/19/glQAuckf01 _story.html?utm_term=.218e43008328, accessed August 5, 2016.

2. Milbank, "The New Party of Reagan."

3. Milbank, "The New Party of Reagan."

4. I use the term *conservative purists* to describe conservatives, many of whom were part of the New Right in the 1980s, who are socially conservative, opposed to immigration reform, hostile toward the "establishment." They decry compromise and represent a populist strand of conservatism that has more in common with Pat Buchanan than Ronald Reagan. Some prominent examples include Richard Viguerie, Phyllis Schlafly, Ann Coulter, Sean Hannity, Rush Limbaugh, Ted Cruz, and others. They also are the greatest proponents of the belief that Reagan succeeded because of his unwillingness to compromise conservative principle. As with any group of individuals, there is a wide range of beliefs among conservative purists.

5. Two excellent examples of how conservative purists viewed the 2000s are Richard A. Viguerie's *Takeover: The 100 War for the Soul of the GOP and How Conservatives Can Finally Win It* (Washington, DC: WND Books, 2014) and Phyllis Schlafly's *A Choice Not an Echo: 50th Anniversary Edition* (New York: Regnery, 2014).

6. An emerging literature discusses the origins of the Tea Party. For a complete analysis consult Ronald P. Formisano's *The Tea Party: A Brief History* (Baltimore: Johns Hopkins University Press, 2012); Theda Skocpol and Vanessa Williamson's *The Tea Party and the Remaking of Republican Conservatism* (Oxford: Oxford University Press, 2012); Kate Zernike's *Boiling Mad: Inside Tea Party America* (New York: Times Books, 2010); Paul Street and Anthony DiMaggio's *Crashing the Tea Party: Mass Media and the Campaign to Remake American Politics* (London: Paradigm Books, 2011); Lawrence Rosenthal and Christine Trost's excellent compilation *Steep: The Precipitous Rise of the Tea Party* (Berkeley: University of California Press, 2012); Christopher S. Parker and Matt A. Barreto's *Change They Can't Believe In: The Tea Party and Reactionary Politics in America* (Princeton, NJ: Princeton University Press, 2013), and Melissa Deckman's *Tea Party Women: Mama Grizzlies, Grassroots Leaders, and the Changing Face of the American Right* (New York: New York University Press, 2016). There have also been several new attempts to explain the overarching narrative of conservatism from the mid-twentieth century to the present. Among these works are E. J. Dionne Jr.'s *Why the Right Went*

Wrong: Conservatism from Goldwater to the Tea Party and Beyond (New York: Simon & Schuster, 2016); and Geoffrey Kabaservice's *Rule and Ruin: The Downfall of Moderation and the Destruction of the Republican Party, from Eisenhower to the Tea Party* (Oxford: Oxford University Press, 2013).

7. I label those who desired to take conservative ideas and apply them to contemporary problems in new and innovative ways as pragmatic conservatives. Just as with conservative purists, pragmatic conservatives disagree on many issues and points of policy, but they tend to agree that the GOP needs to broaden its appeal to people of color and millennials to be successful. Rand Paul, "Exclusive Rand Paul: Stop Warping Reagan's Foreign Policy," *Breitbart News*, March 10, 2014, http://www.breitbart.com/national-security/2014/03/10/rand-paul-reagans-foreign-pol icy/; Michael Reagan, *The New Reagan Revolution: How Ronald Reagan's Principles Can Restore America's Greatness* (New York: Thomas Dunne Books, 2010), 95–97.

8. Ted Cruz, *A Time for Truth: Reigniting the Promise of America* (New York: Broadside Books, 2015), 129; Morton Blackwell, "Please Join Me in Supporting Ted Cruz," *Red State*, January 11, 2016, http://redstate.com/diary/ Morton_C_Black well/2016/01/11/please-join-supporting-ted-cruz; "Glenn Beck Declares Ted Cruz the Second Coming of Ronald Reagan," *Mediaite*, December 18, 2013, http://me diaite.com/online/glenn-beck-declares-ted-cruz-the-second-coming-of-ronald -reagan, accessed august 7, 2016.

9. David Frum, *Comeback: Conservativism That Can Win Again* (New York: Broadway Books, 2008); Arthur C. Brooks, *The Conservative Heart: How to Build a Fairer, Happier, and More Prosperous America* (New York: Broadway Books, 2015); Matt K. Lewis, *Too Dumb to Fail: How the GOP Betrayed the Reagan Revolution to Win Elections (and How It Can Reclaim Its Conservative Roots)* (New York: Hachette Books, 2016); "Rand Paul: GOP Needs to Become 'Bigger' Party," *CBS News*, May 31, 2013, http://www.cbsnews.com/news/rand-paul-gop-needs-to-be come-a-bigger-party/; "Rand Paul Tells Tea Party: Be More Inclusive," *CBS News*, February 27, 2014, http://www.cbsnews.com/news/rand-paul-tells-tea-party-be -more-inclusive/; Paul Ryan, Eric Cantor, and Kevin McCarthy, *Young Guns: A New Generation of Conservative Leaders* (New York: Threshold Editions, 2010); Paul Ryan, *The Way Forward: Renewing the American Idea* (New York: Hachette Book Group, 2014).

10. Although these conservatives have many differences, they all believe that the GOP should stick to its conservative principles in order to win elections. They also tend to emphasize Reagan as a conservative purist and do not believe that Republicans need to expand the base by appealing to African Americans, Latinos, and more socially inclusive millennials. Ann Coulter, *Treason: Liberal Treachery from the Cold War to the War on Terrorism* (New York: Crown, 2003); Ann Coulter, *Slander: Liberal Lies About the American Right* (New York: Crown, 2002); Rush

Limbaugh, "The Great One," *National Review* 56, no. 12 (June 28, 2004): 36–37; Sean Hannity, *Conservative Victory: Defeating Obama's Radical Agenda* (New York: Harper, 2010); Schlafly, *50th Anniversary Edition*; Viguerie, *Takeover*; Laura Ingraham and Craig Shirley, "Ronald Reagan's Words Remain Relevant Today," *Chicago Tribune*, October 28, 2014, http://www.chicagotribune.com/news/opinion /commentary/chi-ronald-reagan-goldwater-speech-reaganism-20141028-story .html. Coulter even went so far in 2015 as to assert that it was delusional to try to court minority voters. Instead, she insisted that "the GOP's only move is to run the table on white voters, as Reagan did . . . by unapologetically opposing the transformation of America into a Third World country, the GOP would sweep the white vote." Ann Coulter, *Adios, America! The Left's Plan to Turn Our Country into a Third World Hellhole* (Washington, DC: Regnery, 2015).

11. There was so much doubt that Republicans would be effective after winning control of both Houses of Congress in the 2014 midterms that Senate Majority Leader Mitch McConnell (R-KY) and Speaker of the House John Boehner (R-OH) wrote an op-ed in the *Wall Street Journal* decrying "the skeptics" who said "nothing will be accomplished in the next two years." John Boehner and Mitch McConnell, "Now We Can Get Congress Going," *Wall Street Journal*, November 5, 2014, http://www.wsj.com/articles/john-boehner-and-mitch-mcconnell-now-we -can-get-congress-going-1415232759. "So How's that 'Showing the GOP Can Govern' Thing Going?," *Washington Post*, May 25, 2015, https://www.washingtonpost .com/blogs/plum-line/wp/2015/05/25/so-hows-that-showing-the-gop-can-gov ern-thing-going/?utm_term=.0608a4892a6b.

12. Rory Carroll, "The Myth of Ronald Reagan: Pragmatic Moderate or Radical Conservative?," *Guardian*, September 19, 2015, https://www.theguardian.com /us-news/2015/sep/19/political-myth-ronald-reagan-republican-moderate-con servative; Faith Whittlesey, "President Reagan and Young Mr. Trump," *Huffington Post*, June 29, 2016, http://www.huffingtonpost.com/ambassador-faith-whitt lesey/president-reagan-and-youn_b_10713678.html.

13. For a complete analysis of how conservative media, especially Rush Limbaugh, created a right-wing echo chamber that presented Reagan as a dogmatic conservative, see Kathleen Hall Jamieson and Joseph N. Cappella's *Echo Chamber: Rush Limbaugh and the Conservative Media Establishment* (Oxford: Oxford University Press, 2008).

14. Jane C. Timm, "Trump Campaign Struggles to Pull Off Minority Outreach Events," *NBC News*, July 29, 2016, http://www.nbcnews.com/politics/2016-election /trump-campaign-struggles-pull-minority-outreach-events-n619191.

15. It is difficult to find an ideological explanation for Trump's success. Trump is a populist politician who appeals to many Americans' hostility toward minorities, immigrants, and the effects of globalization. His candidacy is similar to Patrick

Buchanan's 1992 and 1996 campaigns, and Trump has even adopted Buchanan's slogan of "America First" to describe his worldview. There are also some similarities between Trump and billionaire businessman Ross Perot, who mounted a relatively successful third-party bid in 1992. Far from being conservatives' first choice, Trump seems to have appealed to the darkest elements of the American Right, similar to elements that William F. Buckley was able to separate mainstream conservatism from in the 1960s. For a detailed analysis on the far-Right in American politics, consult George Hawley's *Right-Wing Critics of American Conservatism* (Lawrence: University Press of Kansas, 2016), and Hawley's *Making Sense of the Alt-Right* (New York: Columbia University Press, 2017). A good primary source to better understand how some members of the alternative right understand conservatism is Richard E. Gottfried and Richard B. Spencer's compilation *The Great Purge: The Deformation of the Conservative Movement* (Whitefish, MT: Washington Summit Publishers, 2015). For a detailed history of conservative opposition to capitalism, consult Peter Kolozi's *Conservatives against Capitalism: From the Industrial Revolution to Globalization* (New York: Columbia University Press, 2017).

16. "First Reagan, Now His Stunt Double," *New York Times*, June 13, 2004, AR1.

17. Ron Reagan, "Eulogy for Father Ronald Reagan," June 14, 2004, http://americanrhetoric.com/speeches/ronreaganeulogyfordad.htm.

18. Dinesh D'Souza, "The Secret of His Success," *National Review* 56, no. 12 (June 28, 2004): 30–31.

19. Lawrence Kudlow, "Reaganomics," *National Review* 56, no. 12 (June 28, 2004): 28–29.

20. Rush Limbaugh, "The Great One," *National Review* 56, no. 12 (June 28, 2004): 36–37.

21. William F. Buckley, "Ronald Reagan 1911–2004: The Keynote Address," *National Review* 56, no. 12 (June 28, 2004): 14–17.

22. "Reagan for Today," editorial, *National Review* 56, no. 12 (June 28, 2004): 10.

23. Victor Davis Hansen, *National Review* 56, no. 12 (June 28, 2004): 20–22.

24. "Republican National Convention, Day 3," *C-Span*, September 1, 2004, http://c-span.org/video/?182730-1/republican-national-convention-day-3.

25. "Republican National Convention, Day 3."

26. "Republican National Convention, Day 3."

27. "Republican National Convention, Day 3."

28. In all, the book contained fifty-four contributions from Bob Dole, Robert Bartley, Martin Anderson, Rick Santorum, Trent Lott, Edwin Meese III, Henry Hyde, Phil Gramm, Paul Weyrich, Grover Norquist, Orrin G. Hatch, Mona Charen, Paul Ryan, Michael Deaver, and Robert Novak, among others. Michael Deaver, ed., *Why I Am a Reagan Conservative* (New York: William Marrow, 2005).

29. Deaver, *Why I Am a Reagan Conservative*, xv.

30. Robert D. Novak, "Government: Problem or Solution?," in Deaver, *Why I Am a Reagan Conservative*, 7.

31. Ken Mehlman, "I Believe in Freedom," in Deaver, *Why I am a Reagan Conservative*, 126–127. For an excellent description of how conservatives tied Reagan to Churchill, consult Niels Bjerre-Poulsen's chapter "The Road to Mount Rushmore: The Conservative Commemoration Crusade for Ronald Reagan," in *Ronald Reagan and the 1980s: Perceptions, Policies, Legacies*, ed. Cheryl Hudson and Gareth Davies (New York: Palgrave Macmillan, 2008), 210–227, especially 217–219. For a look at how conservatives connected Churchill and Reagan, see Steven F. Hayward's *Greatness: Reagan, Churchill, and the Making of Extraordinary Leaders* (New York: Crown, 2005).

32. Donald J. Devine, "All Other Political Philosophies Have Failed," in Deaver, *Why I Am a Reagan Conservative*, 115.

33. Edwin Meese III, "A Just and Prosperous Society," in Deaver, *Why I Am a Reagan Conservative*, 44.

34. Martin Anderson, "A Ringing Melody of Ideas," in Deaver, *Why I Am a Reagan Conservative*, 24–26.

35. Bush's proposal would have increased border security, provided a path to legal status for illegal immigrants who had lived in the United States for an extended period, and increased the number of guest workers allowed in the country. For a complete summary of the bill, see: "Summary: S.2611—109th Congress (2005–2006)," Library of Congress, *Congress.gov*, https://www.congress.gov/bill /109th-congress/senate-bill/02611.

36. Kyle Mantyla, "What Would Reagan Do?," *Right Wing Watch*, July 11, 2006, http://rightwingwatch.org/content/what-would-reagan-do. In many ways, the Bush proposal was similar to what Reagan signed into law in 1986. After the passage of the Immigration Reform and Control Act of 1986, the Reagan administration viewed the legislation as a success. Ed Meese received a memo detailing the achievements of Immigration and Naturalization Services in May 1988, which listed the act as a major accomplishment. In addition to granting citizenship to millions of undocumented immigrants, the memo described the creation of more than 1,800 new border agents from 1985 to 1988 and $3.3 million invested in new facilities, equipment, and technology for border enforcement. Only later did conservatives begin to view the measures taken in 1986 as a failure—largely because they failed to end illegal entry into the United States despite increased funding for border security. "Major INS Accomplishments: February 25, 1985 to the Present, Enhanced Border Enforcement," Ed Meese Papers, box 113, "INS Accomplishments, 1985–1988" folder, Hoover Institution Archives, Stanford University, Stanford, California. Reagan's bill was not soft on control measures as future conservatives would claim. Indeed, it was the 1986 legislation that made it so that

"for the first time, Americans will be required to prove who they are before they are allowed to work." Much of the burden was placed on employers, who were required to have new employees fill out a new form—the I-9. According to the *Christian Science Monitor*, "immigration experts consider" the INS draft rules to be "tough." Ultimately, many employers got around the new measures by using subcontractors for hiring. "New Immigration Law Sweeps Wide: Anyone in US Seeking a Job Has to Have Proof of Legal Status," *Christian Science Monitor*, January 22, 1987, 3, Ed Meese Papers, box 113, "INS/Hiring Practices" folder, Hoover Institution Archives.

37. Edwin Meese, "Reagan Would Not Repeat Amnesty Mistake," *Human Events*, December 13, 2006,http://humanevents.com/2006/12/13/Reagan-would -not-repeat-amnesty-mistake, August 8, 2016. Interestingly, following the Immigration Reform and Control Act of 1986, undocumented immigration flows from Mexico to the United States declined and did not increase significantly until after the financial crisis in Mexico in 1995. My analysis is based on the charts from the US Department of Homeland Security provided by Federico. S. Mandelman in "The Slump in Undocumented Immigration in the United States," October 5, 2016, http://economistview.typepad.com/economistview/2016/10/the-slump-in-un documented-immigration-to-the-united-states.html, accessed August 10, 2016. To his credit, Meese seemed to be aware that further measures might be necessary to secure the southern border, which was becoming more of a problem during the late 1980s and 1990s. In 1986, Meese asserted, "The large number of non-Mexican illegal aliens being apprehended illustrates the fact that our southern border is becoming an area of preference among those seeking to enter the United States illegally from around the world." "Record Number of Illegal Aliens Captured," *Washington Post*, September 20, 1986, A12, Ed Meese Papers, box 113, "INS/Apprehension of Illegal Aliens" folder, Hoover Institution Archives.

38. Meese, "Reagan Would Not Repeat Amnesty Mistake." Meese is correct that it is impossible to know how Reagan would have viewed comprehensive immigration reform in 2006. On signing the Immigration Reform and Control Act of 1986, Reagan declared:

> In 1981 this administration asked Congress to pass a comprehensive legislative
> package, including employer sanctions, other measures to increase enforcement of the
> immigration laws, and legalization. The act provides these three essential components.
> The employer sanctions program is the keystone and major element. It will remove
> the incentive for illegal immigration by eliminating the job opportunities which draw
> illegal aliens here. We have consistently supported a legalization program which is
> both generous to the alien and fair to countless thousands of people throughout the
> world who seek legally to come to America. The legalization provisions in this act

will go far to improve the lives of a class of individuals who now must hide in the shadows, without access to many of the benefits of a free and open society. Very soon many of these men and women will be able to step into the sunlight and, ultimately, if they choose, they may become Americans.

Reagan concluded that the bill was the result of long and "difficult" negotiations but was ultimately "a bipartisan effort" in which "both parties" worked together. He insisted that "future generations of Americans will be thankful for our efforts to humanely regain control of our borders and thereby preserve the value of one of the most sacred possessions of our people: American citizenship." Ronald Reagan, "Statement on Signing of Immigration Reform and Control Act of 1986," November 6, 1986, http://reaganlibrary.archives.gov/archives/speeches /1986/110686B .htm, accessed August 11, 2016.

39. "Conservative Leadership Declaration Opposing Amnesty/'Guest Worker' Proposals," June 19, 2006, http://howardphillips.com/archive0606.htm; "Conservative Leadership Declaration Opposing Amnesty/'Guest Worker Proposals," June 19,2006,http://eagleforum.org/topics/amnesty/final-declaration.pdf;KevinCarter, "Some Conservatives Making Immigration Their Top Concern," June 29, 2006, http://www.vdare.com/posts/some-conservatives-making-immigration-their -top-concern.

40. Meese, "Reagan Would Not Repeat Amnesty Mistake."

41. "House Minority Leader John Boehner Calls Immigration Bill 'Piece of S---,'" *Fox News*, May 23, 2007, http://foxnews.com/story/2007/05/23/house-mi nority-leader-john-boehner-calls-immigration-bill-piece-s.html, accessed August 13, 2016.

42. Viguerie, *Takeover*, 155.

43. Viguerie, *Takeover*; Richard A. Viguerie, *Conservatives Betrayed: How George W. Bush and Other Big Government Republicans Hijacked the Conservative Cause* (Los Angeles: Bonus Books, 2006); Patrick J. Buchanan, *Where the Right Went Wrong: How Neoconservatives Subverted the Reagan Revolution and Hijacked the Bush Presidency* (New York: St. Martin's Press, 2004); Michael D. Tanner, *Leviathan on the Right: How Big-Government Conservatism Brought Down the Republican Revolution* (Washington, DC: Cato Institute, 2007). There are also several examples in Deaver, *Why I am a Reagan Conservative*. Bruce J. Schulman and Julian E. Zelizer touch on conservative discontent with Bush in the epilogue to *Rightward Bound: Making America Conservative in the 1970s* (Cambridge, MA: Harvard University Press, 2008), 289–293.

44. Ann Coulter, "What Would Reagan Do?," September 21, 2005, http://www .anncoulter.com/columns/2005-09-21.html.

45. Rebecca Hagelin, "What Would Reagan Do?," January 9, 2008, http://

townhall.com/columnists/rebeccahagelin/2008/01/09/what_would_reagan_do, accessed August 20, 2016.

46. Patricia Cohen, "Conservative Thinkers Think Again," *New York Times*, July 20, 2008, http://www.nytimes.com/2008/07/20/weekinreview/20cohen.html ?pagewanted=&_r=2, accessed August 20, 2016.

47. Jennifer Hoar, "What Does 'Reagan Republican' Mean in '07?," *Weekly Standard*, May 25, 2007, http://www.cbsnews.com/news/what-does-reagan-repub lican-mean-in-07/.

48. Hagelin, "What Would Reagan Do?"

49. Hagelin, "What Would Reagan Do?"

50. Hoar, "What Does 'Reagan Republican' Mean in '07?"

51. Patricia Cohen, "Conservative Thinkers Think Again," *New York Times*, July 20, 2008, http://www.nytimes.com /2008/07/20/weekinreview/20cohen.html?pagewanted=&_r=2.

52. Frum, *Comeback*, 4–5.

53. Frum, *Comeback*, 16.

54. Frum, *Comeback*, 29.

55. For more on how conservative commentators link their political opponents and their opinions to the "mainstream media" see Jamieson and Cappella's *Echo Chamber*.

56. Hannity, *Conservative Victory*, 151.

57. Hannity, *Conservative Victory*, 153–154.

58. Hannity, *Conservative Victory*, 69. Indeed, the first half of the book is dedicated to outlining how radical President Barack Obama was and demonstrating his ties to Marxists and other left-wing radicals.

59. Hannity, *Conservative Victory*, 148.

60. Hannity, *Conservative Victory*, 151–154.

61. Hannity, *Conservative Victory*, 4. Time has seemingly confirmed Hannity's claims. From 2010 to 2016, Republicans dominated the Democrats at the local, state, and federal level. Although President Obama won reelection in 2012, his party lost power at all levels of government during his presidency. "GOP Dominates across America: Just 4 States Have Dem Legislature, Governor," *Conservative News*, November 14, 2016, http://www.conservativenews.com/article /609/gop -dominate-across-america, accessed August 21, 2016; Sheryl Gay Stolberg, Michael D. Shear, and Alan Blinder, "In Obama Era, G.O.P. Bolsters Grip in the States," *New York Times*, November 12, 2015, http://www.nytimes.com/2015/11/13/us/politics /obama-legacy-in-state-offices-a-shrinking-democratic-share.html?_r=0.

CHAPTER 14. RESURRECTING REAGAN: THE TEA
PARTY MOVEMENT AND THE MANIFESTATION OF THE
REAGAN MYTH, 2008–2016

1. Ronald P. Formisano, *The Tea Party: A Brief History* (Baltimore: Johns Hopkins University Press, 2012), 9–13; Rand Paul, *The Tea Party Goes to Washington* (New York: Center Street, 2011), 7.

2. The activists who were, and are, a part of the Tea Party movement were a diverse set of individuals who shared a common concern about the direction of the country. Kate Zernike's *Boiling Mad: Inside Tea Party America* (New York: Times Books, 2010), details these differences by providing specific examples of Tea Party activists from Seattle to Philadelphia. For a nuanced portrayal of Tea Party activists, see Theda Skocpol and Vanessa Williamson's *The Tea Party and the Remaking of Republican Conservatism* (Oxford: Oxford University Press, 2012).

3. For a full video of Santelli's denunciation of the Homeowner Affordability and Stability Plan see "Rick Santelli's 'Rant of the Year,'" *The Chattanooga Tea Party*, April 6, 2009, http://www.chattanoogateaparty.com/rick-santellis-rant-of-the-year/. Quoted in Michael Reagan's *The New Reagan Revolution: How Ronald Reagan's Principles Can Restore America's Greatness* (New York: Thomas Dunne Books, 2010), 47.

4. Formisano, *The Tea Party*, 27; Alan I. Abramowitz, "Grand Old Tea Party: Partisan Polarization and the Rise of the Tea Party Movement," in Lawrence Rosenthal and Christine Trost, *Steep: The Precipitous Rise of the Tea Party* (Berkeley: University of California Press, 2012), 195. The extent to which the Tea Party was a grassroots movement is at the center of the emerging historiography on the movement. This issue is explored at length in Street and DiMaggio's *Crashing the Tea Party* and in Clarence Y. H. Lo's "Astroturf versus Grass Roots: Scenes from Early Tea Party Mobilization," in Rosenthal and Trost, *Steep*, 98–129. Lawrence Rosenthal and Christine Trost's compilation offers the most comprehensive analysis of the Tea Party. It includes articles on race, women, political polarization, and religion and their place in the Tea Party movement.

5. Richard Viguerie, *Takeover: The 100 Year War for the Soul of the GOP and How Conservatives Can Finally Win It* (Washington, DC: WND Books, 2014), 189–190.

6. Formisano, *The Tea Party*, 39.

7. Alexandra Moe, "Just 32% of Tea Party Candidates Win," *NBC News*, November 3, 2010, http://firstread.nbcnews.com/_news/2010/11/03/5403120-just -32-of-tea-party-candidates-win. Senators Marco Rubio and Rand Paul offer their perspective on how they defeated the Republican establishment in their primaries and went on to become senators in their memoirs: Marco Rubio, *An*

American Son: A Memoir (New York: Sentinel, 2012); Paul, *The Tea Party Goes to Washington*.

8. Viguerie, *Takeover*, 194–195.

9. E. J. Dionne Jr., *Why the Right Went Wrong: Conservatism from Goldwater to the Tea Party and Beyond* (New York: Simon & Schuster, 2016), 321.

10. Warner Todd Houston, "Ronald Reagan: Father of the Tea Party," *Right Wing News*, February 6, 2011, rightwingnews.com/republicans/ronald-reagan-father-of-the-tea-party.

11. Michael E. Reagan, "Ronald Reagan Was the Tea Party," *Michael E. Reagan.Com*, October 27, 2010, http://michaelereagan.com/ronald-reagan-was-the-tea-party.

12. Steven F. Hayward, "Would Reagan Vote for Sarah Palin," *Washington Post*, March 7, 2010, http://washingtonpost.com/wp-dyn/content/article/2010/03/05/AR2010030501553.html?sid=st2010030502844.

13. Alex Seitz-Wald, "Huckabee: Reagan Would Have a 'Very Difficult, if Not Impossible Time Getting Nominated Today," *Think Progress*, May 6, 2011, https://thinkprogress.org/huckabee-reagan-would-have-a-very-difficult-if-not-impossible-time-getting-nominated-today-d4d2b108c054#.nslvy83he.

14. Lee Fang, "Rep. Duncan Hunter: Ronald Reagan 'Would Never Be Elected Today' Because He's a 'Moderate/Former Liberal,'" *Think Progress*, July 5, 2011, https://thinkprogress.org/rep-duncan-hunter-ronald-reagan-would-never-be-elected-today-because-he-s-a-moderate-former-liberal-a84f97ad6159#.obfgbqm24.

15. "Sen. Bennett Loses GOP Nomination," *Politico*, May 8, 2010, http://www.politico.com/story/ 2010/05/sen-bennett-loses-gop-nomination-036960, accessed September 21, 2016; Seitz-Wald, "Huckabee."

16. Newt Gingrich, "Like Father, Like Son," foreword to Michael Reagan's *The New Reagan Revolution*, xiii–xiv.

17. Michael Reagan, *The New Reagan Revolution*, 63.

18. Michael Reagan, *The New Reagan Revolution*, 93.

19. Michael Reagan, *The New Reagan Revolution*, 96–97.

20. Michael Reagan, *The New Reagan Revolution*, 66–67.

21. Paul Ryan, Eric Cantor, and Kevin McCarthy, *Young Guns: A New Generation of Conservative Leaders* (New York: Threshold Editions, 2010).

22. Formisano, *The Tea Party*, 2.

23. Dionne, *Why the Right Went Wrong*, 321–322; Bob Woodward, "Bob Woodward: The Inside Story of How Obama and Boehner Negotiate," *Washington Post*, September 6, 2013.

24. Ironically, the Tea Party under John Boehner's leadership was tremendously successful, even if many Tea Party conservatives did not realize or appreciate it. As

of 2012, federal spending growth under President Obama was at its slowest pace since President Dwight D. Eisenhower was in office. The fiscal conservatism of the Obama administration was largely forced upon the president by Speaker Boehner. Despite the Tea Party's dislike for Boehner, he was successful in forcing President Obama to accept caps and cuts to federal spending in 2011, and his refusal to fund the government to the levels that administration requested slowed the budget deficit. Furthermore, the Speaker helped make the Bush tax cuts permanent for most Americans—fighting off what would have been a dramatic tax increase by the Obama administration. The Foundation for Economic Education, in an article detailing Boehner's speakership after he resigned, concluded: "So was Boehner a pushover, a failure, a weak-negotiator? Hardly. He took the president to the wall numerous times over spending restraint. What's more, he actually managed to get real spending cuts for the first time in decades." Daniel Bier, "John Boehner Really Did Beat Obama on Budget Cuts," *Foundation for Economic Education*, September 28, 2015, https://fee.org/articles/john-boehners-biggest-accomplish -fighting-obama-on-spending/; "Who Is the Smallest Government Spender Since Eisenhower? Would You Believe It's Barack Obama?," *Forbes*, May 24, 2012, http:// www.forbes.com/sites/rickungar/2012/05/24/who-is-the-smallest-government -spender-since-eisenhower-would-you-believe-its-barack-obama/#1d29b3fe57ec.

25. "Ronald Reagan Myth Doesn't Square with Reality," *CBS News*, February 4, 2011,http://cbsnews.com/news/ronald-reagan-myth-doesn't-square-with-reality, accessed September 23, 2016.

26. "GOP Aims to Tame Benefits Programs," *Wall Street Journal*, March 4, 2011, http://www.wsj.com/articles/SB10001424052748703752404576178910828355914. For the most detailed analysis of how President Obama and Speaker Boehner negotiated see Bob Woodward's *The Price of Politics* (New York: Simon & Schuster, 2013).

27. Dionne, *Why the Right Went Wrong*, 327.

28. The commission ultimately failed to do so, thus triggering the sequester— automatic spending cuts to both domestic and military spending—in 2013. Dionne, *Why the Right Went Wrong*, 331.

29. Thomas E. Mann and Norman J. Ornstein, "Let's Just Say It: The Republicans Are the Problem," *Washington Post*, April 27, 2012, https://www.washington post. com/opinions/lets-just-say-it-the-republicans-are-the-problem/2012/04/27/gI QAxCVUlT_story.html?utm_term=.c809d51a5a57, accessed September 23, 2016.

30. Viguerie, *Takeover*, 207.

31. John Bresnahan, "Dysfunctional Congress 'Worse' Than Ever?," *Politico*, June 11, 2012, http://www.politico.com/news/stories/0611/58076_Page2.html, accessed September 25, 2016.

32. "Mitt Romney Channels Ronald Reagan," *Washington Post*, June 2, 2011,

https://www.washingtonpost.com/blogs/the-fix/post/mitt-romney-channels
-ronald-reagan/2011/06/02/ AGxiQOHH_blog.html, accessed September 25, 2016.

33. "Mitt Romney in Talks over Nationwide Version of Tough State Immi-gration Laws," *Guardian*, February 24, 2012, https://www.theguardian.com/world/2012/feb/24/kris-kobach-immigration-law-mastermind.

34. Mona Charen, "Why Romney Lost the Hispanic Vote," *National Review*, November 9, 2012, http://www.nationalreview.com/article/333033/why-romney-lost-hispanic-vote-mona-charen.

35. Charen, " Why Romney Lost the Hispanic Vote."

36. John Parkinson, "Boehner: Raising Tax Rates 'Unacceptable,'" *ABC News*, November 8, 2012, http://abcnews.go.com/Politics/boehner-exclusive-raising-tax-rates-unacceptable-revenue-table/story?id=17672947.

37. Shushannah Walshe, "RNC Completes 'Autopsy' on 2012 Loss, Calls for Inclusion Not Policy Change," *ABC News*, March 18, 2013, http://abcnews.go.com/Politics/OTUS/rnc-completes-autopsy-2012-loss-calls-inclusion-policy/story?id=18755809. For the full autopsy see the "Growth and Opportunity Project," Republican National Committee, March 17, 2014, http://goproject.gop.com/.

38. Principled conservatives such as Phyllis Schlafly condemned the autopsy. Schlafly decried "the chatter about 'growth' and 'opportunity,'" explaining that "the need to be more 'inclusive' . . . did not extend to those who want to talk about the right to life or traditional marriage." Schlafly added that "the most insuffer-able part of the Autopsy's advice is the admonition to embrace comprehensive immigration 'reform.'" She concluded that "massive evidence collected by Eagle Forum from the leading pollsters proves that endorsing or legislating any form of amnesty will produce votes for Democrats, not Republicans." Phyllis Schlafly, *A Choice Not an Echo: 50th Anniversary Edition* (New York: Regnery, 2014), 256–257.

39. Rachel Weiner, "Sean Hannity: I've 'Evolved' on Immigration," *Washington Post*, November 8, 2012, https://www.washingtonpost.com/news/post-politics/wp/2012/11/08/sean-hannity-ive-evolved-on-immigration/; Mackenzie Weinger, "Hannity: I've 'Evolved' on Immigration and Support a 'Pathway to Citizenship,'" *Politico*, November 8, 2012, http://www.politico.com/blogs/media/2012/11/hannity-ive-evolved-on-immigration-and-support-a-pathway-to-cit izenship-149078; Liz Goodwin, "Sean Hannity, John Boehner Say GOP Should Tackle Immigration Reform," *Yahoo News*, November 9, 2012, https://www.yahoo.com/news/blogs/ticket/sean-hannity-john-boehner-gop-tackle-immigration-re form-142212570--election.html.

40. Anna Navarro, "Monkeys evolved into humans. Hannity has evolved on immigration. Keeping hope alive." *Twitter*, November 8, 2012, https://twitter.com/ananavarro/status/ 266697131782467584, accessed September 28, 2016; Weinger, "Sean Hannity."

41. In 2014, President Obama used Hannity's words against opponents of comprehensive immigration reform. Obama recalled that "in 2012, Latinos voted in record numbers. The next day, even Sean Hannity changed his mind and decided reform was a good idea." Although what the president said was largely correct, Hannity took exception to Obama's implying that Hannity had supported the specific policies that were on the table in 2014. The conservative commentator declared, "That's not what I said. Interview after interview, I've said what I've said for years: Secure the border first. And I said, this is being used as a weapon by the left and take it out of their hands by securing the borders, and then you deal with the 11 million people after. An no one has ever supported, ever, executive orders, which is what he is planning." "Sean Hannity Calls Out Obama for Citing Him on Immigration Reform Pitch: 'That's Not What I Said,'" *Blaze*, October 3, 2014, http:// www.theblaze.com/stories/2014/10/03/sean-hannity-calls-out-obama-after-he -cited-him-in-immigration-reform-pitch-thats-not-what-i-said/, accessed September 28, 2016.

42. Jeffrey Lord, "When Conservatism Is a Second Language," *American Spectator*, November 8, 2012, http://spectator.org/34459_when-conservatism-second -language/, accessed October 3, 2016.

43. Rush Limbaugh, "Why Did Three Million Republicans Stay Home?," November 8, 2012, http://www.rushlimbaugh.com/daily/2012/11/08/why_did_three _million_republicans_stay_hom.

44. Andrew C. McCarthy, "The Voters Who Stayed Home," *National Review*, November 10, 2012, http://www.nationalreview.com/article/333135/voters -who-stayed-home-andrew-c-mccarthy; "What Went Wrong in 2012? The Case of the 4 Million Missing Voters," *Red State*, November 14, 2012, http://www.red state.com/diary/griffinelection/2012/11/14/what-went-wrong-in-2012-the-case-of -the-4-million-missing-voters/. Other conservatives dismissed these claims and demonstrated that they are based on faulty math. Karl Rove, "The Myth of the Stay-at-Home Republicans," *Wall Street Journal*, April 1, 2015, http://www.wsj .com/articles/karl-rove-the-myth-of-the-stay-at-home-republicans-1427930037; Dan McLaughlin, "The Myth of '4 Million Conservative Voters Stayed Home in 2012,'" *Red State*, November 26, 2015, http://www.redstate.com/dan_mclaugh lin/2015/11/26/myth -4-million-conservative-voters-stayed-home-2012/.

45. Erik Eckholm, "A Republican Voice with Tea Party Mantle and Intellectual Heft," *New York Times*, August 1, 2012, http://www.nytimes.com/2012/08/02/us /politics/republican-senate-candidate-in-texas-is-known-as-an-intellectual -force.html?_r=0.

46. Viguerie, *Takeover*, 236–237.

47. Ted Cruz, *A Time for Truth: Reigniting the Promise of America* (New York: Broadside Books, 2015), 129.

48. Morton C. Blackwell, "An Open Letter to U.S. House and Senate Republicans," *Red State*, November 30, 2012, http://www.redstate.com/diary/morton_c_blackwell/2012/11/30/an-open-letter-to-u-s-house-and-senate-republicans/. Over 140 conservative activists signed the letter including Morton Blackwell, president of the Leadership Institute; Ed Meese, Conservative Action Project; Phyllis Schlafly, president of Eagle Forum; Erick Erickson, editor at Red State; Brent Bozell, For America; Gary Bauer, president of America Values; and Richard Viguerie, chairman of Conservative HQ.

49. For a complete analysis of the negotiations, see Bob Woodward's *The Price of Politics* (New York: Simon & Schuster, 2013).

50. Peter Wehner, "The Jacobin Right," *Commentary*, November 13, 2014, https://www.commentarymagazine.com/politics-ideas/conservatives-republicans/the-jacobin-right/.

51. Alexander Mallin, "Ronald Reagan: Dead for a Decade, 'Alive and Well' at CPAC," *ABC News*, March 7, 2014, http://abcnews.go.com/blogs/politics/2014/03/ronald-reagan-dead-for-a-decade-alive-and-well-at-cpac/.

52. "Cruz Tell CPAC: 'Stand on Principle,'" *Politico*, March 3, 2014, http://www.politico.com/story /2014/03/ted-cruz-cpac-2014-104345, accessed October 4, 2016.

53. Emily Schultheis, "Rubio: No Global Power for Obama," *Politico*, March 6, 2014, http://www.politico.com/story/2014/03/marco-rubio-cpac-2014-104364.

54. Andrew Kirell, "Rand Paul's Starkly Libertarian CPAC Speech: We Must Defend the Rights of All," *Mediaite*, March 7, 2014, http://www.mediaite.com/tv/rand-pauls-starkly-libertarian-cpac-speech-we-must-defend-the-rights-of-all/.

55. Lindsey Boerma, "Rand Paul Still on Top, and Other Takeaways from CPAC 2014," *CBS News*, March 8, 2014, http://www.cbsnews.com/news/rand-paul-still-on-top-and-other-takeaways-from-cpac-2014/.

56. Evan McMurry, "Cruz Bashes Obama, Rand Paul: 'When U.S. Doesn't Stand for Freedom, Tyrants Notice,'" *Mediaite*, March 9, 2014, http://www.mediaite.com/tv/cruz-bashes-obama-rand-paul-when-u-s-doesnt-stand-for-freedom-tyrants-notice/.

57. Rand Paul, "Exclusive Rand Paul: Stop Warping Reagan's Foreign Policy," *Breitbart*, March 10, 2014, http://www.breitbart.com/national-security/2014/03/10/rand-paul-reagans-foreign-policy/.

58. Matt K. Lewis, *Too Dumb to Fail: How the GOP Betrayed the Reagan Revolution to Win Elections (and How It Can Reclaim Its Conservative Roots)* (New York: Hachette Books, 2016), 33–34.

59. Lewis, *Too Dumb to Fail*, 118–121.

60. Arthur C. Brooks, *The Conservative Heart: How to Build a Fairer, Happier, and More Prosperous America* (New York: Broadway Books, 2015), 74, 193.

61. Brooks, *The Conservative Heart*, 192.

62. Brooks, *The Conservative Heart*, 171.

63. Michael Scherer, "The Most Interesting Man in Politics: The Reinventions of Rand Paul," *Time*, October 27, 2014, 30.

64. Morton C. Blackwell, "Please Join Me in Supporting Ted Cruz," *Red State*, January 11, 2016, http://www.redstate.com/diary/Morton_C_Blackwell/2016/01/11/please-join-supporting-ted-cruz/.

65. Media Matters Staff, "Sean Hannity: Ted Cruz is 'A Reagan-Conservative Constitutionalist . . . How Could I Not Admire That,'" *Media Matters*, February 22, 2016, http://mediamatters.org/video/2016/02/22/sean-hannity-ted-cruz-is-a-reagan-conservative/208729.

66. Anna Giaritelli, "Nancy Reagan Inspires Mark Levin's Presidential Pick," *Washington Examiner*, March 9, 2016, http://www.washingtonexaminer.com/nancy-reagan-inspires-mark-levins-presidential-pick/article/2585408.

67. "Glenn Beck Explains Why He Is Endorsing Ted Cruz, Reacts to Trump's Attacks," *Fox News*, January 25, 2016, http://www.foxnews.com/transcript/2016/01/25/glenn-beck-explains-why-is-endorsing-ted-cruz-reacts-to-trump-attacks/, accessed October 5, 2016.

68. Kyle Mantyla, "Beck: Ted Cruz 'May Be Our Ronald Reagan,'" *Right Wing Watch*, December 18, 2013, http://www.rightwingwatch.org/content/beck-ted-cruz-may-be-our-ronald-reagan.

69. James Forsythe, "Glenn Beck Weeps and Tells Crowd That Ted Cruz Will Get Them through the Rapture," *Dead State*, February 14, 2016, http://www.deadstate.org/glenn-beck-weeps-and-tells-crowd-that-the-ted-cruz-will-get-them-through-the-rapture/.

70. "Glenn Beck Just Told His Listeners That Americans Will Be Guilty of This if They Don't Elect Ted Cruz," *Western Journal*, March 19, 2016, http://www.westernjournal.com/glenn-beck-just-told-his-listeners-that-americans-will-be-guilty-of-this-if-they-dont-elect-ted-cruz/, accessed October 5, 2016.

71. Ross Douthat, "The Defeat of True Conservatism," *New York Times*, May 5, 2016, http://www.nytimes.com/2016/05/04/opinion/campaign-stops/the-defeat-of-true-conservatism.html?comments&_r=1.

72. Michelle Ye Hee Lee, "Donald Trump's False Comments Connecting Mexican Immigrants and Crime," *Washington Post*, July 8, 2015, https://www.washingtonpost.com/news/fact-checker/wp/2015/07/08/donald-trumps-false-comments-connecting-mexican-immigrants-and-crime/. Indeed, a large number of conservatives embraced the "Never-Trump" movement and even ran ads against the billionaire businessman. One of these ads, titled "Follow Your Conscience," juxtaposed Reagan calmly and presidentially addressing issues to Trump's erratic behavior. Delegates Unbound, "Follow Your Conscience," *YouTube.com*, June 26,

2016, https://www.youtube.com/watch?feature=player_embedded&v=tFlgP1hnU
10&app=desktop.

73. Nick Gass, "O'Reilly Attacks Trump for Boosting 'Operation Wetback,'"
Politico, November 12, 2015, http://www.politico.com/story/2015/11/donald-trump
-immigration-deportation-215783; Sandra Lilley, "Trump's Immigration Solution: Bring Back Controversial 'Operation Wetback,'" *NBC News*, November 12,
2015, http://www.nbcnews.com/news/latino/trumps-immigration-solution-bring
-back-controversial-operation-wetback-n461381; M. J. Lee, "Why Some Conservatives Say Trump Talk is Fascist," *CNN Politics*, November 25, 2015, http://www
.cnn.com/2015/11/24/politics/donald-trump-fascism/index.html; "Trump Pushes
Expanded Ban on Muslims Entering the U.S.," *Washington Post*, June 13, 2016,
https://www.washingtonpost.com/politics/trump-pushes-expanded-ban-on
-muslims-and-other-foreigners/2016/06/13/c9988e96-317d-11e6-8ff7-7b6c1998
b7a0_story.html?utm_term=.cc556f51f10b, accessed October 5, 2016.

74. John McCormack, "Would Donald Trump Be a Pro-Abortion President?," *Weekly Standard*, January 17, 2016. http://www.weeklystandard.com
/would-donald-trump-be-a-pro-abortion-president/article/2000619; Matt Vespa,
"Trump Pretty Much Says He Supports Universal Health Care during 60 Minutes Interview," *Townhall*, September 28, 2015, http://townhall.com/tipsheet
/mattvespa/2015/09/28/trump-60-minutes-interview-n2057986; Michael Patrick Leahy, "Exclusive: Donald Trump Pushes Back against Critics of His Eminent Domain Position," *Breitbart*, October 8, 2015, http://www.breitbart.com/big
-government/2015/10/08/exclusive-donald-trump-pushes-back-critics-eminent
-domain-position/; Damon Root, "Donald Trump Trashes the Constitution,
Endorses Eminent Domain Abuse," *Reason*, October 8, 2015, https://reason.com
/blog/2015/10/08/donald-trump-trashes-the-constitution-en; Betsy Woodruff,
"Christians Cringe at Donald Trump's Sexy Past," *Daily Beast*, January 26, 2016,
http://www.thedailybeast.com/articles/2016/01/27/christians-cringe-at-donald
-trump-s-sexy-past.html; Jeremy Diamond and Daniella Diaz, "Trump on Sex
Assault Allegations: 'I am a Victim,'" *CNN*, October 15, 2016, http://www.cnn
.com/2016/10/14/politics/donald-trump-sexual-assault-allegations/index.html.

75. Although most conservatives did not embrace Trump during the primaries, many of them embraced him in the general election against Secretary Clinton. Ann Coulter, Phyllis Schlafly, Sarah Palin, Senator Jeff Sessions, Reverend
Jerry Falwell Jr., former Speaker of the House Newt Gingrich, and Jeffery Lord
were prominent exceptions. Both Coulter and Schlafly wrote books endorsing
Trump. Ann Coulter, *In Trump We Trust: E Pluribus Awesome!* (New York: Sentinel, 2016); Phyllis Schlafly, Ed Martin, and Brett M. Decker, *The Conservative Case
for Trump* (Washington, DC: Regnery, 2016).

CONCLUSION. BEYOND REAGAN?

1. Maxwell Tani, "Donald Trump Shocks World, Wins Presidential Election in Biggest Upset in Political History," *Business Insider*, November 9, 2016, http://www.businessinsider.com/donald-trump-wins-election-results-2016-11.

2. Zoe Szathmary and Jay Akbar, "Trump Takes Over the Manhattan Skyline," *Daily Mail*, November 9, 2016, http://www.dailymail.co.uk/news/article-3918754/Lighting-election-Empire-State-Building-turns-live-results-tracker-dazzling-display-Hillary-Trump-face-race-White-House.html?ITO=1490.

3. "Hillary Clinton Supporters Leave New York Election Night Party in Tears," *Huffington Post*, November 9, 2016, http://www.huffingtonpost.com/entry/hillary-clinton-supporters-election_us_5822aad3e4b0d9ce6fbfe13c, accessed November 20, 2016.

4. Adam DeRose, "Experts Review What Went Wrong with Presidential Polling," *Arizona Daily Sun*, November 12, 2016, http://azdailysun.com/news/local/experts-review-what-went-wrong-with-presidential-polling/article_99be1786-b68d-53fb-8c3e-78ed9d4d9c60.html; Matt Taibbi, "President Trump: How America Got it So Wrong," *Rolling Stone*, November 10, 2016, http://www.rollingstone.com/politics/features/president-trump-how-america-got-it-so-wrong-w449783.

5. Ruadhán Mac Cormaic, "Republicans Now Falling into Line behind President-Elect," *Irish Times*, November 11, 2016, http://www.irishtimes.com/news/world/us/republicans-now-falling-into-line-behind-president-elect-1.2866551.

6. Lee Edwards, "Trump's Victory Present's a Golden Opportunity for Conservatism," *Daily Signal*, November 10, 2016, http://dailysignal.com/2016/11/10/trumps-victory-presents-a-golden-opportunity-for-conservatism/.

7. Chriss W. Street, "Stock Market Crash Anticipating Trump's Win: Just Like Reagan," *Breitbart*, November 9, 2016, http://www.breitbart.com/2016-presidential-race/2016/11/09/stock-market-crash-trumps-win-just-like-reagan/.

8. "Krauthammer: 'This Is an Electoral Revolution Not Seen since Reagan,'" *Fox News Insider*, November 8, 2016, http://insider.foxnews.com/2016/11/08/krauthammer-big-trump-night-electoral-revolution-not-seen-reagan; Ian Schwartz, "Krauthammer: Trump an Ideological Revolution Not Seen Since Reagan, Part of 'Worldwide Brexit Movement,'" *Real Clear Politics*, November 9, 2016, http://www.realclearpolitics.com/video/2016/11/09/krauthammer_trump_an_ideologically_revolution_not_seen_since_reagan_part_of_worldwide_brexit_movement.html.

9. The most glaring difference was Trump's opposition to free trade, and the North Atlantic Free Trade Agreement, which Reagan supported. Trump's tone was often dark and menacing compared to Reagan's optimistic approach. Likewise, Trump's insistence on deporting millions of "illegal aliens" who beyond

entering the country illegally were law-abiding Americans was very different from Reagan's insistence that the United States grant those living in the shadows legal status in 1986.

10. "READ: Donald Trump's Acceptance Speech," *U.S. News*, July 21, 2016, http://www.usnews.com/news/articles/2016-07-21/read-donald-trumps-nomina tion-acceptance-speech-at-the-republican-convention.

11. "Hillary Clinton DNC Speech: Full Text," *CNN*, July 29, 2016, http://www .cnn.com/2016/07/28/politics/hillary-clinton-speech-prepared-remarks-tran script/index.html.

12. "Transcript: President Obama's Democratic National Convention Speech," *Los Angeles Times*, July 27, 2016.

13. Katie Glueck, "Clinton Decries Trump's 'Midnight in America,'" *Politico*, July 28, 2016, http://www.politico.com/story/2016/07/dnc-2016-hillary-clinton -speech-exerpts-226394.

14. Margaret Hartmann, "Obama Taunts GOP on Iran Deal by Comparing Himself to Reagan," *New York Magazine*, July 14, 2015, http://nymag.com/daily/in telligencer/2015/07/obama-taunts-gop-on-iran-with-reagan-reference.html; Rory Carroll, "The Myth of Ronald Reagan: Pragmatic Moderate or Radical Conserva- tive?," *Guardian*, September 19, 2015, https://www.theguardian.com/us-news/2015 /sep/19/political-myth-ronald-reagan-republican-moderate-conservative.

15. Carroll, "The Myth of Ronald Reagan." For images of the posters that the Clinton campaign produced see: Guardian reporter Sabrina Siddiqui, "Clinton Camp HQ Contrasting Reagan vs. Current GOP Candidates on the Issues at Its Debate Filing Center," *Twitter*, September 16, 2015, https://twitter.com/Sabrina Siddiqui/status/644292379713904641, accessed November 21, 2016.

16. Erik Wemple, "Jeffrey Lord, CNN's Very Own Trump Apologist, Strikes Again," *Washington Post*, September 18, 2015, https://www.washingtonpost.com /blogs/erik-wemple/wp/2015/09/18/jeffrey-lord-cnns-very-own-trump-apologist -strikes-again/?utm_term=.5f5a054a07fe.

17. Jeffrey Lord, "Trump and the Reagan-Bush Divide," *American Spectator*, August 6, 2015, http://spectator.org/63706_trump-and-reagan-bush-divide/.

18. Elizabeth F. Ralph, "'Look in the Mirror Fatboy:' Ronald Reagan's Sons Discuss Donald Trump and 2016," *Politico*, September 16, 2016, http://www.po litico.com/magazine/story/2015/09/reagan-sons-interview-donald-trump-213149.

19. Peter Wehner, "The Party of Reagan Is No More," *Time Magazine*, March 9, 2016, http://time.com/4253747/the-party-of-reagan-is-no-more/. Some com- mentators also asserted that Trump's nomination marked the end of the Tea Party Movement. In August 2016, Paul Jossey declared that "the Tea Party move- ment is pretty much dead now . . . it was murdered—and it was an inside job." Jossey asserted that "greedy super PACS drained the movement with endless

pleas for money to support 'conservative' candidates—while instead using the money to enrich themselves." Paul H. Jossey, "How We Killed the Tea Party," *Politico*, August 14, 2016, http://www.politico.com/magazine/story/2016/08/tea-party -pacs-ideas-death-214164.

20. George Will, "Who Will Follow Trump off the Cliff," *Washington Post*, May 6, 2016, https://www.washingtonpost.com/opinions/who-will-follow-trump-off -the-cliff/2016/05/06/752678a6-12dc-11e6-93ae-50921721165d_story.html?utm _term=.aabea3c68edd.

21. Wehner, "The Party of Reagan Is No More"; Conor Friedersdorf, "Rush Limbaugh's Ultimate Betrayal of His Audience," *Atlantic*, August 30, 2016, http:// www.theatlantic.com/politics/archive/2016/08/the-ultimate-rush-limbaugh -betrayal-of-his-audience/497996/.

22. Wehner, "The Party of Reagan Is No More." The true reasons for Trump's success will be debated for decades to come. An alternative explanation that emphasizes that Trump voters were more educated and better off financially than many believed is presented in Nate Silver's "The Mythology of Trump's 'Working Class' Support," *FiveThirtyEight*, May 3, 2016, http://fivethirtyeight.com/fea tures/the-mythology-of-trumps-working-class-support/. For a detailed analysis of Trump's nationalist/populist politics see Jonathan T. Rothwell's working paper "Explaining Nationalist Political Views: The Case of Donald Trump," September 4, 2016, http://papers.ssrn.com/sol3/papers.cfm?abstract_id=2822059.

23. Tami Luhbi, "College Grads Are Getting Nearly All the Jobs," *CNN Money*, June 30, 2016, http://money.cnn.com/2016/06/30/news/economy/college-grads -jobs/index.html.

24. Part of Trump's success with minority voters (in comparison to Romney) may have been due to President Obama not being on the ballot. "Exit Polls," *CNN Politics*, http://www.cnn.com/ election/results/exit-polls/national/president, accessed November 25, 2016.

25. "Reince Priebus' Moment," *Politico*, November 10, 2016,http://www.polit ico.com/story/2016/11/ reince-priebus-trump-victory-231159, accessed November 25, 2016; Brett Michael Dykes, "It Appears as Though Hillary Clinton Was Ultimately Done in by Low Democratic Voter Turnout," *Uproxx*, November 9, 2016, http://uproxx.com/news/hillary-clinton-democratic-voter-turnout/; "Michigan Donald Trump Supporters in Their Own Words," *Detroit Free Press*, November 12, 2016, http://www.freep.com/story/news/local/michigan/2016/11/12/donald-trump -supporters-michigan/93609178/; "Trump's Voters Don't Support Deportation: And Other Surprises from the 2016 Exit Polls," *Slate*, November 9, 2016, http://www .slate.com/articles/news_and_politics/politics/2016/11/debunking_myths_about _trump_voters_with_exit_polls.html, accessed November 25, 2016; "Trump Didn't Win Because He's Trump. He Won Because Clinton Is Clinton," *Reason*,

November 9, 2016, http://reason.com/blog/2016/11/09/ an-anti-mandate-for-clin ton, accessed November 25, 2016: "The County-by-County Data on Trump Vot- ers Shows Why He Won," *Washington Post*, November 19, 2016, https://www .washingtonpost.com/news/monkey-cage/wp/2016/11/19/the-country-by-county -data-on-trump-voters-shows-why-he-won/; "Critical Counties: How Trump Seized the Map and Clinton Lost it," CNN, November 19, 2016, http://www.cnn .com/2016/11/19/politics/critical-counties-election-results/index.html.

26. Indeed, there have already been some scholarly works on the subject. For instance, John Fea explores why evangelicals supported Trump despite his per- sonal behavior in *Believe Me: The Evangelical Road to Donald Trump* (Grand Rap- ids, MI: William B. Eerdmans, 2018).

Bibliography

MANUSCRIPT COLLECTIONS

Bob Barr Papers—Annie Belle Weaver Special Collections, University of West Georgia:
  Office Files
Foundation for Economic Education Archives, Irvington-on-Hudson, New York:
  General Files, Correspondence
  People Files
Hoover Institution Archives, Stanford University, Stanford, California:
  Annelise Anderson Papers
  Edwin Meese Papers
  Lyn Nofziger Papers
  William J. Casey Papers
Liberty University Archives, Lynchburg, Virginia:
  Cal Thomas Papers
  Correspondence of Howard Phillips
  Falwell Family Papers
  Moral Majority Papers
  Papers of the Conservative Caucus
Library of Congress, Washington, DC:
  Jack Kemp Files
National Library of Medicine, Bethesda, Maryland:
  C. Everett Koop Papers
Ronald Reagan Museum Exhibits
  Vertical Files
  Webber Hildred Files
Ronald Reagan Presidential Library, Simi Valley, California:
  Anne Higgins—Mail Sample Files
  David Gergen Files
  Elizabeth Dole Files
  Franklin Lavin Files
  Michael McKee Files
  Morton Blackwell Files
  Presidential Handwriting Files

University of Kansas Archives, Lawrence, Kansas:
    Robert J. Dole Presidential Campaign Papers

BOOKS AND OTHER PUBLISHED SOURCES

Abramowitz, Alan I. "Grand Old Tea Party: Partisan Polarization and the Rise of the Tea Party Movement." In Rosenthal and Trost, *Steep*, 195–211.

Abrams, Herbert L. *"The President Has Been Shot": Confusion, Disability, and the 25th Amendment in the Aftermath of the Attempted Assassination of Ronald Reagan.* New York: W. W. Norton, 1992.

Adelman, Ken. *Reagan at Reykjavik: Forty-Eight Hours That Ended the Cold War.* New York: Broadside Books, 2014.

Aldous, Richard. *Reagan and Thatcher: The Difficult Relationship.* New York: W. W. Norton, 2012.

Allitt, Patrick. *The Conservatives: Ideas and Personalities Throughout American History.* New Haven, CT: Yale University Press, 2009.

Altman, Nancy J. *The Battle for Social Security: From FDR's Vision to Bush's Gamble.* New York: Wiley, 2005.

Anderson, Martin. *Revolution: The Reagan Legacy.* Stanford, CA: Hoover Institute Press, 1988.

———. "A Ringing Melody of Ideas." In Deaver, *Why I Am a Reagan Conservative*, 24–26.

Andrew, Christopher, and Oleg Gordievsky. *KGB: The Inside Story.* New York: Harper Perennial, 1990.

Baker, James A. III. *The Politics of Diplomacy: Revolution, War and Peace, 1989–1992.* New York: G. P. Putnam, 1995.

———. *Work Hard, Study . . . and Keep Out of Politics! Adventures and Lessons from an Unexpected Public Life.* New York: G. P. Putnam's Sons, 2006.

Barth, James R., Suzanne Trimbath, and Glenn Yago, eds. *The Savings and Loan Crisis: Lessons from a Regulatory Failure.* New York: Springer, 2004.

Bartlett, Frederick. *Remembering: A Study in Experimental Social Psychology.* Cambridge: Cambridge University Press, 1932.

Bartley, Robert L. *The Seven Fat Years: And How to Do It Again.* New York: Free Press, 1992.

Beck, Glenn. *Cowards: What Politicians, Radicals, and the Media Refuse to Say.* New York: Threshold Editions, 2012.

———. *Glenn Beck's Common Sense: The Case Against an Out-of-Control Government, Inspired by Thomas Paine.* New York: Threshold Editions, 2009.

Béland, Daniel. *Social Security: History and Politics from the New Deal to the Privatization Debate.* Lawrence: University Press of Kansas, 2005.

Bennett, David H. *The Party of Fear: The American Far Right from Nativism to the MilitiaMovement.* New York: Vintage Books, 1995.

Bennett, William J. *America, The Last Best Hope.* Vol. 3: *From the Collapse of Communism to the Rise of Radical Islam.* Nashville, TN: Thomas Nelson, 2009.

Berkowitz, Edward D. *America's Welfare State from Roosevelt to Reagan.* Baltimore: Johns Hopkins University Press, 1991.

———. *Something Happened: A Political and Cultural Overview of the Seventies.* New York: Columbia University Press, 2006.

Berman, William C. *America's Right Turn: From Nixon to Clinton.* Baltimore: John Hopkins University Press, 1994.

Bernanke, Ben S. *The Courage to Act: A Memoir of a Crisis and Its Aftermath.* New York: W. W. Norton, 2015.

Bianchi, Anne. *C. Everett Koop: The Health of the Nation.* Brookfield, Connecticut: Millbrook Press, 1992.

Bimes, Terri. "Reagan: The Soft-Sell Populist." In Brownlee and Graham, *The Reagan Presidency*, 61–81.

Birnbaum, Jeffrey. *Showdown at Gucci Gulch: Lawmakers, Lobbyists, and the Unlikely Triumph of Tax Reform.* New York: Vintage, 1988.

Biven, W. Carl. *Jimmy Carter's Economy: Policy in the Age of Limits.* Chapel Hill: University of North Carolina Press, 2002.

Bjerre-Poulsen, Niels. "The Road to Mount Rushmore: The Conservative Commemoration Crusade for Ronald Reagan." In Hudson and Davies, *Ronald Reagan and the 1980s*, 210–227.

Black, David. *The Plague Years: A Chronicle of AIDS the Epidemic of Our Times.* New York: Simon & Schuster, 1985.

Black, Earl, and Merle Black. *The Rise of Southern Republicans.* Cambridge, MA: Belknap Press, 2002.

Blatti, Jo, ed. *Past Meets Present: Essays about Historic Interpretation and Public Audience.* Washington, DC: Smithsonian Institution Press, 1987.

Blumenthal, Sidney. *The Rise of the Counter-establishment: The Conservative Ascent to Political Power.* New York: Union Square Press, 1986.

Board, William. *Teller's War: The Top Secret Story behind the Star Wars Deception.* New York: Simon & Schuster, 1992.

Bodnar, John. *Remaking America: Public Memory, Commemoration, and Patriotism in the Twentieth Century.* Princeton, NJ: Princeton University Press, 1992.

Bogus, Carl T. *Buckley: William F. Buckley Jr. and the Rise of American Conservatism.* New York: Bloomsbury Press, 2011.

Bourne, Peter G. *Jimmy Carter: A Comprehensive Biography from Plains to Post-Presidency.* New York: Scribner, 1997.

Bowker, Michael, and Phil William. *Superpower Détente: A Reappraisal.* New York: SAGE Publications, 1988.

Boyd, Nancy. *Wide-Open Town: A History of Queer San Francisco to 1965.* Berkeley: University of California Press, 2003.

Brands, H. W. *Reagan: The Life.* New York: Doubleday, 2015.

Brandt, Allan M. "AIDS: From Public History to Public Policy." In Hannaway, Harden, and Parascandola, *AIDS and the Public Debate: Historical and Contemporary Perspectives,* 124–131.

Brinkley, Alan. "The Problem of American Conservatism." *American Historical Review* 99, no. 2 (April 1994): 409–429.

Brinkley, Douglas. *The Boys of Pointe Du Hoc: Ronald Reagan, D-Day, and the U.S. Army 2nd Ranger Battalion.* New York: Harper Perennial, 2005.

———, ed. *Ronald Reagan, The Notes: Ronald Reagan's Private Collection of Stories and Wisdom.* New York: HarperCollins, 2011.

———. *The Unfinished Presidency: Jimmy Carter's Journey to the Nobel Peace Prize.* New York: Penguin, 1998.

Brookhiser, Richard. *Right Time, Right Place: Coming of Age with William F. Buckley Jr. and the Conservative Movement.* New York: Basic Books, 2009.

Brooks, Arthur C. *The Conservative Heart: How to Build a Fairer, Happier, and More Prosperous America.* New York: Broadway Books, 2015.

Brown, Mary Beth. *Hand of Providence: The Strong and Quiet Faith of Ronald Reagan.* Nashville: WND Books, 2004.

Brownlee, W. Elliot, and Hugh Davis Graham, eds. *The Reagan Presidency: Pragmatic Conservatism and Its Legacies.* Lawrence: University Press of Kansas, 2003.

Brownlee, W. Elliot, and C. Eugene Steuerle. "Taxation." In Brownlee and Graham, *The Reagan Presidency,* 155–181.

Bruce, Steve. *The Rise and Fall of the Christian Right: Conservative Protestant Politics in America, 1979–1988.* Oxford: Oxford University Press, 1988.

Bruner, Jerome S. *Acts of Meaning.* Cambridge, MA: Harvard University Press, 1990.

Bryant, Anita. *The Anita Bryant Story: The Survival of Our Nation's Families and the Threat of Militant Homosexuality.* Old Tappan, NJ: Fleming H. Revell, 1977.

Buchanan, Patrick J. *Where the Right Went Wrong: How Neoconservatives*

Subverted the Reagan Revolution and Hijacked the Bush Presidency. New York: St. Martin's Press, 2004.

Buckaloo, Derek N. "Carter's Nicaragua and Other Democratic Quagmires." In Schulman and Zelizer, *Rightward Bound: Making America Conservative in the 1970s*, 246–264.

Buckley, William F. Jr. *Flying High: Remembering Barry Goldwater.* New York: Basic Books, 2008.

———. *On the Firing Line: The Public Life of Public Figures.* New York: Random House, 1989.

———. *The Reagan I Knew.* New York: Basic Books, 2008.

Bunch, Will. *Tear Down This Myth: The Right-Wing Distortion of the Reagan Legacy.* New York: Free Press, 2009.

Burgin, Angus. *The Great Persuasion: Reinventing Free Markets since the Depression.* Cambridge, MA: Harvard University Press, 2015.

Burns, Jennifer. *Goddess of the Market: Ayn Rand and the American Right.* Oxford: Oxford University Press, 2009.

Burstein, Andrew. *Democracy's Muse: How Thomas Jefferson Became an FDR Liberal, a Reagan Republican, and a Tea Party Fanatic, All While Being Dead.* Charlottesville: University Press of Virginia, 2015.

Busby, Robert. *Reagan and the Iran-Contra Affair: The Politics of Presidential Recovery.* New York: St. Martin's Press, 1999.

Busch, Andrew E. *Reagan's Victory: The Presidential Election of 1980 and the Rise of the Right.* Lawrence: University of Kansas Press, 2005.

Bush, George H. W. *All the Best: My Life in Letters and Other Writings.* New York: Simon & Schuster, 1999.

Bush, George H. W., and Brent Scowcroft. *A World Transformed.* New York: Alfred A. Knopf, 1998.

Bush, George W. *Decision Points.* New York: Crown, 2010.

Bush, George W. *41: A Portrait of My Father.* New York, Crown, 2014.

Butler, Thomas. *Memory: History, Culture and the Mind.* New York: Blackwell, 1989.

Byrne, David T. *Ronald Reagan: An Intellectual Biography.* Lincoln, NE: Potomac, 2018.

Campbell, Sue, ed. *Our Faithfulness to the Past: The Ethics and Politics of Memory.* Oxford: Oxford University Press, 2014.

Canaday, Margot. *The Straight State: Sexuality and Citizenship in Twentieth-Century America.* Princeton, NJ: Princeton University Press, 2011.

Cannon, Lou. *Ronald Reagan: The Presidential Portfolio.* New York: Public Affairs, 2001.

————. *Ronald Reagan: The Role of a Lifetime.* New York: Public Affairs, 2000.

Cannon, Lou, and Carl M. Cannon. *Reagan's Disciple: George W. Bush's Troubled Quest for a Presidential Legacy.* New York: Public Affairs, 2008.

Cannon, Lou, and Time Contributors. *The Reagan Paradox: The Conservative Icon and Today's GOP.* New York: Time Books, 2014.

Carter, Dan. *From George Wallace to Newt Gingrich: Race in the Conservative Counterrevolution, 1963–1994.* Baton Rouge, Louisiana State University Press, 1996.

————. *The Politics of Rage: George Wallace, The Origins of the New Conservatism, and the Transformation of American Politics.* Baton Rouge: Louisiana State University Press, 1995.

Carter, David. *Stonewall: The Riots That Sparked the Gay Revolution.* New York: St. Martin's Griffin, 2010.

Charen, Mona. *Useful Idiots: How Liberals Got It Wrong in the Cold War and Still Blame America First.* New York: Perennial, 2003.

Chauncey, George. *Gay New York: Gender, Urban Culture, and the Making of the Gay Male World, 1890–1940.* New York: Basic Books, 1994.

Cheney, Dick. *In My Time: A Personal and Political Memoir.* New York: Threshold, 2011.

Chen Jian. *Mao's China and the Cold War.* Chapel Hill: University of North Carolina Press, 2001.

Clendinen, Dudley, and Adam Nagourney. *Out for Good: The Struggle to Build a Gay Rights Movement in America.* New York: Simon & Schuster, 1999.

Clinton, Bill. *My Life.* New York: Alfred A. Knopf, 2004.

Cohen, Lizabeth. *A Consumers' Republic: The Politics of Mass Consumption in Postwar America.* New York: Vintage Books, 2003.

Colachello, Bob. *Ronnie and Nancy: Their Path to the White House, 1911 to 1980.* New York: Warner Books, 2004.

Collins, Robert M. *Transforming America: Politics and Culture During the Reagan Years.* New York: Columbia University Press, 2007.

Confino, Alon, and Peter Fritzsche, *The Work of Memory: New Directions in the Study of German Society and Culture.* Chicago: University of Illinois Press, 2002.

Connerton, Paul. *How Societies Remember.* Cambridge: Cambridge University Press, 1989.

Corrigan, Matthew T. *Conservative Hurricane: How Jeb Bush Remade Florida.* Gainesville: University Press of Florida, 2014.

Coulter, Ann. *Adios, America! The Left's Plan to Turn Our Country into a Third World Hellhole.* Washington, DC: Regnery, 2015.

———. *In Trump We Trust: E Pluribus Awesome!*. New York: Sentinel, 2016.

———. *Slander: Liberal Lies About the American Right*. New York: Crown, 2002.

———. *Treason: Liberal Treachery from the Cold War to the War on Terrorism*. New York: Crown, 2003.

Courtwright, David T. *No Right Turn: Conservative Politics in Liberal America*. Cambridge, MA: Harvard University Press, 2010.

Cowie, Jefferson. *Stayin' Alive: The 1970s and the Last Days of the Working Class*. New York: New Press, 2010.

Crane, Susan A., ed. *Museums and Memory*. Stanford, CA: Stanford University Press, 2000.

Crawford, Alan. *Thunder on the Right: The 'New Right' and the Politics of Resentment*. New York: Pantheon Books, 1980.

Crespino, Joseph. *In Search of Another Country: Mississippi and the Conservative Counterrevolution*. Princeton, NJ: Princeton University Press, 2007.

———. *Strom Thurmond's America*. New York: Hill and Wang, 2012.

Critchlow, Donald T. *The Conservative Ascendancy: How the Republican Right Rose to Power in Modern America*. Lawrence: University Press of Kansas, 2011.

———. *Intended Consequences: Birth Control, Abortion, and the Federal Government in Modern America*. Oxford: Oxford University Press, 1999.

———. "Mobilizing Women: The 'Social' Issues." in Brownlee and Graham, *The Reagan Presidency*, 293–326.

———. *Phyllis Schlafly and Grassroots Conservatism*. Princeton, NJ: Princeton University Press, 2005.

———. *When Hollywood Was Right: How Movie Stars, Studio Moguls, and Big Business Remade American Politics*. New York: Cambridge University Press, 2013.

Critchlow, Donald T., and Nancy MacLean. *Debating the American Conservative Movement: 1945 to the Present*. New York: Rowman & Littlefield, 2009.

Cromartie, Michael, ed. *Disciples and Democracy: Religious Conservatives and the Future of American Politics*. Washington, DC: Ethics and Public Policy Center, 1994.

Cruz, Ted. *A Time for Truth: Reigniting the Promise of America*. New York: Broadside Books, 2015.

Daigle, Craig. *The Limits of Détente: The United States, the Soviet Union, and the Arab-Israeli Conflict, 1969–1973*. New Haven, CT: Yale University Press, 2012.

Dallek, Matthew. "Not Ready for Mt. Rushmore: Reconciling the Myth of Ronald Reagan with the Reality." *American Scholar* 78, no. 3 (June 2009): 13–23.

———. *The Right Moment: Ronald Reagan's First Victory and the Decisive Turning Point in American Politics*. New York: Free Press, 2000.

Dallek, Robert. *Nixon and Kissinger: Partners in Power*. New York: HarperCollins, 2007.

———. *Ronald Reagan: The Politics of Symbolism*. Cambridge, MA: Harvard University Press, 1999.

Dallin, Alexander. *Black Box: KAL 007 and the Superpowers*. Berkeley: University of California Press, 1985.

D'Antonio, Michael. *Fall from Grace: The Failed Crusade of the Christian Right*. New York: Farrar, Straus and Giroux, 1989.

Deaver, Michael K. *Behind the Scenes: In Which the Author Talks about Ronald and Nancy Reagan . . . and Himself*. New York: William Morrow, 1987.

———. *A Different Drummer: My Thirty Years with Ronald Reagan*. New York: Perennial, 2001.

——— ed. *Why I Am a Reagan Conservative*. New York: William Marrow, 2005.

Deckman, Melissa. *Tea Party Women: Mama Grizzlies, Grassroots Leaders, and the Changing Face of the American Right*. New York: New York University Press, 2016.

DeFrank, Thomas M. *Write It When I'm Gone: Remarkable Off-the-Record Conversations with Gerald R. Ford*. New York: G. P. Putnam's Sons, 2007.

De Groot, Jerome. *Consuming History: Historians and Heritage in Contemporary Popular Culture*. New York: Routledge, 2009.

Derthick, Martha, and Steven M. Teles. "Riding the Third Rail: Social Security Reform." In Brownlee and Graham, *The Reagan Presidency*, 182–208.

Devine, Donald J. "All Other Political Philosophies Have Failed." In Deaver, *Why I Am a Reagan Conservative*, 111–116.

———. *Reagan's Terrible Swift Sword: An Insider's Story of Abuse and Reform Within the Federal Bureaucracy*. Ottawa: Jameson Books, 1991.

Diamond, Sarah. *Roads to Dominion: Right-Wing Movements and Political Power in the United States*. New York: Guilford Press, 1995.

Diggins, John Patrick. *The Rise and Fall of the American Left*. New York: W. W. Norton, 1992.

———. *Ronald Reagan: Fate, Freedom, and the Making of History*. New York: W. W. Norton, 2007.

Dionne, E. J. Jr. *Why the Right Went Wrong: Conservatism from Goldwater to the Tea Party and Beyond*. New York: Simon & Schuster, 2016.

Dobrynin, Anatoly. *In Confidence: Moscow's Ambassador to America's Six Cold War Presidents*. New York: Times Books, 1995.

Dochuk, Darren. *From Bible Belt to the Sunbelt: Plain-Folk Religion, Grassroots Politics, and the Rise of Evangelical Conservatism*. New York: W. W. Norton, 2010.

Doherty, Brian. *Radicals for Capitalism: A Freewheeling History of the Modern American Libertarian Movement.* New York: Public Affairs, 2007.

Domitrovic, Brian. *Econoclasts: The Rebels Who Sparked the Supply-Side Revolution and Restored American Prosperity.* Wilmington, DE: ISI Books, 2009.

———, ed. *The Pillars of Reaganomics: A Generation of Wisdom from Arthur Laffer and the Supply-Side Revolutionaries.* San Francisco: Laffer Center, 2014.

D'Souza, Dinesh. *The End of Racism: Principles for a Multiracial Society.* New York: Free Press, 1995.

———. *Illiberal Education: The Politics of Race and Sex on Campus.* New York: Vintage Books, 1991.

———. *Ronald Reagan: How an Ordinary Man Became an Extraordinary Leader.* New York: Free Press, 1997.

Dueck, Colin. *Hard Line: The Republican Party and U.S. Foreign Policy since World War II.* Princeton, NJ: Princeton University Press, 2010.

Dunn, Charles W., ed. *American Exceptionalism: The Origins, History, and Future of the Nation's Greatest Strength.* New York: Rowman & Littlefield, 2013.

———, ed. *The Enduring Reagan.* Lexington: University Press of Kentucky, 2009.

———, ed. *The Future of Conservatism: Conflict and Consensus in the Post-Reagan Era.* Wilmington, DE: ISI Books, 2007.

Eakin, Paul John. "Autobiography, Identity, and the Fictions of Memory." In Schacter and Scarry, *Memory, Brain, and Beliefs.*

Easton, Nina J. *Gang of Five: Leaders at the Center of the Conservative Crusade.* New York: Simon & Schuster, 2000.

Ebenstein, Alan. *Friedrich Hayek: A Biography.* Chicago: University of Chicago Press, 2003.

Ebenstein, Lanny. *Milton Friedman: A Biography.* New York: Palgrave MacMillan, 2007.

Edsall, Thomas, and Mary Edsall. *Chain Reaction: The Impact of Race, Rights, and Taxes on American Politics.* New York: W. W. Norton, 1992.

Edwards, Lee. *A Brief History of the Modern American Conservative Movement.* Washington, DC: Heritage Foundation, 2004.

———. *The Conservative Revolution: The Movement That Remade America.* New York: Free Press, 1999.

———. *Educating for Liberty: The First Half-Century of the Intercollegiate Studies Institute.* Washington, DC: Regnery Publishing, 2003.

———. *The Essential Ronald Reagan: A Profile in Courage, Justice, and Wisdom.* New York: Rowman & Littlefield, 2004.

———. *Goldwater: The Man Who Made a Revolution.* Washington, DC: Regnery Publishing, 1995.

———. *Just Right: A Life in Pursuit of Liberty.* Wilmington, DE: ISI Books, 2017.

————. *Reagan: A Political Biography*. San Diego: Vintage Books, 1967.

————. *To Preserve and Protect: The Life of Edwin Meese III*. Washington, DC: Heritage Foundation, 2005.

————. *William F. Buckley Jr.: The Maker of a Movement*. Wilmington, DE: ISI Books, 2010.

Ehrman, John. *Neoconservatism: Intellectuals and Foreign Affairs 1945–1994*. New Haven, CT: Yale University Press, 1995.

Eland, Ivan. *Eleven Presidents: Promises vs. Results in Achieving Limited Government*. Oakland: Independent Institute, 2017.

Eliot, Marc. *Reagan: The Hollywood Years*. New York: Harmony Books, 2008.

Ely, Bert, and Vicki Vanderhoff. *Lessons Learned from the S&L Debacle: The Price of Failed Public Policy*. Lewisville, TX: Institute for Policy Innovation, 1991.

Epstein, Benjamin R., and Arnold Forster. *The Radical Right: Report on the John Birch Society and Its Allies*. New York: Random House, 1966.

Evans, Rowland, and Robert Novak. *The Reagan Revolution: An Inside Look at the Transformation of the U.S. Government*. New York: E.P. Dutton, 1981.

Evans, Thomas W. *The Education of Ronald Reagan: The General Electric Years and the Untold Story of His Conversion to Conservatism*. New York: Columbia University Press, 2008.

Falwell, Jerry. *Armageddon and the Coming War with Russia*. Self-published, 1980.

————. *Falwell: An Autobiography*. Lynchburg, VA: Liberty, 1997.

————. *How You Can Help Clean Up America*. Lynchburg, VA: Liberty, 1978.

————. "Introduction." In Richard Viguerie, *The New Right: We're Ready to Lead*. Falls Church, VA: Viguerie Company, 1980.

————. *Listen America!*. New York: Bantam, 1980.

————. *Strength for the Journey*. New York: Simon & Schuster, 1987.

Farris, Scott. *Reagan and Kennedy: Why Their Legacies Endure*. Guilford, CT: Lyons Press, 2013.

Fea, John. *Believe Me: The Evangelical Road to Donald Trump*. Grand Rapids, MI: William B. Eerdmans Publishing Company, 2018.

Feldstein, Martin, ed. *American Economic Policy in the 1980s*. Chicago: University of Chicago Press, 1994.

Fetner, Tina. *How the Religious Right Shaped Lesbian and Gay Activism*. Minneapolis: University of Minnesota Press, 2008.

Filkins, Dexter. *The Forever War*. New York: Alfred A. Knopf, 2008.

Fiorina, Morris P., Samuel J. Abrams, and Jeremy C. Pope. *Culture War? The Myth of a Polarized America*. New York: Longman, 2011.

Fischer, Beth A. "Reagan and the Soviets: Winning the Cold War?" In Brownlee and Graham, *The Reagan Presidency*, 113–132.

————. *The Reagan Reversal: Foreign Policy and the End of the Cold War.* Columbia: University of Missouri Press, 1997.

FitzGerald, Frances. *Way Out There in the Blue: Reagan, Star Wars and the End of the Cold War.* New York: Simon & Schuster, 2000.

Foley, Michael Stewart. *Front Porch Politics: The Forgotten Heyday of American Activism in the 1970s and 1980s.* New York: Hill and Wang, 2013.

Forbes, Steve, and Elizabeth Ames. *Freedom Manifesto: Why Free Markets are Moral and Big Government Isn't.* New York: Crown Business, 2012.

Fordham, Benjamin. *Building the Cold War Consensus: The Political Economy of U.S. National Security Policy, 1949–51.* Ann Arbor: University of Michigan Press, 1998.

Formisano, Ronald P. *The Tea Party: A Brief History.* Baltimore: Johns Hopkins University Press, 2012.

Frederickson, Kari. *The Dixiecrat Revolt and the End of the Solid South, 1932–1968.* Chapel Hill: University of North Carolina Press, 2000.

Friedlander, Saul, ed. *Probing the Limits of Representation: Nazism and the "Final Solution".* Cambridge, MA: Harvard University Press, 1992.

Friedman, Max Paul, and Padraic Kenney. *Partisan Histories: The Past in Contemporary Global Politics.* New York: Palgrave MacMillon, 2005.

Friedman, Milton. *Capitalism and Freedom.* Chicago: University of Chicago Press, 1962.

Friedman, Milton, and Rose Friedman. *Two Lucky People: Milton and Rose D. Friedman.* Chicago: University of Chicago Press, 1988.

————. *Tyranny of the Status Quo.* New York: Harcourt Brace Jovanovich, 1984.

Frisk, David B. *If Not Us Who? William Rusher, National Review, and the Conservative Movement.* Wilmington, DE: ISI Books, 2012.

Frum, David. *Comeback: Conservatism That Can Win Again.* New York: Broadway Books, 2008.

Gaddis, John Lewis. *The Cold War: A New History.* New York: Penguin Books, 2005.

————. *The United States and the End of the Cold War: Implications, Reconsideration, Provocations.* Oxford: Oxford University Press, 1992.

Gamble, Richard M. *In Search of the City on a Hill: The Making and Unmaking of an American Myth.* New York: Continuum, 2012.

Gates, Robert. *From the Shadows: The Ultimate Insider's Story of Five Presidents and How They Won the Cold War.* New York: Simon & Schuster, 2007.

Gergen, David. *Eyewitness to Power: The Essence of Leadership Nixon to Clinton.* New York: Simon & Schuster, 2000.

Gillis, John R. *Commemorations: The Politics of National Identity.* Princeton, NJ: Princeton University Press, 1994.

Gillon, Steven. *The Pact: Bill Clinton, Newt Gingrich, and the Rivalry That Defined a Generation.* Oxford: Oxford University Press, 2008.

Gingrich, Newt. *Lessons Learned the Hard Way: A Personal Report.* New York: HarperCollins, 1998.

———. "Like Father, Like Son." Foreword to Michael Reagan, *The New Reagan Revolution*, xiii–xiv.

———. *A Nation Like No Other: Why American Exceptionalism Matters.* Washington, DC: Regnery, 2011.

———. *To Renew America.* New York: HarperCollins, 1995.

———. *To Save America: Stopping Obama's Secular-Socialist Machine.* Washington DC: Regnery, 2010.

———. *Winning the Future: A 21st Century Contract with America.* Washington, DC: Regnery, 2005.

Glad, Betty. *Jimmy Carter: In Search of the Great White House.* New York: W. W. Norton, 1980.

Gleijeses, Piero. *Conflicting Missions: Havana, Washington, and Africa, 1959–1976.* Chapel Hill: University of North Carolina Press, 2002.

———. *Visions of Freedom: Havana, Washington, Pretoria, and the Struggle for Southern Africa, 1976–1991.* Chapel Hill: University of North Carolina Press, 2013.

Goldwater, Barry. *Why Not Victory? A Fresh Look at American Foreign Policy.* Washington, DC: MacFadden Capitol Hill Books, 1963.

Gorbachev, Mikhail. *Memoirs.* New York: Bantam Books, 1995.

Gorbachev, Mikhail, and Zdenek Mlynar. *Conversations with Gorbachev.* New York: Columbia University Press, 2001.

Gottfried, Richard E., and Richard B. Spencer. *The Great Purge: The Deformation of the Conservative Movement.* Whitefish, MT: Washington Summit Publishers, 2015.

Gould, Lewis L. *The Republicans: A History of the Grand Old Party.* Oxford: Oxford University Press, 2014.

Graubard, Stephen. *Command of Office: How War, Secrecy and Deception Transformed the Presidency, From Theodore Roosevelt to George W. Bush.* New York: Basic Books, 2004.

Greenberg, David. *Nixon's Shadow: The History of an Image.* New York: W. W. Norton, 2003.

Greenya, John, and Anne Urban. *The Real David Stockman.* New York: St. Martin's Press, 1983.

Greider, William. *The Education of David Stockman and Other Americans.* New York: E.P. Dutton, 1981.

Gromyko, Andrei. *Memoirs.* New York: Doubleday, 1989.

Hahn, Peter L. *Mission Accomplished? The United States and Iraq since World War I.* Oxford: Oxford University Press, 2012.

Haig, Alexander M. *Caveat: Realism, Reagan and Foreign Policy.* New York: Scribner, 1984.

Hanhimaki, Jussi. *The Rise and Fall of Détente: American Foreign Policy and the Transformation of the Cold War.* New York: Potomac Books, 2012.

Hannaford, Peter. *Recollections of Reagan: A Portrait of Ronald Reagan.* New York: William Morrow, 1997.

Hannaway, Caroline, Victoria A. Harden, and John Parascandola, eds. *AIDS and the Public Debate: Historical and Contemporary Perspectives.* Washington, DC: IOS Press, 1995.

Hannity, Sean. *Conservative Victory: Defeating Obama's Radical Agenda.* New York: Harper, 2010.

Harden, Victoria A. *AIDS at 30: A History.* Washington, DC: Potomac Books, 2012.

Harris, John F. *The Survivor: Bill Clinton in the White House.* New York: Random House, 2005.

Hart, Jeffrey. *The Making of the American Conservative Mind: National Review and Its Times.* Wilmington, DE: ISI Books, 2005.

Hawley, George. *Making Sense of the Alt-Right.* New York: Columbia University Press, 2017.

———. *Right-Wing Critics of American Conservatism.* Lawrence: University Press of Kansas, 2016.

Hayek, F.A. *Hayek on Hayek: An Autobiographical Dialogue.* Chicago: University of Chicago Press, 1994.

———. *Individualism and Economic Order.* Chicago: University of Chicago Press, 1948.

———. *The Road to Serfdom.* London: University of Chicago Press, 2007 .

Hayward, Steven F. *The Age of Reagan: The Conservative Counterrevolution, 1980–1989.* New York: Crown Forum, 2009.

———. *The Age of Reagan: The Fall of the Old Liberal Order, 1964–1980.* New York: Three Rivers Press, 2001.

———. *Greatness: Reagan, Churchill, and the Making of Extraordinary Leaders.* New York: Crown, 2005.

———. *The Real Jimmy Carter: How Our Worst Ex-President Undermines American Foreign Policy, Coddles Dictators, and Created the Party of Clinton and Kerry.* Washington, DC: Regnery, 2004.

Hazlitt, Henry. *Economics in One Lesson: 50th Anniversary Edition.* Baltimore: Laissez Faire Books, 1996.

Heale, M. J. "Epilogue: Ronald Reagan and the Historians." In Hudson and Davies, *Ronald Reagan and the 1980s,* 249–261.

Heller, Anne C. *Ayn Rand and the World She Made.* New York: Doubleday, 2009.

Hemmer, Nicole. *Messengers of the Right: Conservative Media and the Transformation of American Politics.* Philadelphia: University of Pennsylvania Press, 2016.

Hersh, Seymour M. *The Target Is Destroyed: What Really Happened to Flight 007 and What America Knew about It.* New York: Random House, 1986.

"HIV/AIDS and U.S. History." *Journal of American History* 104, no. 2 (September 1, 2017): 431–460.

Hoeveler, J. David Jr. *Watch on the Right: Conservative Intellectuals in the Reagan Era.* Madison: University of Wisconsin Press, 1991.

Howe, Joshua P. *Behind the Curve: Science and the Politics of Global Warming.* Seattle: University of Washington Press, 2014.

Hudson, Cheryl, and Gareth Davies, eds. *Ronald Reagan and the 1980s: Perceptions, Policies, Legacies.* New York: Palgrave Macmillan, 2008.

Hülsmann, Jörg Guido. *Mises: The Last Knight of Liberalism.* Auburn, AL: Ludwig von Mises Institute, 2007.

Hyman, Louis. *Debtor Nation: The History of America in Red Ink.* Princeton, NJ: Princeton University Press, 2011.

Irwin, Neil. *The Alchemists: Three Central Bankers and a World on Fire.* New York: Penguin Books, 2013.

Jackson, William D. "Soviet Reassessment of Ronald Reagan, 1985–1988," *Political Science Quarterly* 113, no. 4 (Winter 1998–1999): 617–644.

Jacobs, Meg. *Panic at the Pump: The Energy Crisis and the Transformation of American Politics in the 1970s.* New York: Hill & Wang, 2016.

Jamieson, Kathleen Hall, and Joseph N. Cappella. *Echo Chamber: Rush Limbaugh and the Conservative Media Establishment.* Oxford: Oxford University Press, 2008.

Jarvis, Howard. *I'm Mad as Hell.* New York: Times Books, 1979.

Jeffers, Thomas L. *Norman Podhoretz: A Biography.* New York: Cambridge University Press, 2010.

Johnson, Paul. *Modern Times: The World from the Twenties to the Nineties.* New York: Harper Collins, 1991.

Johnson, R. W. *Shootdown: Flight 007 and the American Connection.* New York: Viking, 1986.

Jones, Seth G. *A Covert Action: Reagan, the CIA, and the Cold War Struggle in Poland.* New York: W. W. Norton, 2018.

Jones, Stedman. *Masters of the Universe: Hayek, Friedman, and the Birth of Neoliberal Politics.* Princeton, NJ: Princeton University Press, 2012.

Jurdem, Laurence R. *Paving the Way for Reagan: The Influence of Conservative Media on US Foreign Policy.* Lexington: University Press of Kentucky, 2018.

Kabaservice, Geoffrey. *Rule and Ruin: The Downfall of Moderation and the Destruction of the Republican Party, from Eisenhower to the Tea Party.* Oxford: Oxford University Press, 2013.

Kalman, Laura. *Right Star Rising: A New Politics, 1974–1980.* New York, W. W. Norton, 2010.

Kammen, Michael. *Mystic Chords of Memory: The Transformation of Tradition in American Culture.* New York: Vintage Books, 1991.

Karaagac, John. *Between Promise and Policy: Ronald Reagan and Conservative Reformism.* New York: Lexington Books, 2000.

Karnow, Stanley. *Vietnam: A History.* New York: Penguin, 1983.

Kean, Thomas H., and Lee H. Hamilton. *The 9/11 Report: The National Commission on Terrorist Attacks Upon the United States.* New York: St. Martin's, 2004.

Kelly, Daniel. *Living on Fire: The Life of L. Brent Bozell Jr..* Wilmington, DE: ISI Books, 2014.

Kelman, Steven. "The Grace Commission: How Much Waste in Government?" *Public Interest,* no. 39 (Winter 1985): 62–82.

Kemp, Jack. *The American Idea: Ending Limits to Growth.* Washington, DC: American Studies Center, 1984.

———. *An American Renaissance: A Strategy for the 1980s.* New York: Harper & Row, 1977.

Kengor, Paul. *The Crusader: Ronald Reagan and the Fall of Communism.* New York: Harper Perennial, 2007.

———. *11 Principles of a Reagan Conservative.* New York: Beaufort Books, 2014.

———. *God and Ronald Reagan: A Spiritual Life.* New York: HarperCollins, 2005.

———. *A Pope and a President: John Paul II, Ronald Reagan, and the Extraordinary Untold Story of the 20th Century.* Wilmington, DE: ISI Books, 2017.

Kengor, Paul, and Patricia Clark Doerner. *The Judge: William P. Clark, Ronald Reagan's Top Hand.* New York: Ignatius Press, 2007.

Kengor, Paul, and Robert Orlando. *The Divine Plan: John Paul II, Ronald Reagan, and the Dramatic End of the Cold War.* Wilmington, DE: ISI Books, 2019.

Kengor, Paul, and Peter Schweizer, eds. *The Reagan Presidency: Assessing the Man and His Legacy.* New York: Rowman & Littlefield, 2005.

Klatch, Rebecca E. *A Generation Divided: The New Left, the New Right, and the 1960s.* Berkeley: University of California Press, 1999.

Kleinknecht, William. *The Man Who Sold the World: Ronald Reagan and the Betrayal of Main Street America.* New York: Nation Books, 2009.

Knott, Stephen, and Jeffrey L. Chidester. *At Reagan's Side: Insiders' Recollections from Sacramento to the White House.* New York: Rowman and Littlefield, 2009.

Kolozi, Peter. *Conservatives Against Capitalism: From the Industrial Revolution to Globalization.* New York: Columbia University Press, 2017.

Kondracke, Morton, and Fred Barnes. *Jack Kemp: The Bleeding-Heart Conservative Who Changed the World.* New York: Sentinel, 2015.

Koop, C. Everett. *The Memoirs of America's Family Doctor.* New York: Random House, 1991.

Kotkin, Stephen. *Armageddon Averted: The Soviet Collapse, 1970–2000.* Oxford: Oxford University Press, 2008.

Kristol, Irving. *Neoconservatism: The Autobiography of an Idea.* Chicago: Ivan R. Dee, 1995.

Kristol, William, ed. *The Weekly Standard, A Reader: 1995–2005.* New York: HarperCollins, 2005.

Kruse, Kevin M. *One Nation Under God: How Corporate America Invented Christian America.* New York: Basic Books, 2015.

———. *White Flight: Atlanta and the Making of Modern Conservatism.* Princeton, NJ: Princeton University Press, 2005.

Kudlow, Lawrence, and Brian Domitrovic. *JFK and the Reagan Revolution: A Secret History of American Prosperity.* New York: Portfolio, 2016.

Kuhn, Jim. *Ronald Reagan in Private: A Memoir of My Years in the White House.* New York: Sentinel, 2004.

Kwon, Heonik. *The Other Cold War.* New York: Columbia University Press, 2010.

LaCapra, Dominick. *History and Memory after Auschwitz.* Ithaca, NY: Cornell University Press, 1998.

LaFeber, Walter. *America, Russia, and the Cold War, 1945–1996.* New York: McGraw-Hill, 1997.

Laffer, Arthur B., and Jan P. Seymour. *The Economics of the Tax Revolt: A Reader.* New York: Harcourt Brace Jovanovich, 1979.

Laham, Nicolas. *Ronald Reagan and the Politics of Immigration Reform.* Westport, CN: Praeger, 2000.

LaHaye, Tim. *The Unhappy Gays: What Everyone Should Know about Homosexuality.* Wheaton, IL: Tyndale House, 1978.

Langdale, John J. III. *Superfluous Southerners: Cultural Conservatism and the South, 1920–1990.* Columbia: University of Missouri Press, 2012.

Lassiter, Matthew D. *The Silent Majority: Suburban Politics in the Sunbelt South.* Princeton, NJ: Princeton University Press, 2006.

Leffler, Melvyn P. *For the Soul of Mankind: The United States, the Soviet Union, and the Cold War.* New York: Hill & Wang, 2007.

Lettow, Paul. *Ronald Reagan and His Quest to Abolish Nuclear Weapons.* New York: Random House, 2006.

Levin, Mark. *Plunder and Deceit: Big Government's Exploitation of Young People and the Future.* New York: Threshold Editions, 2015.

Levin, Yuval. *The Fractured Republic: Renewing America's Social Contract in the Age of Individualism.* New York: Basic Books, 2016.

Lewis, Matt K. *Too Dumb to Fail: How the GOP Betrayed the Reagan Revolution to Win Elections (and How It Can Reclaim Its Conservative Roots).* New York: Hachette Books, 2016.

Lichtman, Allan J. *White Protestant Nation: The Rise of the American Conservative Movement.* New York: Grove Press, 2008.

Light, Paul. *Artful Work: The Politics of Social Security Reform.* New York: Random House, 1985.

Limbaugh, Rush. "The Great One." *National Review* 56, no. 12 (June 28, 2004): 36–37.

Linenthal, Edward T. *The Unfinished Bombing: Oklahoma City in American Memory.* New York: Oxford University Press, 2001.

Linenthal, Edward T., and Tom Engelhardt, *History Wars: The Enola Gay and Other Battles for the American Past.* New York: Henry Holt, 1996.

Link, William A. *Righteous Warrior: Jesse Helms and the Rise of Modern Conservatism.* New York: St. Martin's Press, 2008.

Lo, Clarence Y. H. "Astroturf versus Grass Roots: Scenes from Early Tea Party Mobilization." In Rosenthal and Trost, *Steep*, 98–129.

Longley, Kyle. "When Character Was King? Ronald Reagan and the Issues of Ethics and Morality." In Longley et al., *Deconstructing Reagan*, 90–119.

Longley, Kyle, Jeremy D. Mayer, Michael Schaller, and John W. Sloan. *Deconstructing Reagan: Conservative Mythology and America's Fortieth President.* New York: M. E. Sharpe, 2007.

MacMillan, Margaret. *Nixon and Mao: The Week That Changed the World.* New York: Random House, 2007.

Mamdani, Mahmood. *Good Muslim, Bad Muslim: America, the Cold War, and the Roots of Terror.* New York: Pantheon Books, 2004.

Maney, Patrick J. *Bill Clinton: New Gilded Age President.* Lawrence: University Press of Kansas, 2016.

Mann, James. *The Obamians: The Struggle Inside the White House to Redefine American Power.* New York: Viking, 2012.

———. *The Rebellion of Ronald Reagan: A History of the End of the Cold War.* New York: Penguin Books, 2009.

———. *Rise of the Vulcans: The History of Bush's War Cabinet.* New York: Penguin, 2004.

Marlo, Francis. *Planning Reagan's War: Conservative Strategists and America's Cold War Victory.* New York: Potomac Books, 2012.

Martin, William C. *With God on Our Side: The Rise of the Religious Right in America.* New York: Broadway Books, 1996.

Mason, David L. *From Buildings and Loans to Bail-Outs: A History of the American Savings and Loan Industry.* New York: Cambridge University Press, 2004.

Massie, Suzanne. *Trust but Verify: Reagan, Russia and Me.* Rockland, ME: Maine Authors Publishing, 2013.

Matlock, Jack Jr. *Autopsy on An Empire: The American Ambassador's Account of the Collapse of the Soviet Union.* New York: Random House, 1995.

———. *Reagan and Gorbachev: How the Cold War Ended.* New York: Random House, 2005.

Matthews, Chris. *Tip and the Gipper: When Politics Worked.* New York: Simon & Schuster, 2013.

May, Elaine Tyler. *Homeward Bound: America Families in the Cold War Era.* New York: Basic Books, 2008.

Mayer, Jeremy D. "Reagan and Race: Prophet of Color Blindness, Baiter of the Backlash." In Longley et al., *Deconstructing Reagan,* 82–83.

McAllister, Ted V. "Reagan and the Transformation of American Conservatism." In Brownlee and Graham, *The Reagan Presidency,* 40–60.

McFarlane, Robert C. *Special Trust.* New York: Cadell & Davies, 1994.

McGirr, Lisa. *Suburban Warriors: The Origins of the New American Right.* Princeton, NJ: Princeton University Press, 2001.

Meese, Edwin III. "A Just and Prosperous Society." In Deaver, *Why I Am a Reagan Conservative,* 41–46.

———. *With Reagan: The Inside Story.* Washington, DC: Regnery Gateway, 1992.

Mehlman, Ken. "I Believe in Freedom." In Deaver, *Why I am a Reagan Conservative,* 126–127.

Mendell, David. *Obama: From Promise to Power.* New York: HarperCollins, 2007.

Micklethwait, John, and Adrian Wooldridge. *The Right Nation: Conservative Power in America.* New York: Penguin, 2004.

Middendorf, J. William II. *A Glorious Disaster: Barry Goldwater's Presidential Campaign and the Origins of the Conservative Movement.* New York: Basic Books, 2006.

Mises, Ludwig von. *Human Action: A Treatise on Economics.* New Haven, CT: Yale University Press, 1949.

Moen, Matthew C. *The Christian Right and Congress.* Tuscaloosa: University of Alabama Press, 1989.

Mohr, James C. *Abortion in America: The Origins and Evolution of National Policy.* Oxford: Oxford University Press, 1978.

Monaghan, David. *The Falkland's War: Myth and Countermyth.* New York: Palgrave MacMillan, 1998.

Moreton, Bethany. *To Serve God and Wal-Mart: The Making of Christian Free Enterprise.* Cambridge, MA: Harvard University Press, 2009.

Morris, Edmund. *Dutch: A Memoir of Ronald Reagan.* New York: Random House, 1999.

Mosse, George L. *Fallen Soldiers: Reshaping the Memory of the World Wars.* Oxford: Oxford University Press, 1990.

Nash, George H. *The Conservative Intellectual Movement in America: Since 1945.* Wilmington, DE: ISI Books, 1976.

———. *Reappraising the Right: The Past and Future of American Conservatism.* Wilmington, DE: ISI Books, 2009.

———. "Ronald Reagan's Legacy and American Conservatism." In Dunn, *The Enduring Reagan,* 61–69.

Neisser, Uric, and Robyn Fiyush. *The Remembering Self: Construction and Accuracy in the Self-Narrative.* Cambridge: Cambridge University Press, 1994.

Nesmith, Robert. *The New Republican Coalition: The Reagan Campaigns and White Evangelicals.* New York: Peter Lang, 1994.

Nguyen, Lien-Hang T. *Hanoi's War: An International History of the War for Peace in Vietnam.* Chapel Hill: University of North Carolina Press, 2012.

Niskanen, William A. *Reaganomics: An Insider's Account of the Policies and the People.* New York: Oxford University Press, 1988.

Nofziger, Lyn. *Nofziger.* Washington, DC: Regnery, 1992.

Noonan, Peggy. *What I Saw at the Revolution: A Political Life in the Reagan Era.* New York: Random House, 1990.

———. *When Character Was King: A Story of Ronald Reagan.* New York: Penguin, 2002.

Nora, Pierre. *Realms of Memory: The Construction of the French Past.* New York: Columbia University Press, 1992.

Norquist, Grover G. *Rock the House.* Ft. Lauderdale, FL: VYTIS Publishing, 1995.

North, Oliver. *Under Fire: An American Story.* Grand Rapids, MI: Zondervan, 1991.

Novak, Robert D. "Government: Problem or Solution?" In Deaver, *Why I Am a Reagan Conservative,* 7–8.

Obama, Barack. *The Audacity of Hope: Thoughts on Reclaiming the American Dream.* New York: Crown, 2006.

Oberdorfer, Don. *From the Cold War to a New Era: The United States and the Soviet Union, 1983–1991.* Baltimore: Johns Hopkins University Press, 1998.

———. *The Turn: From the Cold War to a New Era.* New York: Poseidon Press, 1991.

O'Brien, David. "Federal Judgeships in Retrospect." In Brownlee and Graham, *The Reagan Presidency*, 327–353.

Olick, Jeffrey K. *The Politics of Regret: On Collective Memory and Historical Responsibility.* New York: Routledge, 2007.

Olick, Jeffrey K, Vered Vinitzky-Seroussi, and Daniel Levy, eds. *The Collective Memory Reader.* Oxford: Oxford University Press, 2011.

Olsen, Henry. *The Working Class Republican: Ronald Reagan and the Return of Blue-Collar Conservatism.* New York: Broadside Books, 2017.

O'Neill, Tip. *Man of the House: The Life and Political Memoirs of Tip O'Neill.* New York: Random House, 1987.

Osgood, Kenneth, and Derrick E. White. *Civil Rights, the Conservative Movement, and the Presidency from Nixon to Obama.* Gainesville: University Press of Florida, 2014.

O'Sullivan, John. *The President, the Pope, and the Prime Minister.* Washington, DC: Regnery, 2006.

Pach, Chester J. Jr. "Sticking to His Guns: Reagan and National Security." In Brownlee and Graham, *The Reagan Presidency*, 85–112.

Palin, Sarah. *America By Heart: Reflections on Family, Faith, and Flag.* New York: Harper Collins, 2010.

———. *Going Rogue: An American Life.* New York: HarperCollins, 2009.

———. *Sarah Palin Uncut: Palin's Fight for American Freedom, Family Values, and Passion for Democracy Presented without Interruption, in Her Own Words.* Pacific Publishing Studio, 2011.

Parker, Christopher S., and Matt A. Barreto. *Change They Can't Believe In: The Tea Party and Reactionary Politics in America.* Princeton, NJ: Princeton University Press, 2013.

Patterson, James T. *Restless Giant: The United States from Watergate to Bush v. Gore.* Oxford: Oxford University Press, 2007.

Paul, Rand. *The Tea Party Goes to Washington.* New York, Center Street, 2011.

Paul, Ron. *End the Fed.* New York: Grand Central Publishing, 2009.

Peacock, Margaret. *Innocent Weapons: The Soviet and American Politics of Childhood in the Cold War.* Chapel Hill: University of North Carolina Press, 2014.

Pemberton, William E. *Exit with Honor: The Life and Presidency of Ronald Reagan.* New York: M.E. Sharpe, 1998.

Perlstein, Rick. *The Invisible Bridge: The Fall of Nixon and the Rise of Reagan.* New York: Simon & Schuster, 2014.

———. *Nixonland: The Rise of a President and the Fracturing of America.* New York: Scribner, 2008.

Peterson, Merrill D. *The Jefferson Image in the American Mind.* Charlottesville: University Press of Virginia, 1998.

———. *Lincoln in American Memory.* Oxford: Oxford University Press, 1994.

Phillips, Kendall R., ed. *Framing Public Memory.* Tuscaloosa: University of Alabama Press, 2004.

Phillips, Kevin. *The Politics of Rich and Poor: Wealth and the American Electorate in the Reagan Aftermath.* New York: Random House, 1990.

Phillips-Fein, Kim. "'If Business and the Country Will Be Run Right': The Business Challenge to the Liberal Consensus, 1945–1964." *International Labor and Working Class History* 72, no. 1 (Fall 2007): 192–215.

———. *Invisible Hands: The Making of the Conservative Movement from the New Deal to Reagan.* New York: W. W. Norton, 2009.

Plokhy, Serhii. *The Last Empire: The Final Days of the Soviet Union.* New York: Basic Books, 2015.

Podhoretz, Norman. *The Bloody Crossroads: Where Literature and Politics Meet.* New York: Simon & Schuster, 1986.

———. *Breaking Ranks: A Political Memoir.* New York: Harper and Row, 1979.

Powell, Colin, with Joseph E. Persico. *My American Journey.* New York: Ballantine Books, 1995.

Raboy, David G,, ed. *Essays in Supply-Side Economics.* Washington, DC: Institute for Research on the Economics of Taxation, 1982.

Rae, Nicol C. *Conservative Reformers: The Republican Freshman and the Lessons of the 104th Congress.* New York: M.E. Sharpe, 1998.

Raphael, Timothy. *The President Electric: Ronald Reagan and the Politics of Performance.* Ann Arbor: University of Michigan Press, 2009.

Rapoport, Ronald B., and Walter J. Stone. *Three's A Crowd: The Dynamic of Third Parties, Ross Perot, and Republican Resurgence.* Ann Arbor: University of Michigan Press, 2005.

Ratnesar, Romesh. *Tear Down This Wall: A City, A President, and the Speech That Ended the Cold War.* New York: Simon & Schuster, 2009.

Reagan, Michael. *The City on a Hill: Fulfilling Ronald Reagan's Vision for America.* New York: Thomas Nelson, 1997.

———. *The New Reagan Revolution: How Ronald Reagan's Principles Can Restore America's Greatness.* New York: Thomas Dunne Books, 2010.

Reagan, Nancy. *My Turn: The Memoirs of Nancy Reagan.* New York: Random House, 1989.

Reagan, Ron. *My Father at 100.* New York: Viking, 2011.

Reagan, Ronald. *Abortion and the Conscience of the Nation.* New York: Thomas Nelson Publishers, 1984.

———. *Actor, Ideologue, Politician: The Public Speeches of Ronald Reagan.* Edited by David W. Houck and Amos Kiewe. London: Greenwood Press, 1993.

———. *An American Life: The Autobiography.* New York: Threshold, 1990.

———. *I Love You, Ronnie: The Letters of Ronald Reagan to Nancy Reagan*. New York, Random House, 2000.

———. *Reagan: A Life in Letters*. Edited by Kiron K. Skinner, Annelise Anderson, and Martin Anderson. New York: Free Press, 2003.

———. *Reagan at CPAC: The Words That Continue to Inspire a Revolution*. Edited by Matt Schlapp. Washington, DC: Regnery, 2019.

———. *The Reagan Diaries*. Edited by Douglas Brinkley. New York: HarperCollins, 2007.

Reagan, Ronald, and Richard G. Hubler. *Where's the Rest of Me? The Autobiography of Ronald Reagan*. New York: Karz-Segil Publishers, 1965.

Reeves, Richard. *President Reagan: The Triumph of Imagination*. New York: Simon & Schuster, 2005.

Regan, Donald T. *For the Record: From Wall Street to Washington*. San Diego: Harcourt Brace Jovanovich, 1988.

Remnick, David. *Lenin's Tomb: The Last Days of the Soviet Empire*. New York: Vintage Books, 1994.

Republican National Committee. *Contract with America: The Bold Plan by Rep. Newt Gingrich, Rep. Dick Armey, and the House Republicans to Change the Nation*. New York: Random House, 1994.

Richardson, Heather Cox. *To Make Men Free: A History of the Republican Party*. New York: Basic Books, 2014.

Rieder, Jonathan. *Canarsie: The Jews and Italians of Brooklyn Against Liberalism*. Cambridge, MA: Harvard University Press, 1985.

Roberts, Paul Craig. *The Supply-Side Revolution: An Insider's Account of Policy-Making in Washington*. Cambridge, MA: Harvard University Press, 1984.

Rodgers, Daniel T. *Age of Fracture*. New York: Belknap Press, 2010.

Rogin, Michael. *Ronald Reagan, The Movie: And Other Episodes in Political Demonology*. Berkeley: University of California Press, 1987.

Rohde, Joy. *Armed with Expertise: The Militarization of American Social Research During the Cold War*. Ithaca, NY: Cornell University Press, 2013.

Romney, Mitt. *No Apology: Believe in America*. New York: St. Martin's Griffin, 2010.

Rosebush, James. *True Reagan: What Made Ronald Reagan Great and Why It Matters*. New York: Center Street, 2016.

Rosenberg, Emily S. *A Date Which Will Live: Pearl Harbor in American Memory*. Durham, NC: Duke University Press, 2003.

Rosenthal, Lawrence, and Christine Trost. *Steep: The Precipitous Rise of the Tea Party*. Berkeley: University of California Press, 2012.

Rove, Karl. *Courage and Consequence: My Life as a Conservative in the Fight*. New York: Threshold Editions, 2010.

Rubio, Marco. *An American Son: A Memoir.* New York: Sentinel, 2012.

Rumsfeld, Donald. *Known and Unknown: A Memoir.* New York: Sentinel, 2011.

Ryan, Paul. *The Way Forward: Renewing the American Idea.* New York: Hachette Book Group, 2014.

Ryan, Paul, Eric Cantor, and Kevin McCarthy. *Young Guns: A New Generation of Conservative Leaders.* New York: Threshold Editions, 2010.

Saltoun-Ebin, Jason. *The Reagan Files: The Untold Story of Reagan's Top-Secret Efforts to Win the Cold War.* Middletown, DE: Self-published, 2010.

Santa Cruz, Paul H. *Making JFK Matter: Popular Memory and the Thirty-Fifth President.* Denton: University of North Texas Press, 2015.

Sarotte, M. E. *Dealing with the Devil: East Germany, Détente, and Ostpolitik, 1969–1973.* Chapel Hill: University of North Carolina Press, 2001.

Schacter, Daniel L. *Memory Distortion: How Minds, Brains, and Societies Reconstruct the Past.* Cambridge, MA: Harvard University Press, 1995.

———. *Searching for Memory: The Brain, the Mind, and the Past.* New York: Basic Books, 1996.

Schacter, Daniel L., and Elaine Scarry, eds. *Memory, Brain, and Beliefs.* Cambridge, MA: Harvard University Press, 2000.

Schaeffer, Frank. *Crazy for God: How I Grew Up as One of the Elect, Helped Found the Religious Right, and Lived to Take All (or Almost All) of It Back.* New York: Carroll & Graf Publishers, 2007.

Schaller, Michael. "Reagan and the Cold War." In Longley et al., *Deconstructing Reagan*, 3–40.

Scheer, Robert. *With Enough Shovels: Reagan, Bush, and Nuclear War.* New York: Random House, 1982.

Schieffer, Bob, and Gary Paul Gates. *The Acting President: Ronald Reagan and the Supporting Players Who Helped Him Create the Illusion That Held America Spellbound.* New York: E.P. Dutton, 1989.

Schlafly, Phyllis. *A Choice Not an Echo.* Pere Marquette Press, 1964.

———. *A Choice Not an Echo: 50th Anniversary Edition.* New York: Regnery, 2014.

Schlafly, Phyllis, Ed Martin, and Brett M. Decker. *The Conservative Case for Trump.* Washington, DC: Regnery, 2016.

Schlesinger, Arthur M. Jr. "Rating the Presidents: Washington to Clinton." *Political Science Quarterly* 112, no. 2 (Summer 1997): 179–190.

Schneider, Gregory L. *Cadres for Conservatism: Young Americans for Freedom and the Rise of the Contemporary Right.* New York: New York University Press, 1998.

———, ed. *Conservatism in America since 1930: A Reader.* New York: New York University Press, 2003.

————, ed. *The Conservative Century: From Reaction to Revolution.* New York: Rowman & Littlefield, 2009.

Schulman, Bruce J., and Julian E. Zelizer, eds. *Rightward Bound: Making America Conservative in the 1970s.* Cambridge, MA: Harvard University Press, 2008.

Schwarz, Fred. *Beating the Unbeatable Foe: One Man's Victory Over Communism, Leviathan, and the Last Enemy.* Washington, DC: Regnery, 1996.

Schweizer, Peter, ed. *The Fall of the Berlin Wall: Reassessing the Causes and Consequences of the End of the Cold War.* Stanford, CA: Hoover Institution Press, 2000.

————. *Reagan's War: The Epic Story of His Forty-Year Struggle and Final Triumph over Communism.* New York: Doubleday, 2002.

————. *Victory: The Reagan Administration's Secret Strategy That Hastened the Collapse of the Soviet Union.* New York: Atlantic Monthly Press, 1994.

Scoblic, J. Peter, *U.S. vs. Them: Conservatism in the Age of Nuclear Terror.* New York: Penguin Books, 2008.

Scott, James M. *Deciding to Intervene: The Reagan Doctrine and American Foreign Policy.* Durham, NC: Duke University Press, 1996.

Self, Robert O. *All in the Family: The Realignment of American Democracy since the 1960s.* New York: Hill and Wang, 2012.

Service, Robert. *The End of the Cold War, 1985–1991.* New York: Public Affairs, 2015.

Settje, David E. *Faith and War: How Christians Debated the Cold and Vietnam Wars.* New York: New York University Press, 2011.

Shilts, Randy. *And the Band Played On: Politics, People, and the AIDS Epidemic.* New York: St. Martin's Griffin, 1987.

————. *The Mayor of Castro Street: The Life and Times of Harvey Milk.* New York: St. Martin's Griffin, 2010.

Shirley, Craig. *Citizen Newt: The Making of a Reagan Conservative.* New York: Nelson Books, 2017.

————. *Last Act: The Final Years and Emerging Legacy of Ronald Reagan.* New York: Nelson Books, 2015.

————. *Rendezvous with Destiny: Ronald Reagan and the Campaign That Changed America.* Wilmington, DE: ISI Books, 2009.

Shultz, George P. *Turmoil and Triumph: My Years as Secretary of State.* New York: Scribner's, 1993.

Simon, William. *Time for Truth.* New York: Berkley, 1978.

Skinner, Kiron K., Annelise Anderson, and Martin Anderson, eds. *Reagan in His Own Hand.* New York: Free Press, 2001.

Skocpol, Theda, and Vanessa Williamson. *The Tea Party and the Remaking of Republican Conservatism.* Oxford: Oxford University Press, 2012.

Skousen, Mark. *Vienna & Chicago, Friends or Foes? A Tale of Two Schools of Free-Market Economics.* Washington, DC: Capital Press, 2005.

Sloan, John W. "The Economic Costs of Reagan Mythology." In Longley et al., *Deconstructing Reagan*, 41–69.

Smith, Gaddis. *Morality, Reason, and Power: American Diplomacy in the Carter Years.* New York: Hill and Wang, 1986.

Speakes, Larry. *Speaking Out: The Reagan Presidency from Inside the White House.* New York: Charles Scribner's Sons, 1988.

Stahl, Jason. *Right Moves: The Conservative Think Tank in American Political Culture since 1945.* Chapel Hill: University of North Carolina Press, 2016.

Steele, Meili. *Hiding from History: Politics and Public Imagination.* Ithaca, NY: Cornell University Press, 2005.

Stein, Judith. *Pivotal Decade: How the United States Traded Factories for Finance in the Seventies.* New Haven, CT: Yale University Press, 2010.

Steinberg, Arnold L. *Whiplash: From JFK to Donald Trump, a Political Odyssey.* New York: Jameson Books, 2017.

Stelzer, Irwin, ed. *The Neocon Reader.* New York: Grove Press, 2004.

Street, Joe. *Dirty Harry's America: Clint Eastwood, Harry Callahan, and the Conservative Backlash.* Gainesville: University Press of Florida, 2016.

Street, Paul, and Anthony DiMaggio. *Crashing the Tea Party: Mass Media and the Campaign to Remake American Politics.* London: Paradigm Books, 2011.

Strober, Deborah Hart, and Gerald S. Strober. *Reagan: The Man and His Presidency.* New York: Houghton Mifflin, 1998.

Stockman, David. *The Triumph of Politics: How the Reagan Revolution Failed.* New York: Harper & Row, 1986.

Suri, Jeremi. "Détente and Its Discontents." In Schulman and Zelizer, *Rightward Bound: Making America Conservative in the 1970s*, 227–245.

———. *Power and Protest: Global Revolution and the Rise of Détente.* Cambridge, MA: Harvard University Press, 2003.

Sutton, Matthew A. *Jerry Falwell and the Rise of the Religious Right: A Brief History with Documents.* New York: Bedford & St. Martin's, 2013.

Tanner, Michael D. *Leviathan on the Right: How Big-Government Conservatism Brought Down the Republican Revolution.* Washington, DC: CATO Institute, 2007.

Taylor, Jay. *The Generalissimo: Chiang Kai-shek and the Struggle for Modern China.* Cambridge, MA: Belknap Press, 2009.

Taylor, John B. "Changes in American Economic Policy in the 1980s: Watershed or Pendulum Swing?" *Journal of Economic Literature* 33, no. 2 (June 1995): 777–784.

Thatcher, Margaret. *The Downing Street Years.* New York: Harper Press, 1993.

Thompson, C. Bradley and Yaron Brook. *Neoconservatism: An Obituary for an Idea.* London: Paradigm Publishers, 2010.

Thompson, Michael J., ed. *Confronting the New Conservatism: The Rise of the Right in America.* New York: New York University Press, 2007.

Thrift, Bryan Hardin. *Conservative Bias: How Jesse Helms Pioneered the Rise of Right-Wing Media and Realigned the Republican Party.* Gainesville: University Press of Florida, 2014.

Troy, Gil. "Toward a Historiography of Reagan and the 1980s: Why Have We Done Such a Lousy Job?" In Hudson and Davies, *Ronald Reagan and the 1980s,* 229–247.

Trump, Donald J. *Crippled America: How to Make America Great Again.* New York: Threshold Editions, 2015.

Tygiel, Jules. *Ronald Reagan and the Triumph of American Conservatism.* New York: Pearson, 2006.

Tyrrell, R. Emmett Jr. *The Conservative Crack-Up.* New York: Simon & Schuster, 1992.

Updegrove, Mark K. *The Last Republicans: Inside the Extraordinary Relationship between George H. W. Bush and George W. Bush.* New York: Harper, 2017.

Vaïsse, Justin. *Neoconservatism: The Biography of a Movement.* Cambridge, MA: Belknap Press, 2010.

Viguerie, Richard. *Conservatives Betrayed: How George W. Bush and Other Big Government Republicans Hijacked the Conservative Cause.* Los Angeles: Bonus Books, 2006.

———. *The Establishment vs. the People: Is a New Populist Revolt on the Way?* Chicago: Regnery Gateway, 1983.

———. *The New Right: We're Ready to Lead.* Falls Church, VA: Viguerie Company, 1980.

———. *Takeover: The 100 Year War for the Soul of the GOP and How Conservatives Can Finally Win It.* Washington, DC: WND Books, 2014.

Viguerie, Richard, and David Franke. *America's Right Turn: How Conservatives Used New and Alternative Media to Take Power.* Los Angeles: Bonus Books, 2004.

Vivian, Bradford. *Public Forgetting: The Rhetoric and Politics of Beginning Again.* University Park: Pennsylvania State University Press, 2010.

Volcker, Paul, and Toyoo Gyohten. *Changing Fortunes: The World's Money and the Threat of American Leadership.* New York: Random House, 1992.

Von Domm, Helene. *At Reagan's Side: Twenty Years in the Political Mainstream.* New York: Doubleday, 1988.

Wall, Wendy. *Inventing the "American Way": The Politics of Consensus from the*

New Deal to the Civil Rights Movement. Oxford: Oxford University Press, 2008.

Wallison, Peter J. *Ronald Reagan: The Power of Conviction and the Success of His Presidency.* Boulder, CO: Westview Press, 2004.

Wanniski, Jude. *The Way the World Works: How Economies Fail and Succeed.* New York: Basic Books, 1978.

Wapshott, Nicholas. *Keynes, Hayek: The Clash That Defined Modern Economics.* New York: W. W. Norton, 2011.

———. *Ronald Reagan and Margaret Thatcher: A Political Marriage.* New York: Sentinel, 2007.

Warner, Judith, and Max Berley. *Newt Gingrich: Speaker to America.* New York: Signet, 1995.

Weinberger, Casper. *Fighting for Peace: Seven Critical Years in the Pentagon.* New York: Grand Central Publishing, 1990.

Wells, Samuel F. "Reagan, Euromissiles, and Europe." In Brownlee and Graham, *The Reagan Presidency*, 133–154.

Westad, Odd Arne. *The Global Cold War: Third World Interventions and the Making of Our Times.* New York: Cambridge University Press, 2007.

Weyrich, Paul M. and William S. Lind. *The Next Conservatism.* South Bend, Indiana: St. Augustine Press, 2009.

White, C. Todd. *Pre-Gay L.A.: A Social History of the Movement for Homosexual Rights.* Chicago: University of Illinois Press, 2009.

White, John Kenneth. *What Happened to the Republican Party?: And What It Means for American Presidential Politics.* New York: Routledge, 2015.

White, Lawrence J. *The S&L Debacle: Public Policy Lessons for Bank and Thrift Regulation.* Oxford: Oxford University Press, 1991.

Wilber, Del Quentin. *Rawhide Down: The Near Assassination of Ronald Reagan.* New York: Henry Holt, 2011.

Wilcox, Clyde. *God's Warriors: The Christian Right in Twentieth-Century America.* Baltimore: Johns Hopkins University Press, 1992.

Wilentz, Sean. *The Age of Reagan: A History 1974–2008.* New York: Harper Perennial, 2001.

Williams, Daniel K. *God's Own Party: The Making of the Christian Right.* Oxford: Oxford University Press, 2010.

Williams, William Appleman. *The Tragedy of American Diplomacy.* New York: W. W. Norton, 1959.

Wilson, James Graham. *The Triumph of Improvisation: Gorbachev's Adaptability, Reagan's Engagement, and the End of the Cold War.* Ithaca, NY: Cornell University Press, 2015.

Winter, Jay. *Sites of Memory, Sites of Mourning: The Great Wars in European Cultural Memory*. Cambridge: Cambridge University Press, 1995.

Winters, Michael. *God's Right Hand: How Jerry Falwell Made God a Republican and Baptized the American Right*. New York: Harper, 2012.

Wirls, Daniel. *Buildup: The Politics of Defense in the Reagan Era*. Ithaca, NY: Cornell University Press, 1992.

Woodward, Bob. *Five Presidents and the Legacy of Watergate*. New York: Simon & Schuster, 1999.

———. *Obama's Wars*. New York: Simon & Schuster, 2010.

———. *Plan of Attack: The Definitive Account of the Decision to Invade Iraq*. New York: Simon & Schuster, 2004.

———. *The Price of Politics*. New York: Simon & Schuster, 2013.

Young, Neil J. *We Gather Together: The Religious Right and the Problem of Interfaith Politics*. Oxford: Oxford University Press, 2016.

Zelizer, Julian E. "Conservatives, Carter, and the Politics of National Security." In Schulman and Zelizer, *Rightward Bound*, 265–287.

Zernike, Kate. *Boiling Mad: Inside Tea Party America*. New York: Times Books, 2010.

Zerubavel, Eviatar. *Time Maps: Collective Memory and the Social Shape of the Past*. Chicago: University of Chicago Press, 2003.

Zubok, Vladislav M. *A Failed Empire: The Soviet Union in the Cold War from Stalin to Gorbachev*. Chapel Hill: University of North Carolina Press, 2007.

Index